FROMMER'S

BUDGET TRAVEL GUIDE

New Zealand from $45 a Day

6th Edition

by Elizabeth Hansen
Assisted by Richard Adams

MACMILLAN • USA

ABOUT THE AUTHORS

Elizabeth Hansen has lived and worked in both Australia and New Zealand. She is the author of *Bed and Breakfast New Zealand, The Woman's Travel Guide to New Zealand,* and *Frommer's Australia.* Her articles have appeared in such magazines as *Travel-Holiday* and *Travel & Leisure.* **Richard Adams** is a photographer as well as co-researcher, navigator, and map enthusiast. When Elizabeth and Richard are not traveling, they live in La Jolla, California.

MACMILLAN TRAVEL

A Prentice Hall Macmillan Company
15 Columbus Circle
New York, NY 10023

ISBN 0-02-860465-2
ISSN 1045-9111

Editor: Ron Boudreau
Map Editor: Douglas Stallings

Design by Michele Laseau
Maps by Ortelius Design and Devorah Wilkenfeld

SPECIAL SALES

Bulk purchases (10+ copies) of Frommer's Travel Guides are available to corporations at special discounts. The Special Sales Department can produce custom editions to be used as premiums and/or for sales promotion to suit individual needs. Existing editions can be produced with custom cover imprints such as corporate logos. For more information write to: Special Sales, Simon & Schuster, 1230 Avenue of the Americas, New York, NY 10020.

Manufactured in the United States of America.

Contents

9 Wellington 225

10 Marlborough, Nelson & the West Coast 248

11 Queenstown & Environs 293

12 Southland 330

List of Maps

For Rick, for being there—again.

Acknowledgments

The author gratefully acknowledges the assistance of the New Zealand Tourism Board. Thanks are also due to Californian-cum-Kiwi Carol Glen for introductions to the country's kindest hosts and to Kate Stanton for her organizing efforts. My helpers—Helen Irvine, Craig Boddington, and Suzanne Osborne—are much appreciated, too.

What the Symbols Mean

★ **Frommer's Favorites** Accommodations, restaurants, attractions, and entertainments you should not miss.

$ **Super-Special Values** Really exceptional value.

In Hotel & Other Listings

The following symbols refer to the standard amenities available in all rooms:

A/C air conditioning
TEL telephone
TV television
MINIBAR refrigerator stocked with beverages and snacks

The following abbreviations are used for credit or charge cards:

AE American Express
BC Bankcard
DC Diners Club
MC MasterCard
V Visa

Trip Planning with This Guide

USE THE FOLLOWING FEATURES

What Things Cost In To help you plan your daily budget

Calendar of Events To plan for or avoid

Suggested Itineraries For seeing the country

What's Special About Checklist A summary of each region's or city's highlights

Easy-to-Read Maps Regional attractions, walking tours, city sights, accommodation and restaurant locations—all referring to or keyed to the text

Fast Facts All the essentials at a glance: currency, embassies, emergencies, mail, taxes, telephone information, and more

OTHER SPECIAL FROMMER FEATURES

Family-Friendly Accommodations & Restaurants Where the whole family will feel at home

Did You Know . . . ? Offbeat, fun facts

Famous New Zealanders The country's greats

Impressions What others have said

An Invitation to the Reader

When researching this book, I discovered many wonderful places—hotels, restaurants, shops, and more. I'm sure you'll find others. Please tell us about them so we can share the information with your fellow travelers in upcoming editions. If you were disappointed with a recommendation, we'd love to know that, too. Please write to:

Elizabeth Hansen
Frommer's New Zealand from $45 a Day, 6th Edition
Macmillan Travel
15 Columbus Circle
New York, NY 10023

An Additional Note

Please be advised that travel information is subject to change at any time—and this is especially true of prices. We therefore suggest that you write or call ahead for confirmation when making your travel plans. The authors, editors, and publisher cannot be held responsible for the experiences of readers while traveling. Your safety is important to us, however, so we encourage you to stay alert and be aware of your surroundings. Keep a close eye on cameras, purses, and wallets—all favorite targets of thieves and pickpockets.

1

Saving Money in New Zealand

If you're headed to New Zealand in the near future, you're in for the time of your life. This small "down under" nation has just completed an amazing economic recovery, and the signs of success are everywhere.

Tourist facilities have been spruced up and expanded. In the new-and-improved New Zealand you'll find more than 70 visitor information centers—most open every day—with staff eager to help you. You'll also find that provincial liquor-licensing laws are a thing of the past: Moderately priced cafés, bistros, and brasseries offering beer, wine, and spirits are now *the* places to dine and drink.

In addition, longer store hours mean that you have more time to shop for bargains; nonsmokers will appreciate the abundance of no-smoking sections in restaurants; and the upgraded roads and excellent signposting will make your travels so much easier.

On my most recent visit I was pleased to see that New Zealand's native people—the Maori—have become more involved in tourism, providing visitors with ample opportunities to experience their culture.

Another discovery delighted me: Bed-and-breakfast inns, guesthouses, and homestays are now readily available in all parts of the country. These economical lodging options have been a favorite of mine since I wrote *The Woman's Travel Guide to New Zealand* in 1984; however, they were hardly plentiful back then. In 1987 when I wrote my second book, *Bed and Breakfast New Zealand,* I had to search and search to find 100 qualifying spots. In 1994 I got a wonderful surprise: For this guide I faced the challenge of sifting through 1,000 or more B&B listings to find the very best. I hope you'll agree with my choices and find these places as charming and affordable as I have.

As a personal note, I'd like to mention that although lots of things have changed in New Zealand, the most important aspect of the country remains the same: The people are still the kindest, nicest folks in the world. After about a dozen trips there over the past two decades, I'm happy to report that car phones, personal computers, and microwave ovens haven't changed Kiwi hospitality.

I look forward to sharing "my" New Zealand with you and helping you have a reasonably priced and rewarding holiday.

1 The $45-a-Day Premise

Is it actually possible to enjoy New Zealand for $45 a day? You bet it is! Remember that this amount is in U.S. dollars—at the time of this writing, $45 U.S. is equivalent to NZ$69.25. And as with all Frommer budget guides, the dollar amount is intended to cover only the basic daily expenses for *one* person: three meals and a night's lodging. On the $45-a-day budget, each pair of travelers would have approximately NZ$138.50 to spend.

Two people traveling together could spend NZ$80 (U.S. $52) for a motel room, NZ$6 (U.S. $3.90) each for lunch, NZ$20 (U.S. $13) each for dinner, and still have NZ$6.50 (U.S. $4.20) to spend on muffins and fresh fruit for breakfast. Tea, coffee, milk, and sugar are provided free in all New Zealand lodgings, with the possible exception of hostels and motor camps. And, of course, should you wish to take advantage of the cooking facilities found in most Kiwi motels, your dinner will cost much less than NZ$20 per person.

Am I implying that the $45-a-day premise works only for two people traveling together? Absolutely not. Most of my trips to New Zealand have been solo ventures, so I'm keenly aware of the needs of single travelers. Since moteliers tend to set their rates as if they were renting rooms on the ark, B&Bs tend to be a better deal for those on their own. For instance, you can stay at a cozy guesthouse for NZ$45 (U.S. $29.25) and enjoy a hearty breakfast shared with other travelers. This will leave you with NZ$20 (U.S. $13) for dinner and enough for lunch.

The accommodations and dining figures I used above are for midprice options. Staying at one of the country's attractive hostels would bring your lodging cost down to about NZ$16 (U.S. $10.40) per person; a camping ground or motorhome spot in a motor camp would be even less. The average B&B homestay costs NZ$45 (U.S. $29.25) single and NZ$70 (U.S. $45.50) double, and most B&B guesthouses charge about NZ$45 (U.S. $29.25) single and NZ$75 (U.S. $48.75) double. On the other hand, the price of a B&B inn can be as high as NZ$100 (U.S. $65) single and NZ$160 (U.S. $104) double. Note that although motel rates range from NZ$70 to NZ$100 (U.S. $45.50 to $65) single or double, hotels are not a good option for thrifty travelers. Rates at modern tourist hotels usually start at NZ$200 (U.S. $130) per night and go up to figures that give this value-conscious author the shivers.

As for dining, the NZ$20 (U.S. $13) I've suggested for dinner should be more than adequate for a main course and dessert or an appetizer and a main course at most of the country's cafés and moderately priced eateries. You'll find it'll be even less expensive to eat at food courts, where NZ$5 (U.S. 3.25) will fill a plate, or to cook at your motel as mentioned above.

2 Forty Money-Saving Tips

AIR TRAVEL

1. Consider traveling off season—April through August—when airlines offer their lowest fares.
2. Take advantage of the free stopovers allowed on many airfares.
3. Reserve your flight sufficiently far ahead of departure to quality for advance-purchase fares.

ACCOMMODATIONS

4. Stay at bed-and-breakfasts, where the rates include breakfast—as well as lots of personal attention.
5. Remember that in addition to dorms, hostels usually have private rooms with twin or double beds. New Zealand hostels—both private ones and those affiliated with Youth Hostel—are way above average in quality.
6. Don't overlook the economically priced motel units and tourist apartments located in motor camps.
7. Farmstay hosts usually offer a tour of their properties at no charge.
8. If you stay in a hotel, try to avoid sampling the contents of the minibar (if there's one in the room), using the telephone, sending faxes, requesting the laundry and/or dry-cleaning service, and ordering room-service meals.

9. Be aware that most things in New Zealand are subject to a 12.5% Goods and Services Tax. When requesting an accommodations rate, ask if the GST is included.
10. Throughout New Zealand, many vacation homes (known as *baches* or *cribs*) are available for rent when they're not in use by the owners. These are great values. If interested, see "Accommodations Choices" in Chapter 3.
11. Before reserving a hotel room, ask if you can take advantage of any long-stay rates, off-season rates, corporate rates, senior-citizen rates, weekend discounts, or automobile-club discounts.

DINING

12. Remember that B&B homestays, guesthouses, and inns offer complimentary coffee and tea.
13. B&B hosts are great sources of good-value dining recommendations.
14. Cooking dinner or "picnicking" in your motel room is a thrifty alternative to dining out.
15. Eat at restaurants that allow you to bring your own wine.
16. Buy your wine at wholesale liquor stores.
17. Avoid the cost of a hotel or motel breakfast by traveling with a stash of your favorite muffins and fresh fruit purchased at a supermarket.
18. Many B&B hosts offer dinner at a small extra cost, an extremely good value.
19. Don't feel compelled to tip. Kiwis rarely do.

LOCAL TRANSPORTATION

20. In cities, take local tours rather than rent a car for sightseeing and take city buses rather than taxis.
21. If you rent a car for intercity transportation, save gas by requesting a small vehicle that gets good mileage.
22. Check the rates offered by local, independent agencies before renting a car. They're usually less expensive than the internationally known companies.
23. Check all one-way car-rental contracts for possible drop-off charges and confirm the time of day the car is due to be returned.
24. Make sure your car-rental agreement includes unlimited free kilometers.
25. If you have another policy covering you, save money by declining the insurance offered by car-rental agencies.
26. Take your home-country auto-club membership card with you to New Zealand since it'll entitle you to Automobile Association (AA) member discounts and excellent free maps.
27. Holders of YHA membership cards and VIP (backpackers) discount cards, as well as those over age 60, are entitled to up to a 30% discount on InterCity and Mount Cook coaches.
28. Mount Cook's Kiwi Coach Pass and the Kiwi Air Pass are good-value options. See "Getting Around" in Chapter 3 for details.

RECREATION & ENTERTAINMENT

29. B&B hosts can recommend affordable fishing guides and adventure activities they are personally familiar with.
30. If you're fit and adventurous, you can walk the country's famous hiking trails without a guide.
31. If you want to catch a film, go on Tuesday night, when all Hoyts cinemas charge only NZ$5 (U.S. $3.25)—the regular price is NZ$8.50 to NZ$10 (U.S. $5.55 to $6.50). Discount tickets for any night can be purchased at Shell service stations.

SHOPPING

32. Search for souvenirs in local department stores rather than at tourist shops.
33. When shopping for gifts to take home, consider buying tea or shortbread biscuits (cookies) from a supermarket.
34. Buy New Zealand books at the Automobile Association (AA), where members of auto clubs around the world receive a discount.
35. Purchases sent overseas are not subject to New Zealand's 12.5% Goods and Services Tax.

INFORMATION & COMMUNICATIONS

36. Long-distance calls within New Zealand are expensive. Be aware that the cheapest time to phone is between 10pm and 7am. The next-best time is during the "economy" period: Monday through Friday from 7 to 8am and 6 to 10pm and Saturday, Sunday, and holidays from 7am to 10pm.
37. Use toll-free numbers whenever possible.
38. The cheapest way for Americans to call home is to use USA Direct. For details, see "Fast Facts: New Zealand" in Chapter 3.
39. Take advantage of the free services offered at the more than 70 Visitor Information Network offices all over the country. These services include making accommodations reservations.
40. One of the best sources for information are B&B hosts, who will know where the bargains are in meals, shopping, nightlife, and so on.

3 Best Bets on a Budget

The role of a guidebook author is not dissimilar from that of a shopper looking for the best produce at a fruit-and-vegetable market. While researching this book I compared untold numbers of dining and lodging options and considered numerous sightseeing, shopping, and recreation possibilities. I passed over products that didn't seem fresh, had obvious bad spots, and failed the aroma test. Only the best got past my discerning eye and onto these pages.

Here's a sampling of the crème de la crème:

New Zealand's Top Attractions for Free

1. I love walking along the **Auckland waterfront.** The variety of boats always amazes me—everything from America's Cup competitors to old ferries. For

details of my favorite jaunt, see "What to See and Do" and "Walking Tour: Along the Wharf" in Chapter 5.

2. One of my favorite viewpoints in the whole country is Auckland's **Savage Memorial Park.** From here you can see the harbor—almost always dotted with white sailboats—and the gulf islands. It might be a windy spot, but the view is fantastic. See "What to See and Do" in Chapter 5 for more information.
3. New Zealand's **craft industry** is especially strong in and around Nelson. You can browse through the region's pottery shops and even watch the artisans at Hoglunds Glassblowing Studio at Korurangi Farm near Richmond.
4. The **road between Te Anau and Milford Sound** winds through some of the prettiest scenery on the South Island. Waterfalls, lofty peaks, and running streams make this drive memorable. See Chapter 11 for more information about Fiordland.
5. **Mount Egmont**—or Taranaki, as the Maori call it—is a beautiful cone-shaped peak on the North Island's west coast. Hiking trails crisscross Mount Egmont National Park. It's possible to reach the summit and return in one day. See Chapter 8 for coverage of New Plymouth and Mount Egmont/Taranaki.
6. Even if you're not a chocaholic, the tour at the **Cadbury Confectionery Ltd.'s factory** in Dunedin is a fun experience, with free samples as a bonus. Note that this tour needs to be reserved well in advance. See "What to See and Do" in Chapter 13 for details.
7. The **Auckland Museum** contains extensive displays explaining various aspects of the Maori culture. Time you spend here before setting out for the rest of the country will give extra meaning to later explorations and experiences. For more information, see "What to See and Do" in Chapter 5.
8. The **Wizard of Christchurch** is a local institution. Too outrageous for an ordinary soapbox, he stands on a ladder in Cathedral Square Monday through Friday at 1pm and shares his opinions with the crowd that gathers to see him. Other free Christchurch activities include strolling along the peaceful Avon River and admiring the cathedral's interior. See "What to See and Do" in Chapter 14 for details.
9. The historic **Puhoi Pub** is one of New Zealand's most interesting old public licensed hotels. Even though the beer isn't free, the atmosphere is—and it couldn't be better. Puhoi is just off State Highway 1, about an hour's drive north of Auckland. Look for details under "The Bay of Islands" in Chapter 5.
10. The popularity of **wine tasting** in the area around Blenheim has grown right along with the quality of Marlborough District wines. For more information, See "In Nearby Blenheim" under "What to See and Do" in the Picton section of Chapter 10.

Best Budget Accommodations

1. **The Gables** in Picton is a cozy B&B where hosts Dick and Ann Smith go out of their way to make guests feel welcome. Imagine paying only NZ$40

(U.S. $26) single or NZ$75 (U.S. $48.75) double and being served scrambled eggs with salmon for breakfast. For full information, see "Picton" in Chapter 10.

2. Heather and Brian Oberer are probably the most popular farmstay hosts on the North Island, so if you want to stay at **Te Ana Farm,** just south of Rotorua, be sure to reserve well ahead. Heather's incredible gourmet meals are just one of the reasons this property is so popular. Rates (including breakfast) are NZ$60 ($39) single and NZ$90 ($58.50) double, with three-course evening meals with wine costing NZ$25 ($16.25) per person. See "Rotorua" in Chapter 7 for details.
3. **Club Nelson** in Nelson is a hostel with a difference. Hosts Linley Rose and Peter Richards offer dorm rooms, shared rooms, and double rooms in a historic 1902 house set on 2 1/2 acres. Guests pay NZ$16 (U.S. $10.40) per person in a dorm or NZ$19.50 (U.S. $12.70) per person in a double room. For more information, see "Nelson" in Chapter 10.
4. The **North Shore Caravan Park, Cabins, and Motel** near Auckland offers tent sites, motorhome sites, cabins, and motel units. The sites cost NZ$16 (U.S. $10.40) for one person or NZ$23 (U.S. $14.95) for two. Cabins start at NZ$37 (U.S. $24.05) for two. See "Where to Stay" in Chapter 5 for details.
5. You wouldn't know from looking at it, but the **Warkworth Inn** is almost 150 years old. At this historic hotel none of the rooms has a bath, but each does have a sink and tea- and coffee-making facilities. Rates (including continental breakfast) are NZ$30 (U.S. $19.50) single, NZ$47 (U.S. $30.55) double, and NZ$60 (U.S. $39) triple. For full information, see "Easy Excursions from Auckland" in Chapter 5.
6. How's this for good value? Lloyd and Betty White welcome guests to **Solitare Homestay,** their historic kauri house on State Highway 12 at Waimamaku, and charge only NZ$50 (U.S. $32.50) single and NZ$90 (U.S. $58.50) double for breakfast, dinner, and a bed for the night. For full information, see "The Bay of Islands" in Chapter 6.
7. At **Farry's Motel** in Dunedin, each unit comes with a fully equipped kitchen and sleeps up to four. The rate is NZ$86 (U.S. $55.90) single or double. See "Where to Stay" in Chapter 13.
8. **Mount Vernon Lodge** offers several types of accommodation in a rustic environment on the Banks Peninsula east of Christchurch. Kids will love the free-roaming lambs and chickens, and horse trekking and a swimming pool are available on site. Rates are NZ$40 (U.S. $26) for two. See "An Easy Excursion from Christchurch" in Chapter 14 for details.
9. **The Briars** is a rural homestay about an hour's drive from Mount Cook. Marylou and Don Blue welcome guests to their attractive modern house furnished with antiques, lots of books, and a collection of Mackenzie Country paintings. Rates (including breakfast) are NZ$35 (U.S. $22.75) single and NZ$65 (U.S. $42.25) double. For more information, see "Mount Cook" in Chapter 11.
10. The **YMCA** in Christchurch is well located across from the Arts Centre and near the Botanic Gardens. Singles range from NZ$33 to NZ$52 (U.S. $21.45 to $33.80), and doubles cost NZ$45 to NZ$70 (U.S. $29.25 to $45.50). See "Where to Stay" in Chapter 14 for details.

Best Budget Dining

1. Christchurch's **Main Street Cafe & Bar,** serving tasty vegetarian cuisine, is understandably popular. Light meals cost about NZ$5 (U.S. $3.25), and something more substantial is available for NZ$12 to NZ$14 (U.S. $7.80 to $9.10). See "Where to Eat" in Chapter 14 for details.
2. On a recent visit to **La Casa Italiano,** on the Devonport ferry wharf, my husband and I shared a standard-size Super La Casa pizza. It was delicious and set us back all of NZ$8.50 (U.S. $5.55). For more information, see "Where to Eat" in Chapter 5.
3. **The Bank,** on The Octagon in Dunedin, really was the ANZ bank until 1993. Now it's a licensed café offering buffet lunches and dinners for NZ$5 to NZ$7 (U.S. $3.25 to $4.55). See "Where to Eat" in Chapter 13 for details.
4. Because Queenstown is so popular with tourists, the dining options there tend to be a little more expensive than in other parts of the country. However, **Giuseppe's** is an exception. Located in a suburb and catering to locals, this spot offers superb dinners for NZ$11 to NZ$16 (U.S. $7.15 to $10.40). See "Queenstown" in Chapter 11 for more information.
5. I happen to love pumpkin soup, and the best I've ever tasted was at **Vino-Vino Bar & Cafe** on Waiheke Island. This place also serves up great cozy atmosphere, 17 New Zealand beers, 9 imported beers, and numerous wines by the bottle or glass. Meals cost about NZ$10 (U.S. $6.50). For details, see "Where to Eat" in Chapter 5.
6. **Kebab Kid** on Parnell Road in Auckland serves a pita pocket filled with delicious marinated lamb for NZ$6.75 (U.S. $4.40). Other options are similarly priced. See "Where to Eat" in Chapter 5 for details.
7. Wonderful Mediterranean food is served at **Sirocco** in Rotorua. Prices for appetizers range from NZ$4.50 to NZ$8.75 (U.S. $2.90 to $5.70); main courses cost NZ$9.50 to NZ$11.95 (U.S. $6.20 to $7.80). For more information, see "Rotorua" in Chapter 7.
8. Wanganui's **Rutland Arms Inn** is a café/bar located in a hotel dating from 1846. The atmosphere is that of an upmarket pub; farm implements and horse brasses hang on the walls. The cuisine is English, with English beers available. Lunch costs NZ$3 to NZ$8 (U.S. $1.95 to $5.20); dinner main courses range from NZ$11 to NZ$19 (U.S. $7.15 to $12.35). See "Wanganui" in Chapter 8 for all the details.
9. Like all food courts, **Gourmet Lane** in Wellington is a boon to budget travelers. Main courses run NZ$5 to NZ$6 (U.S. $3.25 to $3.90). There's even lunchtime entertainment quite often. For full information, see "Where to Eat" in Chapter 9.
10. At **Broccoli Row,** a seafood and vegetarian café in Nelson, diners sit at tables in a large outdoor courtyard or in one of two cozy rooms inside. The chalkboard menu changes daily and offers appetizers for about NZ$7 (U.S. $4.55) and main courses for NZ$13.50 to NZ$14.50 (U.S. $8.80 to $9.40). See "Nelson" in Chapter 10 for details.

4 How This Guide Can Save You Money

All the ingredients for a great affordable trip to New Zealand are between the covers of this book. I've selected the best sights and the best values in accommodations and dining, so all you need to do is decide what interests you the most and what works within your budget.

The following sample 14-day itinerary includes three meals per day, lodging, and some sightseeing and will give you an idea of how you can plan your trip and approximately how much it will cost. You will have to decide if you want to fly, drive, or take a bus between destinations (see "Getting Around" in Chapter 3 for details on these costs).

For each day's meals and accommodations (per person, based on double occupancy) I've given you choices in three price categories: **Thrifty,** for those who want to be extra careful to save every penny; **Frommer,** for those who want to follow the Frommer budget and spend about $45 U.S. a day; and **Splurge,** for those who want to spend a little extra but still get great value.

Day 1: Arrive Auckland

Breakfast On flight.

Accommodations
Thrifty: Auckland Central Backpackers—NZ$18.50 (U.S. $12.05)
Frommer: Aachen House—NZ$41 (U.S. $26.65)
Splurge: Barrycourt Motor Inn—NZ$62 (U.S. $40.30)

Sightseeing Take self-guided walking tour of the waterfront—free.

Lunch
Thrifty: Downtown Centre Food Court—NZ$4 (U.S. $2.60)
Frommer: The Loaded Hog—NZ$6 (U.S. $3.90)
Splurge: Cin Cin on Quay—NZ$12 (U.S. 7.80)

Sightseeing Visit Auckland Museum—free.

Dinner
Thrifty: Kebab Kid—NZ$7 (U.S. $4.55)
Frommer: Angus Steak House—NZ$21 (U.S. $13.65)
Splurge: Sails—NZ$33 (U.S. 21.45)

Day 2: In Auckland

Breakfast
Thrifty: At Auckland Central Backpackers (prepared in communal kitchen)—NZ$4 (U.S. $2.60)
Frommer: At Aachen House—included in room rate
Splurge: At Barrycourt Motor Inn—NZ$10 (U.S. $6.50)

Accommodations Same as for Day 1.

Sightseeing Take ferry to Devonport—NZ$7 (U.S. $4.55) round-trip.

Lunch
Thrifty: La Casa Italiano—NZ$5 (U.S. $3.25)
Frommer: Carpe Diem—NZ$8 (U.S. $5.20)
Splurge: The Left Bank—NZ$12 (U.S. $7.80)

Dinner
Thrifty: Masonic Tavern—NZ$7 (U.S. $4.55)
Frommer: The Left Bank—NZ$21 (U.S. $13.65)
Splurge: Porterhouse Blue—NZ$32 (U.S. $20.80)

Day 3: To Bay of Islands

Breakfast Same as for Day 2.

Accommodations
Thrifty: Aimeo Cottage—NZ$25 (U.S. $16.25)
Frommer: Ounuwhao—NZ$38 (U.S. $24.70)
Splurge: Quality Resort Waitangi—NZ$75 (U.S. $48.75)

Lunch
Thrifty: A picnic—NZ$5 (U.S. $3.25)
Frommer: Strand Cafe—NZ$8 (U.S. $5.20)
Splurge: Duke of Marlborough—NZ$14 (U.S. $9.10)

Sightseeing
Visit Bay of Islands Visitor Centre and Christ Church—free.
Visit Russell Museum—NZ$2.50 (U.S. $1.65).

Dinner
Thrifty: Strand Cafe—NZ$8 (U.S. $5.20)
Frommer: Only Seafood—NZ$25 (U.S. $16.25)
Splurge: The Gables—NZ$31 (U.S. $20.15)

Day 4: In Bay of Islands

Breakfast
Thrifty: At Aimeo Cottage (prepared in unit)—NZ$3 (U.S. $1.95)
Frommer: At Ounuwhao—included in room rate
Splurge: At Quality Resort Waitangi—NZ$13 (U.S. $8.45)

Accommodations Same as for Day 3.

Sightseeing Take day trip to Cape Reinga—by bus (NZ$59–NZ$79/U.S. $38.35–$51.35) or by rental car.

Lunch En route—NZ$10 (U.S. $6.50) as part of bus tour or NZ$5 (U.S. $3.25) for picnic as part of drive.

Dinner **Thrifty:** At Aimeo Cottage (prepared in unit)—NZ$7 (U.S. $4.55)
Frommer: Bistro 40—NZ$26 (U.S. $16.90)
Splurge: Esmae's—NZ$29 (U.S. $18.85)

Day 5: To Rotorua

Breakfast Same as for Day 4.

Accommodations **Thrifty:** Ivanhoe Lodge—NZ$18 (U.S. $11.70)
Frommer: Te Ana Farm—NZ$45 (U.S. $29.25)
Splurge: Regal Geyserland Hotel—NZ$76 (U.S. $49.40)

Lunch (in Cambridge) **Thrifty:** Cambridge Country Store Cafe—NZ$5 (U.S. $3.25)
Frommer: Cambridge Country Store Cafe—NZ$6 (U.S. $3.90)
Splurge: The Grapevine—NZ$10 (U.S. $6.50)

Dinner **Thrifty:** Legends Bar & Cafe—NZ$7 (U.S. $4.55)
Frommer: At Te Ana Farm—NZ$25 (U.S. $16.25), including wine
Splurge: Lewisham's—NZ$35 (U.S. $22.75)

Day 6: In Rotorua

Breakfast **Thrifty:** At Ivanhoe Lodge (prepared in communal kitchen)—NZ$4 (U.S. $2.60)
Frommer: At Te Ana Farm—included in room rate
Splurge: At Regal Geyserland Hotel—NZ$10 (U.S. $6.50)

Accommodations Same as for Day 5.

Sightseeing Tour Whakarewarewa Thermal Reserve—NZ$10 (U.S. $6.50).

Lunch **Thrifty:** Chez Suzanne Coffee Shop—NZ$5 (U.S.$3.25)
Frommer: Sirocco—NZ$8 (U.S. $5.20)
Splurge: THC Rotorua Hotel—NZ$24 (U.S. $15.60), buffet

Sightseeing Visit Rainbow Springs and Rainbow Farm—NZ$13.50 (U.S. $8.80).

Dinner	**Frommer:** Maori concert and hangi dinner at THC Rotorua Hotel—NZ$45 (U.S. $29.25) **Splurge:** Maori concert and hangi dinner on an authentic *marae* (meeting place)—NZ$52 (U.S. $33.80)

Day 7: To Wellington

Breakfast	Same as for Day 6.
Accommodations	**Thrifty:** Trekkers Hotel—NZ$25 (U.S. $16.25) **Frommer:** Tinakori Lodge—NZ$43 (U.S. $27.95) **Splurge:** Harbour City Motor Inn—NZ$68 (U.S. $44.20)
Sightseeing	En route: Visit Craters of the Moon thermal area, Wairakei geothermal power station, Lake Taupo—free.
Lunch	**Thrifty:** Picnic en route—NZ$5 (U.S. $3.25) **Frommer:** Picnic en route—NZ$6 (U.S. $3.90) **Splurge:** Picnic en route—NZ$8 (U.S. $5.20)
Dinner	**Thrifty:** Backbenchers Pub & Cafe—NZ$11 (U.S. $7.15) **Frommer:** Ford's Cafe—NZ$16 (U.S. $10.40) **Splurge:** The Tug Boat—NZ$32 (U.S. $20.80)

Day 8: To Christchurch

Breakfast	**Thrifty:** At Trekkers Hotel—NZ$6 (U.S. $3.90) **Frommer:** At Tinakori Lodge—included in room rate **Splurge:** At Harbour City Motor Inn—NZ$10 (U.S. $6.50)
Accommodations	**Thrifty:** YMCA—NZ$23 (U.S. $14.90) **Frommer:** Alexandra Court Motel—NZ$48 (U.S. $31.20) **Splurge:** Cashmere House—NZ$95 (U.S. $61.75)
Transportation	Ferry from Wellington (North Island) to Picton (South Island)—NZ$38 (U.S. $24.70) normal fare, NZ$30 (U.S. $19.50) off-season
Lunch (in Picton)	**Thrifty:** Toot 'n' Whistle—NZ$5 (U.S. $3.25) **Frommer:** Toot 'n' Whistle—NZ$8 (U.S. $5.20) **Splurge:** Stokers—NZ$16 (U.S. $10.40)

Dinner
Thrifty: Main Street Cafe—NZ$12 (U.S. $7.80)
Frommer: Dux de Lux—NZ$21 (U.S. $13.65)
Splurge: Michael's—NZ$30 (U.S. $19.50)

Day 9: In Christchurch

Breakfast
Thrifty: At YMCA ("picnic" in room with food from Boulevard Bakehouse Cafe)—NZ$3 (U.S. $1.95)
Frommer: At Alexandra Court Motel ("picnic" as above)—NZ$3 (U.S. $1.95)
Splurge: At Cashmere House—included in room rate

Accommodations
Same as for Day 8.

Sightseeing
Visit Botanic Gardens and walk along Avon River—free.

Lunch
Thrifty: Cashel Street food court—NZ$5 (U.S. $3.25)
Frommer: Main Street Cafe—NZ$6 (U.S. $3.90)
Splurge: Dux de Lux—NZ$12 (U.S. $7.80)

Sightseeing
Listen to Wizard of Christchurch in Cathedral Square, visit Christchurch Cathedral, browse shops, and admire architecture of the Arts Centre—free.

Dinner
Thrifty: Italia Cafe—NZ$12 (U.S. $7.80)
Frommer: The Mythai—NZ$21 (U.S. $13.65)
Splurge: Pedro's—NZ$32 (U.S. $20.80)

Day 10: To Dunedin

Breakfast
Same as for Day 9.

Accommodations
Thrifty: Sahara Guesthouse—NZ$37 (U.S. $24.05)
Frommer: Farry's Motel—NZ$43 (U.S. $27.95)
Splurge: Southern Cross Hotel—NZ$70 (U.S. $45.50)

Sightseeing
Visit International Antarctic Visitor Centre—NZ$10 (U.S. $6.50).

Lunch (in Ashburton)
Thrifty: Mill House Cafe at Ashford Craft Shop—NZ$6 (U.S. $3.90)
Frommer: Mill House Cafe at Ashford Craft Shop—NZ$7 (U.S. $4.55)
Splurge: Mill House Cafe at Ashford Craft Shop—NZ$9 (U.S. $5.85)

Dinner
Thrifty: The Bank—NZ$6 (U.S. $3.90)
Frommer: Joseph Mellor—NZ$17 (U.S. $11.05)
Splurge: Bell Pepper Blues—NZ$36 (U.S. $23.40)

Day 11: In Dunedin

Breakfast — **Thrifty:** At Sahara Guesthouse—included in room rate
Frommer: At Farry's Motel ("picnic" in room)—NZ$3 (U.S. $1.95)
Splurge: At Southern Cross Hotel—NZ$10 (U.S. $6.50)

Accommodations — Same as for Day 10.

Sightseeing — Visit Otago Museum—free.

Lunch — **Thrifty:** Potpourri—NZ$4 (U.S. $2.60)
Frommer: The Bank—NZ$6 (U.S. $3.90)
Splurge: Joseph Mellor Restaurant—NZ$10 (U.S. $6.50)

Sightseeing — Tour Cadbury Confectionery Ltd. factory—free.

Dinner — **Thrifty:** Albert Arms Tavern—NZ$10 (U.S. $6.50)
Frommer: Golden Harvest—NZ$18 (U.S. $11.70)
Splurge: High Tide—NZ$26 (U.S. $16.90)

Day 12: To Milford

Breakfast — Same as for Day 11.

Accommodations — **Thrifty:** Milford Sound Lodge—NZ$23 (U.S. $14.95)
Frommer: THC Milford—NZ$42 (U.S. $27.30)
Splurge: THC Milford—NZ$107 (U.S. $69.55)

Lunch — **Thrifty:** Picnic en route—NZ$4 (U.S. $2.60)
Frommer: Picnic en route—NZ$5 (U.S. $3.25)
Splurge: Picnic en route—NZ$6 (U.S. $3.90)

Dinner — **Thrifty:** THC Public Bar—NZ$7 (U.S. $4.55)
Frommer: At THC Milford—NZ$30 (U.S. $19.50)
Splurge: At THC Milford—NZ$36 (U.S. $23.40)

Day 13: To Queenstown

Breakfast — **Thrifty:** At Milford Sound Lodge—NZ$4 (U.S. $2.60)
Frommer: At THC Milford ("picnic" in room)—NZ$4 (U.S. $2.60)
Splurge: At THC Milford—NZ$14 (U.S. $9.10)

Accommodations — **Thrifty:** Bumbles—NZ$20 (U.S. $13)
Frommer: Autoline Motel—NZ$43 (U.S. $27.95)
Splurge: The Stone House—NZ$77 (U.S. $50.05)

Sightseeing — Take boat trip on Milford Sound—NZ$38 (U.S. $24.70).

Lunch	**Thrifty:** Milford Cafe—NZ$5 (U.S. $3.25) **Frommer:** THC Public Bar—NZ$7 (U.S. $4.55) **Splurge:** At THC Milford—NZ$27 (U.S. $17.55), buffet
Dinner	**Thrifty:** The Cow—NZ$19 (U.S. $12.35) **Frommer:** Giuseppe's—NZ$20 (U.S. $13) **Splurge:** Solera Vino—NZ$30 (U.S. $19.50)

Day 14: To Auckland via Christchurch for Departure

Breakfast	**Thrifty:** At Bumbles—NZ$4 (U.S. $2.60) **Frommer:** At Autoline Motel ("picnic" in room)—NZ$4 (U.S. $2.60) **Splurge:** At The Stone House—included in room rate
Lunch (at Mount Cook)	**Thrifty:** The Hermitage coffee shop—NZ$5 (U.S. $3.25) **Frommer:** The Hermitage coffee shop—NZ$6 (U.S. $3.90) **Splurge:** Alpine Room at The Hermitage—NZ$29 (U.S. $18.85), buffet
Transportation	Drive to Christchurch, then fly to Auckland.
Dinner	On flight.

Total Estimated Cost per Person

Thrifty = NZ$762 (U.S. $495.30)
Frommer = NZ$1,176 (U.S. $764.40)
Splurge = NZ$1,962 (U.S. $1,275.30)

2

Getting to Know New Zealand

THERE ARE PROBABLY AS MANY MISCONCEPTIONS ABOUT NEW ZEALAND AS THERE ARE people who have never been there, and one that's particularly popular with Americans is the notion that New Zealand is virtually a suburb of Australia. Don't you believe it! True, both countries are in the Southern Hemisphere and on any map they appear to be close South Pacific neighbors. However, 1,000 miles of Tasman Sea separate them, and their separations are by no means limited to those of a watery nature.

One of the most basic differences between the two countries is also one of the most visible—the land itself. Australia presents a dramatic, hot landscape of brilliant reds and oranges ringed by splendid white beaches shading out to the deep blue of its oceans. New Zealand, on the other hand, offers the striking contrast of lush semitropical rain-forest greenery, cascading waterfalls, playful geysers, wondrous thermal grounds sporting halos of live steam, and thousands of miles of glorious coastline winding in and out of island-studded bays and harbors. In fact, there's such a wealth of blessings here that even the most hidebound urbanite will find it difficult to escape nature's lures—New Zealand is, above all else, the perfect place for getting back in touch with the harmony that should exist between humans and the environment.

1 The Lay of the Land

Surely one of the world's most beautiful countries, New Zealand is composed of two major islands—the North Island and the South Island—plus little Stewart Island pointing off toward Antarctica. It's bounded on the north and east by the South Pacific, on the west by the Tasman Sea, and on the south by the Southern Ocean. From tip to tip, New Zealand measures 1,000 miles, although at its widest it's no more than 280 miles across.

New Zealand's land area is comparable to that of the U.S. state of Colorado: 104,000 square miles. Its population totals 3.5 million—with 822,000 concentrated in Auckland; 326,000 in the capital of Wellington; 307,000 in the South Island's largest city, Christchurch; and 110,000 in Dunedin. Hamilton, with 149,000 inhabitants, is the largest inland city.

Within this country's perimeters is such an astounding array of natural beauty, sporting activities, and sightseeing "musts" that you should banish any thoughts of "doing" New Zealand in a few days or even a week—you couldn't even scratch the surface in that short a time.

It would be best to allow at least 10 days just for sampling the highlights—and I should warn you that once you're there, you'll want to stay months so you can see it all. Since you're not likely to have months to spare, in Chapter 3 you'll find suggested itineraries to help you use whatever time you have to see the sights and do the activities that interest you most (also see the 14-day itinerary, geared toward three budget levels, in Chapter 1). No matter what your itinerary, I'd be willing to bet that you'll be impressed with New Zealand.

For example, the North Island's riches begin with the Bay of Islands, rich in history and a special haven of tranquillity. Then there's the eastern "Sunrise Coast," where the first light of day illuminates beautiful headlands; Rotorua's steamy thermal hotspot; and Wellington's spectacular harbor and hills. And add to that Auckland's surprisingly sophisticated urban scene.

The South Island is reached via a marvelous ferry ride across Cook Strait and through the Marlborough Sounds. Here the Southern Alps cover more territory than the entire country of Switzerland; glaciers stretch toward the sea; Stewart Island dares you to come close to the South Pole; every day's drive is an education in the definition of *sheep station;* Dunedin unfolds its Scottish charms; and Christchurch waits to show you its "down under" version of England.

And this is just a taste of what New Zealand has to offer.

Geological Fault or Maui's Fish?

You have your choice of two theories about how New Zealand came to be.

Geologists say that its islands are the relatively young remnants of a continental mass separated by violent shifts in the earth's crust. Its location on a major fault line accounts for frequent earthquake activity, volcanic mountains, the drowned glacial valleys of Fiordland, and the string of mountain ranges that stretches (with a few interruptions) from the alpine peaks of the South Island up to the blunted headland at Cape Reinga.

However, the Maori have a far different story. According to Maori legend, in the days of the gods and demigods the frail fifth son of a woman named Taranga was thrown into the sea by his mother, who felt that the infant was too weak to survive. He was rescued by Rangi, the Sky Father, who raised him through childhood, then returned him to his amazed mother, complete with a full set of magical abilities and the enchanted jawbone of his grandmother. The overjoyed mother doted on Maui, her restored offspring, to such an extent that his brothers soon developed intense sibling jealousy, which really wasn't eased much when Maui pulled off such astonishing feats as snaring the sun in the pit from which it rose each morning, then smashing its face with that all-powerful jawbone until it was too weak to do anything but creep across the sky. This gave all the people longer days in which to fish and elicited abundant gratitude and respect for Maui.

When Maui set off to fish, his was always the record catch, while his nonmagical brothers barely brought home enough to feed their families—much to the consternation of their wives, who duly complained to Maui. With a condescending (and irritating) wave of his hand, Maui promptly promised his sisters-in-law one load of fish so large it would spoil before they could eat it all. They were delighted, but their husbands were frustrated, angry, and determined to beat Maui to the punch with one last fishing expedition, which they launched at dawn.

The clever (and probably obnoxious) Maui hid under the flooring mats of his brothers' canoe, armed with a special fish hook whose point was fashioned from a chip of the precious jawbone. It wasn't until they were well out to sea that he made his appearance, which sent his brothers into a rage. However, their luck was running true to form, so they grumpily agreed with Maui when he assured them that their luck would turn if they'd only sail out of sight of any land.

Sure enough, they soon filled the canoe with fish. It became so full, in fact, that they began to take on water, and the brothers suggested returning home. To their

IMPRESSIONS

One superstition seems general with all the tribes respecting the formation of the world; or, rather, of their own island. . . . They say a man, or a god, or some great spirit was fishing in his war-canoe, and pulled up a large fish, which instantly turned into an island; and a lizard came upon that, and brought up a man out of the water by his long hair; and he was the father of all the New Zealanders.

—Agustus Earle, 1832

consternation, the arrogant Maui insisted they sail still farther into the unknown waters and calmly produced his magic hook. The brothers then sailed on—bailing and complaining—until at last Maui struck his nose until it bled, smeared his blood on the hook as bait, and threw his line overboard while chanting an incantation for the "drawing up of the world."

What Maui hooked turned out to be a gigantic fish, as large as the gable of a *whare runanga* (meetinghouse), whose very size rendered it *tapu* (sacred). With the fish came the large wedge of land we know today as New Zealand's North Island. Maui, respectful of the tapu, quickly departed for home to get a priest, leaving his brothers with strict orders not to cut up the fish until his return. He was no sooner out of sight than they started scaling and cutting the huge fish.

The gods were much angered at such flagrant disregard for tapu, and they set that great fish to lashing about, throwing cut-up chunks in all directions—which is a perfect explanation for the existence of the North Island's mountains and offshore islands. And though we may call it the North Island, any Maori knows it's really Te Ika a Maui, "the Fish of Maui."

The South Island is actually Maui's canoe, with Stewart Island as its anchor stone. And up in Hawke's Bay that famous fish hook has been transformed into Cape Kidnappers.

As you travel around New Zealand, inquire about the history of local natural attractions—mountains, lakes, and so forth. Chances are there are Maori explanations for their existence that beat scientific theory hands down.

2 New Zealand: One Huge Botanical Garden

New Zealand has been, in a sense, one huge botanical garden during its relatively short life. Undisturbed for the most part by the destructive influence of humankind, its forests and plant life have flourished, regulated by no forces save those of nature. Luxuriant ground covering, ferns ranging from tiny plants attached to mossy tree trunks all the way to tree-size pongas, more than 100 species of trees, and garlands of starry white clematis and blossoms of other flowering vines have created hundreds of miles of cool, dim, tree-vaulted "cathedrals."

The first humans to arrive, themselves closely attuned to nature, accorded the forests due reverence, with just the proper mix of awe and fear. As Peter Hooper, one of New Zealand's best writers and a leading conservationist, says in his excellent book *Our Forests, Ourselves* (John McIndoe Ltd.), "Landscape possesses *mauri*—soul or mind—and it is the outward and visible form of an inward invisible power." An acute awareness of that quality is inescapable when you walk the present-day forests of New Zealand, and its effect can be profound. As Hooper goes on to say, "The tonic wildness of natural spaces is essential to the physical/mental/spiritual wholeness of the individual."

IMPRESSIONS

The day was the perfection of New Zealand weather, which is the perfection of all climates—hot, but rarely sultry; bright but not glaring, from the vivid green with which the earth is generally clothed.

—Bishop George Augustus Selwin, 1843

As if to reinforce the above, New Zealand's Department of Conservation stresses low-impact tourism and environmentally sensitive outdoor recreation.

Native Trees & Plants

In the northern quarter of the North Island you'll find the surviving stands of tall, stately kauri trees, whose hardwood trunks—unblemished by knots or other imperfections—were so prized for shipbuilding by early settlers. Replacement planting is now under way to bring back these magnificent trees for future generations.

During December and January, North Island cliffs and lakeshores are a mass of scarlet when the *pohutukawa* (or Christmas tree) bursts into bloom, while its kinsman, the *rata*, is doing likewise down on the South Island. In early spring, the *kowhai*, which makes no distinction between north and south but grows almost everywhere, is a profusion of large golden blossoms. The *totara* has always been much loved by the Maori, who find its light, durable timber just right for making canoes, as well as for their magnificent carvings. Then there are the pines, including the *rimu* (red), *matai* (black), *kahikatea* (white), and *Dacrydium laxifolium* (pigmy). And the beeches—red, black, and silver. Almost all are evergreen, and seasonal color changes are subtle.

New Zealand also has an astounding array of flowering plants, a full 80% of which are not to be found anywhere else in the world. The undisputed queen of blossoms has to be the world's largest buttercup: the Mount Cook lily. There are almost 60 varieties of mountain daisies, plus a curious "vegetable sheep," which grows in mountainous terrain and has large, cushiony blooms that look like sheep even when you take a close look. Bright orange-and-yellow "red hot pokers" look like just that. Up to a dozen fringed, saucer-shaped white blooms adorn a single flower stalk of the *hinau*, and the golden *kumarahou* bloom has been used over the years in medicinal herb mixtures.

Native & Imported Wildlife

An added joy in tramping through the forests is that you never have to be afraid to put your foot down—there's not one snake in the entire country. Nor are there any predatory animals. In fact, there's only one poisonous spider, and it's rarely found anywhere except on a few scattered sand dunes.

Most of New Zealand's animals did not originate here but were imported by various settler groups. The Maori brought dogs and rats. Captain Cook released a pig whose wild descendants are still about. Other importees include red deer, opossum, hedgehogs, weasels, and rabbits (which were brought over for skins and meat, yet became so numerous and destructive that another animal, the stoat, had to be brought in to control the burgeoning population).

As for birds, you'll see many curious species. The kiwi, whose name New Zealanders have adopted as their own, is one of the oddest. Wingless and about the size of a chicken, it lives in hollow trunks or holes in the ground, emerges only at night to forage for insects and worms with a long curved beak that has nostrils at its tip, and emits a shrill, penetrating whistle. Odder still is the fact that the female kiwi lays one gigantic egg, then leaves the hatching to the male. These days it's rare to see the kiwi in the wild, but you'll find them around the country in special kiwi houses that simulate nocturnal lighting so you can view them during "business" hours.

Down in the mountains of the South Island is a comical mountain parrot that's as bold as the kiwi is shy. The kea nests among the rocks but keeps an eye on the main

Oh Deer!

Homesick British colonists imported a number of animals to New Zealand. Some of these, like sheep and cattle, became the backbone of the economy. Others, such as rabbits, had no predators to contend with and so multiplied and became a serious threat to farmers. Six rabbits could—and often did—eat as much grass as one sheep. In 1893, 16 million rabbit skins were exported, but it wasn't until the Rabbit Destruction Council resorted to large-scale trapping and poison airdrops after World War II that the problem was brought under control.

The tale of the imported deer is even stranger. First introduced for sport in 1851, they, too, multiplied and caused widespread erosion by damaging and devouring back-country vegetation. Amateur hunters couldn't keep the population under control, so the government paid professional cullers to do the job. Many of these used helicopters to find the deer and as a platform from which to shoot.

During a visit to New Zealand in the late 1970s, I was invited to go flying with an American helicopter pilot who was culling deer on the west coast of the South Island. I took the spotter's seat, but—push come to shove—failed to report any sightings. Shoot Bambi? Not me.

Imagine my surprise when I returned to New Zealand a few years later and found deer being treated like members of the royal family. It seems someone had figured out that Asians would pay top dollar for antler velvet, from which they make medicine and aphrodisiacs. Deer farms sprang up everywhere and are today a major component of the agricultural industry. Venison and skins are exported to Western Europe and several Asian nations, but antler velvet is still the most-prized commodity.

roads and is quick to investigate newcomers. It's not unusual, for instance, to see as many as three camped alongside the road to Milford Sound. If you stop, keep a sharp eye on them—those cunning cut-ups are quick to steal jewelry or other shiny objects and to attack with their strong curved beaks such formidable targets as auto parts. In-the-know campers and trampers are careful to keep their gear well beyond the reach of the mischievous little kea.

If you hear a series of pure bell-like sounds pouring through the forest air, it's likely to be the song of the lovely bellbird. Only slightly different in sound is the handsome tui. Around swampy areas, those ear-piercing screams you hear in the night will be coming from the pukeko. And the forest-dwelling morepork's call (often heard at dusk or after dark) may give you a start—it sounds just like its name. The graceful gannet is found only on offshore islands, with one exception, Cape Kidnappers near Napier; there are white herons at Okarito, a unique albatross colony out from Dunedin, and penguins in many spots around the country.

As curious as are some New Zealand birds, however, none of them holds a candle to the tuatara, a reptilian "living fossil" whose prehistoric ancestors became extinct

IMPRESSIONS

The man who introduced the rabbit was banqueted and lauded, but they would hang him now if they could get him.

—Mark Twain, 1890

100 million years ago. It's completely harmless—that is, if its looks don't scare you to death. Shaped like a miniature dinosaur, complete with a spiny ridge down the back and a thick tail, it's protected by law and confined to offshore islets.

Prominent among marine animals that call New Zealand waters home are whales, dolphins, and seals.

The richness of New Zealand flora and fauna will be within easy reach wherever you find yourself around the country, and if you should miss some particular species, there are excellent zoos as well.

3 New Zealand Now

New Zealanders tend to be so . . . well, civilized. Generally speaking, their manners are impeccable and their innate sense of decency often sends them rushing to the aid of strangers. New Zealanders, above all, possess a strong respect for order in their daily lives. Things work as they're supposed to work—and if they don't, somebody fixes them. In short, all the human virtues you so rarely see elsewhere are in abundant supply in New Zealand. It shouldn't take you long to realize the truth in the oft-heard remark that the country is "20 years behind the times."

The Maori & Pakeha Cultures

In modern New Zealand, it's to the credit of both the Maori and the Pakeha (white-skinned people) that their widely differing cultures and a history encompassing long years of cruel warfare have been at least partially overcome, generating an environment that's peaceful though not entirely trouble-free. The difficult journey has been similar to that of 20th-century indigenous people in other parts of the world. Today Maori and Pakeha goodwill is being tested as they debate the provisions of the 155-year-old Treaty of Waitangi, which functions as a Bill of Rights for Maori New Zealanders. By asserting their rights, the Maori are regaining confiscated land and fishing rights as well as making gains to have more emphasis on their culture and language placed in the country's educational system.

The Maori have seen their numbers increase from a low of 42,000 at the turn of the century to more than 350,000 today, about 10% of the population. Once a people suffering from the imported alcoholism and diseases that produced a depression afflicting the race as a whole with a debilitating lethargy, they have become a largely urban people, participating in the middle-class benefits of the Pakeha while holding fast to as much of their traditional culture as has survived those early years of European settlement.

They have demonstrated a surprising adaptability to the ways of democracy and have improved and honed to expertise the skills they acquired from mission schools, making more and more additions as industrial development moved across the country.

The political arena has afforded the Maori access to power acquired through the oratorial prowess and widespread popularity of such leaders as Apirana Ngata, Te Rangi Hiroa, and Maui Pomare—all of whom were knighted and served as cabinet members—and their Young Maori Party. Because of their political, educational, and professional achievements, Maori candidates often are elected by substantially Pakeha constituencies. And they have managed to imbue most of the Pakeha population with an appreciation for their ancient culture.

To experience that culture in its purest form, visitors these days must travel to Rotorua (a Maori center) or stumble on a communal village. It's here you'll find wood carvers and mat weavers demonstrating the arts that adorn their great meetinghouses (whare runanga) with such stylized masterpieces and their bodies with such colorful garb.

Yet even deep in the heart of New Zealand's largest cities (which are home for some 76% of the Maori population), it's easy to observe the traditional lifestyle rhythm that supersedes the Pakeha alarm clock. When a Maori loved one dies, respect must be shown with attendance at the *tangi,* or funeral, no matter how far away it is. Ancient tribal celebrations also demand time off work, and one's family always comes first. And while the old war *hakas* (complete with foot stomping and protruding tongues) and graceful *poi* dance are mainly performed in shows staged for visitors, most Maori city dwellers have a large repertoire of such melodies as the world-famous "Now Is the Hour" (or, Maori Farewell), which was actually written by an Englishman before World War I. And in national elections, they are free to vote in the Pakeha district in which they reside or in one of the four official Maori electorates.

One sad by-product of the Maori move from rural to urban areas, however, has been a gradual weakening of those tribal and family ties that have always been at the very heart of their culture. When there is no *marae* in which to gather at the end of the day, youngsters tend to lose contact with their elders, and even the elders are less closely bound together. In some of the North Island cities (where the Maori

Did You Know . . . ?

- Two-thirds of New Zealanders live north of Lake Taupo.
- New Zealand's 3.5 million human population takes a numerical back seat to its animal population of 62 million sheep and 9 million cattle.
- *Lion New Zealand* won the Whitbred Around-the-World sailing race in 1986, *Steinlager II* won this prestigious international competition in 1990, and *New Zealand Endeavour* won in 1994.
- Look carefully when you pull the plug in a New Zealand washbasin or bathtub—chances are the water will drain out counterclockwise rather than clockwise as you're accustomed to in the Northern Hemisphere.
- The eruption that created Lake Taupo in A.D. 186 was a hundred times greater than that of Mount St. Helens in 1980.
- New Zealand is located between latitudes 34° south and 47° south—the equivalent of Mediterranean Europe.
- To publicize the new sporting activity he'd invented, New Zealander A. J. Hackett bungee-jumped off the Eiffel Tower in 1987.
- New Zealand is a nuclear-free zone.
- Until they became a popular export, kiwifruit were known in New Zealand as Chinese gooseberries.
- New Zealand's public school teachers under age 30 must serve three years teaching in rural schools before they can be considered for raises.
- New Zealand has no native land mammals and no snakes.

concentration is heaviest), social problems have developed that can be traced directly to the feeling of isolation that has developed among a younger generation adrift without strong identity support systems. To counteract that trend, the Maori are establishing urban marae, which are used daily by numerous groups. The ancient ties are gaining strength, as are the ancient teachings, which are passed down to the young from their elders.

You'll also find most of New Zealand's Pakeha living in the cities. Or at least working in cities. More and more, as such centers as Auckland grow larger and larger, the people who work there go home at night to the same sort of small suburban satellite communities popular in the United States. Those miles of dual-lane motorways leading into Auckland, and the sprawling shopping malls in the dozen or so communities that surround it, will have a surprising familiarity.

LIFE ON THE FARM

Most visitors are fascinated by the unfamiliar lifestyle of those who live and work on New Zealand's farmlands. From high-country "stations," which concentrate on wool production, to lower pastures, which fatten up lamb and mutton on the hoof, you'll certainly click your cameras at lovable sheep that seem to have been born with a one-track mind—a fun game when you're traveling is to try to find the sheep that's *not* eating!

For farmers this is a hardworking life of comparative isolation, with socializing more or less relegated to the occasional drop-in at the local tavern. Some of your own best socializing may very well come from just such a drop-in if your timing is good enough to coincide with that of one or two of the farmers. Or, better yet, try to be in a tavern when a gaggle of shearers comes in at the end of a busy day.

On the North Island, the cattle that supply rich cream, butter, and milk—as well as the extra 10 pounds you'll probably carry home—spend winters and summers in the pastures, for grass grows year round in this perfect climate. The New Zealand dairyman is more likely to be found in city or small-town watering holes, since his grazing lands are not very spread out and towns are more plentiful up north.

Actually, about three-quarters of the people in the cities depend on the output of these country folk for prosperity, so involved are they in the processing and marketing of farm products.

THE MAORI LANGUAGE

The Maori came very close to losing their language, with its colorful and vivid imagery. Living in a predominantly European culture, they were forced by circumstance and education to use the English language. However, the growth of *kohanga reo,* or language nests, has resulted in thousands of Maori preschoolers' and their parents' learning the beautiful Maori language from tribal elders, and it's being heard increasingly in homes, schools, and universities. It's also often heard on the radio, and the traditional Maori greeting, *Haere Mai,* is sometimes used to begin evening TV newscasts.

You'll always be surrounded by Maori words and phrases, in both names of places and names of objects always identified by their Maori names. It's a lot more fun to travel around New Zealand if you know, for example, that *roto* is the Maori word for "lake" and *rua* is the word for "two"—hence the name Rotorua. Bear in mind that in the Maori language some words may be both singular and plural, thus such words as *Maori, Pakeha,* and *Kea* never need an *s* to denote the plural (like the English words *deer* and *fish*).

The following are a few of the most commonly used prefixes and suffixes for place names:

Ao Cloud
Ika Fish
Nui Big, or plenty of
Roto lake
Rua Cave, or hollow, or two (Rotorua's two lakes)
Tahi One, single
Te The
Wai Water
Whanga Bay, inlet, or stretch of water

These are other frequently used words:

Ariki Chief or priest
Atua Supernatural being, such as a god or demon
Haka Dance (war, funeral, etc.)
Hangi An oven made by filling a hole with heated stones; and the feast roasted in it.
Karakia Prayer or spell
Kereru Wood pigeon
Kumara Sweet potato
Mana Authority, prestige, psychic force
Marae Courtyard, village common
Mere War club made of greenstone (jade)
Pa Stockade or fortified place
Pakeha White-skinned person; primarily used to refer to those of European descent
Poi Bulrush ball with string attached twirled in action song
Tangi Funeral mourning or lamentation
Tapu Under religious or superstitious restriction ("taboo")
Tiki Human image, sometimes carved of greenstone
Whare House

Politics

In 1852 the British Parliament passed the New Zealand Constitution Act, and self-government was administered through a governor appointed in London, a Legislative Council appointed by the governor, and an elected House of Representatives. It should be of little surprise that these representatives were elected by Pakeha landowners, for the vote was extended only to "individual landowners"—the Pakeha successfully argued that the Maori communal landownership disenfranchised them. That situation was corrected in 1867, and women were granted the right to vote in 1893, a full quarter of a century before it happened in Britain or America.

The government also pioneered such social reforms as minimum-wage laws, old-age pensions, paid vacations, labor arbitration, and child-welfare programs. New Zealand thus became in many respects a "welfare state," its economy based on the export of lamb, mutton, butter, and eggs to England. Throughout the ups and downs of economic developments since, New Zealanders have retained their humanitarian approach to government.

New Zealand's parliamentary form of government recognizes Elizabeth II as head of state, and she's represented by a governor-general, with a locally elected prime minister and members of Parliament. At the present the prime minister is Jim Bolger, and the governor-general is Dame Catherine Tizard. The two main political parties are National and Labour. In the capital, Wellington, all government business is conducted in the Beehive—a building named for its shape.

Religion

Missionary efforts in New Zealand were spearheaded by the Rev. Samuel Marsden, who arrived in 1814. It took the missionaries years to make the first Maori convert. It shouldn't be surprising that it took so long, for deeply imbedded in the indigenous culture were such practices as cannibalism, infanticide, and the worship of war gods. By embracing the doctrines of Christianity they relinquished much of the sensual beauty embodied in their complex, age-old religious traditions. Naked bodies had to be covered, symbolic carvings of fertility gods had to be destroyed, and the reverence and fear once accorded a tribe's chief had to be transferred to their new god.

Today, only artistic vestiges of the ancient pagan gods remain. A majority of New Zealanders—Maori and Pakeha—practice the Protestant religions, with most denominations represented and the Church of England first numerically. Catholic congregations may also be found around the country.

Art

MAORI ART

Much of New Zealand's most distinctive art originates with Maori traditions, dating back to the Archaic Maori (or moa-hunters), whose bone carvings and stone work are essentially superb sculpture. The Classic Maori who came later glorified the valor of their warriors in the ornamentation of bone, wood, and stone weapons, as well as war canoes and artistic tattoos and garments.

Dating from the Historic Maori period, communal meetinghouses (whare runanga) hold some of the finest Maori art, with tikis (human forms of wood, bone, or greenstone representing ancestors or gods); *manaia* (beaked-headed "birdman" figures with human forms, whose meaning and origins remain a mystery); *pakake* (stylized whales and other creatures of the deep); and symbols of religious or powerful supernatural beings (often represented by trees and other natural objects they were believed to inhabit).

The Modern Maori period actually dates from the mid-19th century, and during the 20th century it has featured more abstract and stylized applications of traditional Maori art from all periods, thanks in large part to Sir Apirana Ngata and Sir Peter Buck (Te Rangi Hiroa), who spearheaded the revival and modernization of ancient art forms.

Many outstanding examples of Maori art are found in the Auckland Museum's Maori Court and in the Bay of Plenty and Rotorua areas of the North Island.

PAKEHA ART

Since the earliest arrival of Europeans, painters have worked to capture New Zealand's magnificent light and landscape on canvas. One of the most popular of today's traditional landscape painters is Peter McIntyre, while Gordon Walters concentrates on abstractions of such ancient symbols as the *koru* (whose stylized interpretation has been adopted by Air New Zealand) in a style reminiscent of Mondrian or Klee.

Works of these leading New Zealand painters command substantial prices, but there are many fine—unknown—painters working away in virtually every region of the country, and some of my most prized New Zealand souvenirs are paintings picked up around the country for very low prices. I also make it a practice to keep an eye out for pottery and ceramics—many such items are works of art as well as functional.

Architecture

Although on every visit I find Auckland, Wellington, Christchurch, and Dunedin dotted with more and more glass-and-steel skyscrapers, even in these cities you're likely to experience a rush of recognition (especially if you're a fan of westerns) at the sight of colonial-style homes, shopfronts, and roofed sidewalks that could've been imported from America's Wild West. Indeed, this architectural style arrived in New Zealand in the early 1800s, at the same time settlers were building similar structures in the western United States.

Along with those modern high-rises you'll find a smattering of Mediterranean and ultramodern residences, most located along waterfront drives or in resort areas. Dunedin, on the other hand, is a treasure trove of Victorian, Edwardian, and Flemish Renaissance architecture, with public buildings boasting towers and turrets, spires and gables.

Literature

Short-story writer Katherine Mansfield and novelist Janet Frame are two of New Zealand's literary giants. Both have written from the perspective of a love-hate relationship with their native country, as did poet/satirist A. R. D. Fairburn. The work of James K. Baxter, New Zealand's most gifted poet, concerns religion and social injustices. Dame Ngaio Marsh was an internationally known mystery writer. And the late Sylvia Ashton-Warner was both a respected novelist and an educator.

Novelist and naturalist Peter Hooper celebrates the South Island's West Coast, where he lives and teaches, interweaving legend and myth with historical fact. Maurice Gee is one of the country's most popular contemporary novelists, and Maurice Shadbolt is another favorite storyteller.

In recent years more and more writing of high literary quality has emerged from the Maori community. Writing in English, such authors as Keri Hulme, Rowley Habib, Witi Ihimaera, and Patricia Grace have brought to life the Maori experience in New Zealand.

For specific titles by these authors, see "Famous New Zealanders" and "Recommended Books and Films," later in this chapter.

Cuisine

FOOD

Ask almost anyone about New Zealand's food and the response will likely be "lamb." Well, I'm told by my Kiwi friends that the best lamb gets shipped out to Britain and America. Nonetheless, I've had excellent lamb in New Zealand—as well, alas, as some that wasn't very good. No matter what the quality, it's served as a roast more often than not, and a well-done roast at that. Quite frankly, I've become very fond of roast hogget (that's sheep a little older than lamb and a little younger than mutton), and I suspect that's what often comes to the table under the "lamb" label. What's not very

IMPRESSIONS

> *The longer I live the more I turn to New Zealand, I thank God I was born in New Zealand. A young country is a real heritage, though it takes time to recognize it. But New Zealand is in my very bones.*
>
> —Katherine Mansfield, 1922

well known outside New Zealand is its beef—superb. Steaks and roasts are plentiful and inexpensive. In the last few years venison has also appeared in many restaurants.

The star of Kiwi cuisine, as far as I'm concerned, is seafood—always fresh and of a wide variety. Bluff oysters are a treat—they're large and tangy, with a strong taste of the sea. Then there are the tiny whitebait, usually served in fritters, sometimes crisply fried. The crayfish (you'll recognize the taste as that of the New Zealand rock lobster you can buy frozen in the States) may be more expensive than other seafood, but they're worth every penny. And a fish with which I'm on a first-name basis—the John Dory—is as sweet and succulent as any I've ever tasted.

Up in the north of the North Island you can sometimes find toheroa soup, a delicacy made from a small shellfish much like a cockle that's served in a rich chowder. Trout, of course, abound in New Zealand rivers and lakes, but they're not sold commercially (seems Kiwis adhere to the theory that for such a sporting fish it'd be a deep indignity to be eaten by anyone who hadn't landed it in a fair fight).

Dairy products, too, play a featured role in the New Zealand diet, and you'll know why after your first taste of rich, creamy milk, butter, and ice cream. The first two are served in generous portions in restaurants and guesthouses, so enjoy. New Zealand cheeses are also delicious and relatively inexpensive. A loaf of Vogel bread (rich whole-grain bread that you'll find in almost any health-food store and many supermarkets), a selection of cheeses, and some fresh fruit make the perfect picnic lunch.

You'll find meat pies everywhere—from lunch counters in railway and bus stations to pubs to take-out shops. These thick-crusted little pies filled with chunks of meat and gravy can be delicious if they're the homemade variety, with light, flaky crusts and just the right combination of mild spices and herbs. Keep an eye out for the HOMEMADE sign, which will be more prevalent than you might imagine—avoid whenever you can the tasteless factory-made pies. When it comes to fast food, for better or worse, McDonald's is very popular in New Zealand.

The traditional New Zealand dessert is pavlova (named after the prima ballerina Anna Pavlova): a large meringue shaped like a large cake, baked slowly at a low temperature to form a crusty outside and a tender inside. Its top is usually filled with whipped cream and fruit (kiwifruit when available)—marvelous!

DRINK

Beer is the closest thing to a national drink, and you'll have to do a bit of sampling to find your favorite brew among the many brands—friends of mine spend a lot of time debating the merits of DB (Dominion Breweries), Lion, Steinlager, and a few others. Be cautious, however, when testing those labeled "export"—they're more than twice as potent as American beer. If you're a dedicated beer drinker or have a large party, you'll save money by ordering a "jug of draft," which holds about five 8-ounce glasses.

Every year, New Zealand's vineyards produce better and better **wines.** McWilliams, Montana, Mission, Corbans, and Penfolds—big companies that started producing bulk wine about 30 years ago—have now been joined by boutique wineries that yield small amounts of world-class vintages. My favorite wineries to visit are in the Marlborough District: Hunter's, Cloudy Bay, and Cellier Le Brun—the last the only *méthode champenoise* specialist in the country.

The Hawkes Bay region also produces some great chardonnays and cabernets that compare favorably with their Napa Valley counterparts. While, in general, New Zealand's white wines are of a higher standard than its reds, Te Mata in the Hawkes Bay area has produced some award-winning cabernet sauvignons.

At the 1994 Sydney International Wine Competition, where there were 1,030 entries, New Zealand won 15 of the 19 gold medals. The top New Zealand entrant was Villa Maria Reserved Barrique Chardonnay 1991.

Alcohol is sold in licensed premises, bottle shops, and wholesale bottle stores (the best bargains are found in the last). Wholesale does not mean they won't sell individual bottles (though some have minimum-purchase requirements), so look for that name, usually in city-center shopping areas. Licensed hotels serve drinks in their bars and lounges, and most cafés and restaurants are also licensed—some to sell alcohol and some to let you bring your own.

Note: New Zealand's drinking-and-driving laws are *strictly* enforced. The wise visitor will do as the locals do and take a taxi home after imbibing.

Evening Entertainment

Except in larger cities, nightlife is pretty quiet. New Zealand will have little appeal for travelers who like a regular routine of swinging nightlife that goes on into the wee hours. In Auckland and Wellington there are plenty of nightspots or other entertainment possibilities, and Christchurch has a busy casino. And, of course, there are the Maori concerts in Rotorua and nighttime visits to Waitomo's glowworm grotto.

In a more cultural vein, there's quite good theater around the country, often featuring works by local playwrights. Check out the Mercury Theatre in Auckland, Downstage and Circa in Wellington, and the Court in Christchurch. Musically, the Aotea Centre in Auckland is a major venue for concerts, opera, and ballet. In addition, in large cities look for performances of the New Zealand Symphony, Auckland's Philharmonia, and the New Zealand String Quartet, plus the Royal New Zealand Ballet.

Lucky you if you happen to be in Wellington in a year of that city's biennial International Festival of the Arts, featuring internationally known overseas and local artists. Usually held in March, the festival in next scheduled for 1996.

My very best advice, however, is to do as the Kiwis do—enjoy full, bracing days of outdoor activity, followed by a satisfying evening meal, followed by quiet visits with friends or a little time in front of the TV, followed by an early bedtime. It makes a refreshing change from our frenetic pace at home, and you may be surprised to find how ready you are for those early evenings after a day or so of heavy sightseeing.

Sports & Recreation

SPECTATOR SPORTS

RUGBY On the sports scene rugby dominates from Easter through September, with Saturday matches featuring Kiwi males from schoolboys to businessmen to members of the national team, the All Blacks. International matches are held in Auckland's Eden Park, Wellington's Athletic Park, Dunedin's Carisbrook Park and Christchurch's Lancaster Park. If you're a football nut at home and think U.S. players are pretty tough hombres, be sure to take in at least one match to watch the lads rough-and-tumble around the oval in knee pants—with nary a padded shoulder to be seen.

HORSE RACING After rugby, it's horse racing that claims national affection. There are 271 days of licensed racing (133 of trotting) during the year, and races take place in informal beach settings or open fields with the same degree of enthusiasm as those at the larger tracks around the country. In January is the New Zealand Cup, a highlight of the racing year—if you're here and overcome by gambling fever, go ahead and indulge: Betting is perfectly legal, both on and off the track.

RECREATION

FISHING Angling for rainbow and brown trout can put dinner on the table as well as provide a day in the open. Rotorua and Taupo are trout-fishing centers, but it's hard to fish any river or lake in the country without coming up with a good catch. The season is long—from the first Saturday in October through the end of April (year round at Rotorua and Taupo), and you can buy a special one-month Tourist Fishing License from most fishing-tackle or sporting-goods stores.

Kiwis Play for Keeps

New Zealand's sporting statistics are nothing short of amazing. Not only does the country continually win more medals in the Olympics than nations with many times its population, but also it has proven itself a serious competitor in numerous other international events.

The explanation for this depends, of course, on whom you ask. One popular opinion is that Kiwi kids work hard to develop their skills because their families faithfully attend all their events and enthusiastically support their interests. Those who subscribe to this theory are worried that the introduction of weekend shopping hours will be the beginning of the end of New Zealand's sports prowess.

I've also heard that New Zealanders are passionate about sports because their inherited British reserve inhibits them from expressing their emotions in other arenas. While that may or may not be true, there certainly is a common belief in New Zealand that the way to recognizable achievement is through athletic effort.

Runners Peter Snell and Murray Halberg won gold medals in the 1960 Olympics, and John Walker won gold for his 1,500-meter run in 1976. In the 1984 Olympics, kayaker Ian Ferguson won three golds and Mark Todd brought home New Zealand's first equestrian gold medal.

Both Rod Dixon and Alison Roe have set records in the New York City Marathon. Chris Lewis made his mark in tennis; Bob Charles's game is golf.

Richard Hadlee became a hero on the cricket pitch. The All Blacks, the country's rugby team, inspire nothing less than religious zeal in their followers. Cricket remains popular, and the nation's netball team is world-class.

New Zealand's first America's Cup participation was in Fremantle, Australia, in 1986. They captured international attention then and continue to earn the respect of the yachting community. In 1987, *KZ-7* won the World Championship in Sardinia.

Superlative sailor Peter Blake won the 1986 Whitbred Around-the-World Race in *Lion New Zealand* and outdid himself by winning a second time in 1990 in *Steinlager II.* Grant Dalton followed in Blake's path and won the 1994 Whitbred in *New Zealand Endeavour.*

New Zealand's women sailors excel, too. Two female Kiwis were chosen for the 1995 all-women America's Cup team: Jane Oetking and Leslie Egnot. Egnot won a silver medal in the 1992 Olympics and led her team to second place in the 1994 World Championship.

Deep-sea fishing comes into its own along some 300 miles of the North Island's coastline. Waters less than an hour from shore hold such trophies as marlin, shark (mako, thresher, hammerhead, tiger), five species of tuna, broadbill, and yellowtail. The season runs from mid-January through April, and you'll find well-equipped bases at the Bay of Islands, Whitianga in Mercury Bay, Tauranga, and Whakatane. No license is required.

For more information on fishing, see Chapter 4.

GOLF There are over 300 registered golf clubs in New Zealand, and members of overseas clubs are granted guest privileges at most private clubs. Clubs and a "trundler" (don't expect motorized carts) can be rented, and greens fees are low. One of the most outstanding courses is 50 miles south of Rotorua at Wairakei. You may find courses crowded on weekends, much less so during the week.

HIKING Trekking, or tramping, is another popular sport, and as you move around the country you'll find good tracks almost always at hand. The 10 national parks, which cover more than five million acres, all have well-defined trails, and many provide bunkhouses or huts for overnight stops. Even when you're based in a city there'll be scenic walks in the vicinity; I'll tell you about some of them in the chapters to come, and tourist offices can furnish brochures for their areas.

In fact, it's possible to hike most of the 1,000-mile length of New Zealand along both regional and local trails. The most famous walk—and one of the most splendid—is the guided four-day Milford Track in Fiordland National Park, which draws trekkers from around the world. Other popular trails include the Routeburn, Hollyford, Abel Tasman, and Heaphy. You can make a reservation for a guided walk through tourist offices—or, if you'd like to strike out on your own, contact the Department of Conservation.

For information on the best hikes in New Zealand, see Chapter 4.

Tramping is best in New Zealand from late November through April, when temperatures are their most moderate.

SKIING New Zealand has some of the best ski terrain in the world. The season runs from mid-July through September, picking up when the North American ski season is ending. Major South Island ski fields are at Queenstown, Tekapo, Wanaka, Mount Hutt, and—for advanced skiers—famed Mount Cook. At Mount Cook you fly by skiplane to the 8,000-foot-high head of the Tasman Glacier and ski down the 12-mile run. Good North Island skiing can be found at Whakapapa and Turoa.

For more information on skiing trips and snowboarding, see Chapter 4.

IMPRESSIONS

Lo! Here where each league hath its fountains
In isles of deep fern and tall pine,
And breezes snow-cooled on the mountains,
Or keen from the limitless brine,
See men to the battlefield pressing
To conquer one foe—the stern soil,
Their kingship in labor expressing
Their lordship in toil.
—William Pember Reeves, 1893

WATER SPORTS New Zealanders are water bugs! Anytime they're not slaving away in an office or on a farm or in some other workplace, you'll find them in the water, on the water, or fishing the waters. Visitors can participate in all kinds of water sports. There are pleasant beaches in the Bay of Islands, in the Gisborne area, in the Marlborough Sounds area, and around Nelson. Surfing is especially good around the Bay of Plenty, with Tauranga offering what a Kiwi friend assures me is the best surf of any New Zealand beach. Sailing is available to visitors in the Bay of Islands, where you can indulge in deep-sea fishing as well.

For more information on boating trips and other water sports, see Chapter 4.

4 New Zealand Then

Dateline

- **950** Estimated date of first New Zealand landfall by Maori.
- **Mid-1300s** First great influx of Maori settlers.
- **1642** Abel Tasman becomes first European to discover South Island.
- **1769** Capt. James Cook begins six-month mapping of North and South Islands.
- **1773** Cook's second visit to New Zealand.
- **1777** Cook's third and final visit to New Zealand.
- **1792** First sealers and whalers arrive in New Zealand waters.
- **1814** First Christian missionary, Rev. Samuel Marsden, arrives in Bay of Islands.
- **1833** James Busby named as "British Resident" under jurisdiction of New South Wales.
- **1839–43** New Zealand Company sends out 57 ships carrying 19,000 settlers.
- **1840** Treaty of Waitangi with Maori chiefs signed in Bay of Islands.

➤

MAORI SETTLEMENT

When it comes to New Zealand's first inhabitants, there's more than one theory as to how they settled here. From the mists of prehistory comes the Maori legend of Kupe, who sailed from the traditional homeland of the Polynesians, Hawaiki, around A.D. 950. Even legend doesn't tell us exactly where Hawaiki was located in the vast South Pacific, but present-day authorities believe it was one of the Society Islands group that includes Tahiti. One version of Kupe's adventures has it that he murdered the carver Hoturapa and with the murdered man's wife and canoe set off on a long, wandering voyage, which eventually brought the pair to the place he named Aotearoa, which means "land of the long white cloud." Another says that he was in pursuit of a mammoth octopus when he happened onto New Zealand. Both versions agree that he returned to Hawaiki, taking with him sailing instructions for reaching the uninhabited "Fish of Maui." From some historians comes another explanation—that the first Maori canoes to reach New Zealand came by accident, after having been blown off course at sea.

In the 12th century, two more Maori canoes are said to have touched the shores of Aotearoa. A young Polynesian, Whatonga, was swept out to sea during canoe races, and his grandfather, Toi, went in search of him. When the two were reunited somewhere in the Whakatane region in the Bay of Plenty, they found people already living there; the newcomers intermarried with those we know simply as moa-hunters because they hunted a meaty, wingless bird by that name, which reached heights of up to 13 feet. Nothing more is known about them, and they are sometimes referred to as the Archaic Maori. Descendants of the two Polynesian canoers and moa-hunters now form the basis of two of today's Maori tribes.

It was not until the mid-14th century that Maori arrived in great numbers. They came from Hawaiki because of the devastating tribal wars that had erupted in the wake of overpopulation and severe food shortages. According to Maori tradition, seven oceangoing canoes sailed in a group, which has come to be known as "the fleet." Others sailed in groups of one or two; some came singly. On making landfall, canoe groups kept together, settling in various parts of the country, and it is to these first canoes that most modern-day Maori trace their roots.

By the time "the fleet" arrived, the moa had been hunted to extinction, along with other bird species, such as giant rails, swans, and geese. There were, however, bounteous supplies of fish and seafood to be had for the taking, as well as berries and a few other edible plants, which were supplemented by such tropical plants as taro, yams, and kumara (a kind of sweet potato) that had come in the canoes from Hawaiki. Dogs and rats had also been canoe passengers and became an important source of protein. The cultivation of these imported vegetables and animals gradually led the Maori to become an agricultural society living in permanent villages centered around a central marae (village common or courtyard) and whare runanga (meetinghouse). It was in these villages that the distinctive Maori art forms of wood carving and tattooing evolved, along with a strong sense of family loyalty and total harmony with their environment. It was this culture that thrived at the time of Capt. James Cook's first contact with New Zealand's Maori.

EUROPEAN DISCOVERY

The first recorded sighting of New Zealand by Europeans came on December 13, 1642, when Abel Tasman, scouting new trade territory for the Dutch East India Company, spied what he described as "a great high, bold land" in the Hokitika region of the South Island's west coast. Sailing north in his two tall-masted ships, the *Heemskirk* and *Zeehaen,* he entered Golden Bay on December 18 and encountered the Maori without ever setting foot on land. As the two ships lay at anchor in the peaceful bay, several war canoes put out from shore and their occupants shouted challenges from a safe distance. The next day, however, they were bolder and attacked a cockboat rowing from one of Tasman's ships to the other, killing four sailors in the brief battle before withdrawing. Tasman, dismayed at this hostility and disinclined to

Dateline

- **1844** Maori Chief Hone Heke chops down British flagpole in Bay of Islands, beginning a 20-year revolt centered around land rights.
- **1852** New Zealand Constitution Act passed by British Parliament.
- **1860s** Discovery of gold on South Island's west coast and North Island's east coast, creating several boomtowns.
- **1860–81** Second Maori War over land rights.
- **1882** Refrigeration introduced; first shipment of lamb to England.
- **1893** Voting rights extended to women.
- **1914–18** 100,000 New Zealanders join Australia–New Zealand Army Corps to fight in World War I; New Zealand loses more soldiers per capita than any other nation.
- **1939** New Zealand enters World War II.
- **1947** Statute of Westminster adopted by government; New Zealand gains full independence from Britain.
- **1951** New Zealand ratifies Australia–New Zealand–United States (ANZUS) mutual security pact.
- **1960s** New Zealand begins monitoring radioactivity in region as France accelerates nuclear testing in its Polynesian possessions.
- **1965** New Zealand troops sent to Vietnam.

➤

seek reprisals, fired at the retreating canoes and put out to sea. For many years afterward, lovely Golden Bay was known as Murderer's Bay, as it was christened by Tasman on that December day.

As it turned out, this was his only glimpse of the Maori since bad weather forced him to proceed up the west coast of the North Island. He failed to find a suitable landing spot so he left what he charted as a vast southern continent to sail on to Tonga and Fiji. But for that bad weather and the hostile Maori, the first European exploration of New Zealand would almost certainly have been Dutch. However, that distinction was left for an Englishman more than a century later.

THE COMING OF CAPTAIN COOK

When Capt. James Cook left England in 1768 on the 368-ton bark *Endeavour,* he was under orders from George III to sail to Tahiti to observe the transit of the planet Venus across the sun, a once-a-century happening. But the Yorkshireman carried "secret additional orders," which he opened only when his initial duty was accomplished. King George had directed him to sail southwest in search of the "continent" reported by Tasman. If he found it uninhabited, he was to plant the English flag and claim it for the king; if not, his instructions were to take possession of "convenient situations"—but only with the consent of the indigenous people. In addition, he was to study the nature of the soil, to examine the flora and fauna, and to make charts of the coastal waters.

It was on October 7, 1769, that New Zealand was first sighted by the surgeon's boy, Nicholas Young, from his perch in the mast. Naming the headland (in the Gisborne area) Young Nick's Head, Captain Cook sailed into a crescent-shaped bay and put down anchor. A rather kindly man, Captain Cook made every effort to cultivate Maori friendship, communicating by way of a young Tahitian chief named Tupea who had come along as guide and interpreter. The Maori, although they understood and could converse with Tupea, remained hostile even in the face of gifts the captain offered. Nor would they permit him to put aboard the food and water his men so badly needed. Disappointed and bitter, Cook weighed anchor after claiming the country for King George and naming the beautiful bay Poverty Bay because, as he noted in his journal, "it afforded us no one thing we wanted."

Sailing north, Captain Cook rounded the tip of the North Island and went on to circumnavigate both

Dateline

- **1973** Britain joins European Economic Community (Common Market), with subsequent disastrous reduction in imports from New Zealand.
- **1981** A tour by the South African rugby team causes violent protest in New Zealand.
- **1982** As a move against deep economic recession, New Zealand signs Closer Economic Relations (CER) agreement with Australia.
- **1984** New Zealand begins economic and social restructuring (privatization).
- **1985** All nuclear-armed and nuclear-powered vessels banned from New Zealand ports; Greenpeace *Rainbow Warrior* sunk by French terrorists in Auckland harbor, killing a crew member.
- **1986** New Zealand competes in the America's Cup races for the first time.
- **1987** The New Zealand yacht *KZ-7* wins the World Championship in Sardinia; at home, the sharemarket crashes.
- **1990** New Zealand hosts the Commonwealth Games and the visit of Elizabeth II adds to the festivities commemorating the 150th anniversary of the Treaty of Waitangi.
- **1991** Relations between the United States and

➤

islands during the next six months, charting them with amazing accuracy, missing only such details as the entrance to Milford Sound (which is quite invisible from the open sea) and the fact that Stewart Island was not a part of the mainland (he mistakenly believed Foveaux Strait to be a bay). In addition, he recorded the flora and fauna as instructed and brought back sketches of the indigenous people, who grew more friendly as word of the gift-bearing Pakeha (fair-skinned men) spread. He also recorded details of Maori customs and described the "Indians" as "a brave, open, warlike people." Even today, the journal he kept so meticulously makes fascinating reading.

Captain Cook returned to New Zealand for a month in 1773 and again in 1777. Until his death at the hands of indigenous people in Hawaii on February 14, 1779, he ranged the length and breadth of the South Pacific, sailing as far north as the Arctic Circle and as far south as Antarctica. He and the *Endeavour* have in fact become as mucha part of New Zealand legend as those early Maori chiefs and their mighty canoes.

Dateline

New Zealand, strained by the 1985 antinuclear ban, begin to thaw.

- **1993** New Zealand celebrates 100 years of women's sufferage.
- **1994** The decade of belt-tightening starts to pay off and New Zealand's economy declared one of the world's most competitive; South African rugby team tours New Zealand without protest.
- **1995** New Zealand's population reaches 3.5 million; economic growth continues.

EUROPEAN SETTLEMENT

Organized European settlement in New Zealand did not get under way with any success until 1840, and the unorganized settlement that preceded it was, for the most part, a disaster.

Sealers began arriving in 1792 and virtually denuded South Island waters of what had been flourishing colonies of seals through their policies of killing cows and pups and allowing no closed seasons or limit on skins (some ships carried off as many as 60,000 per year). By 1820 they moved on to more profitable waters.

Whalers, too, discovered rich hunting grounds in New Zealand waters and arrived in droves. Oil vats soon dotted the Bay of Islands, where safe anchorage was an added attraction. Their unscrupulous methods were much like those of the sealers, and New Zealand's coastal waters were no longer a natural haven for the mammoth animals. Unlike the sealers, however, the whalers brought in their wake a multitude of land-based evils in the form of an attendant population, which Charles Darwin described after his 1835 visit as "the very refuse of Society." Consisting of escapees from Australia's penal colonies, ex-convicts, runaway sailors, and a motley collection of "beachcombers," and concentrated in the Kororareka settlement (now known as Russell)—their grogeries (drinking spots), brothels, and lawlessness earned it the nickname "hellhole of the Pacific." Ships that would have normally called in at the port stayed away in

IMPRESSIONS

There is nothing soft about New Zealand, the country. It is very hard and sinewy, and will outlast many of those who try to alter it.
—John Mulgan, 1947

fear of the widespread practice of shanghaiing sailors for whaling vessels that were shorthanded.

Legitimate traders and merchants, attracted by the wealth of flax and such trees as the kauri—which were ideal for shipbuilding—as well as the lucrative trade in muskets and other European goods with the Maori, while law-abiding (that is, observing such law as there was), were little better than the sealers and whalers in respecting the country's natural resources. Great forests were felled with no eye to replanting, luxuriant bushlands disappeared in flames to clear hills and valleys for man's encroachment, and when a commercial value was placed on the tattooed and preserved heads that were a part of Maori culture, even the native population was threatened for a time as chiefs eager to purchase muskets lopped off more and more heads, both friend and foe. The latter was a short-lived trade, but quite lively while it lasted.

The immigration of Europeans had a devastating impact on Maori culture. Most destructive were the introduction of liquor, muskets, and European diseases against which the Maori had no immunity. Muskets in particular set off decimation of the Maori on a grand scale, for they intensified the fierce intertribal warfare that for centuries had been a part of the Maori lifestyle—tens of thousands were killed off by the fire-spouting sticks until the availability of muskets became so general that no one tribe had superiority in firepower; by about 1830 chiefs began to realize that the weapon was literally destroying all tribes.

Missionaries were the one benign group to arrive during this period, spearheaded by the Rev. Samuel Marsden, who arrived in the Bay of Islands in 1814 and preached his first sermon to the Maori on Christmas Day with the help of a young chief he had befriended. His was a practical brand of Christianity; and when his duties as chaplain to the convict settlement in Sydney demanded his return, he left behind a carpenter, a shoemaker, and a schoolteacher to instruct the Maori. Most of those men of the cloth who followed were of the same persuasion, and they were responsible for setting down the Maori language in writing (largely for the purpose of translating and printing the Bible), establishing mission schools (by the 1840s large numbers of Maori could both read and write), and upgrading agricultural methods through the use of plows and windmills, for instance.

On the religious front, their progress was slow—to their credit, they were determined not to baptize any Maori until he had a full understanding of the Christian faith—and it was some 11 years before they made the first Maori convert. That the missionaries went about their conversions in much too puritanical a manner is illustrated by the fate of one who admonished a chief for fishing on Sunday: "You are a wicked, bad man. . . . You have broken the Sabbath . . . you and your people will all go to hell and be burnt with fire for ever and ever." As the chief's great-grandson reported many years later, "To have put up with insult without avenging it according to its nature would have been fatal to a chief occupying a leading position and injurious to the tribe, as it would render it contemptible to its neighbors." Accordingly, "in less time than it takes to remove the feathers from a fat pigeon, the man of incantation was in an oven and prevented from creating further mischief."

By the late 1830s, however, Maori were ready to accept the concept of a god of peace, undoubtedly influenced greatly by the vastly changed nature of warfare since the coming of the musket. They were also a literal-minded, practical people, much impressed by the missionaries' ability to cure diseases that resisted all efforts by their own healers, as well as the white man's imperviousness to Maori witchcraft.

Christianity was in fact the beginning of the end of many aspects of Maori tribal society as it had existed for centuries.

As the number of British in New Zealand grew, so, too, did lawlessness, with many atrocities committed against both Maori and settlers. The missionaries were foremost among those who complained to the British government, which was by no means anxious to recognize the faraway country as a full-fledged colony, having already experienced difficulties with America and Canada, and struggled through the Napoleonic Wars and revolts on various other fronts. As a substitute, in 1833 the Crown placed New Zealand under the jurisdiction of New South Wales and sent James Busby as "British Resident," with full responsibilities for enforcing law and order, but with such laughable means of meeting those responsibilities that he was nicknamed "the man-of-war without guns." Needless to say, he was completely ineffectual.

THE TREATY OF WAITANGI

Back in Britain, the newly formed New Zealand Company began sending out ships to buy land from the Maori and establish permanent settlements. Their methods were questionable, to say the least, and caused increasing alarm in London. It must be noted, however, that between 1839 and 1843 the New Zealand Company sent out 57 ships carrying 19,000 settlers, the nucleus of a stable British population. In 1839 Capt. William Hobson was sent out by the government to sort things out, and by catering to the Maori sense of ceremony (and some mild arm-twisting), he arranged an assembly of chiefs at the Busby residence in the Bay of Islands. There, on February 6, 1840, the famous Treaty of Waitangi, after lengthy debate, was signed with much pomp.

The treaty guaranteed the Maori "all the Rights and Privileges of British Subjects" in exchange for their acknowledgment of British sovereignty, while granting the Crown exclusive rights to buy land from the Maori. The fact that many of the chiefs had no idea of the treaty's meaning is clear from one chief's later explanation that he had merely signed a receipt for a blanket sent by the queen as a gift! Nevertheless, 45 of the Maori chiefs at the assembly did sign, and when it was circulated around the country, another 500 also signed. Instead of easing things, however, the Treaty of Waitangi ushered in one of the bloodiest periods in New Zealand's history.

The British were eager to exercise that exclusive right to purchase Maori land, and while some chiefs were just as eager to sell, others wanted only to hold on to their native soil. As pressures were brought to bear to force them to sell, revolt quickly surfaced, and when Chief Hone Heke (ironically, the first to sign the treaty) hacked down the British flagpole at Kororareka (Russell) in 1844, it signaled the beginning of some 20 years of fierce fighting.

The Maori, always outnumbered and outarmed, won the unqualified respect and admiration of the British as brave and masterful warriors. The British, on the other hand, were regarded with the same degree of respect by the chiefs, who had not expected that the Pakeha could put up any sort of real fight. At last the British emerged as victors, but out of the bloody confrontations came the basis of a relationship, which to this day is based on that same mutual respect as well as on many of those same tensions.

Today, New Zealand's population base is 3.5 million: 10% are Maori, 4% are Pacific Island Polynesian, 1% are Chinese, and the rest are of European origin (Pakeha).

5 Famous New Zealanders

Jane (Jean) Gardner Batten (1909–82) An internationally known native of Rotorua, Batten is still honored for her record-breaking solo flights. From her early twenties, this intrepid aviatrix conquered the skies in aircraft considered crude by today's standards. In 1933 she flew solo from England to India; in 1934 from England to Australia, returning to England in 1935 to become the first woman to fly both ways; in 1935 from England to Brazil; and in 1936 from England to New Zealand, the first-ever solo flight, establishing a new solo record on her return in 1937. In *Alone in the Sky* she paints a vivid picture of her solo flight around the world. A recluse in later life, she was interred in a pauper's grave.

Walter Godfrey Bowen (1922–93) Familiarly known as Godfrey to New Zealanders and sheepshearers around the world, Bowen began his career at 16. His first world record came in 1953 for shearing 456 sheep in nine hours; he bettered this in 1960 when he sheared 559 sheep in Wales. He was one of the driving spirits behind the founding of the Agrodome agricultural exhibition center near Rotorua.

Janet Paterson Frame (b. 1924) Born in Dunedin, Frame is one of New Zealand's most brilliant writers. After emerging from a youth spent largely in mental institutions because she had been incorrectly diagnosed as schizophrenic, she found her first international success with *Owls Do Cry* in 1957. She has since produced a steady stream of novels and enjoyed accolades both at home and abroad. *An Angel at My Table,* part of her three-volume autobiography, has been televised in the United Kingdom as well as New Zealand, and her awards include two New Zealand Book Awards, the Hubert Church Award, the New Zealand Scholarship in Letters, and the Robert Burns Fellowship.

Charles Frederick Goldie (1870–1947) An Aucklander, Goldie studied painting in Paris for six years, and on returning to New Zealand he embarked on the series of Maori portraits for which he is best known. *The Arrival of the Maori in New Zealand,* painted in collaboration with L. J. Steele, is one of the most widely reproduced paintings in the country. His moving depictions of Maori subjects are the result of much time over 10 years spent photographing and sketching in Rotorua.

Sir Edmund Percival Hillary (b. 1919) Revered in his native country, Auckland-born Hillary was the first to conquer the heights of Mount Everest, the world's highest mountain. He undertook two sessions of climbing in the area before reaching the summit in 1953, on the eve of the coronation of Elizabeth II, who promptly knighted him. Another of his achievements was his trans-Antarctic dash that made his the first vehicle party to reach the South Pole overland. He has been involved in building hospitals and schools for the Sherpa people of the Himalayan region, and in 1975 he wrote the compelling *Nothing Ventured, Nothing Won.*

Keri Hulme (b. 1947) Born in Christchurch of Maori, English, and Orkney ancestry, Hulme is one of her country's finest novelists and poets. Her 1983 novel, *The Bone People,* won the 1984 New Zealand Book Award for Fiction and the Pegasus Prize for Maori writing, then Britain's prestigious Booker Prize for Fiction in 1985. Having settled into the remote southern West Coast village of Okarito, she continues to produce sensitive novels of the highest literary standards.

Katherine Mansfield (1888–1923) Widely regarded as one of the finest short-story writers in English, Wellington-born Mansfield is probably the best known and most respected internationally of New Zealand's writers. She began writing for publication at age nine. After living a rather bohemian life in London for several years, she returned to New Zealand, drawing on that country and its people for some of her finest and most mature work. Her outstanding stories include "Prelude," "At the Bay," and "The Garden Party." Several collections of them, as well as omnibus collections of her works and letters, have been published. She died at 34 of tuberculosis while in France, where she had lived for some years.

Lord Rutherford (1871–1937) The father of nuclear physics was born in Brightwater, near Nelson, and educated at Canterbury University before leaving for Cambridge. Rutherford was the first man to split the atom and won a Nobel Prize for his scientific achievements.

Dame Kiri Te Kanawa (b. 1944) One of the world's leading operatic sopranos, Te Kanawa was born in Gisborne and educated in Auckland. In 1966 she was awarded a bursary (scholarship) for study in London, and in 1971 she made her debut at London's Covent Garden in *The Marriage of Figaro,* the first of many performances that have won her international acclaim. In addition to being featured in many operatic recordings, she sang at the wedding of Prince Charles and Princess Diana. She is currently based in London.

6 Recommended Books & Films

BOOKS

MAORI WRITINGS If Maori legend and language catch your imagination, you may want to look for *The Caltex Book of Maori Lore* (A. H. & A. W. Reed Ltd.) by James Cowan, who spent much time among the Maori; and *A Dictionary of the Maori Language* by H. W. Williams, grandson of Bishop William Williams, who compiled the first dictionary at Paihia in 1844.

The Coming of the Maori (Whitcombe and Tombs) by Sir P. Buck, a distinguished Maori and Pacific authority, is an account of the first Polynesian migration, and J. Metge's *The Maori of New Zealand* (Rutledge) is one of the best introductions to Maori life before and after European settlement. An excellent collection is *Into the World of Light: An Anthology of Maori Writing* (Heinemann), edited by Witi Ihimaera and D. S. Long.

NONFICTION One of my own most treasured reference books is the *New Zealand Encyclopedia* (David Bateman Ltd.), edited by Gordon McLauchlan, which covers every aspect of the country. I also frequently refer to my *Mobil New Zealand Travel Guide—North Island* and *Mobil New Zealand Travel Guide—South Island,* both by Diana and Jeremy Pope (Reed Books).

Depending on your interests, you may want to read *Lifestyles of New Zealand Forest Plants* (Victoria University Press) by John Dawson and Rob Lucas, Michael Cooper's *The Wines and Vineyards of New Zealand* (Hodder & Stoughton), and/or *Standing in the Sunshine* (Viking) by Sandra Cooney. The last book focuses on the many achievements made by New Zealand women over the past century.

In addition, I highly recommend *The Best of New Zealand,* published by Jason Publishing Co., P.O. Box 9390, Newmarket, Auckland, New Zealand 1031 (☎ **09/520-6155**; fax 09/524-6114). Overseas orders cost NZ$59.95 (U.S. $39), including packaging and air parcel post.

FICTION & POETRY *Owls Do Cry* (W. H. Allen), *A State of Siege* (Pegasus Press), and *Living in the Maniototo* (Braziller) are three representative novels by New Zealand's most distinguished living novelist, Janet Frame. Collections of Katherine Mansfield's short stories include *Prelude, Bliss and Other Stories* and *The Garden Party and Other Stories.*

A favorite New Zealand novel is Peter Hooper's *Song of the Forest* (McIndoe). Dame Ngaio Marsh wrote more than 30 whodunits, the best of which is *Photo Finish* (Little). And *Greenstone* (Simon & Schuster) is one of the late Sylvia Ashton-Warner's most popular books. You might also enjoy Maurice Gee's *Going West* (Faber and Faber) and Maurice Shadbolt's *One of Ben's* (David Ling).

Two excellent collections of contemporary poetry, both published by Oxford University Press, are *Anthology of Twentieth Century New Zealand Poetry* and *Oxford Book of Contemporary New Zealand Poetry.* In addition, *100 New Zealand Poems,* chosen by Bill Manshire, is published by Godwit Press.

FILMS

Older outstanding films produced in New Zealand are *Sleeping Dogs,* featuring handsome Kiwi actor Sam Neill; *Smash Palace,* a compelling look at marital relations in New Zealand, featuring Roger Donaldson; *Utu,* a look at Maori and Pakeha relations in the last century; and *Goodbye Pork Pie,* about a minicar that takes over its one female and two male passengers. (Be aware that if you find videos of these films in New Zealand, they may not play on U.S. VCRs—New Zealand uses the PAL system, while the United States uses NTSC.) A more recent New Zealand film is *Desperate Remedies,* set in an outpost of the British Empire.

Perhaps the best-known Kiwi film is *The Piano,* directed by Jane Campion—the epic story of a colonial-era mute woman (Holly Hunter) whose father marries her to an insensitive New Zealander (Kiwi Sam Neill). She has her piano with her when she immigrates to her new land. Her husband leaves the piano on the beach and later sells it to another settler (Harvey Keitel), who is intrigued by the woman and requests that she give him lessons. Soon they fall in love. Anna Paquin plays the woman's savvy young daughter.

The Piano was awarded the Palme d'Or at the Cannes Film Festival and went on to win three 1994 Academy Awards: Best Actress for Holly Hunter, Best Supporting Actress for Anna Paquin, and Best Original Screenplay for Jane Campion. Anna Paquin became the second-youngest person (the youngest was Tatum O'Neal) and the first New Zealander to win an Oscar.

Released in early 1995 was the powerful *Once Were Warriors,* based on a novel by Alan Duff and directed by Lee Tamahori (who's part Maori). This disturbing film is about a violent working-class Maori family—the novel focuses particularly on the husband/father, but the movie shifts the focus to the wife/mother, played magnificently by half-Maori actress Rena Owen.

Due out from Miramax Films in mid-1995 is *Heavenly Creatures,* which promises to be a "guided tour" of Christchurch as well as the story of the notorious 1950s Pauline Parker/Juliet Hulme affair. Filmed on location, the movie stars Melanie Linskey from New Plymouth and Kate Winsley from England.

3

Planning a Trip to New Zealand

THIS CHAPTER MAY WELL BE SOME OF THE MOST IMPORTANT READING YOU'LL DO before setting off on your New Zealand trip. It deals with the preplanning "homework" that can make the difference between returning home with pleasant memories or with a feeling of frustration and bewilderment.

What I'll be talking about here are the details that'll help you plan as carefree a trip as possible. You'll need to know about such things as currency and the rate of exchange, how long your trip should be so you get the most out of New Zealand, which upcoming events you wouldn't want to miss and which don't matter to you, what sort of clothes and provisions you should pack, and what you may expect in terms of accommodations, restaurants, shopping, and things to see and do.

1 Information, Entry Requirements & Money

Sources of Visitor Information

One of the most useful things you can do when planning a New Zealand visit is contact the nearest **New Zealand Tourism Board** for its comprehensive publication, *The New Zealand Vacation Planner.* Included with the planner will be helpful brochures on sightseeing highlights, sports, and other special interests. Travel consultants in each office are available to help with any queries.

North American locations of the New Zealand Tourism Board include 501 Santa Monica Blvd., Suite 300, Santa Monica, CA 90401 (☎ **310/395-5453,** or toll free **800/388-5494** in the U.S.; fax 310/395-5453); and 888 Dunsmuir St., Suite 1200, Vancouver, BC, V6C 3K4 (☎ **604/684-2117**).

Other locations include Level 8, 35 Pitt St., Sydney, NSW 2000, Australia (☎ **02/247-5222**); New Zealand House, Haymarket, SW1Y 4TQ, London, England (☎ **0171/973-0360**); Friedrichstrasse 10–12, 6000 Frankfurt am Main 1, Germany (☎ **069/971-2110**); and 3414 Jardine House, 1 Connaught Place, Central, Hong Kong (☎ **852/526-0141**).

When you arrive in New Zealand, you'll find more than 70 local **Visitor Information Network** offices around the country with friendly staff members who are experts in all aspects of your holiday and eager to help. Look for the identifying ***"i"*** that makes visitor information offices easy to spot.

You'll find local Visitor Information Network addresses listed for each destination in this book. They're also listed in *The New Zealand Vacation Planner* (see above). Before your trip, you might also want to look at one or two **travel videos** about New Zealand. They really make the country, its diversity, and its people come alive and help you decide on the places you most want to visit. Several good ones—and hopefully one or more of them will be available in the travel section of your local video store—include *New Zealand: A World on Its Own* (25 minutes), *New Zealand on My Mind* (produced by the New Zealand Tourism Board, 25 minutes), and *Utterly New Zealand* with Leeza Gibbons (40 minutes).

Entry Requirements

DOCUMENTS

You'll need a passport for entry to New Zealand, and it must be valid for no less than three months beyond the date you plan to depart. A travel tip about passports: It's a good idea to make two photocopies of the identification page of your passport (the one with your photo), as well as any other travel documents, then leave one copy at home and carry the other with you. You'll save yourself a lot of hassle in case you and those vital papers part company and you need them replaced. The photocopies will not serve as valid documents, but they'll furnish the information necessary to cut through miles of red tape to get new ones.

For a stay of less than three months, you won't need a visa (providing you don't intend to work, study, or undergo medical treatment) if you're a citizen of the United States, Canada, Great Britain (allowed a six months' stay), Australia, Austria, Belgium, Denmark, Finland, Federal Republic of Germany, France, Greece, Iceland, Ireland, Italy, Japan, Liechtenstein, Luxembourg, Malta, Monaco, the Netherlands, Norway, Portugal, Spain, Sweden, Switzerland, and Singapore.

VISAS If you wish to stay beyond the limits stated above, or if your nationality is not listed, consult your nearest New Zealand Embassy, High Commission, or consulate for information on obtaining the appropriate visa. Americans who want to stay longer than three months may obtain a visa application from the consular office nearest their home. The **New Zealand Embassy** is located at 37 Observatory Circle NW, Washington, DC 20008 (☎ **202/328-4880**); and there are consular offices in Los Angeles and New York. Still other consulates may be found at the New Zealand Tourism Board addresses shown above. No fee, but you'll need a photograph. For information on working-holiday visas, inquire at one of the consulates for current regulations. Count on about four weeks for processing by mail.

VACCINATIONS No certificate of vaccination is currently required of any traveler arriving in New Zealand. However, officials are quick to point out that should you develop an illness or skin rash, you should see a doctor and say that you've recently arrived in the country.

CUSTOMS

Three things visitors must show before entry permission is granted: a confirmed outward or round-trip ticket; enough money for their New Zealand stay—figure NZ$1,000 (U.S. $650) per person per month, or NZ$400 (U.S. $260) with accommodation already paid (credit or charge cards are acceptable as evidence of funds); and the necessary documents to enter the next country on their itinerary or to reenter the country from which they came.

There is no Customs duty on any personal effects you bring into the country and intend to take away with you. Also duty-free are 200 cigarettes or half a pound of tobacco or 50 cigars, as well as 4.5 liters of wine or beer, one bottle of spirits or liqueur (up to 1.125 liters), and goods up to a total combined value of NZ$500 (U.S. $390) for your own use or that you're bringing as a gift. If you plan to take in anything beyond those limits, best contact the New Zealand Customs Department, Head Office, Wellington, New Zealand, or the nearest embassy or consulate office, *before* you arrive. Ask for the publication *Customs Guide for Travelers.*

Money

CURRENCY

You won't have any trouble at all with New Zealand's currency: The **New Zealand dollar (NZ$)** is based on the decimal system with 100 cents to the dollar. There are coins in denominations of 5, 10, 20, and 50 cents and $1 and $2, as well as banknotes in $5, $10, $20, and $100 amounts.

For American Readers At this writing $1 U.S. = approximately NZ$1.54 (or NZ$1 = 65¢), and this was the rate of exchange used to calculate the dollar values given in this book (rounded up to the nearest nickel).

For British Readers At this writing £ 1 = approximately NZ$2.44 (or NZ$1 = 41p), and this was the rate of exchange used to calculate the pound values in the accompanying table.

Note: International exchange rates fluctuate from time to time depending on complicated political and economic factors. Thus the rates given in the accompanying table

The New Zealand Dollar, the U.S. Dollar & the British Pound

NZ$	U.S.$	U.K.£
.25	.16	0.10
.50	.33	0.21
.75	.49	0.31
1	.65	0.41
2	1.30	0.82
3	1.95	1.23
4	2.60	1.64
5	3.25	2.05
6	3.90	2.46
7	4.55	2.87
8	5.20	3.28
9	5.85	3.69
10	6.50	4.10
15	9.75	6.15
20	13.00	8.20
25	16.25	10.25
30	19.50	12.30
35	22.75	14.35
40	26.00	16.40
45	29.25	18.45
50	32.50	20.50
60	39.00	24.60
70	45.50	28.70
80	52.00	32.80
90	58.50	36.90
100	65.00	41.00

may not be the same when you travel to New Zealand, and so this table should be used only as a guide.

TRAVELER'S CHECKS

Most of your money should be in traveler's checks, not in cash. But because exchange rates of foreign currencies against the U.S. dollar have fluctuated more radically recently than in past years, the best advice is to start watching the daily exchange rates as soon as you know you'll be going to New Zealand. A variation of only a few cents can sometimes net you considerably more buying power. Of course, for safety's sake, you won't want to convert all your precious travel dollars, no matter what the rate.

I should also remind you that it's a good idea to keep the record of your traveler's checks separate from the checks themselves and to be sure to record each one you cash. If the worst should happen and you lose checks, replacement will depend on your having those uncashed numbers.

CURRENCY EXCHANGE

Banks, of course, offer the best exchange rates, *not* hotels, department stores, or restaurants.

CREDIT & CHARGE CARDS

Major credit and charge cards—American Express, Bankcard, Diners Club, MasterCard, and Visa—are widely accepted throughout New Zealand, even in remote areas, and can be a real convenience when you're traveling. Be aware, however, that you may be billed at an exchange rate that differs from the one in effect when you made the charge, and this may prove to be to your advantage or disadvantage.

What Things Cost in Auckland	U.S.$
Taxi from airport to city center	22.75
Airport bus to city center	6.50
Double room at the Aachen House (Frommer budget)	53.30
Double room at Auckland Central Backpackers (Thrifty budget)	24.10
Lunch for one at Carpe Diem (Frommer budget)	5.20
Lunch for one at La Casa Italiano (Thrifty budget)	3.25
Dinner for one, without wine, at the Left Bank (Frommer budget)	13.65
Dinner for one, without wine, at the Masonic Tavern (Thrifty budget)	4.55
Can of beer	2.30
Cup of coffee	1.95
Roll of ASA 100 Kodacolor film, 36 exposures	6.20
Admission to the Auckland Museum	Free
Movie ticket	6.50
Concert or theater ticket	13.00

What Things Cost in Dunedin	U.S.$
Taxi from airport to city center	26.00
Airport minibus to city center	6.50
Double room at Farry's Motel (Frommer budget)	55.90
Double room at the Sahara Guesthouse (Thrifty budget)	48.10
Lunch for one at the Bank (Frommer budget)	3.90
Lunch for one at Potpourri (Thrifty budget)	2.60
Dinner for one, without wine, at the Golden Harvest (Frommer budget)	11.70
Dinner for one, without wine, at the Albert Arms Tavern (Thrifty budget)	6.50
Can of beer	1.95
Cup of coffee	1.65
Roll of ASA 100 Kodacolor film, 36 exposures	6.50
Admission to the Otago Museum	Free
Movie ticket	5.55
Concert or theater ticket	9.75

2 Timing Your Trip—Climate, Holidays & Events

Climate

Weatherwise, you're safe to visit New Zealand any time of the year. Temperatures are never extreme, although I've experienced days warmer than those midsummer averages and a degree or two below the midwinter averages quoted. One thing to keep in mind, however, is that on a visit that takes you to both islands, you'll be going from a subtropical climate in the north of the North Island to the coolness (sometimes coldness) of the South Island.

Nor is there a specific rainy season, although the west coast of the South Island can experience up to 100 inches or more of rain a year on its side of the Southern Alps, while just over those mountains to the east rainfall will be a moderate 20 to 30 inches. Rain is heavier in the west on the North Island as well, with precipitation on the whole ranging from 40 to 70 inches annually. Milford Sound holds the record as the wettest spot in the country (and also perhaps the most beautiful) with an annual downpour of 365 inches; fortunately, it doesn't rain every day or all day long.

As for sunshine, you'll find more in the north and east of both islands, with the Bay of Islands and the Nelson/Marlborough Sounds area leading sun spots. Frost and snow in the North Island are mainly confined to high country such as Mount Egmont/Taranaki and the peaks in Tongariro National Park, so if it's snow or snow-related sports you're after, look for them on the South Island. Even there, skiing is not a year-round activity, so a little research on specific destinations is in order before you set your dates.

SEASONS

In New Zealand, seasons are those of the Southern Hemisphere, thus the exact opposite of those in North America. There just isn't a bad season to travel, so your own schedule and interests will set your timing priorities. A fundamental guideline, however, is that during Kiwi holiday times, accommodations can be very tight. So if you plan to come between mid-December and January 30, when New Zealand families are traveling about their country on annual "hols," or during the Easter, May, or midterm school holidays (see below), reservations are an absolute must.

SPRING September, October, November. This is one of the best times to visit, since Kiwis are going about their business activities, schools are in full session, innkeepers will greet you with delight—with or without a booking—and the countryside is bright with blossoming fruit trees and brand-new baby lambs.

SUMMER December, January, February. Beaches and boats are primary preoccupations of the natives during these months, and resorts are booked to capacity. Advance planning will let you share these sun-filled days, although you should be prepared for slightly higher accommodation rates. It's a fun time to visit if you get your reservations under way early enough.

FALL March, April, May. In my opinion, this is a great time to visit New Zealand. The weather is pleasant and just cool enough in southern parts to remind you that winter is on its way, while in the Bay of Islands region midday and early afternoons are still shirt-sleeve warm. Poplars are a brilliant gold, and more subtle foliage changes can be seen in the forests. Just remember those Easter and midterm school holidays, when bookings may be tight.

WINTER June, July, August. Okay, you ski buffs—this is the time when your ski calendar goes on a year-round basis. From about mid-June on, the slopes are a skier's dream. Making advance reservations at major ski resorts is certainly advisable, but you can nearly always count on finding accommodations within an easy drive even if you arrive with nothing confirmed. Around the rest of the country, this is another season you can pretty much amble around without booking ahead—except, of course, for that aforementioned two-week school holiday in late August to early September (August 21 to September 8, 1995).

Holidays

Statutory holidays in 1995 are January 1 (New Year's), January 2 and 3 (New Year Holiday), February 6 (Waitangi Day), April 14 (Good Friday), April 17 (Easter Monday), April 25 (Anzac Day), June 5 (Queen's Birthday), October 23 (Labour Day), December 25 (Christmas Day), and December 26 (Boxing Day).

In 1996, holidays include January 1 and 2 (New Year's), February 6 (Waitangi Day), April 5 (Good Friday), April 8 (Easter Monday), April 25 (Anzac Day), June 3 (Queen's Birthday), October 28 (Labour Day), December 25 (Christmas Day), December 26 (Boxing Day), and January 1 and 2, 1997 (New Year's).

Holidays celebrated locally are January 23 (Wellington), January 30 (Auckland), January 30 (Northland—that is, Bay of Islands), January 30 (Nelson), March 13 (Taranaki), March 20 (Otago and Southland—that is, Dunedin, Queenstown, Invercargill), October 20 (Hawkes Bay and Marlborough), November 10 (Canterbury), and December 4 (Westland).

Midterm school holidays last for two weeks, and December holidays last six weeks (through the end of January). That's when Kiwi families are on the move holidaying it up, so be sure of your reservations during those months. School holidays for 1996 are March 30 to April 14, June 29 to July 14, September 14 to 29, and December 17 to January 26, 1997.

New Zealand Calendar of Events

January

- **Summer City Festival,** Wellington. Daily cultural, entertainment, and recreational events in the capital city. January and February.
- **Fiordland Festival Week,** Te Anau. Arts and crafts, food stalls, and street entertainment. Mid-January.
- **Wellington Cup,** Wellington. Leading horse-racing event (galloping). Late January.
- **National Yearling Sales,** Wellington. Held in conjunction with Wellington Cup. Late January.

February

- **Waitangi Day Celebrations,** Bay of Islands. New Zealand's national day, celebrating signing of treaty with Maori, February 6.
- **Martinborough Country Fairs,** Martinborough. Popular gathering of crafts artisans from around the country. First Saturday in February and March.
- **Floral Festival,** Christchurch. Garden visits, floating gardens, floral carpets in the "Garden City" of the South Island. First two weeks in February.

March

- **Festival of Arts,** Wellington. Important festival of the performing arts, by both internationally known artists and street entertainers. First three weeks of March in even-numbered years.
- **Martinborough Country Fairs.** First Saturday in February and March. See February, above.
- **International Shearing Contest,** Masterton. Three-day contests for wool handling, lamb and goat shearing. Early March.
- **Dukes International Billfish Tournament,** Bay of Islands. Draws the fishing crowd from around the world. Early March.
- **Summer Festival Week,** Dunedin. Street entertainment, cultural and sporting events. Mid-March.
- **Ngaruawahia River Regatta,** Turangawoewoe Marao, Ngaruawahia. Canoe races, Maori songs and dances performed by cultural groups. Mid-March.
- **Hokitika Wild Foods Festival,** Hokitika. Wild pig, venison, possum pâté, goat, all sorts of wild herbs, honey, and fish from local waters star in this one-day West Coast celebration. Great fun. Third or fourth week in March.

April

- **Rugby Season,** Countrywide. April through September.
- **Arrowtown Autumn Festival,** Arrowtown. Week of market days, miners'

band, and street entertainment celebrating the gold-mining era. Early April.

- **Bluff Oyster Festival,** Bluff Township. Celebrating opening of oyster season, with shucking and eating contests. Early April.
- **Highland Games,** Hastings. Contestants from all over the country and Australia vie for championships in tossing the caber, sheaf throwing, and other field games. Mid-April.
- **Mackenzie Highland Show,** Fairlle. One of New Zealand's largest agricultural and produce shows, featuring horses, sheep, cattle, dog trials, wood chopping, and Highland dancing. Easter Saturday.
- **National Jazz Festival,** Tauranga. Youth bands and overseas acts join with local professionals. Easter weekend.

May

- **Fletcher Challenge Marathon,** Rotorua. Grueling footrace. Early May.
- **Hot Air Balloon Fiesta,** Hamilton. Three-day competitions in New Zealand's ballooning capital. First weekend in May.

June

- **DB Draught Marathon,** Christchurch. Hotly contested by runners from around the country. Early June.
- **National Agricultural Field Days,** Hamilton. Largest field day in Australasia, covering every type of rural activity, as well as stock sales that reach astronomical prices. Mid-June.

July

- **Queenstown Winter Festival,** Queenstown. Boisterous, fun-filled celebration of winter season, with ski events and street entertainment. Early July.

August

- **Wanaka Snowfest,** Wanaka and Treble Cone Ski Field. Lots of skiing events in this winter festival. Late August.

September

- **Alexandra Blossom Festival,** Alexandra. Floral parade, displays of local arts and crafts, garden tours, and entertainment. Late September to early October.

October

- **Rhododendron Week,** Dunedin. Fun-filled days highlighted by garden tours and cultural events to celebrate this city's magnificent displays of rhododendron blooms. Mid-October.
- **Lifespan Mountains to Sea Multi-Sports Event,** Tongariro and Whanganu National Park. Labour Day Weekend, late October.
- **Maritime Mardigras,** Stewart Island. A lively festival of the sea. Late October.

November

- **Whangamomona Republic Day,** Whangamomona. Passports are issued and entry visas sold to visitors when borders are closed around this self-styled republic formed after boundary changes moved Whangamomona from the Tarankai region to that of Wanganui-Manawatu. All sorts of street entertainment and food stalls, with proceeds going to charity.

Nearest Saturday to November 1.

- **International Trout Fishing Competition,** Rotorua. International anglers gather to compete with the locals, fishing 14 lakes in four days. Mid-November.
- **Christchurch A & P Show,** Christchurch. This agricultural and pastoral show is the South Island's largest and includes thoroughbred and standard-bred racing. Even those who don't attend watch the running of the New Zealand Cup on TV. Second week in November.

December

- **BP National Tennis Championships,** Wellington. International-class men's tournament. Late December to early January.

Auckland Calendar of Events

January

- **Auckland Cup Horse Racing.** One of the country's richest horse races. January 1.
- **Anniversary Day Regatta.** Colorful sailing event, with local and international entrants. Last Monday in January.
- **Men's International Tennis Tournament.** Late January to early February.
- **Women's International Tennis Tournament.** Late January to early February.

February

- **Polo.** Check locally for dates throughout the month.
- **Cricket.** Various dates throughout the month.

March

- **World Carnival of Harness Racing.** A two-week schedule of races and related events. First two weeks in March.
- **Savile Polo Cup,** Auckland Pologround, Clevedon. One of New Zealand's oldest sporting trophies, the Savile pits domestic teams against international contenders. Mid-March.
- **Round the Bays Run.** Great fun, with runners from around the South Pacific participating, ending with a barbecue in one of the city's parks. Late March.

April

- **Auckland Racing Club Easter Festival.** Annually attracts more than 1,000 competitors and incorporates elements of an agricultural and pastoral show. Mid-April.

May

- **New Zealand Brass Band Championships.** Soloists, small groups, and large bands compete in marching events as well as other performances. Mid-May.

June

- **Great Northern Steeplechase.** The country's leading steeplechase event, run over Auckland's Ellerslie Racecourse's famous "Hill." Early June.

August

- **Bledisloe Rugby Cup.** Fiercely competitive rugby series between New Zealand and Australia. Late August.

September

- **World's Trampoline Championships.** Competitors from more than 30 countries gather in Auckland's ASB Stadium. Early September.

December

- **Horse Racing (NZ Derby, Queen Elizabeth Auckland Handicap, and others).** Check locally for specific dates of individual events during the month.

3 Health & Insurance

BEFORE YOU GO

HEALTH PREPARATIONS If you take any form of medication, it's a good idea to bring along prescriptions (written in the generic form, not the brand name) from your doctor in case you need refills. This also applies to prescriptions for eyeglasses or contact lenses.

INSURANCE Check to be sure your property insurance is in good order, with premium payments up-to-date and full coverage for fire, theft, and so on. It's also a good idea to have health and accident insurance when traveling. If your present policy doesn't provide coverage when you're out of the country, check with your insurance carrier about temporary medical coverage for the duration of your trip. Most travel agents can arrange this, along with travel-delay or cancellation and lost-luggage insurance.

IN NEW ZEALAND

ACCIDENT REHABILITATION & COMPENSATION As a visitor to New Zealand, you have access to the same no-fault **accident rehabilitation and compensation plan** as Kiwis and are covered from the time you arrive until the time you leave—and it doesn't cost you one penny. Benefits include compensation for *reasonable*—though not necessarily all—expenses directly resulting from the accident, such as medical and hospital expenses, as well as lump-sum payments for permanent incapacity. It doesn't matter if the accident was your fault or not.

The ACC will not, however, cover loss of earnings in your country of origin, nor will it pay the cost of medical or rehabilitation treatment outside New Zealand. Extra travel costs incurred as a result of your injury (such as canceling bookings and rescheduling travel plans) and ordinary sickness will also not be covered. Because the ACC plan is no-fault, you have no right to sue.

For more information, contact your nearest New Zealand Tourism Board office (see "Information, Entry Requirements, and Money," earlier in this chapter). Benefits are determined by the **Accident Rehabilitation and Compensation Insurance Corporation,** whose head office is at Shamrock House, 81–83 Molesworth St., Wellington (☎ **04/473-8775**). Contact them immediately if you should happen to have an accident.

MEDICAL ATTENTION This is *not* free like accident rehabilitation and compensation, so it's important that you make sure your medical insurance covers you in New Zealand. Medical facilities there are excellent and health care is of a very high standard.

A Case of Packing

There's one basic tenet: No matter when you plan to go or what you plan to do, dress in New Zealand is, for the most part, informal.

When you plan to arrive will, of course, play a big part in your wardrobe decisions—remember that the seasons will be those in the Southern Hemisphere. There are, however, few temperature extremes either in the subtropical tip of the North Island or in the cooler South Island. Auckland, for example, has an average midsummer maximum temperature of 73°F, with 56° the midwinter average high. Queenstown's summer average maximum is 72°F, with a winter high of 50°. Generally, you can look for mild days in the Bay of Islands, cool to cold down in the Southern Alps. That translates into layering your clothes.

One item I wouldn't be without during a winter visit is my spencer—a lightweight lambswool undershirt I bought on one of my first trips to New Zealand. I'd suggest that after arrival you buy one in the lingerie section of a department store (such as Ballantines in Christchurch, where I got mine) or in a specialty store (such as the Wool Shed in Taupo).

What you plan to do will also determine what you pack. New Zealand offers some of the best tramping in the world, so if that's what you want to do, bring suitable clothing, sturdy boots, a backpack, and the necessary utensils if you'll be camping overnight. Note that you needn't bring boots and a heavy coat if the extent of your tramping will be an organized trek on the glaciers—both will be provided by your guide.

Now for one bit of advice that stems from my own experience of returning with an overstuffed suitcase that was nice and light when I left: I doubt you're going to be able to resist buying those terrific natural-wool sweaters (especially the handknits), so I'd suggest leaving all your sweaters at home and picking up one or two in New Zealand to wear during your trip and then back home. In warm weather, men will no doubt be tempted to adopt the universal Kiwi male dress of walking shorts, high socks, and a short-sleeve shirt—all of which you can pick up after arrival. In other words, you'll end up wearing some of your nicest souvenirs.

Here are a few other carry-alongs: a washcloth in a plastic bag since they're seldom furnished in New Zealand motels; dual-voltage appliances (such as a hairdryer); adapter plugs for New Zealand's three-pronged outlets; insect repellent; prescriptions for your medications (in generic, not brand-name, form) or glasses or contact lenses; a small calculator or currency converter; a flashlight if you'll be driving after dark; cassette tapes if you'll be doing a lot of driving; a camera and more film than you think you'll need; and all other items too obvious to list here.

Sports enthusiasts may want to bring favorite fishing rods, golf clubs, or skis, all of which are allowed through Customs; however, these are readily available in New Zealand. Many fishing guides furnish equipment, and you can rent clubs at most golf courses. If hostels will be your accommodations choice, you might bring along a sleeping bag or sheets and a pillowcase. Blankets and linens can be rented, though.

4 Tips for the Disabled, Seniors, Singles, Families & Students

FOR THE DISABLED

Recognizing that all too often wheelchair travelers, as well as their companions, are excluded from guesthouse and other accommodations because of narrow doors, steps, and inaccessibility of toilets, the New Zealand accommodations industry has encouraged accommodation design to circumvent these problems. Since 1975 every new public building and every major reconstruction in the country has been required to provide reasonable and adequate access for the disabled. Accommodations with nine or more units must also provide one or more accessible facilities.

Driving in New Zealand is possible for the handicapped traveler since **Budget Rent a Car** offers vehicles especially adapted to meet the needs of disabled drivers. You can get advance information on reservations through the **New Zealand Tourism Board,** 501 Santa Monica Blvd., Suite 300, Santa Monica, CA 90401 (☎ **310/395-7480,** or toll free **800/388-5494** in the U.S.), or through travel agents.

An essential part of every disabled visitor's before-travel plans should be the comprehensive ***Access: A Guide for the Less Mobile Traveler,*** available from New Zealand Tourism Board offices. Included are an up-to-date list of hotels, motels, and guesthouses that provide accommodations designed for the comfort and convenience of the disabled; a list of sightseeing attractions that provide such facilities; and even a list of New Zealand thermal pools equipped for easy access. Thermal pools, which New Zealand has in abundance, have long been thought to bring relief to some disabled people; however, recent years have seen the growth of those devoted solely to recreational purposes—making the *Access* guide extremely valuable when selecting those to visit.

General information and news are also available from the **Travel Industry and Disabled Exchange (TIDE),** 5435 Donna Ave., Tarzana, CA 91356 (☎ **818/343-6339**). You can also contact **Nautilus Tours,** operators of tours for the disabled, at this address and phone number.

FOR SENIORS

Accommodations discounts for those over 65 are becoming more and more frequent in New Zealand, although most apply almost exclusively to off- or low-season rates. Be sure to inquire about these when you call for a reservation. If you're booking through an agent, stress that the discount should be requested since it may not be offered voluntarily.

Some sightseeing attractions offer senior-citizen prices—so, again, inquire when you pay your admission fee. Anyone over age 60 is entitled to a discount on InterCity and Mount Cook coaches. Members of the **American Association of Retired Persons (AARP)** (☎ **202/434-2277**) are eligible for discounts on car rentals and hotels.

FOR SINGLES

Almost all of my traveling in New Zealand has been done alone, and I can tell you from firsthand experience that being a single traveler has never been a problem. On the social scene, there just aren't many places I hesitate to go on my own, and restaurants have yet to stick me next to the kitchen door or at the most undesirable table in the place. As for motel and guesthouse hosts, they unfailingly go out of their way to make me feel at home, often taking great pains to see that I know as much as they themselves know about the location and what's on at the moment.

Having said all that, I must add a cautionary note about hitchhiking or wandering around city streets in the wee hours on your own—although New Zealand still enjoys a relatively low crime rate, you are well advised to team up with someone else if you plan to do either.

It's also true that in New Zealand, as in most of the rest of the world, I frequently (but I hasten to say, not *always*) pay a slightly higher per-person rate for accommodations than if I were half of a couple—one of the realities of travel. The only tip I can offer in this regard is to look about for another single traveler and team up as roommates.

FOR FAMILIES

Go ahead, bring the kids! New Zealand is especially well suited to memorable family holidays. Even in these turbulent times, the family unit is still very much the core of Kiwi life, and visiting families are welcomed with open arms. And, unlike many other cultures, New Zealanders don't frown on children in restaurants.

An increasingly popular family holiday with our readers is that spent in New Zealand farmhouses—children and parents alike are utterly delighted to walk the fields with the farmer and, more often than not, lend a helping hand with the farm chores. For the city-bred, that's a lovely treat. See "Accommodations Choices," later in this chapter, for details.

On the budgetary front, motel units usually come complete with kitchen facilities, and easily prepared meals are a money-saving device when you have so many mouths to feed. If the thought of all that cooking and washing up brings groans from the distaff side of the family, there is the consoling counterthought that marketing in New Zealand—be it in small neighborhood "dairies" or supermarkets much like those at home—is loads of fun. You'll see many familiar products, plus a host of unfamiliar brands, cuts of meat, and canned products. Any shopkeeper or grocery clerk, however, will delight in telling you all about them and how they should be used or cooked.

You might also consider using New Zealand's excellent YHA hostel accommodations. There's no membership requirement for children under 18 traveling with families of adult members. Since not all hostels have suitable rooms—and since those that do, have them in limited number—you should write for their handbook (see "For Students," below) and book as far in advance as possible.

When it comes to keeping the children amused, what child wouldn't be happy exploring sheep farms, glowworm caves, wide beaches with weird rock formations, forests alive with exotic birds, and small towns that smack of their image of America's "Wild West." Sports, music, dancing, and a host of other activities are also geared for the young and available wherever you go in the country. White-water rafting, glacier walking, and the like will not only delight youngsters but also provide lifelong memories of unique experiences. Parents will be happy to know that virtually every sightseeing attraction admits children at half price, and many have family prices as well.

After dark, older children will enjoy such entertainments as Maori dinner shows (don't be surprised if you hear your offsprings' rendition of the fierce war *haka* for months after your return home!). Most guesthouses, motels, and hotels have babysitters on hand for the small fry when an adult night out is called for.

FOR STUDENTS

The **International Student Identity Card** opens doors to dollarwise events and activities aimed only at students and also offers substantial discounts on almost every facet of travel. You must, however, arm yourself with this valuable document before you leave home. The cost is $16 U.S., and you can obtain your card through the Council on International Educational Exchange (CIEE), 205 E. 42nd St., New York, NY 10017 (☎ **212/661-1414**), or at any of the 30 Council Travel offices or 440 campus issuing offices across the country.

Students should also know about the **Student Travel Network** (also known as STA Travel), with its West Coast headquarters at 7202 Melrose Ave., Los Angeles, CA 90046 (☎ **213/934-8722, 212/477-7166** in New York, or toll free **800/777-0112** in the rest of the U.S.; **071/737-9921** in London; **604/682-9136** in Vancouver). It offers discounted international airfares on the major carriers for students under 26. These favorable rates sometimes extend to recent graduates or academic staff. The New Zealand headquarters is at 10 High St., Auckland (☎ **09/309-9995**).

For economical accommodations, as well as a great way to meet other travelers, join **Hostelling International–American Youth Hostels (HI–AYH),** 733 15th St. NW, Suite 840, Washington, DC 20005 (☎ **202/783-6161,** or toll free **800/444-6111** in the U.S.). HI–AYH membership cards give you access to 55 HI–New Zealand hostels, plus many travel and sightseeing discounts. Should you arrive in New Zealand without a membership card, you may obtain an International Guest Card costing NZ$4 (U.S. $2.60) per night or NZ$24 (U.S. $15.60) for your entire stay. International Guest Cards can be obtained at HI–New Zealand hostels or YHA Holiday Shoppes in Auckland (Customs and Gore streets), Wellington (corner of Cambridge Terrace and Wakefield Street), and Christchurch (corner of Glouster and Manchester streets). For more information, contact **YHA New Zealand,** P.O. Box 436, Christchurch (☎ **03/379-9970;** fax 03/365-4476).

YHA members can buy travel insurance at discounted rates in New Zealand and receive discounts on the domestic services of Air New Zealand, Ansett New Zealand, InterCity Coachlines and rail travel, as well as Mount Cook and Newmans Coaches. For details, contact YHA New Zealand at the address above.

One of the leading travel tour operators for students 18 through 35 is **Contiki Holidays,** 300 Plaza Alicante, Suite 900, Garden Grove, CA 92640 (☎ toll free **800/466-0610** in the U.S.) (for details, see "Getting There," below).

Student unions at universities can also be helpful to traveling students. Remember to ask about student discount admission to attractions.

5 Getting There

In this section I'll be dealing with the single largest item in any budget for New Zealand travel—the cost of getting there. While not nearly as costly as it once was, transportation across the South Pacific is the first financial hurdle in your planning. Once you arrive, you'll have a number of options as to how much or how little to spend on transport around New Zealand.

By Plane

You *could* go by ship, of course—one of the luxury liners that sail maybe twice a year, or a freighter making stops all across the Pacific—but for most of us the only practical way to go is by jet. And although air travel cannot be called cheap, it can be called a travel bargain if you utilize the options wisely.

The most important part of your holiday planning begins with predeparture research on airfares. There are differences in the types of fares and seasonal charges, and there are differences in airlines. Your first task should be to study these differences, decide on the one best suited to your needs, then telephone or visit a qualified travel agent or the individual airline offices. Be forearmed with a list of the specific information you need so that answers to your questions can be as direct as possible.

THE AIRLINES

All other things being equal (fares, schedules, and so forth), there is much to be said for choosing any country's national airline, since flying with the locals enables you to encounter en route the people you'll be visiting. In the case of Air New Zealand, the additional reason is that the ever-gracious flight attendants offer in-flight service reminiscent of a bygone era's. Naturally they're friendly and kind—they're New Zealanders, after all—but the fact that there's a hot towel offered before each meal and that tea is served from a pot are impressive in these days of bad attitudes and crumby tea bags.

The combination of these factors undoubtedly accounts for Air New Zealand's topping international passenger polls year after year. Those who sing the praises know what they're singing about—and, as I said, flying this airline is a great way to begin experiencing New Zealand before you land.

Incidentally, if you're curious about the symbol that adorns the tail of every Air New Zealand plane: It's the *koru,* an ancient Maori motif first seen on the prows of those mighty canoes that navigated the Pacific many centuries ago.

All Air New Zealand direct flights to New Zealand from the United States depart from Los Angeles (LAX, Terminal 2) and Honolulu, with Canadian service departing from Toronto and Vancouver. All fly to Auckland International Airport (flights between Australia and New Zealand also fly into Wellington and Christchurch). In addition, Air New Zealand flies to Auckland from London (Heathrow, Terminal 2), Frankfurt, Tokyo, Seoul, Singapore, Bangkok, Bali, Taipei, and Hong Kong.

These are the principal airlines offering service to New Zealand:

- **Air New Zealand** (☎ toll free **800/262-1234** in the U.S., **800/663-5494** in Canada)
- **British Airways** (☎ toll free **800/247-9297** in the U.S., **800/668-1080** in Canada)
- **Canadian Airlines** (☎ toll free **800/426-7000** in the U.S., **800/665-9933** in Canada)
- **Qantas** (☎ toll free **800/227-4500** in the U.S. and Canada)
- **United Airlines** (☎ toll free **800/241-6522** in the U.S. and Canada)

AIRLINE FARES

Set out below are the various types of fares available and their costs as this book is going to press. Remember, however, that these figures are far from cast in stone—as are the fare types, for that matter. Fares can change in a matter of days as airlines rush to introduce new and more competitive fare structures. Use the following as a guide, then shop around carefully.

Note: When you leave New Zealand, you'll have to pay a departure tax of NZ$20 (U.S. $13).

SEASONAL SAVINGS When you travel can have a real impact on your airline costs. Low season runs from April through August, shoulder season includes March and September through mid-November, and peak season is late November through February.

FREE TICKETS Don't overlook the possibility of getting a free ticket through an airline mileage club. Domestic carriers have partner airlines that fly to New Zealand: For instance, American Airlines is partners with Qantas. Members of American's AAdvantage Program accrue AA frequent-flier miles not only every time they fly that airline but also every time they use their American Airlines/Citibank credit card (one mile for each dollar spent). Mileage credits can be used to fly to New Zealand on Qantas.

BEST-FOR-THE-BUDGET FARES As I've said previously, getting to New Zealand can hardly be called cheap. However, if you choose one of the fare classifications that permit en-route stopovers, you'll be purchasing transportation to multiple destinations for the same fare you would pay to get to New Zealand only. And a bit of preliminary research will reveal further savings in package deals that include reduced land costs. So along with exploring New Zealand you could stop over in Tahiti, the Cook Islands, Western Samoa, Tonga, Fiji, and/or Hawaii before returning home.

One possibility is to go through a firm that specializes in "down under" fares, such as **Discover Australia Marketing** of Sacramento, California (☎ toll free **800/637-3273** in the U.S.). This company often offers airline tickets at discount prices to New Zealand as well as Australia.

All fares listed below provide reductions for children.

Promotional Fares Every airline comes up with annual special bargain fares for limited time periods. Savings can be considerable, although many times there are restrictions you must meet to qualify for the fare. Before you make reservations be sure to check for any of these fares.

Coral Direct As we go to press, the lowest round-trip fare on Air New Zealand from Los Angeles to Auckland is $948 U.S. This is the low-season 21-day advance-purchase ticket. During shoulder season this fare is $1,048 U.S., during peak season it's $1,248 U.S. No stopovers are permitted; the minimum stay in New Zealand is seven days, the maximum one month. Tickets must be paid for within seven days of making reservations. No changes are permitted, and there's a penalty for cancellation. Children 2 to 11 fly for 67% of the adult fare.

Coral Experience This fare is $1,048 U.S. in low season, $1,148 U.S. in shoulder season, and $1,348 U.S. in peak season. One free stopover is permitted, and additional stops cost $150 each. The minimum stay is 7 days; the maximum, three months. Reservations and ticketing must be completed 14 days before departure; a cancellation penalty applies. Children 2 to 11 are charged 67% of the adult fare.

Coral Adventure Airpass This fare is $1,419 U.S. in low season, $1,519 U.S. in shoulder season, and $1,719 U.S. in peak season, and it allows three free stopovers. Reservations and ticketing must be completed 14 days before departure; a cancellation penalty applies. Children 2 to 11 travel for 67% of the adult fare.

Coral Explorer Airpass This fare is $1,858 U.S. in low season, $1,958 U.S. in shoulder season, and $2,158 U.S. in peak season. It includes six free stopovers.

The maximum stay is six months, and a cancellation penalty applies. Children 2 to 11 are charged 67% of the full fare.

REGULAR FARES Budget travelers should probably disregard this section entirely—except, of course, for comparison to the savings you'll get by reserving one of the special fares.

Although it's the costliest way to travel, flying in **first class** carries many extras—such as no advance-purchase requirement, virtually unlimited stopovers en route, no penalty for changes or cancellations, a maximum stay of one year, and many in-flight comfort and service perks. The nonstop round-trip first-class fare is $7,200 U.S.

Called Pacific Class on Air New Zealand flights, **business class** differs from first class chiefly in in-flight comfort and service (seats are not as wide, menu choices not as varied). Other conditions are the same as for first class. The round-trip business-class fare is $4,518 U.S.

Regular **economy class** is the next rung down on the comfort and service ladder yet includes the same provisions as the two classes above. The round-trip economy-class fare is $3,066 U.S.

A TRAVEL FANTASY: AROUND THE WORLD

Well . . . why not! After all, you'll have come virtually halfway around the world by the time you travel from North America to New Zealand. Instead of backtracking across the Pacific, this is the perfect time to circle the globe.

I must admit that this fantasy has nagged at me on each trip to New Zealand, and while I haven't yet managed the free time, it's definitely in my future. Air New Zealand makes this dream trip available on an individual basis (interlining with other airlines), with some restrictions, for around $3,000 U.S. Other carriers also give flight to around-the-world fantasies. It's certainly worth thinking about.

Package Tours

There are several excellent package plans on the market that offer good value to the budget traveler. In addition to air travel, they include transportation, lodging, and some sightseeing discounts.

Air New Zealand (☎ **310/615-1111,** or toll free **800/262-1234** in the U.S.), for example, often offers a hotel accommodation package for a mere pittance above its promotional fares. That's hard to beat, as are other money-saving packages, including Hotpac and Lodgepass accommodations vouchers in good-quality motels and lodges at reduced rates. There's a good range of fly/drive, farm and homestay, and ski packages—for details, contact Air New Zealand. Arrangements paid for in the United States prior to departure are *not* subject to the 12.5% GST.

For those in the 18-to-35 bracket, **Contiki Holidays,** 300 Plaza Alicante, Suite 900, Garden Grove, CA 92640 (☎ toll free **800/466-0610** in the U.S.), offers great South Pacific holidays. While travel is with a group, these trips could hardly be called group tours—schedules are such that ample free time is allowed, and for every planned activity there's at least one option. Transportation and accommodations are top-notch, and activities include such unusual events as beachside barbecues, white-water rafting, and ballooning. In short, these are fun tours that appeal to those lively souls who are young at heart as well as in years. Best of all, they offer one of the best-value bargains in the business. For details of the current offerings, contact Contiki Holidays.

Jetset Tours, 5120 W. Gold Leaf Circle, Suite 310, Los Angeles, CA 90056 (☎ toll free **800/453-8738** in the U.S.), operates in Australia, New Zealand, and most of the South Pacific. It offers well-organized group tours and fly/drive tours. Details may be obtained through travel agents or directly from Jetset Tours.

Two other long-established operators in the South Pacific are **Islands in the Sun,** 2381 Rosecrans Ave., Suite 325, El Segundo, CA 90245 (☎ **310/536-0051,** or toll free **800/828-6877** in the U.S.; fax 310/536-6266); and **Austravel,** 51 E. 42nd St., Suite 616, New York, NY 10017 (☎ **212/972-6880,** or toll free **800/633-3404** in the U.S.).

6 Getting Around

When it comes to getting around New Zealand, you can pick and choose your modes of transportation, mixing and matching at your discretion. As I've said, things *work* in this country: Bus and rail transportation are reliable, car-rental firms are dependable, and airlines furnishing domestic service cover longer stretches with ease. Driving, of course, affords the most flexibility, as you're tied to no one's schedule except your own. However, public transportation is an economical, pleasant way to go and, in one form or another, will reach any destination in New Zealand.

By Plane

Air New Zealand National, Mount Cook Airline, Ansett New Zealand, and several other smaller airlines fly internal routes in New Zealand. Schedules are frequent and

Beating the Dreaded Jet Lag

No matter which airline you choose, if you fly nonstop it's going to be a *long* 12-hour flight during which you cross the international date line and lose one whole calendar day (which you gain, of course, on the return trip), go through four time zones, and turn the seasons upside down. There's no way your body isn't going to suffer the pangs of jet lag.

There are as many ways to minimize that malady of long-distance travel and make time fly as there are long-distance travelers, but here are some strategies to consider:

- Walk around the plane to keep your legs and feet from swelling.
- Try to stick to nonalcoholic beverages (very hard when faced with those complimentary New Zealand wines). Drink lots of water.
- If you're one of the many people who swear by those inflatable neck pillows, don't forget yours.
- Either wear comfortable loose clothing or wear something chic to board and bring a sweatsuit or something similar to change into once on board.
- Reserve your seat well ahead, asking for aisle, window, bulkhead, exit row, or whatever suits you best.
- Request special meals ahead of time.
- Bring an engrossing book.
- Make sure you get pillows, a blanket, and a sleep mask from the flight attendant before they're all spoken for.
- Find out which movies will be playing and don't see them beforehand.
- Consider breaking your journey with a South Pacific stopover.

convenient, and the equipment is modern and comfortable. All domestic flights are nonsmoking.

DISCOUNT FARES

All three airlines mentioned below give significant discounts to holders of VIP (backpackers) cards and YHA members.

AIR NEW ZEALAND For those whose time is limited (or those who simply want to vary their modes of travel), the **Explore New Zealand Airpass** offered by Air New Zealand (☎ toll free **800/262-1234** in the U.S.) is a great deal. You purchase three to eight flight coupons for a set price. For NZ$450 (U.S. $292.50) you purchase three coupons good for any 3 of their 460 daily flights; six coupons cost NZ$850 (U.S. $552.50). Fares for children 4 to 11 are 67% of the adult fare. These coupons (good for 60 days from the date of your first flight and accepted on all Air New Zealand National, Link, and Mount Cook Airline services) *must be purchased before you reach New Zealand* and be bought in conjunction with international travel. You don't have to reserve individual flights, however, until you actually reach New Zealand, and unused coupons may be turned in for a refund before you leave for home.

MOUNT COOK AIRLINE Mount Cook Airline (☎ **310/648-7066** in Los Angeles, or toll free **800/468-2665**) links New Zealand's major tourist areas to each other and to Auckland and Christchurch. Schedules are designed to connect with Air New Zealand's domestic service, as well as with international flights.

Mount Cook also provides some of the most spectacular flightseeing tours in the world. If you splurge on a glacier flight, you may fly on Mount Cook Airline. And if your stay must be short, you'll find it's Mount Cook that can get you around to the sightseeing points topping your list. In that case, you should definitely consider the **Kiwi Air Pass,** which *must be purchased before you arrive in New Zealand.* For $549 you can take a circle trip around New Zealand, with stops at any point. Travel must be within 30 consecutive days and must be in one direction—no backtracking. The pass is also valid on Mount Cook Line's bus service if it's substituted for air travel. You can purchase it through a qualified travel agent or by calling Mount Cook Airline.

ANSETT NEW ZEALAND An offshoot of an Australian airline and now operating throughout New Zealand, Ansett New Zealand (☎ toll free **800/366-1300** in the U.S. and Canada) offers several **Good Buy Special Fares** and the **New Zealand Airpass** (which is priced similarly to Air New Zealand's Explore New Zealand Airpass). This airpass *can be purchased prior to departure for New Zealand or after your arrival*—but note that the 12.5% GST will apply if you purchase the pass in New Zealand. No children's discounts are offered.

By Bus

For the budget traveler, buses offer the best way of getting around New Zealand. Consider the following:

- You travel with New Zealanders who aren't touring but merely going about their business—a chance to rub elbows in the most elementary way.
- On many of the buses drivers give an excellent commentary on the countryside—not for tourists, mind you, but for Kiwis who may travel the route frequently but seem as interested as those who are traveling through for the first time.

- When you leave the driving to someone else, there's no need to worry about getting used to driving on the left, keeping one eye glued to the map, or looking for road signs rather than all those scenic splendors.
- All buses are comfortable; some are carpeted and most have individual reading lights. Smoking is not permitted.
- Frequent stops for tea and refreshments are scheduled.
- In rural areas, buses often pull up in front of T-bars alongside the road so the driver can lean out to collect mail sacks to be dropped off at the next post office. All sorts of other freight travels along with you as well—giving you a close-up look at Kiwi life outside the cities.

In addition to regularly scheduled services, New Zealand bus lines run excellent **sightseeing and excursion day trips.** Details are supplied in the appropriate chapters to follow.

DISCOUNT FARES

The three major bus companies in New Zealand are InterCity, Mount Cook, and Newmans, all offering discounts; InterCity and Mount Cook offer money-saving passes as well. Information on any of these passes is available through New Zealand Tourism Board offices.

You should know that *all bus and rail journeys must be booked in advance*—this is particularly important during peak travel periods. Though I've never seen anyone just show up without a reservation and be refused a seat, I wouldn't recommend your taking the chance. Sometimes there's only one bus per day.

NEWMANS COACH LINES With an extensive service network on the North Island only, Newmans Coach Lines (☎ **09/309-9738** in Auckland) offers a 30% discount to holders of YHA cards, New Zealand Backpackers Passes, and the Independent Traveller Discount Cards. A 30% discount is also given to anyone over 65, and a 20% discount is offered to valid full-time students (or anyone with an International Student Identity Card).

INTERCITY InterCity (☎ **09/357-8400** in Auckland) also gives a 20% discount to students and a 30% discount to anyone over 60 and YHA members, plus a 30% discount to VIP (backpackers) card holders.

InterCity has two dollarwise passes: The **Travelpass** provides unlimited rail, coach, and ferry travel for 8 days in a 22-day period for NZ$425 (U.S. $276.25), 15 days in a 35-day period for NZ$530 (U.S. $344.50), or 22 days in a 56-day period for NZ$650 (U.S. $422.50). In addition, InterCity offers a coach pass that includes one trip on the Interislander Ferry. The **Tiki Tours Coach Pass** price is NZ$395 (U.S. $256.75) for 7 days over two weeks, NZ$495 (U.S. $321.75) for 14 days over four weeks, and NZ$595 (U.S. $386.75) for 21 days over six weeks.

MOUNT COOK LANDLINE Mount Cook (☎ toll free **0800/800-287** in New Zealand or **800/468-2665** in the U.S.) gives a 30% discount to all the card holders mentioned above, anyone over 60, and all students over 15. Mount Cook's **Kiwi Coach Pass** provides for 7 days of travel in a 14-day period for NZ$418 (U.S. $271.70), 10 days of travel in a 21-day period for NZ$501 (U.S. $325.65), 15 days of travel in a 35-day period for NZ$580 (U.S. $377), 25 days of travel in a 60-day period for NZ$692 (U.S. $449.80), and 33 days of travel in a 90-day period for NZ$735 (U.S. $477.75). Also included with this pass is a one-way air sector or return ferry trip across Cook Strait.

By Train

All operated by **InterCity,** New Zealand's trains are quite comfortable, although the equipment can be anything from older suburban cars to very good overnight sleepers to sleek, modern rail cruisers.

Trains run along coastlines and mountain gorges with fantastic views, which are sometimes hidden from highways that run farther inland or on higher ground.

These are the major rail services and fares:

AUCKLAND–WELLINGTON The ***Northerner,*** a night train, has normal seated carriages, plus a licensed buffet car where drinks and food are served. The one-way fare is NZ$109 (U.S. $70.85).

The day trip is via the ***Overlander,*** and you'll hear an informative commentary as you pass through fern forests, sacred Maori burial grounds, and volcanic peaks. Free morning and afternoon tea is served by uniformed hostesses and stewards, who also provide newspapers and magazines and will take orders for drinks to be served at your seat. The one-way fare is NZ$129 (U.S. $83.85).

CHRISTCHURCH–DUNEDIN–INVERCARGILL The ***Southerner,*** an overnight nonsleeper, makes this run, one train in each direction. A buffet car serves drinks and food, and drinks may also be ordered from the service staff in your carriage. You're given an illustrated map of the route, which passes some spectacular coastal scenery as well as pastoral scenes of grazing sheep and wheat fields. The one-way fare is NZ$88 (U.S. $57.20). The **TranzAlpine Express** travels between Christchurch and Greymouth for NZ$69 (U.S. $44.85).

These trains are the showpieces of the system. They're carpeted, attractive in decor, and well heated, air-conditioned, or well ventilated. Other comfortable trains include the daylight ***Bay Express,*** between Wellington and Napier (NZ$63/U.S. $40.95); and the ***Coastal Pacific,*** between Christchurch and Picton, connecting with the Picton–Wellington ferry (NZ$59/U.S. $38.35). For details, contact New Zealand Rail (☎ toll free **0800/802-802** in New Zealand).

By Car

New Zealand is a driver's paradise. You can wander at will over roads that (outside the larger cities) carry light traffic. Better yet, you can stop to take a closer look at an inviting seascape or lush fern forest. When lunchtime arrives, you can picnic at whichever scenic spot takes your fancy.

New Zealand roads are exceptionally well maintained, except for a few mountainous stretches on the South Island, where you sometimes wonder how they managed to carve out a road in the first place. And speaking of mountains, let me say—as one who has driven for donkeys' years in all sorts of terrain—that if you're not accustomed to mountain driving, you should consider using public transportation.

RENTALS

Nearly all New Zealand car-rental firms offer unlimited-mileage rates, a decided plus for budgeteers. One of the best bargains I've been able to unearth is through **Maui Econocar Rentals** (☎ toll free **800/351-2323** in the U.S.), which provides the latest-model cars—all under six months old—at low daily rates ranging from NZ$33 to NZ$137 (U.S. $21.45 to $89.05), depending on the car size you rent (from 2- to 10-passenger vehicles). That's with unlimited mileage—insurance is about NZ$15 (U.S. $9.75) per day. With offices in Auckland and Christchurch, they don't even charge for pickup in one island and drop-off in the other. They also have terrific rates for caravans (more about that later). You can book through New Zealand Tourism Board offices in North America or the telephone number given above, or you can contact them directly at Maui Econocar Rentals, Richard Pearse Drive, Mangere, Auckland (☎ **09/275-3013;** fax 09/275-9690); or 430–544 Memorial Ave., Christchurch (☎ **03/358-4159,** or toll free **0800/651-080** in New Zealand), both open daily from 8:30am to 5pm.

The wise traveler will compare the rates and services of several rental-car companies before making a decision. Other possibilities include **Affordable Rental Cars,** 12 Kenyon Ave., Mt. Eden, Auckland (☎ **09/630-1567;** fax 09/630-3692). Daily rates here range from NZ$35 to NZ$38 (U.S. $22.75 to $24.70) off-season (May through September) and are NZ$45 (U.S. $29.25) the rest of the year. Minibuses cost more. These prices include GST, insurance, unlimited mileage, airport transfers, and maps.

Another good alternative to the higher-priced multinational companies, **Apex Car Rentals,** 160 Lichfield St., Christchurch (☎ **03/379-6897;** fax 03/379-2647), offers late-model cars from NZ$40 (U.S. $26) per day (all-inclusive).

You may also be interested to know that **Avis, Hertz,** and **Budget** (reserve in advance through U.S. offices) have branches in all major cities and airports, with daily costs averaging from about NZ$100 (U.S. $65) for economy models up to NZ$150 (U.S. $97.50) for larger models. All offer reductions for longer rental periods.

TOURIST BUY BACK

If your New Zealand stay will be for a long period, you may be interested in the guaranteed tourist buy-back plan offered by **North Harbour Hyundai,** 175 Wairau Rd., Takapuna (☎ **09/444-7795;** fax 09/444-7099). This car dealership on Auckland's North Shore sells used Toyotas, Nissans, Hondas, and similar cars to visitors with a written agreement to purchase the vehicle after a stipulated time period. You might, for instance, buy a 10-year-old car for NZ$5,000, drive it for three months, and sell it back for NZ$3,000. Cars come with a nationwide warranty; owner pays insurance.

CAR SHARING

Another alternative to renting a car is getting a lift from someone who's going your way. **Travelpool** (☎ **09/307-0001**in Auckland) puts people who want a ride in touch with those who have a car and vice versa. The system operates throughout the country. The person getting a ride pays a small commission and something toward gas, which works out to cost about half the price of a bus ticket.

READERS RECOMMEND

The Automobile Association. *"We came to the conclusion that we could get better rental-car deals by waiting until we were there and not trying to make arrangements from the States. Of course, we were not traveling in high season either. . . . We found the AA in New Zealand was exceptional in giving us timely and plentiful information that helped make our trip very enjoyable."*—W. Svirsky, Longwood, Fla., U.S.A.

The Automobile Association. *"We rented a car through the AA in Auckland. Don't forget your American Triple A card as I did! The lady at the Auckland AA found us a rental for NZ$70 a day; if I had had my AAA card, it would have been NZ$35 to NZ$40, she said."*—V. Wright, Gig Harbor, Wash., U.S.A.

DRIVING RULES & MAPS

You must be at least 21 to rent a car in New Zealand and must possess a current driver's license that you've held for at least one year from the United States, Australia, Canada, the United Kingdom, and a few other countries, or an International Driving Permit. You drive on the left and must—by law—buckle that seat belt when the car is moving. The speed limit on the open road is 60 m.p.h. (100kmph); in congested areas, towns, and cities it's 30 m.p.h. (50kmph). Drive with extreme caution when an area is signposted LSZ (Limited Speed Zone). Signposting, incidentally, is very good all through the country—there's little chance of losing your way. Fuel prices vary from area to area but are currently about NZ$.95 (U.S. 60¢) per liter (that's about $2.45 U.S. per gallon).

You'll be given a set of maps when you pick up your rental car, and if you're a member of the Automobile Association in the United States, Australia, Britain, or some European countries, you'll have some reciprocal privileges with the New Zealand AA, which includes their very good maps, plus "strip maps" of your itinerary and comprehensive guidebooks of accommodations (some of which give discounts to AA members). Be sure to bring your home-country membership card. You can contact the **New Zealand Automobile Association** at 99 Albert St., Auckland (☎ **09/377-4660**); 343 Lambton Quay, Wellington (☎ **04/473-8738**), or 210 Hereford St., Christchurch (☎ **03/379-1280**). **Wises Mapping,** 360 Dominion Rd., Mt. Eden, Auckland (☎ **09/638-7146**), produces one of the best maps of New Zealand, available from newsstands and bookshops.

Other Ways to Get Around

BY TAXI

Taxi stands are located at all terminals and on major shopping streets, and you may not hail one on the street within a quarter mile of a stand. They're on call 24 hours a day; their telephone numbers are in local directories, though there's an additional charge if you phone for one. Rates vary from place to place, but all city taxis are metered (in smaller localities there's often a local driver who'll quote a flat fee). Drivers don't expect a tip just to transport you, but if they handle a lot of luggage or perform any other special service, it's very much in order.

BY RV

If you want to take advantage of New Zealand's budget motor camps—or if you're simply a caravaner at heart—**Maui Rentals** (☎ toll free **800/351-2323** in the U.S.), **Mount Cook Line** (☎ toll free **800/262-0248** in the U.S., **800/999-9306** in Canada), and **Newmans** (☎ **09/302-1582** in Auckland) offer minivans and motorhomes at seasonal prices ranging from NZ$80 to NZ$135 (U.S. $52 to $87.75) for two berths, NZ$107 to NZ$189 (U.S. $69.55 to $122.85) for four berths, and NZ$120 to NZ$205 (U.S. $78 to $133.25) for larger vehicles. You can make reservations through New Zealand Tourism Board offices or telephone numbers in North America listed above. In New Zealand, caravans may be booked at any local office of these firms.

BY INTER-ISLAND FERRY

Even if you fly the better part of the trip, try to plan a crossing of Cook Strait on the Wellington–Picton ferry in at least one direction. You'll get a look at both islands from the water, as well as the near-mystical Marlborough Sounds, just as those early Maori and Europeans did. The crossing is one of New Zealand's best travel experiences. *If you plan to bring a car by ferry, you need a confirmed reservation.* Buy your ticket ahead to avoid a potential delay of a day or more. The rate for taking the car or caravan with you is NZ$114 to NZ$150 (U.S. $74.10 to $97.50), depending on size. For more information, check the details under "Crossing Between the North and South Islands," in Chapter 9.

7 Suggested Itineraries

Deciding how long to stay can be a problem, for New Zealand has so much to see and do you'll have a hard time fitting in everything. But it is possible to plan itineraries that will hit the high spots. Travel counselors at New Zealand Tourism Board offices are most helpful in this respect. Here are a few sample itineraries as well. You'll note that you'll have to cover some of the longer stretches by flying. Those flights, however, will be on rather small, low-flying planes, with breathtaking views of the countryside below and awesome mountain peaks that ring the landscape.

All these itineraries are possible, but I strongly recommend that, if there's any way you can manage it, you plan a minimum of three weeks to see both islands at something like a leisurely pace. Some of New Zealand's beauty spots simply invite (almost demand) lingering, and there are several you'll have to omit on a shorter visit. A month would be even better. Failing that, I would stick to one island per visit for the shorter time periods and take in such memorable extras as the Bay of Islands and the Coromandel Peninsula on the North Island and the Banks Peninsula and Stewart Island in the south. You'll have come a long way to see New Zealand, and it would be a shame to get around at too fast a trot.

CITY HIGHLIGHTS On the North Island, Auckland, Rotorua, and Wellington are absolute "must sees," and if it is in any way possible, include Coromandel Peninsula, Bay of Islands, Napier, and Wanganui.

Any South Island itinerary should include Christchurch, Mount Cook, Dunedin, Queenstown (with a trip to Milford Sound), and Nelson.

HISTORIC SITES TOUR New Zealand's varied history can form the basis of an interesting itinerary. You might begin at the top of the North Island, with the oldest surviving building in all of New Zealand, Kemp House (1821–22) in the Kerikeri Basin, the reconstructed Maori village of Keri Park near Kerikeri, Russell's Pompallier House, and the Treaty House in Waitangi. Auckland, of course, bristles with historic sites, as does Wellington. That's just a small sample of historic sightseeing. There are a host of other North and South Island historic sites that will leave you with a deeper, more vivid impression of this country's background and the elements that have shaped its people.

For help in planning an itinerary to suit your particular historical interests, contact The Director, **New Zealand Historic Places Trust,** P.O. Box 2629, Wellington.

If You Have One Week

TOURING THE NORTH ISLAND ONLY

Day 1 Arrive in Auckland in the early morning; sightsee in the afternoon.

Day 2 Drive from Auckland (or take a tour bus, which allows time for sightseeing) to Waitomo, tour the caves and glowworm grotto, then drive on through wooded hills and pastureland dotted with sheep and cattle to Rotorua (356km/221 miles).

Day 3 Full day of sightseeing; Maori concert or hangi in evening.

Day 4 Early-morning flight to the Bay of Islands; launch cruise in the afternoon.

Day 5 Entire day of sightseeing, or take the day-long bus excursion to Cape Reinga and the Ninety-Mile Beach.

Day 6 Drive from the Bay of Islands to Auckland via the west coast (377km/234 miles, about 6 1/2 hours), with sightseeing stops at Waipoua Kauri Forest and Dargaville.

Day 7 Sightseeing most of day; early-evening departure for overseas destination.

TOURING THE SOUTH ISLAND ONLY

Day 1 Arrive in Auckland in the early morning; fly to Christchurch; sightsee in afternoon.

Day 2 Drive along the east coast from Christchurch to Dunedin (362km/225 miles, about 5 hours), across part of the Canterbury Plains and through the seaside resort of Timaru and the "White Stone City" of Oamaru.

Day 3 Entire day of sightseeing in Dunedin, with drive or tour-bus excursion to the Otago Peninsula to see Larnach Castle, Southlight Wildlife, and the Royal Albatross Colony.

Day 4 Early start for the drive from Dunedin to Queenstown (283km/176 miles, about 4 hours) through pleasant farmland; sightsee in the late afternoon.

Day 5 Day-long excursion to Milford Sound (bus in, fly out), including launch cruise to Tasman Sea. (If you're pressed for time, fly in and out.)

Day 6 Allow about 8 hours for the drive from Queenstown to Christchurch (486km/302 miles), which passes through beautiful Kawarau Gorge, then north past breathtaking views of Mount Cook at Lake Pukaki and on across the Canterbury Plains. (Another option is an early-morning flight to Mount Cook, with flightseeing in the afternoon, flying on to Christchurch and Auckland on Day 7.)

Day 7 Sightseeing in the morning; midafternoon flight to Auckland, arriving in time for your evening overseas departure.

If You Have 10 Days

Day 1 Arrive in Auckland in the early morning; sightsee in the afternoon.

Day 2 Drive or take a tour bus to Rotorua via the Waitomo caves and glowworm grotto.

Day 3 Full day of sightseeing in Rotorua; Maori concert or hangi in evening.

Day 4 Early-morning flight from Rotorua to Christchurch, sightseeing in the afternoon.

Day 5 Early-morning flight to Mount Cook; flightseeing over glaciers, icefields, and mountains in the afternoon.

Day 6 Early-morning flight to Queenstown; sightseeing in the afternoon.

Day 7 Day-long trip to Milford Sound (by tour bus and/or plane) for a launch cruise to the Tasman Sea.

Day 8 Early-afternoon flight to Dunedin; sightseeing in late afternoon.

Day 9 Drive or take a tour-bus excursion to the Otago Peninsula to see Larnach Castle, Southlight Wildlife, and the Royal Albatross Colony.

Day 10 Sightseeing in the morning; early-afternoon flight to Auckland (with plane change in Christchurch), arriving in time for your evening overseas departure.

If You Have Two Weeks

Day 1 Arrive in Auckland in the early morning; fly to Christchurch; spend the afternoon sightseeing.

Day 2 Early-morning flight over the Canterbury Plains to Mount Cook, in the heart of the Southern Alps; flightseeing in the afternoon.

Day 3 Early-morning flight to Queenstown; sightseeing in the afternoon.
Day 4 Day-long tour-bus excursion to Milford Sound for a launch cruise to the Tasman Sea.
Day 5 Drive from Queenstown to Dunedin (283km/176 miles, about 4 hours), through pleasant farming country.
Day 6 Drive or take a tour-bus excursion to the Otago Peninsula to visit Larnach Castle, Southlight Wildlife, and the Royal Albatross Colony.
Day 7 Scenic early-morning flight from Dunedin to Wellington, following the east coastline and crossing Cook Strait; sightseeing in the afternoon.
Day 8 Sightseeing in Wellington.
Day 9 Drive or take a bus from Wellington to Napier (327km/203 miles, about 5 hours) through the rugged—and scenic—Manawatu Gorge.
Day 10 Sightseeing in the Hawkes Bay area around Napier; then drive to Taupo (155km/96 miles) and on to Rotorua (88km/55 miles).
Day 11 Full day of sightseeing in Rotorua; Maori concert or hangi in the evening.
Day 12 Drive or take a tour bus to Waitomo to tour the caves and glowworm grotto; then drive on to Auckland (356km/221 miles, about 5$^1/_2$ hours).
Day 13 Full day of sightseeing in Auckland.
Day 14 Depart Auckland for your overseas destination.

If You Have Three Weeks

Day 1 Arrive in Auckland in the early morning; fly to Christchurch; spend the afternoon sightseeing.
Day 2 Early-morning flight over the Canterbury Plains to Mount Cook, in the heart of the Southern Alps; flightseeing in the afternoon, returning to Christchurch.
Days 3–7 Train to Picton, pick up a car and drive to Nelson and down the West Coast to Greymouth and Hokitika; drive to Fox and Franz Josef Glaciers; drive to Wanaka and Queenstown.
Day 8 Sightseeing and lake cruise.
Day 9 Day-long tour-bus excursion to Milford Sound for a launch cruise to the Tasman Sea.
Day 10 Drive from Queenstown to Dunedin (283km/176 miles, about 4 hours), through pleasant farming country.
Day 11 Drive or take a tour-bus excursion to the Otago Peninsula to visit Larnach Castle, Southlight Wildlife, and the Royal Albatross Colony.
Day 12 Scenic early-morning flight from Dunedin to Wellington, following the east coastline and crossing Cook Strait; sightseeing in the afternoon.
Day 13 Sightsee in Wellington.
Day 14 Drive or take a bus from Wellington to Napier (327km/203 miles, about 5 hours) through the rugged—and scenic—Manawatu Gorge.
Day 15 Sightseeing in the Hawkes Bay area around Napier; then drive to Taupo (155km/96 miles) and on to Rotorua (89km/55 miles).
Day 16 Full-day of sightseeing in Rotorua; Maori concert or hangi in the evening.
Days 17 and 18 Drive or take a tour bus to Waitomo to tour the caves and glowworm grotto; overnight in Waitomo; then go on to Auckland (356km/221 miles, about 5$^1/_2$ hours).
Day 19 Full day of sightseeing in Auckland.
Day 20 Drive to Thames, on the Coromandel Peninsula.
Day 21 Depart Auckland for your overseas destination.

If You Have a Month

To the three-week itinerary above, add two days to Day 20, for a full exploration of the Coromandel Peninsula; another four days, the first to drive to the Bay of Islands, with one full day of sightseeing and a second for cruising the bay, and another for the return drive to Auckland.

8 Accommodations Choices

More than any other factor, where you stay will influence your overall impression of New Zealand. Because I want you to love my home away from home the way I do, I'm adding this section on the lodging options. Some "down under" definitions can be confusing, so I want to make sure you pick the right digs.

HOTELS

In New Zealand, *hotel* refers to modern tourist hotels and older public-licensed hotels. The former are usually outside the reach of budget travelers (unless it's time for a splurge), but the latter can be very good value. This is particularly true in small towns, where pubs offer a small number of rooms—generally with shared bathrooms down the hall. As reader P. A. McCauley of Baltimore, Md., points out: "For those who are on a budget but don't have backpacking gear, they can be a life-saver."

MOTELS

In New Zealand, motel rooms (known here as units) frequently come with cooking facilities and a living room (referred to as a lounge), as well as a bedroom. Even if there aren't cooking facilities, you'll always find an electric kettle (called a "jug"), tea, coffee, milk, sugar, and so forth, plus frequently a small refrigerator. The majority of rooms have in-room TVs and telephones and on-premises laundry facilities. Motel rates range from NZ$70 to NZ$100 (U.S. $45.50 to $65) single or double. A motel room without a separate bedroom is called a bed-sitter (studio).

MOTOR INNS

These are basically upmarket motels, often with a restaurant on the premises.

COUNTRY LODGES

Originally these lodges catered to hunters and other sport-minded folk; nowadays they've become exclusive haunts where gourmet meals are as important as fishing. These lodges generally do not offer good value and are well outside a budget traveler's realm.

HOLIDAY HOMES OR BACHES

When they're not being used by their owners, holiday homes throughout New Zealand can be rented by the night or longer. Known as *baches* (or *cribs* on the South Island), these are very good value for independent travelers. You can buy *Baches & Holiday Homes to Rent,* which lists the details on 430 properties, from bookstores or the AA in New Zealand—or contact Mark and Elizabeth Greening, P.O. Box 3107, Richmond, Nelson, New Zealand (☎ and fax **03/544-4799**). The price is NZ$14.95 (U.S. $9.75).

HOSTELS

Even if you've never hosteled before, you may want to try it in New Zealand. In addition to dorm rooms, most hostels offer single and double quarters. Hostels are great for budget travelers who want to fend for themselves in the communal kitchens and don't mind shared bathroom facilities.

See "For Students" under "Tips for the Disabled, Seniors, Singles, Families, and Students," earlier in this chapter, for information on YHA hostels. Also keep in mind that in New Zealand, **YHA hostels** are open 24 hours a day and do not impose curfews or duties—and having a glass of wine with your meal is quite acceptable. Kitchens at these hostels are fully equipped.

Other popular hostels are part of the **VIP network.** While you don't need a VIP card, you get a discount on each of the more than 60 hostels in the group when you have one, as well as other significant discounts. See "By Plane" and "By Bus" under "Getting Around," earlier in this chapter. VIP Discount Cards cost NZ$25 (U.S. $16.25) and are valid for 12 months. Contact **Backpackers Resorts of New Zealand Ltd.,** Box 991, Taupo, New Zealand (☎ and fax **07/377-1157**) for details. Hostels cost about NZ$16 (U.S. $10.40) per person.

MOTOR CAMPS

Not only for those traveling by campervan (RV) or with a tent, motor camps also offer cabins, flats, and motel units. All of these are "self-contained"—with a kitchen and bathroom. Occupants of cabins sometimes must supply their own linens. Only motel units are serviced—receive daily maid service. Campers share communal kitchens and bathrooms.

BED-&-BREAKFASTS

This is the most confusing term, because it means something different in nearly every country in which it's used. In New Zealand, properties offering accommodation and breakfast for one set price include homestays, farmstays, guesthouses, and inns.

Homestays range from the-kids-are-in-boarding-school-and-we've-got-two-spare-rooms to we-love-meeting-people-and-we-purposely-built-this-house-to-comfortably-accommodate-guests. Luckily for you, I've sorted out one from the other. Homestays are a wonderful way to meet people and see how they live. The hosts are a font of knowledge about local attractions and dining options; the breakfasts are usually very good, and dinners (when they're offered) are especially good value. The average homestay, not booked through an agency, costs NZ$70 (U.S. $45.50) double and NZ$45 (U.S. $29.25) single.

Farmstays, essentially homestays on a farm, present an ideal opportunity for learning what makes New Zealand tick and for savoring some of the beautiful Kiwi countryside. A firsthand knowledge of just what it takes to raise all those sheep and cattle and kiwifruit will give you more insight into New Zealand life than you could gain in any other way.

In addition to specific farmstays listed in this book, several companies will help you find a farm. One of these is **New Zealand Farm Holidays,** P.O. Box 256, Silverdale, Auckland, New Zealand (☎ **09/307-2024;** fax 09/426-8474). The cost, including dinner and breakfast, begins at about NZ$79 ($51.35) per person. **Hospitality Plus Ltd.,** P.O. Box 56175, Auckland 3, New Zealand (☎ **09/810-9175;** fax 09/810-9448), offers homestays and farmstays from NZ$60 (U.S. $39) for bed and breakfast to NZ$90 (U.S. $58.50) for dinner, bed, and breakfast. This rate is per person, based on two people sharing. Home-hosted dinners without accommodation cost NZ$50 (U.S. $32.50) per person for three courses with wine.

Guesthouses present another bed-and-breakfast option. Offering good value and modest prices, guesthouses have simply furnished rooms (often without en suite baths), and there's almost always a guest lounge with a TV and tea- and coffee-making facilities. For more information, contact **New Zealand's Federation of Bed &**

Breakfast Hotels, Inc., 52 Armagh St., Christchurch, New Zealand (☎ **03/366-1503**). Guesthouses cost about NZ$75 (U.S. $48.75) double and NZ$45 (U.S. $29.25) single.

Bed-and-breakfast inns, with their attractive decors and superb morning meals, are my personal favorite type of accommodation in New Zealand. They cost a bit more: up to NZ$160 (U.S. $104) double and NZ$100 (U.S. $65) single, but I'd rather skimp on something else and splurge on a wonderful B&B. As with homestays and farmstays, the hosts are helpful and gracious, but in the case of most New Zealand inns you get a bonus of historic ambience and old-world charm. Sometimes it's hard to tell the difference between a homestay and a bed-and-breakfast inn; generally inns have more rooms than homestays and guests have less interaction with the hosts.

Fast Facts: New Zealand

American Express The American Express Travel Service office is at 101 Queen St., Auckland (☎ **09/379-8240**). Other agencies (mostly travel-agent offices) around the country are located in Christchurch, Dunedin, Lower Hutt (near Wellington), Napier, Nelson, Queenstown, Rotorua, Wellington, and Whangarei. They accept mail for clients (you're a client if you have an American Express card or traveler's checks), forward mail for a small fee, issue and change traveler's checks, and replace lost or stolen traveler's checks and American Express cards.

Business Hours Banks in international airports are open for all incoming and outgoing flights; others are open from 9am to 4:30pm Monday through Friday. Shops are usually open from 9am (sometimes 8am) to 5:30pm Monday through Thursday, until 9pm on either Thursday or Friday. Increasingly, shops are open all day Saturday; most, but not all, shops are closed Sunday.

Camera/Film Film is expensive in New Zealand, so bring as much as you can with you. You're not limited by Customs regulations, just by baggage space. Most brands are available in larger cities. There is also same-day developing service in most cities.

Cigarettes You can bring in 200 cigarettes per person, as allowed by Customs regulations. Most brands for sale in New Zealand are English or European, although more and more American brands are appearing on the market.

Climate See "Timing Your Trip," earlier in this chapter.

Crime See "Safety," below.

Currency See "Information, Entry Requirements, and Money," earlier in this chapter.

Customs See "Information, Entry Requirements, and Money," earlier in this chapter.

Documents Required See "Information, Entry Requirements, and Money," earlier in this chapter.

Driving Rules See "Getting Around," earlier in this chapter.

Drug Laws Because of its long, indented coastline, New Zealand has been easy prey for drug traffickers. As a result, laws are not only among the world's strictest, they're also stringently enforced. Don't even be tempted!

Drugstores Pharmacies observe regular local shop hours, but each locality usually will have an Urgent Pharmacy, which remains open until about 11pm every day except Sunday, when there will be two periods during the day when it's open. You'll find them listed in local telephone directories. There's a minimal extra charge for prescriptions filled during nonshop hours.

Electricity New Zealand's voltage is 230 volts, and plugs are the three-pin flat type. If your hairdryer or other small appliances are different, you'll need a transformer/adapter. Most motels and better hotels have built-in wall transformers for 110-volt, two-prong *razors,* but if you're going to be staying in hostels, cabins, homestays, or guesthouses, better bring a transformer or dual-voltage appliances.

Embassies/Consulates In Wellington, the national capital, you'll find embassies for the United States and Canada, as well as the British High Commission (see "Fast Facts: Wellington" in Chapter 9). In Auckland are consulates for the United States, Canada, and Ireland (see "Fast Facts: Auckland" in Chapter 5).

Emergencies Dial **111** anyplace in New Zealand for the police, an ambulance, or to report a fire. Should you need a doctor, either consult the nearest visitor information office or prevail on your motel or guesthouse host to direct you to one. Even most small towns have medical centers.

Etiquette Mind your manners! They're highly valued in New Zealand, and the Kiwis are among the most mannerly people on the face of the earth. If you're uncertain what to do in a social situation, just hold on to the rudiments of common courtesy and you'll be fine.

Holidays See "Timing Your Trip," earlier in this chapter.

Information See "Information, Entry Requirements, and Money," earlier in this chapter.

Language English is spoken by all New Zealanders—Maori and Pakeha. You'll hear Maori spoken on some TV and radio programs and in some Maori settlements, but it's seldom used in conversation in the presence of overseas visitors.

Laundry No matter whether you'll be staying in hostels or motels, there will usually be a well-equipped laundry on the premises for your use. Cities have commercial laundries, but most visitors have little need for them.

Liquor Laws The minimum drinking age is 20 in pubs, 18 in licensed restaurants or with parent or guardian. Children are allowed in pubs with their parents.

Mail New Zealand post offices will receive mail for you and hold it for one month. Just have it addressed to you c/o *Poste Restante* at the Chief Post Office of the city or town you'll be visiting. American Express will receive and forward mail for its clients. Allow 10 days for delivery from the United States. It costs NZ$1.50 (U.S. $1) to send an airmail letter to the United States or Canada and NZ$1.80 (U.S. $1.20) to the United Kingdom or Europe. Overseas airmail postcards and aerograms cost NZ$1 (U.S. 65¢). "Fast Post" mail within New Zealand costs NZ80¢ (U.S. 55¢) per card or letter.

Maps Wises Mapping, 360 Dominion Rd., Mt. Eden, Auckland (☎ **09/638-7140**), produces one of the best maps of New Zealand, available at newsstands and bookshops. Rental-car firms furnish a map with every car rented.

Newspapers/Magazines New Zealand has no national newspapers, although most large-city newspapers carry national and international, as well as local, news. Leading newspapers are the *New Zealand Herald* (Auckland) and *Dominion* (Wellington).

Passports See "Information, Entry Requirements, and Money," earlier in this chapter.

Pets Because of its dependence on a disease-free agricultural environment, New Zealand has restrictions on the importation of most animals. If you must bring a pet, check first with the Ministry of Agriculture and Fisheries, P.O. Box 12-108, Wellington, or any New Zealand embassy or consulate.

Radio/TV The BCNZ (Broadcasting Council of New Zealand) is the major broadcaster in New Zealand, operating TV Channel 1 and TV Channel 2, and Radio New Zealand. The majority of TV productions come from Britain and America. For current scheduling, check the listings in daily newspapers. And to hear the country's beautiful national anthem, "God Defend New Zealand," sung in both English and Maori, tune in to Channel 1 at sign-off time.

Restrooms There are "public conveniences" strategically located and well signposted in all cities and many small towns. You'll find public restrooms at most service stations.

Local Plunket Rooms are a real boon to mothers traveling with small children, for they come with a "Mother's Room," where you can change diapers and do any necessary tidying up. The Plunket Society is a state-subsidized organization, which provides free baby care to all New Zealand families, and their volunteers are on duty in the Plunket Rooms—no charge, but they'll welcome a donation.

Safety Whenever you're traveling in an unfamiliar city or country, stay alert. Be aware of your immediate surroundings. Wear a moneybelt and don't sling your camera or purse over your shoulder. This will minimize the possibility of your becoming a victim of crime. Every society has its criminals. It's your responsibility to be aware and alert even in the most heavily touristed areas.

Taxes There's a 12.5% Goods and Services Tax (GST). And be sure to save enough New Zealand currency to pay the departure tax of NZ$20 (U.S. $13).

Telephone/Telegram/Fax There are three main kinds of public telephones in New Zealand: card phones, credit-card phones, and coin phones. **Local calls** cost NZ20¢ (U.S. 13¢). Reader W. Svirsky of Longwood, Fla., found the use of card phones almost mandatory because in many areas the only public phones were card phones. "Fortunately," he wrote, "the magnetic-strip PhoneCards are available just about everywhere in NZ$5 (U.S. $3.25), NZ$10 (U.S. $6.50), NZ$20 (U.S. $13), and NZ$50 (U.S. $32.50) denominations. The digital readout on the phones shows the current value of the card and the decrease in value as you use the phone."

The telephone area code in New Zealand is known as the STD (subscriber toll dialing). To call **long distance** within New Zealand, dial the STD—**09** for Auckland and Northland, **07** for the Thames Valley, **06** for the East Coast and Wanganui, **04** for Wellington, or **03** for the South Island—then the local number. (If you're calling from outside New Zealand, omit the "0.") For operator assistance within New Zealand, dial **010;** for directory assistance, **018.**

The most economical way to make **international phone calls** from New Zealand is to charge them to an international calling card (they're available free from your long-distance company at home, so get one before you go). All calls, even international ones, can be made from public phone booths (long-distance calls made from your hotel or motel often have hefty surcharges added). To reach an international operator, dial **0170;** for directory assistance for an international call, dial **0172.** You can also call the United States via AT&T's USA Direct service by dialing **000-911.**

For more information about lowering telephone costs, see "Information and Communications" under "Forty Money-Saving Tips," in Chapter 1.

All **telegrams** are sent through the post office, either by telephone or in person. The lowest rate is "Letter Rate," which takes about 24 hours for delivery. Telegrams sent after regular post office hours can cost twice as much.

You'll find **fax** facilities at many hotels and motels, as well as in some local post offices, Visitor Information Network offices, and photocopy centers.

Time New Zealand is located just west of the international date line, and its standard time is 12 hours ahead of Greenwich mean time. Thus when it's noon in New Zealand, it's 7:30am in Singapore, 9am in Tokyo, 10am in Sydney; and—all the previous day—4pm in San Francisco, 7pm in New York, and midnight in London. In New Zealand, daylight saving time starts the first weekend in October and ends in mid-March.

Tipping Most New Zealanders don't tip wait persons unless they've received extraordinary service—and then only 5 to 10%. I suggest you follow suit. Also, I'd give taxi drivers about 10% and porters NZ$1 or $2, depending on how much luggage you have.

Tourist Offices See "Information, Entry Requirements, and Money," earlier in this chapter.

Visas See "Information, Entry Requirements, and Money," earlier in this chapter.

Water Drink away—New Zealand tap water is pollution free and safe to drink anywhere you develop a thirst. In the bush you should boil, filter, or chemically treat water from rivers and lakes to avoid contracting giardia.

4 The Active Vacation Planner

WHEN IT COMES TO RECREATIONAL ACTIVITIES, I CAN'T THINK OF ANYWHERE more accommodating than New Zealand. The clean green environment of this relatively small country offers many perfect places for stress-busting sojourns and exhilarating exercise. Surrounded by beautiful forests, majestic fiords, and secluded beaches, you can stretch your muscles as you clear your mind. And you'll be in good company: Kiwis consider recreation a way of life and welcome visitors to join them.

This chapter covers New Zealand's most popular active vacation choices, providing you with details on the best places to go and the best contacts for information, equipment, and supplies. Of course, it's only a sampling of what New Zealand offers. In addition, you can enjoy golf on many great courses found from one end of the country to the other and soaring near Omarama, where the conditions are excellent (this tiny town hosted the World Gliding Championships in January 1995). Other popular pastimes include caving, cave rafting, white-water rafting, mountain biking, mountaineering, horse trekking, rock climbing, abseiling, hunting, and running. Check with the nearest visitor information center if any of these options appeals to you.

For information on a variety of active vacation trips, contact the New Zealand Tourism Board nearest you for a copy of the 18-page **"Naturally New Zealand Holidays"** brochure. If the tourism board happens not to have the brochure, contact Naturally New Zealand Holidays, P.O. Box 33-940, Takapuna, New Zealand (☎ **09/486-5327;** fax 09/486-5328).

If you want to know all the recreational options, you might want to buy the ***New Zealand Adventure Annual & Directory*** from New Zealand Adventures Agencies Ltd., P.O. Box 737, Christchurch, New Zealand (☎ **03/326-7516;** fax 03/326-7518). The directory costs NZ$19.95 (U.S. $13.00), plus NZ$12.50 (U.S. $8.15) for economy postage or NZ$19 (U.S. $12.35) for air mail.

1 Skiing & Snowboarding

New Zealand attracts dedicated **skiers** like a magnet—its "down under" ski season (usually late June through October) allows those from the Northern Hemisphere to hit the slopes year round.

On the North Island, the two major commercial ski fields are Whakapapa and Turoa, both on the slopes of Mount Ruapehu in the Tongariro National Park; Ruapehu, with a simmering crater lake, is an active volcano that soars some 9,200 feet high, making it the North Island's highest peak. **Whakapapa** (☎ **07/892-3738;** fax 07/892-3732), the largest ski field, offers a range of facilities for beginners to the most advanced. **Turoa** (☎ **06/385-8456**), on Mount Ruapehu's south side, is appreciated for its long spring season lasting into late October.

On the South Island, **Mount Hutt** ski field (☎ **03/302-8811;** fax 03/302-8697), located only about an hour and a half from Christchurch, offers both traditional downhill skiing and heliskiing. Farther south are four ski areas that lure both New Zealanders and overseas visitors to the Southern Lakes Ski Region between Queenstown and Wanaka. You can take your pick from the internationally respected **Remarkables, Cardrona, Treble Cone,** and **Coronet Peak.** Among them, they offer downhill skiing, cross-country skiing, and heliskiing, plus equipment rental, private and group lessons, and terrain for all levels of skier.

Lift prices in New Zealand range from NZ$48 to NZ$58 (U.S. $31.20 to $37.70); skis, boots, and pole rentals cost from NZ$25 to NZ$35 (U.S. $16.25 to $19.50); and lessons are about NZ$32 (U.S. $20.80) for two hours. Costs for kids are lower.

At **Mount Cook,** skiers can catch a ride on a helicopter or skiplane and then schuss down the famous—and *very* challenging—Tasman Glacier. For full details on this not-exactly-budget activity, see "Mount Cook" in Chapter 11.

Mount Cook Line operates the skiplanes at Mount Cook, owns The Remarkables and Coronet Peak ski areas, and offers a number of good-value ski packages that include accommodations, lift tickets, and transfers to and from the slopes. Contact Mount Cook Line at toll free **0800/800-737** in New Zealand, **008/221-134** in Australia, **800/999-9306** in Canada, or **800/262-0248** in the United States.

The top **snowboarding** destination in New Zealand is the **Temple Basin Ski Area** in Arthur's Pass National Park, two hours from Christchurch. Helisnowboarding is offered in the Southern Lakes region.

If the skiing bug should bite you after you're in New Zealand, head for one of Mount Cook Line's extensive network of Travel Centres in major cities and tourist centers.

2 Fishing

New Zealand is one of the top spots in the world (if not *the* top spot) for **trout fishing**—both rainbow and brown. An interesting fact is that the ova for these big rainbow trout came from California in the United States—from the Russian River, to be specific. Except for in Rotorua and Taupo, the season is limited from about October to April. The Tongiriro River, near Turangi, is one of the best trout-fishing rivers in the world. The best time to fish there is from May to October.

Note: It's illegal to sell trout in New Zealand, so if you want to eat any you'll have to catch it yourself.

Both the North Island and the South Island have trout in streams and lakes, but salmon fishing is limited to the South Island. The Rakaia River is a favorite spot, and January through March is the best time.

Writer Zane Grey called the Bay of Islands the "anglers El Dorado" because of its plentiful **big-game fishing.** There are also areas on the Coromandel Peninsula and the Bay of Plenty where this is a popular sport. The best months to try for big game are January through May.

You'll find details about **fishing guides** under each "Sports and Recreation" heading in this book. Dedicated budget travelers should be aware, however, that these guides are far from inexpensive.

3 Boating & Other Water Sports

BOATING

Of course, boating is a major summer pastime (December through February) in a country with 1,597 kilometers (992 miles) of coastline. There are countless possibilities—from exploring the thousands of secluded inlets and tranquil bays to sailing to uninhabited islands, even heading out to the high seas.

Auckland, known as the City of Sails, is said to contain more boats per capita than any other city in the world. Once you see the Waitemata Harbour dotted with white sails on a Sunday afternoon you'll have no trouble believing this. **Sailing** is extremely popular in the harbor and the adjacent Hauraki Gulf. Other beautiful places to sail are the Bay of Islands and the Marlborough Sounds.

Both bareboat and skippered charters are available. If this interests you, contact **Moorings Rainbow Yacht Charters,** Opua Wharf, Opua, Bay of Islands (☎ **09/402-7821,** fax 09/402-7546; in Auckland, ☎ **09/378-0719,** fax 09/378-0931). Other reliable operators include **Marlborough Sounds Charters Ltd.,** P.O. Box 71, Picton (☎ **03/573-7726**); and **Charter Link,** 2 Aratai St., Bucklands Beach, Auckland (☎ **09/535-8710;** fax 09/537-0196).

If paddling around is more what you're looking for, you'll find a lot of **kayaking** and **canoeing** enthusiasts in New Zealand. Sea kayaking is popular in the Bay of Islands, in the Hauraki Gulf, around the Coromandel Peninsula, in the Marlborough Sounds, and even in Milford Sound. The Rangitikei River, between Wanganui and Palmerston North, is ideal for those who prefer river paddling.

For more information, contact **Coastal Kayakers,** P.O. Box 325, Paihia, Bay of Islands, New Zealand (☎ **09/402-8105;** fax 09/404-0291); **Auckland Canoe Centre,** 302A Dominion Rd., Auckland, New Zealand (☎ and fax **09/638-6773**); or **Marlborough Sounds Adventure Co.,** P.O. Box 195, Picton, New Zealand (☎ **03/573-6078;** fax 03/573-8827).

OTHER WATER SPORTS

If you saw the film *Endless Summer II,* you probably know that Raglan, on the North Island, in a truly hot **surfing** spot. And it isn't the only place to ride the waves. Oakura, near New Plymouth, claims to have world-class surfing and **windsurfing.** If you arrive in New Zealand sans board, inquire at the nearest visitor information center about where you can rent one.

Diving is popular in the Bay of Islands and around Northland's Poor Knights Islands. Visibility here ranges from 66 to 230 feet in the best months—February through June. It gets pretty cold, but hardy folks even dive in Milford Sound and at Stewart Island.

Feel like checking out a wreck or two? The remains of the *Rainbow Warrior* lie on the white-sand bottom among Northland's Cavalli Islands, and the Russian cruise ship *Mikhail Lermontov* sits where it sunk in the Marlborough Sounds.

For details on diving, contact **Bay Guides,** 12 Marsden Rd., Paihia, Bay of Islands (☎ **09/402-8428;** fax 09/402-8346), or the visitor center in Picton (see Chapter 10).

4 Cycling

Cycle touring is popular with New Zealand visitors because it provides a great way to see the wonders of the country at a relaxed pace. The South Island's West Coast is probably the area most frequently covered, though it's possible to cycle almost anywhere. Two other good areas are Christchurch and the Canterbury Plains.

Several operators organize cycling trips: Contact **New Zealand Pedaltours,** P.O. Box 37-575, Parnell, Auckland, New Zealand (☎ **09/302-0968;** fax 09/302-0967), or **Cycling Downunder,** P.O. Box 10-180, Christchurch, New Zealand (☎ and fax **03/366-4318**).

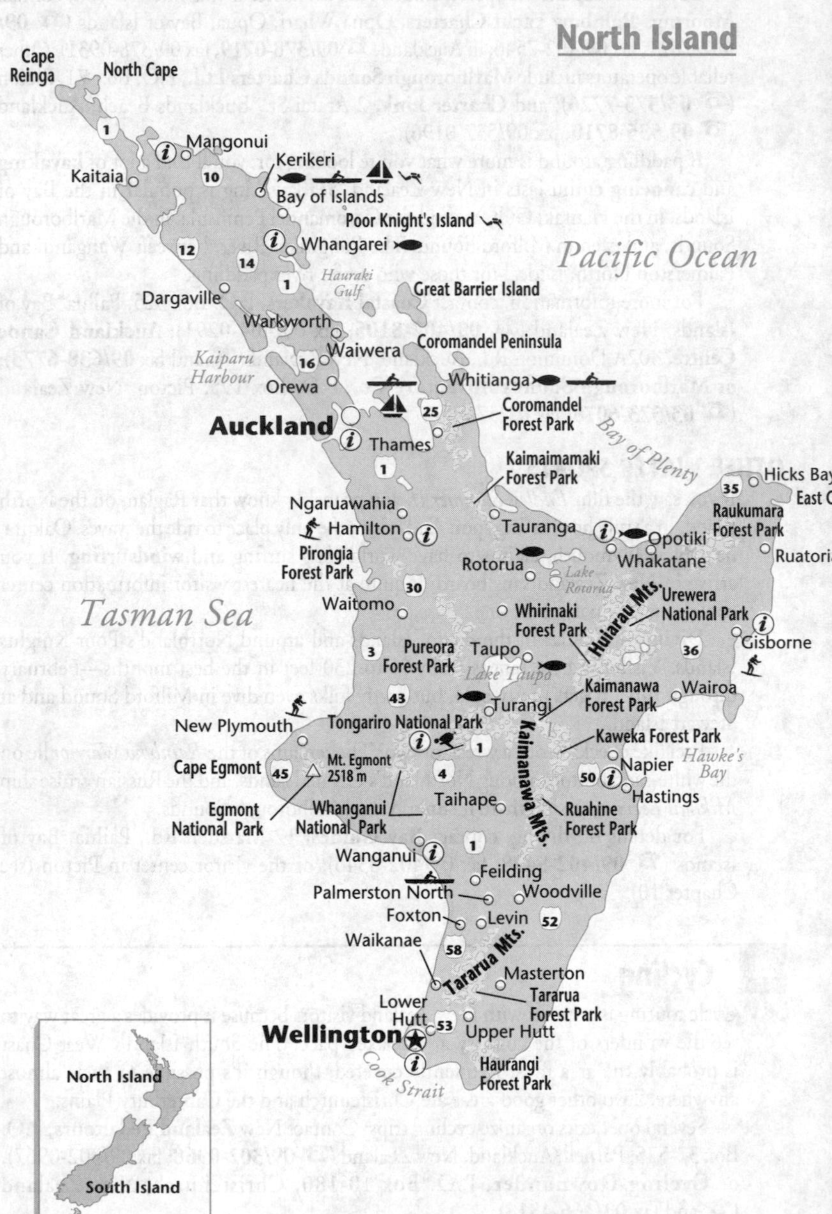

North Island
Cape Reinga
North Cape
Mangonui
Kaitaia
Kerikeri
Bay of Islands
Poor Knight's Island
Whangarei
Pacific Ocean
Hauraki Gulf
Great Barrier Island
Dargaville
Warkworth
Waiwera
Coromandel Peninsula
Kaiparu Harbour
Orewa
Whitianga
Coromandel Forest Park
Auckland
Thames
Bay of Plenty
Kaimaimamaki Forest Park
Hicks Bay
East Ca
Raukumara Forest Park
Ngaruawahia
Hamilton
Tauranga
Opotiki
Whakatane
Ruatoria
Pirongia Forest Park
Rotorua
Lake Rotorua
Waitomo
Whirinaki Forest Park
Huiarau Mts.
Urewera National Park
Tasman Sea
Gisborne
Taupo
Pureora Forest Park
Lake Taupo
Kaimanawa Forest Park
Wairoa
Turangi
Kaimanawa Mts.
New Plymouth
Tongariro National Park
Kaweka Forest Park
Cape Egmont
Mt. Egmont 2518 m
Napier
Hawke's Bay
Hastings
Taihape
Egmont National Park
Whanganui National Park
Ruahine Forest Park
Wanganui
Feilding
Palmerston North
Woodville
Foxton
Levin
Waikanae
Tararua Mts.
Masterton
Tararua Forest Park
Lower Hutt
Wellington
Upper Hutt
Cook Strait
Haurangi Forest Park
North Island
South Island
1
10
12
14
16
25
1
35
30
3
36
43
1
4
45
50
1
52
58
53
9628

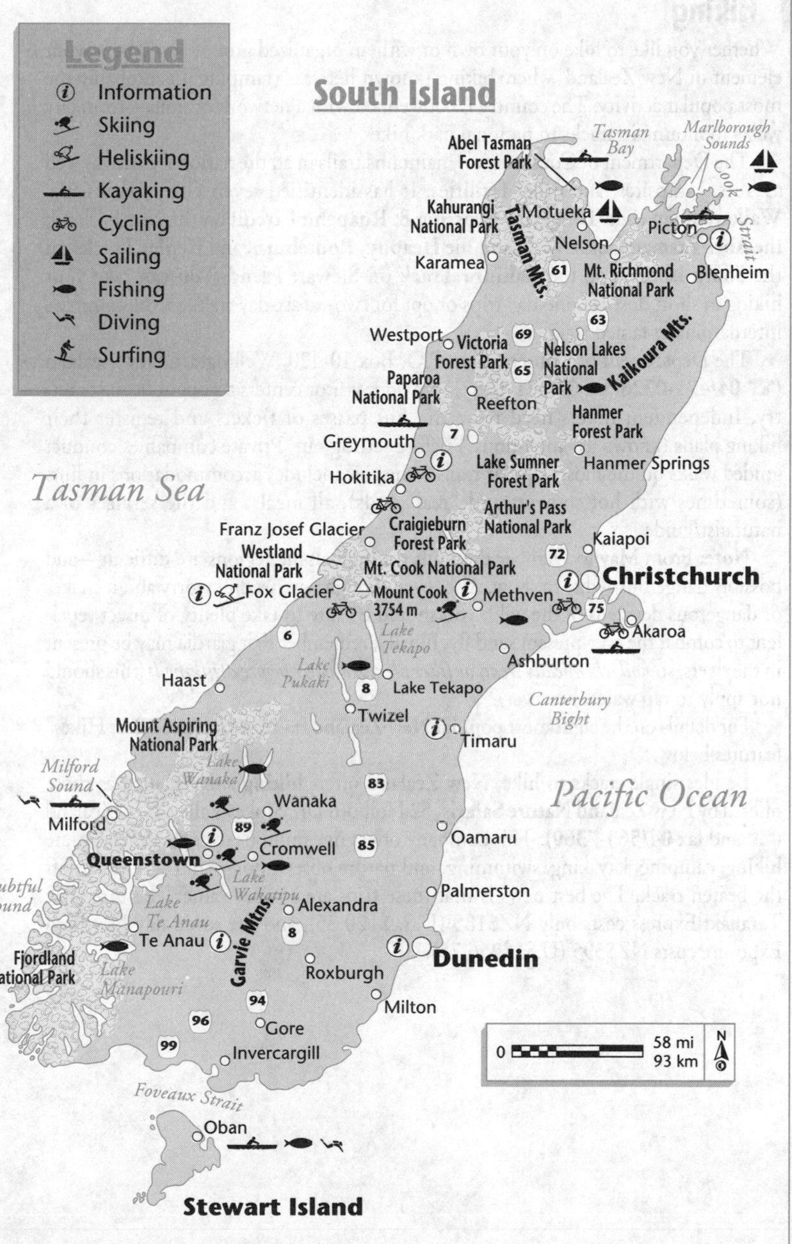
Legend
Information
Skiing
Heliskiing
Kayaking
Cycling
Sailing
Fishing
Diving
Surfing
South Island
Tasman Bay
Marlborough Sounds
Abel Tasman Forest Park
Cook Strait
Kahurangi National Park
Tasman Mts.
Motueka
Picton
Nelson
Karamea
Blenheim
Mt. Richmond National Park
61
63
69
65
Westport
Victoria Forest Park
Nelson Lakes National Park
Kaikoura Mts.
Paparoa National Park
Reefton
Hanmer Forest Park
Hanmer Springs
7
Greymouth
Lake Sumner Forest Park
Hokitika
Tasman Sea
Arthur's Pass National Park
Craigieburn Forest Park
Franz Josef Glacier
Kaiapoi
72
Westland National Park
Mt. Cook National Park
Christchurch
Fox Glacier
Mount Cook 3754 m
Methven
75
Akaroa
Lake Tekapo
6
Ashburton
Lake Pukaki
Haast
8
Lake Tekapo
Canterbury Bight
Twizel
Mount Aspiring National Park
Timaru
Lake Wanaka
Milford Sound
83
Pacific Ocean
Wanaka
Milford
89
85
Oamaru
Cromwell
Queenstown
Lake Wakatipu
Doubtful Sound
Lake Te Anau
Palmerston
Alexandra
Garvie Mtns.
Te Anau
8
Dunedin
Fjordland National Park
Lake Manapouri
Roxburgh
94
Milton
96
Gore
99
Invercargill
0
58 mi
93 km
N
Foveaux Strait
Oban
Stewart Island

5 Hiking

Whether you like to hike on your own or with an organized group, you'll be in your element in New Zealand, where hiking (known here as "tramping") is probably the most popular activity. The country is cobwebbed with a network of trails—from city walks to mountain tracks to national park hikes.

The Department of Conservation maintains trails in all the national parks, as well as huts, campsites, and other facilities. It has identified seven Great Walks: the **Waikaremoana** and **Tongariro Crossing & Ruapehu Circuit** on the North Island; the **Abel Tasman Coast Walk** and the **Heaphy, Routeburn,** and **Kepler Tracks** on the South Island; and the **Rakiura Track** on Stewart Island. You can take your hiking in short doses of one-day trips or opt for two- to six-day treks on the country's internationally famed trails.

The Department of Conservation, P.O. Box 10-420, Wellington, New Zealand (☎ **04/471-0726;** fax 04/471-1082), provides visitor centers throughout the country. Independent hikers need to secure hut passes or tickets and register their hiking plans (known as "intentions") before setting out. Private companies conduct guided walks on the most popular trails—the cost includes accommodations in huts (sometimes with hot showers and "real" beds), all meals, and the services of a naturalist/guide.

Note: From May to October the trails through alpine regions are difficult—and possibly dangerous—due to snow. Also, even though you needn't worry about snakes or dangerous denizens of the wild, you should be sure to take plenty of insect repellent to combat the ever-present sand fly. Finally, remember that giardia may be present in the rivers, so *boil, chemically treat, or filter all river water before drinking it* (this should not apply to tap water, however).

For details on the eight most popular New Zealand trails, see the two "Best Hikes" features below.

Besides single tracks to hike, New Zealand offers **hiking safaris,** such as those offered by **New Zealand Nature Safaris,** 52 Holborn Dr., Stokes Valley, New Zealand (☎ and fax **04/563-7360**). This company offers five minibus trips that incorporate hiking, camping, kayaking, swimming, and nature observation—and stay *strictly* off the beaten track. The best news is that these trips are a super value: The three-day Taranaki Express costs only NZ$185 (U.S. $120.25), and the seven-day Northern Exposure costs NZ$395 (U.S. $256.75).

The Best Hikes
Marlborough, Nelson & Beyond

QUEEN CHARLOTTE WALKWAY

This walk passes through lush coastal forest, around coves and inlets, and along ridges offering spectacular views of the Queen Charlotte and Kenepuru Sounds. Access to Ship Cove is by boat or float plane. One-day walks are possible.

DURATION/DISTANCE 4 days/67km (42 miles)

START Ship Cove (Marlborough Sounds)

END Anakiwa (Marlborough Sounds)

OPEN Year round. Guided walks given November through May only.

CONTACT • **Department of Conservation** Picton Field Centre, Picton, New Zealand (☎ **03/573-7582;** fax 03/573-8362).

• **Guided Walk** Marlborough Sounds Adventure Company, P.O. Box 195, Picton, New Zealand (☎ **03/573-6078;** fax 03/573-8827).

COST • **Independent Walk** NZ$2 (U.S. $1.30) per night camping fee or lodgings at various price levels—plus transfers.

• **Guided Walk** NZ$550 (U.S. $357.50) for four-day package covering 45km (28 miles) from Ship Cove to Punga Cove.

ABEL TASMAN COAST TRACK

This walk is well known for its views of gorgeous shoreline. You pass through coastal forests and walk along beautiful beaches. Access to Marahau is by bus or boat. Launches make it convenient to do one-day walks. Buses pick you up at the end of the trail.

DURATION/DISTANCE 3 to 5 days/51km (32 miles)

START Marahau (Abel Tasman National Park)

END Wainui Bay (Abel Tasman National Park)

OPEN Year round. Guided walks given year round.

CONTACT • **Department of Conservation** King Edward and High streets (P.O. Box 97), Motueka, New Zealand (☎ **03/528-9117;** fax 03/528-6751).

• **Guided Walk** Abel Tasman National Park Enterprises, Old Cederman House (R.D. 3), Motueka, New Zealand (☎ **03/528-7801;** fax 03/528-6087).

COST • **Independent Walk** NZ$6 (U.S. $3.90) per night hut fee or camping fee—plus transfers. Lower price for children.

• **Guided Walk** NZ$550 (U.S. $357.50) for three-day package; NZ$850 (U.S. $552.50) for five-day package. Lower prices for children.

HEAPHY TRACK

This exciting walk takes you from the junction of the Brown and Aorora rivers, across tussock-covered flats, and finally to the wild sea on the West Coast. Bus and taxi transfers are available to both ends of the track.

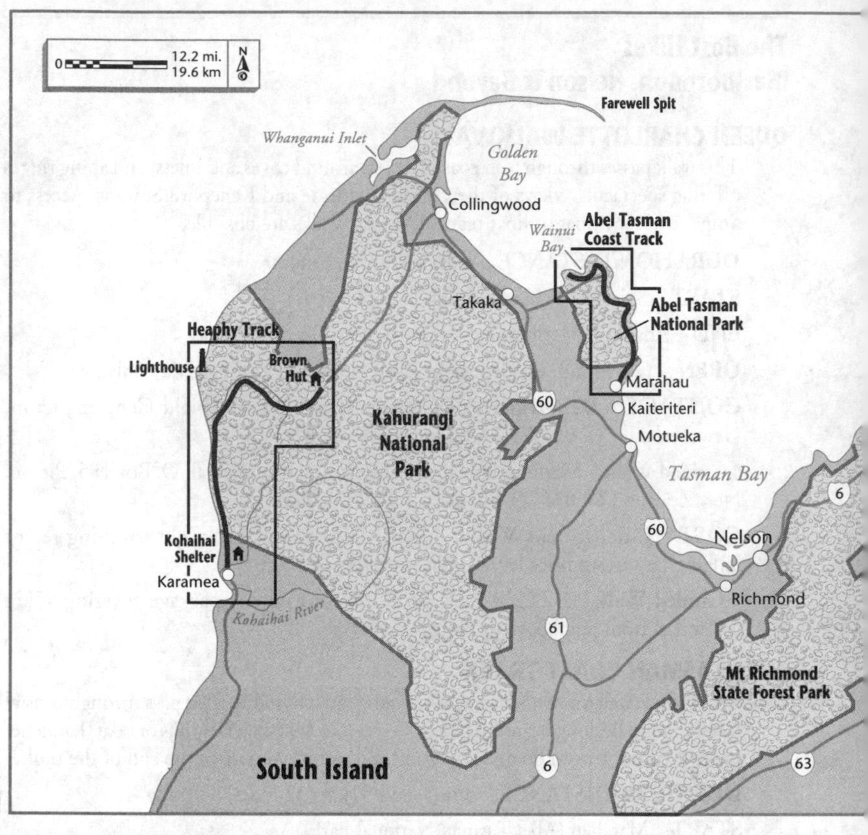

DURATION/DISTANCE 4 to 6 days/77km (48 miles)

START Brown Hut (Kahurangi National Park)

END Kohaihai River mouth (Kahurangi National Park)

OPEN Year round. Guided walks not available.

CONTACT • Department of Conservation 1 Commercial St. (P.O. Box 53), Takaka, New Zealand (☎ **03/525-8026;** fax 03/525-8444).

COST • Independent Walk NZ$8 (U.S. $5.20) per night hut fee; NZ$6 (U.S. $3.90) per night camping fee—plus transfers. Lower prices for children.

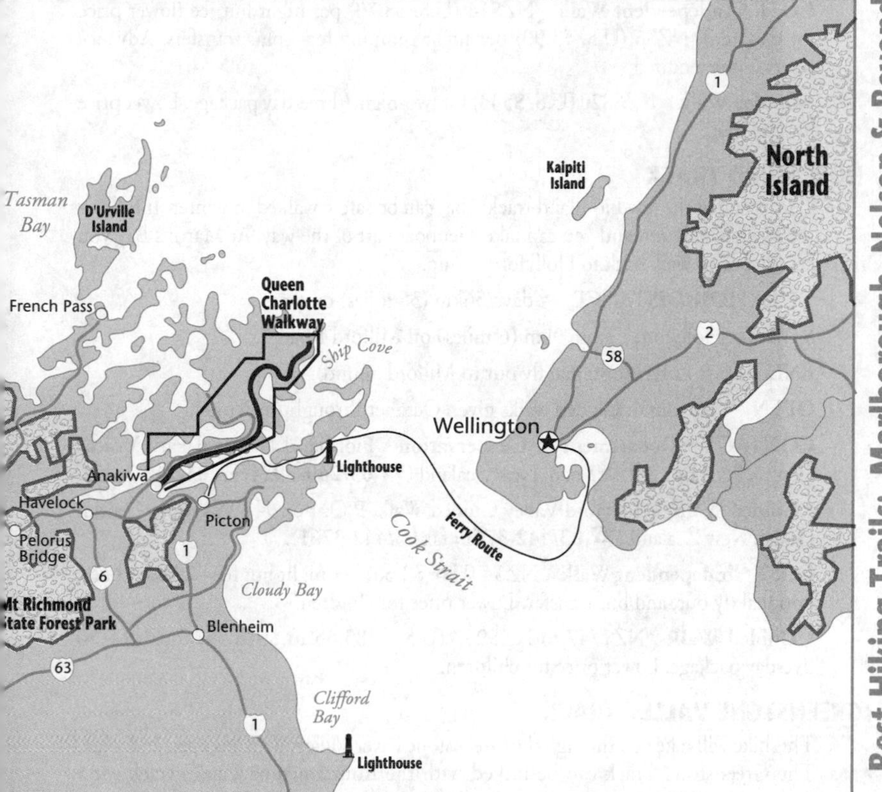

The Best Hikes

Queenstown & Fiordland

ROUTEBURN TRACK

On this track you'll cross the Harris Saddle and pass through parts of both Mount Aspiring and Fiordland National Parks. Bus transfers are available. Along the way are waterfalls, forested valleys, and spectacular mountain scenery.

DURATION/DISTANCE 2 to 3 days/39km (24 miles)

START Routeburn Shelter, 75km (47 miles) from Queenstown via Glenorchy

END "The Divide" Shelter, 80km (50 miles) from Te Anau on the Milford road

OPEN Late October through mid-April.

CONTACT • Department of Conservation Fiordland National Park Visitor Centre, P.O. Box 29, Te Anau, New Zealand (☎ **03/249-7924;** fax 03/249-7613).

• Guided Walk Routeburn Walk Ltd., P.O. Box 568, Queenstown, New Zealand (☎ **03/442-8200;** fax 03/442-6072).

COST • Independent Walk NZ$14 (U.S. $8.70) per night hut fee (lower price for children); NZ$6 (U.S. $3.90) per night camping fee—plus transfers. Advance reservations required.

• Guided Walk NZ$820 (U.S. $533) for two-night/three-day package. Lower price for children.

HOLLYFORD TRACK

This is one of the few Fiordland tracks that can be safely walked in winter. It follows the Hollyford River, and you can take a jet boat part of the way. At Martins Bay you can fly out or walk back to Hollyford Camp.

DURATION/DISTANCE 4 days/56km (35 miles) one way

START Hollyford Camp, 9km (6 miles) off Milford Road

END Martins Bay (optional fly out to Milford Sound)

OPEN Year round. Guided walks given October through April only.

CONTACT • Department of Conservation Fiordland National Park Visitor Centre, P.O. Box 29, Te Anau, New Zealand (☎ **03/249-7924;** fax 03/249-7613).

• Guided Walk Hollyford Valley Guided Walk, P.O. Box 94, Wakatipu, Central Otago, New Zealand (☎ **03/442-3760;** fax 03/442-3761).

COST • Independent Walk NZ$4 (U.S. $2.60) per night hut fee—plus jet boat, optional fly out, and bus transfer. Lower price for children.

• Guided Walk NZ$747 to NZ$957 (U.S. $485.55 to $628.55) for three- to five-day package. Lower price for children.

GREENSTONE VALLEY TRACK

This hike will take you through the Greenstone River Valley, which is open and wide. The Greenstone Track can be linked with the Routeburn or Caples track for a four- or five-day round-trip. Boat transfers are available to Elfin Bay.

DURATION/DISTANCE 2 days/40km (25 miles)

START Elfin Bay on Lake Wakatipu, 86km (53 miles) from Queenstown via Glenorchy

END Lake Howden, 80km (50 miles) from Te Anau

OPEN November through April.

CONTACT • Department of Conservation 37 Shotover St., Queenstown, New Zealand (☎ **03/442-7933;** fax 03/442-7932).

• Guided Walk Routeburn Walk Ltd., P.O. Box 568, Queenstown, New Zealand (☎ **03/442-8200;** fax 03/442-6072).

COST • Independent Walk NZ$8 (U.S. $5.20) per night hut fee—plus transfers. Lower price for children.

• Guided Walk NZ$720 (U.S. $468) for two-night/three-day package. Lower price for children.

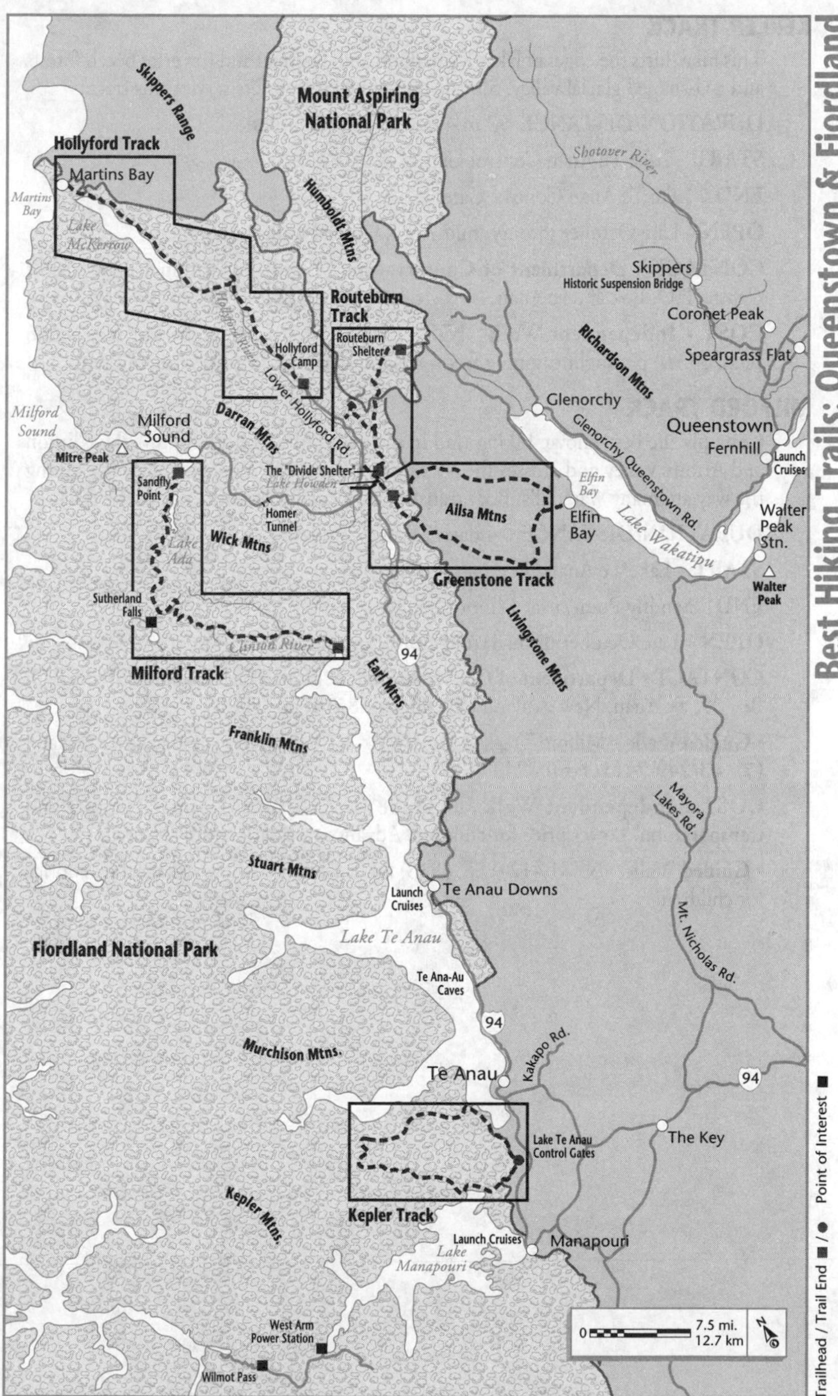

Best Hiking Trails: Queenstown & Fiordland

Trailhead / Trail End ■/● Point of Interest ■

KEPLER TRACK

This hike skirts the edges of lakes Manapouri and Te Anau and traverses beech forests and a U-shaped glacial valley. Shuttle bus and boat transfers service this track.

DURATION/DISTANCE 3 to 4 days/67km (42 miles)

START Lake Te Anau Control Gates

END Lake Te Anau Control Gates

OPEN Late October through mid-April. Guided walks not offered.

CONTACT • Department of Conservation Fiordland National Park Visitor Centre, P.O. Box 29, Te Anau, New Zealand (☎ **03/249-7924;** fax 03/249-7613).

COST • Independent Walk NZ$14 (U.S. $8.70) per night hut fee; NZ$6 (U.S. $3.90) per night camping fee—plus transfers. Lower prices for children.

MILFORD TRACK

Certainly the best-known hiking trail in the world, the Milford follows the Clinton and Arthur Valley and crosses the Mackinnon Pass (1,073 meters/3,520 ft.). Along the way are many waterfalls. Boat transfers are available at both ends of the track.

DURATION/DISTANCE 4 days/54km (33 miles)

START Lake Te Anau (Te Anau Downs)

END Sandfly Point, near Milford Sound

OPEN Late October through mid-April.

CONTACT • Department of Conservation Milford Track Booking Office, P.O. Box 29, Te Anau, New Zealand (☎ **03/249-8514;** fax 03/249-8515).

• Guided Walk Milford Track Guided Walk, P.O. Box 185, Te Anau, New Zealand (☎ **03/249-7411;** fax 03/249-7947).

COST • Independent Walk NZ$188 (U.S. $122.20)—includes huts and transportation. Lower price for children. Advance reservations are required.

• Guided Walk NZ$1,412 (U.S. $918) for five-night/six-day package. Lower price for children.

5

Auckland

New Zealand's largest city was its capital until 1864, and now it holds a full 24% of the entire population; adds many thousands each year, making it the nation's fastest-growing city; and has the largest Polynesian population of any city in the world. Auckland's international airport is most often the overseas visitor's introduction to this delightful land and its people.

Straddling a narrow, pinched-in isthmus created by the activity of some 60 volcanoes over a period of more than 50,000 years, Auckland is said by Maori legend to have been inhabited by giants in the days before the moa-hunters. Its present-day giants are commerce and industry, but the attraction for both ancient and latter-day Goliaths was probably the same—its excellent twin harbors. Europeans arrived in Auckland in 1839, and when the Waitangi treaty was signed in 1840 negotiations with the Maori transferred the isthmus to British ownership. The flag was hoisted on September 18, 1840, an event marked annually by the Anniversary Day Regatta (celebrated in January because of better sailing conditions). The thriving town served as New Zealand's first capital until 1864, when the seat of government was transferred to Wellington because of its central location.

Today's Auckland is nestled among volcanic peaks that have settled into gently rounded hills, minor mountains, and sloping craters. North Head and Bastion Point stand like sentinels on either side of Waitemata Harbour's entrance, and Rangitoto, the largest and more recently active volcano (last eruption was in the 13th century), sits in majestic splendor just offshore. Mount Eden's eastern slopes are marked by Maori earthworks, and One Tree Hill has become an archeological field monument because of the large Maori *pa* (fort) that once existed there.

What is possibly the world's finest collection of Maori artifacts can be seen in the Auckland Museum, along with a display of the moa, the giant bird that stood 10 feet from beak to tail and has been extinct for centuries. Colonial-style homes and a fair number of towering high-rises in the city center are monuments to its Pakeha development. Side by side with reminders of its history are modern Auckland's diversions—outstanding restaurants, more entertainment than you'll find in other parts of the country, and an ambience that grows more cosmopolitan every year. The city warrants a few days of your time, with much to offer that'll enhance the remainder of your New Zealand trip.

1 From a Budget Traveler's Point of View

BUDGET BESTS & DISCOUNTS Otto and Joan Spinka have operated **Touristop** since 1978, located in Auckland's Downtown Airline Terminal, 86–94 Quay St. (☎ **09/377-5783**; fax 09/377-6325). This knowledgeable couple specializes in offering value-for-dollar services such as bookings for accommodations, tours, rental cars, sightseeing tours, harbor cruises, and just about anything else associated with New Zealand–wide travel at the best possible price. They are also agents for Newmans coachlines nationwide network, with coaches departing just outside. They issue one- and multiday coach passes, as well as all backpacker coach passes. They even offer international airfares at "unbeatable prices" and there's never any booking fee. They're open daily from 7:30am to 6pm (until 9pm on Friday), and you'll also find magazines, maps, film, candies, coins, and a nice selection of New Zealand souvenirs at Touristop—but most of all, you'll find a warm, friendly helping hand.

What's Special About Auckland

Museums

- Auckland Museum, with perhaps the best collection of Maori and South Pacific artifacts in the world.
- New Zealand National Maritime Museum, where state-of-the-art exhibits show the role boats have played in the nation's history.

Harbor Spectacles

- The Devonport Ferry, a short ferry ride to the Devonport suburb, with splendid views of the city from the water.
- Harbor cruises, ranging from trips to outlying islands to dinner harbor cruises.
- Anniversary Day Regatta, the last Monday in January, when the harbor is alive with colorful sailing craft of all sizes and shapes, both local and international.

City Spectacles

- One Tree Hill, site of an ancient Maori fort, with marvelous views over the city and harbor.
- Waterfront Promenade, from Princess Wharf around the harbor to Kelly Tarlton's Underwater World.
- Kelly Tarlton's Underwater World, a world-class aquarium featuring New Zealand sea creatures.

Markets

- Victoria Park Market, with over 50 stalls and several cafés and restaurants.
- Parnell Village, a collection of colonial-style boutiques, craft shops, and restaurants.

Great Neighborhood

- Devonport, a colonial-style suburb with a waterfront promenade, views from Mount Victoria, and a colony of craftspeople.

Parks & Gardens

- Winter Garden, tropical hothouse in the Auckland Domain, with some 10,000 varieties, including New Zealand's unusual ferns.
- Parnell Rose Garden, with splendid rose displays and terrific views of the city and harbor.

2 City Specifics

Arriving

BY PLANE

The **Auckland International Airport** lies 21km (13 miles) south of the city just behind Manukau Harbour. You'll find the **Downtown Airline Terminal** at 86–94 Quay St., at the corner of Albert Street (☎ **379-6056**), next to the Travelodge Hotel.

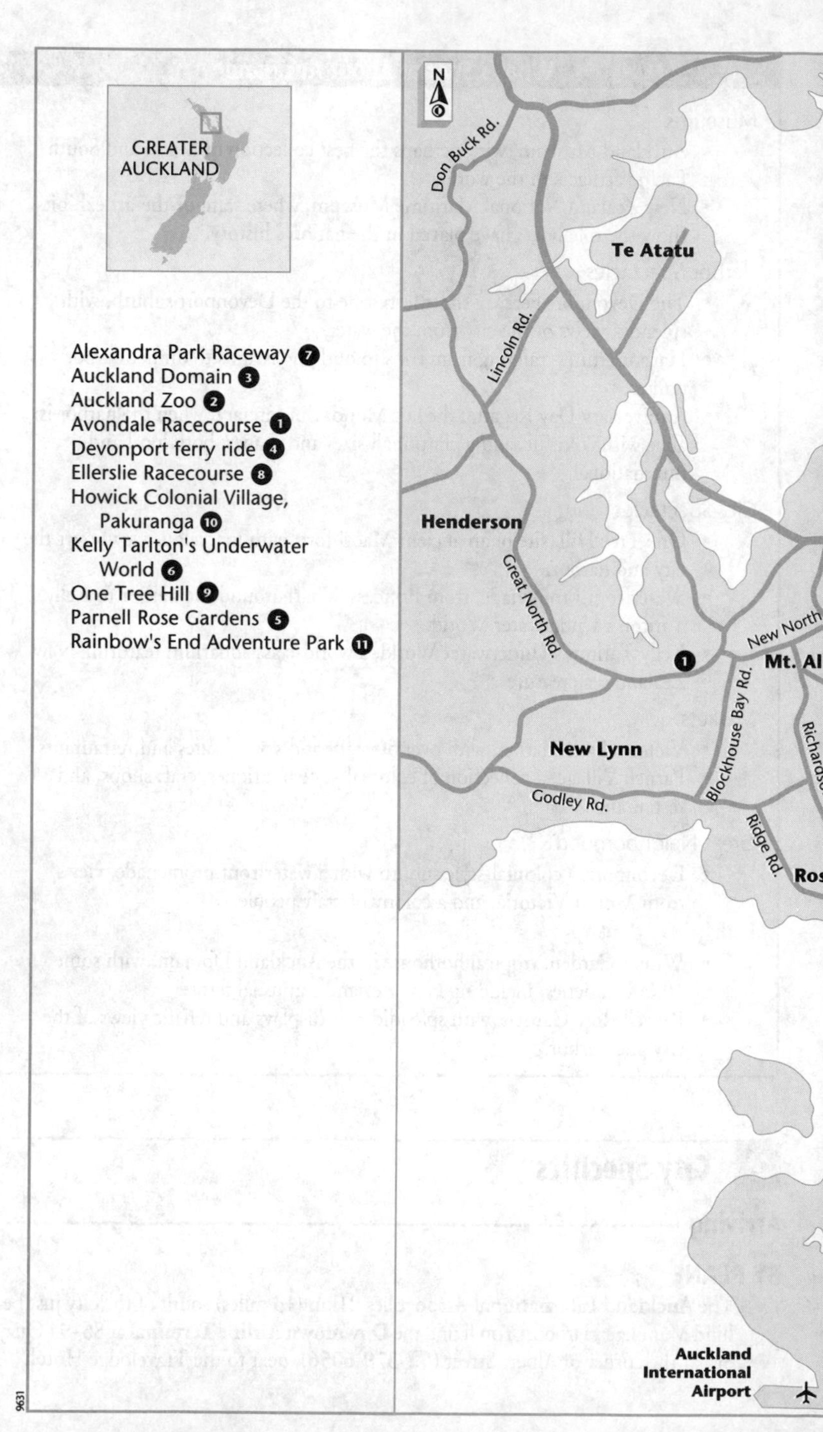
GREATER AUCKLAND
Alexandra Park Raceway 7
Auckland Domain 3
Auckland Zoo 2
Avondale Racecourse 1
Devonport ferry ride 4
Ellerslie Racecourse 8
Howick Colonial Village, Pakuranga 10
Kelly Tarlton's Underwater World 6
One Tree Hill 9
Parnell Rose Gardens 5
Rainbow's End Adventure Park 11
N
Don Buck Rd.
Te Atatu
Lincoln Rd.
Henderson
Great North Rd.
New North Rd
Mt. Albe
Blockhouse Bay Rd.
Richardson Rd.
New Lynn
Godley Rd.
Ridge Rd.
Rosk
Auckland International Airport
9631

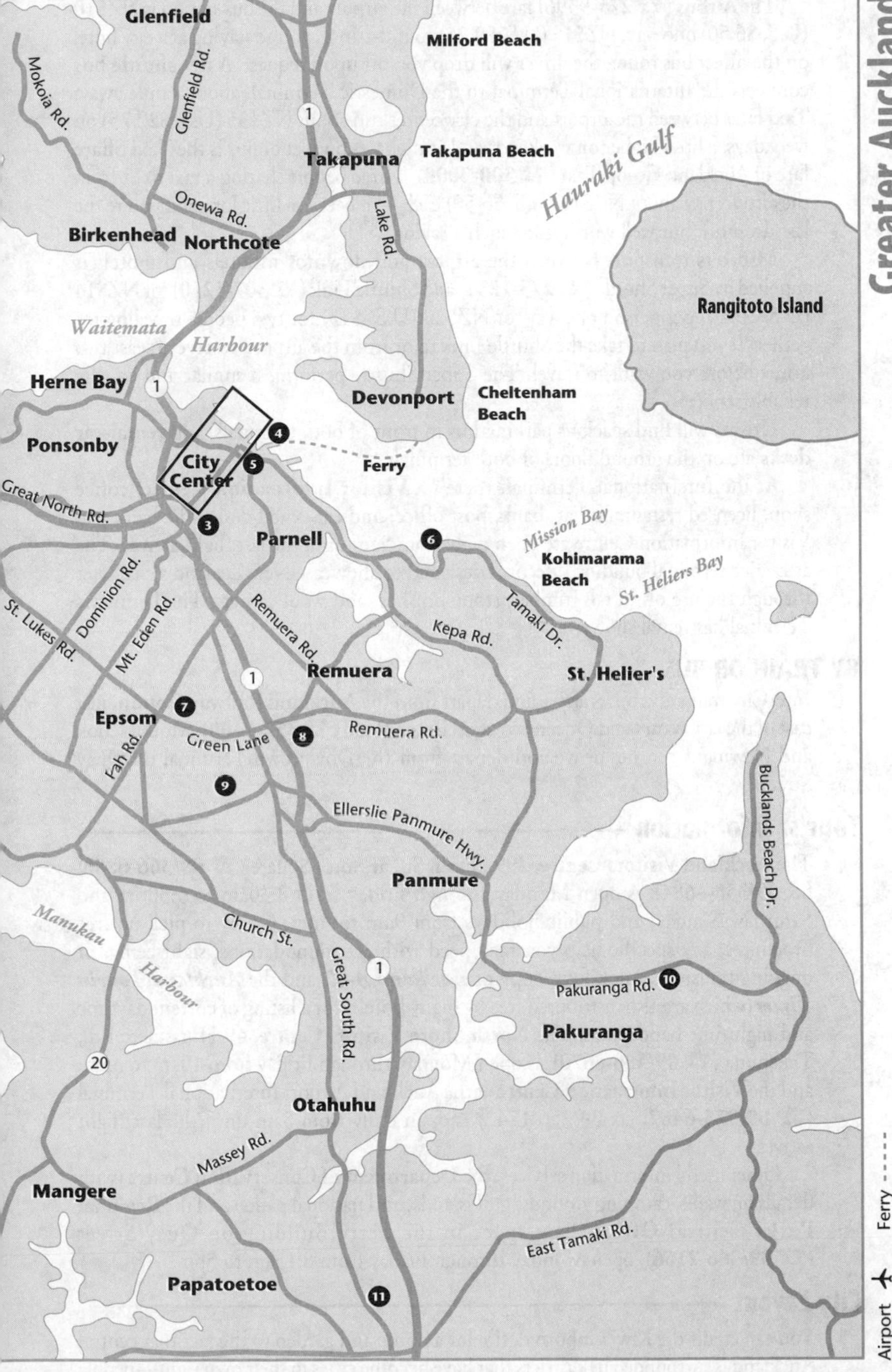
Greater Auckland
Glenfield
Milford Beach
Mokoia Rd.
Glenfield Rd.
1
Takapuna
Takapuna Beach
Hauraki Gulf
Onewa Rd.
Lake Rd.
Birkenhead
Northcote
Rangitoto Island
Waitemata
Harbour
Herne Bay
1
Devonport
Cheltenham
Beach
4
Ponsonby
City
Center
5
Ferry
Great North Rd.
3
Parnell
6
Mission Bay
Kohimarama
Beach
St. Heliers Bay
Dominion Rd.
St. Lukes Rd.
Mt. Eden Rd.
Remuera Rd.
Tamaki Dr.
Kepa Rd.
1
Remuera
St. Helier's
7
Epsom
8
Remuera Rd.
Green Lane
Fah Rd.
9
Bucklands Beach Dr.
Ellerslie Panmure Hwy.
Panmure
Manukau
Church St.
Harbour
Great South Rd.
1
10
Pakuranga Rd.
Pakuranga
20
Otahuhu
Massey Rd.
Mangere
East Tamaki Rd.
Papatoetoe
11
Airport
Ferry

The **Airbus** (☎ **275-9396**) fare between the airport and the bus station is NZ$10 (U.S. $6.50) one way, NZ$15 (U.S. $9.75) round-trip. If you're staying at a city hotel on the direct bus route, the driver will drop you off upon request. A free **shuttle bus** connects the International Terminal to the Domestic Terminal, about a mile away. **Taxi** fares between the airport and the city center run about NZ$35 (U.S. $22.75) on weekdays, a little higher on weekends and at night. A budget bonus is the **Taxi Share** fare of Auckland Co-op Taxi (☎ **300-3000**). Three people sharing a taxi to or from the airport pay about NZ$10 (U.S. $6.50) each—may take a little longer if you're the last drop-off, but well worth it for such a saving.

Minibus transport between the airport and downtown hotels and motels is supplied by Super Shuttle (☎ **275-1234**) and Shuttle Link (☎ **307-5210**) for NZ$14 (U.S. $9.10) per person one way, or NZ$20 (U.S. $13) for two people traveling together. If you plan to take the Shuttle Link to or from the airport, reserve at least two hours before you want to travel. The Super Shuttle performs a similar and equally reliable service.

Drivers will find spacious parking lots in front of both terminals, and **rental-car desks** are on the ground floors of both terminals.

At the International Terminal, there's a **Visitor Information Centre,** coffee shop, licensed restaurant, bar, bank, post office, and car-rental desk. The bank and Visitor Information Centre are open daily from 5am until the last flight arrives. The attractive terminal building's decor is designed to showcase New Zealand's character through the use of murals, timber, stone finishes, and wool carpets. The Domestic Terminal has rental showers.

BY TRAIN OR BUS

InterCity trains and buses arrive and depart from the **Auckland Railway Station,** just east of the city center and Queen Street on Beach Road (☎ **357-8400**). Mount Cook and Newmans coaches arrive and depart from the Downtown Terminal on Quay Street.

Tourist Information

The **Auckland Visitors Centre,** 299 Queen St., at Aotea Square (☎ **09/366-6888**; fax 09/358-4684), is open Monday through Friday from 8:30am to 5:30pm and Saturday, Sunday, and public holidays from 9am to 4pm. Go by to pick up free brochures, any specific help you may need with accommodations, sightseeing, or ongoing transport. Look for a copy of ***Auckland A–Z*** and the ***Auckland Tourist Times*** (which are also distributed free by many hotels) for a listing of current daytime and nighttime happenings. The **North Shore Visitors Centre,** 49 Hurstmere Rd., Takapuna (☎ **09/486-8670**), is open Monday through Friday from 10am to 3pm; and the **Visitor Information Centre** at the Auckland Airport International Terminal (☎ **09/275-6467**; fax 09/256-1742) is open daily from 5am until the last flight arrives.

Other useful information services, the **Department of Conservation Centre** (with details on walks, camping grounds, gulf islands, and national parks) and the **Regional Parks Central Office** share space in the Ferry Building on Quay Street (☎ **09/366-2166**), open Monday through Friday from 8:15am to 5pm.

City Layout

You can credit the Kiwi's inborn desire for a home and garden to the fact that central Auckland is surrounded by districts that have become cities in their own right—people

A Note on Neighborhoods

Parnell, an inner suburb, lies just east of Auckland Central. The cafés and shops here make this a great area for a stroll punctuated by morning or afternoon tea.

Mission Bay and **St. Heliers** are attractive waterfront suburbs with views of Waitemata Harbour and Rangitoto Island. There's a footpath along the shore for walkers and joggers.

Remuera, known locally as "Remmers," is Auckland's most affluent suburb. This is where the "ladies who lunch" live, and real estate carries big price tags.

Herne Bay and **Ponsonby,** inner suburbs to the west of Auckland Central, were once considered undesirable but are now popular with Yuppies, who are restoring the neighborhoods' fine old homes. Ponsonby hosts some of Auckland's most interesting restaurants.

North Shore City is really an amalgam of several small towns: Devonport, Takapuna, Birkenhead, and others. They lie beyond the north end of the Harbour Bridge and are popular places to live as well as visit. Access is by bus, car, and ferry.

Mangere is where you'll find Auckland International Airport; don't be surprised if you hear local folks substitute the name of the suburb for the name of the place—"What time are you due out at Mangere?"

Otara, to the south, is witness to Auckland's growing cosmopolitan population, where Pacific Islanders constitute 45%, Maori 26%, Europeans/Anglos 23%, and Asians, Indians, and others 6%.

may *work* in the inner city, but when evening comes, they're off to wider spaces. And the homeward journey will take them over at least one of the many bridges (they cross the harbor, rivers, creeks, and bays) and possibly onto the speeding motorway that runs north-south through the city. That motorway can be a blessing for the visitor unfamiliar with the territory and driving on the left, for it virtually eliminates the possibility of losing your way when you set out for the Bay of Islands, Rotorua, or other major points.

MAIN ARTERIES The city itself is also fairly straightforward. The main street is **Queen Street,** which ends in Queen Elizabeth's Square at **Quay Street.** Quay Street runs along the Waitemata harborfront. At the other end of Queen Street is **Karangahape Road** (pronounce it "Ka-ranga-happy," or simply call it "K Road" as Aucklanders do), a mere 2km ($1^1/_4$ miles) from Quay Street. Within that area you'll find most of the city's shops, restaurants, nightspots, and hotels, as well as bus, rail, and air terminals.

STREET MAPS Pick up a map at the Visitor Information Centre or at the Automobile Association (if you remembered to bring your home-country membership card).

3 Getting Around

BY BUS

The city's bus system is quite good, reaching all districts with convenient and frequent schedules. You can pick up route maps and timetables from **The Bus Place,** on Victoria

Street West, or the **Downtown Bus Terminal,** on Commerce Street. Airport and sightseeing buses depart from the Downtown Airline Terminal, on Quay Street. For schedule and fare information, call Buz-a-Bus (☎ **366-6400**).

Fares are by zone, running from NZ40¢ to NZ$4 (U.S. 25¢ to $2.60). Children 4 to 15 are charged half fare and children under 4 ride free. You must have exact change. If you're going to be using the buses a lot, you can purchase a one-day **Busabout Pass** for unlimited bus travel at NZ$8 (U.S. $5.20) for adults or NZ$4 (U.S. $2.60) for children. There's also a **Family Pass** for NZ$12 (U.S. $7.80). Buy them on the buses or at the Downtown Bus Terminal.

An **Inner City Shuttle** bus (it's the one painted yellow, with a red band and the destination "000"—(yes, that's how it's marked!) runs every 10 minutes from the Railway Station along Customs Street, up Queen Street to Karangahape Road, then back to the station by way of Mayoral Drive and Queen Street for a fare of NZ40¢ (U.S. 25¢), no matter how far you ride.

The **Explorer Bus** (☎ **360-0033**) is a double-decker tourist bus departing from the Ferry Building, Quay Street, on the hour from 10am to 4pm daily. There are drop-offs and pickups at five major Auckland attractions and in general it's a convenient way to get around for a set fare of NZ$10 (U.S. $6.50).

One word of caution when you're planning evening activities: Auckland buses stop running around 11:30pm Monday through Saturday and 10pm on Sunday, so if your evening is going to be a late one, plan on taking a taxi home.

BY TAXI

Taxi stands are at all terminals and on the corner of Customs Street West at Queen Street, or you can phone for a taxi (☎ **300-3000**). At flag fall, the fare is NZ$2 (U.S. $1.30), with the meter rising NZ$1.28 (U.S. 85¢) per kilometer. Waiting time costs 38¢ per minute.

BY BICYCLE

Well, I suppose you *could.* Still, what with Auckland's up-and-down terrain, it might be pretty tiring. Bikes are, of course, wonderful for harborfront rides and a few other level stretches, but all in all, you're better off on foot or using the bus.

BY CAR

Auckland has a high percentage of drivers per capita, and driving in the city can be a real hassle. My best advice is to park the car and use that excellent bus system as much as possible. If you must drive into the city, you can park the car for the day in parking lots (called car parks hereabouts) operated by the City Council. They're on Beresford Street, just off Karangahape Road; near the waterfront on Albert Street, west of Queen; on Victoria Street, just east of Queen; Britomart, off Customs Street to the east of Queen Street; downtown to the east of Queen Street; downtown to the west of Queen Street with an entrance from Customs Street West; Civic Underground on Mayoral Drive; and Victoria Street East. All are open 24 hours daily, and rates are quite reasonable.

BY BOAT

The **Devonport Ferry** departs regularly from Queen's Wharf on Quay Street (☎ **367-9125**). The round-trip (return) fare is NZ$7 (U.S. $4.55).

You could also travel around the harbor on **Fuller's Harbor Explorer** (☎ **367-9111**), which goes to Devonport, Kelly Tarlton's, and Rangitoto Island. This all-day boat pass costs NZ$22 (U.S. $14.30) for adults, half price for children.

Fast Facts: Auckland

Airlines Air New Zealand flights can be booked at Air New Zealand House, Quay Street (☎ **357-3000**). For flight arrival information, dial **357-3030;** for departure information, **367-2323.**

American Express You'll find the American Express Travel Services office at 101 Queen St. (P.O. Box 2412), Auckland (☎ **09/379-8243**).

Area Code Auckland's STD (area) code is **09.**

Babysitters Most hotels and motels can furnish babysitters. The following Child Care Centers can also provide daytime child care and help in arranging babysitters for the evening: Community Child Care Centres, Princes Street (☎ **302-2629**); and Freemans Bay Child Care, Pratt Street (☎ **376-7282**).

Currency Exchange Cash traveler's checks and exchange any other currency at city-center banks and most neighborhood branches. Hotels and restaurants will usually cash traveler's checks in another currency, but you'll get a much better rate at banks. A currency exchange in the Ferry Building on Quay Street is open daily.

Dentist For emergency and/or after-hours dental service, call **520-6609** or **579-9099.**

Disabled Services For information on ramps, toilets, car parks, telephones, and so forth, contact the Disability Resource Centre, 14 Erson Ave. (P.O. Box 24-042), Royal Oak, Auckland (☎ **625-8069**).

Doctor For emergency medical service, call **524-5943** or **579-9909;** for emergency ambulance service, dial **111.**

Embassies/Consulates All embassies are in Wellington, the national capital (see "Fast Facts: Wellington" in Chapter 9). Auckland has consulates of the **United States,** at Shortland and O'Connel streets (☎ **303-2724**); **Canada,** at 44–48 Emily Place (☎ **309-3690**); and **Ireland,** in the Dingwall Building at 87 Queen St. (☎ **302-2867**).

Emergencies In an emergency, dial **111.**

Hospitals The major hospitals are Auckland Hospital, Park Road, Grafton (☎ **379-7440**); Green Lane Hospital, Green Lane Road, Epsom (☎ **638-9909**); the National Women's Hospital, Claude Road, Epsom (☎ **638-9919**); and the North Shore Hospital, Shakespeare Road, Takapuna (☎ **486-1491**).

Hotlines Call the Citizens Advice Bureau (see the telephone directory for the local number), Drug Dependency (☎ **276-7193**), Life Line (☎ **522-2999**), or the Salvation Army (☎ **379-4150**).

Libraries The Auckland Central Library, Lorne Street (☎ **377-0209**), is open Monday through Thursday from 9:30am to 8pm, Friday until 9pm, Saturday from 10am to 1:30pm, and Sunday from 1 to 5pm.

Lost Property Contact the Central Police Station (☎ **379-4240**) or any local police station.

Luggage Storage/Lockers There are "left luggage" facilities at the Visitor Information Centre in the International Terminal of Auckland Airport, open 24 hours daily; and at the Downtown Airline Terminal, Quay Street, open daily from 7am to 8:30pm.

Newspapers/Magazines The morning *New Zealand Herald* and the afternoon *Auckland Star* are published Monday through Saturday; the *Sunday Star, Sunday Times,* and *Sunday News* are Sunday-morning publications.

Police In an emergency, dial **111.** For other matters, call the Central Police Station (☎ **379-4240**).

Post Office The Chief Post Office (CPO), in the CML Mall, on Queen Street at Wyndham Street, is open Monday through Thursday from 8:30am to 5pm, until 6pm on Friday, and Saturday from 9am to noon. For *Poste Restante* pickup, go to the Post Shop in the Bledisloe Building on Wellesley Street.

Religious Services Go to the Holy Trinity Cathedral (Anglican), Parnell Road, Parnell; the Tabernacle (Baptist), 429 Queen St.; the Aotea Chapel (Methodist), opposite Town Hall; St. Andrews (Presbyterian), 2 Symonds St.; the Meeting House (Society of Friends/Quaker), 113 Mt. Eden Rd., Mt. Eden; or St. Patrick's Cathedral (Roman Catholic), 43 Wyndham St.

Restrooms Public restrooms are situated in handy locations throughout the city, some in multistory parking garages. Those in the Downtown Bus Terminal and Albert Park are open 24 hours daily.

Taxes The national 12.5% Goods and Services Tax (GST) applies across the board.

Telegrams/Telex/Fax All telegrams are sent through the post office, either by telephone or in person. Fax and telex facilities are available through hotels and motels, as well as in the main post office (see "Post Office," above).

Telephone See "Telephone" under "Fast Facts: New Zealand," in Chapter 3.

Weather Information For Auckland regional forecasts, call **009-9909** (it's a 24-hour service, but not a free call).

4 Where to Stay

The most important thing to remember about accommodations in Auckland is that you should book your first night accommodation *before you leave home*—I can think of few things worse than arriving *anywhere* after a 12-hour flight and having to look for a room. A reservation is especially important on weekends, when Auckland can be very tightly booked. If you should arrive without a room already reserved, however, turn immediately to the nearest Visitor Information Centre (there's one in the International Arrivals Building at the airport). Just keep in mind that you'll be in no position to do much shopping around for budget accommodations.

The rates quoted below include the 12.5% GST.

Motels

Domain Lodge, 155 Park Rd., Grafton, Auckland. ☎ **09/303-2509.** Fax 09/358-0677. 14 rms (all with bath). TV TEL

Rates: NZ$73.13 (U.S. $47.55) bed-sitter (studio) for one, NZ$84.38 (U.S. $54.85) bed-sitter for two; NZ$84.38 (U.S. $54.85) one-bedroom unit for one; NZ$95.63 (U.S. $62.15) one- or two-bedroom unit for two. Additional person NZ$11.25 (U.S. $7.30) extra. AE, MC, V.

At this lodge, a location convenient to the city center comes along with a rare opportunity to do a good deed with your travel dollars. Beautifully situated overlooking the 200-acre Domain (park), it's owned by the Auckland Division of the Cancer Society (patients being treated at Auckland Hospital stay free), and superior accommodations are offered to the public on an as-available basis, including bed-sitter units with tea and coffee facilities. Best of all, your room rent goes directly to help the society's work. There's good public bus transportation.

Mt. Eden Motel, 47 Balmoral Rd., Mount Eden, Auckland 3. ☎ **09/638-7187.** Fax 09/630-9563. 25 units (all with bath). TV TEL

Rates: NZ$67–NZ$75 (U.S. $43.55–$48.75) unit for one, NZ$75–NZ$85 (U.S. $48.75–$55.25) unit for two. Additional person NZ$12 (U.S. $7.80) extra. AE, DC, MC, V.

Only a short, pleasant walk from Mount Eden and Mount Eden Village shops, the motel in a quiet residential location is set back from the road, eliminating traffic noise. In fact, with off-street parking just outside your unit you can forget driving into the city, since there's good bus service just a few minutes away. There are one- and two-bedroom units, as well as bed-sitters (studios) with double and twin beds, all with full kitchens and radios. Some units sleep up to eight people, and no-smoking rooms are available. Facilities include an outdoor pool, an indoor Jacuzzi, a guest laundry, a car wash, and a barbecue area. Breakfast is available, and there are many restaurants nearby. Laurel and Bruce Waters, the owner/operators, will help with your sightseeing and ongoing itinerary.

Raceway Motel, 67 St. Vincent Ave., Remuera, Auckland. ☎ **09/524-0880** or **520-0155.** Fax 09/520-0155. 10 units (all with bath). TV TEL **Directions:** Take the Greenlane exit on the motorway toward Ellerslie Racecourse and it's the second left.

Rates: NZ$75 (U.S. $48.75) unit for one or two. AE, DC, MC, V.

In a tranquil spot yet handy to the city center, this motor lodge is near Ellerslie Racecourse and Alexandra Park, only a short walk from a good shopping center and licensed restaurants. All units have complete kitchens and radios, and there's a guest laundry, as well as covered parking. Cots and highchairs are available, and both continental and cooked breakfasts are available through room service. Public bus transportation is nearby. The hosts are Chris and Heather Barber.

Ranfurly Evergreen Lodge Motel, 285 Manukau Rd. (near Ranfurly Rd.), Auckland. ☎ **09/638-9059.** Fax 09/630-8374. 12 units (all with bath). TV TEL

Rates: NZ$73–NZ$85 (U.S. $47.45–$55.25) unit for one or two. AE, DC, MC, V.

This two-story hostelry has a pleasant setting of manicured lawn, roses, and hedges. The lovely one-bedroom units each accommodate two to five people. Each unit has one full window wall, is nicely decorated, and comes equipped with color TV and electric blankets. There's a guest laundry, as well as car-wash facilities, on the premises, and a shopping center is just 100 yards away. Although the units have kitchens, a continental breakfast is available for NZ$6 (U.S. $3.90). On the direct airport bus route, the lodge is 5km (3 miles) from the city center; a public bus stops at the door.

ON THE NORTH SHORE

Green Glade Motel, 27 Ocean View Rd., Northcote, Auckland. ☎ **09/480-7445.** Fax 09/480-7439. 13 units (all with bath). A/C TV TEL **Transportation:** The owner will pick you up at the Downtown Airline Terminal.

ACCOMMODATIONS
Aspen Lodge 20
Auckland Central Backpackers 18
Auckland Youth Hostel 15
Domain Lodge 25
Parnell Youth Hostel 21
DINING
All Blacks Club 19
Angus Steak House 6
Cheers Cafe and Bar 8
Cin Cin on Quay Brasserie & Bar 3
Fortuna 17
Fraser's Place 22
Harbourside Seafood Bar & Grill 2
The Hard to Find Cafe 13
Konditorei Boss 24
The Loaded Hog 4
Mai Thai Restaurant 12
Nicholas Nickleby Coffee Lounge 9
Rick's Cafe Americain 11
Shakespeare Tavern 7
Tops Brasserie 5
Union Fish Co. 16
ATTRACTIONS
Auckland City Art Gallery 14
Auckland Museum 26
Ewelme Cottage 27
National Maritime Museum 1
Parnell Village 23
Victoria Park Market 10
0
500 m
547 y
N
Freemans Bay
St. Marys Bay
Western Viaduct
Princess Wharf
Air New Zealand
Queen Elizabeth II Sq.
Pakenham Rd.
Poore St.
Beaumont St.
Gaunt St.
Halsey St.
Market Place
Customs St. West
Wolfe St.
Fanshawe St.
Hardinge St.
Wyndham St.
St. Patrick's Sq.
Swanson St.
Queen St.
Victoria Park
Kingston St.
Durham St. West
Durham St. East
Victoria St. West
Drake St.
Nelson St.
Hobson St.
Federal St.
Albert St.
Elliot St.
Wellesley St. West
Lorne St.
Kitchener St.
Cook St.
Visitors Information Centre
Aotea Sq.
Rutland St.
Mayoral Dr.
Vincent St.
Union St.
St. Paul St.
White St.
Airedale St.
Greys Ave.
Myers Park
Turner St.
Pitt St.
Liverpool St.
City Rd.
Karangahape Rd.
Upper Queen St.
Cemetery
Cemetery
Grafton Bridge
South St.
West St.
9632

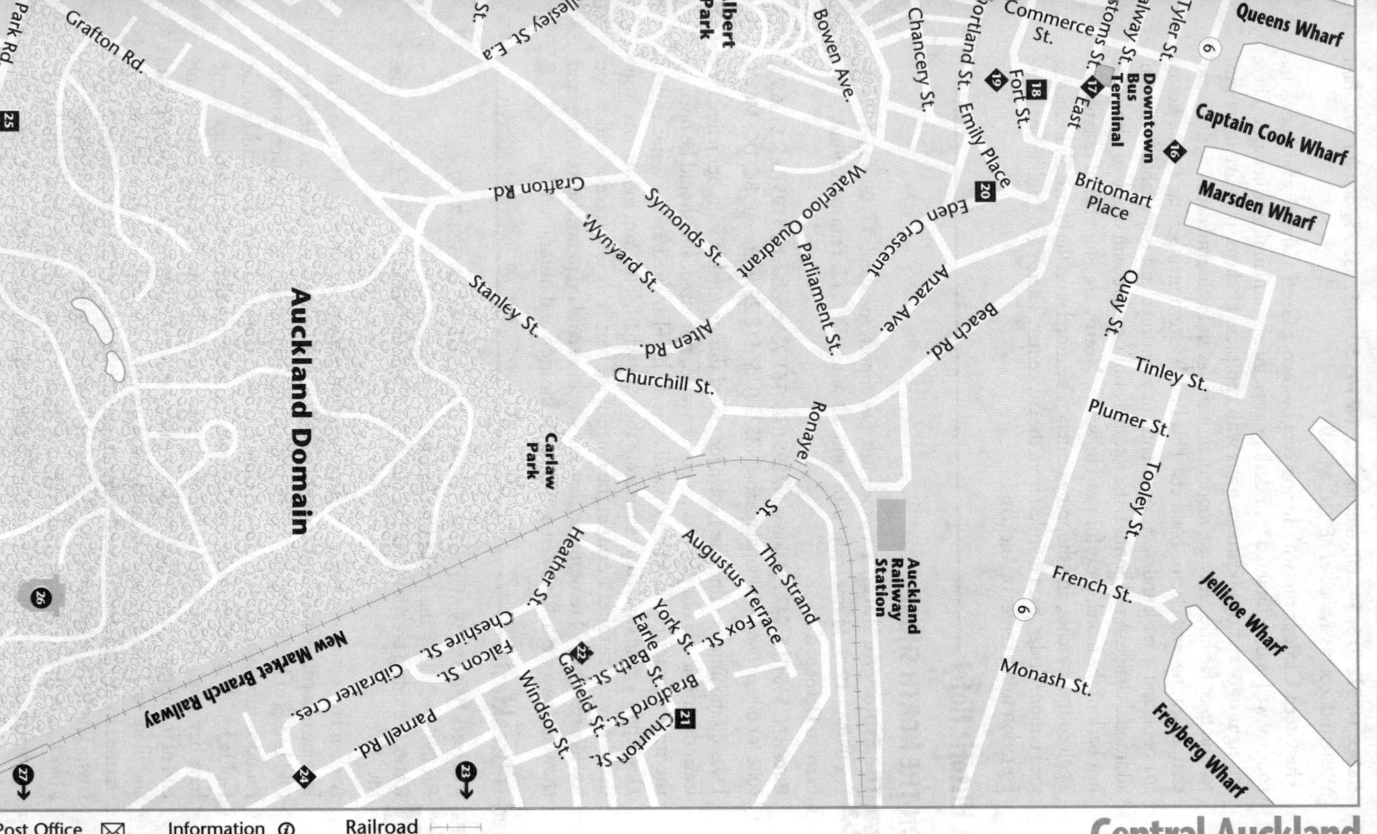
Queens Wharf
Captain Cook Wharf
Marsden Wharf
Jellicoe Wharf
Freyberg Wharf
Tyler St.
Downtown Bus Terminal
Commerce St.
East
Fort St.
Britomart Place
Quay St.
Tinley St.
Plumer St.
Tooley St.
French St.
Monash St.
Emily Place
Chancery St.
Eden Crescent
Anzac Ave.
Beach Rd.
Auckland Railway Station
Bowen Ave.
Waterloo Quadrant
Parliament St.
Ronaye St.
The Strand
Augustus Terrace
Fox St.
York St.
Earle St.
Bath St.
Bradford St.
Churton St.
Garfield St.
Windsor St.
Heather St.
Cheshire St.
Falcon St.
Parnell Rd.
Gibralter Cres.
New Market Branch Railway
Symonds St.
Alten Rd.
Churchill St.
Wynyard St.
Grafton Rd.
Stanley St.
Carlaw Park
Auckland Domain
Park Rd.
Post Office
Information
Railroad
Central Auckland

Rates: NZ$72 (U.S. $46.80) unit for one; NZ$85.50 (U.S. $55.75) unit for two. Best Western discounts available. AE, DC, MC, V.

The Green Glade is run with loving care by owner Geoff Calvert, who knows his country well and maintains a tour desk to assist guests in planning itineraries. There are eight one- and two-bedroom units with complete kitchens, plus five units with tea and toast facilities. All have modern furnishings and a cheerful decor, with a radio, central heating, and electric blankets. This Best Western member has a pool, heated spa pool, and guest laundry. A continental or a hot breakfast is available for a small additional charge. A real bonus is the forested public reserve with stands of white pine just back of the motel, great for peaceful walks. Nearby are a number of restaurants, a golf course, beaches, and shopping centers. The motel is on the North Shore, across the Harbour Bridge, 8km (5 miles) from the city center. There's good public bus transportation to the center of Auckland.

A Historic Hotel

ON THE NORTH SHORE

The Esplanade Hotel, 1 Victoria Rd., Devonport, Auckland. ☎ **09/445-1291.** Fax 09/445-1999. 14 rms (none with bath), 12 suites. TV TEL **Transportation:** Ferry to Devonport.

Rates: NZ$65 (U.S. $42.25) single; NZ$95 (U.S. $61.75) double; NZ$195 (U.S. $126.75) suite for one or two. Additional person NZ$25 (U.S. $16.25) extra. AE, BC, DC, MC, V.

I was disappointed to find the Esplanade closed during my last visit, but relieved to learn that the lovely old pub was being renovated, not razed, and should be open by the time you get there. The Edwardian-style hotel is sited at the water end of Devonport's main street, only steps from the ferry wharf. The front rooms have wonderful views. The suites are out of the range of the cost-conscious traveler (unless you feel like splurging). I recommend that you stay in a standard room, use the toilets and showers down the hall, and enjoy the prime location and historic ambience.

Bed-&-Breakfasts

Aachen House, 39 Market Rd., Remuera, Auckland. ☎ **09/520-2329.** Fax 09/524-2898. 7 rms (none with bath).

Rates (including breakfast): NZ$58 (U.S. $37.70) single; NZ$82 (U.S. $53.30) double. MC, V.

Aachen House sits on a hill in a charming neighborhood, overlooking Hobson Park. It's one of a pair of two-story residences built in 1905 that were known as the "Two Old Ladies of Market Road." There's a decided Victorian air about the place, with its rounded turret wing off to one side and lots of gingerbread trim. Jean and Donald Goldschmidt are the friendly, helpful hosts. The rooms all have high ceilings, some have bay windows looking out onto nice views, and all share the three baths at one end of the upstairs hall. A hot English breakfast is served in a quaint old dining room, and there's a TV lounge with tea and coffee makings. On cool evenings, the lounge is warmed by an open fire. In good weather, guests often play croquet on the large back lawn. The B&B is located 4km (2½ miles) from downtown, with public bus service a block away (from the airport, take the shuttle). Smoking is not permitted in the house.

Aspen Lodge, 62 Emily Place, Auckland. ☎ **09/379-6698.** Fax 09/377-7625. 26 rms (none with bath).

Family-Friendly Accommodations

Green Glade Motel (see p. 97) Swimming at nearby beaches and romps through the pine forest just back of the motel are sure to appeal to youngsters.

Karin's Garden Villas (see p. 103) The large lawn here is a perfect place for kids to stretch their legs, and the beach is nearby.

Rates (including breakfast): NZ$45 (U.S. $29.25) single; NZ$65 (U.S. $42.25) double. Lower winter rates May–Sept. AE, DC, MC, V.

This small, neat establishment is a short walk from Queen Street in the city center and also from the main rail and bus station. The rooms are small but clean, and the breakfasts are more than adequate. Facilities include tea- and coffee-making equipment and a guest laundry. The helpful staff can arrange car and campervan rentals, as well as sightseeing tours. Aspen Lodge is on the airport shuttle route, and there's good city bus service. Several readers have criticized the spartan decor, so I now recommend the Aspen only to dedicated budgeteers.

Bavaria Bed and Breakfast Hotel, 83 Valley Rd., Mount Eden, Auckland. ☎ **09/638-9641.** Fax 09/638-9665. 11 rms (all with bath).

Rates (including breakfast): NZ$59 (U.S. $38.35) single; NZ$89 (U.S. $57.85) double. AE, MC, V.

In a quiet residential area on the western slope of Mount Eden, close to restaurants, shops, and banks, the Bavaria is owned and operated by Rudi and Ulrike Stephan, who came to New Zealand as tourists and stayed as permanent residents. The colonial-style house is surrounded by private gardens, and the guest rooms—singles, doubles, and family size—are spacious and attractively furnished. The TV lounge opens to a sun deck, and the sunny breakfast area overlooks the gardens. The Bavaria is located 2km (1 mile) from the city center and 15 minutes from the airport; a bus stop is nearby.

Chalet Chevron Bed & Breakfast Hotel, 14 Brighton Rd., Parnell, Auckland. ☎ **09/309-0290.** Fax 09/373-5754. 12 rms (all with bath). TEL

Rates (including breakfast): NZ$55 (U.S. $35.75) single; NZ$95 (U.S. $61.75) double; NZ$130 (U.S. $84.50) triple. AE, DC, MC, V.

John and Judy Dufty, the enthusiastic and informative hosts, have a genuine interest in their guests' enjoyment of Auckland and New Zealand, as well as in their comfort. The guest rooms are pleasant and comfortable, and there is one family room. Three rooms have bathtubs, the rest have showers, and several serve up harbor views. A TV is provided in the lounge. The hotel is a short walk from Parnell Village, and there's good bus service to the city center.

Janet and Jim Millar, 10 Ngaroma Rd., Epsom, Auckland. ☎ **09/625-7336.** 2 rms (both with bath).

Rates (including breakfast): NZ$40 (U.S. $26) single; NZ$60 (U.S. $39) double. Dinner (available upon request) NZ$20 (U.S. $13) extra. No credit cards.

Janet and Jim Millar's bungalow is almost 80 years old. One of the rooms here has a private sitting area with extra bedding for families. (The Millars' grandchildren are frequent and welcome visitors, so little ones are no problem.) There's a path at one end of the street leading directly to Maungakiekie (One Tree Hill Domain). Both experienced travelers, the Millars enjoy talking about travel with their guests. Early arrivals are welcome. There's nearby bus service into the city center.

Remuera House, 500 Remuera Rd., Remuera, Auckland. ☎ **09/524-7794** or **520-3175.** 9 rms (none with bath). **Bus:** 635, 645, or 655.

Rates (including hot breakfast): NZ$39 (U.S. $25.35) single; NZ$58 (U.S. $37.70) double. AE, MC, V.

"Old world" best describes Remuera House, which dates from 1901 and has a big bay window—in fact, large windows everywhere—and wisteria growing in the backyard. Pictures of the grandparents of host Ray King, who has an avid interest in genealogy, hang on the dining room wall. The house offers comfortable rooms, a sun porch, a TV lounge with tea and coffee facilities, and a laundry. Guests share separate men's and women's toilets and baths. Remuera House is in a quiet neighborhood 10 minutes from downtown Auckland. Readers have commented on Ray's helpfulness and the delicious breakfast offered here.

Sedgwick Kent Lodge, 65 Lucerne Rd., Remuera, Auckland. ☎ **09/524-5219.** Fax 09/520-4825. 4 rms (1 with bath). TV

$

Rates (including breakfast): NZ$70 (U.S. $45.50) double without bath, NZ$100 (U.S. $65) double with bath. AE, MC, V.

I envy the lucky readers who stay in this beautifully restored turn-of-the-century homestead. It looks like something out of *Architectural Digest,* and Louisa Hobson-Corry entertains in Martha Stewart style. There's kauri (native timber) paneling in the bath, and superior-quality linens on all beds. Breakfast is served in front of the fireplace during the winter and on the patio in summer. Louisa is happy to take visitors shopping in Parnell, and her husband, Cliff, likes to lead walks in the nearby Waitakere Ranges. Two spa pools, a piano, a fax, a computer, and a very friendly cat named Oscar are all available for guests' enjoyment.

ON THE NORTH SHORE

Cheltenham-by-the-Sea, 2 Grove Rd., Devonport, Auckland. ☎ or fax **09/445-9437.** 3 rms (none with bath).

Rates (including breakfast): NZ$45 (U.S. $29.25) single; NZ$65–NZ$70 (U.S. $42.25–$45.50) double. No credit cards.

Joyce and Harry Mossman's large home is set amid shade trees and a spacious lawn, only a minute from Cheltenham Beach and just a little farther from shops, restaurants, and bus transportation. Joyce and Harry offer three bedrooms, two with twin beds and one with a queen-size bed. Guests share two bathrooms when the house is full, but the hosts prefer to have only one or two rooms in use at any time. There's a TV in the lounge. Located on the North Shore, the house is 20 minutes from the city center via the Harbour Bridge or Devonport Ferry and is served by the airport shuttle bus. The Mossmans can arrange local tours.

READERS RECOMMEND

Heathmaur Lodge, 75 Argyle St., Herne Bay, Auckland. ☎ **09/376-3527.** *"We stayed with Geoff and Pat at Heathmaur Lodge. He's English; she's Kiwi—both very friendly and helpful to their guests. We can certainly recommend this establishment to any traveler from any country."*—Harry and Gladys Waters, Bournemouth, England. [**Author's Note:** This guesthouse has 13 rooms (7 with bath)].

Karin's Garden Villas, 14 Sinclair St., Devonport, Auckland. ☎ or fax **09/445-8689.** 4 rms (1 with bath), 1 studio cottage. **Transportation:** Take the airport shuttle, or the host will meet you at the ferry.

Rates (including continental breakfast): NZ$55 (U.S. $35.75) single without bath, NZ$75 (U.S. $48.75) single with bath; NZ$85 (U.S. $55.25) double without bath, NZ$95 (U.S. $61.75) double with bath; NZ$95 (U.S. $61.75) studio cottage (without breakfast, three-night minimum). Dinner NZ$20 (U.S. $13) extra. No credit cards.

Karin Loesch's homey old villa has a large lawn and fruit trees at the end of a cul-de-sac, just a few minutes' walk from the beach, golf, restaurants, shops, and the bus line. She and her two teenage children are multilingual and welcome visitors, especially families, from all over the world. Guests can use the laundry and use the kitchen to cook their own meals or enjoy Karin's dinners. Breakfast includes "good German coffee." The bright, airy two-story studio cottage has a double bed, a sofa sleeper, cooking facilities, a telephone, and a shower.

Villa Cambria, 71 Vauxhall Rd., Devonport, Auckland. ☎ **09/445-7899.** 4 rms (none with bath). **Transportation:** Take the shuttle bus to the door, or the host will provide a courtesy car from the ferry.

Rates (including breakfast): NZ$75 (U.S. $48.75) single; NZ$95 (U.S. $61.95) double. Lower winter rates. BC, MC, V.

Host Noel Allen welcomes guests to Villa Cambria, which he recently restored and opened as a B&B guesthouse. The house was built in 1905 and is surrounded by landscaped grounds and gardens. The lounge is furnished with antiques, and breakfast is served on a kauri kitchen table. Cheltenham Beach is nearby, as are golf, shops, and dining spots. Smoking is not allowed in the bedrooms or kitchen but is permitted in designated areas. Laundry facilities are available.

ON WAIHEKE ISLAND

Waiheke Island is a sparsely populated retreat 35 minutes by ferry from Auckland.

Gulf Haven, 49 Great Barrier Rd., Enclosure Bay, Waiheke Island. ☎ **09/372-6629.** 2 rms (neither with bath), 2 units (both with bath). **Transportation:** The hosts pick up guests from the ferry.

Rates (including continental breakfast): NZ$50 (U.S. $32.50) single; NZ$75 (U.S. $48.75) double; NZ$90 (U.S. $58.50) twin; NZ$130 (U.S. $84.50) self-contained unit (two-night minimum). Dinner NZ$25 (U.S. $16.25) extra. No credit cards.

I don't use superlatives loosely, but I have to tell you that the garden surrounding this homestay is jaw-dropping, drop-dead gorgeous. Besides surrounding the house, the garden fills terrace after terrace between the house and the rocky coastline about 100

READERS RECOMMEND

Colleen Gray Homestay, 23 Auld St., Torbay, Auckland. ☎ **09/473-9558.** *"One of the nicest B&Bs I've ever stayed at. . . . Many tourists might be put off staying so far out of town, but it's only a 40-minute bus ride away and the beauty of the place really justifies it. Colleen Gray takes guests on lovely local bush walks. She's one of the few New Zealanders who know how to make proper coffee, and her kiwi muffins are second to none. I have a three-crown highly commended B&B in England, so I think I know a little about the trade."*—Eileen Finn, Northumberland, England.

feet below. Happily, hosts Alan Ramsbottom and Lois Baucke have large windows throughout their home, so the view is easily visible.

The house is modern, with a restful ambience. The hosts will pick up guests at the ferry and provide complimentary transport to restaurants. Visitors who don't have a car, but would like to explore more, can join the rural postman when he makes his rounds (NZ$10/U.S. $6.50). No smoking is permitted inside the house, and children are not accepted.

Hostels

Auckland Central Backpackers, 9 Fort St., Auckland. ☎ **09/358-4877.** Fax 09/358-4872. 110 rms (none with bath). **Transportation:** Free transport from the airport to the hostel.

Rates: NZ$16 (U.S. $10.40) single; NZ$40 (U.S. $26) double; NZ$10 (U.S. $6.50) bunk (with no linen supplied). BC, MC, V.

This centrally located hostel gets rave reviews from readers and has recently won the New Zealand Tourism Board's top award for best budget accommodation. With 308 beds, this place isn't tiny, but guests still comment that the staff are "helpful and courteous." All beds except 20 are made up with sheets and duvets. There's a bar, restaurant, movie theater, travel agency, and convenience store on site. Auckland Central Backpackers is a VIP hostel.

Auckland Youth Hostel, City Rd. and Liverpool St., Auckland. ☎ **09/309-2802.** Fax 09/373-5083. 142 beds (no rooms with bath). **Bus:** All Queen Street buses. **Transportation:** 24-hour airport shuttle service.

Rates: NZ$19 (U.S. $12.35) per person for YHA members, NZ$23 (U.S. $14.95) for non-members. MC, V.

Centrally located off Queen Street, this is one of Auckland's top hostels. Separate male and female bathrooms are provided on each floor. All rooms are attractively decorated and most have a good view of the harbor; there are also a limited number of family units. On premises are a guest lounge and a separate TV lounge, as well as a good moderately priced restaurant. Laundry service is available, and if your itinerary calls for it, you can arrange early check-in or late checkout. The friendly 24-hour staff can also book ongoing travel and accommodations and arrange discounts. This is a YHA hostel.

Parnell Youth Hostel, 2 Churton St., Parnell, Auckland. ☎ **09/379-3731.** Fax 09/358-4143. 81 beds in 11 dorms. **Transportation:** Bus service between the airport and the city from 7am to 10pm, pickup service from the airport after 10pm; city bus service, a 10-minute walk from the City Bus Station.

Rates: NZ$16 (U.S. $10.40) per person. MC, V.

Within walking distance of the city center, this youth hostel near Parnell Village draws positive comments for the cheerful colors used throughout, the inviting dining room with pine tables and chairs, the yard (three-quarters of an acre) filled with fruit trees and picnic tables, and the view of the harbor from the upstairs rooms. It also has a TV room, a large lounge downstairs, a smaller one upstairs filled with books and games, a laundry, baggage storage, showers and toilets for the disabled, and supplies of brochures on New Zealand. One self-contained dorm is available as a family room. Videos about the country are shown throughout the day, and all your ongoing travel bookings can be made right in the hostel. They'll hold your mail while you're traveling. This is a YHA hostel.

ON WAIHEKE ISLAND

Waiheke Island Backpackers (Hekerua House), 11 Hekerua Rd., Waiheke Island. ☎ **09/372-8371.** Fax 09/372-7174. 5 rms (none with bath), 20 dorm beds. **Transportation:** Eight daily ferries from Auckland's Ferry Building to Matiatia Wharf on the island; then the local Palm Beach bus to Hekerua Road.

Rates: NZ$17.50 (U.S. $11.40) per person double; NZ$15 (U.S. $9.75) per person in a dorm; NZ$10 (U.S. $6.50) tent site. Third night half price if paid in advance. No credit cards.

Take a short ferry ride across Auckland's harbor to the island and you'll find this sunny private hostel set amid trees, close to good beaches and shops. The large lounge opens to the sun deck, a pool, and summer barbecues; the beach is only five minutes away. Other island activities include fishing, swimming, horse riding, tramping, and windsurfing.

Palm Beach Backpackers Lodge, 54 Palm Rd., Palm Beach, Waiheke Island. ☎ **09/372-8662.** Fax 09/379-2084. 15 dorm, twin, and double rms (most without bath), 30 campsites. **Transportation:** The ferry from Auckland takes 35 minutes; then there's a free bus to Palm Beach.

Rates: NZ$18.50 (U.S. $12.05) per person double; NZ$16 (U.S. $10.40) dorm bed.

This VIP hostel is just 50 yards from the water's edge and is an ideal spot for activity-oriented guests. Sea kayaking, sailing, horse riding, mountain biking, fishing, snorkeling, and bush walks all happen here. There's even a nudist beach nearby, plus barbecues, kitchen facilities, storage lockers, and a TV room. VIP card holders can buy a discount ferry ticket.

Camping & Cabins

ON THE NORTH SHORE

$ **North Shore Caravan Park, Cabins, and Motel,** 52 Northcote Rd., Takapuna, Auckland (P.O. Box 36139, Auckland 9). ☎ **09/419-1320** or **418-2578.** Fax 09/480-0435. 4 motel rms (all with bath), 29 cabins, 8 tourist flats, 130 caravan sites, 30 tent sites. **Transportation:** Frequent bus service is nearby.

Rates: NZ$66 (U.S. $42.90) single rm; NZ$80 (U.S. $52) double rm; NZ$37–NZ$55 (U.S. $24.05–$35.75) cabin for two; NZ$62 (U.S. $40.30) flat for one, NZ$68 (U.S. $44.20) flat for two; NZ$16 (U.S. $10.40) caravan/tent site for one, NZ$23 (U.S. $14.95) caravan/tent site for two. Additional person in caravan/tent site NZ$11.50 (U.S. $7.50) extra. AE, MC, V.

A member of the Top 10 Group of Holiday Parks, this spot boasts a first-rate location, accessible to downtown Auckland via the Harbour Bridge. All communal facilities, including the kitchen, are kept very clean. I particularly like the pink Italian tile baths. Other facilities include a large laundry with dryers and a TV room. A Pizza Hut is adjacent.

Worth the Extra Money

There was a time, not so long ago, when Auckland's luxury or near-luxury accommodations were almost nonexistent. Not so today, however. As New Zealand has become more and more attractive to corporations as well as tourists, upscale hotels, motor inns, and even bed-and-breakfast accommodations have sprung up to meet a growing demand. Those listed below are, I believe, not only posh enough to provide every ounce of pampering your splurge dollars should buy, but offer the best value in every respect for those hard-earned dollars.

Ascot Parnell, 36 St. Stephens Ave., Parnell, Auckland 1. ☎ **09/309-9012.** Fax 09/309-3729. 11 rms (all with bath). TEL **Bus:** The airport bus stops in front; city bus service is one block away.

Rates (including breakfast): NZ$76.50 (U.S. $49.75) single; NZ$108 (U.S. $70.20) double. Additional person NZ$24 (U.S. $15.60) extra for adults, NZ$13.50 (U.S. $8.80) extra for children under 12. AE, DC, MC, V.

This bed-and-breakfast is one of Auckland's most pleasant and atmospheric lodgings—a short walk from Parnell Village, the Auckland Museum, and the Rose Gardens and a hilly walk (about 1½ miles) from the city center. The grounds feature lovely shrubbery and flowers, many native to New Zealand, with a gigantic century-old pin oak that's registered as a "historic tree." The house dates from 1910 and, under the loving care of Bart and Therese Blommaert, it's maintained to preserve an informal elegance. The guest rooms are spacious, each with an individual decor, and one family room will accommodate up to four. There's a pretty dining room, a TV lounge (where complimentary coffee, tea, and juice are offered), and off-street parking. I've had nothing but good reports from readers, many of whom have commented on the hosts' friendly, personalized travel advice. Because the Ascot is so popular, reserve as far in advance as possible.

Barrycourt Motor Inn, 10–20 Gladstone Rd., Parnell, Auckland. ☎ **09/303-3789,** or toll free **800/528-1234** in the U.S., **0800/504-466** in New Zealand. Fax 09/377-3309. 40 rms (all with bath), 62 studios and suites, 5 budget units. A/C TV TEL **Bus:** The city bus stops at the door; the Explorer Bus stops every hour; the airport bus stops every half an hour; the airport shuttle stops on request.

Rates: NZ$99–NZ$142 (U.S. $64.35–$92.30) single or double; NZ$175.50 (U.S. $114.10) studio for two or three; NZ$142–NZ$194 (U.S. $92.30–$126.10) one-bedroom suite for two to four; NZ$180–NZ$221 (U.S. $117–$143.65) two-bedroom suite for two to six; NZ$86–NZ$97 (U.S. $55.90–$63.05) budget unit for two. AE, DC, MC, V.

This Best Western motor inn is a personal favorite not only because of the quality of the units but also because the staff is unfailingly friendly and helpful—a reflection of owner Norm Barry's business philosophy. It's also conveniently located less than a mile from the CPO and within easy walking distance of Parnell Road's quaint shopping district. The original part of the inn consists of 22 units in a modern brick building: bed-sitters (studios) and one- and two-bedroom units sleeping two to five people, with well-equipped kitchens and ample closets (both features throughout the Barrycourt). The Executive Block holds 80 units, most with private balconies and harbor views. All units have tea- and coffee-making facilities, radios, and refrigerators; many also have complete kitchens, and two-bedroom suites have their own clothes washer and dryer. The suites and units with private balconies boast marvelous views of Auckland's harbor. The best bets for budgeteers are five units in a lodge at the bottom of the property. Some rooms have oak paneling, beamed ceilings, stained-glass panels, and leaded-glass windows. TV reception includes U.S. and Australian satellite channels.

Facilities include four spa pools, a sunbed solarium, a pool, a self-service laundry, same-day dry cleaning and laundry; photocopying; rental cars and cycles; foreign-currency exchange; and a Victorian building that houses the excellent Gladstones restaurant (see "Where to Eat," below). There's ample parking, and there's a separate building to store any luggage you won't need while exploring the rest of New Zealand.

ON THE NORTH SHORE

Devonport Villa, 46 Tainui Rd., Devonport, Auckland. ☎ **09/445-2529.** Fax 09/445-9766. 5 rms (all with bath). Transportation: The hosts will pick up arriving guests at the ferry.

Rates (including full breakfast): NZ$95 (U.S. $61.75) single; NZ$117.50–NZ$160 (U.S. $76.40–$104) double. AE, MC, V.

What a delightful base from which to do your exploration of the area! Hosts Yvonne Lambert and Philip Brown make guests feel welcome and provide them with sightseeing information as well as ideas for onward travels. In addition, Yvonne serves delicious breakfasts that include homemade muffins and muesli (granola). The house is a restored villa dating from 1903. Each room has a high ceiling, an armoire made from native timbers, a quilt made by Yvonne's sister, and fresh flowers. Every inch is tastefully appointed and immaculate. Guests are welcome to enjoy the lounge and dining room; some even buy fish and chips from a nearby shop and bring them to the B&B for supper. Crab Apple, their lovely cat, is only too happy to help clean up the leftovers. Devonport Villa is a 15-minute walk from the wharf, but a minibus taxi meets every ferry and transports guests to the inn for NZ$1 (U.S. 65¢). Cheltenham Beach is two minutes' walk away. No smoking is permitted in the villa.

The Peace & Plenty Inn, 6 Flagstaff Terrace, Devonport, Auckland. ☎ **09/445-2925.** Fax 09/445-2901. 4 rms (2 with bath).

Rates (including full breakfast): NZ$160 (U.S. $104) double with bath, NZ$135 (U.S. $87.75) double without bath. AE, MC, V.

Hosts Carol and Bruce Hyland have lived and traveled in various parts of the world, and they called on this experience when it came time to restore and decorate the house that's now their inn. The Bahama Room acknowledges the island where they lived on their boat; Canada is a tribute to Bruce's nationality; Provence is a favorite destination. The house was built in 1888 for the manager of a kauri timber mill and thus is built of the prized (and pricey) native wood. Each room is outfitted with superb linens, fluffy robes, bottles of spring water, and toiletries; fresh flowers abound. Carol's breakfasts include homemade yogurt and muesli (granola), as well as free-range eggs and edible flowers. Complimentary tea, coffee, sherry, and cookies are always available in the lounge. The Garden Suite, the only room where children are accepted, has a bath, a telephone, and a private entrance. The inn is less than a block from the ferry. Smoking is not permitted.

5 Where to Eat

Eating out in Auckland can be just about anything you want it to be. There are scads of small attractive and moderately priced cafés, a wide range of cuisine at reasonable prices, and an impressive array of posh restaurants serving international dishes. They're scattered all over the city, but there are interesting concentrations along Parnell Road in Parnell and Ponsonby Road in Ponsonby. You'll find examples of each in these pages, but you should also pick up a copy of the free *Auckland Dining Guide,* published quarterly and available at many hotels, as well as Visitor Information Centres. Its listings are quite complete, and there's a city map included showing restaurant locations.

$ **Angus Steak House,** 35 Albert St., at Swanson St. ☎ 379-7815.

Cuisine: STEAK. **Reservations:** Recommended.
Prices: Steak and salad bar NZ$21 (U.S. $13.65). AE, DC, MC, V.
Open: Lunch Mon–Fri noon–2pm; dinner daily 5–11pm.

This perennial Auckland favorite features a central location, generous portions of good food, and very reasonable prices. Seven kinds of steak are offered, as well as chicken and ham. All prices include a trip to the extensive salad bar, and the portions are large enough that many couples split the steak and pay NZ$6.80 (U.S. $4.40) for the second person's trip to the salad bar. The wooden tables are a little too close together and the low beamed ceiling in the cellar seems to invite tall travelers to bump their heads—so be careful. Licensed for beer and wine and BYO.

★ $ **Annabelle's,** 409 Tamaki Dr., St. Heliers. ☎ **575-5239.**

Cuisine: BURGERS/PASTA/OMELETS. **Reservations:** Not accepted.
Prices: Appetizers NZ$7–NZ$12 (U.S. $4.55–$7.80); main courses NZ$8–NZ$19 (U.S. $5.20–$12.35). AE, MC, V.
Open: Mon–Fri 11:30am–10pm, Sat–Sun 8am–11pm.

The specialties here are seven kinds of burgers, available in two sizes—quarter or half pound. Chicky Weber is named for owner Thomas Weber; New Zealand Weber is topped with beetroot (sliced beets), raw onion, and fried egg. Other dishes include pastas and omelets and some very tasty (and very hot) lamb curry. Beverage choices range from juices, milkshakes, and soft drinks to beer and specialty coffees. Named after the owners' young daughter, Annabelle's is very popular with locals, so be prepared to wait for a table. BYO and licensed. No smoking.

Cheers Cafe & Bar, 12 Wyndham St., just off Queen St. ☎ **309-8779.**

Cuisine: MODERN CAFE. **Reservations:** Not required.
Prices: Appetizers NZ$5.20–NZ$9.50 (U.S. $3.40–$6.20); main courses NZ$8.95–NZ$14.50 (U.S. $5.80–$8.20). AE, DC, MC, V.
Open: Daily 11am–1am.

This licensed café in the city center is a bright, airy place with lots of blond wood, greenery, and a fountain. The tempting menu includes chicken or beef satay on basmati rice with spicy peanut sauce, stir-fried lamb with garlic and mint, fresh fish filets or steaks (choose either blackened or baked with beurre blanc), and chicken thighs pan-fried with tomato pesto and fresh chiles. You can also order nachos, a burger, an omelet, or pasta. Cheers is well known for its inventive cocktails, large range of beers, and wide selection of local and imported wines. There's also an "On the Wagon" assortment of freshly squeezed juices, teas, and cappuccinos. Happy hour is Monday through Friday from 5 to 6pm and Saturday and Sunday from 11am to 6pm.

The Fish Pot, 99B Tamaki Dr., Mission Bay. ☎ **528-4097.**

Cuisine: FISH & CHIPS/SEAFOOD. **Reservations:** Not required weekdays, recommended Fri–Sat for dinner.

Prices: Fish and chips NZ$14 (U.S. $9.75); full meals NZ$13–NZ$17 (U.S. $8.45–$11.05); children's menu NZ$5–NZ$8 (U.S. $3.25–$5.20). AE, DC, MC, V.
Open: Daily noon–"late."

The Fish Pot eateries have rapidly become favorite gathering places for Auckland residents as well as visitors. You can't beat them for superb seafood—whether you go for fish and chips (better than any you've had before, I'll wager) or a main course that comes with a side salad and crisp fries. The super fish and chips use the catch of the day with a light, crisp batter, the secret of which they refuse to divulge, and I'm partial to the papilottes, a parcel of the day's catch wrapped in phyllo pastry and served with spinach sauce. Wine and beer are moderately priced; also BYO. Take-out is available.

Another Fish Pot is located at 283 Remuera Rd., Remuera, Auckland (☎ **524-5309**), a BYO, and the chain is also represented in Taupo, Tauranga, Rotorau, Hamilton, and Paihia.

Fortuna, 55 Customs St. E. ☎ **373-2421.**
Cuisine: CANTONESE. **Reservations:** Recommended.
Prices: Main courses NZ$10–NZ$13 (U.S. $6.50–$8.45); 20-course buffet lunch NZ$12 (U.S. $7.80). Children under 11 eat free if accompanied by an adult. AE, DC, MC, V.
Open: Lunch daily noon–2:30pm; dinner Mon–Sat 6–11pm, Sun 6–9:30pm.
Closed: Christmas Day.

The menu in this attractive family-run restaurant is mostly Cantonese, with choices from Malaysia and Singapore as well. All five chefs trained in top Hong Kong restaurants. Eat your fill at lunch from selections of seafoods, poultry, beef, pork, lamb, and a choice of soups and desserts—terrific value for money. An especially good value is the Saturday and Sunday yum char lunch. The sumptuous Sunday smorgasbord dinner offers even more choices. A great favorite with locals, it's on the waterfront in the center of the city.

Fraser's Place, 116 Parnell Rd. ☎ **377-4080.**
Cuisine: DELI/SALADS/INTERNATIONAL. **Reservations:** Not required. **Bus:** Good city bus service in this Parnell area.
Prices: Deli NZ$2 (U.S. $1.30); lunch NZ$6–NZ$12.50 (U.S. $3.90–$8.15). No credit cards.
Open: Mon–Sat 9am–4pm.

This is one of the special places beloved by local residents and so seldom found by visitors. Ian Fraser left a successful business career to follow his heart into the kitchen of this sparkling deli/restaurant. You enter through the deli displaying such unexpected treasures as those melt-in-your-mouth Greek spinach-and-cheese pies and miniquiches, to be eaten at the pine-stool counter just back of the shop or to take home for that late-night snack when you don't want to go out. There are all sorts of sausages, cheeses, salads, and rolls as well. Upstairs are three distinctly different dining rooms: the Graffiti Room (you can leave your mark if you can find a spot on the wall), the Piaf Room, and the Conversation Room. The decor throughout is a treat, but it's the food that makes this place special. Ian was brought up in the East, and you'll find on the menu several spicy dishes like goulash, chili con carne, and mustard veal. Salad platters include smoked salmon, coppa and paw paw, shrimp and avocado, spanakopita Greek salad, and assorted cheese and fruit platters. Pâtés are homemade and out of this world. No wine license, but there are four special liqueur coffees. BYO.

The Hard to Find Cafe, 47 High St. ☎ **373-4681.**

Cuisine: MEXICAN. **Reservations:** Not required.
Prices: Main dishes NZ$11.50–NZ$16.50 (U.S. $7.50–$10.75). AE, DC, MC, V.
Open: Lunch Mon–Fri noon–2:30pm; dinner daily 5:30–10pm.

The menu and prices make this an Auckland favorite. Les and Eva Moricz serve some of the best Mexican food I've had anywhere in the world (including my favorite San Diego spot). Their tacos come with all kinds of fillings, including vegetarian, and the nachos are really crispy. Although the hearty soup alone makes a good lunch, for something even more filling try the enchilada and taco with rice and salad. There are chalkboard specials, a nice selection of desserts, and several special coffees. No alcohol is served, but you're welcome to bring your own beer or wine.

$ **Kebab Kid,** 363 Parnell Rd., Parnell. ☎ **373-4290.**

Cuisine: GREEK/MIDDLE EASTERN.
Prices: Light meals NZ$6–NZ$7 (U.S. $3.90–$4.55). AE, DC, MC, V.
Open: Sun–Mon noon–10pm, Tues–Thurs and Sat noon–11pm, Fri noon–2am.

This place is casual, so if you're thinking of a flashy night out, skip this listing. The 20-something crowd who run Kebab Kid provide half a dozen wooden tables in a small room, magazines for reading while you're waiting, and very tasty food. You might enjoy charwarma, a toasted whole-meal bun with spiced lamb, lettuce, tomatoes, and sauces; or grilled chicken in pita bread with tsatsiki sauce. There's also a selection of Moroccan salad, hummus, tsatsiki, and falafel for two. Customers order at the counter, and meals are prepared in the open kitchen in one corner. The baklava comes with hokey pokey ice cream (New Zealand's favorite—vanilla ice cream with chunks of hard candy). Not licensed and not BYO. Also does take-out.

Konditorei Boss, 305 Parnell Rd. ☎ **377-8953.**

Cuisine: QUICHE/SALADS/PASTRIES. **Reservations:** Not required.
Prices: Average lunch NZ$3.50–NZ$10 (U.S. $2.30–$6.50). AE, BC, MC, V.
Open: Daily 8am–5pm.

This Parnell Village place is cafeteria style yet quite stylish. It's a grand spot for breakfast—you can sit and read the newspaper or plot the day's activities. The front porch is inviting, and it's handy for those in wheelchairs, who can just wheel right up. You can order everything from danish and coffee (or cappuccino) to fruit cups to meat-filled croissants to cheese pies. Everything is homemade, including good, hearty German-style bread. Pastries are terrific, as is their Black Forest cake.

Mai Thai, 57B Victoria St. W., near Albert St. ☎ **303-2550.**

Cuisine: THAI. **Reservations:** Recommended.
Prices: Appetizers NZ$8–NZ$10 (U.S. $5.20–$6.50); main courses NZ $14.50–NZ$22 (U.S. $9.45–$14.30). AE, MC, V.
Open: Lunch Mon–Fri noon–2:30; dinner Mon–Sat 6–10:30pm.

A small restaurant that's big on service, this is one of the best Asian eateries in Auckland. It's in a city–center location, but the decor and ambience are comparatively peaceful. Thai service staff proffer their country's traditional cuisine—some of which is very spicy. Fully licensed with a good wine list. Also BYO.

Nicholas Nickleby Coffee Lounge, 9 High St. ☎ **373-4604.**

Cuisine: SALADS/QUICHES/LIGHT MEALS. **Reservations:** Not required.
Prices: Main dishes NZ$4–NZ$10 (U.S. $2.60–$6.50). No credit cards.
Open: Mon–Fri 7am–2:30pm.

This is a real find for budgeteers. It's a small, unpretentious, cozy, downstairs eatery in the city center where everything is homemade and of the very freshest ingredients, and it's a great favorite with office workers (which means you'll do well to go earlier or later than regular office meal hours). The self-service counter always includes a nice variety of salads, small quiches, meat pies, meat rolls, soups, lasagne, and melt-in-your-mouth muffins and other pastries. Desserts, too, are exceptionally good. A cooked breakfast of bacon and eggs is also available in the morning.

Rick's Cafe Americain, Victoria Park Market, Victoria St. W. ☎ **309-9074.**

Cuisine: BURGERS/PASTA/SALADS/SEAFOOD. **Reservations:** Not required.
Prices: Appetizers NZ$7–NZ$10 (U.S. $4.55–$6.50); main courses NZ$11–NZ$17 (U.S. $7.15–$11.05). AE, DC, MC, V.
Open: Mon–Fri 7:30am–1am, Sat–Sun 9am–1am (breakfast daily until noon).

It doesn't look much like its *Casablanca* counterpart, but this is a terrific drop-in place in the city center for snacks, light lunches, and moderately priced dinners. Offerings range from potato skins with sour cream to chili to spareribs to fresh fish. Prices are moderate and light meals can be very inexpensive. It's licensed, of course, and sometimes there's live music.

Tops Brasserie, in the Parkroyal Hotel, Queen and Customs sts. ☎ **377-8920.**

Cuisine: SNACKS/LIGHT MEALS. **Reservations:** Not required.
Prices: Snacks NZ$4–NZ$6 (U.S. $2.60–$3.90); average two-course meal NZ$12–NZ$18 (U.S. $7.80–$11.70). AE, MC, V.
Open: Daily 6:30am–midnight.

On the ground floor of the Parkroyal Hotel in the city center, this handy pit stop is conveniently located near shopping and sights. The menu has a wide variety of offerings—from snacks to light lunches to two-course meals, all at moderate prices. It's fully licensed and serves counter lunches and take-aways from its delicatessen on the corner.

Union Fish Company, 16 Quay St. ☎ **309-6593.**

Cuisine: SEAFOOD. **Reservations:** Required.
Prices: Appetizers NZ$9.50–NZ$13 (U.S. $6.20–$8.45); main courses NZ$17.50–NZ$24 (U.S. $11.40–$15.60). AE, DC, MC, V.
Open: Lunch Mon–Fri noon–2:30pm; dinner daily 6–10pm.

This one-time marine repair warehouse on the waterfront has been converted into a nautical dining room that features a bar in the prow of a boat, a ship's figurehead, touches of brass, original maritime memorabilia, old maritime and early Auckland pictures, and a menu that calls itself a "bill of lading." Many Aucklanders consider this the best place for seafood Japanese style. Choose your own crayfish from the tank, to be prepared any way you like, or select from such specialties as sashimi (raw fish with wasabi mustard), Bluff oysters, Nelson salmon (fresh or smoked), scallops, green-lipped mussels, or a choice of fish from the daily menu. Licensed.

Wings Restaurant, 71 Tamaki Dr., Mission Bay. ☎ **528-5419** or **528-6398.**

Cuisine: STEAK/SEAFOOD. **Reservations:** Recommended Fri–Sat nights.
Prices: Appetizers NZ$4–NZ$10 (U.S. $2.60–$6.50); main courses NZ$16–NZ$20 (U.S. $10.40–$13); less at lunch. AE, DC, MC, V.
Open: Lunch Mon–Fri noon–2:30pm; dinner daily 6–11pm.

On the waterfront in Mission Bay, Wings specializes in steak, but the menu also includes fine seafood as well as chicken dishes. Drivers will find ample parking, and the thoughtful owners have provided access ramps and table room for wheelchairs. There's good city bus service to the restaurant.

Pub Meals

All Blacks Club, 47–51 Fort St. ☎ **309-2450.**

Cuisine: PUB MEALS. **Reservations:** Not required.
Prices: Sandwiches NZ$2 (U.S. $1.30); average meal NZ$7 (U.S. $4.55). No credit cards.
Open: Lunch only, Mon–Fri noon–2:30pm. (Pub, Mon–Sat 10am–11pm.)

One of the most economical meals in town is the pub counter lunch at this small club just a few blocks from Queen Street in the city center. The menu includes fish and chips or roast beef on rye, oysters, prawns, and lasagne. An assortment of sandwiches and rolls is also available. A unique collection of rugby memorabilia covers the walls. Licensed.

The Loaded Hog, on Viaduct Quay, 104 Quay St., near Customs St. W. ☎ **366-6491.**

Cuisine: PUB MEALS. **Reservations:** Accepted only Mon–Thurs.
Prices: Snacks NZ$2.50–NZ$7 (U.S. $1.65–$4.55); light meals NZ$5–NZ$7 (U.S. $3.25–$4.55); main courses NZ$10.50–NZ$14 (U.S. $6.85–$9.10). AE, BC, DC, MC, V.
Open: Daily noon–9pm or a little later.

This smart pub, which opened in late 1993, is best known for its microbrewery and the nightlife crowds that congregate here. However, it's also a viable dining option, as steak, pasta, venison, and fish main courses and a variety of snacks are served at reasonable prices. The decor is appealing: Farm implements hang from the walls, bar stools and chair seats are covered in either red or blue plaid, and there are wood floors. Large windows overlook the dock, where you might just see an America's Cup boat or two. Fully licensed.

Shakespeare Tavern & Hathaway's Brasserie, 61 Albert St. ☎ **373-5396.**

Cuisine: PUB MEALS. **Reservations:** Not required.
Prices: Under NZ$15 (U.S. $9.75). AE, DC, MC, V.
Open: Mon–Wed 11am–7:45pm, Thurs 11am–9:45pm, Fri–Sat 11am–10:45pm, Sun noon–9:45pm. (Tavern, daily 11am–7pm.)

If it's pub grub you savor, visit this spot, located in the city center. It makes lager, ale, stout, and even ginger beer (if you try them all, you leave with a certificate). The winsome publican, Peter Barraclough, has been here since 1975, and his friendly daughter, Karen, is often on duty in the lounge upstairs. Hathaway's, the restaurant located downstairs, offers moderately priced fare. You'll probably come away with a T-shirt or mug as a souvenir—it's that kind of place. Licensed, of course.

READERS RECOMMEND

Kwan's Thai Restaurant, at Jervois and St. Mary's roads, Ponsonby. *"This restaurant deserves very high marks for food and service."*—Gordon Mears, Seattle, Wash., U.S.A.

Quayside Cafe, Quay Street. *"This was the best, and possibly cheapest, restaurant we experienced in all of New Zealand. It was also one of the few places to serve regular brewed coffee (not instant). The Quayside Cafe is located across the street from the Ferry Building, on one side of Queen Elizabeth II Square. It was just the best food we encountered."* —Tim Nelson, Petaluma, Calif., U.S.A.

Nearby Dining

ON THE NORTH SHORE

In addition to the places mentioned below, fans of Mexican food should check out **Taco Pronto,** 5 Clarence St., Devonport. As we go to press, this inexpensive eatery is being opened by successful former San Diego restaurateur Dean Betts. I don't know many details (like the meal hours) but, based on his track record in my hometown, I can promise you it'll be the best Mexican food in New Zealand.

Carpe Diem, 49 Victoria Rd., Devonport. ☎ **445-7732.**

Cuisine: MODERN NEW ZEALAND. **Reservations:** Not accepted.

Prices: Lunch NZ$5.50–NZ$12 (U.S. $3.60–$7.80); dinner NZ$12.50–NZ$15.50 (U.S. $8.15–$10.10). BC, DC, MC, V.

Open: Mon 9am–5pm, Tues–Thurs and Sun 9am–9pm, Fri–Sat 9am–10pm.

This café is popular with both locals and the many visitors who either stay in Devonport or take the ferry over for the day. The food is great and the casual decor appealing. For lunch you could have a tomato, mozzarella, and pesto focaccia sandwich; homemade soup with grilled bruschetta; or tandoori chicken with naan bread. Dinner main courses include chicken breast stuffed with feta and pesto on roasted provençal vegetables or fresh spaghetti with sautéed scallops, mussels, capers, and parmesan. Depending on the time of day, you might prefer just to have a cappuccino or espresso and one of the many available desserts. Unfortunately, the service staff aren't as friendly as most New Zealanders, but just ignore them and enjoy your meal. Licensed and BYOW (bring your own wine).

Catch 22 Fish Shop, 19 Victoria Rd., Devonport. ☎ **445-2225.**

Cuisine: FISH AND CHIPS. **Reservations:** Not accepted.

Prices: Average meal NZ$4–NZ$5 (U.S. $2.60–$3.25). No credit cards.

Open: Sun–Mon noon–8pm, Tues–Wed 9:30am–8pm, Thurs–Fri 9:30am–9pm, Sat 10:30am–9pm.

I realize that this is a fish shop, not a restaurant, but I'm including it because you might want to buy fish and chips and take them across the road to Windsor Reserve. I can't think of many nicer spots for a picnic. However, don't buy the paua fritters; my husband and I did and ended up feeding them to a golden retriever with an indiscriminate palate. Catch 22 sells juice and cold sodas but no alcohol.

La Casa Italiana, Shop 9, the Devonport Ferry Wharf. ☎ **445-9933.**

Cuisine: PIZZA/PASTA. **Reservations:** Not accepted.

Prices: Appetizers NZ$5 (U.S. $3.25); main courses NZ$7–NZ$9 (U.S. $4.55–$5.85). No credit cards.

Open: Daily 10am–8:30pm.

This little quick-food counter on the Devonport Ferry Wharf is one of my favorite places to eat. Delicious pizzas come in two sizes and with 13 toppings. On a recent lunch visit, my husband and I shared a standard-size Super La Casa (tomato, cheese, mushrooms, ham, salami, bacon, capers, prawns, olives, and more for NZ$8.50/U.S. $5.55). There are tables and chairs nearby—inside and outside. La Casa's owners are brothers Tony and Jafar, who immigrated to New Zealand nine years ago. They make their pizza dough and all the desserts on the premises. Cappuccino and espresso are available, as is wine.

The Left Bank Restaurant, 14 Victoria Rd., Devonport. ☎ **445-2615.**

Cuisine: MODERN MULTI-ETHNIC. **Reservations:** Recommended.
Prices: Snacks NZ$6.50–NZ$8.50 (U.S. $4.25–$5.55); salads NZ$14 (U.S. $9.10); main courses NZ$14–NZ$22 (U.S. $9.10–$14.30). AE, DC, MC, V.
Open: Mon–Sat noon–11pm, Sun 9:30am–11pm.

This congenial café has a menu that includes tapas (everything from marinated mushrooms to charcoal-grilled garlic chicken kebabs); avocado, bacon, and banana salad; fettuccine; fish of the day; and a sinful chocolate cake with chocolate sauce, almonds, and whipped cream. It's the perfect place for grazing. It's an easy walk from the ferry landing; if driving, take the Harbour Bridge. Licensed. More than 15 wines are available by the glass.

The Masonic Tavern, King Edward Parade at Church St., Devonport. ☎ **445-0485**

Cuisine: PUB MEALS.
Prices: Bistro meal NZ$5–NZ$14 (U.S. $3.25–$9.10). No credit cards.
Open: Lunch daily noon–2pm; dinner daily 5–9pm.

If you're at all interested in an authentic, atmospheric working-man's pub that dishes up helpings of good grub at inexpensive prices, don't miss the Masonic Tavern. Hot meals, as well as light snacks, all go for reasonable prices. Burgers, sandwiches, and other traditional dishes are offered.

ON WAIHEKE ISLAND

★ **Vino-Vino Bar & Cafe,** Oceanview Mall, Oneroa, Waiheke Island. ☎ **372-9888.**

Cuisine: MODERN NEW ZEALAND. **Reservations:** Not accepted.
Prices: Snacks NZ$3.50–NZ$8.50 (U.S. $2.30–$5.55); lunch or dinner NZ$7.50–NZ$12 (U.S. $4.90–$7.80). AE, BC, DC, MC, V.
Open: Mon–Thurs 11am–10pm, Fri–Sat 11am–11pm, Sun 11am–8pm.

This wine bar/café has four things going for it: a menu that's actually fun to read, a great atmosphere, a wonderful view, and very good food. I stopped in here recently and had the best pumpkin soup I've ever tasted. Other menu offerings include Vino's hot roast lamb on rye with beetroot-and-mint chutney ("wrap your laughing gear around this"), white-onion and rosemary pizza bread with cheese, egg, and green-olive pâté ("wow, try this"), and salad with sesame-tofu balls and peanut-and-coriander dressing. There's an open fire in winter and outdoor seating on a sun deck in summer. A dozen wines are available by the glass (more by the bottle), and Guinness is on tap.

Worth the Extra Money

With Auckland's wealth of fine dining, it almost seems obligatory to indulge in at least one "big splurge" while you're there. The following are among those I consider worthy of that extra expenditure.

Cin Cin on Quay Brasserie & Bar, in the Ferry Building, 99 Quay St. ☎ **307-6966.**

Cuisine: NEW ZEALAND/PACIFIC. **Reservations:** Recommended for lunch.
Prices: Appetizers NZ$7.50–NZ$14.90 (U.S. $4.90–$9.70); main courses NZ$18.50–NZ$24.50 (U.S. $12.05–$15.95). AE, DC, MC, V.
Open: Breakfast daily 8–11am; lunch/dinner daily until "very late." (Bar, open "very late" also.)

This eclectic, stylish waterfront eatery in the old Ferry Building is a focal point for ferrygoers—but, more than that, for Aucklanders who know that this spot is the winner of many New Zealand restaurant awards. A wood-burning pizza oven, wood-fired grill with mesquite wood, and open kitchen are a few of the unusual features. The chef oversees a menu that includes Italian, French, Chinese, and Japanese cuisine. The large bar serves drinks outside all day, specializing in imported beers and wines by the glass. Inside, marble floors add a touch of elegance to the large casual dining area, and soft colors dominate the the decor. Upstairs, there's mezzanine dining with a more formal ambience. Prices are surprisingly moderate. Light meals and snacks of Italian pastries and the like are also served.

Gladstones, in the Barrycourt Motor Inn, 10–20 Gladstone Rd., off St. Stephens Ave., Parnell. ☎ **303-3789**

Cuisine: NEW ZEALAND. **Reservations:** Recommended.

Prices: Appetizers NZ$8–NZ$17.50 (U.S. $5.20–$11.40); main courses NZ$17.50–NZ$26 (U.S. $11.40–$16.90); less at lunch. AE, DC, MC, V.

Open: Daily 7am–10pm.

Gladstones is Barrycourt's light and airy eatery set in an extension to a turn-of-the-century home. The menu includes rack of lamb, loin of pork Italiana, and seafood linguine. The wine list is impressive. Save room for the great desserts, including blueberry crumble, warm chocolate cake, and Norm's delight—homemade ice cream on a fruit coulis. Licensed. There's good city bus service to the restaurant's Parnell address.

Harbourside Seafood Bar & Grill, in the Ferry Building, 94 Quay St. ☎ **307-0486** or **307-0556.**

Cuisine: SEAFOOD. **Reservations:** Recommended.

Prices: Appetizers NZ$11–NZ$13.50 (U.S. $7.15–$8.80); main courses NZ$16–NZ$32 (U.S. $10.40–$20.80)

Open: Daily 11:30am–10pm. **Closed:** Christmas Day.

This stylish second-floor restaurant on the waterfront in the city center has a terrific view of the harbor—ask for a table near a window. Seating is both indoors and out. The decor is modern, with paintings, dividing screens, a marbled entrance, and a crayfish tank. Seafood dishes have won their fair share of kudos, and there's an extensive wine list. The menu features a charcoal-gilled seafood platter, grilled John Dory, and baked salmon filet. My favorite is the risotto, in which prawns, scampi, scallops, squid, and fish are tossed with a Tuscan sauce. Four token meat dishes are offered for nonseafood diners. An excellent brunch is served on Saturday, Sunday, and holidays. Licensed.

Sails Restaurant, The Anchorage, Westhaven Marina, off Fanshawe St. ☎ **378-9890.**

Cuisine: SEAFOOD/NEW ZEALAND SPECIALTIES. **Reservations:** Required.

Prices: Appetizers NZ$7–NZ$14 (U.S. $4.55–$9.10); main courses NZ$14–NZ$20 (U.S. $5.20–$7.15) at lunch, NZ$20–NZ$25 (U.S. $7.15–$9.10) at dinner. AE, DC, MC, V.

Open: Lunch Mon–Fri noon–2pm; dinner Mon–Sat 6:30–10:30pm.

For a water-level view of Auckland's beautiful harbor, head for Sails, nestled beside the approaches to the Auckland Harbour Bridge. The large, light, and airy dining room is decorated in cool shades of green, white, and gray, but its most impressive decor is just outside its wall of windows, where hundreds of private sailboats are anchored in the harbor. The menu features—what else?—seafood, and I could make a meal just from the starters listed (a seafood terrine of scallops and crab, smoked fish with horseradish cream, oysters grilled with spinach and cheese or champagne and cream, fresh pasta with a garlicky tomato sauce, etc.). Main courses include orange roughy, seafood mornay, fresh crayfish, and nonfishy specialties of lamb, chicken, and pork. Desserts are excellent, and there's a good selection of cheeses. Sails is fully licensed. Coffee lovers will like to know that Twinings Grosvenor roast is served here. A delightful place and very popular.

ON THE NORTH SHORE

The Low Flying Duck, 99 Victoria Rd., Devonport. ☎ **445-8133.**

Cuisine: MODERN NEW ZEALAND. **Reservations:** Recommended.
Prices: Appetizers NZ$9.50 (U.S. $6.20); main courses NZ$19.50 (U.S. $12.70). AE, DC, MC, V.
Open: Dinner only, Mon–Sat 6–10:30pm.

Jan Pace, who runs the Low Flying Duck, uses high-quality New Zealand seafood, beef, lamb, and fowl to create innovative dishes, such as crisp duck thigh oven baked and served with grilled banana; and brazil and nut ravioli served with pumpkin–and–sour cream sauce. All main dishes come with fresh seasonal vegetables, and there's delightful courtyard dining in summer months. BYO. The High Flying Grapes Wine Shop is next door.

Porterhouse Blue, 58 Calliope Rd., Devonport. ☎ **445-0309.**

Cuisine: NEW ZEALAND. **Reservations:** Recommended.
Prices: Appetizers NZ$9.50–NZ$14 (U.S. $6.20–$9.10); main courses NZ$18.50–NZ$25 (U.S. $12.05–$16.25). AE, BC, DC, MC, V.
Open: Dinner only, Mon–Sat 6:30–10pm.

An open fire and candles contribute to the cozy atmosphere here, as do lots of green plants, terra-cotta–colored walls, and a pretty stained-glass window. The menu includes boned leg of rabbit, braised lamb shanks, ocean-fresh fish, and wild venison medallions. My only gripe is the offensive practice of charging NZ$2 (U.S. $1.30) per person for bread. On the other hand, the restaurant offers free transportation within Devonport and someone will meet the ferry if prearranged. Licensed or BYOW. (Save NZ$10/U.S. $6.50 or more by picking up your wine at the High Flying Grapes on Victoria Road.)

Specialty Dining

LUNCH OR DINNER AFLOAT

A lunch or dinner cruise is a terrific way to explore Auckland's spectacular harbor, and the city views are impressive, to say the least, especially in the evening, when the city lights are reflected along the shoreline. The freshest of seafoods are served on most cruises, along with beef and other nonseafood dishes. It's a bit pricey—about NZ$40 (U.S. $26) for lunch, NZ$75 (U.S. $48.75) for dinner—but well worth every New Zealand cent. Hours for luncheon cruises are 12:30 to 2:30pm; dinner, 6 to 9pm. Reserve with **The Pride of Auckland Company,** in the Downtown Airline Terminal at the corner of Quay and Albert streets (☎ **373-4557**).

BREAKFAST

See my full recommendations above for details on the following restaurants, all of which serve breakfast as early as 7am to 7:30pm. Best get there before 10am, however, when most begin lunch preparations: **Konditorei Boss,** 305 Parnell Rd. (☎ **377-8953**); **Cin Cin on Quay Brasserie & Bar,** 99 Quay St. (☎ **307-6966**); **Nicholas Nickleby Coffee Lounge,** 9 High St. (☎ **373-4604**); and **Tops Brasserie,** in the Parkroyal Hotel at Queen and Customs streets (☎ **377-8920**).

LATE-NIGHT DINING

See my full recommendations above for details on these late-serving eateries: **Cheers Cafe & Bar,** 12 Wyndham St., just off Queen Street (☎ **309-8779**); **Cin Cin on Quay Brasserie & Bar,** 99 Quay St. (☎ **307-6966**); and **The Fish Pot,** 99B Tamaki Dr., Mission Bay (☎ **528-4097**).

DINING COMPLEXES

Be sure to pay a visit to the **China Oriental Markets,** 2 Britomart Place (☎ **302-0678**). It's down near the waterfront, and you can't miss the lavender, blue, lime, and yellow facade. Inside are 130 stalls featuring every type of food (and merchandise) imaginable. It was created in late 1989 and is open daily.

Victoria Park Market, on Victoria Street West, also has an International Food Hall, as well as several fully licensed restaurants and a McDonald's.

FOOD COURTS

These provide another inexpensive dining option in Auckland. The most popular is located on the second level of the **Downtown Shopping Centre** at Queen Elizabeth II Square on Quay Street. It's open Monday through Saturday from 7am to 6:30pm. **Food Alley** on Albert Street, across from the Regent Hotel, is another good one. Here nine different kinds of ethnic food are served. Food Alley is open daily from 10am to 10pm, and it's licensed to serve alcohol. And at the **Viaduct Quay Food Court** at the west end of Quay Street across from the Maritime Museum you'll find Wholey Mackerel, Hey Pesto, and Killer Tortilla. The average meal in any of these food courts costs NZ$5 (U.S. $3.25).

LOCAL BUDGET BETS

One of the most inexpensive ways to eat, of course, is to stop by a deli and pick up the makings of a meal in your motel—you'll be getting full value then from that lovely fridge, stove, pots and pans, and dishes.

An alternative, especially on those days when you're absolutely pooped from sightseeing and don't want to face any sort of food preparation, is to order a delicious pizza and have it delivered piping hot right to your door. **Dial-A-Dino's Pizza** (☎ **576-1180**) delivers from 4:30 to 11pm Sunday through Thursday and 4:30pm to 1am on Friday and Saturday. There's a wide variety of pizza toppings from which to choose: ham, salami, pepperoni, diced beef, mushrooms, onions, olives, prawns, smoked oysters, bacon, anchovies, capers . . . well, that's part of their list. They also offer crusty garlic bread and soft drinks, and delivery is usually within 30 minutes. Pizzas come in 6-, 8-, and 12-slice pies.

6 What to See & Do

If your time in Auckland is going to be limited and you can't figure out how you'll work in everything you'd like to see, you should consult the Visitor Information Centre (see "Tourist Information" under "City Specifics," earlier in this chapter). Just call or go by and tell them what you want to see and how much time you have. The following are sightseeing *suggestions,* but you should fit your own time to your own special interests.

SIGHTSEEING SUGGESTIONS

Day 1 You'll need at least half the day to see and fully appreciate the Auckland Museum. Kelly Tarlton's Underwater World will fill the afternoon, and a nice ending for the day is a dinner cruise on the harbor.

Day 2 Focus your second day on the waterfront. Visit the National Maritime Museum on Hobson Wharf and take the walking tour at the end of this section.

Day 3 Take the ferry over to Devonport, on Auckland's North Shore, and spend the day exploring its streets lined with colonial-style bungalows, with a stop at one of its fine beaches.

Day 4 Use this day for an excursion to Waiheke Island or the Waitakeres.

Day 5 Visit the ancient Maori fort on One Tree Hill, then plan an afternoon at the Auckland Zoo or shopping at Victoria Park Market or Parnell Village.

The Top Attractions

Before you set out to explore Auckland, arm yourself with the money-saving **Explorer Bus Pass** or a **Busabout Pass** for traveling between major attractions (see "Getting Around," earlier in this chapter).

Auckland Museum, Auckland Domain. ☎ **309-0443,** or **377-3932** for recorded information.

A visit to this museum is a virtual necessity for a full appreciation of the Maori culture you'll be exposed to in other parts of the country. The imposing gleaming-white museum, surrounded by the sweeping lawns and flower gardens of the Domain, houses the world's largest collection of Maori artifacts, providing you with a rich background from which to understand the Maori of today. Be sure to pick up a free guide map as you enter the museum.

In the **Maori Court,** the most impressive exhibit is probably the 82-foot war canoe chiseled from one enormous totara trunk and covered with intricate, symbolic

Frommer's Favorite Auckland Experiences

Taking a Harbor Cruise Anytime of Day But especially spectacular in the evening, when city lights add a special magic to the sight.

Browsing Through Shops in Parnell Village Many feature New Zealand and other South Pacific crafts housed in colonial-style bungalows.

Spending a Day in Devonport I really enjoy taking the ferry to Devonport and spending time in this seaside suburb. The view of the Auckland skyline from the water is great, and it's fun to watch the various vessels in the harbor. Once on the North Shore, I go up to a lofty lookout point on Mount Victoria for a more expansive vista and then into the village for lunch at one of the many cute cafés.

Driving Along the Water Tamaki Drive starts in the city and follows the coastline out to suburban St. Heliers. This is a popular jogging route, but when I'm short of time (or energy) I drive—slowly—taking in the view of sailboats and windsurfers on the harbor. The Michael Savage Memorial Park, above Tamaki Drive, is a good view point.

carvings. You'll see that same artistic carving in the 85-foot meetinghouse, whose painted rafters and carved and painted wall panels are a wonder of red, black, and white scrollwork. The wall panels also feature tribal-motif carvings interspersed with traditional woven flax patterns. The meetinghouse sits between two storehouses raised on stilts to protect community goods from predators. Also in the museum are displays of gorgeous feather cloaks (each feather knotted in by hand) worn by high-ranking men, as well as a display of jade tikis. Look for the greenstone *mere* (war club), such a lordly weapon that it was reserved for the slaying of only the highest-ranking captives (who considered it an honor to meet their end with such a club). Look also for the Maori portraits, the life's work of famed New Zealand artist C. F. Goldie, a Pakeha who captured on canvas not only the ornate tattoos of chieftains and common folk, but their fierce tribal pride as well.

Twice a day, **Maori concerts** bring to life the culture and history of New Zealand's native people. These performances include action songs, a poi ball demonstration, and an explanation of the use of greenstone and making *piu piu* (flax) skirts. Guided tours of the Maori gallery take place 45 minutes before every show. Check with the museum for times.

Another not-to-be-missed feature is the exciting **Caltex Volcanoes & Giants Exhibition,** which is running until January 1996. Here, multimedia presentations tell the story of New Zealand's natural history—including giant extinct birds, dinosaurs, and volcanoes. (The interactive nature of this area is in contrast to the static collections in other parts of the museum. Happily, there are plans under way to revitalize the whole place.)

If you're traveling with youngsters 2 to 12, I suggest that you take them to **Weird and Wonderful,** a children's discovery center that provides a wealth of imaginative hands-on experiences.

Elsewhere in the museum are the **Hall of South Pacific Art,** the **Hall of Asian Art,** the **Pacific Canoe Hall,** native bird displays (including that giant moa exhibit), and much, much more.

The shop near the entrance of the museum is worth a little browsing time for publications on Maori art and New Zealand flora and fauna, as well as reproductions and replicas of some of the exhibits—a good place to pick up mementos to carry home. There's also a coffee lounge (open from 10am to 3:45pm), which serves sandwiches, salads, desserts, and beverages.

Admission: Permanent collection, free; Maori concert, NZ$6.50 (U.S. $4.25); Weird and Wonderful, NZ$1 (U.S. 65¢); Volcanos and Giants, NZ$7 (U.S. $4.55) adults, less for children.

Open: Daily 10am–5pm; children's discovery center, daily 1–4:30pm. **Closed:** Good Friday and Christmas Day. **Bus:** 635 from the Downtown Bus Terminal.

Auckland City Art Gallery, Kitchener and Wellesley sts., at the intersection of Albert Park. ☎ **309-0831** for recorded information.

New Zealand's oldest and largest art gallery, this is one of the most active art museums in the South Pacific. Its permanent collection ranges from European masters to contemporary international art, plus the most comprehensive collection of New Zealand fine art in the country. Works by New Zealand artists date from 1770 to the present and include a display of fine Maori portraits. The Gallery Cafe offers refreshment, and there's good browsing in the bookshop. Free guided tours are given Wednesday through Sunday at 2pm.

Admission: Free, except for periodic special exhibitions.

Open: Daily 10am–4:30pm.

Kelly Tarlton's Underwater World, Orakei Wharf, 23 Tamaki Dr., Orakei. ☎ **528-0603.**

This is the inspiration and last work of the late Kelly Tarlton, the famed diver whose legacy to the country also includes the outstanding Museum of Shipwrecks in the Bay of Islands. His careful planning literally puts you inside an underwater environment by way of a moving walkway that passes through a clear tunnel surrounded by hundreds of native New Zealand fish swimming freely, apparently paying no mind to their gaping visitors. The experience is much the same as that of an actual dive—after passing through heavy "surf," you'll move over a sandy ocean bottom, through forests of waving seaweed, into mysterious underwater caves, and along rocky reefs. Look for sea creatures ranging from tiny sea horses to the leggy octopus, and don't miss the magnificent shark tank with its toothy inhabitants and huge stingrays. In the **Antarctic Encounter** there are live penguins, Snow Cats, and plenty of ice. There's good wheelchair access from the parking lot, and Kelly's Cafe offers snacks and buffet meals at reasonable prices as well as a dynamite over-the-water location.

Admission: NZ$16 (U.S. $10.40) adults, NZ$8 (U.S. $5.20) children 4–12, free for children under 4; special rates for family groups and senior citizens.

Open: Daily 9am–9pm. **Transportation:** Mission Bay city bus, Explorer Bus, or Fullers Harbour Explorer.

Auckland Zoo, Motions Rd., Western Springs. ☎ **378-1620.**

One of the few places to observe the kiwi, that flightless bird that has become New Zealand's national symbol, is the Nocturnal House here at the zoo. The birds are exhibited daily in natural bush settings, which resemble a moonlit forest floor. You can watch them foraging, their long beaks seeking food in the leaf-covered ground. Don't plan a quick run out to the zoo just to look at the kiwis, however—more than 2,000 other birds, mammals, fish, and reptiles (representing some 200 species) will entice you from one area to another in the beautifully tended park surroundings. For instance, you can also take a look here at the tuatara, Earth's oldest reptile.

Admission: NZ$9 (U.S. $5.85) adults, NZ$4.50 (U.S. $2.95) children 5–15, free for children under 5; NZ$24 (U.S. $15.60) family ticket for two adults and up to four children.

Open: Daily 9:30am–5:30pm (last admission 4:15pm). **Closed:** Christmas Day. **Bus:** 45, leaving every 10 minutes from Customs Street.

★ **New Zealand National Maritime Museum,** Hobson Wharf, Quay St. ☎ **358-3010.**

Encompassing 1,000 years of maritime history, this interactive museum tells the story of the early Polynesian explorers, the immigrant ships that brought "new" New Zealanders from many countries, and the yachting successes of a nation obsessed by the water. The Big Boat, *KZ-1,* is out front. Inside, visitors can sit in oral-history chairs, trace their ancestors on computers, and note the amazingly accurate map created on Captain Cook's first voyage to New Zealand in 1769. Be sure to notice the Moth Class dinghy designed by Kiwi schoolboy Bruce Farr—now one of the world's leading yacht designers—and don't skip the audiovisual presentation in the theater near the entrance. The scow *Ted Ashby* provides rides at 1pm daily. There's a good museum store, and Launchman's is a great spot for lunch or tea. Allow plenty of time for your visit; there's *a lot* here.

Did You Know . . . ?

- Auckland and its environs is New Zealand's largest urban area, home to one-third of its population.
- The city has two harbors, sprinkled with more than 20 islands, with over 100 beaches, and 2,000 hours of sunshine annually.

Admission: NZ$9 (U.S. $5.85) adults, half price for children; NZ$18 (U.S. $11.70) family ticket.

Open: Daily 10am–5pm (later during the summer).

More Attractions

Parnell Rose Garden, Gladstone Rd., Parnell. ☎ **307-0136** or **302-1252.**

If it's rose-blooming time when you visit, be sure to stop to see this garden. Thousands of traditional roses are set in color-coordinated beds. The Rose Garden Lounge serves lunches on weekdays.

Admission: Free.

Open: Nov–Mar, daily during daylight hours. **Bus:** 702 from the Downtown Bus Terminal.

The Auckland Domain, bounded by Grafton Rd., Park Rd., Titoki St., and the railway line.

This green expanse near the city center offers walking paths and massive sweeping lawns—perfect for picnics. Ducks swim on ponds formed by natural springs. If you're interested in plants, don't miss the Winter Garden and the Fernery, both contained in glasshouses. The stately Auckland Museum, the focal point of the Domain, is described under "The Top Attractions," above.

Admission: Free.

Open: Winter Garden, daily 10am–4pm.

Museum of Transport and Technology, and New Zealand Science Centre, 825 Great North Rd., Western Springs. ☎ **846-0199.**

There's a fascinating collection of vehicles, trains, trams, aircraft, steam engines, and pioneer artifacts at the MOTAT, as it's best known. There you'll find New Zealand's only full-time publicly operating tramway, including Auckland's first electric tram (ca. 1902). In the Pioneers of Aviation Pavilion, special tribute is paid to Richard Pearse, who on March 31, 1902, flew an aircraft on the South Island. Life in 1840–90 New Zealand is re-created in the Victorian Village, where the church is still used for weddings and christenings. There are several food facilities on the grounds, but the 120-year-old Colonial Arms Restaurant is rather special, serving Devonshire teas and à la carte meals. The museum is just 3 miles from the city center.

Admission: NZ$8.50 (U.S. $5.55) adults, NZ$6.50 (U.S. $4.25) senior citizens, NZ$4.50 (U.S. $2.95) children; NZ$23 (U.S. $14.95) family ticket for two adults and up to four children.

Open: Daily 10am–4pm. **Closed:** Christmas Day. **Bus:** 145 from Customs Street East.

Ewelme Cottage, 14 Ayr St. ☎ **379-0202.**

This cottage was built by the Rev. Vicesimus Lush (somehow, I find humor in that surname for a minister) and named for Ewelme Village in England. It has been authentically preserved, right down to 19th-century furnishings and as much of the original wallpaper as could be salvaged.

Admission: NZ$2.50 (U.S. $1.65) adults, NZ50¢ (U.S. 35¢) children.

Open: Daily 10:30am–noon and 1–4:30pm. **Closed:** Good Friday and Christmas Day. **Bus:** 635, 645, or 655 from the Downtown Bus Terminal.

Howick Historical Village, Lloyd Elsmore Park, Bells Rd., Pakuranga. ☎ **576-9506.**

More than 25 buildings in a flowering garden setting take you back to village life in colonial New Zealand. Based on the local military, the village faithfully depicts the 1840–80 period.

Admission: NZ$8 (U.S. $5.20) adults, NZ$3 (U.S. $1.95) children.

Open: Mid-Mar to Dec 24, daily 10am–4pm; Dec 26 to mid-Mar, daily 10am–5pm. **Bus:** Howick and Eastern bus to Fortunes Road, Pakuranga. **Directions:** Drive 30 minutes on the Pakuranga Highway.

OTHER AUCKLAND SIGHTS

The historical **Old Auckland Customhouse** on Customs Street West is an outstanding example of 1880s architecture. It's a massive but graceful-looking building whose halls once rang with waterfront commerce. Today it has been beautifully restored and houses craft shops, two bookshops, Brandy's cocktail bar, and restaurants. Well worth a stop, both inside and out.

Parnell Village is actually a row of restored colonial houses along Parnell Road between St. Stephens Avenue and York Street in what is one of Auckland's oldest suburbs. Nowadays, those quaint old homes hold boutiques so fashionable they border on the trendy, art galleries, eateries, and pubs. But despite the bustle of shoppers, you'll get a real feeling of old Auckland just by ambling along the sidewalks and down tiny alleyways.

With or without binoculars, the view is nothing short of spectacular from the summit of **Mount Eden,** Auckland's highest point. An extinct volcano, which was fortified by the Maori, Mount Eden looks down on the city, both harbors, and Hauraki Gulf. The no. 274 bus from Customs Street East will get you there, or it's a lovely drive.

One Tree Hill (Cornwall Park, Mount Eden) is also an extinct volcano and was also the site of a large Maori *pa* (fort). There's an obelisk on the summit as a memorial to that race. The views are terrific, and the adjoining parkland is great for long walks.

A FERRY RIDE TO DEVONPORT

One of the nicest ways I know to see Auckland is from the ★ **harbor ferry,** which crosses to the North Shore. Usually you'll be aboard the zippy catamaran *Kea,* but from time to time the much-beloved and semiretired steam ferry MV *Kestrel* makes the journey. As the city recedes, you're treated to a focused look at big-city growth: The old red-brick Ferry Building with its clock tower stands in marked contrast to streamlined high-rises, and the stately white Auckland Museum looks down on it all with the dignity born of historical perspective. You pass the naval base, then if you plan it right and return in the evening, the sparkling city lights turn big-city sprawl into diamond-studded magic. You catch the ferry (☎ **367-9125**) at the Queens Wharf terminal on Quay Street (its North Shore destination is Devonport), leaving every half hour (on the hour and half hour) from 7am to 7pm on Monday through Friday, and every hour (on the hour) from 7 to 11pm on Monday through Friday and from 7am to 11pm on Saturday and Sunday. The round-trip fare is NZ$7 (U.S. $4.55).

The little suburb of **Devonport** is where the Maori say their great ancestral canoe *Tainui* first touched land in this area, somewhere around the 14th century. You'll see a stone memorial to that event on the grassy strip along the King Edward Parade foreshore—the bronze sculpture is an orb topped by a *korotangi* (weeping dove), one of the birds the Maori brought with them from their homeland. There are four white-sand beaches in Devonport, as well as Mount Victoria, which sits near the business center and is now topped by a harbor signal station (great views from up there). You can also walk up to North Head and explore the old military fort with its tunnels and gun sites. Devonport Tours (☎ **445-9880**) will take you there on a one-hour minibus tour.

Stroll along **King Edward Parade** and look for no. 7, where one of New Zealand's most talented writers—he was also an artist and a poet—Rex Fairburn (1904–57) once lived. A little farther along you'll come to the Masonic Hotel at the corner of Church Street. It was built in 1866, and this is where you'll find the **Masonic Tavern** (see "Where to Eat," earlier in this chapter). Just across the way, **Art by the Sea** (☎ **445-6665**) is in what was once the Duder Brothers' mercantile store; it's open daily from 10am to 5pm. The crafts of New Zealand artists are sold.

Other good places to shop include **The Glass House,** 61 Victoria Rd. (☎ **445-0377**); look for the Tony Sly pottery. I also really like **Flagstaff Gallery,** 25 Victoria Rd. (☎ **445-1142**), where most of the works of art are by New Zealand artists and they will ship your purchases. (Remember: You don't pay GST on things shipped out of the country.) You may also find some interesting items at **Abigail's Country Store,** 43 Victoria Rd. (☎ **445-3072**). Many shops in Devonport are open seven days a week. For more information, call the **Devonport info line** (☎ **445-7600**).

It's not imperative, but you may want to visit the **Royal New Zealand Navy Museum** on Spring Street (☎ **445-5186**), five blocks from the ferry wharf. It's open daily from 10am to 4:30pm, and admission is free. You also might like to visit the **Devonport Museum and Gardens,** at 31-A Vauxhall Rd. (☎ **445-2661**), between 2 and 4pm on weekends. Devonport is full of interesting houses that survive from the 1800s and early 1900s—no. 9 Mays St. is a marvel of cast-iron decoration, and virtually every house on Anne Street is a museum piece. The **Esplanade Hotel,** one of the first things you'll see as you debark from the ferry, dates from 1902.

There are an increasing number of good eateries in Devonport (see the North Shore sections in "Where to Eat," earlier in this chapter) if you should decide to stay for dinner.

Day-Trip Destinations

Wineries, islands, and ranges all lie within a comfortable day-trip distance of Auckland. They can be visited as part of an escorted tour (see "Organized Tours," below) or independently.

Waiheke Island is only 35 minutes from the city by ferry and affords a good place for hiking, kayaking, and cycling. The hilly island has a permanent population of 6,000, 700 of whom commute into Auckland daily. About 70% is open farmland and alternative lifestyles flourish here. Oneroa, the main village, is a 15-minute walk from the ferry. Call Fullers (☎ **367-9111**) for information on their *Quickcat* service to Waiheke Island. (Accommodation and dining options are included in "Where to Stay" and "Where to Eat," earlier in this chapter.)

Rangitoto is another popular day-trip destination. The volcanic island has miles of walking tracks and offers great views of Auckland and the Hauraki Gulf. There are also pohutukawa forests, fern groves, and a black-backed-gull colony. Fullers's (☎ **367-9111**) *Manu* provides regular service.

To the west of Auckland are numerous **wineries** that welcome visitors. These can be reached in a rental car, providing you don't do too much tasting. For a complete list, pick up the brochure "Winemakers of West Auckland" at the Visitors Information Centre.

The **Waitakere Ranges** are also west of Auckland and, along with the **west coast surf beaches** at Piha and Muriwai, present another day-trip destination. Bush walking, scenic drives, board surfing, hang gliding and picnicking are all popular activities. The **gannet colony** at Muriwai Beach is one of only two mainland nesting sites in the world.

Especially for Kids

In addition to the attraction listed here, don't forget the **Weird and Wonderful** children's discovery center at the Auckland Museum.

Rainbow's End Adventure Park, Great South and Wiri Station rds., Manukau City. ☎ **262-2030.**

This leisure park boasts all sorts of action rides, video games, mini-golf, a roller coaster, and the Zim Zam Zoo (you'll have to see it!). The kids—of any age—will love it!

Admission: All-day Super Pass (including all rides), NZ$29 (U.S. $18.85) adults, NZ$19 (U.S. $12.35) children 4–13, free for children under 4; Mini Pass (including three rides), NZ$15 (U.S. $9.75), plus NZ$4 (U.S. $2.60) for each additional ride.

Open: Summer, Sun–Fri 10am–5pm, Sat 10am–10pm; winter, hours vary.

Special-Interest Sightseeing

One of Auckland's (and indeed, New Zealand's) very best attractions is offered by the **Auckland Tourist Hospitality Scheme,** and it doesn't cost a penny. Do this at the beginning of your trip if possible—it will give more meaning to every Kiwi contact you make thereafter. This group of enthusiastic volunteers will arrange for you to spend a morning, afternoon, or evening with an Auckland family for absolutely no other reason than to have an opportunity to talk on a one-to-one basis in the informal, relaxed atmosphere of a private home. It's a terrific chance to learn about New Zealand daily life firsthand and to exchange views from our different parts of the world. They'll try to match you by profession or hobby from among the 80 Auckland families who participate. They don't arrange overnight stays—just friendly visits. You can call them when you arrive, or better yet, write in advance to any of the following: Mrs. Polly Ring, 775 Riddell Rd., Glendowie, Auckland 5 (☎ **575-6655**); Mrs. Jean Mahon, 2/17 Arundel St., Hillsborough, Auckland (☎ **624-3398**); Mrs. Eve Williamson, 170 Cook St., Howick, Auckland (☎ **535-8098**); Mrs. Trevor Holloway, 126 Puhinui Rd., Papatoetoe, Auckland (☎ **278-8434**); Mrs. Valerie Blackie, Flat 3, 16 Orakau Ave., Epsom, Auckland (☎ **625-9373**); and Mrs. Meryl Revell, 60 Prince Regent Dr., Half Moon Bay, Auckland (☎ **535-5314**).

Walking Tour

Along the Wharf

Start In front of the Maritime Museum at the west end of Quay Street.
Finish At The Loaded Hog, between Quay Street and Customs Street West.

Time The walk itself is about 20 or 30 minutes long, but with stops at the Maritime Museum, at the China Oriental Markets, and for shopping, it could easily consume half a day.
Best Times Any day will do, but it's more interesting when lots of cargo ships are in port.
Worst Times When the Maritime Museum is closed.

The fact that Auckland is known as the City of Sails is indicative of the fact that water and boats are of paramount importance here. Hence a walk along the wharf is really the best possible way to get a sense of the city.

Begin your tour at the:

1. **Maritime Museum,** specifically under *KZ-1* ("kay-zed one" to Kiwis), the biggest racing sloop ever built. This giant monohull tried to capture the America's Cup in San Diego in 1988. Unfortunately for New Zealand, Dennis Conner sailed a catamaran and left the "big boat" in his wake. A plaque on the boat recaps the battle—most of which was fought in the courtroom. Sir Michael Fay donated the vessel to the Maritime Museum. Allow at least an hour, and more likely several hours, to visit the museum (fully described in "The Top Attractions," earlier in this chapter).

Take a Break

In the Maritime Museum, the **Launchman's Cafe** is a good spot to fortify yourself with something tasty. Indoor seating and outdoor seating overlooking the harbor and boats are provided.

When you leave the museum, head east on Quay Street and walk past the:

2. **Ports of Auckland Building.** Until this building was constructed, the rooms in the Travelodge Hotel across the road had harbor views. Now guests look out on the headquarters for all Auckland port business. This includes handling more 300,000 containers a year—more cargo than any other New Zealand port. What you see here is a vital economic link between New Zealand and the 73 countries with which it does business. The contemporary design of this building is a stark contrast to the:
3. **red iron railing** that runs along the footpath (sidewalk). Note the traditional appearance, including cast-iron figures on the gates and gaslights perched on top. You'll pass two harbor-cruise ticket counters at Launchman's Landing before reaching the:
4. **Ferry Building.** This picturesque landmark is the hub of the city's passenger ferry service. Here are also the Auckland Regional Parks Visitor Centre (including the Department of Conservation), a currency exchange, and a couple of nice shops. Cin Cin on Quay Brasserie and Harbourside Seafood Bar & Grill are described in "Where to Eat," earlier in this chapter.

   When you leave the Ferry Building, look across the street and observe the view of Queen Elizabeth II Square and Queen Street, Auckland's main thoroughfare. As you continue walking east, you should be able to see cargo ships from many different international ports. Continue to:
5. **Marsden Wharf,** and look to see if *The Spirit of Adventure* and *The Spirit of New Zealand* are there. These two- and three-masted vessels are used for

youth-development programs. Selected young people ages 15 to 19 from all over New Zealand take a turn at sailing on the ships.

Cross the road and enter the:

6. **China Oriental Markets,** where goods from all over the world are sold. Like any flea market or swap meet, you'll have to peruse a lot of marginal items before finding a gem.

   Cross Britomart Place and you'll see:

7. **Breen's Sheepskins,** which is not a glamorous store but has long been the best place in Auckland to buy sheepskins, leather jackets, wool slippers, wool blankets, and the like. A few doors farther, the:

8. **Union Fish Co.** has been in this location for more than a dozen years. This restaurant has one of the few licenses to buy directly off the fishing boats.

   Cross Commerce Street and continue to:

9. **Queen Elizabeth II Square.** The Quayside Cafe, on your left as you look up Queen Street, is highly touted by a reader in "Where to Eat," earlier in this chapter. The fate of the magnificent old CPO building is still undecided at press time—as is the future of the temporary information center in the square. The statue of a Maori figure in a kaitaka cloak was sculptured by Molly Macalister. The:

10. **Downtown Shopping Centre** is convenient if you need a postcard or a snack from the extensive food court one level up from ground. You might also want to cross Lower Albert Street and stop at the:

11. **Downtown Airline Terminal,** where there are scads of tour-booking offices. Continue across Hobson Street to Viaduct Quay and treat yourself to a cold beer at The Loaded Hog. (This pub-in-a-microbrewery also serves tea and coffee.) Admire the view of fishing boats and—sometimes—America's Cup boats in the harbor.

Organized Tours

From the **Visitors Information Centre,** you can book several half- and full-day tours of the city and its environs. Half-day tours, morning or afternoon, cover sightseeing highlights, and an all-day tour usually includes the eastern and western suburbs, the zoo, and vineyards. Half-day tours run about NZ$35 (U.S. $22.75) for adults, half that for children.

Fullers Cruise Centre, Ferry Building, Quay Street (☎ **367-9111**), has a cruise and vineyard tour to Waiheke Island that includes a wine tasting. It's half a day, and the price is about NZ$35 (U.S. $22.75).

Bush & Beach Ltd., 13 Nereus Place, Mairangi Bay, Auckland (☎ **478-2882**), are outdoor specialists offering a range of small-group (one- to eight-passenger) tours around the Auckland region, traveling in a minibus. Led by experienced guides, the tours are flexible and focus on the unique aspects of each route. Among the offerings: a half-day (1:30 to 5pm) Waitakere Range tour that visits surf beaches, rocky headlands, and a subtropical rain forest, with time to explore; a full-day (9:30am to 5pm) west coast tour, passing through farmlands, vineyards, and orchards, with opportunities for walking; a half-day (9:30am to 12:30pm) tour to a mainland gannet colony that's one of only two in the world and 2 miles of black iron sand surf beach (August to April only). Prices range from NZ$50 to NZ$80 (U.S. $32.50 to $52).

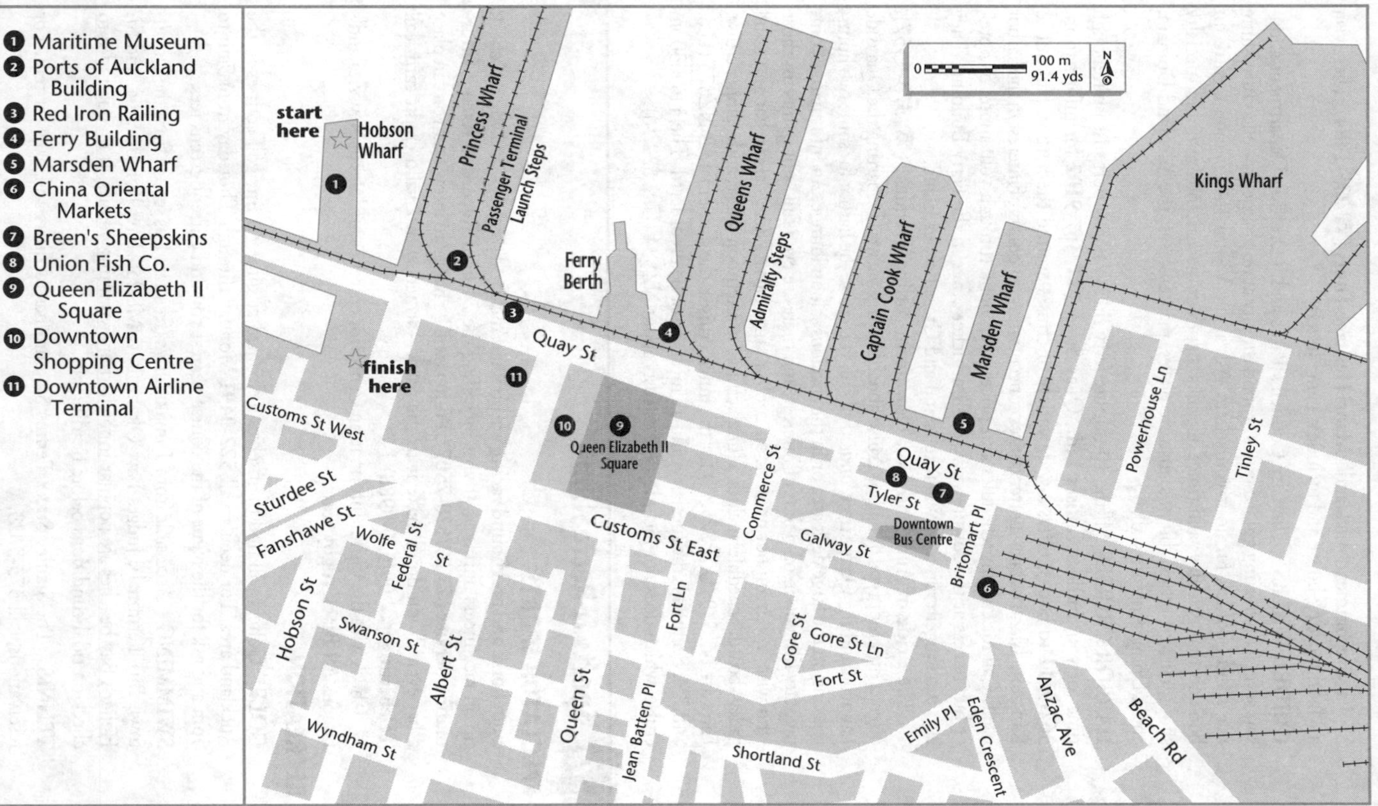

Walking Tour—Along the Wharf

I also recommend Auckland's **Maori Heritage Tours** (☎ **235-1384**). These visit a Maori meeting house and include a hangi lunch.

GUIDED WALKS The City Council's Parks and Recreation Department sponsors several interesting guided walks around the city at no charge, as well as furnishing maps and booklets for do-it-yourselfers. Ask at the Visitor Information Centre for booklets that give days and times of walks that examine arts and crafts and specialty shops, current art exhibitions, historic places, marketplaces, the Auckland Domain, and a Domain nature walk.

HARBOR CRUISES If the 10-minute ferry ride to Devonport just isn't enough time for you, **Fullers Cruises Ltd.,** Quay Street (☎ **367-9102** for information, **367-9111** to book), offers a wide variety of cruises around the harbor. Sail out to Rangitoto Island or take shorter cruises concentrating on points of interest in the harbor itself. Call for current schedules and prices, then book through your motel or hotel, or buy tickets at the downtown waterfront ticket office in the Ferry Building. They also run longer cruises to Waiheke Island and Great Barrier Island.

The Pride of Auckland Co., Downtown Airline Terminal (☎ **373-4557**), offers a different type of harbor cruise aboard luxury yachts. Departing the Quayside Launch Landing, Quay Street, under full sail, you cruise the harbor for some two hours, relaxing on the large deck area or in the spacious saloon lounge. An informative commentary fills you in on points of interest, and there are even full sailing suits for those who wish to remain out on deck on cool or rainy days. There's also a bar and a full galley aboard. Schedules include a lunch cruise, an afternoon cruise, and a dinner cruise. Fares are NZ$39 (U.S. $25.35) for the lunch cruises; the dinner fare is NZ$75 (U.S. $48.75). Seafood is the specialty, and all meals must be preordered. The 3 to 4:30pm cruise, which does not include a meal, costs about NZ$34 (U.S. $22.10).

7 Sports & Recreation

SPECTATOR SPORTS

Both **horse and greyhound racing** are popular Auckland pastimes, and you can check up on race meets during your visit by calling the 24-hour **Recorded Racing Information Service** (☎ **09/520-7507**). Punters will be happy to know that you can place a bet even if you don't make it to the track—armed with a valid credit card, call **Telebetting** (☎ **09/520-9988**).

Check with the Visitor Information Centre for current schedules of New Zealand's famous **All Black rugby team.**

RECREATION

GOLF Golfers will find themselves welcomed at some 30 fine golf courses in the Auckland area. For details, call **522-0491** Monday through Thursday from 9am to 5pm and ask for the name of the course nearest you and current greens fees.

SWIMMING Accessible from Tamaki Drive (frequent bus service from the Downtown Bus Terminal), Judges Bay, Okahu Bay, Mission Bay, Kohimarama, and St. Helier's Bay beaches are popular inner-harbor swimming venues. It's a good idea to check on tidal conditions before heading out.

TENNIS The Stanley Street Tennis Stadium has racquets and balls for rent. For reservations, call **373-3623.**

CYCLING You can rent a bike from Adventure Cycles, 1 Fort Lane (☎ **309-5566**).

8 Savvy Shopping

THE SHOPPING SCENE

Plan to spend at least half a day shopping or just browsing or sightseeing in **Parnell Village.** That's the stretch of Parnell Road between York Street and St. Stephens Avenue. In restored colonial homes and stores, there are boutiques, art galleries, craft shops, antiques stores, restaurants, and pubs. It's great people-watching territory, and a place where you just may pick up that one-of-a-kind souvenir. Most shops, restaurants, and pubs are open daily.

Victoria Park Market, Victoria Street West (☎ **309-6911**), is a lively gathering place for shoppers interested in fashion to wood items, lingerie to glassware. It's open daily from 9am to 7pm (restaurants have later hours).

China Oriental Markets, at the corner of Quay Street and Britomart Place (on the waterfront), has no less than 140 stalls, selling a wide variety of European and Asian goods.

Some of the best craft shops in Auckland are in the beautifully restored old **Customhouse,** 22 Customs St. W., which dates from 1888. You'll find pottery, quilts, hand-woven wall hangings, hand-knit sweaters, glasswear, porcelain, wood works, and a very good bookshop (which mails books home, saving you the GST). Shop hours are 9am to 5pm Monday through Thursday, until 5:30 on Friday and Saturday, and noon to 5:30pm on Sunday. There is also shopping seven days a week in the Ferry Building.

Out in the Newmarket section, **Two Double Seven Shopping Center,** 277 Broadway, is one of Auckland's newest shopping complexes. Housed in a sprawling, five-story block-long building, the center houses specialty stores that include sportswear, jewelry, giftware, music, high-fashion shops, and an International Foodcourt. Drivers will find a covered parking area, and others can take any bus number beginning with 30 or 31 and marked ONEHUNGA or FAVONA, departing from Victoria Street East (just off Queen Street, outside the A.M.P. Insurance Building.)

DUTY FREE At **Regency Duty Free Stores,** they stock an amazing variety of international brands, as well as top-quality New Zealand handcrafts and souvenirs. All purchases will be held until your departure from the country. They have three locations in Auckland at Auckland International Airport (☎ **275-6893**), 25 Victoria St. W. (☎ **308-9014**), and 25 Queen St. (☎ **358-1111**).

SPECIALTY SHOPPING

CHINA At **Tanfield Potter,** 287 Queen St. (☎ **309-0935**), they have been importing fine china, crystal, glassware, cutlery, and high-quality giftware since 1861. Probably the best selection in Auckland. Open Monday through Thursday from 9am to 5:30pm, Saturday from 9:30am to 12:30pm.

CRAFTS Auckland is fairly broken out with craft shops, and I found **Parnell Elephant House,** 237 Parnell Rd. (☎ **309-8740**), to be outstanding among the lot. It's a large shop, set back from Parnell Road—follow the elephant footprints (printed, of course, not the real thing) down a little alleyway. I can't begin to enumerate all the craft items, both from New Zealand and countries around the world: wood (carved, turned, and sliced), rocking horses, patchwork, weaving, pottery, batik and silk clothing, stained glass, and jewelry are just a very few. This is a special shop, with value-for-money prices. They accept credit/charge cards and traveler's checks, and are happy to mail overseas. Open daily from 10am to 5pm.

One of the city's most unusual craft shops is **Radical International,** 285 Parnell Rd. (☎ **377-2193**). It carries exquisite hand-carvings and other crafts from Thailand at unbelievably low prices. Lovely delicate colors on the carved pieces are created by vegetable dyes, and sizes vary from tiny to quite large. Not to worry, however, if you just can't resist one of the larger items—they will gladly ship overseas. They accept most credit and charge cards, and hours are 9:30am to 5pm Monday through Friday, 10am to 4pm Saturday and Sunday.

JEWELRY If you're looking for upmarket silver items, dress jewelry, or watches, go by **Queens Arcade Jewellers,** 20 Queens Arcade, Queen Street (☎ **373-5435**). Friendly service and a good selection. They also do watch repairs. Hours are 10am to 5pm Monday through Friday.

LEATHER The purveyors at **Leather Fashions Ltd.,** 530 Ellerslie/Panmure Hwy., Panmure, Auckland (☎ **527-3779** or **570-4789**), have won accolades from readers over the years—and with good reason. For budget travelers looking for real value for money, Leather Fashions prices represent one of the *best* bargains I have found in all my New Zealand travels. Savings run from $100 to several times that on all sorts of leather and suede apparel and handbags, in classic as well as trendy designs (no sheepskin—see below). "Buttery soft" isn't really adequate to describe the lovely smoothness of fine deerskin or polished suede with a leather finish. If a jacket, coat, skirt, slacks—and even jumpsuits—you fancy from the racks is the wrong size or color, owner Gwen Hewett, together with her experienced, friendly staff, will duplicate it in the leather, size, and color of your choice. And if you're good enough at sketching a design, they'll execute it faithfully, right down to the last little detail. They furnish complimentary taxi service from the city center, accept all major credit/charge cards, and will gladly ship overseas. Hours are 8:30am to 5pm Monday through Friday and 9am to 3pm Saturday.

SHEEPSKIN At **Breen's Sheepskins,** 8 Quay St. (☎ **373-2788**), they boast of having the largest range of sheepskins in New Zealand. There's such a wide variety of styles, colors, and prices that I must confess the terrific assortment of coats and jackets, rugs in several sizes, bed underlays (wonderful for a good night's sleep!), car seats, boots, hats, etc., etc., etc., kept me entranced for most of a morning. Grant Barlow and his staff have specialized in New Zealand sheepskin products for almost 20 years, and they can offer good advice and guidance for what may well be some of your most valued purchases in the country. Open Monday through Friday from 9am to 6:30pm and Saturday and Sunday from 9:30am to 4pm.

9 Evening Entertainment

For current cultural and entertainment events in Auckland, the **Bass Booking Agency,** Aotea Centre (☎ **307-5000**), provides easy credit-card booking with next-day courier delivery of tickets. They can also make bookings around the country—a good way to save time and avoid disappointment by leaving it until you reach your ongoing destinations. In addition to the listings here, you'll find current goings-on in the *Tourist Times.*

THE PERFORMING ARTS

For cultural offerings that include dance, concerts, and theater, check out what's happening at the **Aotea Centre,** 299 Queen St. at Aotea Square (☎ **307-5050**); the ASB

Theatre here seats 2,240. The **Mercury Theatre,** on Mercury Lane (☎ **366-1536**), has just been sold and its future is uncertain. The **Watershed Theatre,** on Customs Street West (☎ **358-4028**), is a legitimate theater offering fringe dramatic works.

THE PUB & CLUB SCENE

Live music is on tap Wednesday through Saturday evenings at the **Queen's Head,** 404 Queen St. (☎ **302-0223**), a pretty pub that serves inexpensive light meals. It's open from 11am to 10pm on Monday through Thursday, until 11pm on Friday and Saturday. The original facade of a hotel dating from 1890 has been retained, a small architectural jewel that escaped the bulldozer.

Jazz buffs will be happy to know there are jazz cruises in summer—book at Fullers's office in the Ferry Building. **Governor Grey's,** in the Sheraton Auckland, 83 Symonds St. (☎ **379-5132**), is an elegant, sophisticated nightspot that features an Irish night on Monday and jazz on Wednesday, from 7pm. **The Blues Barn,** 510 Queen St., features live bands Wednesday through Sunday nights; **Jimmy Rocket's,** in the Old Customhouse, Customs and Albert streets (☎ **308-9137**), is Auckland's only 1950s-style American café and serves burgers, hot dogs, nachos, and other light eats; and the **Shakespeare Tavern,** at the corner of Albert and Wyndham streets (☎ **373-5396**), has country music Monday nights in downstairs Hathaway's Brasserie and live entertainment in the Bard Lounge on Friday (see "Where to Eat," earlier in this chapter).

My favorite Auckland watering hole is **The Loaded Hog,** on Quay Street near Customs Street West (☎ **366-6491**). This is one of the city's few microbreweries, and it enjoys a waterfront location near Hobson Wharf. It's open Monday through Wednesday from 11am to 1am, Thursday through Saturday from 10am to 3am, and Sunday from 10am to 1am. Free brewery tours are given from 2 to 4pm on Saturday. A DJ plays music for dancing Thursday through Saturday nights, and the line to get in snakes out the door and around the corner. (See also "Where to Eat," earlier in this chapter.)

Kitty O'Brien's Tavern, 2 Drake St. (☎ **303-3936**), is another spot you might enjoy. This Irish pub offers music nightly with a band every Friday and Saturday. Stand-up comics also sometimes appear here. All New Zealand beers are served, as well as Guinness. Kitty's is open Tuesday through Sunday until midnight.

10 Easy Excursions from Auckland

In addition to the places mentioned here, be sure to note "Day-Trip Destinations," under "What to See and Do," earlier in this chapter, and those destinations covered in Chapter 6.

Cambridge

153km (95 miles) SE of Auckland

GETTING THERE Cambridge makes an ideal stop when traveling from Auckland to Rotorua. It's on the route of Newmans, Mount Cook, and InterCity coaches.

ESSENTIALS The **Cambridge Information Office,** at the corner of Queen and Victoria streets (☎ **07/827-6033**; fax 07/827-3505), is open Monday through Friday from 8am to 4:30pm. The **STD (area code)** for Cambridge is **07.**

Cambridge (pop. 10,533) is a pretty little town on the Waikato River. Its village green, stately trees, and old churches give it an English air.

WHAT TO SEE & DO

I'd like to say it was the historic buildings that attracted me to Cambridge, but in truth it was the **Cambridge Country Store,** 92 Victoria St. (☎ **07/827-8715**). A wide selection of New Zealand crafts is sold here, and there's a good café upstairs. It's housed in a 100-year-old church and open daily from 9am to 5pm. Nearby on Empire Street, boutiques and antiques stores await. Serious shoppers should plan to be here in September or April when there are antiques fairs.

The **Cambridge Museum,** in the Old Courthouse, Victoria Street (☎ **07/827-3319**), is open Tuesday through Saturday from 10am to 4pm and Sunday and holidays from 2 to 4pm. Be sure to notice **St. Andrews Church**; it's the pretty white one on the corner of Victoria Street and State Highway 1.

Some of New Zealand's best race horses are bred in Cambridge, and the area is well known for its studs. Tours of some of these properties can be arranged through **Cambridge Thoroughbred Stud Tours** (☎ **07/827-3295**). This is also a popular area for **jet boating.** Contact the Visitor Information Office for details.

WHERE TO STAY

Birches, Maungatautari Rd. (P.O. Box 194), Cambridge. ☎ **07/827-6556.**

2 rms (both with bath).

Rates (including breakfast): NZ$45 (U.S. $29.25) single; NZ$75 (U.S. $48.75) double. Three-course evening meal with wine NZ$25 (U.S. $16.25) extra. BC, MC, V.

Hosts Sheri Mitchell and Hugh Jellie welcome guests to their 30-acre farm a short distance out of Cambridge and take them on walks to see cows and sheep. Their property has two guest rooms: one in the house with its bath across the hall and the other in a tiny adjacent cottage. Both contain heaters, tea- and coffee-making facilities, and electric blankets. Everyone shares the sitting room, tennis court, and pool. Hugh's a veterinarian, so this is the place to get your farming questions answered. Olivia is their cute young daughter.

WHERE TO EAT

The Grapevine Winebar, 72 Alpha St. ☎ **827-6699.**

Cuisine: MODERN NEW ZEALAND. **Reservations:** Recommended.

Prices: Appetizers NZ$8–NZ$10.50 (U.S. $5.20–$6.85); main courses NZ$15–NZ $19.50 (U.S. $9.75–$12.70); lunch NZ$5.50–NZ$17.50 (U.S. $3.60–$11.40). AE, BC, DC, MC, V.

Open: Lunch daily noon–2pm; dinner daily 6–9pm.

In the Old Power Board Building, the Grapevine has a convivial, casual atmosphere. There's live music on weekends, and the bar stays open until the wee hours. For lunch you could have pizza and salad or mushroom-and-parmesan fettuccine. Dinner main courses include boneless lamb loins served with tamarillo sauce, venison steaks with plum sauce, and vegetable parcels with fruit coulis. Licensed.

The Hibiscus Coast/Kowhai Coast

48km (30 miles) N of Auckland

GETTING THERE The Hibiscus Coast, comprising the communities of Silverdale, Whangaparaoa, Orewa, Waiwera, and Puhoi, is only about 45 minutes by car from central Auckland. For folks with limited time, a trip up here provides a great glimpse into rural life. It's also a convenient stop en route to the Bay of Islands. InterCity coaches and Auckland city buses provide regular service.

ESSENTIALS Tourist information is available from **Geographics/The Outdoor Shop and Information Centre,** Hibiscus Coast Highway, Orewa (☎ **09/426-7496**). The **STD (area code)** for the Hibiscus Coast is **09.**

Waiwera's hot springs have been drawing visitors for almost 150 years. Orewa is a tiny seaside town (pop. 5,600) with a beautiful beach. Puhoi has a popular pub and retains the flavor of its Bohemian settlers.

WHAT TO SEE & DO

There are few things as relaxing as soaking in the hot water at the **Waiwera Thermal Pools,** State Highway 1 (☎ **09/302-1684**). Twenty-two indoor and outdoor pools are kept at 28° to 45°C (80° to 115°F), and there are private pools as well as larger ones—also a water slide. The complex is open Monday through Thursday and Sunday from 9am to 10pm and Friday and Saturday from 9am to 11pm. It costs NZ$9 (U.S. $5.85) for adults and NZ$5 (U.S. $3.25) for children 5 to 13; free for children under 5. If you forgot yours, a shop on the premises sells "togs" (swimsuits).

It's a slight detour off the highway, but if history interests you, take a look at the **Puhoi Hotel,** or "pub" as it's known. The two-story white frame building holds the district's first liquor license, issued in 1879. Farm implements and saddles are suspended from the walls, and the place is a treasure trove of old photos. If history doesn't interest you, you could do as the locals do on a sunny day: Order a pitcher of Lion Red and lounge on the lawn.

WHERE TO STAY

Angel Valley, 42 Manuel Rd. (R.D. 2), Silverdale. ☎ **09/426-6175.** 2 rms (none with bath), 1 studio unit (with bath).

Rates (including breakfast): NZ$35 (U.S. $22.75) single; NZ$65 (U.S. $42.25) double; NZ$85 (U.S. $55.25) self-contained unit for two. Dinner with wine NZ$20 (U.S. $13) extra. Transfer from Auckland NZ$30 (U.S. $19.50) extra. MC, V.

This country homestay affords you a chance to wake up to sheep outside the window and admire a spectacular view of rolling green hills. Ute Engel lives on this 4-acre farmlet, five minutes off State Highway 1. She offers two rooms in her cozy no-smoking home and an adjacent studio unit with cooking facilities. The hostess is a very sensitive and caring person, and the atmosphere at Angel Valley is noticeably peaceful. Children are welcome, but stairs make this homestay a poor choice for less mobile people. Vegetarian meals are available.

Marco Polo Backpackers Inn, 2d Hammond Ave., Hatfields Beach, Orewa. ☎ **09/426-8455.** 24 beds (no rooms with bath).

READERS RECOMMEND

Hibiscus Country Homestay, 819 Whangaparaoa Rd., Whangaparaoa. ☎ **09/424-5467.** *"This B&B could only be described as outstanding. We were welcomed with a tray of tea and biscuits . . . and there's a huge terrace overlooking the garden and glorious views of the Hauraki Gulf. Doreen and Ray Blaber served a delicious dinner and breakfast. It was just astounding value for money."*—Mrs. Gloria Phillips, Wilts., England.

Rates: NZ$25 (U.S. $16.25) single; NZ$34 (U.S. $22.10) double; NZ$13 (U.S. $8.45) bed in a dorm; NZ$8 (U.S. $5.20) tent site. MC, V.

Hosts Jan and Marleen Bastiaanssen get rave reviews from guests for their friendliness and helpfulness. They even organize coastal walks and volleyball games on the beach. This hostel, just north of Orewa, offers a fully equipped kitchen, as well as a homey atmosphere.

The Warkworth Inn, Queen St., Warkworth. ☎ **09/425-8569.** Fax 09/425-9696. 8 rms (none with bath).

Rates (including continental breakfast): NZ$30 (U.S. $19.50) single; NZ$47 (U.S. $30.55) double; NZ$60 (U.S. $39) triple. AE, BC, DC, MC, V.

This is one of New Zealand's best bargains. All quarters in this 132-year-old property have tea- and coffee-making facilities, sinks, clocks, and heaters. High ceilings are all that belie the otherwise youthful appearance of the accommodations. Guests share a TV lounge opening onto a veranda. There's a restaurant on the premises, and bistro meals are available in the bar. Although this inn is in the town center, little traffic noise exists because Highway 1 bypasses Warkworth—however, this could be a noisy spot on Thursday and Friday nights, where there's a band in the bar.

6

Farther Afield from Auckland

FROM AUCKLAND, MOST TOURISTS HEAD SOUTH TO WAITOMO AND ITS GLOWWORMS, then on to Rotorua and its concentration of Maori culture. And rightly so. Nowhere else in the world will you find anything to compare with the mystical, silent glow of Waitomo's grotto. Nowhere else can you duplicate Rotorua's thermal steaminess or lakes, hills, and valleys alive with myth and legend, along with a Polynesian race who revere those tales of long ago and follow an ancient lifestyle while perfectly at home in the modern culture surrounding them. If push comes to shove and it comes down to north or south, then by all means opt for the southern route.

However, if you can work in an extra two days, which will let you go north *then* south, you're in for one of this world's travel treats. Take the long route up and experience the shady "cathedral" created by centuries-old kauri forests; cut across the northern end of the North Island to Waitangi in the Bay of Islands and walk where the British negotiated with Maori chieftains to establish their first official New Zealand foothold; relive this country's history as you visit its first Christian mission, then the splendidly carved Maori meetinghouse; discover private beaches, some on uninhabited islands that account for the naming of this lovely spot; head out to the open sea for some of the finest deep-water fishing in the world; enjoy sunny days and balmy evenings as well as a friendly and hospitable local populace. You can plan on two days, but chances are you'll alter plans to extend your stay—or leave looking over your shoulder and wishing you had!

Add that extra day or two before or after the journey north, and a short drive east will bring you to one of New Zealand's nooks and crannies that is all too often overlooked by visitors, although much loved by Auckland area residents. The Coromandel Peninsula, where the Coromandel mountain range forms the spiky spine of this clawlike region that juts out between the Hauraki Gulf and the Pacific, is rich in unspoiled terrain and its coastline is incredibly beautiful.

1 The Coromandel Peninsula

119km (74 miles) E of Auckland

GETTING THERE • By Bus Murphy Buses and InterCity run regular schedules from Auckland to the entry town of Thames. (InterCity's Travel Pass and Tiki Tours Coach Pass are valid for travel on Murphy Buses.)

• By Car Drive south from Auckland on State Highway 1 for about 50km (31 miles), then turn east on State Highway 2. About 34km (22 miles) later you'll pick up Highway 25 to Thames.

ESSENTIALS Thames (pronounced "Tems") is the first town of any size as you reach the peninsula from Auckland. The **information center** is on Queen Street (☎ **07/868-7284**); other area information offices are located at Albert Street, Whitianga (☎ **07/866-5555**); and Whitaker Street, Te Aroha (☎ **07/884-8052**). They can furnish a wealth of information on the area, along with such helpful guides as "The Coromandel Craft Trail" and "The Coromandel Dictionary." Coromandel Peninsula phone numbers are in the **07 telephone area code** (STD).

The peninsula is one of the most beloved holiday spots for Aucklanders, and that's easy to understand. For city dwellers, it's a haven of natural beauty that is a world apart from urban hassles, and for the visitor, it provides a capsule version of the North Island's history and glorious scenery.

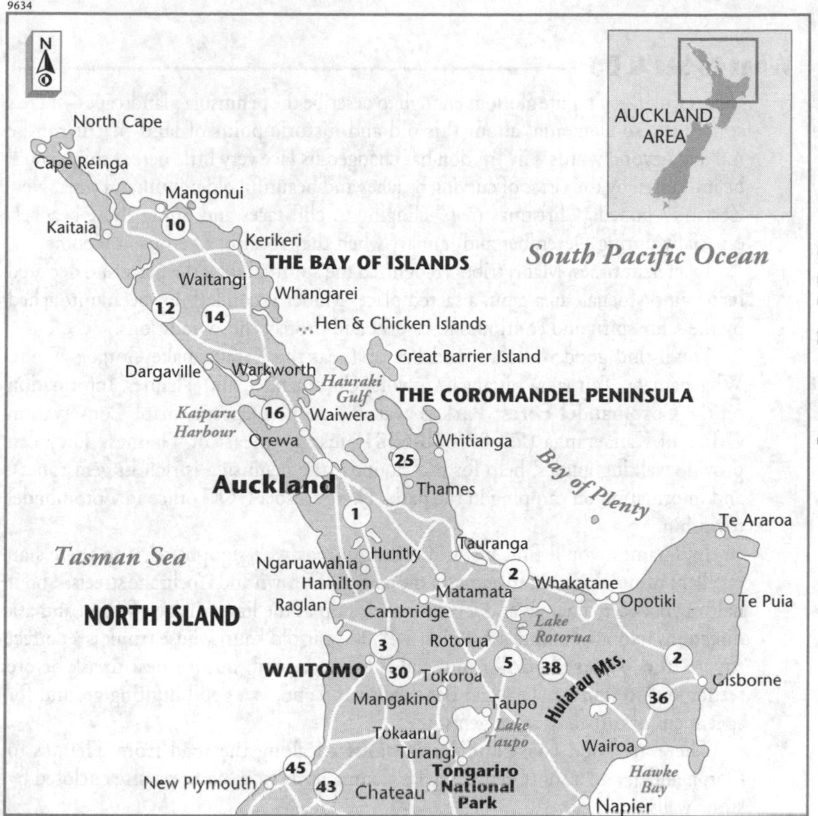

The $1^{1}/_{2}$-hour drive from Auckland is rewarded by dramatic land- and seascapes; wide sandy beaches; wild and rugged mountain peaks; quaint villages hugging both coastlines; relics of logging, gold mining, and gum fields; and the crafts of talented artisans who have found an idyllic lifestyle on the peninsula.

While it's certainly possible to make a day trip to the Coromandel Peninsula from Auckland, let me urge you to spend at least one overnight in order to more fully appreciate the area. At the end of your Auckland stay, try to plan two days on the peninsula before pressing on—you'll have explored a very special, little-known-to-outsiders part of New Zealand, and you'll travel on refreshed by the experience.

GETTING AROUND This is a rugged, wild region you've come to, and you should know right off that the only easy driving you can count on is the excellent paved road that runs some 56km (35 miles) from Thames to Coromandel. North of Coromandel, and on routes crossing the width of the peninsula, you'll find everything from partially paved roads to graveled roadbeds that—in the words of one of my Auckland friends—are "little more than tracks." That by no means implies that you should miss any of the spectacular forest and mountain scenery, only that you should drive with caution, or that you should consider letting **Murphy Buses** (**☎ 07/867-6829**) act as your personal chauffeur for this portion of your holiday. Their peninsula loop service runs daily in summer, six days a week in winter.

What to See & Do

"Spectacular" isn't quite glorious enough to describe the peninsula's landscape—there's something so elemental about this old and historic point of land that it can be moving beyond words. Civilization has changed its face very little here. I think you'll be impressed by the vistas of curving beaches and beautiful old pohutkawa trees, New Zealand's famed "Christmas tree," clinging to cliff faces and lining those beaches, especially during December and January when they're a riot of crimson blooms.

In ancient times, Maori tribes recognized the spirituality of the place and declared its Mount Moehau area tapu, a sacred place. Modern man has not been untouched by the same spirit and continues to respect and protect those traditions.

You'll find good **walks** around Paeroa (near the Karangahake Gorge), Waihi, Whangamata, Tairua, Whitianga, Colville, Coromandel, and Thames. Information on the **Coromandel Forest Park** is available at the Department of Conservation Office in Kauaeranga (☎ **07/868-6381**) just southeast of Thames. They can provide walking guides, help for rockhounds (the peninsula is rich in gemstones), and information on camping in the park. There's also a DOC office in Coromondel township.

In Thames, you'll find historic **mining areas** well signposted, and there's an excellent **mineralogical museum** on the corner of Brown and Cochrane streets. About halfway between Thames and Coromandel, stop at the little village of Tapu and ask directions to one of nature's oddities, a 2,500-year-old kauri whose trunk is a perfect square (the **"square kauri"** is out the Whitianga road, but it's best to ask before setting out to find it). Te Mata Beach, also at Tapu, is a good hunting ground for specimens of carnelian-agate gemstones.

There are good **coast and bush walks** all along the road from Thames to Coromandel, and a short detour to Te Kouma leads to a Maori **pa site** enclosed by stone walls.

Coromandel is where gold was first discovered in New Zealand, in 1852, and the **School of Mines Museum** (☎ **866-8545**) contains many relics of those early gold-fever days. It's open Monday through Friday from 10am to 3pm and free to those under 15, with NZ$2 (U.S. $1.30) admission for adults. Take time to visit the **True Colours Craft Co-op** near the post office, a space shared by several craftspeople. Incidentally, the town, peninsula, and mountain range take their names from the timber-trading ship HMS *Coromandel,* which called into this harbor for kauri spars in 1820.

Also in Coromandel, the **Driving Creek Railway** (☎ **866-8703**) is another popular attraction. Barry Brickell owns New Zealand's only narrow-gauge mountain railway, which passes through replanted native forest. There are usually *at least* two departures daily (at 2 and 4pm), but call to confirm. Tickets cost NZ$7 (U.S. $4.55) for adults and NZ$4 (U.S. $2.60) for kids.

If you plan to drive to the northern tip of the peninsula, you'll find the last gasoline ("petrol") pumps at Colville, along with a good collection of arts-and-crafts studios. (Be sure your rental-car agreement permits driving here—some don't.)

On the peninsula's east coast, Whitianga has a excellent **historical museum** and many **arts and crafts studios,** and is a major center for **boating and charter fishing.** Across the inlet at Ferry Landing is the country's oldest stone wharf. At Hot Water Beach, ask the time of the next low tide—that's when you can dig a hole in the beach, settle in, and soon find yourself immersed in hot sea water—your own private spa pool.

While you're in the neighborhood, stop at the **Colenso Herb Garden,** between Coroglen and Tairua and a five-minute drive from the Hot Water Beach. Orchard owners Ruth and Andy Pettit serve Devonshire tea, fresh juice, homemade scones and muffins with cream and jam, or soup and toast. You can eat on the porch or inside, where strains of classical music set just the right scene. The tearoom, which has a tempting gift shop, is open daily from 10am to 5pm.

Where to Stay

North Islanders flock to the Cormandel Peninsula during December and January, so if you're coming then, be sure to reserve ahead. If you arrive during other months, you'll usually be able to find accommodations through the local information centers. The rates given below include GST.

IN OR NEAR THAMES

A Historic Hotel

Brian Boru Hotel, Pollen and Richmond sts., Thames. ☎ **07/868-6523.** Fax 07/868-9760. 47 rms (37 with bath).

Rates: NZ$45 (U.S. $29.25) single without bath, NZ$59 (U.S. $38.35) single with bath, NZ$96 (U.S. $62.40) single with spa bath; NZ$66 (U.S. $42.90) double without bath, NZ$88 (U.S. $57.20) double with bath, NZ$150 (U.S. $97.50) double with spa bath. All-inclusive Agatha Christie weekends NZ$355 (U.S. $230.75) per person. Off-season, backpackers are charged from NZ$15 (U.S. $9.75). AE, BC, DC, MC, V.

In the center of town, this two-story kauri building with a veranda dates back to 1874 and is a focal point for locals, who love the bar and the fine dining room, which serves great seafood and pub meals for moderate prices. Barbara Doyle, the managing director here, runs some lively Agatha Christie–style weekends twice a month, and if you're in a sleuthing mood, you might check to see if one is scheduled during your visit—they're great fun and value, since the fee covers accommodation, meals, and sleuthing from Friday night to Sunday lunch.

Motels

Puru Park Motel, West Crescent and Main Rd., Te Puru (P.O. Box 439, Thames). ☎ and fax **07/868-2686.** 6 units (all with bath) TV TEL **Directions:** Take Coromandel Road 11km (6½ miles) north of Thames.

Rates: NZ$60 (U.S. $39) single; NZ$70 (U.S. $45.50) double. AE, DC, MC, V.

Set in landscaped grounds in Puru Bay, these recently refurbished motel units are spacious and comfortably furnished. Each sleeps two to four and has a fully equipped kitchen. There's a self-service laundry, a children's play area, and tennis courts next door. The beach and a boat ramp are nearby. Readers report that hosts June and Peter Fullerton are most helpful.

Seaspray Motel, 613 Coast Rd., Waiomu Bay (P.O. Box 203, Thames). ☎ and fax **07/868-2863.** 5 units (all with bath). TV TEL **Directions:** Go 14km (8½ miles) north of Thames on the coast road.

Rates: NZ$55 (U.S. $35.75) single; NZ$68 (U.S. $44.20) double. MC, V.

At the Seaspray, Waiomu Bay is so close you feel you're sleeping on an ocean liner. There are one- and two-bedroom units, a self-service laundry on the premises, and out back a stately Norfolk pine and a picnic area. Hosts Paul and Joanna Whiteman provide breakfast at an extra charge.

A Bed-&-Breakfast

Glenys and Russell Rutherford, 110 Hape Rd., Thames. ☎ and fax **07/868-7788.**
2 rms (1 with bath).

Rates (including breakfast): NZ$35 (U.S. $22.75) single without bath; NZ$60 (U.S. $39) double with bath. No credit cards.

Glenys and Russell Rutherford's comfortable home overlooks the lovely Firth of Thames. They have a double room with private facilities and a single room without, and there's a games room and a lounge as well as a pool. This engaging couple really know their area and some of the potters and painters who live here, and they're always glad to direct their guests to studios, as well as to the historic and scenic points of interest.

IN OR NEAR COROMANDEL

Motels

Anglers Lodge & Caravan Park, Amodeo Bay, Coromandel. ☎ **07/866-8584.**
7 units (all with bath). TV

Rates: NZ$74 (U.S. $48.10) single; NZ$89 (U.S. $57.85) double. MC, V.

Merv and Lois Groucott's pleasant beachfront complex includes one- and two-bedroom apartments, all with complete cooking facilities (you can buy provisions from the small store right on the premises). Other amenities include a pool, a spa pool in a glass geodesic dome, a tennis court, a play area with a trampoline, a barbecue kiosk, a lounge with a billiard table, and boats for rent. Good bush and coastal walks are right at hand. The site is 18km (11 miles) north of the town of Coromandel.

Coromandel Colonial Cottages, Ring Rd., Coromandel. ☎ and fax **07/866-8857.**
8 units (all with bath). TV TEL

Rates: NZ$65 (U.S. $42.25) single; NZ$75 (U.S. $48.75) double. Additional person NZ$15 (U.S. $9.75) extra for adults, NZ$11 (U.S. $6.90) extra for children. AE, MC, V.

All units here have two bedrooms and sleep up to six. Each has its own carport, and the restful rural setting on the outskirts of town (there's a creek at the back of the

READERS RECOMMEND

Coromandel Hotel, Kapanga Rd., Coromandel (☎ **07/866-8760**). *"I was especially impressed with the Coromandel Hotel in Coromandel. The room was nicely decorated with hot and cold running water. It was one of the few places I stayed that had a bathtub in a* decorated *room, and it cost only NZ$25 (U.S. $16.25)."*—P. A. McCauley, Baltimore, Md., U.S.A.

Spellbound Homestay, 77 Grange Rd., Hanei Beach (R.D. 1), Whitianga (☎ **07/866-3543**). *"This place stood out: clean as an operating room; lovely, well-informed hosts; and world-class views fitting the name. It's walking distance to Cathedral Cove. Truly, Alan and Barbara's is one of the gems of the Coromandel."*—John W. Behle, Cincinnati, Ohio, U.S.A.

property) includes such amenities as a spa pool, children's playground, barbecue area, billiard room, and swimming pool. Their rental four-wheel-drive bush vehicle is a great way to go exploring, and beaches, golf courses, and shops are close by. A good restaurant is just two minutes away and a courtesy car is provided. Families are preferred.

NEAR BUFFALO BEACH

A Motor Lodge

 **Mercury Bay Beachfront Resort,** 111 Buffalo Beach Rd. N. (P.O. Box 9), Whitianga. ☎ **07/866-5637.** Fax 07/866-4524. 8 two-room suites. TV TEL

Rates: NZ$70–NZ$165 (U.S. $45.50–$107.25) suite for one or two. Rate depends on season and unit. AE, DC, MC, V.

This place sits right on the edge of Buffalo Beach, with wonderful sea views and fully equipped units, a laundry with dryers, and a car wash; it gives you a delicious sense of having your own private beach just outside your door. There's a spa pool, plus a windsurfer and sailing catamaran for your use. The folks here, Liz and Tom True, are especially helpful in arranging boat trips, fishing expeditions, and bush walks; she's a Kiwi and he's a Floridian who gave up a career in the oil business for a more tranquil lifestyle.

TE AROHA

A Hostel

There's a delightful small **YHA Hostel** on Miro Street (P.O. Box 72), Te Aroha (☎ **07/884-8739**). Nestled in the foothills of Mount Te Aroha, it's only five minutes away from the famous hot-spring baths of Te Aroha. Rates are NZ$10 (U.S. $6.50) per person.

CAMPGROUNDS ON THE PENINSULA

Van and caravan sites are available on a first-come, first-served basis in **Conservation Lands and Farms Parks** around the peninsula. Camping fees are NZ$3 (U.S. $1.95) per adult, NZ$2 (U.S. $1.30) for school-age children, free for preschoolers. For details, contact the Department of Conservation, P.O. Box 78, Thames (☎ **07/868-6381**).

Buffalo Beach Resort, Eyre Street (P.O. Box 19), Whitianga (☎ **07/866-5854**), is adjacent to the beachfront, within easy walking distance of six beaches, the wharf, and the shopping center. There are powered caravan sites, as well as tent sites, and a lodge for international backpackers. Owners Trudi and Alan Hopping are very helpful. Rates run NZ$8.50 (U.S. $5.55) per adult for tent and caravan sites, NZ$14 (U.S. $9.10) per person for backpackers, and NZ$34 (U.S. $22.10) double. Hot pools in a garden setting are under construction.

Where to Eat

You'll find small, local eateries in good supply around the peninsula, and your best bet is to look to the locals for pointers on the right choice. Failing that, look for hotel dining rooms, few though they are in number, to provide good, plain food at moderate prices. And give a thought to picnicking along the way—even peanut-butter sandwiches would taste elegant in a setting of such natural splendor!

In Thames

Brian Boru Hotel, Pollen and Richmond sts. ☎ **868-6523.**

Cuisine: GRILLS/SEAFOOD. **Reservations:** Not required.

Prices: Breakfast NZ$14 (U.S. $9.10); bistro lunches NZ$12–NZ$15 (U.S. $7.80–$9.75); dinner NZ$15–NZ$25 (U.S. $9.75–$16.25). AE, DC, MC, V.

Open: Breakfast daily 7:30–10am; lunch daily 11:30am–2:30pm; dinner daily 5:30–10pm.

This marvelous old hotel in the center of Thames is so evocative of the past that you get a trip back in time thrown in for free. The small bar is one of the most attractive on the peninsula. The breakfast menu is quite varied and features freshly perked coffee. All three meals are served daily, and the à la carte menu features fresh local seafood at modest prices. Mussel soup is the house specialty. Licensed.

In Coromandel

Coromandel Hotel, Kapanga Rd., Cormandel. ☎ **866-8760.**

Cuisine: BISTRO/NEW ZEALAND. **Reservations:** Not required.

Prices: Breakfast NZ$12 (U.S. $7.80); lunch NZ$5–NZ$10 (U.S. $3.25–$6.50); dinner NZ$10–NZ$18 (U.S. $6.50–$11.70). AE, MC, V.

Open: Breakfast daily 8–9am; lunch Mon–Sat noon–1:30pm; dinner Mon–Sat 6–8:30pm.

In the center of Cormandel, this is a pleasantly old-fashioned kind of place, well worth a stop for a pint or a simple meal. The hotel dates from the 19th century. Licensed.

WORTH THE EXTRA MONEY

In Whitianga

Doyles Restaurant, 21 The Esplanade, Whitianga. ☎ **866-5209.**

Cuisine: SEAFOOD/GRILLS. **Reservations:** Recommended.

Prices: Appetizers NZ$10–NZ$20 (U.S. $6.50–$13); main courses NZ$16–NZ$35 (U.S. $10.40–$22.75). AE, BC, DC, MC, V.

Open: Breakfast and lunch Dec–Apr 8am–2:30pm; dinner daily (year round) 5:30pm–midnight.

Superbly sited overlooking Buffalo Beach and Mercury Bay, this dining option offers a wide range of fresh seafood, steaks, a roast of the day, and pasta dishes. You might order mussel soup, rock oysters, or scallops—all local. The proprietors are Barbara Doyle, who also owns the Brian Boro Hotel in Thames, and Stjepan Hrestak, a well-trained chef/butcher from Croatia. The seaside building housing the restaurant was built by Barbara's father in 1946. If the weather's good, ask to sit on the balcony. Licensed.

2 The Bay of Islands

For New Zealanders, this is where it all began. "Civilization" in the guise of British culture, that is. But long before Capt. James Cook anchored the *Endeavour* off Motuarohia Island in 1769, civilization of the Maori sort existed in perfect harmony with the soft forces of nature, often at considerable *disharmony* with their tribal neighbors. Maori history tells of the arrival of Kupe and Ngahu from Hawaiki, then of Whatonga and Toi, and later of the great chiefs Ruatara, Hongi Hika, and Tamati Waaka Nene. It speaks of the waterfront settlement at Kororareka, already well established when Captain Cook appeared and gave the region its Pakeha name. Be that as it may, New Zealand's modern history also begins here in the Bay of Islands.

British settlers first set foot on New Zealand soil in 1804, and a whole litany of British "firsts" follows that date: 1814, the first Christian sermon (today, you'll find a large Celtic cross memorial planted on that very spot, a stretch of beach on the north side of Rangihoua Bay); 1820, the first plow introduced; 1831, the first European marriage; 1835, the first printing press; 1839, the first bank; and 1840, a whole slew of important "first" events—post office, Customs House, and official treaty between the British and Maori chieftains. After that, the British brand of civilization was in New Zealand to stay.

The Bay of Islands you'll encounter today is a happy blend of all that history—pride in those important happenings—and relaxed contentment in the natural attributes, which make this (as any resident is quick to tell you) "the best spot in the country to live—or play." And play they do, for recreation is the chief industry up here. Setting and climate combine to create about as ideal a resort area as you could wish. Imagine a deeply indented coastline whose waters hold some 150 islands, most with sandy stretches of beach. Imagine waters so filled with sporting fish like the kingfish (yellowtail) that every world record for their capture has been set here. Imagine, too, a climate with average temperatures of 85°F (70°F is considered a cooler-than-usual winter day!), maximum humidity of 40%, and cool bay breezes every day of the year. Imagine all that and you'll know what to expect in the Bay of Islands!

However, you won't find a local transportation system in any form other than the delightful little ferry that delivers schoolchildren, businesspeople, tourists, and freight from one shore to the other. Nor will you find any sort of wild nightlife. Toting up the "wills" and "won'ts," I'd have to say you come up with a balance in favor of a perfect place in which to soak up sun and sea and fresh air, and put the frenetic pleasures of big city life on hold.

GETTING THERE

BY PLANE Eagle Airways has daily flights between Auckland and Kerikeri, with a shuttle bus into Paihia. Make reservations through Air New Zealand.

BY BUS Both InterCity and Northliner Express have daily bus service between Auckland and Paihia. Both companies charge NZ$41 (U.S. $26.65) one way, but Northliner (☎ **09/307-5873** in Auckland) offers a 30% discount to backpackers and anyone over age 50.

BY CAR It's an easy, beautiful drive to the Bay of Islands from Auckland. Along the way you'll pass through rolling green hills dotted with sheep and cows, and you'll see lots of huge ponga ferns and pine trees, as well as cabbage trees, poplars, and toi toi. The coastal views and tranquil beaches are also gorgeous. You might want to stop along the Hibiscus Coast (see "Easy Excursions from Auckland" in Chapter 5), in Warkworth or Whangarei, or even take a longer route through the kauri forest on the west coast (see "En Route to Auckland, by Way of the West Coast," below). The straight shot from Auckland can be accomplished in three hours, but I suggest you forget about hurrying and enjoy your introduction to Northland.

BY TOUR Several companies in Auckland offer one-, two-, and three-day tours to the Bay of Islands. For good value and personal service, you might want to contact Henry and Lorna at **Best Deal Sights** (☎ **09/818-7799**).

ORIENTATION

There are three distinct resort areas in the Bay of Islands: **Paihia, Russell,** and **Kerikeri.** If you've come for the fishing, you'll want to be based in Russell, on the eastern shore and home of most charter boats; for almost every other activity, Paihia, across on the western shore, is the central location; and Kerikeri is the center of a thriving citrus-growing industry as well as a small, interesting "don't miss" sightseeing side trip.

ESSENTIALS The STD (**telephone area code**) for Paihia and Russell is **09**.

Information You'll find the **Bay of Islands Information Centre** on Marsden Road on the waterfront in Paihia (☎ **09/402-7426**). The staff will arrange accommodations reservations throughout the entire Bay of Islands—bed-and-breakfast room, motel unit, motor camp, or tent site. They also keep up-to-the-minute information on all sightseeing and other activities. The office is staffed daily from 8am to 6pm.

Fullers Northland (☎ **09/402-7811**), locally known simply as Fullers, operates a Holiday Shoppe in the Maritime Building in Paihia. They're the ones you'll turn to for any area cruises or coach tours, all InterCity bookings, passenger and car-ferry reservations, and airline information and reservations (including international flights).

GETTING AROUND

BY CAR Driving is easy and parking seldom a problem in the Bay of Islands. If you arrive via air or bus, **rental cars** are available through Budget Rent-A-Car, Maritime Building, Paihia (☎ **402-8568**).

ON FOOT Shanks' mare is actually the *best* way to move around each location in the Bay of Islands, since towns are small and distances short between attractions. It's when you move from the Paihia/Russell area to Kerikeri, etc., that you may yearn for wheels.

BY TAXI For taxi service, call the Fullers office shown above. The **Island Water Taxi** (book at Fullers or the Visitor Information Centre) offers 24-hour service, and fares depend on the hour and number of passengers.

BY FERRY No matter where you settle, you're going to come to know that neat little ferry intimately—unless you have your own boat, that's the only inexpensive way to get from one shore to another (well, there is a long-way-round drive, but it's much too time-consuming). Personally, I have a real fondness for that 15-minute voyage—for that little space of time, you're in close contact with the daily lives of the locals as you cross with women returning from a supermarket run, school kids as rambunctious on the after-school run as on schoolbuses the world over, and all sorts of daily-living goods being transported. It runs at hourly intervals beginning at 7am (on the hour from Russell, on the half hour from Paihia) and ending at 7:30pm (from Paihia). In summer, crossings are extended to 10:30pm. Fares are NZ$6 (U.S. $3.90) round trip for adults, NZ$3 (U.S. $1.95) for children 5 to 15; children under 5 free. You'll soon have that schedule firmly fixed in your mind—it's important to be on the same side of the water as your bed when the service shuts down! If you should find yourself stranded, however, all is not lost—just considerably more expensive via water taxi.

About 15 minutes south of Paihia, at **Opua,** there's a flat-bottom car-ferry for drivers that crosses the narrow channel to Okiato Point, a 10-minute drive from Russell. Crossings are every 10 minutes from 6:40am to 9pm, and the one-way fare for car and driver is NZ$7 (U.S. $4.55) plus NZ$1 (U.S. 65¢) for each adult passenger, half price for children.

What to See & Do

The very first thing on your agenda should be to go by the **Bay of Islands Information Centre** and pick up brochures outlining the various bay cruises and setting out schedules and prices for each. The information center can furnish specific information on just about any of the other activities listed in this section.

SIGHTS & ATTRACTIONS

There's a wealth of sightseeing to be done on land in the Bay of Islands, but nothing compares with the bay itself. All those islands are set in a bay so sheltered that it's known to mariners as one of the best hurricane anchorages in the South Pacific. And if you do no other sightseeing during your stay, you should take one of the **bay cruises** that circumnavigate these islands. There's the 4-hour ★ **Cape Brett cruise,** with its breathtaking passage through the **"Hole in the Rock"** when the weather is right; the price is NZ$49 (U.S. $31.85) for adults, NZ$25 (U.S. $16.25) for children. Then there's the longer (5½-hour) ★ **Cream Trip,** which retraces the route used in years gone by to collect cream for market from the islands and inlets around the bay. Along this route, your knowledgeable skipper will point out Captain Cook's first anchorage in 1769; the spot where Rev. Samuel Marston preached the first Christian sermon on the beach; island locales of violence, murder, and cannibalism; and Otehei Bay, on Urupukapuka Island, which was the site of Zane Grey's camp so well written of in his *The Angler's El Dorado.* The price of the Cream Trip is NZ$55 (U.S. $35.75) for adults, NZ$27 (U.S. $17.55) for children. See "Organized Tours," below.

If time permits (it will take an entire day) I heartily recommend the trip to ★ **Cape Reinga.** There's something intriguing about being at the very top of New Zealand (and if you visit Stewart Island down south, you'll have seen the country from stem to stern!). And besides, there's a mystical aura about the cape, since the Maori believed that it was from a gnarled pohutukawa tree in the cliffs here that souls jumped off for the return to their Hawaiki homeland after death. Then there's the drive along hard-packed golden sands of the **Ninety-Mile Beach** (which measures 52 miles at low tide). The tour leaves Paihia at 7:30am, returns at 6:30pm, and costs NZ$89 (U.S. $57.85) for adults, NZ$51 (U.S. $33.15) for children.

On land, your sightseeing will be divided between Russell and Waitangi. At the top of your "must see" list should be the **Treaty House** in Waitangi. It's the birthplace of modern New Zealand.

In Waitangi

Lucky you if your visit coincides with the February 6 celebration of **Waitangi Day.** It's like being in the United States on the Fourth of July. The center of activity is the Treaty House lawn, scene of the Waitangi Treaty signing, with a re-creation of that event, lots of Maori song and dance, and Pakeha officials in abundance, dressed to the nines in resplendent uniforms of yesteryear and today. The Royal New Zealand Navy is there in force, as are crowds of vacationing Kiwis. Book way ahead, then get set to join in the festivities.

Treaty House, Waitangi National Reserve, Waitangi. ☎ **402-7437.**

It was in this Georgian-style house that the British Crown succeeded in having its first treaty ratified by enough chieftains to assure its acceptance by major Maori leaders throughout the country. Set in parklike grounds, this was the home of James Busby from 1832 to 1880, and its broad lawn was the scene of the colorful meeting of Pakeha and Maori during the treaty negotiations over 150 years ago on February 6, 1840. Inside, there's a museum display of a facsimile of the treaty written in Maori, other mementos of those early days, and rooms with period furnishings. An audiovisual presentation of the treaty's history may be seen at the Visitors Centre. On the grounds stands one of the most magnificent whare runangas (meetinghouses) in the country, constructed for the 1940 centennial celebration, containing elaborately carved panels from all the Maori tribes in New Zealand. Just below the sweeping lawn, on Hobson's Beach, there's an impressive 117-foot-long **Maori war canoe,** also made for the centennial, from three giant kauri trees.

Admission: NZ$7 (U.S. $4.55) adults, free for children.

Open: Daily 9am–5pm.

Kelly Tarlton's Museum of Shipwrecks. ☎ 402-7018.

As this is written, this wonderful museum ship is awash (you should pardon the pun) in plans for its future. Look for it in its old location near the Paihia–Waitangi bridge, the Treaty House in Waitangi, or (as present plans project) near the Maritime Building in Paihia. Whatever you do, don't miss it, for if you've an ounce of romance in your soul, you'll treasure a visit to this three-masted bark, the *Tui.* The late Kelly Tarlton, a professional diver, made this the focus of his life's work, excavating treasure from the many ships that have perished in the waters off New Zealand. Beside each display of treasure he brought up from the deep, there's a photograph of the ship from which it was recovered. There's a continuous slide show depicting Kelly going about his work underwater, and realistic sound effects of storms, the creaking of timbers, and the muffled chant of sea chanteys.

Admission: NZ$5 (U.S. $3.25) adults, NZ$2 (U.S. $1.30) children.

Open (tentative in view of the above): Daily 9am–5pm. **Closed:** Christmas Day.

In Russell

Russell is a veritable concentration of historical sites. It was here that the great Maori leader Hone Heke burned everything except mission property at a time when most of what was there *should* have been burned in the interest of morality and environmental beauty, since the town seethed with all sorts of European vices, diseases, and injustices against the indigenous people. The old Anglican church and headstones of sailors buried in its graveyard bear to this day bullet holes from that long-ago battle.

On the highest elevation in Russell stands the **flagstaff** Hone Heke chopped down four times in defiance of British rule. It is reached by auto or on foot, and the lookout up there affords one of the best views of the bay.

Bay of Islands Maritime Park Headquarters and Visitors Centre, The Strand, on the waterfront in Russell. **☎ 403-7685.**

Stop here and watch the 15-minute audiovisual presentation *The Land Is Enduring* to get a grasp of the Maori and English history of this area. The center, operated by the Department of Conservation, has camping information and maps and sells a variety of books, prints, cards, T-shirts, and sweatshirts.

Admission: Free.

Open: Mon–Fri 8:30am–4:30pm, Sat–Sun 9am–4:30pm.

Pompallier, The Strand, on the waterfront in Russell. ☎ **403-7861.**

This house was built in 1841 by the French Bishop Pompallier for the Roman Catholic Mission to house a printing press used from 1842 to 1849 to print religious documents in the Maori language. That press is still here today, and there's also a working tannery and a book bindery.

Admission: NZ$5 (U.S. $3.25) adults, free for children.

Open: Daily 10am–5pm.

Russell Museum, York St., Russell. ☎ **403-7701.**

This local history museum records the earliest years of Maori–European contact. Highlights are the one-fifth-scale model of the Captain Cook's *Endeavour,* the Hansen-King Collection of historic costumes, and 10-minute video on Russell's beginnings.

Admission: NZ$2.50 (U.S. $1.65) adults, NZ50¢ (U.S. 35¢) children.

Open: Daily 10am–4pm.

Christ Church, at Church St. and Robertson Rd., Russell.

Dating from 1836, this is not only the oldest surviving church in New Zealand but also the oldest building in the country still used for its original purpose. Among those who contributed funds for its construction was Charles Darwin, who visited New Zealand on *The Beagle* while making the observations that resulted in *The Origin of Species.* The church has been the site of numerous turning points in history, including Captain Hobson's proclamation prior to the signing of the Treaty of Waitangi. Be sure to notice the needlepoint pew cushions crafted by local residents.

Admission: Free.

Open: Daily 9am–5pm.

In Kerikeri

You really should take time to make the 20-minute drive to Kerikeri, a small town that figured prominently in the country's early history. It holds the oldest masonry building in New Zealand, the **Stone Store,** built between 1832 and 1835 as a mission supply center, which is now a museum and general store. (However, at press time there is some talk of closing the Stone Store because it's unsafe.)

Kerikeri is also an **arts-and-crafts center,** and you can watch many of the artisans at their work in small shops. A direct descendant of Hone Heke constructed the replica Maori village of **Keri Park** without hammer or nails, as his ancestors built their own dwellings. Another authentic reconstruction of a pre-European Maori settlement is **Rewa's Village.**

ORGANIZED TOURS

Fuller Northland (☎ **402-7421** in Paihia, **403-7866** in Russell) is the largest and most visible tour operator in the Bay of Islands as well as the 1990 and 1992 winner of the New Zealand Tourism Award as the country's best tour operator. Kings (☎ **09/402-8288,** or toll free **0508/888-282** in New Zealand) conducts similar trips for slightly lower prices. Among the half dozen cruises and outings offered, the most popular are the ★ **Cape Brett Hole-in-the-Rock** cruise and the ★ **Cream Trip bay cruise.** Both trips offer an island stopover. The coach trip to ★ **Cape Reinga via Ninety-Mile Beach** is also a great experience.

A new attraction gives you a chance to see dolphins in their natural habitat and, conditions permitting, you can swim with them. Fullers calls their trip **Dolphin Encounters** (NZ$65/U.S. $42.25 for adults, NZ$35/U.S. $22.75 for children), but they aren't the only company offering this experience.

SPORTS & RECREATION

There are beaches galore for good **swimming** from November through March. They're lined up all along the town waterfronts, and delightful little coves with curving strands are just awaiting your discovery down almost any side road along State Highway 10 headed north—if you pass through privately owned land to reach the water, you may be asked to pay a small fee, something like NZ$1 (U.S. 65¢).

You can arrange to play **golf** at the beautiful 18-hole waterfront course at Waitangi Golf Course, where clubs are for hire.

Deep-sea fishing is at its best up here. In fact, world records for yellowtail, marlin, shark, and tuna have been set in these waters. There are a couple dozen big-game fishing charter boats operating out of Russell, but I might as well warn you that it can be an expensive proposition unless you can form your own group (or fall in with a group that has a vacancy) to share the NZ$700 to NZ$800 (U.S. $455 to $520) cost for 10 hours of fishing. With a party of four (the maximum), the per-person cost becomes more manageable, but is still pretty hefty. If the fact that some 600 striped, blue, and black marlin were landed in these waters makes this an irresistible expense, **Game Fishing Charters,** in the Maritime Building in Paihia, may be able to help you line something up.

Light-line fishing is much more affordable, and the Visitors Information Centre in Paihia can furnish a list of fishing charters available. Most supply rods and bait and run three- to five-hour trips.

There's good **scuba diving** in these waters, and **Paihia Dive, Hire and Charters Ltd.,** on Williams Road, can provide all equipment and arrange dives.

The Bay of Islands is rich in excellent ★ **scenic and historic walks,** and the park rangers at the following addresses can furnish details of all trails, as well as a very good booklet called "Walking in the Bay of Islands Maritime and Historic Park." Go by the Park Visitor Centre in Russell (P.O. Box 134; ☎ **403-7685**) or the Ranger Station in Kerikeri (P.O. Box 128; ☎ **407-8474**) for their friendly assistance. There are also beautiful camping sites, some of them on uninhabited islands in the bay, with nominal per-night fees. You must reserve with the park rangers at Russell—you might write ahead and ask for their useful booklet, "Huts and Camping." Send $1 U.S. for each booklet.

If the idea of a couple of days of **sailing** aboard a fully equipped yacht appeals to you, get in touch with the people at **Moorings Rainbow Yacht Charters** (☎ **09/378-0719;** fax 09/378-0931). You get to be the skipper, your family or friends

READERS RECOMMEND

Dolphin Discoveries, P.O. Box 21, Russell (☎ **09/403-7350**). *"We found this to be the highlight of our holiday and would certainly recommend it to any other travelers. Although we are middle-aged, we were just as excited as the younger people on the boat. We swam next to the wild dolphins, and the magic of this trip will stay with me forever."* —Elspeth Dennett, Lancastershire, England.

the crew. The yachts accommodate four to eight people and may be chartered for a minimum of two days, at prices *starting* at NZ$260 (U.S. $169) in peak season or NZ$150 (U.S. $97.50) in low season. If you're not ready to venture out on your own, rent the yacht at the usual rate and pay an additional NZ$395 (U.S. $256.75) for three days of instruction. For full details, contact the company in the States at South Pacific Sailing Adventures, 2610 S. Harbor Blvd., Suite 201, Oxnard, CA 93035 (☎ toll free **800/815-9499;** fax 805/985-2170).

SHOPPING

Take some time from other activities in the Bay of Islands to browse around the several very good shops in the area. I have lugged home some of my best New Zealand handcrafts from up here, including a gorgeous natural-wool hand-knit sweater from **Dalrymples,** The Strand, Russell, where Peter Dalrymple keeps an assortment of good-quality gifts and souvenirs at reasonable prices. Over on the Paihia side, **Classique Souvenirs** is a good bet for good buys; you'll find exceptional craft items at **Katoa Crafts** (pottery, weaving, woodwork, paintings, etc.); and a very good selection is at **Waitangi Crafts and Souvenirs** on Marsden Road. Prices, far from being resort-area-inflated, are competitive with city shops and in many cases lower—and it's fun to shop with the friendly Bay of Islands proprietors, who take a personal interest in seeing that you find what you want. Most are open daily during peak season, and weekdays plus Saturday mornings at other times.

EVENING ENTERTAINMENT

Pub pickings are limited to the **Duke** in the Duke of Marlborough Hotel on the Strand in Russell, where conversation is likely to center around fishing, and the Quality Resort **Waitangi Pub** and **Anchorage Bar,** where you'll bend an elbow with residents of the Paihia side of the bay and vacationing visitors. Other possibilities include the **Lighthouse Tavern,** upstairs in the Selwyn Mall in Paihia; the **Roadrunner Tavern,** 2 1/2 miles south of town; and the **Terrace Nightclub,** on Kawakawa Road in Opua, open nightly from 10pm until late.

Where to Stay

The Bay of Islands is a budget traveler's dream: The area abounds in excellent inexpensive accommodations, and more are being built all the time. Most are of modest size, earning a moderate but adequate income for couples or families who seem far more interested in their guests' having a good time than in charging "what the traffic will bear." Rates do fluctuate according to season, however, with a slight increase during holidays and a slightly higher jump during the peak summer months of December through February. Those are also the times it is absolutely essential to reserve well in advance, since the Bay of Islands is tops on just about every Kiwi family's holiday list, and many book from year to year. If you're planning a visit during any of these seasons, you can either contact one of the hostelries you see listed here, or the Visitors Information Centre.

Several renders have suggested that staying on the Paihia side of the bay is more convenient because of late-night crossing difficulties. Having stayed in both Paihia and Russell, I can honestly express no personal preference. However, you may want to consider carefully just where you'll want to be in the wee hours.

The rates quoted below include GST.

IN RUSSELL

A Historic Hotel

The Duke of Marlborough Hotel, The Strand (P.O. Box 191), Russell. ☎ **09/403-7829.** Fax 09/403-7828. 29 rms (all with bath), 1 suite. TV TEL

Rates: NZ$68–NZ$80 (U.S. $44.20–$52) single; NZ$68–NZ$120 (U.S. $44.20–$78) double; NZ$127 (U.S. $82.55) suite. Lower rates off-season. DC, MC, V.

The Duke of Marlborough has watched the comings and goings of generations of residents and visitors from its waterfront perch since it opened as New Zealand's very first hotel. It has suffered major fires three times and three times been rebuilt. Grand it may be—stuffy it isn't. Just a few steps from the Russell wharf, its covered veranda is the natural gathering place for fishermen at the end of a day on the water in pursuit of those deep-sea fighters. The conversation tends to be lively, attracting locals as well as hotel guests. The Duke, in fact, could be called the social hub of Russell (if Russell could, in fact, be said to have a social hub).

Regulars come back to the Duke year after year for its old-worldliness and also for the comfort of its rooms. Some beds have wicker headboards, the floors are carpeted, the walls are wood paneled, and tea- and coffee-making facilities are in each room. There's a dining room serving all meals (see "Where to Eat," below), a TV lounge, and a charming guest lounge with wicker furniture, a colonial-style bar, and a fireplace.

Chalets

Wairoro Park, P.O. Box 53, Russell. ☎ **09/403-7255.** 7 chalets (all with bath). TV TEL **Directions:** Go about a mile from the ferry, then turn left on a hilly dirt road and follow the signs.

Rates: NZ$80 (U.S. $52) chalet for two. Minimum charge of NZ$130 (U.S. $84.50) per chalet during the Christmas holidays. Additional person NZ$12 (U.S. $7.80) extra for adults, NZ$6 (U.S. $3.90) extra for children. BC, MC, V.

The hospitality here could probably be labeled Kiwi-Dutch-English, since owner Yan Boerop is Dutch, his wife, Beryl, is English, and they're both now dyed-in-the-wool Kiwis. They've settled in on the Russell side of the Opua car-ferry in an absolutely idyllic setting of some 160 acres on the shores of a sheltered bay cove. They use a great many of those acres to run cattle, and in the midst of an orchard just steps away from the beach they have three two-story A-frame chalets and three one-bedroom luxury chalets. The first level of each holds a large lounge and fully equipped kitchen. There are two bedrooms upstairs, and with the three divans in the lounge, the units accommodate up to eight. Facilities include a covered carport and decks looking out to gorgeous views. A large three-bedroom chalet is set in its own 18 acres of bushland, with private water access and marvelous sea views—call for rates and availability. The Boerops thoughtfully provide a dinghy or motorboat, a 12-foot catamaran, two kayaks, and a windsurfer at no charge for guests. Regulars book from one holiday season to the next—which means, of course, that it's a good idea to write as far in advance as possible, no matter when you're coming.

A Hostel

Arcadia Lodge, Florence Ave., Russell. ☎ **09/403-7756.** 9 backpacker beds, 4 units.

Rates: NZ$32–NZ$38 (U.S. $20.80–$24.70) double; NZ$14 (U.S. $9.10) backpacker bed. No credit cards.

Linley and Bill Shatwell spent many holidays in the Bay of Islands area before buying this lodge, which includes four attractive, inexpensive units that are spotless and comfortable, and look out onto great views of the bay. Actually they're an extension of the main house. Each is a self-contained unit with kitchen and will sleep four. Three double and two single rooms are available upstairs in the house. They also have a dinghy and old bikes for guest use. This is a very popular place with budget travelers, both in New Zealand and among overseas travelers who've heard about it by word of mouth, so it's a good idea to book ahead if you can. It's located on the outskirts of town.

Bed-&-Breakfasts

Aimeo Cottage, Okiato Point Rd. (R.D. 1), Russell. ☎ **09/403-7494.**
Fax 09/403-7516. 1 rm (with bath), 1 self-contained unit (with bath).

Rates (including cooked breakfast): NZ$65 (U.S. $42.25) double. Dinner NZ$20 (U.S. $13) extra. No credit cards.

Annie and Helmuth Hormann arrived in New Zealand by way of Tahiti on their 35-foot sailboat. Their home, located near the Opua car-ferry, has a fabulous water outlook and a fair number of Tahitian artifacts. She works at the Duke of Marlborough Hotel, and he's home during the day. (A native of Berlin, the host refers to their picnic table as his "beer garden.") They offer one double room with bath and one self-contained apartment with bath and kitchen, the latter being a great bargain. A restaurant, gallery, and store are within walking distance.

Ounuwhao–Harding House, Matauwhi Bay, Russell. ☎ **09/403-7310.**
5 rms (1 with bath).

$ **Rates** (including breakfast): NZ$45 (U.S. $29.25) single without bath; NZ$75 (U.S. $48.75) double without bath, NZ$90 (U.S. $58.50) double with bath. No credit cards. **Closed:** June–July.

No, I haven't misspelled the name of this B&B—it's pronounced "oo-noo-*fow*" and it means "fighting with spears." Allan and Marilyn Nicklin bought this 1894 house in Dargaville and had it shipped here by land and sea. Only Kiwis would be so industrious! Their efforts are evident: The house has high ceilings, tall windows, imported English floral tile in the bath, and beautiful wallpaper throughout. Guests enjoy the lounge where a TV, tea- and coffee-making facilities, and a fireplace are for their use. Three rooms have sinks; all have quilts, cushions, and curtains made by Marilyn, plus brass headboards. In the words of reader Meg Gammon of Kailua, Hawaii, "It is perfect in every way." No smoking is permitted in the house.

IN PAIHIA

Motels

Bay of Islands Motel, 6 Tohitapu Rd., Te Haumi Bay (P.O. Box 131), Paihia.
☎ **09/402-7348.** Fax 09/402-8257. 19 cottages (all with bath). TV TEL

Rates: NZ$60 (U.S. $39) cottage for one; NZ$75–NZ$135 (U.S. $48.75–$87.75) cottage for two. AE, MC, V.

Set in spacious grounds off Seaview Road, these self-contained colonial-style cottages have a lounge, separate bedrooms, a bath, and a full kitchen. Privacy is assured, since the cottages are placed at angles so the windows of one don't face those of another—the whole effect is that of a charming minivillage. Other facilities include a swimming pool, a spa pool, a laundry, and a playground for the small fry, who will also enjoy nearby beaches (close enough to hoof it). There's also a licensed restaurant. The managers can supply cooked or continental breakfasts on request and are happy to book tours, cruises, and fishing trips right from their office. Readers have commented on the "spotless" accommodations.

Best Western Casa-Bella Motel, McMurray Rd., Paihia. ☎ **09/402-7387.** Fax 09/402-7166. 21 units (all with bath), 1 suite. TV TEL

Rates: NZ$75 (U.S. $48.75) unit for one; NZ$85 (U.S. $55.25) unit for two; NZ$95 (U.S. $61.75) suite. Best Western discounts available. AE, DC, MC, V.

This charming red-tile-roofed sparkling-white Spanish-style complex is close to shops, restaurants, and the beach. There is a variety of nicely furnished apartments, each with full kitchen facilities, in-house video, and electric blanket. Some of the superior units have water beds, others have *firm* queen-size beds, and one is a very special honeymoon suite. On the premises are both a heated swimming and a hot-spa pool, as well as full laundry facilities. Umbrella-shaded picnic tables and benches are set about on the landscaped grounds. Hosts Stefan and Darryl Vohan are very helpful. It's located on the first street on the left after the Beachcomber.

A Bed-&-Breakfast

Wairoa Homestays, Bayly Rd. (P.O. Box 36), Paihia. ☎ **09/402-7379.** 2 rms (neither with bath).

Rates (including breakfast): NZ$40 (U.S. $26) single; NZ$80 (U.S. $52) double; NZ$28 (U.S. $18.20) per person, bed only. Dinner NZ$38 (U.S. $24.70) extra. No credit cards.

Dorothy Bayly extends visitors a warm welcome to her seaside two-story country home. She will do your washing and take you for a drive around the farm; for a small additional charge she'll arrange pickup in Paihia. Her three-course dinner includes wine and a before-dinner drink. There's a spa bath and tennis court on the property, with good beach walks and a golf course nearby.

A Hostel

Centabay Backpackers Hostel, Selwyn Rd., Paihia. ☎ **09/402-7466.** 3 units (all with bath), 18 rms (none with bath).

Rates: NZ$17 (U.S. $11.05) per person double; NZ$14 (U.S. $9.10) per dorm bed. Family and group rates available in low season. MC, V.

This is the most centrally located hostel in town and quite appealing. It's run by the ever-helpful Brita and Heinz Marti, who arrange sailing, horseback riding, sea kayaking, fishing, and overnight camping trips to Cape Reinga. In addition to dormitories with two to six beds, there are three studio units with toilet and shower, toaster, tea- and coffee-making facilities, and a balcony. There are no chores, and the place is very clean. Two lounges have a TV, and there are kitchens, a games room, and bike rental. The booking office can also arrange sightseeing cruises and trips, sometimes with discounted fares.

Worth the Extra Money

Quality Resort Waitangi, Tau Henare Dr., Waitangi (P.O. Box 150, Paihia). ☎ **09/402-7411,** or toll free **0800/808-228** in New Zealand. Fax 09/402-8200. 145 rms (all with bath). MINIBAR TV TEL

Rates: NZ$150 (U.S. $97.50) single or double. AE, MC, V.

This lovely hotel is actually set in the parklike grounds of the Waitangi National Trust, with superb land and water views. It's a tranquil, relaxing base for sightseeing in the entire region. There's 24-hour room service, piano music in the lounge on summer evenings, a good restaurant, and a heated pool. It's a stone's throw from the Treaty House, the Maori war canoe, and an excellent golf course, and about a mile from Paihia.

CABINS & CAMPGROUNDS

Bay of Islands Holiday Park, Lily Pond, Puketona Rd. (P.O. Box 393), Paihia. ☎ **09/402-7646.** Fax 09/402-7408. 200 tent sites, 100 powered sites, 3 on-site caravans, 11 cabins, 66-bed lodge.

Rates: NZ$8.50 (U.S. $5.55) per person site; NZ$35 (U.S. $22.75) double, cabin or on-site caravan. Additional adult NZ$8 (U.S. $5.20) extra. Lower rates off-season. BC, MC, V.

This is a big place, offering a communal kitchen and bath, laundry facilities, linen rental, a camp store, a games room, and a children's playground. It's about 4 miles to the beach and boat ramp and 5 miles to Paihia. The hosts are Linda Stewart and Maurice Biddington.

Falls Motor Inn & Caravan Park, Puketona Rd., Haruru Falls (P.O. Box 14, Paihia). ☎ and fax **09/402-7816.** 14 studio and two-bedroom units (all with bath), 45 caravan sites (10 powered).

Rates: NZ$65 (U.S. $42.25) studio for one; NZ$77 (U.S. $50.05) studio for two; NZ$95 (U.S. $61.75) two-bedroom unit for two (additional person NZ$12 U.S. $7.80 extra); NZ$7.50 (U.S. $4.90) per adult and NZ$5 (U.S. $3.25) per child powered site. Rates 20% higher Christmas–Easter. AE, DC, MC, V.

In addition to sites for campers and caravaners and two sizes of unit, the Falls Motor Inn offers a pool with a view of the Waitangi River, a small sandy beach, a dinghy, an outdoor spa pool, and shared kitchen, laundry, and bathroom facilities. The activities board will keep you up-to-date on current area happenings. Hosts Peter and Ramona Lucie-Smith are happy to point out nearby walks and and other nature-oriented options. A licensed restaurant is just 100 yards away. Haruru Falls is 4km (2½ miles) west of Paihia.

IN KERIKERI

A Hostel

Kerikeri YHA Hostel, Main Rd. (P.O. Box 62), Kerikeri. ☎ **09/407-9391.** 3 rms (none with bath), 32 dormitory beds.

Rates: NZ$32 (U.S. $20.80) double; NZ$13 (U.S. $8.45) dorm bed. MC, V.

Set in 2½ acres, this hostel consists of nine dormitory rooms, some with five beds, some with four, plus three double rooms. Other facilities include a communal kitchen and laundry, a lounge and recreation/games room, and a volleyball court. There's river swimming just a five-minute walk from the hostel, and many of the area's historic sites are within easy walking distance. The hostel is located on the main road just north of the village.

FARTHER AFIELD IN NORTHLAND

A Bed-&-Breakfast

Siesta Homestay, Tasman Heights Rd. (P.O. Box 67), Ahipara.
☎ and fax **09/409-4565.** 2 rms (both with bath). TV

Rates (including breakfast): NZ$70 (U.S. $45.50) single; NZ$95 (U.S. $61.75) double. Dinner with wine NZ$25 (U.S. $16.25) extra; individualized day tour for up to four people NZ$200 (U.S. $130) extra; pickup service from Auckland NZ$500 (U.S. $325) extra. MC, V.

Siesta is an out-of-the-ordinary homestay, so even if you don't normally like B&Bs, I think you should consider this place. The house was built in 1988 specifically to accommodate visitors. The two guest bedrooms are in a separate wing, and each has a bath, a TV, a balcony, a writing desk, a sitting area, tea- and coffee-making facilities, and a heater. The house sits high on a hill overlooking the Tasman Sea and Ninety-Mile Beach, with views from every window. Hosts Rolf and Hanna Stump have embraced Northland enthusiastically since emigrating from Switzerland over 15 years ago and are a mine of information on the area. I highly recommend you arrive in time for afternoon tea so you can enjoy one of Hanna's homemade treats. Ahipara is 15km (9 miles) west of Kaitaia and makes a convenient overnight stop after a day trip to Cape Reinga.

Where to Eat

As you'd expect in such a popular resort area, the Bay of Islands has many good places to eat. Seafood tops the list of menu offerings, with fish coming to your table just hours after it was swimming in the waters offshore.

IN RUSSELL

The Duke of Marlborough, The Strand, Russell. ☎ **403-7829.**

Cuisine: SEAFOOD/NEW ZEALAND. **Reservations:** Recommended.
Prices: Appetizers NZ$7–11 (U.S. $4.55–$7.15); main courses NZ$19–NZ$24 (U.S. $12.35–$15.60). Half-price meals for children under 10. AE, DC, MC, V.
Open: Breakfast daily 7:30–9:30am; lunch daily 11:30am–2:30pm; dinner daily 6:30–9pm.

The Duke serves à la carte meals in its old-world dining room. They've added a salad bar and a dining deck overlooking the bay. Main courses are fresh seafood and roasts of lamb or sirloin, pork, and chicken. The Duke is fully licensed, with an excellent wine cellar.

READERS RECOMMEND

McBain's "A" Frame, Te Ngaere Beach, Wainui Bay Rd., Kaeo (☎ **09/405-0249**). *"Christine and John McBain have a beach homestay that we think merits inclusion in your next edition. The hosts are avid botanists and Te Ngaere has some of the most spectacular scenery to be seen anywhere. There are miles of quiet coastline and secluded bays nearby."*—Timothy M. Rastello, Denver, Colo., U.S.A. [**Author's Note**: Kaeo is about 35km (22 miles) north of Kerikeri.]

 **The Gables,** The Strand, Russell. ☎ **403-7618.**

Cuisine: SEAFOOD/NEW ZEALAND. **Reservations:** Required.
Prices: Appetizers NZ$8–NZ$14 (U.S. $5.20–$9.10); main courses NZ$18–NZ$26 (U.S. $11.70–$16.90). AE, DC, MC, V.
Open: Dinner only, daily 7–11pm. **Closed:** Mon–Tues in winter.

This was one of the first buildings on the waterfront, built in 1847, and was a riotous brothel in the days of the whalers. Its construction is pit-sawn kauri on whalebone foundations (in fact, there's a huge piece of whale vertebra, discovered during the renovation, now on display in the bar). The decor is early colonial, with a kauri-paneled ceiling in the bar, kauri tables, and in winter, the cheerful warmth of open fires. The restaurant enjoys beautiful sunsets and a bay view. The menu changes regularly, but seafood, beef, lamb, game, and fresh seasonal produce are a mainstay. The Gables is fully licensed, with a respectable wine list. The Gables has won several awards and has a widespread reputation, so book early.

Quarterdeck, The Strand, Russell. ☎ **403-7761.**

Cuisine: SEAFOOD. **Reservations:** Recommended.
Prices: Appetizers NZ$7–NZ$9; main courses NZ$17–NZ$25 (U.S. $11.05–$16.25). MC, V.
Open: Dinner only, daily 6–9pm (later in high season). **Closed:** July.

Freshness is something you can count on at the Quarterdeck. In a setting of early Bay of Islands prints and photographs and high-backed booths, there's a terrific seafood platter, as well as snapper or whatever the latest catch has brought in, plus steaks, chicken, and light meals. A salad comes with all meals. In fine weather, there's delightful outdoor dining on the waterfront. Licensed and BYOW.

 **Strand Cafe,** The Esplanade, Russell. ☎ **403-7589.**

Cuisine: CAFE. **Reservations:** Not accepted.
Prices: Light lunch or dinner NZ$7.50 (U.S. $4.90). No credit cards.
Open: Summer, daily 7:30am–9pm. Winter, Tues–Sun 8:30am–4pm.

Barbara Tunbridge bakes wonderful scones, and the atmosphere she and her husband, Chris, create is very welcoming. I could sit here all day and admire the water view, drink one of the five kinds of tea, and read the newspaper they provide. There's inside and outside seating, checkers and dominos, and eight kinds of coffee as well. Lunch or dinner choices include blackened squid and green leaf salad, warm chicken salad, "real man's vegetable quiche," and farmhouse pâté. Not licensed and not BYO. Their ice-cream parlor is adjacent.

IN OR NEAR PAIHIA

If you can't muster the energy to go out at the end of the day, in addition to the listings below, there's always **Dial-a-Pizza** (☎ **402-7536**).

Bistro 40 Restaurant and Bar, 40 Marsden Rd. ☎ **402-7444.**

Cuisine: MODERN NEW ZEALAND. **Reservations:** Required.
Prices: Appetizers NZ$9–NZ$13 (U.S. $5.85–$8.45); main courses NZ$15–NZ$24 (U.S. $9.75–$15.60). AE, MC, V.
Open: Dinner only, daily 6–11pm.

This charming 1884 white frame house overlooks the bay. Meals are served in a bright sunny front room, and from mid-December through March there's also service on a small terrace shaded by a passionfruit-vine-laden trellis. Specialties are fresh local seafood, poultry, meat, and game. Go early and enjoy a before-dinner drink in their garden setting. Licensed.

Esmae's, 41 Williams Rd. ☎ **402-8400.**

Cuisine: NEW ZEALAND. **Reservations:** Recommended.
Prices: Appetizers NZ$7–NZ$9 (U.S. $4.55–$5.85); main courses NZ$17–NZ$22 (U.S. $11.05–$14.30). AE, DC, MC, V.
Open: Dinner only, daily 5:30pm–"late." **Closed:** Sun in winter.

Named after its consummate hostess, this restaurant in the center of town features home-style New Zealand cooking, and the menu even tells you where the fish or meat comes from. Esmae Dally will meet, greet, and seat you. There are fresh Kerikeri oysters, scallops, local fish, crayfish, and mussels. Nonseafood lovers are catered to, and I'm fond of marinated lamb steak, grilled and served with emerald sauce. Vegetarians will find at least one offering, such as the vegeroni crêpe, a combination of local vegetables and pasta with a mustard-cream sauce. Licensed

La Scala Restaurant, in the Selwyn Road Shopping Center. ☎ **402-7031.**

Cuisine: SEAFOOD/STEAKS. **Reservations:** Required.
Prices: Main courses NZ$15–NZ$30 (U.S. $9.75–$19.50); children's menu NZ$10 (U.S. $6.50). MC, V.
Open: Dinner only, Tues–Sun 6–10pm.

Located upstairs, La Scala has a pretty garden atmosphere, with window walls, green carpet, light-wood tables, cane-back chairs, and greenery everywhere. Fresh seafood is the specialty, as well as New Zealand steaks. In addition to the fish of the day, scallops, oysters, and crayfish, there are such items as honey prawns (shrimp battered, dipped in honey, and sprinkled with sesame seeds). Fully licensed, it's in the town center.

Only Seafood, 40 Marsden Rd. ☎ **402-6066.**

Cuisine: SEAFOOD. **Reservations:** Not accepted.
Prices: Appetizers NZ$8–NZ$15 (U.S. $5.20–$9.75); main courses NZ$13.50–NZ$25 (U.S. $8.80–$16.25). AE, BC, MC, V.
Open: Dinner only, daily from 5pm.

Located upstairs from the Bistro 40 Restaurant and Bar (see above), this attractive dining spot has a casual atmosphere and serves, as the name suggests, only fresh local seafood. You might like the hot calamari salad, fish pie, or fresh pan-fried fish with Cajun spices. The interior is plain—wooden floor, white walls, and white tables; outside, you can eat on the veranda overlooking the water. Licensed.

Taylors Licensed Cafe-Restaurant, State Hwy. 10, between Paihia and Kerikeri. ☎ **407-8664.**

Cuisine: NEW ZEALAND. **Reservations:** Required during the season and on weekends.
Prices: Appetizers NZ$8–NZ$12 (U.S. $5.20–$7.80); main courses NZ$16–NZ$21 (U.S. $10.40–$13.65); average lunch NZ$12 (U.S. $7.80). MC, V.
Open: Lunch daily noon–2pm; dinner daily 6:30pm–late.

Taylors looks like a roadhouse on the outside, an Olde English restaurant on the inside. The low-beamed ceiling, fireplaces, ornaments, and paintings make this a cozy, relaxed setting for the good food that comes to the table. The far-ranging menu features such specialties as lamb loin flamed in kiwifruit liqueur and mint jelly with a creamy sauce. Fresh seafood is served, and there's a wide selection of steaks. Fully licensed, with a good selection of wines. In summer, there's poolside dining in a picturesque garden setting.

En Route to . . .

AUCKLAND, BY WAY OF THE WEST COAST

If you came up to the Bay of Islands from Auckland on Highway 1, you may want to return on a longer, less direct route that takes in the **Waipoua Kauri Forest,** the **Trounson Kauri Park,** and the town of **Dargaville.** The kauri is the giant of the New Zealand native forest, and at Waipoua the largest trees are over 1,000 years old. Look for *Tane Mahuta* (God of the Forest), the largest known kauri in the country and *Te Matua Ngahere* (Father of the Forest), by volume the second-biggest known tree in New Zealand. These and other special trees are signposted on the tourist drive through the forest.

As you pass through Dargaville, you may want to stop at the **Dargaville Maritime Museum,** Harding Park (☎ **09/439-7555**). Here are the relics salvaged from numerous wrecks around the west coast and the mast from the Greenpeace flagship *Rainbow Warrior,* which was blown up by the French in Auckland Harbour in 1985. The museum is open daily from 9am to 4pm; admission is NZ$3 (U.S. $1.95). The **Dargaville Information Centre,** Normanby Street (☎ **09/439-8360**), can answer questions.

Another possible stop is the **Matakohe Kauri Museum,** Church Road, Matakohe (☎ **09/431-7417**). This is the place to learn all about the big trees and the early years of New Zealand's history when so many of them were cut down. It's open daily from 9am to 5pm; admission is NZ$5 (U.S. $3.25).

Where to Stay

If you want to stop overnight en route, try one of the following two B&Bs.

Awakino Point Lodge, State Hwy. 14 (P.O. Box 168), Dargaville. ☎ **09/439-7870.** 3 units. TV

Rates (including continental breakfast): NZ$57 (U.S. $37.05) single. Additional person NZ$13 (U.S. $8.45) extra. AE, DC, MC, V.

June Birch welcomes guests to her 5-acre farmlet surrounded by attractive gardens and orchard. She offers three self-contained units: One has a small kitchen, a separate lounge, log fire, and two bedrooms; the second also has two bedrooms; the third has one bedroom and a separate lounge. June rates high marks from readers.

$ **Solitaire Homestay,** State Hwy. 12, Waimamaku, South Hokianga. ☎ **09/405-4891.** 4 rms (none with bath).

Rates (including breakfast and dinner): NZ$50 (U.S. $32.50) single; NZ$90 (U.S. $58.50) double. No credit cards.

It's hard to say what's best about this place. The lovely 1912 kauri house has high ceilings and the other earmarks of colonial villas. Lloyd and Betty White are warm and caring people who go out of their way to look after their guests. She prepares picnic lunches to take into the nearby kauri forest, and on request they organize horseriding and trekking. Meals include home-grown vegetables and the pork, beef, and lamb they raise. It isn't surprising that many travelers stay longer than they had originally intended—and leave as friends. The four guest rooms share two baths. No smoking is permitted in the house.

WAITOMO

If you're going from the Bay of Islands directly to Waitomo, count on a long day's drive, shortened considerably if you return to Auckland via the short route, Highway 1 (about a three-hour drive). Along the way, you might stop by the town of **Warkworth,** once the center of extensive sawmilling of kauri spars to furnish masts for the Royal Navy. There are the remains of several Maori pas (fortified villages) in the area. About 7km (4 miles) away, at the coastal town of **Sandspit,** you can take a launch to Kawau Island to visit **Mansion House,** the restored home of Gov. George Grey. Then there are those beautiful beaches nearer Auckland at **Waiwera** and **Orewa** (see "Easy Excursions from Auckland," in Chapter 5).

From Auckland, the 203km (126-mile) drive to Waitomo passes through rich farm country and horse and cattle farms.

Hamilton is New Zealand's largest inland city and the commercial and industrial center of this agricultural area, as well as the site of the University of Waikato. Several major religions are centered here: It's the see city for the Anglican Diocese of Waikato; the Mormons have their magnificent South Pacific temple headquarters at Temple View, high on a hill at Tuhikaramea, southwest of the city center; and there's a Sikh temple on the northern outskirts of town at Horotiu. Throughout the city, you'll see lovely gardens in both city parks and private lawns.

Raglan, west of Hamilton, is a surf spot of great renown. A scant 16km (10 miles) before you reach Waitomo and the caves, **Kiwi House and Native Bird Centre** is located at Otorohanga. It's open daily from 9:30am to 4pm (to 5pm in summer). Admission is NZ$7 (U.S. $4.55). The remaining distance to Waitomo runs through more rolling farmland.

A Farm Stay for Campervans En Route

On State Highway 3, about halfway between Hamilton and Waitomo, the **Parklands Dairy Farm,** Kio Kio, R.D. 4, Otorohanga (☎ **07/871-1818**), is run by Owen Rountree and family, whose hospitality goes far beyond that of most owners. That is undoubtedly because this is their home, and what they're offering—in addition to power outlets at campervan sites, showers, toilets, and a barbecue—is a real "down home" farm welcome. Guests are invited in for a "cuppa" in the evening, and when it's farm-chore time, guests often go right along. This really is a motor camp with a difference, and it's a convenient base for Waitomo caves sightseeing. Rates, which include GST, are NZ$18 (U.S. $11.70) per person, bed-and-breakfast.

READERS RECOMMEND

Matawha, R.D. 2, Raglan (☎ **07/825-6709**). *"We had a wonderful, restful farm stay in Raglan. It's off the beaten path—the last half hour of travel is on a gravel road, but it's well worth it. Jenny and Peter Thomson have a cattle and sheep farm that overlooks the Tasman Sea and a peaceful black-sand beach. Our girls loved being able to run around on the farm without supervision and play with the cats, see the hens, and try to pet the sheep."* —Meg Barth Gammon, Kailua, Hawaii, U.S.A.

3 Waitomo

204km (126 miles) S of Auckland

GETTING THERE • By Bus or Train There's excellent InterCity and Northliner Express transportation from the Bay of Islands to Auckland, and InterCity and Newmans Coach service leave Auckland at about 8am for Otorohanga. The Waitomo Shuttle Bus (☎ **07/873-8214**) will transfer you to the Waitomo caves. *Reservations are essential,* and the fare is NZ$6 (U.S. $3.90) one way. You could also take the *Overlander* train from Auckland to Otorohanga.

ESSENTIALS The **telephone area code** (STD) for Waitomo is **07**.

The **Museum of Caves Information Centre** is on Main Street (P.O. Box 12), Waitomo (☎ **07/878-7640;** fax 07/878-6184). It's open daily from 8:30am to 5pm. There's a NZ $3.50 (U.S. $2.30) admission charge to the museum on the premises.

Waitomo Village owes its existence to the more than 200,000 visitors who come annually to visit three remarkable limestone caves, and its main street holds a general store, post office, and tavern (which sells tickets to the caves as well as souvenirs and has the usual bottle store, public bar, and bistro restaurant). At the top of a gracefully winding driveway stands the THC Waitomo Caves Hotel. Waitomo Cave, with its splendid Glowworm Grotto, is some 400 yards beyond the tavern, and about $2^1/_2$ miles away are Ruakuri and Aranui caves, both of which rival Wiatomo as sightseeing attractions.

What to See & Do

The caves are *the* attraction at Waitomo, chief among them the Waitomo Cave with its Glowworm Grotto. But you should include the Aranui Cave in your sightseeing if you have the time.

THE TOP ATTRACTION

Forty-five-minute guided tours are run on regular schedules at two caves—tickets are available at the Glowworm Cave Ticket Office (☎ **07/878-8227**). There's a two-cave combination ticket at NZ$25 (U.S. $16.25) for adults; one cave costs NZ$16.50 (U.S. $10.75). Children are charged half price. Be sure to wear good walking shoes and carry a sweater if the weather is a bit cool—it'll be cooler underground.

The best time to visit the **Glowworm Grotto in Waitomo Cave** is in the mid- to late afternoon—crowds are smaller than at midday. Tours run from 9am to 4:30pm (5:30pm in summer).

About 400 yards from the THC Hotel, a guide greets you at Waitomo's entrance to escort you through large antechambers, pointing out limestone formations with names like "The Organ," 8 feet high with a 24-foot base.

The largest cavern in any of the caves is "The Cathedral," which rises 47 feet and is an acoustically perfect auditorium that has seen performances by such recording artists as the Vienna Boys' Choir and Dame Nellie Melba.

Then it's on to a small grotto festooned with glowworms, where your guide fills you in on the glowworm's life and death cycle. A very short cycle it is, for the adult fly lives exactly 4 days, just long enough to produce the next generation. Having done that, it simply dies and becomes food for the next batch of glowworms.

The whole process begins with a tiny egg, which has a 21-day incubation period, then hatches into an inch-long grub. The grub then cloaks itself in a hollow mucous tubelike nest, which is attached to the grotto roof with a multitude of slender threads, each holding minute drops of acid and suspended like fishing lines down from the roof. The bait for those lines is the hypnotic blue-green light that comes from the larva's light organs (and that, of course, is what you see as you pass through the grotto) to attract a night-flying midge, which is "caught" by the threads, paralyzed by the acid, and reeled up and eaten by the larva. After about six months, the larva pupates for about two weeks in a hard, brown cocoon about half an inch long and suspended by a circle of those slender threads. The pupa's flirtatious light show attracts several males, which proceed to help the fly escape her cocoon. Four days of egg laying, then it's time to end it all by diving into the lines cast by new larvae as a main course along with the midges.

Now that you understand how and why the glowworms glow, your guide is ready to take you on an unforgettable boat ride down the underground river, which flows through the 100-foot-long, 40-foot-high, 50-foot-wide Glowworm Grotto. As you board the large, flat-bottomed boat, he will caution you that absolute silence is required, since the glowworms will extinguish their lights at the slightest noise. I must say that the warning is probably unnecessary, since the spectacle of more than 10,000 of those tiny pinpricks of light leaves one awed beyond words, and silence seems the only fitting way in which to view them. The boat glides slowly along what is called the "Milky Way," then returns to the dock, where you climb back up through the cave and are given an opportunity to question your guide on any of the things you have seen. It's a memorable experience.

OTHER ATTRACTIONS

For the adventurous, there's an exciting **black-water rafting** experience on an underground river at a cost of NZ$50 (U.S. $32.50) and an abseiling/rock-climbing thrill called **Lost World Adventures** (NZ$195/U.S. $126.75). **Horse trekking** and **white-water rafting** can also be arranged.

Ask at the Information Centre if you need transportation to the other cave, which is some 3km (2½ miles) away. There's an unusual delicacy about the limestone formations and ivory-colored, translucent stalactites in the **Aranui Cave.**

Where to Stay & Eat

The Information Centre mentioned above can tell you about farm and homestays in the area. The rates quoted below include GST.

THC Waitomo Caves Hotel, Waitomo Village. ☎ **07/878-8227,** or toll free **0800/801-111** in New Zealand. Fax 07/878-8858. 37 rms (all with bath), plus backpacker hostel rooms.

Rates (single or double): NZ$32 (U.S. $20.80) economy; NZ$96 (U.S. $62.40) standard; NZ$135 (U.S. $87.75) premium. AE, BC, DC, V.

This charming 1910 hotel retains much of its stately character. It's nestled in the hills above the village, convenient to the caves. Notable visitors have included Elizabeth II and Prince Philip in 1953, George Bernard Shaw, Zane Grey, and General MacArthur. Premium rooms have telephones and TVs. The economy lodging is an associated YHA hostel—some rooms are in the hotel and some in the adjacent hostel. Lunch is served in the Garden Room; dinner is offered in the Fred Mace licensed restaurant. The Waitomo Caves Tavern is a great spot for a drink.

En Route to Rotorua

It's an easy, three-hour-or-less drive from Waitomo to Rotorua, through rolling farmland and long stretches of bush. Approaching that steamy thermal town, you'll catch glimpses of its gleaming lakes and volcanic peaks. There's an "other world" aspect (and slight sulfuric odor!) about Rotorua and its environs, which will begin to capture your imagination even before you roll into town.

7

Rotorua & the East Coast

Right in the middle of the North Island, Rotorua is also in the center of the most intense thermal field in New Zealand: the 242km-long, 32km-wide (150-mile-long, 20-mile-wide) Taupo Volcanic Plateau. The city and its environs are rife with bubbling mud, silica terraces, and towering geysers. There's also the pervasive, though rather faint, sulfuric odor that comes along with the thermal activity.

This is the very heart of New Zealand's Maori culture, and the city's 54,000 population includes a high percentage of Maori. The city and surrounding area are quite literally soaked with attractions, almost all tied by legend to the Maori.

As for that awesome thermal activity, the Maori are quick to tell you the legend that explains its existence in Maori terms. It seems the great navigator-priest Ngatoroirangi, having reached the summit of Mount Tongariro, suffered greatly from the cold and implored his goddess sisters back in Hawaiki to send along some of their native warmth to this frigid, windswept place. Their response was a generous one—they pitched their gobs of fire across the water, which hopped, skipped, and jumped over the land, touching down at White Island, Rotorua, Wairakei, Taupo, Tokaanu, and Ketetahi, finally reaching the freezing Ngatoroirangi at Mount Tongariro. Geologists, on the other hand, simply say that underground lava or superheated rock heats and pressurizes underground water, sending it spouting up via any escape route it can find—natural fissures and porous rock. Whatever the explanation, today's residents of the area have harnessed that thermal activity to provide heat and hot water for domestic use.

As you can see from all the above, Rotorua should be included on your North Island itinerary. Limited time may well point you from Rotorua to Taupo and points south (see Chapter 8). However, **Tauranga** and **Whakatane** await those who can spare a few days, and there's a glorious drive around the **Sunrise Coast,** the place where the sun is first seen each morning. Here you'll find magnificent seascapes, secluded coves and bays, deserted beaches, tiny Maori settlements, and finally the Poverty Bay town of **Gisborne** and Hawke's Bay's crowning jewel, **Napier.** It's an area alive with history, both Maori and Pakeha. You'll see where the Arawa canoe made landfall; where Capt. James Cook first saw the New Zealand mainland and where he stopped on his second voyage; where ferocious, decisive battles between Maori and Europeans were fought; and along the way there are some of the finest examples of Maori carvings in New Zealand.

This swing around the Sunrise Coast is an off-the-beaten-track digression that I strongly urge you to take if you can fit it into your timetable. It's a bit of New Zealand far too many visitors miss.

1 Rotorua

221km (137 miles) SE of Auckland

GETTING THERE • By Plane Mount Cook Airline, Air New Zealand, and Eagle Airways operate daily flights between Auckland and Rotorua, and Ansett flies up from Wellington and Christchurch.

• By Train The *Geyserland* makes regular runs from Auckland.

• By Bus InterCity, Mount Cook Landline, and Newmans all have daily bus schedules between Auckland and Rotorua, arriving at the Information Centre.

• By Car Drive south from Auckland on Highway 1 to Tirau, then east on Highway 5 to Rotorua; consider stopping in Cambridge (see "Easy Excursions from

What's Special About Rotorua

Concerts & Feasts

- Maori concerts and traditional *hangi* feasts, similar in some ways to the Hawaiian luau, featuring seafood, succulent meats, and local vegetables cooked in an earthen pit—not to be missed.

Thermal Attractions

- Whakarewarewa Reserve, with a silica terrace pierced by seven active water spouts and Pohutu Geyser, which sends spouts of steam and water some 100 feet into the air.
- Waimangu Valley, where lakes boil and hiss, steaming cliff faces are streaked with baking minerals, and—amazingly—native plants flourish in the midst of this hostile landscape.

Cultural Centers

- Maori Arts & Crafts Institute, adjacent to the Whakarewarewa Reserve, where you can see demonstrations of such traditional Maori skills as carving and weaving.

Sporting Activities

- White-water rafting, jet-boat trips, waterskiing, fishing, golf, forest walks, and mountain hikes.

Peaceful Pleasures

- Lake Rotorua, a very pretty place for walking, picnicking, and watching swans.
- Hot pools, where you can soak away stress and strain in thermal water at the Polynesian Pools, among other places.

Auckland," in Chapter 5). If you're coming from Waitomo, the trip will be about 150km (93 miles).

ESSENTIALS • Orientation Rotorua sits in the curve of Lake Rotorua's southwestern shore, spreading inland in a neat pattern so you'll be oriented in a matter of hours. The center of town is not large: A good 10-minute walk will take you from the railway station northward past the post office and Visitor Information Centre to the lovely Government Gardens. Older downtown hotels are also along this route, while more modern hotels are more or less concentrated along the southern end of Fenton Street. This main street runs from the lake for 3km (2 miles) south to the Whakarewarewa (never mind—just call it "Whaka," as the locals do), a thermal reserve owned by the Maori. The post office, on Hinemoa Street (☎ **347-7851**), open Monday through Friday from 8:30am to 4:30pm, is where you can pick up *Poste Restante* mail.

• Information The center of tourist information is the **Tourism Rotorua Visitor Information Centre,** 67 Fenton St. at the corner of Haupapa Street (☎ **07/348-5179;** fax 07/348-6044), open daily from 8:30am to 5pm. It's loaded with tourist information and has a helpful staff who will make reservations. The center also has a licensed café, currency exchange, baggage storage, Department of Conservation office, and postal center. Look for *Thermalair,* a free publication listing current goings-on, which you'll find in many hotels and in the tourist offices, and check the evening newspaper, the *Daily Post,* for day-to-day events. Tourist information is also available at the **AA Travel Centre,** 59 Amohau St. (☎ **07/348-3069**).

• **Telephone** The telephone area code (STD) for Rotorua is **07.**

The first tourists in Rotorua were Maori, members of the Arawa tribe whose seagoing canoe reached the shores of the Bay of Plenty sometime during the 14th century. Pushing inland to Lake Rotorua, they stayed on as settlers. Today's tourist will find some 5,000 of their descendants happily following much of the traditional tribal lifestyle in the largest area in New Zealand that is both preserved and promoted as a showcase for pre-European culture.

Those early arrivals found the area ideally suited to settlement. Nature supplied not only everything they needed for survival, but threw in mysterious volcanic cones, large, deep lakes, and all those steaming thermal pools as natural habitats for innumerable Maori spirit gods who, of course, were unseen passengers in the Arawa canoe as it crossed the Pacific. There's a Maori legend centered on the antics of the gods to be told about almost every one of the natural wonders you'll see in Rotorua.

Because Rotorua sits right in the middle of the most intense activity (that explains the strong smell of sulfur here), overheated water will bubble up all around you in the form of geysers, mud pools, or steam bores. You'll bathe in it, see the locals cooking with it, stay in guesthouses that are heated with it, or simply walk carefully around the boiling mud pools, watching their performance.

Just as fascinating is the gallery of Maori culture through which you'll wander. In song and dance you'll hear some of those legends firsthand; at a hangi feast you'll taste food cooked in a centuries-old manner; in a model Maori village you'll watch the younger generation learning carving and weaving from their elders. And in shops you'll find a good assortment of craft items.

Tours are numerous, well planned, and not too expensive—this is, after all, perhaps the North Island's major tourist town, and you may be sure that whatever you want to do or see, someone will have devised an easy, inexpensive way for you to do it.

GETTING AROUND The **Rotorua Sightseeing Shuttle** (☎ **347-7555** or **025/957-399**) will get you to the major attractions. A half-day pass costs NZ$15 (U.S. $9.75) and a full-day pass is NZ$22 (U.S. $14.30); children are charged half price.

There are city and suburban **buses,** but they're infrequent (about one an hour) on weekdays and nonexistent on weekends. Coach tours are another option for seeing the sights.

You'll find **taxi** stands at the Information Centre and on Fenton Street near the Ansett office, or you can call a cab (☎ **348-5079**).

What to See & Do

SIGHTS & ATTRACTIONS

In & Near Town

Most major attractions are offered on tours, though you can visit them on your own, especially those in downtown Rotorua, such as the Bath-House (formerly known as Tudor Towers), the Government Gardens, and Ohinemutu. Narrowing down your choices of which places to visit is difficult, so it'll really help to go to the Visitor Information Centre and look at their short video of attractions to get an idea of what each is like. Heavy rainfall increases geothermal activity, so showers won't necessarily dampen your sightseeing here.

Government Gardens.

Reigning over this downtown city park is the stately **Bath-House,** one of New Zealand's oldest buildings (1906) and built as a fashionable bathhouse, the largest in the country, along European spa lines. The gardens themselves are a lovely mix of rose gardens (lit at night), croquet and bowling lawns, and steaming thermal pools. They're a delightful in-town resting spot, and the Bath-House provides worthwhile sightseeing. Inside, you'll find the **Rotorua Art and History Museum,** displaying paintings of both local and international artists as well as a significant collection of Maori carvings and artifacts and the unique history of the volcanic plateau.

Admission: NZ$2 (U.S. $1.30).

Open: Gardens, daily dawn–dusk; Bath-House/museum, daily 10am–4:30pm.

Polynesian Pools, in the Government Gardens, Hinemoa St. ☎ **348-1328.**

A chief attraction at the Gardens is the Polynesian Pools, overlooking the lake. Here you can experience the mineral pools at your leisure, for as long as you choose, and can rent a bathing costume (swimsuit) and towel, if necessary. There are pools open to the sky, enclosed pools, and private pools. The soft alkaline water in the large pool maintains a constant temperature of about 100°F, while the smaller pools (reached along wooden walkways) contain water high in sulfur and magnesium—very good for sore muscles—at temperatures of 90° to 110°F. Private pools are available for NZ$8 (U.S. $5.20) per adult for half an hour, as well as gentle water massage for NZ$37.50 (U.S. $24.40). There's a licensed café and a well-stocked souvenir shop. You can rent a swimsuit and towel for NZ$2 (U.S. $1.30) each, plus a locker for NZ$1 (U.S. 65¢). Just beyond the reception area, be sure to take a look at the excellent mural of the migration of Polynesians from Hawaiki.

Admission: NZ$7 (U.S. $4.55) adults, NZ$2 (U.S. $1.30) children.

Open: Daily 6:30am–10pm.

★ **Ohinemutu,** about half a mile north of Rotorua.

This is the suburb where the largest Arawa subtribe, the Ngatiwhakaue, dwells. Although the residences are very much in the Pakeha style—small, everyday bungalows—the lifestyle follows tribal custom. On a *marae* (open courtyard, or clearing) stands the beautifully hand-carved **Tamatekapua meetinghouse.** This is where most tribal matters are discussed and important decisions made; concerts are also held here every night. Homes are thermally heated, and in every backyard you'll see the steam ovens where much of the family cooking is done.

Perhaps the most outstanding structure in Ohinemutu is ★ **St. Faith's Anglican Church,** a remarkable representation of the Pakeha Christian faith as interpreted through Maori art. The Tudor-style church building is a revelation of Maori color, intricate carving, exquisite scrollwork, and even an integration of ancient Maori religions, as represented by the figures of mythical demigods and their primitive subjects, which are carved in the base of the pulpit. There's a lovely, truly spiritual blending of the two cultures in a magnificent plate-glass window looking out to the lake; the window shows a full-size figure of Christ haloed and clad in a Maori cloak of kiwi feathers, appearing to be walking on the lake. It was sandblasted by a local Pakeha artist, Mr. Mowbray, and in the figure's stance he captured the unmistakable dignity and grace of Maori chieftains. A visit to St. Faith's is a touching, memorable experience.

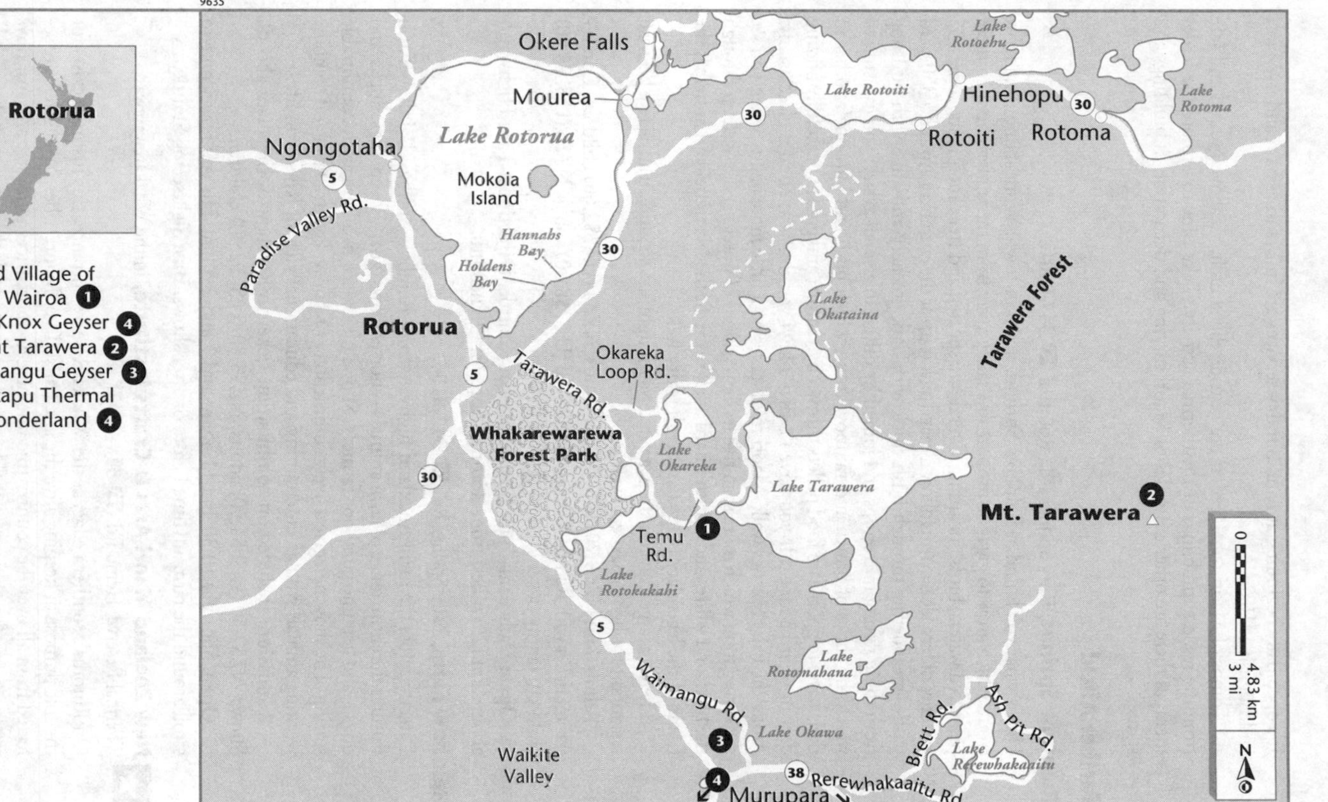

Rotorua & Environs

It's open daily beginning at 8am. Sunday services are in Maori at 8am and in Maori and English at 10am.

Tombs of Maori tribal leaders are outside the church, all above ground and safe from the restless rumblings of the thermal activity. Take time to explore the settlement, as there are other examples of Maori carving and decoration in buildings and statues.

Farther Afield

Rainbow Springs, Fairy Springs Rd., Rotorua. ☎ **347-9301.**

Here's what you'll find at Rainbow Springs, north of town: World-famous rainbow trout, which grow to gigantic proportions safely away from the angler's hook in these protected waters; birds, including several rare species; and trees and plants, some 135 varieties of fern alone. You follow a map (pick it up at the entrance) around a 350-yard path—meandering through bush thick with dark greenery and alive with birdsong from those resting in treetops and joined by others in a small aviary; you can stop to watch the antics of brown and rainbow trout, which push and butt one another in their haste to gobble up food pellets thrown by visitors, and gaze at peacefully grazing deer in their paddock. If you haven't seen a kiwi yet, this is as good a place as any. Along the Fairy Springs walk, Maori myth takes on a little more reality when you see the spring from which more than five million gallons of water per day well up through the black and white sands. It isn't hard at all to credit the Maori belief that here is the home of the legendary Patupaiarehe, the fairy folk.

There's a large souvenir shop, a cafeteria for light snacks, and an attractive licensed restaurant for light, inexpensive meals.

Admission: NZ$9.70 (U.S. $6.30) adults, NZ$4 (U.S. $2.60) children. Combination ticket with Rainbow Farm, NZ$13.50 (U.S. $8.80) adults, NZ$6 (U.S. $3.90) children; family ticket NZ$26 (U.S. $16.90).

Open: Daily 8am–5pm. **Bus:** Sightseeing Shuttle. **Directions:** Take Highway 5 about 4km (2½ miles) from Rotorua, north of Ohinemutu.

Rainbow Farm, Fairy Springs Rd. ☎ **347-8104.**

Directly across the main Auckland highway from Rainbow Springs, Rainbow Farm features the entire range of farm animals—horses, cows, goats, sheep, pigs, ducks, and dogs—and genuine gumboot farmers. Shows take place in a barn with comfortable seating. The showmen give a lively commentary of a busy day on a farm and combine working animals with an entertaining and educational view of Kiwi farm life.

Admission: Included on combination ticket to Rainbow Springs (see above). Shows, NZ$7.50 (U.S. $4.90) adults, NZ$3.50 (U.S. $2.30) children.

Open: Shows at 10:30 and 11:45am and 1 and 2:30pm, but you're welcome to stroll around the farm anytime before or after shows. **Bus:** Sightseeing Shuttle.

New Zealand Maori Arts & Crafts Institute, in the Whakarewarewa Thermal Reserve, Hemo Rd. ☎ **348-9047.**

On Rotorua's southern edge, at the Whaka Reserve entrance, this institute exists for the sole purpose of keeping alive the ancient skills of Maori tribes. Youngsters are selected from all over the country to come here as apprentices to master artisans: Boys study carving for a minimum of three years, after which they may take their newly acquired skills back to their own tribes or stay on to become teachers at the institute; girls learn to weave traditional cloaks and make distinctive flax skirts and intricately

Downtown Rotorua

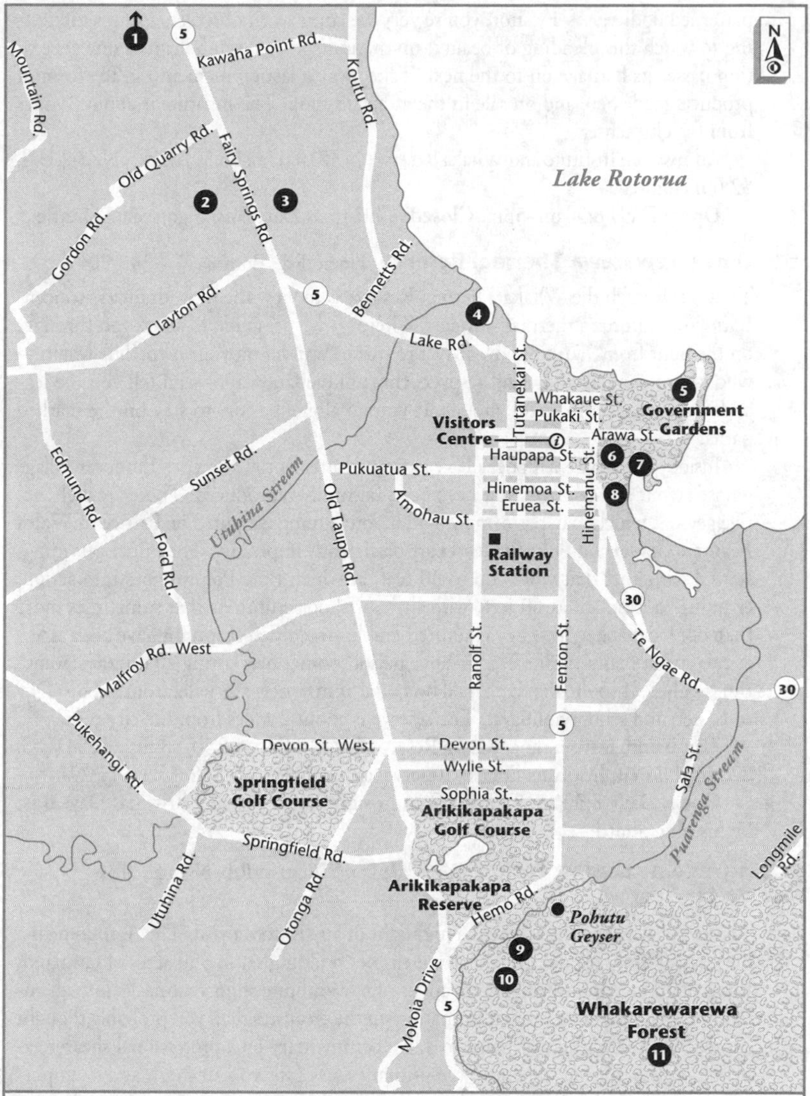

Information ⓘ

- Agrodome Leisure Park 1
- The Bath-House 6
- Government Gardens 5
- New Zealand Maori Arts & Crafts Institute 9
- Ohinemutu 4
- Polynesian Pools 8
- Rainbow Farm 3
- Rainbow Springs 2
- Rotorua Art and History Museum 7
- Whakarewarewa Forest 11
- Whakarewarewa Thermal Reserve 10

patterned bodices. As a visitor, you're very welcome as an observer, and it's interesting to watch this blending of beauty, myth, and spiritual symbolism as one generation passes its heritage on to the next. Take away a lasting memento in the form of products made here and on sale in the attached shop. The institute is about 2 miles from the city center.

Admission: Institute and Whaka Reserve, NZ$10 (U.S. $6.50) adults, NZ$4 (U.S. $2.60) children.

Open: Daily 8:30am–5pm. **Closed:** Christmas Day. **Bus:** Sightseeing Shuttle.

Whakarewarewa Thermal Reserve, Hemo Rd., Rotorua. ☎ **348-9047.**

To walk through the Whaka Thermal Reserve is to view the most dramatic concentration of Rotorua's thermal wonders. There's a Maori guide to show you through, on the hour from 9am to 4pm, or you're free to wander on your own. The Maori—who knows, understands, and respects this unique landscape—can tell you the legends that interpret its many moods. If you go alone, be sure to stay on the marked paths.

Inside the reserve is a model village patterned after Rotowhio, a pre-European village whose layout and construction have been faithfully reproduced. There are eight active geysers, which may perform for you if your timing is right. The **Prince of Wales Feathers Geyser** and **Pohutu Geyser** are particularly impressive. The Prince gets things started with a jet that works up to 30 feet, at which time Pohutu goes into action, erupting to as much as 60 feet, with little offshoot eruptions that sometimes more than double that height. They're unpredictable—recorded eruptions have been as few as two and as many as nine in a 24-hour period, sometimes lasting 20 minutes, sometimes only 5. If you're lucky, there'll be a 12:15pm concert (usually from Labour Day to Easter, and school holidays). The reserve is about 2 miles from the city center.

Admission: Institute and Whaka Reserve, NZ$10 (U.S. $6.50) adults, NZ$4 (U.S. $2.60) children; Institute, Whaka Reserve, and concert, NZ$18 (U.S. $11.70).

Open: Daily 8:30am–5pm (to 6pm in summer). **Closed:** Christmas Day. **Bus:** Sightseeing Shuttle.

Agrodome Leisure Park, in Riverdale Park, Western Rd., Ngongotaha. ☎ **357-4350.**

The award-winning show here is a highlight of any Rotorua visit. The Agrodome is a huge (12,000 sq. ft.) octagonal natural-timber building set in 350 acres of farmland. Rams of 19 breeds of sheep are the focus of a 60-minute show that packs into an entertaining commentary more information on the creatures than you probably thought existed. Each ram walks on stage to a live commentary by a professional shearer explaining the origins of the breed, the primary uses of its wool or meat, and its importance to New Zealand's sheep industry. When all 19 are on stage, the master shearer explains the tricks of his trade and proceeds to demonstrate his skill. The sheep dogs are then whistled in and put through their paces, and the audience is invited to meet the dogs and rams and pose for photos with the stars. Then it's everyone outside for a dog trial by a strong-eye dog and a huntaway dog and three stubborn sheep.

Facilities include a farmyard nursery and licensed restaurant. Also available are horse rides and farm tours to a kiwifruit orchard and deer paddock. Incidentally, the sheepskin shop at the Agrodome has been the source of two of my most-prized New Zealand purchases—both the selection and the prices are excellent. The site is 4 miles north of Rotorua on State Highway 5.

Admission: NZ$9 (U.S. $5.85) adults, NZ$4.50 (U.S. $2.95) children; 10% family discount for adults with schoolage children. Horse rides, NZ$15 (U.S. $9.75) for 30 minutes; farm tours, NZ$8 (U.S. $5.20).

Open: Shows daily at 9:15am, 11am, and 2:30pm (additional shows during heavy tourist seasons). **Bus:** Sightseeing Shuttle.

Whakarewarewa Forest, Long Mile Rd., off Tarawera Rd., Rotorua. ☎ **346-2082.**

This popular forest on the outskirts of town has walking, mountain biking, and horseriding tracks through many types of trees. You'll see majestic California redwoods dedicated to the men of New Zealand's Forest Service who gave their lives in both world wars. Look for the network of color-coded walking tracks throughout, all starting from the Visitors Centre. The center has a helpful staff, interesting displays, and variety of woodcrafts for gifts and souvenirs.

Admission: Free.

Open: Visitors Centre, Mon–Fri 8:30am–5pm, Sat–Sun and holidays 10am–4pm.

Other Activities

For a lofty view of Rotorua, the lakes, and the steamy landscape surrounding them, take the **Skyline Skyride,** Fairy Spring Road (☎ **347-0027**). You ascend some 2,975 feet in a glass-enclosed gondola. The charge is NZ$10 (U.S. $6.50) for adults, NZ$4 (U.S. $2.60) for children.

If you're intrigued by mazes, there's a terrific one about 10 minutes from the city. The **Fairbank Maze,** on Highway 30, near the airport on Te Ngae Road (☎ **345-4089**), has about a mile of pathways—and it's even accessible to wheelchairs. Admission is a mere NZ$3 (U.S. $1.95) for adults, half price for children. It's open daily from 9am to 6pm.

Golf courses in the area include the Springfield Golf Club (☎ **348-2748**), the Lake View Golf Club (☎ **357-1234**), and the Rotorua Golf Club (☎ **348-4051**).

If you've the urge to do as the black swans do and get out on Lake Rotorua, hop aboard the ***Lakeland Queen,*** which offers morning or afternoon tea, lunch, and dinner cruises. The paddlewheeler is fully licensed, and all but the dinner cruise bring you close to Mokoia Island, where legendary lovers Hinemoa and Tutanekai met. The morning tea cruise departs at 9:50am. The luncheon buffet cruise (NZ$25/U.S. $16.25) leaves at 12:30pm, and the dinner buffet cruise (NZ$42.50/U.S. $27.65), including live entertainment, starts at 6 and 8pm. Book at the office on the lakefront (☎ **348-6634**).

You can see the lake in other ways too—consider from a **helicopter, floatplane, small airplane,** or **fishing boat.** It's a splurge, for sure, but to find out more, inquire at the Visitors Centre or at the lakefront. These same sources can help you make contact with a fishing guide.

Other Excursions

You can drive yourself to the thermal areas around Rotorua or take a guided tour. **Carey's** (☎ **347-1199**) operates a wide variety of half- and full-day excursions. Coaches depart from all accommodations and the Visitors Information Centre.

The full-day ★ **Waimangu Round Trip** is the best known and most comprehensive. And even though it entails a 5km (3-mile) walk through steamy Waimangu Valley, unless you're really infirm it shouldn't be too strenuous. Just be sure to wear comfortable walking shoes. Bus departure is from your lodging at various times or the Visitors Information Centre at 8:45am, and you'll return at 5pm. A picnic lunch and entrance to Polynesian Pools are provided. The fare is NZ$125 (U.S. $81.25) for adults, NZ$65 (U.S. $42.25) for children, but you'll cover 42 miles and the better portion of Rotorua's history. Tours operate daily.

Heading south past the Whaka Reserve, you pass **Earthquake Flat** and a crater lake, which changes hue from green to blue every 36 hours, en route to **Waimangu Geyser.** Stilled now, it erupted regularly during the first four years of this century, spewing rocks and earth as far as 1,500 feet and claiming four lives before it fell silent. Its crater gave one gigantic three-day-long gasp in 1917, exploding with such violence that it flung debris as far as 1,000 feet. Two weeks later the crater began to fill with water, and in a short time a 6-acre boiling lake was formed, which has been aptly named **Frying Pan Lake.** Temperatures of the water from subterranean springs that feed it average 210°F at the surface, 315°F in the depths.

From the lake you strike out on foot for 2$^1/_2$ miles to **Mount Tarawera,** which erupted in 1886 to destroy the famous pink and white silica terraces that had been a popular tourist attraction. Six European visitors lost their lives, and the 800-foot-deep hot Rotomahana Lake was formed. A launch takes you out on the lake, past steaming cliffs, which are stratified with brilliant colors. At the end of the launch cruise, there's another half-mile walk to **Lake Tarawera,** one of the largest in the area and famed for its fishing. After a 7-mile cruise across the lake, with clear views of Mount Tarawera's blasted summit, you're met by coach to travel on to the nearby **Buried Village of Te Wairoa,** which perished in the Mount Tarawera eruption and has been excavated and well preserved. You'll also see the **Wairere Falls,** which descend 150 feet in three stages. The drive back to Rotorua passes both the **Green and Blue Lakes** and the **Redwood Grove Forest.** One suggestion: Those soothing, hot Polynesian Pools may be the perfect end to a full and satisfying day.

Carey's other excursions go to Hell's Gate and Waiotapu.

Not as well known perhaps as Waimangu, the **Waiotapu Thermal Wonderland,** 2$^1/_2$ miles beyond Waimangu on Highway 5, is the most colorful of all the thermal areas, sporting hues of yellow, gold, ochre, salmon, orange, and green. It also claims the largest mud pool in the southern hemisphere (you only see about a third of it) and the **Lady Knox Geyser,** which spouts off at 10:15am every day when it's "fed" soap. Some of the highlights include the Champagne Pool, complete with bubbles and fizz; the Artist's Palette, which changes constantly; the Opal Pool, which has a vibrant color; the Terraces, where you'll feel as if you're walking on water; and the Maori Sacred Track—all well marked on the map you're given. This thermal reserve has been a family business since 1931. A snack bar and souvenir shop are on the premises. There's something special about this place—allow time to enjoy it. You can get a local bus to Waiotapu, but it's a bit of a hike into the thermal park. It's open daily from 8:30am to 6pm (to 4pm in winter); admission is NZ$8.50 (U.S. $5.55) for adults and NZ$3 (U.S. $1.95) for children.

SHOPPING

I've already mentioned the excellent shop out at the Agrodome, and you'll find other good shops at Rainbow Springs and Rainbow Farm—in addition to the shopping option offered at the Maori Arts & Crafts Institute. The **Great New Zealand Shop** in the Tourism Rotorua complex is another possibility.

You might also want to look at **Penny's Souvenirs,** at the corner of Hinemoa and Hinemaru streets (☎ **348-5787**), opposite the Quality Resort, for a selection of carvings, greenstone and paua items, sheepskins, and general souvenirs, as well as

T-shirts. Owner Reg Durrant will open after normal hours for a group, a great convenience if you just can't fit shopping into a day of sightseeing. Open daily until 6:30pm.

Where to Stay

Rotorua is replete with accommodations in all shapes, sizes, and price ranges. In addition to major hotels, there are more than 100 motels and 15 motor camps. Those in the budget range are among the best you'll find in this category anywhere in the country. Indeed, don't expect Rotorua to conform to the usual popular resort image of "charging what the traffic will bear for the least service we can get away with"—this is a resort of a different stripe, one where prices are moderate, service is friendly and efficient, and accommodations standards are exceptionally high.

The prices listed below include GST.

MOTELS

Aarangi Lodge Motel, 287 Fenton St. (at Grey St.), Rotorua. ☎ and fax **07/348-5056.** 3 units (all with bath). TV TEL **Transportation:** Courtesy car on request.

Rates: NZ$70 (U.S. $45.50) unit for two; NZ$100 (U.S. $65) unit for four. MC, V.

Readers praise the helpfulness of Alan and Elaine Barker, the owners of this motel, which feels more like a private house. Each apartment unit has a sitting area, two bedrooms, and a kitchen. Facilities include a hot mineral pool and a laundry, and the Barkers will supply continental or cooked breakfast on request. The Aarangi Lodge is close to the town center.

Acacia Lodge Motel, 40 Victoria St., Rotorua. ☎ **07/348-7089.** Fax 07/346-1104. 18 rms (all with bath), 8 suites. TV TEL **Transportation:** Courtesy-car service to/from the airport and bus station.

Rates: NZ$65 (U.S. $42.25) single; NZ$75 (U.S. $48.75) double; NZ$82 (U.S. $53.30) suite. AE, BC, DC, MC, V.

At this pretty motel, Jon and Marie Dehnen offer brick rooms with large picture windows and colorful flower boxes. Each has full kitchen facilities, a radio, and central heat; some have water beds, and there are some family units. Other amenities include a sauna, mineral pools, a nice play area, and laundry facilities. The peaceful location is near the city center and sightseeing attractions, and the Dehnens are happy to arrange tours for their guests.

Ambassador Thermal Motel, Whakaue and Hinemaru sts. (P.O. Box 1212), Rotorua. ☎ **07/347-9581.** Fax 07/348-5281. 19 units (all with bath). TV TEL

Rates: NZ$72 (U.S. $46.80) single; NZ$85.50 (U.S. $55.60) double. Best Western and auto club discounts available. AE, MC, V.

A short walk from the lakefront and town, the Ambassador is an attractive three-story white building with arched covered balconies and apartments, some of which have ceilings with exposed beams. There are two private thermal pools, a swirl pool, an outdoor freshwater pool, and a games room with a pool table. Restaurants and a host of attractions are within easy walking distance in this central but quiet location where John Scott is the friendly host. The motel is opposite the Queen Elizabeth Hospital.

Bel Aire Motel, 257 Fenton St., Rotorua. ☎ and fax **07/348-6076.** 8 units (all with bath).

TV TEL **Transportation:** The owners will pick up and deliver guests to the airport or bus terminal.

Rates: NZ$49.50 (U.S. $32.20) apartment for one; NZ$65 (U.S. $42.25) apartment for two. AE, DC, V.

A reader from Australia wrote to tell me about the Bel Aire, and his recommendation certainly stood the test of close inspection. This centrally located small motel offers spotless, recently renovated one- and two-bedroom apartments that sleep two to seven people, each with a full kitchen, geothermal heating, a radio, and video. There's a hot mineral pool, as well as a guest laundry and drying room, and owner/operators Lois and Brian Aickin can furnish breakfast on request.

Boulevard Motel, Fenton and Seddon sts., Rotorua. ☎ **07/348-2074.** Fax 07/348-2072. 30 rms (all with bath). TV TEL

Rates: NZ$56 (U.S. $36.40) standard apartment for one or two; NZ$81 (U.S. $52.65) apartment with spa pool for one or two. AE, DC, MC, V.

The Boulevard is set on 2 acres of landscaped grounds and is family-owned and -operated by the Bradshaws. The two-story, balconied white motel in the town center also has a restaurant on the premises. The apartment units—accommodating one to nine people—have a separate sitting area and one to three bedrooms; are beautifully furnished, with complete kitchen; and have central heating. There are serviced units (sleeping two), which are smaller and have tea-making facilities and a fridge. Some apartments have water beds; others have spa pools. Those lovely grounds are set about with garden furniture and hold a multitude of recreational facilities: a putting green, a swimming pool, four spa baths, swirl pools, sauna, and games room. There's a laundry, dryer, and steam iron for guest use. Readers have commented on the good restaurant.

Motel Sulphur City, 241 Fenton St., Rotorua. ☎ **07/348-6513.** Fax 07/347-7400. 7 units (all with bath). TV TEL **Transportation:** The owners will pick up guests at the train or bus station.

Rates: From NZ$65 (U.S. $42.25) apartment for one or two. Auto club discount. AE, DC, MC, V.

Owner/operators John and Jan Walker offer standard motel apartments with full kitchen and sitting area, as well as one- and two-bedroom units. There's parking just outside each unit and a private hot pool. Cooked or continental breakfast is available. It's a five-minute walk from the town center.

Studio Motel, 315-A Fenton St., Rotorua. ☎ **07/346-0867,** or toll free **0800/101-966** in New Zealand. Fax 07/347-2822. 5 units (all with bath). TV TEL

Rates: NZ$50–NZ$75 (U.S. $32.50–$48.75) apartment for one or two. AE, DC, MC, V.

This economy-priced motel in town has attractive one- and two-bedroom apartments that can sleep up to four, as well as a spa pool and laundry. The hosts are Len and Diane Berryman. It's a good idea to reserve ahead.

Tom's Motel, 6 Union St., Rotorua. ☎ **07/347-8062.** Fax 07/347-0078. 10 units. TV TEL **Transportation:** Courtesy car available.

Rates: NZ$60–NZ$80 (U.S. $39–$52) unit for one or two. Discount for seniors over age 60. AE, DC, MC, V.

Tidy, quiet, and economical, Tom's Motel has five studios and five one-bedroom units (for up to five people), each with a kitchen. There's also an outdoor pool, an indoor spa pool, a laundry, and car-wash facilities. Breakfast is available on request. This location near the center of town is an ideal sightseeing base for the area, since the longer your stay, the lower the rate. The hosts are Dorothy and John Belton.

BED-&-BREAKFASTS

$ **Eaton Hall,** 39 Hinemaru St., Rotorua. ☎ and fax **07/347-0366.** 8 rms (none with bath).

Rates (including cooked breakfast): NZ$45 (U.S. $29.25) single; NZ$68 (U.S. $44.20) double; NZ$90 (U.S. $58.50) triple. BC, MC, V.

Colin and Maureen Brown have filled this two-story guesthouse in the center of town with comfortable furnishings (some antiques), old china, and lots of bric-a-brac. All the bedrooms have sinks. There's a cozy TV lounge, with coffee and tea available. A bonus here is that the hosts, as ticket agents, can organize and sell tickets for sightseeing attractions, fishing trips, concerts, and sightseeing flights. Colin will take guests on tours for reasonable rates.

$ **Tresco International Guest House,** 3 Toko St., Rotorua. ☎ and fax **07/348-9611.** 7 rms (none with bath). **Transportation:** Courtesy car available.

Rates (including breakfast): NZ$45 (U.S. $29.25) single; NZ$68 (U.S. $44.20) double; NZ$88 (U.S. $57.20) triple. BC, V.

Barrie Fenton and Gay Scott-Fenton own and operate this guesthouse with attractive, sparkling-clean rooms with hot and cold running water and tea- and coffee-making facilities. The guesthouse is only one block from the city center, and there's a homey, happy air about the place. In addition to off-street parking, there's a guest laundry, a TV lounge, and a mineral plunge pool. If you stay here, your day will start with a substantial continental or cooked breakfast.

HOSTELS

Ivanhoe Lodge, 54 Haupapa St. (just off Tutanekai St.), Rotorua. ☎ **07/348-6985.** 65 beds (no rooms with bath).

Rates: NZ$30 (U.S. $19.50) double; NZ$14 (U.S. $9.10) dorm bed. MC, V.

This lodge in the center of town offers budget, hostel-type accommodations. There are single, twin, and double cabins, all heated, plus single, twin, and double rooms. Linen and blankets are available for a small fee. All cabins and rooms are carpeted, with mirrors and dressers. The facilities are all communal: a fully equipped modern kitchen, large dining or common room (with a brilliant mural of the area), hot thermal pool, TV lounge, and games room.

$ **YHA Hostel,** Eruera and Hinemaru sts., Rotorua. ☎ **07/347-6810.** Fax 07/349-1426. 68 beds (no rooms with bath).

Rates: NZ$18 (U.S. $11.70) per person double; NZ$14 (U.S. $9.10) dorm bed. NZ$4 (U.S. $2.60) extra for nonmembers. MC, V.

This hostel is just about the best buy in Rotorua. It's a large, comfortable building, accommodating 68 people in 18 rooms, and there are family rooms. There's a well-equipped kitchen, a provisions shop, laundry facilities and irons, a TV lounge, a recreation room, and a thermal pool. It's situated right in town.

CABINS & CAMPGROUNDS

The $ **Holdens Bay Holiday Park,** 21 Robinson Ave., Holdens Bay (P.O. Box 9), Rotorua (☎ and fax **07/345-9925**), only 6km (3½ miles) from Rotorua, has a pretty setting very near Lake Rotorua. On the extensive grounds, there are tent and caravan sites, tourist cabins (bring your own linens and blankets), and modern tourist apartments (just bring yourself), as well as a swimming pool, volleyball court, hot spa pools, a store, children's play area, laundry, TVs for rent, a barbecue, car wash, and games room. Rates are NZ$10 (U.S. $6.50) per person for tent and caravan sites, NZ$25 (U.S. $16.25) double for standard cabins, NZ$36 (U.S. $23.40) double for tourist cabins, and NZ$55 (U.S. $35.75) for tourist flats for two people, all including GST.

Besides being secluded, right on the lake and only a little over a mile from downtown Rotorua, the **Lakeside Motor Camp,** 54 Whittaker Rd., Rotorua (☎ **07/348-1693**), has an abundance of trees, swings and a trampoline, a games and TV room, mineral pool, showers, laundry, communal kitchen, natural steam cooker, car wash, and camp store. Swimming, boating, fishing, and waterskiing are all at your doorstep. All units have full cooking facilities, and you supply linen and blankets. Tent sites are NZ$8 (U.S. $5.20) per person; van sites, NZ$18 (U.S. $11.70) for two people; on-site caravans, NZ$30 (U.S. $19.50) for two; cabins, NZ$35 (U.S. $22.75) for two; apartments, NZ$49 (U.S. $31.85) for two; and chalets, NZ$55 (U.S. $35.75) for two. The gate to the property closes at 11pm for security reasons.

A FARM STAY

★ **Te Ana Farm,** Poutakataka Rd., Ngakuru (R.D. 1), Rotorua.
☎ and fax **07/333-2720.** 3 rms (2 with bath).

$ **Rates** (including cooked breakfast): NZ$60 (U.S. $39) single; NZ$90 (U.S. $58.50) double. Three-course dinner with wine NZ$25 (U.S. $16.25). No credit cards.

After more than a dozen trips to new Zealand, a few places stand out in my mind as being really exemplary, and Te Ana is one of them. Heather and Brian Oberer have been welcoming guests to their 569-acre dairy, beef, sheep, goat, and deer farm for more than 13 years, and yet they meet each new face with enthusiasm and genuine warmth. Two bedrooms are in the house, adjacent to the guest lounge where there are coffee- and tea-making facilities, a TV, and a good supply of reading material. The room with twin beds has a large bathroom; the queen-size room shares the hosts' bathroom. A cottage in the garden offers another two bedrooms and a bathroom. Heather's gourmet meals are legendary: Dinner might start with an appetizer of salmon mousse, followed by a main course of chicken and apricots in puff pastry accompanied by fresh veggies from the garden. If you're lucky, she'll make pavlova for dessert. Te Ana is situated in a picturesque valley 32km (20 miles) south of Rotorua. It's bounded by Lake Ohakuri, and the Oberers make a canoe and fishing rod available for those who want them. Brian takes folks on four-wheel-drive farm tours and for walks across the property. Guests are also welcome to watch their 145 cows being milked. There's no smoking in the house.

WORTH THE EXTRA MONEY

Hotels

★ **Prince's Gate Hotel,** 1 Arawa St. (P.O. Box 112), Rotorua. ☎ **07/348-1179.**
Fax 07/348-6215. 52 rms and apartments (all with bath). MINIBAR TV TEL

$ **Rates:** NZ$113 (U.S. $73.45) single; NZ$135 (U.S. $87.75) double; NZ$200 (U.S. $130) apartment. Complimentary continental breakfast for guests who are *Frommer's New Zealand* readers. AE, BC, DC, MC, V.

This hotel was constructed in Waihi (95 miles to the north) in 1897 and was a popular spot there until 1909, when the townfolk voted in prohibition and all the pubs were closed. The building sat idle until 1919, when it was dismantled and transported by bullock cart to its present location. Today it's an attractive boutique hotel offering an old-world atmosphere, comfortable accommodations, friendly service, and a central location adjacent to the Government Gardens. Facilities include a guest laundry, health complex, thermal baths, tennis court, sauna, plunge pool, bike rental, and a restaurant, bar, and café with indoor/outdoor seating. A convention center is under construction across the street. No-smoking rooms are available, and all rooms have tea- and coffee-making facilities and hairdryers. Room service is available 18 hours a day. Brett Marvelly is a great host.

Regal Geyserland Hotel, Fenton St., Rotorua. ☎ **07/348-2039.** Fax 07/348-2033. 65 rms (all with bath). A/C TV TEL

Rates: NZ$152 (U.S. $98.80) single or double. Children under 12 stay free in parents' room. Inquire about frequent two-day specials and weekend packages available May–Sept. AE, DC, MC, V.

What makes this place so special is its panoramic view of the Whakarewarewa Thermal Reserve, just outside the windows of most of its rooms. From your room with a window wall facing the reserve, you can watch the Pohutu Geyser shoot up as high as 50 feet in the air, and fascination with those steaming, bubbling mud pools will keep you posted at the window. The hotel itself has the usual luxury hotel trappings, with pretty and comfortable rooms, spa pools, a swimming pool, and a first-class restaurant. If you lean toward luxury hotels, this one is as good as any; but as I said, it's all that steam out there that makes it warrant space in a budget guide, so if you reserve, be sure to specify that you want a room overlooking the thermal reserve, not a poolside room.

THC Rotorua Hotel, Tyron and Froude sts., Rotorua. ☎ **07/348-1189.** Fax 07/347-1620. 124 rms (all with bath). A/C MINIBAR TV TEL

Rates: NZ$120–NZ$160 (U.S. $78–$104) single or double. Special two-day rates available periodically. AE, BC, DC, MC, V.

This hotel overlooks the fascinating thermal activity of the Whakarewarewa. It's also the setting of Rotorua's most popular hotel Maori hangi and concert each night, the only one in town that invites guests to witness the actual lifting of the hangi from its earthen oven. Guest rooms have tea- and coffee-making facilities and fridges. There are two bars and two excellent restaurants, as well as a heated swimming pool, guest laundry, and tour desk. This hotel is a big splurge that offers good value for the dollar.

Motels

Ledwich Lodge, 12–14 Lake Rd. (P.O. Box 2370), Rotorua. ☎ **07/347-0049,** or toll free **0800/730-049** in New Zealand. Fax 07/347-0048. 14 units (all with bath). TV TEL

Rates: NZ$88 (U.S. $57.20) single; NZ$100 (U.S. $65) double. Additional person NZ$15 (U.S. $9.75) extra. AE, DC, MC, V.

This motel is small, with a facade that doesn't draw attention to itself. The lake is its front yard and it's within walking distance of everything in town. It also has exceptionally pretty units with bay windows, bright tropical-print curtains, large baths with spa pools, queen-size beds covered with feather duvets, full kitchens, thermal heating, and lots of wood trim. In addition, there's a small thermally heated pool and a picnic area, and guests have access to a steam box for hangi-style cooking; breakfast is available. There are also two-bedroom units, as well as two apartments for the disabled.

Wylie Court Motor Lodge, 345 Fenton St., Rotorua. ☎ **07/347-7879,** or toll free **0800/100-879** in New Zealand. Fax 07/346-1494. 36 units (all with bath). A/C MINIBAR TV TEL **Transportation:** Courtesy car to/from the airport.

Rates: NZ$85 (U.S. $55.25) single; NZ$126 (U.S. $81.90) double. Flag international discounts available. AE, DC, MC, V.

One of Rotorua's most attractive motels, Wylie Court is set in 2½ landscaped acres on the outskirts of town. The two-story units are decorated in soft colors and have modern, comfortable furnishings. Each unit has a full living room with two convertible sofa beds, full kitchen, and bath on the ground floor; upstairs there's a mezzanine bedroom with a double bed (some have water beds). Each will sleep as many as four in comfort. What wins my heart completely, however, is the pretty roofed and fenced-in patio out back of each unit, with its own private heated plunge pool where you can soak to your heart's content whether or not there's a bathing suit in your luggage—sheer luxury!

Barry and Glen Johnston, their son, Tony, and his wife, Sharon, have provided loads of amenities: a heated swimming pool, a children's playground, a thermal pool, a guest laundry, in-room video, the daily newspaper delivered to your door, and a cooked or continental breakfast at a small additional charge. Highly recommended by readers both for its facilities and its genial hosts.

Where to Eat

Floyd's Café, 44 Haupapa St. ☎ **07/347-0024.**

Cuisine: MODERN NEW ZEALAND. **Reservations:** Not required.
Prices: Appetizers NZ$7–NZ$9 (U.S. $4.55–$5.85); main courses NZ$15–NZ$18 (U.S. $9.75–$11.70); average lunch NZ$10 (U.S. $6.50). AE, BC, DC, MC, V.
Open: Lunch Mon–Fri 11:30am–2:30pm; dinner Mon–Sat 6–9pm.

This place in the town center is hard to beat for moderately priced food that's well prepared and served in a casual atmosphere. The thick, chunky mussel chowder is a standout, as are their seafood crêpe, lasagne, lamb filets, and vegetarian phyllo. BYO.

Freos, at the lake end of Tutanekai St., next door to Lewisham's. ☎ **346-0976.**

Cuisine: MODERN NEW ZEALAND. **Reservations:** Recommended.
Prices: Appetizers NZ$6.50–NZ$9 (U.S. $4.25–$5.85); main courses NZ$8.50–NZ$22 (U.S. $5.55–$14.30). AE, BC, DC, MC, V.
Open: Daily 11am–11pm.

The ultra-plain decor of this modern café is a contrast to the interesting and very good food served here. You might like a Greek or Caesar salad, a venison or satay burger, paella, lamb or vegetable curry, or focaccia sandwich. They also offer three kinds of pasta and three steaks. If you'd like to bring your own, Arawa Wines & Spirits is right across the street. A children's menu is available. Licensed and BYOW.

Gazebo, 45 Pakuatua St. ☎ **348-1911.**

Cuisine: ITALIAN/GERMAN/FRENCH. **Reservations:** Recommended for dinner.
Prices: Main courses NZ$15.50–NZ$22 (U.S. $10.10–$14.30); lunch specials NZ$10 (U.S. $6.50). AE, DC, MC, V.
Open: Daily 10am–10pm.

This is a casual, cozy spot with a chalkboard menu, lots of greenery (as befits its name), and such specialties as vegetarian shashlik, pecan lamb parcels, ginger-lime venison medallions, rigatoni pasta with mushroom sauce, and pork loin continental. If you call in advance, they'll cook the fish you've hooked in local waters. Jazz plays continuously. BYO, but no smoking permitted. It's located in the town center.

$ **Legends Bar & Cafe,** in the Tourism Rotorua Visitor Information Centre Complex, 67 Fenton St. ☎ **349-3735.**

Cuisine: CAFE. **Reservations:** Not required.
Prices: Light meals NZ$2.50–NZ$8.95 (U.S. $1.65–$5.80). AE, BC, DC, MC, V.
Open: Sun–Mon 8am–6pm, Tues–Sat 8am–8:30pm. (Deliveries Tues–Sat 6–8:30pm.)

Rotorua's Visitor Information Centre gets my vote for being the best in the country, and one of the reasons is this attractive café. I think Tourism Rotorua should be congratulated for putting a reasonably priced licensed eatery in such a convenient location. The café is light and bright, with contemporary furnishings. Diners can sit at a bar or one of the 15 or so tables. Meals include lasagne, meat pies, quiche, pizza, fish and chips, and burgers. Legends also does take-out and serves a wide range of coffees and teas.

★ $ **Sirocco,** 86 Eruera St., across from the multiplex cinema. ☎ **347-3388.**

Cuisine: MEDITERRANEAN. **Reservations:** Not accepted.
Prices: Appetizers NZ$4.50–NZ$8.75 (U.S. $2.95–$5.70); main courses NZ$9.50–NZ$11.95 (U.S. $6.20–$7.75). AE, BC, DC, MC, V.
Open: Daily 11am–12:30am (later Fri–Sat).

Sirocco means a hot dry wind—the kind found in the Mediterranean, where most of the dishes served in the cozy coffee bar/café originate. This is really an old house that's been "done up" by the current owners. The bar is made of used brick, and there's a wooden mantel over the fireplace. Sample "entrees" (which I hope you realize by now are what Americans call appetizers) include warm smoked mussels with sun-dried tomato or focaccia bread with ham, cheese, avocado, and tomato. Sample mains courses include vegetarian ravioli, thin-cut scotch filet, and cotoleta Milano (lamb cutlet, tomato, and olive tapenade). Licensed and BYOW.

★ **Zanelli's Italian Cafe,** 23 Amohia St. ☎ **348-4908.**

Cuisine: ITALIAN. **Reservations:** Recommended.
Prices: Appetizers NZ$8.50 (U.S. $5.55); main courses NZ$15–NZ$18 (U.S. $9.75–$11.70). AE, DC, MC, V.
Open: Dinner Mon–Sat 6–10pm; late supper Mon–Sat 10pm–midnight.

Located in town, Zanelli's serves generous portions, and you can easily make do with an appetizer and salad. There's a whole chalkboard devoted to desserts. The atmosphere is lively, and three-quarters of the tables are no-smoking. This is Rotorua's most authentic Italian fare. BYO.

SPECIALTY DINING

TAKE-OUT FOOD For those times when eating in is a good idea either for budget or energy (at the end of a long sightseeing day) reasons, you have two good Rotorua alternatives. If you've a yen for fresh New Zealand specialties like marinated mussels, oysters, clams, or cooked lamb, hie yourself over to **Fenwick's Delicatessen** (☎ **347-0777**), next to the post office in Hinemoa Centre. It's chock-full of ready-to-eat goodies, as well as a wide selection of cheeses, hot barbecued rôtisserie chicken, salads, sweets, and a host of specialty goods, all at very good prices. Hours are 8am to 5:30pm Monday through Friday, until noon on Saturday; closed Sunday.

You'll have trouble passing the window at **Chez Suzanne Coffee Shop,** 61 Hinemoa St. (☎ **348-6495**), next to the *Daily Post* building, without going in. The selection of pastries and sandwiches is excellent, and they are exceedingly fresh. Beverages include cappuccino, espresso, and hot chocolate. This is a small place, with a few booths, a counter, and a few wooden tables with fresh flowers on them. Filled croissants are NZ$2.40 (U.S. $1.55) and sandwiches run NZ$1 to NZ$2.50 (U.S. 65¢ to $1.65). It's open Monday through Friday from 9am to 4pm and Saturday from 9:30am to 12:30pm; closed some Saturdays. Say hello to Sue Morice.

FAST FOOD On the theory that you can drop in for a Big Mac almost anywhere in the world, I don't normally send readers to **McDonald's.** In Rotorua, however, I recommend that you go by the one of the corner of Fenton and Amohau streets to view the exquisite wall-size carvings done by the Maori Arts & Crafts Institute. Best of all, they give you a free booklet beautifully illustrated with photos and Maori legends. Kudos to McDonald's for this recognition of indigenous culture.

WORTH THE EXTRA MONEY

Chapman's Restaurant, in the THC Rotorua Hotel, Froude St. ☎ **348-1189.**

Cuisine: SEAFOOD BUFFET. **Reservations:** Required.

Prices: Seafood buffet NZ$24 (U.S. $15.60) at lunch, NZ$29 (U.S. $18.85) at dinner. AE, DC, MC, V.

Open: Lunch daily noon–2:30pm; dinner daily from 6pm.

Lunch will most assuredly be your main meal of the day if you reserve for the elaborate seafood buffet here, overlooking the Whakarewarewa Reserve. Be sure to reserve early, for this endless supply of the freshest of seasonal seafoods is a great favorite with locals and other visitors alike. You'll leave knowing you've found real value for your dollars. Licensed. Dancing is available after dinner on Friday and Saturday. See "Evening Entertainment," below, for information on the hangi dinners offered here.

Lewisham's, 115 Tutanekai St. ☎ **348-1786.**

Cuisine: AUSTRIAN. **Reservations:** Recommended.

Prices: Main courses NZ$20–NZ$24 (U.S. $13–$15.60); average lunch NZ$15 (U.S. $9.75). AE, DC, MC, V.

Open: Lunch Mon and Wed–Fri noon–2pm; dinner Wed–Mon 6–10pm.

Set in a colonial cottage that was one of the first houses on Tutanekai Street, this cozy restaurant has an interior of exposed-brick fireplaces and antique furnishings. New Zealand specialties include pan-fried terekihi and South Island baby salmon with dill-and-cucumber sauce. Among the continental offerings, I favor both the champignon (mushroom) schnitzel and the Hungarian beef goulash. BYO.

READERS RECOMMEND

Poppy's Villa Restaurant, 4 Marguerita St. (☎ **347-1700**). *"We stumbled across an excellent restaurant in Rotorua. The presentation of the food and the selection of food were magnificent. The desserts were a work of art. We told them that they could compete with any restaurant in San Francisco, and we meant it."*—Nancy H. Bennett, Moraga, Calif., U.S.A.

Evening Entertainment

Check *Thermalair* for dine-and-dance venues or special events, or plan on a Maori concert with or without a hangi dinner.

MAORI CONCERTS & HANGI FEASTS

You'll find some show-stopper Maori concerts in the big hotels (see below), but for authenticity and insight into the Maori musical heritage you can't beat the nightly 8pm concert at the ★ **Tamatekapua meetinghouse** in Ohinemutu (☎ **349-3949**). The surroundings, for one thing, are authentic in this meetinghouse of the Arawa tribe, which opens to the public only at night. The singing group was founded by the elders of the tribe to help their young people learn to sing and perform the traditional songs. The performers are mostly 13 to 18 years old; the younger ones stand at the back and work their way forward over the years. Tickets are NZ$13 (U.S. $8.45) for adults, NZ$5 (U.S. $3.25) for children, and the money goes for the upkeep of the meetinghouse and to transport the youth abroad for singing engagements and festivals.

Hangi (earth oven) cooking is traditional with the Maori in preparing their communal meal. A large pit is filled with a wood fire topped by stones; then when the stones are heated through, baskets of food are placed on top and covered with damp cloths. Earth is then shoveled over all to create a natural steam oven. After about three hours, dinner is unveiled, with intermingling flavors of the various foods lightly touched by wood smoke.

There's a **hangi feast** every night of the year at the **THC Retorua Hotel** on Froude Street, on the edge of the Whakarewarewa Reserve (☎ **348-1189**). The NZ$45 (U.S. $29.25) tab would put this in the splurge category were it not for the fact that it includes an hour-long **Maori concert** featuring first-class performers. Tickets for the concert only cost NZ$15 (U.S. $9.75). Complimentary transport within Rotorua is provided.

Hangi preparations begin long before your scheduled arrival at 6pm. By 3pm the *ngawha* (natural Maori rock steamer) is being filled: Meats like wild pork, lamb, chicken, and venison go in first for longer cooking; vegetables such as pumpkin, kumara, potatoes, and watercress are placed on top. Don't show up any later than 6:15pm or you'll miss the **opening of the ngawha,** when a costumed Maori maiden lifts the food out with all due ceremony and leads a procession of food-bearing followers into the dining room, where it is spread on a buffet table. Accompaniments like marinated mussels, smoked eel, raw marinated fish, salads, Maori bread, and tamarillos (tree tomatoes) with fresh cream complete the eat-as-much-as-you-can-hold feast. The traditional hangi would never include desserts, but the THC provides sweets and Pakeha beverages (tea, coffee, and wine). By 7pm, all is ready for you to dig in. Enjoy!

At 8 o'clock, an outstanding troupe of Maori singers and dancers begins an hour-long concert of Polynesian dances, action songs, and pois. By any standards, this is a "money's worth" splurge.

A third concert option is provided by **Tamaki Tours** (☎ **346-2823**), a Maori-run business. They collect their guests from hotels and motels and transfer them to a *marae* (a sacred meeting place) just outside Rotorua. This evening is very special because of the cultural experiences to which the visitors are introduced. These include a *wero* (challenge), *hongi* (greeting), and *haka* (war dance). A traditional hangi dinner of native foods is served on the marae before the guests are driven back to their lodgings.

The all-inclusive cost is NZ$52 (U.S. $33.80) for adults, half price for children 5 to 12.

En Route to Taupo

The drive to Taupo is a short 84km (52 miles) over excellent roads. The Orakei Korako Geyserland is 45 minutes south of Rotorua. Eight kilometers (5 miles) before you reach Taupo, look for the steamy **Wairakei Geothermal Power Station,** which harnesses all that underground energy to furnish electrical power.

En Route to Gisborne

There are two ways of commencing the splendid East Cape drive from Rotorua: Head northeast on Highway 30 for Whakatane in the Bay of Plenty, a 57-mile drive; or take a detour, driving due north for 55 miles to Tauranga, then turning east on Highway 2 for the 62-mile stretch to Whakatane. I'd say that decision rests on where your own interests lie.

THE LONG ROUTE VIA TAURANGA & EAST CAPE ROAD

Tauranga, and its adjacent beach resort/port of Mount Maunganui, is now a peaceful center of citrus-fruit farming, but its history is one of fierce battles, both in intertribal Maori wars and between the British and Maori.

The **Visitors Information Centre,** on the Strand (☎ **07/578-8103**), can direct you to several interesting historical spots. Fishing trips can be organized easily from the wharf on the Strand.

Tauranga has 71,000 inhabitants; Mount Maunganui, only 11,000. This area is second only to Auckland in popularity among vacationing Kiwis, some 500,000 of whom come here every year, compared to 41,000 international visitors.

The gardens of the ✪ **Elms Mission House,** on Mission Street, built by an early missionary and one of the finest examples of colonial architecture of its time (1847), are open to the public Monday through Saturday from 9am to 6pm. The library dates from 1837 and is probably the oldest in the country. On the carefully tended grounds, you'll see kauri, rimu, and orange trees, along with kiwifruit orchards, a special treat if you haven't gotten to see any before now. It's highly recommended, and there's no admission charge.

If you like poking around old cemeteries, **Otemataha Pa** will be of interest. It was the burial ground for the Church Mission Society from 1835 to 1881, as well as for soldiers and sailors who died in the Land War in 1864–65. It's near the Mission House and just up the hill from **Robbins Park Rose Garden** and picnic area on Cliff Road.

Tauranga Historic Village, 155 17th Ave. W. (☎ **578-1302**), bows to the past with 14 acres of a re-created colonial village, with cobblestone streets, a blacksmith's shop, a military barracks, a Maori village, and much more. Rides by train, double-decker bus, or horse-drawn cart give another perspective. You'll find a tearoom and a licensed restaurant in the village—old-fashioned, of course. It's open daily year round from 10am to 4pm, with an admission of NZ$6 (U.S. $3.90). Weekends, when there's a craft market, are the best time to go.

Mount Maunganui, a leading port 5km (3 miles) from Tauranga, is best known and loved by thousands of Kiwis for its **Ocean Beach,** a stretch of golden sand along what is called the best surfing beach in New Zealand. (**Papamoa Beach,** on the other hand, is quieter.) The ✪ **walking track** around the mount takes about an hour. You can also climb to the top, for which you should allow a couple of hours. At the base of the mount, on Adams Avenue, are **hot saltwater pools** where, for a small admission fee, you can ease your aches away; there's swimsuit and towel rental for those who arrive unprepared. A fresh water supply fills the pools every three hours; open from 8am to 10pm daily year round.

About 19 miles south of Tauranga lies **Te Puke,** the "Kiwifruit Capital of the World," and **Kiwifruit Country (☎ 07/573-6340)**, a popular attraction that you'll recognize by the giant slice of fruit (a camouflaged observation tower) out front. Stop by—there's no admission charge to look around, and you can wander through the grounds and theme orchard, which features 60 different fruits and nuts, from macadamias to feijoas (try this local fruit if you can) to pomegranates. There's also an audiovidual show and children's playground. For a fee, you can take a half-hour tour of the working orchard and listen to a taped commentary. The fruit is harvested in May and June. Kiwifruit Country also has a children's playground; a gift shop featuring kiwifruit products; complimentary tasting of kiwifruit wines, liqueur, and apéritif; and a café featuring kiwi burgers and kiwifruit parfait.

From Highway 2 (a little over 27 miles east of Tauranga) on the drive to Whakatane you can take a short detour to the little settlement of **Maketu** and see the cairn that marks the Arawa canoe landing place, and also the Te Awhi-o-te-rangi meetinghouse, a beautiful example of Maori carvings. Tauranga makes an interesting prelude to the East Cape Drive if time permits.

Where to Stay in Tauranga

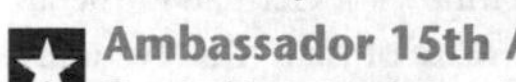

Ambassador 15th Avenue Motel, 9 15th Ave., Tauranga. **☎ 07/578-5665.** Fax 07/578-5226. 8 units (all with bath). TV TEL

Rates: NZ$68 (U.S. $44.20) single; NZ$79 (U.S. $51.35) double. AE, DC, MC, V.

You won't get a more pleasant welcome in Tauranga than at this small motel owned by Brian and Maureen Dudley. Facilities include plenty of flowers and gardens, an outdoor pool, a spa pool, a trampoline, swings, a laundry, and a portable barbecue. There are three studios and five larger units, all quite comfortable, with kitchen facilities and nice, hard mattresses. Breakfast is available daily. The Ambassador is 3½ km (2 miles) south of downtown.

Where to Eat in & Near Tauranga

You can get a good three-course meal in Tauranga at **$ Charley Brown's,** 194 Cameron Rd. (**☎ 07/575-4653**), for about NZ$23 (U.S. $14.95). Portions are large, so you might consider ordering a "half serve." There's a children's menu, and the restaurant is licensed. Open daily from 5:30pm.

In **Katikati,** a little north of Morton Estates on the Thames Highway, do as the locals do and drop by the **Katikati Tavern** for fish and chips from noon to 2pm.

DRIVING TO GISBORNE VIA WHAKATANE

Stop by the **Visitors Information Centre** on Boon Street in Whakatane (**☎ 07/308-6058**) for details on some of the more interesting sights in the town and nearby. This is the legendary settling place of Toi (see "New Zealand Then," in Chapter 2) on his search for his grandson, Whatonga, and the earthworks out on the road to Ohope are traditionally held to be those of this *pa.* It is also the landing place of the great Mataatua canoe, part of the Hawaiki migration fleet. A model of that canoe can be seen next to the imposing rock arch known as **Pohaturoa Rock** (once part of a sacred Maori cave and now a memorial to those who died in World War I). On Mataatua

Street, right in the center of town, you'll see the beautiful **Wairere Waterfall.** Don't miss seeing the beach at **Ohope,** and consider a closer look at ★ **White Island,** the active volcano 32 miles offshore.

Some 37 miles east of Whakatane, Highway 2 brings you to Hoptiki and State Highway 35, known as the ★ **East Cape Road,** which hugs the coastline for most of its 213-mile route up around New Zealand's most easterly point and down to Gisborne on Poverty Bay. The drive—breathtaking in any season—is a heart-stopper during Christmas, when hundreds of pohutukawa trees burst into brilliant scarlet blooms along the cliffs overlooking the sea. All along, you'll find deserted beaches, sea views, and native bush, which combine to make this one of New Zealand's finest scenic drives. This is an area with a predominantly Maori population, and most of the small villages and towns you'll pass through either still are, or once were, Maori centers. Sadly, some of the most exquisite Maori carvings from the area have been removed: The Auckland Museum's Te Toki-a-Tapiri war canoe and Wellington's National Museum's Te Hau-ki-Turanga meetinghouse and Nuku te Whatewha storehouse all came from this region. There are, however, still outstanding examples of the art to be seen along the drive.

I don't want to alarm you, but in recent years the East Cape has become a popular spot for motorcycle gangs. Should you happen upon them, I suggest you use common sense, and steer clear.

Opotiki was once a large Maori settlement, but today is best known for its **Church of St. Stephen the Martyr,** scene of the particularly brutal murder of German Lutheran missionary Carl Sylvius Volkner in 1865. Bloodstained relics of that grim event are on exhibit in the church. At **Te Kaha,** Tu Kaihi meetinghouse in the marae has an elaborately carved lintel you'll be welcome to view *if you ask permission before entering the marae.* A little farther along, **Waihau Bay** has good views across Cape Runaway (so named by Captain Cook as he watched Maori canoes "run away" when shots were fired over their heads), as well as very good beaches. **Whangaparaoa** is where the great migration canoe *Tainui* landed—its captain's wife is credited with bringing the kumara to New Zealand.

Hicks Bay—not quite midway—has marvelous views and one of the finest carved meetinghouses on the East Cape. The community's name comes from one of Captain Cook's officers, who first sighted it, and it was the site of a tragic Maori massacre in which one European was killed and eaten on his wedding night (after which complaints were registered that he was too tough and stringy to be tasty!). Turn left at the general store to reach the **Tuwhakairiora meetinghouse,** whose carvings were done in 1872. It is dedicated to local members of the Ngati Porou tribe who died in overseas wars, and its unique rafter design (found only in this region) is symbolic of the honor of death in battle for the warrior.

A little farther along, the road descends to sea level to follow the narrow bay to where the little town of **Te Araroa** nestles under the cliffs. Thirteen miles east of Te Araroa, along an all-weather road, stands the **East Cape Lighthouse,** in an isolated location. There has been a light here since 1906. The track to the lighthouse must be covered by foot, and it leads up some 600 steps—perhaps a look from afar will suffice. Sunrise is lovely here.

One of New Zealand's most ornate Maori churches is the ★ **Tikitiki Church,** a memorial to Maori soldiers who died in World War I. The carved panels and rafter patterns depict Ngati Porou tribal history, and two war-hero brothers are featured in the east window. Closer to Gisborne, you can view another beautifully carved modern meetinghouse near the wharf at **Tokomaru Bay.** This is where a brave band of women, two warriors, and three whalers successfully defended a headland *pa* from attack by a large enemy force. **Anaura Bay,** just 43 miles from Gisborne, was Captain Cook's landing place on his second New Zealand voyage. The *Endeavour* hung around for two days trying to get water casks beyond the surf before heading south for a better watering place. **Waioeka,** 17 miles away from Gisborne, is a good spot to fill up the gas tank (petrol stations are few and far between in these parts). And Gisborne, of course, was the place Captain Cook *first* sighted the New Zealand mainland (more about that later).

THE SHORT ROUTE FROM WHAKATANE TO GISBORNE

For those who simply wish to reach Gisborne from the Bay of Plenty, there's a shorter, faster way to get there than around the East Cape. Highway 2 is a pleasant, three-hour drive on a winding road through green farmlands, native bush, along rushing mountain rivers, and through **Waioeka Gorge**—not a bad drive, mind you, but nothing to compare with the East Cape.

2 Gisborne

287km (177 miles) SE of Rotorua, 298km (184 miles) SE of Tauranga

GETTING THERE • By Plane There are scheduled flights from all major New Zealand cities.

• By Bus InterCity offers daily bus service to Gisborne from Auckland and Rotorua.

• By Car Gisborne is reached via State Highway 35 (the East Cape Road) from the north, and from Rotorua via Highway 30 to Whakatane, then Highway 2 southeast to Gisborne.

ESSENTIALS • Orientation Gisborne is situated on the northern shore of Poverty Bay where the Waimata and Taruheru rivers come together to form the Turanganui. Riverside park areas abound, and most bridges were built for pedestrian as well as vehicular traffic. The city center is compact, with Gladstone Road a main thoroughfare. The post office is at 74 Grey St. (☎ **867-8869**).

• Information The **Eastland & Gisborne District Information Centre** is located at 209 Grey St. (☎ **06/868-6139**), where the friendly staff offers assistance to visitors. It's open in summer, Monday through Friday from 8:30am to 9pm and Saturday, Sunday, and holidays from 10am to 5pm; in winter, Monday through Friday from 8:30am to 5pm and Saturday, Sunday, and holidays from 10am to 5pm.

• Telephone The telephone area code (STD) for Gisborne is **06.**

GETTING AROUND For taxi service, call the Gisborne Taxi Society (☎ **867-8869**).

Because of its closeness to the international date line, Gisborne (pop. 31,000) is judged to be the most easterly city in the world and the first to see the sun's rays each morning. It's also the place where New Zealand's European history began. Capt. James Cook's *Endeavour* entered these waters in early October 1769, and it fell the lot of the 12-year-old surgeon's boy, Nicholas Young, to be the first to sight land—a fact that must have caused some consternation among the rest of the crew, since the good captain had promised a gallon of rum as a reward, two if the sighting should be at night! True to another promise, Captain Cook named the white bluffs the boy had seen at the southern end of the bay's wide entrance "Young Nick's Head." As for Young Nick, he is also celebrated by a statue at the mouth of the Turanganui River at Waikanae Beach. It was two days later, on October 9, 1769, that a party ventured forth from the ship, and after a series of misunderstandings with Maori over the next two days (during which one Maori was killed when the English thought he was trying to steal a beached longboat, another when he reached toward a sword, and four more when they resisted being taken aboard the *Endeavour* from their canoe), Cook found it impossible to gain Maori cooperation in gathering the fresh water and provisions he needed. Small wonder! At any rate, he left in disgust, writing in his journal that he was sailing "out of the bay, which I have named Poverty Bay because it afforded us not one thing we wanted."

One thing is a virtual certainty: Had Captain Cook gotten off on the right foot with the indigenous people, a name incorporating the word "*poverty*" would never have occurred to him. Gisborne is in fact the very center of one of New Zealand's most fertile areas, with a balmy climate that sees more than 2,215 hours of sunshine annually. It's a gardenland of vegetable farms and orchards bearing citrus fruits, grapes, and kiwifruit. Dairy and sheep farms prosper. That sunny climate, combined with beaches that offer ideal swimming, surfing, and fishing conditions, also make it a holiday resort that's becoming increasingly popular with Kiwis from all over the North Island.

What to See & Do

To get a panoramic view of Poverty Bay, the city, its harbors and rivers, head for ★ **Kaiti Hill Lookout.** It's signposted at the northern end of Gladstone Bridge, and you can drive most of the way, walking the last little bit to a brick semicircular lookout point at the very edge of the hill. There's a statue of Captain Cook there that looks suspiciously like Napoleon (notice the hand in the jacket, so characteristic of "The Little Emperor") looking out toward Young Nick's Head on the opposite side of the bay.

At the foot of Kaiti Hill, you'll pass one of New Zealand's largest Maori meetinghouses, ★ **Poho-o-rawiri.** It's so large that the traditional construction of a single ridgepole supported by pillars had to be abandoned in favor of more modern methods. All its carvings (which are splendid) were done in Rotorua. You'll usually find the side door open; if not, look up the caretaker, who lives just next door.

Also at the bottom of Kaiti Hill, on Kaiti Beach Road, there's a memorial on what is thought to be the spot on which Captain Cook landed, as well as a cannon, which may or may not have been salvaged from the wreck of the *Endeavour* (seems there's some dispute because it's made of iron, while Captain Cook's ship supposedly carried brass cannons).

Canadians will want to go by **Alfred Cox Park** on Grey Street to see the giant totem pole, which the Canadian government presented to New Zealand in 1969 to mark the Cook Bicentenary and to acknowledge the debt both countries owe that great explorer. It's adjacent to the Eastland Information Centre.

This area is filled with historic *pa* sites in the hills behind Poverty Bay Flats—ask at the information center if any meetinghouses are open to the public. There are also some excellent walkways in the area, and the information center can furnish detailed trail booklets.

Swimmers will want to take advantage of the superb surf at both **Waikanae** and **Midway beaches.** Surfers prefer **Wainui and Makarori beaches.** Small-fry (as well as the young at heart) will enjoy the **Adventure Park** and Young Nick's Playground.

There is excellent **fishing** in these waters, both offshore and in the rivers. You can arrange charter boats and guides through the information center. Anglers will want to ask for the *Guide to Trout Fishing in the Gisborne Area,* compiled by the Gisborne Anglers Club.

The ★ **Gisborne Museum & Arts Centre,** 18–22 Stout St. (☎ **867-3832**), has displays depicting Maori and European history along the East Coast, as well as geological and natural history, colonial technology, decorative arts, and maritime history exhibits. The Art Gallery has an ongoing program of changing art and craft exhibitions (local, national, and international). The Museum Complex, which includes the main museum building, two historic houses and associated outbuildings, and a maritime museum, is open from 10am to 4:30pm on Monday through Friday, and 2 to 4:30pm on Saturday, Sunday, and holidays; longer weekend hours during December and January; closed Christmas Day and Good Friday. Adults pay NZ$2.50 (U.S. $1.65); children and students, NZ$1 (U.S. 65¢).

Next door to the museum are **Wyllie Cottage,** built in 1872, and the **Star of Canada Maritime Museum.** The ill-fated *Star of Canada* struck rocks at Kaiti Beach in 1912.

There are four one-hour ★ **walks** (one is actually one to three hours) in Gisborne, all easily mapped out in the brochure "Gisborne Walking Tours," available through the Information Centre, which can also give you information on four longer walks (2 to 5½ hours) in the Eastland area, in Wharerata, Cook's Cove, Anaura Bay, and Otoko.

The **Eastwoodhill Arboretum,** 22 miles due west of Gisborne (☎ **863-9817**), is the largest collection in the Southern Hemisphere of trees and plants native to the northern hemisphere. If you're partial to daffodils, you'll find 2½ acres of them in yellow profusion here in spring, and in fall the oaks, maples, and ash put on a show. Open from August through May (call or inquire at Information Centre for hours); by arrangement other times.

Many of New Zealand's white-wine grapes are grown near Gisborne, so if you're a wine connoisseur, have the Visitors Information Centre direct you to a couple of outstanding **wineries** just outside Gisborne: **Millton Vineyard,** on Papatu Road, Manutuke, Gisborne (☎ **862-8680**), is one.

Where to Stay

The rates given below include GST.

A MOTEL

★ **Teal Motor Lodge,** 479 Gladstone Rd., Gisborne. ☎ **06/868-4019.** Fax 06/867-7157. 3 rms, 21 units (all with bath). TV TEL

Rates: NZ$75–NZ$85 (U.S. $48.75–$55.25) single or double; NZ$85–NZ$99 (U.S. $55.25–$64.25) unit for one or two. AE, DC, MC, V.

This is something a little different—a New Zealand motel with a decidedly Asian flavor, run by Stewart and Lynda Haynes. Set on almost 2 acres of shaded and landscaped lawns, only a short walk to the city center, the spacious rooms have an airy look, with exposed beams and stained timber exteriors, plus restful color combinations in decor throughout. There's a quiet air about the place, not to mention a saltwater swimming pool. The apartments have one or two bedrooms and full kitchens. A continental breakfast is available.

A BED-&-BREAKFAST

Green Gables Travel Hotel, 31 Rawiri St., Gisborne. ☎ **06/867-9872.** 10 rms (none with bath).

Rates (including breakfast): NZ$40 (U.S. $26) single; NZ$58 (U.S. $37.70) double. No credit cards.

This favorite is run by Elizabeth (Betty) Croskery. Green Gables is an old house—set in shaded grounds in town and approached by a rose-bordered walk—that has been renovated without losing one bit of its original charm. The rooms are spacious and nicely furnished (two of them singles), all with hot and cold running water. They share four showers. One, on the ground floor, has a pretty bay window. The old-fashioned lounge contains a fireplace, and the attractive dining room looks out onto the lawn. Betty provides Kiwi hospitality at its best—and one of the best breakfasts you'll find in New Zealand. Dinners are available by arrangement. Readers have described this guesthouse as "delightful."

A HOSTEL

Gisborne YHA Hostel, 32 Harris St. (at Wainui Rd.), Gisborne. ☎ **06/867-3269.** 29 beds (no rooms with bath).

Rates: NZ$14 (U.S. $9.10) per person. MC, V.

This hostel is in a relaxed urban setting close to the city center, beaches, and major sightseeing. There are 29 beds in nine rooms, communal showers, a full laundry facility, and a communal kitchen. A basic food shop is in the hostel, as well as equipment for badminton and volleyball.

CABINS & CAMPGROUNDS

Gisborne has an excellent motor camp run by the City Council. It's handy to good swimming and surfing beaches, spotless, and provides above-average facilities. During high season (summer months), advance reservations are absolutely necessary, as it is extremely popular with Kiwis.

The ★ **Waikanae Beach Holiday Park,** at the beach end of Grey Street, Gisborne (☎ **06/867-5634;** fax 06/867-9765), has brown-wood blocks of cabins arranged U-shape around a grassy courtyard with attractive plantings. There are tourist cabins, which sleep four in two twin-bedded rooms and have private toilet and shower, refrigerator, gas range, crockery, cutlery, and cooking utensils; you supply linen and blankets. Charges range from NZ$12 (U.S. $7.80) for two people for tent sites to NZ$14 (U.S. $9.10) for two for power sites to NZ$48 (U.S. $31.20) for two for tourist cabins. On the premises are a large laundry, kitchen, showers, children's play area, and tennis courts. The beautiful and safe Waikanae Beach is just across the road, and the city center is an easy walk away. The Olympic Pool complex and minigolf are nearby.

Where to Eat

For eating on the fly, you have several choices for basic budget fare: **Captain Morgan's,** at 285 Grey St. (☎ **867-7821**), a BYO restaurant that also has take-away meals and an ice-cream parlor; **Riverdale Fish Shop,** 279 Stout St. (☎ **867-5429**), which offers burgers and toasted sandwiches in addition to the finny specialties; and the **London St. Fish Shop,** on London Street (☎ **868-8475**), with burgers and fish orders.

Marina, Marina Park, Vogel St. ☎ **868-5919.**

Cuisine: SEAFOOD/STEAK/NEW ZEALAND. **Reservations:** Recommended.
Prices: Average dinner NZ$26 (U.S. $16.90). AE, MC, V.
Open: Lunch Mon–Fri noon–2pm; dinner Mon–Sat 6–10pm.

Housed in a three-story white building on the riverbank, the Marina offers excellent fresh local seafood, veal, chicken, and steak. There's more than a little style in both the setting and the food presentation by the friendly, competent staff. It's a favorite with locals, so reserve early. Fully licensed.

★ $ **The Pinehurst Restaurant,** 4 Clifford St. ☎ **868-6771.**

Cuisine: MODERN NEW ZEALAND. **Reservations:** Recommended.
Prices: Appetizers NZ$7–NZ$10 (U.S. $4.55–$6.50); main courses NZ$17–NZ$24 (U.S. $11.05–$15.60). AE, DC, MC, V.
Open: Dinner only, Mon–Sat 6:30pm–"late."

Easily the most elegant restaurant in Gisborne, the Pinehurst Restaurant is an old-style house with rimu paneling and bay windows in a tranquil residential area close to town. Interesting appetizers include spicy lamb kebabs served on a Greek salad as well as shrimp and scallops teriyaki. Main courses range from Cajun T-bone to sun-dried tomato tagliatelle.

En Route to Napier

The 216km (134-mile) drive along Highway 2 from Gisborne to Napier passes through some of the most picturesque natural scenery in the country: rugged hill-country sheep stations, lush native bush, Lake Tutira, and a breathtaking view of Poverty Bay Flats from the top of the Wharerata Hills some 23 miles outside the city. **Morere Springs Scenic Reserve,** between Poverty and Hawke's bays (you'll see the sign along the highway), is a nice stopoff point for forest walks (there are four tracks, from half an hour to three hours, from which to choose), picnicking, or soaking in thermal pools.

3 Hawke's Bay

Hawke's Bay has been called the "Greenhouse of New Zealand" because of its sunny climate and ideal growing conditions for all kinds of vegetables, citrus fruits, and grapes. Indeed, when you see the expanse of vineyards, you may well think of it as the "Winery of New Zealand." Its resort center is Napier (pop. 52,000), one of the country's most delightful holiday spots. It's the ideal base for Hawke's Bay exploring.

Just 13 miles from Napier on Highway 2, Hastings is a town of lovely parks and gardens and Spanish Mission–style as well as art deco architecture—most definitely worth a day trip from Napier. If you're not driving, there is regular bus service between the two towns. Also, the "Getting There" section for Napier, below, applies to both towns, often called the Twin Cities of Hawke's Bay.

Napier

216km (134 miles) SW of Gisborne, 423km (262 miles) SE of Auckland, 228km (141 miles) SE of Rotorua

GETTING THERE • By Plane Air New Zealand, in the Travel Centre at Hastings and Station streets (☎ **06/835-1171**), provides daily service between the Hawke's Bay Airport and Auckland, Wellington, Dunedin, Nelson, and Christchurch, as well as weekday flights to Hokitika and Invercargill. The airport shuttle service into town (☎ **870-0700**) is about NZ$8 (U.S. $5.20).

• By Train There is rail service between Napier and Wellington via the *Bay Express.* There is no train service from the north.

• By Bus There is daily bus service between Napier/Hastings and Auckland, Gisborne, Rotorua, Taupo, Tauranga, and Wellington via InterCity and Newmans coach lines.

• By Car Both Napier and Hastings are on the north-south Highway 2; Highway 5 reaches Napier from the northwest and State Highway 50 from the southwest.

ESSENTIALS • Orientation The pride—and showplace—of Napier is its Marine Parade, a beautiful stretch of waterfront lined with stately Norfolk pines. Many visitor activities center around the Marine Parade, which holds a wide variety of attractions. Kennedy Road, the principal thoroughfare, diagonally bisects the town. The best beach in the area is Westshore Beach, located in Westshore Domain, part of the new-land legacy of the 1931 disaster. The Chief Post Office (CPO) is on Dickens Street.

• Information You'll find the **Visitors Information Centre** at the northern end of the Marine Parade (☎ **06/834-4161**). Hours are 8:30am to 5pm Monday through Friday, 9am to 5pm on Saturday and Sunday and public holidays; closed only on Christmas Day. Racks are filled with helpful brochures, maps (including a scenic drive), and visitor guides. Dianne Chester and her staff can help with accommodations and information on art deco walks, winery tours, and Cape Kidnappers.

• Telephone The telephone area code (STD) for Hawke's Bay is **06.**

GETTING AROUND There is no city bus service. **Taxi** stands are at Clive Square and at the corner of Emerson and Hastings streets by the Bank of New Zealand (☎ **835-7777**). **Taxis for wheelchairs** are available by calling Dan Stothers (☎ **843-2318**).

Spread around the wedge of Bluff Hill (which was virtually an island when Captain Cook described it on his voyage south from Poverty Bay), Napier was founded by whalers in the mid-1800s. You won't find any trace of those early settlers in today's city, however: In 1931 an earthquake of such violence that it was recorded as far away as Cairo and Calcutta demolished the entire city and nearby Hastings, killing hundreds of people. In its aftermath, not only did a completely new city arise, but it arose on new ground, for the quake had lifted the inner harbor floor, creating 10,000 acres of dry land—the site of the present airport, for instance, was under water prior to 1931.

Rebuilt during the Depression, the town opted for the art deco and Spanish Mission architecture so popular in the 1930s. As a result, Napier claims it probably has the world's largest collection of buildings in these styles (see "Art Deco Walk," under "What to See and Do," below).

WHAT TO SEE & DO

Plan to spend most of your time along the Marine Parade's Golden Mile. In addition to the listings below, as you walk north, you'll come to the **Boating Lake,** with paddleboats for children and adult-size bumper boats, as well as small racing cars, which are open from 10am to 9:30pm every day. Other amusements include children's bumper boats, radio boats, putt-putt golf, and roller skating. Stop for a while and soak in the beauty of the **Sunken Gardens,** with their waterwheel and floating white lotus sculpture. Then, on past the **information center,** there's the **Sound Shell,** which is used on summer weekends for an arts and crafts market.

★ **The Aquarium,** Marine Parade. ☎ **834-4196.**

The Aquarium is one of New Zealand's best. Stop for a moment to view the bronze sculpture showing two trawler fishermen hauling a net full of fish. It's so masterfully executed that fishermen have been known to stand and point out each species of fish in the net. The Aquarium's central feature is a huge saltwater oceanarium, which holds over 25 species of ocean-dwelling fish, ranging in size from crayfish to sharks. Feeding time is 3:15pm, when a scuba diver hand-feeds the fish. You'll also get to see a crocodile, turtles, vividly colored tropical fish, sea horses, the lethal piranha, and octopi. The Vivarium, on the top floor, holds the tuatara, a living fossil unique to New Zealand, and also aquatic reptiles like water dragons, turtles, and frogs.

Admission: NZ$6.50 (U.S. $4.25) adults, NZ$3.25 (U.S. $2.10) children.

Open: Daily 9am–5pm (until 9pm Dec 26–Jan). **Closed:** Christmas.

Marineland, Marine Parade. ☎ **835-7579.**

A 45-minute show features dolphins, leopard seals, sea lions, and penguins. Also on hand are cormorants and gannets. Marineland, in the same building as the Aquarium, also houses **Lilliput,** an animated village and model railway with authentic New Zealand rolling stock and locomotives, and offers a "swim with dolphins" experience.

Admission: Marineland show and Lilliput, NZ$7.50 (U.S. $4.90) adults, NZ$3.75 (U.S. $2.45) children.

Open: Daily 10am–4:30pm. Shows are at 10:30am and 2:30pm, with an additional 4pm performance Dec 26 to mid-Jan.

★ **The Stables Colonial Museum and Waxworks,** Marine Parade. ☎ **835-1937.**

This museum re-creates the past with rooms from another era; my favorites depict a man in an outhouse, a doctor taking the blood pressure of a wicker-chair-bound patient, and a prostitute's quarters (this one provokes a bit of speculation about what exactly is going on). But the pìece de résistance of the museum is ***Earthquake 31,*** a documentary about the infamous earthquake; try to see it at the beginning of your sightseeing to best understand the unique history of this place. The 23-minute film includes actual footage of Napier before and after the earthquake and an interview with older citizens who lived through it, two of them teachers. Outside the movie theater, which has a floor that actually moves during footage of the quake, there is a dramatic replica of the collapse of the local nurses' home and the rescue performed by sailors and firefighters. (If you have to choose one, pick the film.) It's the brainchild of owner Kevin Percy, who runs the place with his wife, Judy. The museum is opposite Marineland.

Admission: Museum only, NZ$4.50 (U.S. $2.95); film only, NZ$4.50 (U.S. $2.95); combination museum and film, NZ$6 (U.S. $3.90).

Open: Daily 9am–5pm.

Hawke's Bay Art Gallery and Museum, Marine Parade. ☎ **835-7781.**

The museum and gallery offer a wide range of exhibits, many of which are related to the art and history of the region. A Tourism Design Award–winning exhibition, "Nga Tukemata" (The Awakening), presents the art of the local Ngati Kahungunu tribe and an audiovisual presentation tells the story of the disastrous Hawke's Bay earthquake of 1931. The "Newest City on the Globe" exhibition shows the rebuilding of Napier in the early 1930s in its famed art deco style. Paintings and the decorative arts from this period are also featured.

Admission: NZ$2 (U.S. $1.30).

Open: Daily 10am–4:30pm.

Kiwi House, Marine Parade. ☎ **835-7553.**

This is where you're guaranteed to see kiwi birds. Also on view are owls, night herons, sugar gliders, whistling frogs, and many others. There's a live show at 1pm, and the birds are fed at 2pm. There's also a sheepskin shop in the main entrance. Kiwi House is located at the northern end of the Golden Mile.

Admission: NZ$3 (U.S. $1.95) adults, NZ$1.50 (U.S. $1) children.

Open: Daily 11am–3pm.

Other Sights

The city of Napier itself is virtually an open-air museum of **art deco and Spanish architecture** as a result of massive reconstruction between 1931 and 1933. More than 60 years later, the buildings are remarkably unchanged and no doubt represent one of the world's most concentrated collections of buildings from this period (see "Art Deco Walk," below). Historic **Clive Square,** on Monroe Street between Emerson and Dickens streets, was the village green from the 1860s to the mid-1880s, when it became a public gardens. After the earthquake, it was the site of "Tin Town," a temporary shopping area.

Westshore Domain is Napier's most popular swimming beach, about a mile and a half of gray sand and pebbles. Surf at the **Marine Parade** beach is a bit too rough for good swimming, but it's a good place to get a little sun. There is, however, a saltwater pool at Marine Parade featuring the "Wild Rampage Ride." **Onekawa Park** at Maadi Road and Flanders Avenue has two Olympic-size pools, one indoor, the other outdoor. Small fee.

ART DECO WALK A map outlining a ✪ **self-guided walk** through the downtown deco area and another showing a more extensive scenic drive are available from the information center for NZ$1.50 and NZ$2 (U.S. 98¢ and $1.30), respectively. **Guided walks** leave the Art Deco Shop on Tennyson Street every Wednesday, Saturday, and Sunday at 2pm from December 26 to late February and include slide and video presentations and refreshments. They cost NZ$5 (U.S. $3.25) for adults and are conducted by the Art Deco Trust (P.O. Box 133, Napier; ☎ **06/835-0022**), which promotes the city's architecture.

Nearby Attractions

This is one of only two places in New Zealand where gannets are known to nest on the mainland (they are commonly found on offshore islands). There's a colony of some 6,000 out at ✪ **Cape Kidnappers,** that dramatic line of cliffs that forms Hawke's Bay's southern end some 17 miles south of Napier. The gannet sanctuary is open to the public from late October to April, and the graceful birds are well worth a visit. To reach them, drive 13 miles south to Clifton Domain; then it's a little less than a two-hour walk along 4 or 5 miles of sandy beach. That walk *must* be made at low tide, since high tides come right up to the base of the steep cliffs, which is why private vehicles may not be taken out to the sanctuary. Be sure to check with the Visitors

Information Centre in Napier (☎ **834-4161**) or Hastings (☎ **876-0205**), or the Department of Conservation in Napier (☎ **835-0415**), about the tides or taking a tour there. The best time to view the birds is from early November to late February.

There are two options to going on your own: the tours offered by **Kidnappers Sea Escape** (see the comments in "Readers Recommend," below) and a Land Rover half-day trip operated by **Gannet Safaris** (☎ **875-0511**), which costs about NZ$35 (U.S. $22.75).

There are 25 **wineries** in the Napier area, most open daily. Two offer tours, the Mission Winery and the Church Road Winery. Ask at the information center for brochures about tours and directions for reaching them. Also, Napier is where you can see how a fleece gets transformed into car-seat covers, rugs, and more. You can take a free 25-minute tour through the **Classic Sheepskin Tannery** at 22 Thames St., off Pandora Road (☎ **835-9662**), daily at 11am and 2pm. The shop there sells sheepskin products at factory prices, and they have a fully insured worldwide mailing service. There's also a courtesy car available daily.

WHERE TO STAY

The rates listed below include GST.

Motels

In addition to the listings below, some of the area's best motel apartments are at the **Kennedy Park Holiday Complex,** described under "Camping and Cabins," below.

Blue Dolphin Motel, 371–373 Kennedy Rd., Napier. ☎ **06/843-9129.** Fax 06/843-9227. 9 units (all with bath). TV TEL

Rates: NZ$65 (U.S. $42.25) single; NZ$75 (U.S. $48.75) double. AE, DC, MC, V.

Paul and Jenny Guest, Napier residents for more than 30 years, are the friendly owners of the Blue Dolphin. The units come with full kitchen facilities and separate bedrooms that sleep two to five. All have radio and video. There's a games room, heated outdoor spa pool, and guest laundry. Cooked or continental breakfasts are available.

Reef Motel, 33 Meeanee Quay, Westshore, Napier. ☎ **06/835-4108.** Fax 06/835-4789 . 7 units (all with bath). TV TEL **Transportation:** Courtesy car from/to the rail, bus, and air terminals.

Rates: NZ$55 (U.S. $35.75) single; NZ$65 (U.S. $42.25) double. AE, DC, MC, V.

Lorraine and Stephen Riley are the friendly, helpful hosts at the Reef. The motel's units each sleep two to six, with separate bedrooms and a living area that opens into a

READERS RECOMMEND

Kidnappers Sea Escape, 30 Cedar Rd., Te Awanga, Hastings (☎ and fax **06/875-0556**). *"We wish to report to you an absolutely outstanding opportunity for viewing the gannet colony at Cape Kidnappers. . . . This outfit employs inflatable boats to visit the gannet colony by sea. The views of the gannets are unparalleled. The owner and pilot, Mr. Richard Williams, is conscious of the safety and comfort of passengers, as well as diligent in avoiding disruptions to the gannets themselves. It's a fabulous experience."* —Fredric Chanania, Falls Church, Va., U.S.A. [**Author's Note:** This trip costs NZ$45 (U.S. $29.25).]

kitchen. Upstairs units have great views. There's a spa pool and laundry facilities on the premises. Both cooked and continental breakfasts are available.

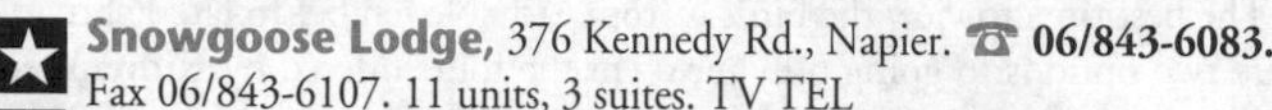

Snowgoose Lodge, 376 Kennedy Rd., Napier. ☎ **06/843-6083.** Fax 06/843-6107. 11 units, 3 suites. TV TEL

Rates: NZ$80 (U.S. $52) single; NZ$90 (U.S. $58.50) double; NZ$90–NZ$100 (U.S. $58.50–$65) suite. Best Western discounts available. AE, DC, MC, V.

You park outside your own unit at the Snowgoose, where Ray and Pierrine Cooper keep things shining, outside as well as in. The front lawn has even won an award for the best motel garden in Napier. The one- and two-bedroom units are all nicely furnished and have radios and electric blankets. Most also are brightened with one or two of Pierrine's growing plants. There's a block of executive suites that have their own spa bath (sheer luxury!). On-premises facilities include a laundry, car wash, children's play area, games room, outdoor swimming pool, and private spa pool—no charge for the use of any. Shops are nearby, and the Coopers can arrange babysitting. All units have full kitchens. The motel is on the main road 2 miles from the town center.

Spanish Lady Motel, 348 Kennedy Rd., Napier. ☎ **06/843-9188.** Fax 06/843-6064. 11 units (all with bath). TV TEL

Rates: NZ$70 (U.S. $45.50) apartment for one; NZ$82 (U.S. $53.30) apartment for two. Best Western discounts available. DC, MC, V.

The unassuming exterior of this small hostelry hides the amenities hard to find in most New Zealand lodgings: washcloths in the bath and a sink with one mixer faucet for both hot and cold water. Add to that good lighting and a firm mattress—heaven! The one- and two-bedroom apartment units are all on the ground floor, eight with wheelchair access. There are also fully equipped kitchens, a pool, a spa pool, a playground, an ice machine, and a cactus garden. The hosts are Dorothy and Ian Finlayson. It's on the main road about 3½km (2 miles) from the center of town.

A Bed-&-Breakfast

Pinehaven Travel Hotel, 259 Marine Parade, Napier. ☎ and fax **06/835-5575.** 6 rms (none with bath).

Rates (including continental breakfast): NZ$38 (U.S. $24.70) single; NZ$60 (U.S. $39) double. MC, V.

The Pinehaven is down the street from the YHA Hostel and across from Marineland. June and Ray Riley have hosted guests from all over the world. The Pinehaven has six comfortably furnished rooms, all with hot and cold running water. The bedrooms are heated and have electric blankets. Downstairs is a TV lounge with tea- and

READERS RECOMMEND

The Masonic Hotel, Tennyson St., Napier (☎ **06/835-8689;** fax 06/835-2297). *"This was one of our best bargain accommodations. A spacious double room overlooking the Esplanade was only NZ$49—including a full breakfast in the Cobb & Co. dining room. We also thought* ***Buck's Great Wall*** *almost next door to the Masonic, served some of the best Chinese food we've ever tasted."*—Sue and Frank Thorne, Fallbrook, Calif., U.S.A. [**Author's Note:** This rate at the Masonic must have been an off-season special, as my sources tell me that NZ$49 (U.S. $31.85) is the room-only tariff.]

coffee-making facilities. The optional cooked breakfast is extra. This guesthouse enjoys a wonderful sea view.

A Hostel

YHA Hostel, 277 Marine Parade, Napier. ☎ **06/835-7039.** 39 beds (no rooms with bath).

Rates: NZ$14 (U.S. $9.10) per person. MC, V.

This hostel couldn't have a better location—it's right on the beachfront, across from Marineland. The former guesthouse has 39 beds in 18 rooms. Front rooms overlook the bay, and facilities include a TV and video room, a pleasant kitchen and dining room, an outdoor barbecue and dining area, a smoking lounge, laundry facilities, and bike rental.

Camping & Cabins

It's hard to find superlatives strong enough for Napier's ★ $ **Kennedy Park Holiday Complex** on Storkey Street, off Kennedy Road, Napier (☎ **06/843-9126;** fax 06/843-6113). If you've been impressed with Kiwi motor camps in general, just wait until you see this one! Set in 17 acres of trees, grass, and colorful flowers (including $1^1/_2$ acres of roses!), with top-grade accommodations, this has to be the "Ritz" of New Zealand camps. Those accommodations run the gamut from tent sites to ungraded cabins to graded (two-star) cabins to tourist flats and motel units. The 110 sites with no power run NZ$16 (U.S. $10.40) for two adults, NZ$4 (U.S. $2.60) for a child; those with power, just pennies more. Ungraded cabins come with beds, tables, and chairs, and you supply cooking and eating utensils, linen and blankets, and use the communal toilet and shower facilities. Rates are NZ$29 (U.S. $18.85) for one or two. The 16 graded cabins sleep four (plus a rollaway bed if needed), have easy chairs, and are furnished with hot- and cold-water sinks, fridge, range, coffee/tea maker, toaster, crockery, cutlery, frying pan, pots, and utensils. You supply linen and blanket, and use the communal toilet and shower facilities. Two people pay NZ$38 (U.S. $24.70). Tourist flats fill that gap between cabins and motel units—they're actually of motel quality, but they're not serviced. These 20 units cost NZ$64 (U.S. $41.60) for two people. Finally, motel units come in varying sizes: bed-sitters (studios) and one- and two-bedroom units. Many have peaked, pine-beamed ceilings, a window wall, and stucco and wood-paneled walls. All are of superior quality, have well-chosen furnishings, look out over lawn and gardens, and are NZ$60 to NZ$74 (U.S. $39 to $48.10) for one or two. American Express, Diners Club, MasterCard, and Visa cards accepted.

WHERE TO EAT

I'm not really sure this item belongs under "Where to Eat," but because New Zealand budget travel is so closely tied to those wonderful motel units and their

READERS RECOMMEND

Providencia, Middle Rd. (R.D. 2, Hastings), Havelock North (☎ and fax **06/877-2300**). *"Just south of Napier, in the beautiful Havelock North area, we came across a charming B&B operated by Janet and Raul Maddison-Mejias. She's from Sydney; he's Chilean. The house dates from about 1903. They are worth seeking out for their truly warm hospitality."*—Lily and Des Morrison, Palm Springs, Calif., U.S.A. [**Author's Note:** This tiny inn offers three rooms (one with bath) as well as all meals.]

kitchens, I think you should know about ■ **Chantal Wholefoods,** 29 Hastings St. (☎ **835-8036**). Even if you're not a strict vegetarian, I think you'll love this store—all sorts of natural foods, dried fruits, nuts, tofu, and, in addition, marvelous whole-grain breads to make any sandwich taste its best. Chantal's is very much like an old-fashioned grocery store. The foods are all in open drums and you package them yourself—it's lots of fun, and prices come out lower than those in supermarkets.

Juices & Ices, Emerson St. ☎ **835-9944.**

Cuisine: ICE CREAM/SNACKS. **Reservations:** Not required.
Prices: Snacks under NZ$10 (U.S. $6.50). No credit cards.
Open: Mon–Fri 8:30am–5pm, Sat 10am–1pm.

This favorite of Napier citizens specializes in homemade ice cream, with a dozen flavors from which to choose. You can also order toasted sandwiches, soup, and fresh fruit juices. Juices & Ices, at Clive Square, has a cheerful ice-cream-parlor ambience.

$ **Mabel's Restaurant,** 204 Hastings St. ☎ **835-5655.**

Cuisine: BREAKFAST/LIGHT LUNCH. **Reservations:** Not required.
Prices: Breakfast under NZ$8 (U.S. $5.20); lunch under NZ$10 (U.S. $6.50). No credit cards.
Open: Mon–Fri 6:30am–3pm.

Early risers will appreciate Mabel's, where breakfast is featured weekdays from 6:30am to 9:30am. You can also get a light, reasonably priced meal of soup, quiche, or salad. Just check the blackboard selections. Mabel's is in the center of town.

★ $ **The Old Flame,** 112 Tennyson St. ☎ **835-6848.**

Cuisine: NEW ZEALAND SMÖRGÅSBORD. **Reservations:** Recommended, especially on weekends.
Prices: Lunch NZ$14 (U.S. $9.10); dinner NZ$22.50 (U.S. $14.65). AE, BC, DC, V.
Open: Lunch daily 11:30am–2pm; dinner daily 5:30–9pm.

This intimate restaurant occupies a single-story house across from the Municipal Theatre. It's strictly smörgåsbord—tables heaped high with tempting New Zealand dishes. The place has a medieval look, rather than deco, for a change. Licensed and BYOW.

EVENING ENTERTAINMENT

After dark, you'll always find folks congregating in the lively **Masonic Hotel** bar and the **Shakespeare Hotel,** Hawke's Bay's major music pub.

Take in a movie at the art deco **State Theatre,** on the corner of Dickens and Dalton streets; or see a show or concert (very inexpensive) at the **Municipal Theatre** on Tennyson Street (if nothing else, try to see the auditorium).

READERS RECOMMEND

Ziebes, 2 White St., Taradale (☎ **06/844-9977**). *"This is a small but very good restaurant just south of Napier. The atmosphere was very pleasant, the service excellent, and the meal for two, for about NZ$50 (U.S. $32.50), included drinks and the best filet mignon I've ever had."*—Lois Churchill, Elkland, Penn., U.S.A.

An Excursion to Hastings

Just 21km (13 miles) south of Napier on Highway 2, Hastings is a town of lovely parks and gardens and Spanish Mission–style as well as art deco architecture—most definitely worth a visit. If you're not driving, there is regular bus service between the two towns. Stop by the **Visitor Information Centre,** on Russell Street North (mailing address: Private Bag 9002, Hastings; ☎ **06/878-0510**), for brochures, information, a Spanish Mission Tour map, and a scenic-drive guide. It's open Monday through Friday from 8am to 5pm and on Saturday, Sunday, and holidays from 10am to 3pm. Inquire at the information center about tours. No matter how you get around, the **scenic drive** is one you really shouldn't miss.

The ★ **Hawke's Bay Exhibition Centre,** Civic Square, Hastings (☎ **876-2077**), is the region's top spot for touring exhibitions of painting, sculpture, craft, and historical material. There's a shop specializing in local craft souvenirs and a fine café. Admission is NZ$2 (U.S. $1.30). It's open Monday through Friday from 10am to 4:30pm and Saturday and Sunday from noon to 4:30pm; closed Christmas Day.

Pick up the "Taste Our Tradition" brochure from the information center for directions on visiting the local wineries. One of the best is the ★ **Vidal Winery,** 913 Aubyns St., near Sylvan Road (☎ **876-8105**). Vidal has a lot to offer, including the Vidal Winery Brasserie right on the premises. They have a rustic, wine-cellar setting, with beamed ceiling, old oak casks lining the walls, and candlelight. There's also a barbecue area outside with umbrella trees and a grape arbor. The menu includes homemade soup, lamb filet souvlaki, gourmet pizza, Cajun prawn salad, and pork French cutlet. Prices are in the NZ$10 to NZ$18 (U.S. $6.50 to $11.70) range. The Brasserie is open for lunch daily from noon and for dinner daily from 6pm.

Be sure to drive up to ★ **Te Mata Peak,** about 11km (7 miles) from the Hastings Information Centre. The view is spectacular, and ask locals or the center about the lovely Maori legend from which it took its name. Take Havelock Road to Te Mata Road to Simla Avenue to Te Mata Peak Road and ascend the 1,310-foot-high peak for a stunning 360° panoramic view.

ESPECIALLY FOR KIDS

Within the 8 acres that make up ★ **Fantasyland,** in Windsor Park, entered via Grove Road (☎ **876-9856**), are enough assorted attractions and amusements to delight any child and all but the most hardened of his or her elders. Each time I go there are new additions, all elaborately but tastefully executed. Who wouldn't be intrigued by a pirate ship complete with cannons, a turreted castle, and a spaceship parked on its moon base! The tree house (open to any and all climbers) is fun, as is the little village with its firehouse, jail, and stores. A terrific array of playground equipment, go-karts, bumper boats, battery-operated cars, and tricycles are available for active youngsters, and, for those of us not so active, there's a miniature train ride around the park, along with miniature golf. Canoes and rowboats compete with swans and ducks on the pretty pond, and the shady, landscaped grounds invite an extended spell of just plain loafing—spreading a picnic on the handy tables set about (easily arranged with food from the take-away bar). The tea shop is a refreshment alternative. Admission is NZ$3 (U.S. $1.95), and children under 15 go in free. Rides cost NZ$1 to NZ$3 (U.S. 65¢ to $1.95) each. Open daily from 9am to 5pm (to 4:30pm April to October).

En Route to Taupo

Your drive from Napier to Taupo via Highway 5 will take less than two hours, but there was a time when it took two days. That was when stagecoach service was first initiated over a route that had been used by Maori in pre-European days on forays to collect seafood from Hawke's Bay.

The landscape you'll be passing through changes from lush vineyards to cultivated farm fields to rugged mountain ranges, and it doesn't take much imagination to picture the arduous journey as it was in the early days. About 3$^1/_2$ miles before you reach Taupo, look for the lonely peak of **Mount Tauhara,** an extinct volcanic cone rising from the plains.

8

Lake Taupo & Beyond

WHETHER YOU COME INTO TAUPO FROM ROTORUA, PAST WAIRAKEI'S STEAMY thermal power complex, or from Napier, under the lonely eye of Mount Tauhara, it's the lake on whose shores the town sits that will draw you like a magnet. Lake Taupo, New Zealand's largest, opens before you in a broad, shimmering expanse, with its far shores a misty suggestion of cliffs, coves, and wooded hills.

The lake was created in A.D. 186 by an enormous volcanic eruption—estimated to have been 100 times greater than that of Mount St. Helens in 1980. The eruption left a hole more than 32km (20 miles) wide, 40km (25 miles) across, and 600 feet deep in some places. Today, that crater contains the sparkling blue water of Lake Taupo.

To the south, three active volcanos are the focal point of **Tongariro National Park.** This was New Zealand's first national park (the world's second, after Yellowstone), and the original 1887 deed from Te Heuheu Tukino IV and other Tuwharetoa tribal chiefs transferred only some 6,500 acres (all the land within a 2km (1-mile) radius of the volcanic peaks), an area that has now been expanded to 30,453 acres.

Wanganui, one of New Zealand's oldest cities, was settled amid much controversy over just how title to the land was obtained by Col. William Wakefield on behalf of the New Zealand Company in 1840. Since those early days, the town has grown and over the years developed into a popular holiday spot.

New Plymouth is an active port city in the lush Taranaki district. It's known for the rhododendron festival held annually in late October or early November. The area is dominated by snow-capped Mount Egmont.

1 Taupo

287km (178 miles) SE of Auckland, 84km (52 miles) S of Rotorua, 155km (96 miles) NW of Napier

GETTING THERE • By Plane Mount Cook Airline provides regular service.

• By Bus There is regular bus service via Mount Cook Landline, InterCity, and Newmans between Taupo and Hamilton, Rotorua, and Wellington. Newmans and InterCity also connect Taupo to Napier and Tauranga.

• By Car Highways 1 and 5 pass through Taupo.

ESSENTIALS • Orientation Taupo is spread along the northeastern tip of the lake, just where the Waikato River, New Zealand's longest, flows out of Lake Taupo's Tapuaeharuru Bay. Its main street is Tongariro Street, named after the largest river flowing into the lake. Perpendicular to Tongariro is another important street, named Heu Heu (the locals pronounce it "hue-hue"). The striking purple-and-salmon post office at the corner of Ruapehu and Horomatangi streets is open Monday through Friday from 8:30am to 4:30pm.

The small settlements of Acacia Bay and Jerusalem Bay are just across on the western shore of the lake.

• Information The **Visitors Information Centre,** in the Great Lake Centre on Tongariro Street (☎ **07/378-9000**; fax 07/378-9003), can book accommodations, tours, and other activities, as well as provide a wide range of informative brochures on area attractions, reserve fishing guides, and sell fishing licenses. It also sells stamps, PhoneCards, and souvenirs. The center is open daily from 8:30am to 5pm.

• Telephone The telephone area code (STD) for the Lake Taupo region is **07.**

GETTING AROUND • By Bus There's no local bus service, but Paradise Tours offers minibus tours.

What's Special About the Lake Taupo Region

Adventurous Activities

- Trout fishing—one of the world's best sites for rainbow and brown trout.
- Pleasure boating and waterskiing—pursued on the lake by large numbers.
- Skiing on an active volcano—a rare opportunity found in Tongariro National Park.
- Golf—the challenging Wairakei International Golf Course, made dramatic by thermal vapors rising in the background.
- Bungee jumping—over the beautiful Waikato River.
- Scenic flights—giving a bird's-eye view of the lake, Hairakei's steaming valley, Huka Falls, and Tongariro National Park.

Pure Pleasure

- The many thermal pools, such as the ones at Tokaanu.

Strange Sights & Sites

- Wairakei Geothermal Power Station, the first to use wet steam, with some 60 bores and over 19km (12 miles) of pipeline.
- The Craters of the Moon and nearby Wairakei Thermal Valley—both weird and wonderful to behold.

Cultural Opportunities

- Go fishing or horse trekking with a member of the Tuwharetoa tribe.

• **By Car** You won't need one in town. For sorties out of town, try Rent-a-Dent (☎ **07/378-2740**).

• **By Taxi** Call Taupo Taxis (☎ **378-5100**).

• **By Bike** For getting around Taupo by bicycle, contact Roy's Cycle World on Ruapehu Street (☎ **378-6117**).

There's a bit of magic at work in Taupo—and it's easy to see its immediate attraction to descendants of the *Arawa* canoe. Present-day Maori will tell you that the lake was created by the magic of Ngatoroirangi, the legendary navigator of that migrating canoe. According to the legend, he stood on the summit of Mount Tauhara and flung down a gigantic tree, which landed here, leaving a vast trough as it plowed through the earth. When water welled up to fill the trough, Lake Taupo was born. Its very name is linked to legend—the Maori called it Taupo-nui-a-Tia (the "Great Cloak of Tia") after one of the Awara chiefs who explored much of this region, naming and claiming choice spots for his tribe. If you don't believe in folklore, you'll accept the Pakeha explanation of its origin: that the lake's crater is the result of an enormous volcanic eruption in A.D. 186 (the resultant orange sky was observed as far away as Rome and China).

Taupo's most appealing aspect to many is the fact that this pleasant, medium-size town of 18,000 people is a *real* place, not just a tourist draw—probably because travelers often rush past it on their way to Rotorua. It certainly welcomes visitors, but you'll also see plenty of people just going about their daily lives, going to work or school, congregating in local cafés, or indulging in an ice-cream cone (half a dozen parlors here encourage just that).

For locals and visitors alike, the lake is as much the central attraction today as it was in those far-off times. The fishing on which the Maori settlers so depended has changed only in the addition of two imported trout species to enhance the native fish population. It was in 1868 that brown trout eggs were introduced from Tasmania, followed by California rainbow trout in 1884. Lake Taupo rainbows are now considered a totally self-supporting wild population. It's the trout that draw anglers here in such numbers that those on shore have been so tightly packed as to be likened to a human picket fence. And there's seldom a time when the lake's surface is not alive with boats trolling lines in their wake.

Pleasure boating is a never-ending diversion in these parts, and waterskiing has gained such popularity that there are now specified ski lanes along the shoreline.

There is also an abundant supply of land-based attractions. Landlubbers have been coming in nearly equal numbers since the late 1870s to visit the thermal pools and view the natural wonders of the lake's environs.

What to See & Do

ACTIVITIES ON THE LAKE

Well, there's ★ **fishing.** Even if you've never cast a line, this may be the very time to join that "picket fence" and experience the singular thrill of feeling a nibble and pulling in a big one. And they do grow *big* in Lake Taupo—the average trout size is 3½ pounds, with 8- and 10-pound catches not unheard of. Just remember that there's a limit of three trout per person per day (you can catch and release as many as you want). The visitors center can fix you up with a license (you can get one for just one day, if you'd like) and fill you in on rules and regulations, as well as help you find a guide if you'd just rather not be a "picket" (however, note that hiring a guide is not exactly a budget choice). Two of my favorite **guides** are Punch Wilson (☎ **378-5596**) and Richard Staines (☎ **378-2736**). Most restaurants are happy to cook up your catch of the day; they aren't allowed to offer it on their menu (which is probably why so many trout live to grow so big).

Ernest Kemp Scenic Tours, at the Taupo Boat Harbour (☎ **378-3218**), runs enjoyable ★ **lake cruises** aboard the steamer *Ernest Kemp* every morning and afternoon. It's a two-hour sail, well worth the fare of NZ$22 (U.S. $14.30) per adult, NZ$12 (U.S. $7.80) per child (there are special family prices on holidays)—a great way to experience the lake itself and get a very different look at its shoreline. It's essential to book, through the visitors center or at the Boat Harbour.

OTHER SIGHTS & ACTIVITIES

The visitors center puts out an excellent booklet, "Walking Trails," outlining city and near-city ★ **walks** as well as tramping trails in the area. There are long walks and short walks, walks close to town and others as far away as Tongariro National Park. What a peaceful interlude to take the 45-minute forest walk, and for sheer scenery excitement there's the contrast of thrilling thermal activity and serene pine plantations along the Craters of the Moon track. The booklet gives clear, concise directions (with maps for most tracks), as well as estimated times and such helpful information as the fact that all of Mount Tauhara is a Maori Reserve and I trust you will treat it with proper respect, leaving only footprints (and perhaps a bit of your heart). A terrific idea is to intersperse sightseeing or other sports activities with a walk into the very soul and being of New Zealand, its forests, mountains, and rivers.

To see firsthand the awesome power of all that steam you've only glimpsed in

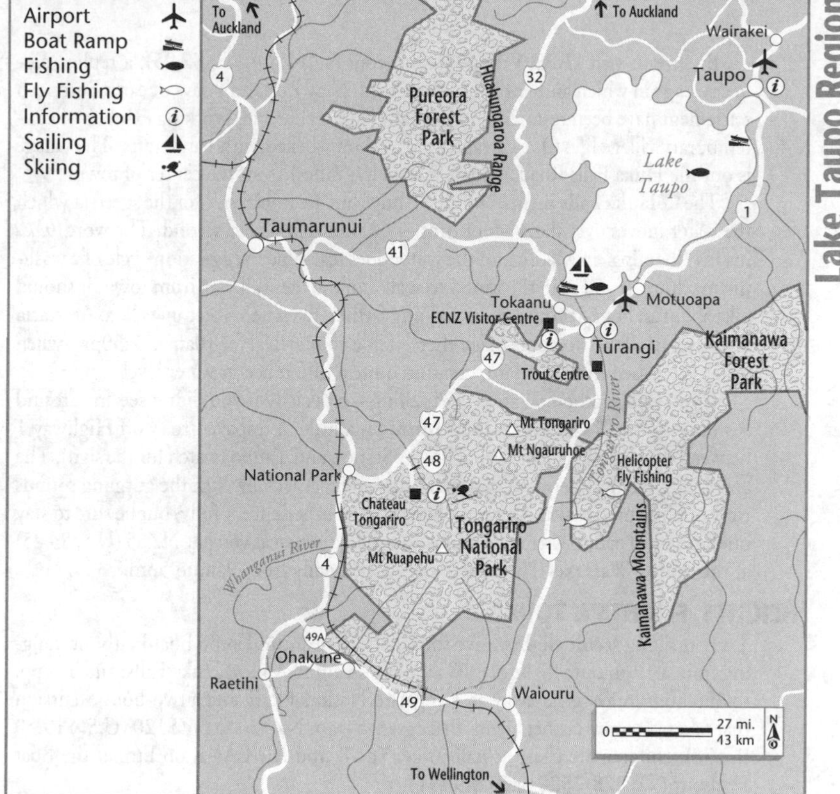

Rotorua, take the 8km (5-mile) drive out to the ★ **Wairakei Geothermal Power Station.** When work began in 1950 to harness all that power, this was the second-largest such project in the world and the first to use wet steam. Scientists from around the globe came to observe. Using some 60 bores and over 19km (12 miles) of pipeline, the project now supplies a great deal of the North Island's electricity requirements. Stop by the Information Centre (on the left as you drive into the valley), which is open daily from 9am to 4:30pm. The display and audiovisual show give a compelling overview of local geothermal activity and furnish answers to all the obvious questions (ask for the sheet titled "Questions Often Asked"). Study the excellent borefield model and drilling-process diagram, then leave the center and follow the marked road, which crosses the borefield itself, to a lookout from which you can view the entire site.

The 18-hole **Wairakei International Golf Course** (☎ **374-8152**) is challenging, not to mention dramatic, with thermal vapors rising in the background. *Golf Digest* rated this course one of the 10 best in the world. Visitors are welcome and rental equipment is available; call ahead.

Just in front of the De Brett Thermal Hotel, a short way out of town on Highway 5, a cut has been made through the pumice on the south side of the road and pumice strata has been marked and dated showing volcanic debris dating as far back as 1480 B.C. and as "recently" as A.D. 131. It's an eerie feeling to gaze on physical evidence of the earth's history! The De Brett, itself, is worth a short visit, since its grounds incorporate the **Onekeneke Valley of Hot Pools.**

Be sure to visit **Huka Village** (admission: NZ$4.50/U.S. $2.95), a replica pioneer village in which authentic buildings from New Zealand's days of early European settlement have been restored and brought back to life with working exhibits of contemporary village life. One cottage holds a shop stocked with handcrafts. The village is out the Huka Falls Road about 2½km (1½ miles) from the center of town.

The ★ **Huka Falls** themselves aren't huge but are impressive for the speed at which the water moves over the 35-foot drop—62,000 gallons per second. The word *huka* means "foaming" in Maori, and the water does resemble the agitation cycle of a washing machine. If you're in the mood to walk, follow the walkway from town; it should take about an hour. If you feel like walking farther, from here you can walk to **Aratiatia Rapids,** but allow two hours to get there. Time your arrival for 10am or 2:30pm, when water is released from the dam, creating quite a difference in water level.

If you find geothermal areas compelling—especially if you didn't see any around Rotorua—visit ★ **Craters of the Moon,** on a mile of unpaved road off Highway 1 between the Wairakei Geothermal Power Station and Taupo (watch for the sign). The area looks like the aftermath of a fire, quite eerie, especially with the gurgling sounds the bubbling mud makes. Get out of your car to experience it fully, but be sure to stay on the marked paths. There's no admission charge, whereas you pay NZ$5 (U.S. $3.25) at the nearby **Wairakei Thermal Valley,** open daily from 9am to 5pm.

HEIGHTS, FLIGHTS & TOURS

Truly thrilling **scenic flights** leave the lakefront near the Taupo Boat Harbour, ranging from a 10-minute flight over Wairakei's steaming valley, Huka Falls, and Taupo, to one-hour forays as far away as Tongariro National Park and a two-hour excursion that takes you even farther afield. Prices range from NZ$30 to NZ$120 (U.S. $19.50 to $78); children are charged half price. You'll find ARK Aviation Ltd. at the Boat Harbour (☎ **378-7500** or **378-9441**).

You may also want to experience **bungee jumping** over the beautiful Waikato River (☎ **377-1135**) for NZ$85 (U.S. $55.25), **tandem skydiving** (☎ **025/428-688**) for NZ$170 (U.S. $111.50), **jet boating** (☎ **374-8572**) for NZ$40 (U.S. $26), or **river rafting** (☎ **377-0419**) for NZ$65 (U.S. $42.25).

Minibus tours of the region around Lake Taupo are given daily by ★ **Paradise Tours** and led by knowledgeable and affable guide Sue King. Book with Sue (☎ **378-9955,** or **025/904-944**). Local tours, given every morning and afternoon, last 2½ hours and cost NZ$24 (U.S. $15.60). She also offers half- and full-day tours to Orakei Korako, Rotorua, and the Waitomo caves. Highly recommended.

Tuwharetoa Tourism, on Tongariro Street (☎ **378-0254**), offers an opportunity to experience fishing, horse trekking, hunting, and other outdoor pursuits with a local Maori as your guide. The Ngati (tribe) Tuwharetoa have exclusive access to some of the best wilderness areas in the Taupo district. They also offer marae stays and authentic concerts and hangi dinners.

SHOPPING

Try not to leave Taupo until you've checked out the wool and sheepskin products at the **Wool Shed,** on Ruapehu Street (☎ **378-9513**). It sells wonderful sweaters, spen-

READERS RECOMMEND

The Super Loo, in the park next to the information kiosk. *"This is the most elegant state-of-the-art ladies and gents conveniences we've ever seen."*—Sue and Frank Thorn, Fallbrook, Calif., U.S.A.

cers, slippers, sheepskins, and knitting wool (yarn). This is also the place to look for wool bush shirts, gloves, and car-seat covers. The hand-knits are all crafted locally.

EVENING ENTERTAINMENT

Nightlife is low-key at best in Taupo. There are sometimes disco nights at varying venues around town—your best bet is to check with the Visitors Information Centre to see what's happening when you're there. It must be said, however, that if you've been fishing for trout on Lake Taupo all day or engaging in any of the wonderful outdoor activities in this area, you'll be more than ready for bed by nightfall anyway.

Where to Stay

Only during the holiday season should it be necessary to reserve very far in advance, since there are more than 3,000 beds available in the immediate vicinity. The efficient, well-run Visitor Information Centre can furnish a list of area accommodations, complete with current prices.

The rates given below include GST.

MOTELS

★ **Adelphi Motel,** 39–41 Kaimanawa St. (P.O. Box 1091), Taupo. ☎ and fax **07/378-7594.** 10 units (all with bath). TV TEL

Rates: NZ$60 (U.S. $39) single; NZ$85 (U.S. $55.25) double. Auto club discounts available. Rates higher during holidays. AE, DC, MC, V.

This attractive in-town motel is presided over by Audrey and Ann Freeman. The only second-floor apartment has views of the lake and mountains. There are one- and two-bedroom units, sleeping two to six, each with a fully equipped kitchen, a radio, and an electric blanket. One is especially designed for the disabled. There are two private spa pools on the premises, as well as a laundry, car-washing facilities, and a trampoline. Breakfast is available for a small charge, as is dinner on request.

Cedar Park Motor Lodge, Two Mile Bay (P.O. Box 852), Taupo. ☎ **07/378-6325.** Fax 07/377-0641. 24 units (all with bath). TV TEL

Rates: NZ$78 (U.S. $50.70) single; NZ$90 (U.S. $58.50) double. Rates higher during holidays and lower off-season. DC, MC, V.

Cedar Park is one of the most attractive accommodations in Taupo, with some two-story units that feature peaked ceilings and picture windows looking out over the lake. Each unit has a separate sitting area, two bedrooms, a complete kitchen, video, a radio, and electric blankets. There's a heated swimming pool, hot spa pools, a children's play area, barbecue, laundry, and car-wash facilities. Also, a very good BYO restaurant is right on the premises. The hostelry is located across Highway 1 from the lakefront, 4km ($2^1/_2$ miles) from the center of town.

READERS RECOMMEND

Delmont Lodge, 115 Shepherd Rd., Taupo (☎ **07/378-3304;** fax 07/378-3322). *"I stayed at this bed-and-breakfast inn, and it's lovely and has magnificent views of the lake and mountains. Jenny Delmont is a great hostess and serves fresh-squeezed orange juice for breakfast. It really is a little piece of magic set at beautiful Lake Taupo."* J. Cozby, Devonport, N.Z. [**Author's Note:** Delmont Lodge offers three rooms, all with private baths. Rates (including breakfast) are NZ$90 (U.S. $58.50) single or NZ$130 (U.S. $84.50) double.]

$ **Dunrovin Motel,** 140 Heu Heu St. (P.O. Box 647), Taupo. ☎ **07/378-7384.** 8 units (all with bath). TV TEL

Rates: NZ$49 (U.S. $31.85) single; NZ$65 (U.S. $42.25) double. AE, DC, MC, V.

The Dunrovin Motel is on a quiet street that's central to the town. Colin and Yenjit Evans offer one- and two-bedroom units, with twin and double beds, sleeping two to eight. All have a complete kitchen and radio. A children's play area and a guest laundry are on the premises, and cooked or continental breakfasts are available for an additional charge.

A BED-&-BREAKFAST

★ $ **Bradshaw's Guest House,** 130 Heu Heu St., Taupo. ☎ **07/378-8288.** 12 rms (7 with bath).

Rates (including breakfast): NZ$35 (U.S. $22.75) single without bath, NZ$40 (U.S. $26) single with bath; NZ$55 (U.S. $35.75) double without bath, NZ$60 (U.S. $39) double with bath. MC, V.

The friendliness of hosts Pete and Sue Howard makes this a popular place. Bradshaw's is a homey white house set on a quiet residential street near the center of town. The rooms are nicely done up, with attractive furnishings and lots of wood paneling. There's a cozy TV lounge (with books for non-tube addicts), a tea-and-coffee room, a laundry, a dining room that faces the lake, and 12 bedrooms, 3 of them singles.

A HOSTEL

★ $ **Rainbow Lodge,** 99 Titiraupenga St., Taupo. ☎ **07/378-5754.** Fax 07/377-1568. 9 rms (none with bath). **Transportation:** Courtesy pickup from the bus station.

Rates: NZ$30 (U.S. $19.50) double; NZ$13 (U.S. $8.45) dorm bed. AE, MC, V.

Rainbow Lodge, near the town center just off Spa Road, is only a short distance from main highways, shops, the bus depot, and the lake. Sue and Mark Dumble offer dormitory rooms and double rooms. Most guests supply their own linens, but they're available for rent. Communal facilities include toilets, bathrooms, the kitchen, the dining room, the lounge, the laundry, the games area, and the sauna. Underfloor heating keeps things cozy. The Dumbles will help you arrange all sorts of activities (fishing, tramping, canoe trips), some at special discounts available only to guests. Mountain bikes and fishing rods can be rented.

READERS RECOMMEND

The Gables Motel, 130 Lake Terrace, Taupo (☎ **07/378-8030**; fax 07/378-8031). *"We stayed at several AA Host hotels that I think deserve special recognition. . . . We found that we received very good value for money. The Gables had lovely units facing Lake Taupo. Several of them, including ours, had a private spa."*—Mrs. Robert Coennen, Nassau Bay, Texas, U.S.A.

Waitahanui Lodge, State Hwy. 1 (R.D. 2), Taupo (☎ **07/378-7183**, or toll free **0800/104-321** in New Zealand). *"I'm enclosing a brochure from the cute lodge my husband and I stayed in at Lake Taupo on our honeymoon in New Zealand. Great fishing and nice family."*—Karen Rydstrom, Evanston, Ill., U.S.A. [**Author's Note:** These self-contained cabins are located 8km (5 miles) south of Taupo. There's a tackle store on the premises. The rates are NZ$60 to NZ$70 (U.S. $39 to $45.50) double.]

CAMPING & CABINS

In a quiet rural setting overlooking the lake, the **Acacia Holiday Park,** Acacia Bay Road (P.O. Box 171), Taupo (☎ **07/378-5159**), offers tent and caravan sites, cabins, and self-contained tourist flats. On the premises are a hot spa pool and recreation room with a pool table, as well as ample picnic tables and barbecues. Best of all, the friendly owners, Keith Ericksen and Glyn and Carolyn Rushby, take much pleasure in providing visitors with information, maps, and brochures on local attractions. The rates for tent and caravan sites are NZ$9 (U.S. $5.85) for adults and NZ$4.50 (U.S. $2.95) for children; for cabins, NZ$26 (U.S. $16.90) double; for tourist flats, NZ$49 (U.S. $31.85) for two people.

WORTH THE EXTRA MONEY

Cottage Mews Motel, Lake Terrace, Taupo. ☎ **07/378-3004.** Fax 07/378-3005. 8 units, 2 suites. TV TEL

Rates: NZ$105 (U.S. $68.25) unit for one or two; NZ$110 (U.S. $71.50) suite for two. AE, DC, MC, V.

The prettiest lodging in town is right beside the lake in a colonial-style motel with black wood siding and white trim (a bit of New England in the South Pacific). A wheelbarrow filled with bright posies sits at the entrance. The impressive split-level apartment units have a kitchen, a balcony, toilets both upstairs and down, a large spa bath, and striking wood trim throughout. Some units have lake views, private patios, and a king or queen-size bed. My favorite is the lake-view accommodation. Breakfast is available at an additional charge. It's located about 1km (1/2 mile) south of the Napier/Taupo turnoff.

Manuels Beach Resort Hotel, Lake Terrace, Taupo. ☎ **07/378-5110.** Fax 07/378-5341. 18 rms (all with bath), 7 suites. TV TEL

Rates: NZ$130 (U.S. $84.50) single; NZ$152 (U.S. $98.80) double; NZ$200 (U.S. $130) suite. AE, DC, MC, V.

For an elegant lakeside stay, try this motor inn that mirrors its owner's love of the Mediterranean. The lobby is welcoming, with a chandelier, a giant mirror, and fresh flowers. The standard rooms have either a balcony or patio; all have sofa beds along with a double bed. The suites include a minibar and coffee and tea facilities. A few of the rooms have bathtubs (a favorite feature of mine). The swimming pool is thermally heated, and the grotto spa pool, complete with glowworms, is Disney-inspired. A lounge with overstuffed chairs overlooks the lake, and wrought-iron tables and chairs on the patio at the lakeshore are conducive to sipping the brandy Alexanders or piña coladas available from the bar. The hotel's Edgewater restaurant (see "Where to Eat," below) is very good.

READERS RECOMMEND

Clearwater Motor Lodge, 229 Lake Terrace, Taupo (☎ and fax **07/377-2071**). *"This was magnificent. Our room, more appropriately a suite, was one of six with lakefront views. It included a kitchenette, a wonderful spa, a very comfortable king-size bed, a small sitting room, and a bathroom with glassed shower stall. Large windows and a door to an outside terrace gave us a wonderful view of Taupo and the lake. The rate was NZ$115 (U.S. $74.75)."*—Edward and Sandra Adler, Painsville, Ohio, U.S.A.

Where to Eat

Echo Cliff, 5 Tongariro St. ☎ **378-8539.**

Cuisine: NEW ZEALAND. **Reservations:** Recommended.
Prices: Appetizers NZ$6–NZ$10 (U.S. $3.90–$6.50); main courses NZ$12–NZ$20 (U.S. $7.80–$13). AE, DC, MC, V.
Open: Lunch Mon–Fri noon–2pm; dinner daily 5:30–9pm.

You'll find good value at Echo Cliff, right at the lake, upstairs over Sullivan's Sports. The menu includes all the New Zealand standards (seafood, lamb, veal, chicken, beef, and so on), plus Dutch Indonesian and continental dishes. Great view. Fully licensed.

Hudders Licensed Cafe, 22 Tuwharetoa St. ☎ **378-5919.**

Cuisine: CAFE. **Reservations:** Not accepted.
Prices: Snacks and light meals NZ$6–NZ$12 (U.S. $3.90–$7.80). AE, DC, MC, V.
Open: Daily noon–"late."

You'll have to fight the locals for a seat in this popular little café. The menu is innovative and competitively priced, and the lively atmosphere enjoyable. If it weren't for those very Kiwi kumara fries on the menu, I'd say the food here is American. Look for Bonanza beef feasts, Ninja burgers, Presley's prawns, E.T.'s BLT, and muchos nachos. Licensed and BYO.

Margarita's Bar and Restaurant, 63 Heu Heu St. ☎ **378-9909.**

Cuisine: MEXICAN. **Reservations:** Recommended.
Prices: Average meal NZ$15–NZ$20 (U.S. $9.75–$13). AE, DC, MC, V.
Open: Dinner only, daily 5pm–1am.

Located above the Real Estate House in the center of town, Margarita's specializes in Mexican and not-so-Mexican food, creative cocktails, inviting atmosphere, and reasonable prices. It's fully licensed, with a complete cocktail bar and live music every night.

WORTH THE EXTRA MONEY

Edgewater Restaurant, in Manuels Beach Resort Hotel, Lake Terrace. ☎ **378-5110.**

Cuisine: FRENCH/NEW ZEALAND. **Reservations:** Required.
Prices: Average dinner (without wine) NZ$40 (U.S. $26). AE, DC, MC, V.
Open: Dinner only, daily 6:30–11pm.

One of the most beautifully prepared meals I've had in New Zealand was at this award-winning restaurant. Sample main courses include lamb pot au feu, lamb tournedos, and white veal with goose-liver mousse. Chef Hennie Silleman has won awards for lamb and venison dishes, as well as for desserts. The dining room is richly decorated in deep green and mauve. The Edgewater is licensed and has an outstanding lake view.

READERS RECOMMEND

Finch's Brasserie and Bar, 64 Tuwharetoa St. (☎ **377-2425**). *"This spot offers a wide range of dinners where the quality is first class and the presentation superb. Customers are encouraged to have a before-dinner drink beside a fireplace in the cozy lounge. Dinner for two, including drinks, cost approximately NZ$50 (U.S. $32.50)."*—E. and S. Adler, Painsville, Ohio, U.S.A.

En Route to Tongariro

The 94km (58-mile) drive from Taupo to Tongariro National Park is an easy one—good roads with changing scenery as you follow Highway 1 along the eastern shore of Lake Taupo through small towns and fishing settlements, around charming bays, always with that vast lake on your right. Look for **Motutaiko Island** (the only one in the lake) as you approach Hatepe. As you near the southern end of the lake, you'll begin to catch glimpses of volcanic cones, which are at the heart of the park. Consider stopping in **Turangi** if trout are your passion. The **Tongariro River** is one of the best-known trout-fishing places in the world. I also recommend a detour to the thermal pools at **Tokaanu.** Even if you don't soak, there's a great nature walk. Highway 47 cuts off from Highway 1 to lead you through plateaulike tussocklands across to Highway 48 and the entrance to park headquarters and the elegant Château. It's clearly signposted, and as you leave Lake Taupo behind, the volcanic nature of this terrain begins to dominate the landscape. By the time you reach the Château, you've entered another world from that of the lake you've left behind.

WHERE TO STAY & EAT EN ROUTE

Bridge Fishing Lodge, State Hwy. 1, Turangi. ☎ **07/386-8804,** or toll free **0800/509-995** in New Zealand. Fax 07/386-8803. 34 rms (all with bath), 2 suites. MINIBAR TV TEL

Rates: NZ$96 (U.S. $62.40) single or double; NZ$134 (U.S. $87.10) family suite. AE, DC, MC, V.

The Bridge Fishing Lodge, at the southern end of Lake Taupo, has rooms for single or double occupancy, seven with fully equipped kitchens. The rooms have tea and coffee facilities, fridges, videos, radios, and heaters. There's a licensed restaurant, a bar, a guest lounge, a sauna, a barbecue, a laundry, and a tour desk. They'll also rent you fishing tackle and waders if the fish in the lake and adjacent Tongariro River prove too great a temptation. Family units sleep six.

The Settlers Motel, State Hwy. 1 and Arahori St. (P.O. Box-30), Turangi. ☎ **07/386-7745.** Fax 07/386-6354. 8 studios and units. TV TEL

Rates: NZ$62 (U.S. $40.30) studio for one; NZ$75 (U.S. $48.75) studio for two; NZ$81 (U.S. $52.65) unit for two. AE, MC, V.

READERS RECOMMEND

Joy Wardell, Omori Rd. (R.D. 1), Turangi (☎ **07/386-7386**). *"Joy lives in a home adjoining her daughter and son-in-law's property. Joy was our principal host, but the entire family enjoys meeting people, and they dropped by frequently for dinner or drinks. Both homes have magnificent views of Lake Taupo, the mountains, and farmlands and are located near the mighty Tongariro River (fishing, jet boating, and rafting) and Mount Ruapehu (skiing and walking). Joy offers one bedroom (twin beds) with a private bath. She's a fun, energetic, and kind woman who enjoys life. She made us feel most welcome."* —Carolann H. Natemeyer, Houston, Texas, U.S.A.

Jack and Betty Anderson, 1 Poto St., Turangi (☎ **07/386-8272**). *"I stayed at seven B&Bs in New Zealand, and these were the most fun hosts. They are a relaxed, happy people. I went fishing and caught some trout, and Jack did a super Cajun-style dinner with the fish. I ended up staying three nights rather than one. They offer two self-contained cottages, as well as rooms in their home."*—John W. Behle, Cincinnati, Ohio, U.S.A.

At the southern end of Lake Taupo, the Settlers offers eight serviced units with kitchens, radios, and heaters, and there's a guest laundry. They can provide fishing guides, and they've even included fish-cleaning facilities so when you catch your dinner you can cook it up in your unit. Licensed restaurants and shops are a short walk away. There are also two-bedroom units, and one with a water bed. The hosts here are Jean and Jim Driscoll.

2 Tongariro National Park

99km (61 miles) SW of Taupo, 141km (87 miles) NE of Wanganui

GETTING THERE • By Train The *Overlander* and the *Northerner* express trains stop at the national park.

• By Bus InterCity provides bus service to the national park.

• By Car Highways 1, 4, 47, and 48 reach the national park.

ESSENTIALS • Information The National Park Headquarters is in the little village of **Whakapapa,** at the end of Highway 48. The Visitors Centre (**☎ 07/892-3729**), the center of information and assistance in planning tramps through the park, is open daily from 8am to 5pm. They keep up-to-date weather data, and provide detailed maps, guide services, camping permission, and hunting permits. They also offer two excellent video presentations—*The Sacred Gift of Tongariro* and *The Ring of Fire*—and have fine displays on the natural and human history of the park. The Visitors Centre also has information on the popular ski fields 7km (4½ miles) above the village.

• Telephone The telephone area code (STD) for the national park area is **07.**

It's a dramatic landscape, dominated by three volcanos that rise with stark beauty from heathlike plains. The Maori consider the volcanos sacred (*tapu*) and have mythical explanations for their origins. In the past, they buried their chiefs in caves along the slopes.

Ruapehu, with its 2,796-meter (9,227-foot) snowcapped summit, is the highest mountain on the North Island and provides its principal skiing facilities while holding in its basin the simmering, ice-ringed Crater Lake. **Ngauruhoe,** rising 2,290 meters (7,557 feet), smolders constantly and from time to time sends showers of ash and lava spilling from its crater (the last in 1975) to alter its shape once again. **Tongariro,** lowest of the three (1,968 meters/6,494 ft), is also the most northerly and the center of Maori legend. There were once, so the story goes, many mountains in the North Island's center, all male with the exception of Pihanga, who was wed to Tongariro and was the object of the other mountains' lustful fantasies. According to one version of the legend, Pihanga's heart belonged only to Tongariro, who defeated the other mountains and exiled them from the region. Another version has Pihanga discovered by Tongariro dallying with Taranaki, which resulted in a fierce fight that ended with a swift, hard kick to Taranaki's backside and his hasty retreat to the west coast, where he stands in solitary splendor today as Mount Egmont, an almost perfect replica of Japan's Mount Fuji. You can follow his trail, which became the Whanganui River, and still see the enormous depression under Mount Egmont's Fantham's Peak put there by Tongariro's kick. When mists surround Egmont today, the Maori will tell you he is weeping for his lost love.

For non-legend-believers, there is the nonlegendary fact that the peaks are at the end of a volcanic chain that extends all the way to the islands of Tonga, 1,000 miles away. Their origin is fairly recent, as these things go, dating back only about two million years.

Tongariro National Park is now a World Heritage Site, but long before this was declared a Maori chief had the wisdom and foresight to preserve it. In 1887, Te Heuheu Tukino, a paramount chief of the Tuwharetoa tribe, in an effort to shield the tapu nature of the Tongariro Mountains, gifted the land to the people of New Zealand. By this act, he guaranteed that it would be protected for all people, for all time. The park became the first national park in New Zealand and the second in the world.

What to See & Do

Skiing is *the* activity during the season, which normally lasts from June to October or November, with three well-developed fields inside the park. The most popular is the **Whakapapa Ski Area,** on the northwestern side of Mount Ruapehu, just 7km (4½ miles) beyond the village. You can call for **snow and ski information** (☎ **07/892-3833** or **892-3738**). The Ski Shop can rent you ski equipment and provide instruction and a current brochure detailing all charges. If you have your own equipment with you, expect to spend about NZ$50 (U.S. $32.50) for lifts and tows for a full day. All facilities operate from 8:30am to 4:30pm unless weather conditions interfere, and there's public bus transportation from the village to the ski field, which I heartily recommend that you use since driving and parking can be a real problem. Whakapapa's "sister resort" is Copper Mountain in Colorado, and there are some reciprocal privileges.

In any other season, there are fascinating ★ **walks** to view more than 500 plant species, the giant rimu trees (some well over 600 years old), and 30 bird species within the park's boundaries. Then there's that hot ★ **Crater Lake** on Mount Ruapehu, the **Ketetahi Hot Springs**, and a pleasant 20-minute **Ridge Track.** Ambitious trackers can take a whack at climbing all three volcanos in one day—but believe me, it takes a lot of ambition, with a healthy dose of stamina thrown in! It's much easier to ride the two chair lifts that operate during summer. Check with the park headquarters for details on all possibilities.

Where to Stay

Accommodations are as scarce as the proverbial hen's teeth! If Tongariro National Park is a big stop on your itinerary, you might consider a night or two at the elegant Grand Château, with "extra-money" prices. There are also accommodations in our budget range, few though they may be. Need I say that early reservations are absolutely necessary during the ski season? You might also consider a Turangi base, only a short drive from the park (see "En Route to Tongariro," at the end of the Taupo section, earlier in this chapter).

CAMPING & CABINS

The **Whakapapa Holiday Park,** Mount Ruapehu (☎ and fax **07/892-3897**), is down the first right turn after you pass park headquarters. Set on the banks of Whakapapanui Stream, it's surrounded by lush bushland. There are tent and caravan sites (all nicely screened by foliage), four six-berth cabins, and two four-berth cabins. Cabins come with two-tier bunks, table and chairs, and electric heating. On the premises are toilets and showers, electric stoves, a laundry with a drying room, and a camp store. Rates for tent or caravan sites are NZ$9 (U.S. $5.85) per adult and NZ$4.50 (U.S. $2.95) per child; cabins run NZ$33 (U.S. $21.45) for two people. Tourist flats are available for NZ$50 (U.S. $32.50) for two. Bunkbed accommodations are available from November to April for NZ$12.50 (U.S. $8.15) per person per night. No credit or charge cards are accepted.

Trampers on the mountain slopes can arrange through the park headquarters to use strategically placed rustic **huts,** which are equipped with bunks and coal stoves.

A LODGE

Ruapehu Skotel, c/o Mount Ruapehu Post Office. ☎ **07/892-3719.** Fax 07/892-3777. 14 rms (some with bath), 45 chalets.

Rates: NZ$36 (U.S. $23.40) double without bath, NZ$82 (U.S. $53.30) double with bath; NZ$110 (U.S. $71.50) deluxe chalet. Rates higher in ski season, lower for solo travelers. AE, DC, MC, V.

This rustic lodge on the lower slopes of Mount Ruapehu, above the Grand Chateau, offers both self-contained chalets and lodge accommodations. The attractive slant-roofed lodge rooms can accommodate two, three, or four people; most have hot and cold running water and many have shower and toilet. There's a large, bright guest kitchen with individual food lockers, stoves, and fridge. Also on the premises are a laundry, a sauna, private spas, a gym, and a large games room. The lounge invites conviviality, and there's a restaurant/bar. The chalets sleep six (four bunks and two single beds); the kitchens are completely equipped, and there's a TV. Outside, views of Ngauruhoe's cone are spectacular. All buildings are centrally heated and have piped-in music. This is a lively place, with movies, hikes, fishing, and botany expeditions. A reader wrote to say that she was "very impressed with the food" here.

WORTH THE EXTRA MONEY

The Grand Chateau, Mount Ruapehu, Tongariro National Park. ☎ **07/892-3809.** Fax 07/892-3704. 64 rms (all with bath). MINIBAR TV TEL

Rates: Summer, NZ$107–NZ$158 (U.S. $69.55–$102.70) single or double. Winter, NZ$160–NZ$250 (U.S. $104–$162.50) single or double. AE, BC, DC, MC, V.

The Grand Chateau, at the end of State Highway 48, is a hotel in the manner of years gone by, but with a 1930s deco-style lounge. The rooms are elegant, and there are such additional comforts as a heated pool and sauna. Also offered here are a nine-hole golf course, tennis courts, and a bowling green. The Chateau justifies its listing in a budget travel guide on two counts: It's an outstanding hotel, internationally famous; and it's one of the scarce places to stay in this neighborhood.

Where to Eat

The Grand Chateau, Mount Ruapehu, Tongariro National Park. ☎ **892-3809.**

You can eat at any price range at the Chateau. For the truly budget-minded, there's the paneled, no-frills **Cafeteria,** open every day from 8am to 5pm, where you'll find meat pies, sandwiches, salads, and such at low prices. The cozy, publike **Carvery** serves a quite nice evening meal with a choice of roasts, fish, grills, and salads. For an elegant—and expensive—dinner, it's the high-ceilinged, chandeliered **Ruapehu**

Room, from 6:30 to 9pm. The à la carte menu features New Zealand specialties, as well as many exotic dishes, which are prepared or flamed at your table.

The Chateau can also supply you with **box lunches** for a day on the slopes, and during ski season there are kiosks and snack bars open at the ski fields. Try the **Knoll Ridge Chalet.**

En Route to Wanganui

The 141km (87 miles) from Tongariro National Park to Wanganui pass through some of the most scenic countryside in the North Island. Indeed, the winding road between Raetihi and Wanganui passes through what has been labeled the "Valley of a Thousand Hills." These are the **Parapara Hills,** formed from volcanic ash, with shell-rock seams and great walls of "papa" rock (a blue clay), which can, incidentally, be quite slippery when landslides put it across the highway. This entire drive, however, is one to be done at a leisurely pace (with an eye out, especially in winter, for patches of that clay across the road) so as to enjoy the spectacular scenery. Sheep farms line your way, with at least one deer farm visible from the highway. There are numerous rest areas en route, offering delightful panoramic views, and in autumn, silver birches dot the landscape with brilliant golds and oranges.

You'll pass the beautiful **Raukawa Falls,** skirt three small lakes whose waters shade from green into red into black during the course of the year and are held sacred by the Maori, then cross the Whanganui River over the Dublin Street Bridge to enter Wanganui.

3 Wanganui

141km (87 miles) SW of Tongariro National Park, 160km (99 miles) SE of New Plymouth, 193km (120 miles) N of Wellington

GETTING THERE • By Bus InterCity, Newmans, and Dominion Coachlines provide services between Wanganui and Auckland, New Plymouth, National Park, and Wellington.

• By Car Wanganui can be reached via Highways 3 and 4.

ESSENTIALS • Information The **Wanganui Visitors Information Centre** is located at 101 Guyton St. (P.O. Box 637), Wanganui (☎ and fax **06/345-3286**). Pick up a copy of their handy "Wanganui, The River City" brochure. The center can also furnish you with other useful brochures, book river tours, and provide maps. Be sure to notice the topographical table map on which you can trace your route through this scenic region. Visitors are sure to get a warm welcome here from Vivian Morris and her staff. They're on hand Monday through Friday from 8:30am to 5pm and Saturday and Sunday from 10am to 2pm.

• Mail The General Post Office is on Ridgeway Street (☎ **345-8349**).

• Telephone The telephone area code (STD) for Wanganui is **06.**

Wanganui (the river and park are spelled "Whanganui") was born amid fierce controversy over the way in which Col. William Wakefield, acting for the New Zealand Company in 1840, took title to the land. It seems he came ashore with an assortment of mirrors, blankets, pipes, and other trinkets and piled them on the site of the present-day Moutoa Gardens. With this offering, he "bought" some 40,000 acres of Maori land. The Maori, however, replaced Wakefield's gifts with 30 pigs and nearly 10 tons of potatoes—their customary "gift for gift"—and had no idea they had transferred title to their lands.

Despite the dispute, settlers began arriving and the town prospered, though constantly caught up in Maori-Pakeha conflicts, some of which were quite violent. It wasn't until 1848 that land problems were laid to rest with the payment of £1,000 for about 80,000 acres clearly defined in a bill of sale from the Maori, which ended with the words "Now all the land contained within these boundaries . . . we have wept and sighed over, bid farewell to and delivered up forever to the Europeans."

It was the Whanganui River (whose riverbed was carved out by Taranaki in his wild flight from Tongariro's wrath) that made this site such a desirable one for the Europeans. It had long served as an important waterway to the interior, as well as affording an excellent coastal harbor. It was said by the Maori that the great explorer Kupe sailed the river. Pakehas soon established regular steamer service between the town and Taumarunui, and because of the magnificent scenery along the riverbank, the three-day journey quickly became an important sightseeing trip for tourists from all over the world. The steamer plied the river until 1934, and it's a pity that fire destroyed the wonderful old hotel and houseboat that provided overnight accommodations to those travelers.

A large portion of the Whanganui River is now part of a national park, with an entrance to its wonderfully wild mix of virgin forest and secondary-growth bush at the historic little settlement of Pipiriki. Set right on the river, this was once the terminus for riverboats, and it nestles among wooded hills, with picnic spots and easily accessible bush reserves. Most of the Whanganui National Park is accessible only by boat or on foot.

What to See & Do

To put first things first, take a good look at Wanganui and its environs, which will bring everything else you see into perspective—it's the look you get from ★ **Durie Hill,** at the south end of the Wanganui Bridge at Victoria Avenue. Pick up the souvenir booklet that tells you the history of this place, then go through a 672-foot tunnel to reach a unique elevator, which takes you to the summit, 216 feet up. The fare is NZ$1 (U.S. 65¢), and you'll count it money well spent. From the platform at the top, Wanganui is spread before you: The historic river's winding path is clear; to the west stretches the Tasman Sea; and to the north rises Mount Egmont (that unlucky lover, Taranaki). If you're game to walk up 176 steps, the top of the nearby **War Memorial** will give you a view that extends from Mount Ruapehu all the way to the South Island (you'll have to take that on faith—as yet, I haven't summoned up the stamina to make the climb!). Even from the ground, the War Memorial Tower is worth a few minutes of your time. It's constructed of shell rock from the riverbanks, which holds two-million-year-old fossils that prove conclusively that Wanganui was once a part of the sea.

There are delightful ★ **walks** in and around Wanganui. Look for the brochure "A Heritage Walk Around Wanganui City" at the information center. Another, the **Atene Skyline Walk,** takes a full day (about eight hours) but rewards you with stunning views of the area and a "meander" around what was once seabed. Trampers who hanker for a several-days trek through **Whanganui National Park** should ask for requirements and other details at the Visitors Information Centre.

Be sure to stroll down **Victoria Avenue,** Wanganui's main drag. A four-block area in the city center has been renovated and sports Victorian-style street lights, park benches, brick paving, and pocket gardens—all very attractive.

If you like raspberries (as I do) and you're in Wanganui between November and January, ask the visitor center for directions to a **pick-your-own berry farm.** What a treat!

Children will enjoy the romp, grownups the respite, at the **Kowhai Park Playground** on Anzac Parade near the Dublin Street Bridge. The Jaycees of Wanganui built it, and its 4 acres now hold a Tot Town Railway (complete with station, tunnel, and overhead bridge), a huge whale, brontosaurus, clock tower, sea-serpent swings, all sorts of storybook characters, and even a mini-volcano to explore. And speaking of parks, save time for a leisurely stroll through the one at **Virginia Lake** (adjacent to Great North Road and St. John's Hill), whose grounds are a haven of trees, flowers, water lilies, ducks, swans, an aviary, and beautiful winter gardens.

The riverside ★ **Moutoa Gardens** historic reserve is where Maori-Pakeha contact was first made and the first controversial "purchase" of Maori land was transacted. There are memorials to Maori war dead, statues, and the city courthouse there now. It's down at Taupo Quay, off Victoria Quay (beside the huge computer center, a vivid contrast between yesterday and today).

You might also enjoy the **Wool Tour** (☎ **343-6131**), which operates Monday through Friday.

OTHER SIGHTS

Whanganui Regional Museum, in the Civic Centre, Watt St. ☎ **345-7443.**

You won't want to miss the Whanganui Regional Museum—it's the largest regional museum in the country, and there's a large Maori collection, a gallery showing Maori portraits by Lindauer, a settler's cottage, natural-history exhibits, and a 75-foot war canoe built in 1810, which is one of the largest in the country and still has bullets from the Maori wars imbedded in its hull.

Admission: NZ$2 (U.S. $1.30) for adults, NZ60¢ (U.S. 40¢) for children over 5, free for children under 5.

Open: Mon–Sat 10am–4:30pm, Sun and public holidays 1–4:30pm. **Closed:** Good Friday and Christmas Day. **Directions:** Walk one block east of Victoria Avenue toward the end of Maria Place.

St. Paul's Anglican Memorial Church, in the suburb of Putiki.

St. Paul's was built in 1936 by Maori and Pakehas working together. The stained-glass Williams Memorial Window features the figure of Christ wearing robes with a Maori-design border, and there's fine carving in the church's interior.

Admission: Free.

Open: Daily 9am–6pm (if the church is locked, inquire at the house next to the church hall).

Holly Lodge Estate Winery, Papaiti Rd., Upper Aramoho, Wanganui. ☎ **343-9344.**

Plan to spend an hour or two at the Holly Lodge Estate Winery. You can drive out Somme Parade to the winery, but the approach by river via the historic paddlewheeler

Otunui is much more fun. The owners will show you around the vineyards and outbuildings where wines are produced, explaining every step of the process as you go. The Wine Shop and Tasting Bar give you a chance to test several of the wines and buy at wholesale prices. Be sure to step into the small craft shop, where most items have been made locally. Papaiti also has several orchards where you can purchase fruit during the season.

Admission: Free. Paddlewheeler fare NZ$14 (U.S. $9.10) adults, NZ$8 (U.S. $5.20) children under 16.

Open: Daily 9am–6pm. **Directions:** Take the Wine Trip aboard the paddlewheeler *Otunui* (☎ **345-0344** or **025/432-997**) from the city marina at the foot of Victoria Avenue or drive out Somme Parade.

★ **Bushy Park,** Hwy. 3, 24km (16 miles) northwest of Wanganui (Kai Iwi, R.D. 8, Wanganui). ☎ **342-9879.**

Bushy Park was originally the homestead of G.F. Moore, who came to Wanganui in the mid-1860s. The fine old home built in 1906 was occupied by his descendants until 1962, when the house and grounds, plus 211 acres of native forest, were bequeathed to the Royal Forest and Bird Protection Society. The large wooden homestead stands in spacious lawns and gardens planted with a large variety of native plants, with a backdrop of some 220 acres of native bush. An Interpretation Centre houses displays devoted to forest ecology, and visitors are free to walk the forest trails and picnic on the extensive grounds. Devonshire teas are available.

There is accommodation in a self-catering bunkhouse for NZ$10 (U.S. $6.50) per person.

Admission: Day visitors, NZ$3 (U.S. $1.95) adults, NZ$1 (U.S. 65¢) children 7–15; children under 7 free.

Open: Daily 10am–5pm. **Directions:** Turn off State Highway 3 at Kai Iwi and drive 8km (5 miles) to the park.

Bason Botanical Reserve, Rapanui Rd.

The Botanical Reserve's Homestead Garden is a delightful place for a stroll among more than 100 camellias and a wide assortment of shrubs, vines, annuals, bulbs, and perennials. The ultramodern conservatory holds the interesting display center and tropical plant house.

Admission: Free.

Open: Gardens, daily 9:30am–dusk; conservatory, Mon–Fri 10am–4pm, Sat–Sun and holidays 2–4pm. **Directions:** Take State Highway 3 about 5½ km (3½ miles) west to Rapanui Road, turn left, and continue to Mowhanau Beach.

RECREATION

Golfers will find the attractive, centrally located nine-hole Gonville Domain Municipal Golf Course on York Street (☎ **344-5808**). The Wanganui Golf Club (☎ **344-4581**) and the Castlecliff course (☎ **344-4554**) are 18-hole courses. **Swimmers** can head for one of two family fun centers, both of which have outdoor pools plus learners' and toddlers' pools, and there are picnic and barbecue areas. The Gonville Complex is on Tawa Street (☎ **345-5990**), and the Wanganui East Complex, which also has an exhilarating water slide, is on Tinirau Street (☎ **343-6650**).

RIVER TOURS

Exploring the river by **jet boat** takes top priority for most visitors to Wanganui, and there are several options for doing it. But let me suggest that before you set out, drop by the information center and purchase the excellent Whanganui River map published by the Department of Lands & Survey—it's an excellent investment, showing the river and its banks in detail, with historical notes on each point of interest. I further suggest that you study the map before you book your river trip—while there is certainly no *un*interesting part of the river, there may be some portion you'd particularly like to see, and you'll want to be certain you choose a jet boat that will take you there. The information center can also give you current details on which jet-boat tours are operating, departure and return times, and prices in effect at the time of your visit (I try, but you know what can happen to prices!).

A lovely two-hour jet-boat tour leaves from the terminal in the city and takes you out to Hipango Park. Your guide is not only informative but entertaining as well, giving interesting anecdotes about the river and the country through which you're passing.

Another excellent way to explore the river is with **Rivercity Tours** (☎ **06/344-2554** or **025/993-347;** fax 06/347-7888). The company offers jet-boat trips on the river, as well as two- to five-day canoe adventures, suitable for people of all ages and experience. Their minibus road tours are highly recommended. The **mailrun** leaves the post office at 7:15am on Monday through Friday and returns in midafternoon; the cost is NZ$22 (U.S. $14.30) and reservations are essential. Best of all, friendly Don and Maree Adams and their staff will design a tour tailormade to your special interests. Call for schedules and prices.

Where to Stay

That famed Wanganui hospitality extends to virtually every owner or manager of accommodations I have met, and you can be sure of a friendly reception no matter where you end up staying. There are good digs both in town and in the suburbs.

GST is included in the rates listed below.

A LICENSED HOTEL

Grand Hotel, Guyton and St. Hill sts., Wanganui. ☎ **06/345-0955.** Fax 06/345-0953. 55 rms (all with bath), 1 suite. TV TEL

Rates: NZ$50–NZ$60 (U.S. $32.50–$39) single or double; add NZ$10 (U.S. $6.50) per person in the two-bedroom suite. AE, DC, MC, V.

Modernization in this older hostelry has been limited strictly to facilities and furnishings, with such holdovers from its beginnings as dark-wood paneling and fireplaces in the spacious public rooms, oil paintings in gold-leafed frames, the old carved-wood staircase, and a bar crammed full of excellent carvings by local Maori. The furniture is modern (huge, comfortable chairs grouped around low tables in the lounge), yet the decor (upholstering, draperies, etc.) retains a period look.

The guest rooms range from those accommodating just one to those sleeping up to five comfortably. Each is individually decorated, a nice departure from the standardized look of most present-day hotel rooms. A two-family suite features two bedrooms, one on each side of the central lounge. There's a Cobb & Co. restaurant on the premises.

MOTELS

Acacia Park Motel, 140 Anzac Parade, Wanganui East. ☎ and fax **06/343-9093.** 12 units (all with bath). TV TEL

Rates: NZ$60 (U.S. $39) single; NZ$70–NZ$75 (U.S. $45.50–$48.75) double. AE, DC, MC, V.

One of Wanganui's prettiest motels, the Acacia is set in 2 acres of parkland overlooking the river, with units spread among magnificent old trees. The attractive units have radios, electric blankets, and electric heating. Eight are fully self-contained, sleeping four to six, with shower, toilet, fridge, electric range, and full kitchen. Five serviced units sleep up to three and have a fridge, tea and coffee facilities, toaster, and electric frying pan. There's a guest laundry, a spa pool, a games room with a pool table, a children's play area, and a trampoline. The more expensive units have a kitchen. The Acacia is 1.5km (1 mile) from the center of town.

Avro Motel and Caravan Court, 36 Alma Rd., Wanganui. ☎ **06/345-5279.** Fax 06/345-2104. 18 studios and units, 10 caravan sites. TV TEL

Rates: NZ$60 (U.S. $39) studio for one; NZ$70 (U.S. $45.50) apartment for two; NZ$18 (U.S. $11.70) caravan site for two. Auto club discounts. Weekly rates available in winter. AE, DC, MC, V.

There's much to choose from at the Avro. The gardenlike grounds hold bed-sitters (studios) and one-, two-, and three-bedroom units, all with kitchens and wide windows overlooking the lawns. There's an outdoor swimming pool, two indoor spa pools, a children's play area, and a laundry. Mary and Harvey Nixon are the hosts at this nice motel about a mile from the town center. There's a licensed restaurant just 100 yards from the motel, with a nine-hole golf course nearby.

Incidentally, the Avro has marvelous caravan facilities: 10 hookups, each with a small cabin enclosing a shower, toilet, and dressing room. Caravan guests may also use the laundry.

A BED-&-BREAKFAST/HOSTEL

The Riverside Inn and YHA Hostel, 2 Plymouth St., Wanganui. ☎ **06/347-2529.** 10 rms (1 with bath), 22 backpacker beds.

Rates (including continental breakfast): NZ$40 (U.S. $26) single without bath; NZ$55 (U.S. $35.75) double without bath, NZ$70 (U.S. $45.50) double with bath; NZ$14 (U.S. $9.10) per bed (without breakfast). No credit cards.

Set back from the street in a flower garden, this rambling 1895 wooden house has been lovingly brought up-to-date through renovation, with due respect for its age and character. The guesthouse accommodations are decorated with lace curtains, fringed lampshades, and potted plants. The parlor is furnished in wicker and cane, and there's a TV lounge and breakfast room with tea and coffee facilities. The backpacker lodgings are in the rear of the building. Cooked breakfast and dinner are available for an extra charge. Patricia Moore is a helpful host.

CABINS & CAMPING

Four miles east of town, on the city side of the river, the $ **Aramoho Holiday Park,** 460 Somme Parade, Aramoho, Wanganui (☎ **06/343-8402**), has spacious, shady grounds on the riverbank. There are bunk cabins, each with four bunks; graded cabins that sleep two to six, with hot and cold running water, small electric stoves, cooking utensils, and heaters; and tourist apartments and chalets that sleep up to seven, with a complete kitchen, china, cutlery, pots and pans, a toaster, an electric coffee pot, and a private toilet and shower. One chalet sleeps nine and is accessible to wheelchairs. You can rent linen, blankets, and irons. The communal kitchen has gas stoves and a fridge, the laundry includes dryers and an ironing board, and the toilets and showers are stainless steel and Formica. Very near the river is a family barbecue, and there's a seven-day grocery store just across the road. Tent and caravan sites are also available in tree-shaded spots. Rates run NZ$8 (U.S. $5.20) per person for tent sites, NZ$10 (U.S. $6.50) for bunks, NZ$30 (U.S. $19.50) for a cabin for two, and NZ$50 (U.S. $32.50) for a chalet for two. Bankcard, MasterCard, and Visa are accepted.

The **Avro Motel** also has caravan and camping facilities (see "Motels," above).

Where to Eat

Capers, Victoria Arcade, Victoria Ave. ☎ **345-8119.**

Cuisine: NEW ZEALAND. **Reservations:** Recommended for dinner.
Prices: Main courses NZ$9–NZ$12 (U.S. $5.85–$7.80); lunch NZ$3.50–NZ$5 (U.S. $2.30–$3.25). No credit cards.
Open: Mon–Thurs 8am–8pm, Fri 8am–9pm, Sat 8am–3pm.

At the rear of Victoria Arcade, Capers offers wholesome fare and very good value prices. The high ceiling and large number of green plants contribute to the pleasant atmosphere. Daily specials are described on a chalkboard menu. The best bet is the NZ$5 (U.S. $3.25) luncheon plate served from noon to 2pm. Dinner is offered from 5pm, and in between meal hours the locals congregate here to enjoy the homemade cakes—especially the Chelsea buns. The hosts are Judith and Peter. (I forgot to ask their last name, but I remember she told me she does all the baking.) Licensed.

Cobb & Co., in the Grand Hotel, Guyton and St. Hill sts. ☎ **345-0955.**

Cuisine: NEW ZEALAND/BISTRO. **Reservations:** Recommended Fri–Sat for dinner.
Prices: Light meals NZ$6–NZ$15 (U.S. $3.90–$9.75). AE, DC, MC, V.
Open: Lunch daily 11:30am–5pm; dinner daily 5:30–10pm.

No matter what your price or appetite range, this Cobb & Co. in the town center comes up with just the right dish. The coffee shop has an attractive light, bright decor and offers both booths and tables. (Be sure to notice the plaster detailing on the ceiling.) The same menu is served for lunch and dinner and features steaks, fish, chicken, and roasts. Fully licensed.

Liffiton Castle, 26 Liffiton St. ☎ **345-7864.**

Cuisine: INDIAN/NEW ZEALAND. **Reservations:** Recommended, especially on Sat.
Prices: Main courses NZ$13.50–NZ$18 (U.S. $8.80–$11.70). AE, DC, MC, V.
Open: Dinner only, Mon–Sat 5:30–10pm.

This is a century-old house that over the last five years has been renovated with loving care spiced up with a generous dollop of humor. You enter over a moat into a bar whose centerpiece is the bar itself, a renovated theater box from the old Majestic Theatre—notice the three jesters behind the bar (no, not the bartenders), also from the Majestic. There are pressed-tin ceilings from the Wanganui Girls College; a dance floor from the Boys Technical College; a handsome hand-carved 17th-century mantel; arched windows from a local church; an antique English sideboard; and an Armoury Room. All that (plus a good bit more) creates an interesting, warm, inviting—and fun—atmosphere.

The food? Superb! Steaks are a specialty, all of superior grades and beautifully cooked, as well as authentic Indian dishes. There's a special children's menu and a good wine list, reasonably priced. The locals love this place. Licensed.

Michael's Restaurant, 281 Wicksteed St. ☎ **345-2690.**

Cuisine: NEW ZEALAND. **Reservations:** Recommended.
Prices: Lunch NZ$15–NZ$20 (U.S. $9.75–$13); dinner NZ$40 (U.S. $26) à la carte, NZ$30 (U.S. $19.50) fixed price. AE, DC, MC, V.
Open: Lunch Tues–Fri noon–3pm; dinner Tues–Sat 6:30–10pm.

This lovely award-winning restaurant is set in a 1911 Victorian villa surrounded by gardens. The house retains its original character, with kauri furniture. Favorites among its specialties are noisette of venison, lamb rump, and filet of salmon. Licensed. Michael's is located in town.

Rutland Arms Inn, Victoria Ave. and Ridgeway St. ☎ **347-7677.**

Cuisine: ENGLISH. **Reservations:** Recommended Thurs–Sat for dinner.
Prices: Appetizers NZ$5.50–NZ$7.50 (U.S. $3.60–$4.90); main courses NZ$11–NZ$19 (U.S. $7.15–$12.35); lunch NZ$3–NZ$8 (U.S. $1.95–$5.20). AE, BC, DC, MC, V.
Open: Lunch Mon–Sat 10am–2pm; dinner daily 5:30–10pm; brunch Sun 10am–2pm.

This atmospheric upmarket pub has an open-beam ceiling, and the walls are decorated with farm impliments and horse brasses. Old bottles line the plate rail above the window, and a large open fireplace keeps things cozy in winter. Built in 1846, the Rutland Arms is only one of the restored 19th-century buildings in this neighborhood. In addition to roast beef and Yorkshire pudding, fish and chips, and a ploughman's platter, there's a wide selection of English beers. If you hail from England and you're homesick, you can even order pea, pie, and pud (steak-and-kidney pie served with mashed potatoes and peas). Licensed.

Shangri-La, St. John's Hill. ☎ **345-3654.**

Cuisine: NEW ZEALAND. **Reservations:** Recommended.
Prices: Appetizers NZ$5 (U.S. $3.25); main courses NZ$7–NZ$11 (U.S. $4.55–$7.15); Devonshire teas NZ$3.60 (U.S. $2.35); sandwiches and light lunches NZ$2–NZ$4 (U.S. $1.30–$2.60). AE, DC, MC, V.
Open: Lunch daily 11:30am–3pm; Devonshire teas daily 9am–5pm.

In a lovely setting—with a window wall overlooking Virginia Lake and the Winter Garden—the Shangri-La is very much a family-run restaurant. Maurice Vige, the French owner/chef, took his training in Paris; his wife, Frances, is English-trained; and daughters Annette and Nicole act as hostesses. Meals here are home-cooked and easy on the budget. Maurice is meticulous in the preparation of all the food appearing on his tables. As a result, everything from basic Kiwi dishes to homemade pies to burgers and fries is well prepared. The morning and afternoon Devonshire teas are a real treat. BYO.

Top-o-Town's Coffee Shop, 198 Victoria Ave. ☎ **345-7615.**

Cuisine: KIWI. **Reservations:** Not required.
Prices: Light meals NZ$3–NZ$9 (U.S. $1.95–$5.85). No credit cards.
Open: Mon–Fri 6:30am–4pm, Sat 8am–2pm, Sun 10am–2pm.

My favorite small, inexpensive eatery in the center of Wanganui is a cozy place with friendly people behind the self-service counter. Everything served is fresh and homemade, and the menu includes morning and afternoon teas and light meals. There are savouries, meat pies, bacon and eggs, steak, salad and chips, ham steak, fish, sandwiches, pies, and some of the best homemade cakes and pastries you're likely to find anywhere.

En Route to Wellington

Following Highway 3 south from Wanganui until it joins Highway 1, you're in for an easy three-hour, 193km (120-mile) drive along excellent roads: pastoral scenes of grazing sheep and cultivated fields at first, smashing sea views later, then a four-lane expressway leading into the beautiful harbor and splendid hills of wonderful, windy Wellington.

If you've got the time and the inclination, you might like to stop for tea at the **Bridge Inn** in Bulls—this tearoom has long been a favorite spot of mine. Look for it outside town at the north end of the bridge adjacent to the Bridge Motor Lodge.

After Bulls, you can decide if you want to turn south on Highway 1 or continue on Highway 3 to **Palmerston North.** This city isn't on most visitors' intinerary unless they have a need to visit Massey University or a penchant for rugby. The **New Zealand Rugby Museum,** at 87 Cuba St. (☎ **06/358-6947**), is open Monday through Saturday from 10am to noon and 1:30 to 4pm, and Sunday from 1:30 to 4pm. You might also like to check with the **Palmerston North Information Centre,** The Square (☎ **06/358-5003;** fax 06/356-9841), about other sights and activities in this city.

Back on Highway 1, my auto-phile spouse would never forgive me if I didn't tell you about the **Southward Car Museum** in Paraparaumu (☎ **04/297-1221**). Here you'll find the largest and most varied collection of motor vehicles in the Southern Hemisphere, including vintage and veteran cars dating from 1895, as well as motorcycles, stationary engines, and a model railway. It's the private collection of Len—make that Sir Len—Southward who started working as a messenger in a Wellington motor house in 1919 and now owns 250 vehicles. He began collecting cars in 1956 when he purchased a Model T for £40 and was knighted in 1986 "for services to community." There's a large cafeteria on the premises for lunch and teas. The museum is open daily from 9am to 4:30pm; closed Good Friday, ANZAC morning (April 25), and Christmas Day. The admission is NZ$4 (U.S. $2.60) for adults and NZ$1 (U.S. 65¢) for children.

The Southward Car Museum is only one of the attractions in the area known as the **Kapiti Coast,** a stretch along Highway 1 about 58km (36 miles) northeast of Wellington. Waikanae is the principal township. If you're particularly interested in birdlife and/or Maori culture, you might want to make arrangements with the Department of Conservation (☎ **04/472-5821,** fax 04/499-0077) to go out to **Kapiti Island,** where there's a nature reserve and a marine reserve. Three boat operators offer transport. The Kapiti Coast also offers Tiger Moth and helicopter scenic flights, golf, bush walks, rafting, fishing, and a flora and fauna reserve called the **Nga Manu Sanctuary.**

WHERE TO STAY EN ROUTE

$ **Waikanae Beach Homestay,** 115 Tutere St., Waikanae. ☎ **04/293-6532.** 3 rms (none with bath).

Rates (including breakfast): NZ$45 (U.S. $29.25) single; NZ$65 (U.S. $42.25) double. Three-course dinner NZ$18 (U.S. $11.70) extra. No credit cards.

If it's genuine Kiwi hospitality you're after, this is the place. Jeanette and Bryce Jones have a comfortable family home on the beach, and they're the kind of people I can only describe as "hugable." Their two-story house has two spare bedrooms downstairs (these share a bath) and one room upstairs with its own toilet and sink (occupants use the shower downstairs). Bryce catches fish, and Jeanette serves it for dinner, along with fresh local vegetables. There's no smoking, and children are welcome. Try to be here from November to March when it's warm enough to swim at the beach.

Waimoana Homestay, 63 Kakariki Grove, Waikanae. ☎ **04/293-7158.** 2 rms (both with bath).

Rates (including breakfast): NZ$60 (U.S. $39) single; NZ$100 (U.S. $65) double. Multicourse dinner with wine NZ$30 (U.S. $19.50) extra. AE, BC, DC, MC, V.

This contemporary custom-designed house has two guest bedrooms, each with a queen-size and a single bed and a bath. An unusual aspect is the indoor swimming pool that's the focus of the living area. Whether eating dinner at the glass-top table in the starkly modern dining room or enjoying a before-dinner drink in the living room, you get a view of the pool. Ian Stewart is a retired life insurance executive; his wife, Phyllis, is an outstanding cook and hostess. Their home is adjacent to a reserve where there are bush walks, and the large windows afford views of Kapiti Island and the South Island. The hosts have a brochure rack in their front hall and a supply of souvenirs for sale. Guests can take the train into Wellington or do local activities. There's no smoking here, and children are not accepted.

4 New Plymouth

164km (102 miles) NW of Wanganui, 369km (229 miles) SW of Auckland

GETTING THERE • By Plane Air New Zealand Link provides daily service from Auckland, Wanganui, and Wellington, with connecting service to other New Zealand cities.

• **By Bus** InterCity and Newmans provide daily coach service.

• **By Car** New Plymouth can be reached by State Highway 3 and State Highway 45.

ESSENTIALS • Orientation New Plymouth (pop. 49,000) is sited on the west coast of the North Island, in the shadow of Mount Egmont/Taranaki. It's a good base from which to explore the beautiful Taranaki district. Devon Street East and Devon Street West are the main thoroughfares. The post office, on Currie Street (☎ **758-2110**), is open Monday through Friday from 8:30am to 5pm.

• **Information** Take your questions to the **New Plymouth Information Centre,** at Liardet and Leach streets (☎ **06/758-6086**; fax 06/758-1395), open Monday through Friday from 8:30am to 5pm and Saturday, Sunday, and holidays from 10am to 3pm. It also sells postage stamps.

• **Mail** New Zealand Post is located on Currie Street (☎ **06/758-2110**). Open Monday through Friday from 8:30am to 5pm.

• **Telephone** The telephone area code (STD) for New Plymouth is **06.**

New Plymouth is New Zealand's energy center, with major reserves of natural gas—both onshore and offshore—as well as an oil- and natural gas–fueled electric power station. It also has a busy port from which cheese and oil condensate are shipped. In contrast to its energy-based industries, the city boasts several beautiful parks and gardens and is the gateway to Egmont National Park, where conical Mount Egmont/

Taranaki dominates. The Taranaki region is also known for its lush farmlands and as a major dairy center.

The city gets its name from Plymouth in Devon, England—former home of the first to settle here.

What to See & Do

New Plymouth has numerous near-perfect swimming and surfing **beaches** in close proximity and is well known for its excellent **Govett-Brewster Art Gallery,** on Queen Street, and the **Taranaki Museum,** on Ariki Street. The dazzling array of rhododendrons and azaleas at ★ **Pukeiti Rhododendron Trust,** on Carrington Road, a 30-minute drive south of the city, draws visitors from all over the country. **Pukekura Park,** only three blocks from the Visitor Centre, also has lovely gardens as well as two lakes. The New Plymouth Information Centre can furnish directions and open hours for these and many other local attractions. You might want to ask for the "Heritage Walkway" brochure.

Some 7km (4 miles) south of New Plymouth, the **Tupare Garden,** 487 Mangorei Rd., has 9 acres of English-style gardens that are some of the finest in the country. The most spectacular season in the gardens is September to November, and if you arrive here in late October to early November, a highlight of your visit will be the annual Rhododendron Festival.

In Hawera, the ★ **Tawhiti Museum,** 47 Ohangai Rd. (☎ **06/278-6837**), is run by local potter Nigel Ogle and his wife, Teresa. Housed in an old dairy factory, this unique museum includes a model of a Maori bush village, a one-twelfth-scale war canoe, and many exhibits tracing Maori and Pakeha histories in this region. Many have lifelike animated figures illustrating everyday activities over the years.

The Taranaki landscape is dominated by the cone-shaped ★ **Mount Egmont/ Taranaki,** a volcano that has been dormant for over 400 years. This is one of the few mountains you can drive completely around, and there are over 300km (180 miles) of walking tracks within **Egmont National Park,** ranging from 10 minutes to five days, with a selection for both inexperienced and veteran walkers. There are inexpensive huts for walkers within the park, maintained by the Department of Conservation (details from the Visitor Information Centre).

WHERE TO STAY

In addition to the places described below, there's a Department of Conservation backpacker hostel at Dawson Falls. For information on **Konini Lodge,** contact the DOC, on Pembroke Road in Stratford (☎ **06/765-5144**) or at the Egmont National Park Visitor/Display Centre at Dawson Falls (open Thursday through Monday from 10am to 4pm). The cost is NZ$12 (U.S. $7.80) for each adult and NZ$8 (U.S. $5.20) per child.

★ **Dawson Falls Tourist Lodge,** Manaia Rd. (P.O. 91), Stratford.
☎ **06/765-5457,** or toll free **0800/651-800** in New Zealand. Fax 06/765-5457.
11 rms (all with bath). TEL

Rates: NZ$80 (U.S. $52) single; NZ$105 (U.S. $68.25) double; NZ$125 (U.S. $81.25) honeymoon room. AE, BC, DC, MC, V.

This is one of my favorite places in New Zealand. I love the feeling of being isolated and cozy amid the Swiss decor and the wonderful print comforters and matching shams. The lodge is 45 minutes south of New Plymouth and 20 minutes west of Stratford, one-third of the way up the forested slopes of Mount Egmont/Taranaki in Egmont

National Park; walking trails start right outside the front door, and the national park visitor/display center is steps away. Those who aren't energetic enjoy lounging in front of the log fire or just staring out the window at the alpine scenery. There are also a sauna and plunge pool on the premises. I can recommend the honeymoon room—whether this is your first, second, or a trial. You might also want to consider Room 8, which has "a loo [toilet] with a view," or Room 7, which has a huge bathtub and a great view of the mountain. Number 4 is a cozy single. There's no smoking in the bedrooms. Hosts Nell and Tom Lilford are super-friendly. The lodge is licensed and offers all meals. Reserve well ahead if you want to stay on a weekend.

Mountain House Motor Lodge, Pembroke Rd. (P.O. Box 303), Stratford. ☎ and fax **06/765-6100,** or toll free **0800/657-100** in New Zealand. 10 rms (all with bath). TV TEL

Rates: NZ$75–NZ$95 (U.S. $48.75–$61.75) single or double. AE, BC, DC, MC, V.

Here are more rooms within Egmont National Park, 10 minutes west of Stratford on the east side of Mt. Egmont/Taranaki, surrounded by natural beauty and close to hiking trails. Six chalets have kitchens, and all the spacious quarters are attractive and have tea- and coffee-making facilities, small refrigerators, and radios. There's a piano and an open fire in the lounge and a sauna. Keith Anderson and his Swiss wife, Berta (they're responsible for the decor of Dawson Falls Lodge; see above), are the hosts here. She's the chef who's earned the dining room several awards and a loyal following. As we go to press, Keith is developing another five-bedroom property. (If you're going to Taranaki, ask him about it; it should be finished by the time you get there.)

$ **Patuha Farm Lodge,** Upper Pitone Rd. (R.D. 4, New Plymouth), Okato. ☎ and fax **06/752-4469.** 10 rms (all with bath). TEL

Rates (including all meals): NZ$70 (U.S. $45.50) per person. BC, MC, V.

Compared to the two lodges described above, this spot lacks atmosphere, but it's a great location for those visiting the gardens at the adjacent Pukeiti Rhododendron Trust 30km (18 miles) from New Plymouth. The 2km ($1^1/_2$-mile) driveway passes some of the 1,000 ewes that graze on these 600 acres. Peter Henderson, with his parents, Morris and Janet, are the hosts here. All rooms have heaters and clock, radios; some have TVs, Tea and coffee facilities are in the hall, and there's a spa tub. The rates are good value. Licensed.

Where to Eat

Chez Beau, Molesworth St., New Plymouth. ☎ **758-9045.**

Cuisine: MODERN NEW ZEALAND. **Reservations:** Recommended.

Prices: Appetizers NZ$7–NZ$13.50 (U.S. $4.55–$8.80); main courses NZ$14.50–NZ$25 (U.S. $9.45–$16.25). AE, MC, V.

Open: Dinner only, daily 4:30–10pm.

I am endebted to my friend Phil Harrington for introducing me to this stylish bar/brasserie where large windows overlook the ocean. It's upstairs in a very modern black building, and I might have missed it were it not for Phil. The decor is director's chairs and wooden picnic tables, some with umbrellas; bar stools face the ocean and a great view. Main courses include venison cutlets, fresh fish, curries, lamb Wellington, and rack of lamb. The portions are large—I don't recommend that you attempt more than one course. "Light mains" are easier on both the wallet and the waistline. These include Thai seafood, salad niçoise, and several pasta dishes. Licensed.

9 Wellington

"WONDERFUL, WINDY WELLINGTON" THIS CITY IS CALLED—WITH DERISION BY Kiwis who don't live here, with affection by those who do. Well, there's no denying that it *is* windy: 60-m.p.h. winds sweep through what is the only substantial gap in New Zealand's mountain chain on an average of 40 days each year. Winds notwithstanding, however, Wellington is easily New Zealand's cultural center and one of its most beautiful cities. Indeed, its magnificent harbor rivals any in the world. Your first view of that harbor, with the city curved around its western and southwestern shoreline and surrounding hills abloom with what appear from a distance to be tiny dollhouses spilling down their sides, is likely to make you catch your breath, even if that view should happen to be in the rain (which is a distinct possibility). On a fine day, there are few city views anywhere to equal it.

This gorgeous place was discovered in A.D. 950 by Kupe, the great Polynesian explorer, and by the time Captain Cook stopped by (but didn't land) in 1773, the harbor was lined with Maori settlements. When New Zealand Company representative Col. William Wakefield's good ship *Tory* arrived on the scene in September 1839, warring between the Maori tribes had become so fierce, and the local tribes were so fearful of their more powerful enemies, that (after a bit of negotiating back and forth, and a few of the usual misunderstandings about land transfers and so forth), they accepted the Pakeha as the lesser of two evils.

By January 1840 settlers began coming in goodly numbers, and after a rather rowdy beginning (when, according to contemporary reports, meetings were held to try to determine how the citizenry could protect themselves from the lawless police force), the town began a growth that has never really stopped. A tug-of-war with Auckland finally resulted in Wellington's being named the colony's capital on the basis of its central location and the belief that the "middle island" (that's the South Island's claim to being the "mainland") might well pull out and establish a separate colony altogether if it were not afforded better access to the capital than faraway Auckland provided.

Wellington today, while peopled mainly by civil servants, diplomats, and corporate home-office staffs, maintains a conservative—but far from stuffy—air. There is perhaps more sheer diversity here than in any of New Zealand's other cities: Narrow streets and Edwardian buildings nudge modern edifices of concrete and glass; massive office buildings embrace colonial-style restaurants; fashionable boutiques are housed in pseudo-colonial-style complexes while craft shops hold sway in avant-garde structures; and the after-dark scene is one of New Zealand's liveliest. The last few years, in fact, have seen even more diversity with the legislative requirement that all major buildings must be brought up to earthquake-resistant standards. Those requirements have resulted in massive demolition of older buildings and the erection of even more modern high-rise structures. Indeed, it is estimated that within the next few years as many as half the office and commercial spaces in the city center will be replaced. The times they are truly a-changing in wonderful, windy Wellington!

What is *not* likely to change—and it's important to us as visitors—is the ebb and flow of the city's population as government workers depart on weekends for visits home, then flood back into town on Monday. That means an abundance of accommodations are available over weekends, very few during the week (more about that later under "Where to Stay").

In short, Wellington has from the first been a cosmopolitan city, and it's growing more so all the time. It is also your port of embarkation for the South Island's wonders—but pray don't embark until you've explored this hub around which New

What's Special About Wellington

Scenic Splendors

- The harbor—one of the world's most sheltered and easily one of the most beautiful.
- The gorgeous views from Mount Victoria—the harbor sparkling in daylight, city lights twinkling around its perimeter after dark.
- The Botanic Gardens, especially the Lady Norwood Rose Gardens and Begonia House.

Museums

- The National Art Gallery and National Museum, with superb collections of international and New Zealand art and South Pacific artifacts.
- The Maritime Museum, at Queens Wharf, to put you in touch with Wellington's long-standing connection with the sea.

A Historic Place

- Old St. Paul's Church, on Mulgrave Street, a lovely old church that provides a peaceful interlude for busy sightseers.

Cultural Events

- Performances by the National Symphony Orchestra, National Ballet, and National Opera Company in the striking Michael Fowler Centre.

Special Attractions

- The Kelburn Cable Car—unique in the Southern Hemisphere.
- The Beehive—one of the Parliament buildings and the symbol of New Zealand government.

Zealand's government revolves. And from a practical point of view, plan your explorations for a weekend when rooms are easier to come by and special rates are offered to fill rooms vacated by that disappearing weekday population.

1 City Specifics

ARRIVING

BY PLANE The **Wellington Airport** (☎ **04/388-8500**) is 10km (6 miles) south of the city center and served by the following international airlines: Air France (☎ **04/472-2460**), Air New Zealand (☎ **04/388-9900**), British Airways (☎ **04/472-7327**), Lufthansa (☎ **09/303-1529**), Qantas Airways (☎ toll free **0800/808-767** in New Zealand), Singapore Airlines (☎ **04/473-9749**), and United Airlines (☎ **04/472-6897**). Leading domestic airlines are Air New Zealand (☎ **04/388-9900** or **385-9922**), Air Nelson (☎ **04/388-2770**), Ansett (☎ **04/471-1146**), Mount Cook Airlines (☎ **04/388-9900**), and several smaller airlines.

The **Wellington Airport Visitors Information Centre** (☎ **04/388-8500**), in the Domestic Terminal, is staffed Monday through Friday from 7:30am to 8:30pm, Saturday from 7:30am to 7:30pm, and Sunday from 8am to 8pm. There's an Information Desk in the International Terminal staffed Monday through Saturday from 5:30am to 7:30pm and Sunday from 9am to 7:30pm.

There's a good medium-priced cafeteria at the airport, serving light meals and snacks, open from 6am to 9pm every day. Also, there are bars, car-rental desks, bookshops, and gift shops in both terminals; a duty-free shop in the International Terminal; and a nursery in the Domestic Terminal. The bank is open normal hours, as well as one hour before any overseas departure and for one hour after each overseas arrival. Ample luggage carts are provided at no charge.

Airport shuttle services are provided Monday through Friday by **Johnstons Shuttle** (☎ **384-7654**) and **Super Shuttle** (☎ **387-8787**). The one-way fare from the airport to the railway station (or vice versa) is NZ$4 (U.S. $2.60) for adults and NZ$2 (U.S. $1.30) for children. A door-to-door service is also provided "on demand" (at a higher fare) by both companies.

A **taxi** between the city center and the airport will cost approximately NZ$20 (U.S. $13) on weekdays, a little more on weekends.

BY TRAIN & BUS The Wellington **Railway Station** is on Waterloo Quay, and most **long-distance** buses depart from that station (☎ **04/498-3413** for long-distance rail information; ☎ **04/472-5111** or **499-3261,** or toll free **0800/800-737** in New Zealand for long-distance bus information). The Mount Cook depot is on Courtenay Place.

BY CAR Wellington is reached via Highways 1 and 2. It's 195km (121 miles) from Wanganui, 460km (285 miles) from Rotorua, and 655km (406 miles) from Auckland.

BY FERRY For information on the **Inter-Island Wellington–Picton Ferry,** call **04/498-3999.**

TOURIST INFORMATION

The **Wellington City Information Centre,** Civic Square, Wakefield Street (☎ **04/801-4000;** fax 04/801-3030), is open daily from 8:30am to 5:30pm. Ask for the monthly *What's On,* as well as "Wellington Great Time Guide" and other brochures, which are plentiful. The free *Capital Times,* also available from the Information Centre and leading hotels, is published weekly, with information on current activities. The center also has information on the entire country, not just Wellington, and sells postage stamps and PhoneCards.

CITY LAYOUT

The main point of reference in the city is, of course, the harbor, with its exciting waterfront Lambton Harbour Project. Willis Street and Lambton Quay are business streets; for shopping, Lambton Quay, Manners Street, Cuba Street, and Courtenay Place are best. The best lookout for a panoramic view of the city is 648-foot Mount Victoria in the southern end of the city (hop the no. 20 bus for the 15-minute ride); the easiest lookout to reach is Kelburn, with its cable car from Lambton Quay.

2 Getting Around

BY BUS There's a good city bus service, and the main city bus terminal, Ridewell, is at the corner of Bunny and Featherston streets (☎ **801-7000** for route information). Eastbourne buses arrive at and depart from the railway station (☎ **562-8154** for schedules). Fares are based on distance traveled, and you can purchase 10-trip concession tickets. The Information Centre will give you a terrific city map that also shows major bus routes, plus timetables for specific routes. Timetables are also available from newsstands.

BY TRAIN Ridewell runs commuter trains to the suburbs on fairly frequent schedules; phone **801-7000** for timetable information.

BY CAR If you're driving, avoid downtown Wellington. Traffic congestion is significant, and parking spaces are scarcer than hen's teeth.

BY TAXI You'll find taxi stands in front of the railway station, in the Lambton Quay shopping area between Grey and Hunter streets; on Bond Street, just off Willis Street; on Dixon Street between Cuba and Victoria streets; and on Cambridge Terrace near Courtenay Place. There's a NZ$1 (U.S. 65¢) surcharge if you telephone for a taxi (☎ **384-4444**), and on weekends and holidays. A so-called "green" (lower) fare applies between 6am and 8pm on weekdays; outside those hours, you'll pay the "red" (higher) fare—you can check the light on the taxi meter to be sure which fare is in effect.

Fast Facts: Wellington

Airlines The Air New Zealand office for domestic and international reservations and information is at the corner of Panama Street and Lambton Quay (☎ **471-1616**).

American Express The American Express office is located in the Sun Alliance Centre, 280–292 Lambton Quay (☎ **473-7766;** fax 473-7765), open Monday through Friday from 8:30am to 5pm.

Area Code Wellington's telephone area code (STD) is **04**.

Babysitters Most hotels and motels can furnish babysitters, or you can call Wellington Nannies Connection (☎ **384-1135**).

Car Rentals Avis Rent a Car, 25 Dixon St. (☎ **801-8106**), is open daily from 8am to 6pm.

Dentist For emergency dental care, call **472-7072.**

Disabled Services Contact the Disabled Person's Advice Bureau, John Kennedy Good Centre, Wobum (☎ **469-3091** or **801-6685**).

Doctor For emergency doctor referrals, call **472-2999.**

Drugstores There are late-hour pharmacies at 17 Adelaide Rd., Wellington (☎ **385-8810**), and 729 High St., Lower Hutt (☎ **567-6725**).

Embassies/Consulates The U.S. Embassy is at 29 Fitzherbert Terrace, Thorndon (☎ **472-2068**); the Canadian Embassy is at 61 Molesworth St. (☎ **473-9577**); the British High Commission is at 44 Hill St. (☎ **472-6049**).

Emergencies Call **111** for police, fire, and ambulance emergencies.

Hospitals Wellington Hospital is on Riddiford Street, Newtown (☎ **385-5999**).

Libraries The National Library, Molesworth Street (☎ **474-3000**), is open Monday through Friday from 9am to 5pm. The Wellington Public Library, 65 Victoria St. (☎ **801-4040**), is open Monday through Thursday from 9:30am to 8:30pm, Friday from 9:30am to 9pm, and Saturday from 9:30am to 5pm.

Luggage Storage/Lockers There are lockers in the Domestic Terminal at the airport self-claim baggage area and at the railway station's Left Luggage Office.

Newspapers Wellington's morning newspaper is *The Dominion,* and in the evening there's the *Evening Post,* both published Monday through Saturday. On Sunday morning, look for *The Dominion Sunday Times.* Overseas newspapers are sometimes available from newsstands and are available in the reading room of the National Library.

Photographic Needs Try the Langwood Photo Centre, 59 Manners Mall, in the Breeze Plaza (☎ **473-1557**).

Police See "Emergencies," above.

Post Office The Information Centre sells stamps. Collect *Poste Restante* mail at the railway station.

Radio Wellington's leading stations are 99 and 100 on the FM dial; Radio Windy Classic Rock is 94.1 and 98.1 on FM.

3 Where to Stay

You'll stand a much better chance of finding budget accommodations on weekends than during the week. It all has to do with the city's resident population tide—in on Monday, out on Friday evening. It's true that there are a lot of bed-and-breakfast listings, but the majority cater to their permanent guests and few are interested in transients like you and me. That tidal flow does, however, create one unique situation in the capital city: Many superior hotels and motels cut prices drastically over the weekends when they have a surplus of rooms, which means that a little shopping around may well net you a budget price in a "splurge" location. More and more restaurants, shops, and sightseeing attractions are remaining open for the weekend, making it quite possible to take advantage of those special rates without sacrificing your usual holiday activities.

The rates given below include GST.

A LICENSED HOTEL

$ **Trekkers Hotel,** 213 Cuba St., Dunlop Terrace (P.O. Box 27-125), Wellington 1. ☎ **04/385-2153.** Fax 04/382-8873. 101 rms (some with bath), 6 units (all with bath). TV

Rates: NZ$40 (U.S. $26) single without bath, NZ$60 (U.S. $39) single with bath; NZ$50 (U.S. $32.50) double without bath, NZ$70 (U.S. $45.50) double with bath; NZ$89 (U.S. $57.85) one-bedroom unit for one or two; NZ$99 (U.S. $64.35) two-bedroom unit for one or two; NZ$15 (U.S. $9.75) backpacker's bunk. AE, DC, MC, V. **Parking:** Free.

This licensed hotel off Vivian Street is very central and offers a variety of accommodations, including small dormitories (two or four bunk beds), singles, and doubles, both with and without private facilities (there's hot and cold running water in those without), six rooms with facilities for the disabled, and six motel units in a separate block. They vary in style from new and modern to older and recently renovated. There's a guest laundry, sauna, and spa pool. The attractive restaurant features exceptionally good meals for around NZ$16 (U.S. $10.40). There's free off-street parking and a travel shop for tours and travel.

MOTELS

Apollo Lodge, 49 Majoribanks St., Wellington. ☎ and fax **04/385-1849.** 25 studios, 8 units. TV TEL

Rates: NZ$100 (U.S. $65) studio or unit for one or two. AE, DC, MC, V.

This would be a real find even if it weren't the most convenient location in Wellington at anything like budget prices. But the superb location is the icing on the cake—it's so close to city center shopping, entertainment, and sightseeing that you can leave the car and walk (a longish but pleasant stroll) or use the convenient city bus transport, and there are several first-rate restaurants right in the neighborhood. I found the staff here extremely friendly and helpful. The attractive units are set in off the street, and eight have separate bedrooms. You have a choice of full kitchen facilities or of serviced units with coffee pot, toaster, and fridge. All are fully carpeted and come with radio, electric blankets, and heaters. Cooked or continental breakfasts are available, and there's a full-service laundry as well as highchairs and a play area for children. If you're traveling with a large party, you might want to book the three-bedroom (sleeps seven) bungalow also on the grounds that goes for the same rate as a motel unit—you'll have to negotiate the price, since it depends on the number of people and length of stay. You should note that the Apollo is popular with regular Kiwi visitors to Wellington, and your best bet here is weekends.

Majoribanks Apartments, 38 Majoribanks St., Wellington. ☎ **04/385-7305** or **385-8879.** Fax 04/385-1849. 14 apartments. TV TEL

Rates: NZ$100 (U.S. $65) apartment for one or two. Additional person NZ$15 (U.S. $9.75) extra per adult, NZ$10 (U.S. $6.50) extra per child. AE, DC, MC, V.

An American from Washington, D.C., greeted me with an unsolicited recommendation—"This place is fantastic, not only for the facilities and comfort, but for the friendliness of the owner." My encounter with owner John Floratos certainly confirmed the traveler's comments, but in addition, I was much impressed with the bright, nicely decorated apartments in this hostelry just across from the Apollo. All have fully equipped kitchen and radio. There are one- and two-bedroom units, and there's good off-street parking. Majoribanks is within walking distance of the city center.

Wellington Motel, 14 Hobson St., Wellington. ☎ **04/472-0334.** Fax 04/472-6825. 3 studios, 2 units. TV TEL

READERS RECOMMEND

Wallace Court Motel, 90 Wallace St., Wellington (☎ **04/385-3935**). *"This motel is worth a recommendation. We had one bedroom with kitchenette (microwave, toaster, etc.) and appreciated the fresh flowers and mints and the free laundry and soap. We also liked the friendly hosts and good location—the motel's a 10-minute walk to downtown and 5 minutes to the excellent National Art Gallery and National Museum."*—Beverly Carr, Toronto, Ontario, Canada.

Quality Inn Hotel, 73 Roxburgh St., Oriental Bay (☎ **04/385-0279**). *"Our room was a splendid, spacious one on the top floor with a gorgeous view of the bay for NZ$110 (U.S. $71.50), weekend rates. The hotel is walking distance to the center of the city and has a very good restaurant and lounge."*—Virginia Wright, Gig Harbor, Wash., U.S.A.

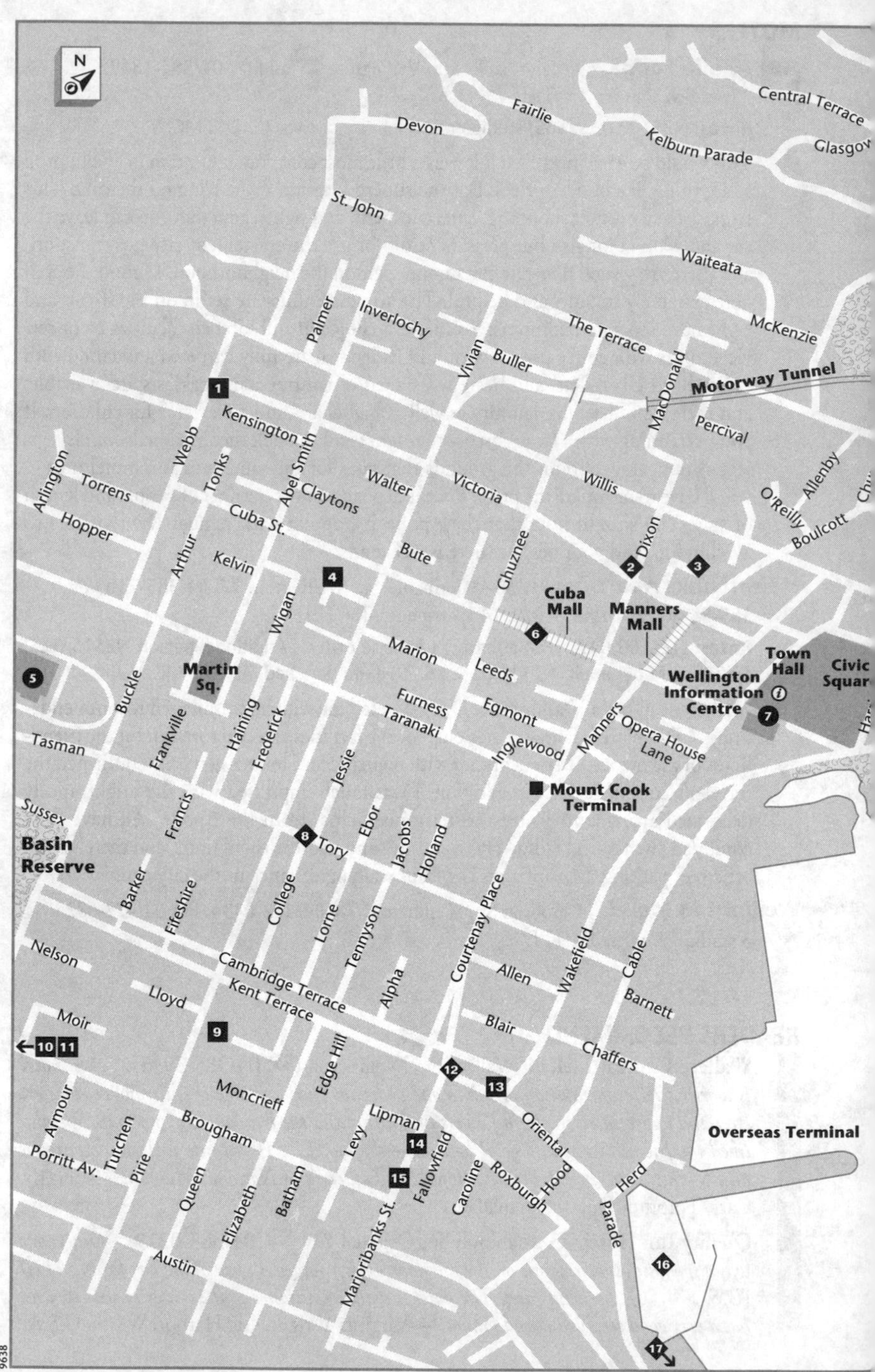
N
Central Terrace
Fairlie
Devon
Kelburn Parade
Glasgow
St. John
Waiteata
Palmer
Inverlochy
The Terrace
McKenzie
Vivian
Buller
MacDonald
Motorway Tunnel
Kensington
Webb
Abel Smith
Percival
Tonks
Walter
Victoria
Willis
Arlington
Torrens
Claytons
Allenby
O'Reilly
Hopper
Cuba St.
Boulcott
Arthur
Kelvin
Bute
Dixon
Ghuznee
Cuba Mall
Manners Mall
Wigan
Marion
Town Hall
Civic Square
Martin Sq.
Leeds
Wellington Information Centre
Buckle
Furness
Egmont
Taranaki
Haining
Frederick
Frankville
Manners
Opera House Lane
Tasman
Inglewood
Jessie
Mount Cook Terminal
Sussex
Francis
Ebor
Basin Reserve
Tory
Jacobs
Holland
Barker
Fifeshire
College
Courtenay Place
Lorne
Tennyson
Cable
Wakefield
Nelson
Cambridge Terrace
Allen
Kent Terrace
Alpha
Lloyd
Barnett
Moir
Blair
Edge Hill
Chaffers
Moncrieff
Armour
Lipman
Oriental
Brougham
Overseas Terminal
Tutchen
Levy
Fallowfield
Porritt Av.
Pirie
Caroline
Roxburgh
Hood
Herd
Queen
Elizabeth
Batham
Marjoribanks St.
Parade
Austin
9638

Wellington

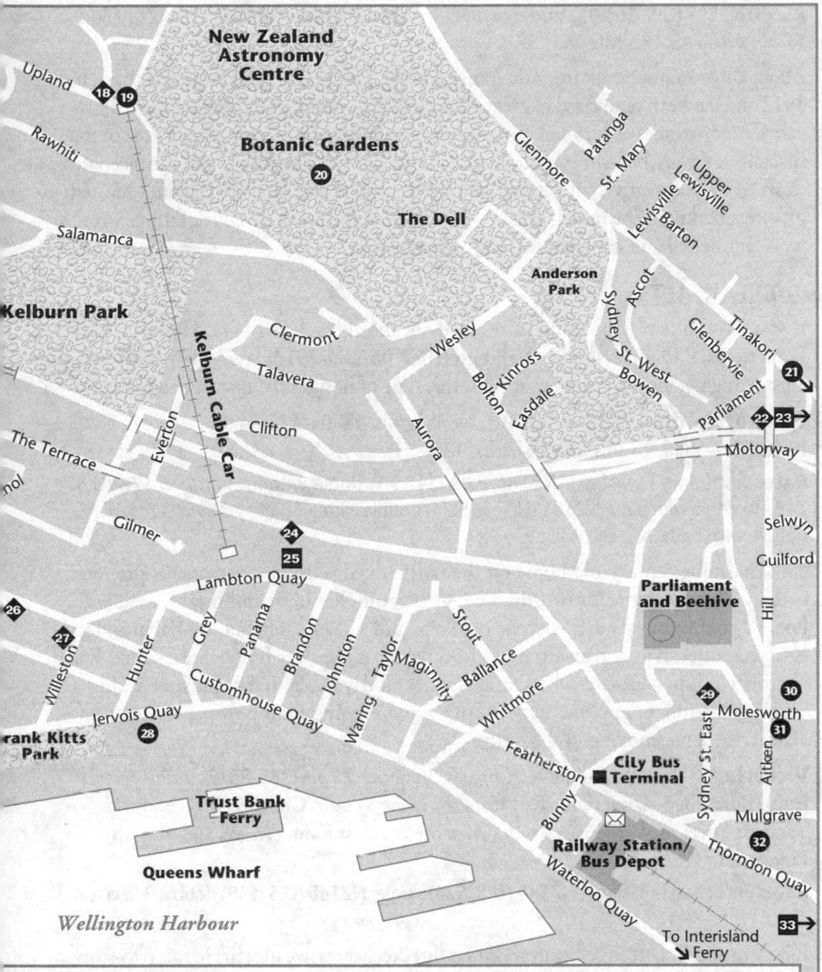

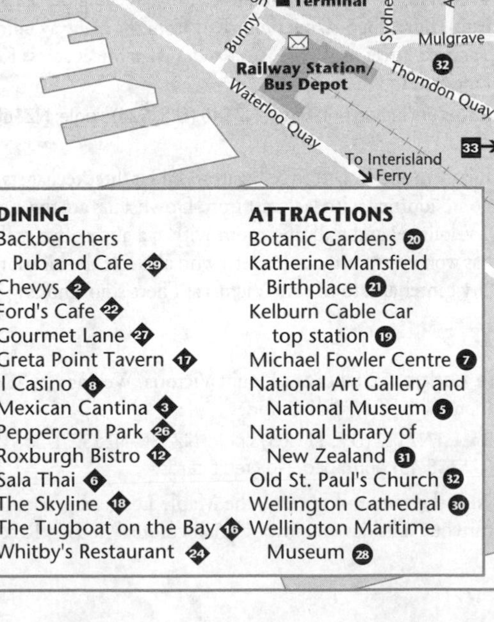

ACCOMMODATIONS

- Apollo Lodge 14
- Harbour City Motor Inn 1
- James Cook Centra Hotel 25
- Marjoribanks Apartments 15
- Maple Lodge 10
- Port Nicholson YHA Hostel 13
- Rowena's Lodge 11
- Tinakori Lodge 23
- Trekkers Hotel 4
- Victoria 9
- Wellington Motel 33

DINING

- Backbenchers Pub and Cafe 29
- Chevys 2
- Ford's Cafe 22
- Gourmet Lane 27
- Greta Point Tavern 17
- Il Casino 8
- Mexican Cantina 3
- Peppercorn Park 26
- Roxburgh Bistro 12
- Sala Thai 6
- The Skyline 18
- The Tugboat on the Bay 16
- Whitby's Restaurant 24

ATTRACTIONS

- Botanic Gardens 20
- Katherine Mansfield Birthplace 21
- Kelburn Cable Car top station 19
- Michael Fowler Centre 7
- National Art Gallery and National Museum 5
- National Library of New Zealand 31
- Old St. Paul's Church 32
- Wellington Cathedral 30
- Wellington Maritime Museum 28

Information · Post Office · Pedestrian Mall

Rates: NZ$97 (U.S. $63.05) studio or unit for one or two. Additional person NZ$12 (U.S. $7.80) extra. AE, DC, MC, V.

About a five-minute walk from the railway station, this large house was built back in 1912 and has been renovated to create five nice accommodations with such charming extras as bay windows, beamed ceilings, and small leaded windowpanes. Three of the spacious units are bed-sitters (studios), and two have one bedroom and can sleep up to six. All are attractively furnished and have showers and kitchens. There's limited off-street parking. The motel is near Davis Street at the northern edge of the city center. Continental and cooked breakfasts are available.

BED-&-BREAKFASTS

If you have difficulty booking into a bed-and-breakfast listed here, **Harbour City Homestays,** P.O. Box 14-345, Wellington (☎ **04/384-7913;** fax 04/385-0408), has a list of high-standard homes that offer this type of hospitality at reasonable rates.

★ **Tinakori Lodge,** 182 Tinakori Rd., Wellington. ☎ **04/473-3478.** Fax 04/472-5554. 10 rms (3 with bath). TV

Rates (including breakfast): NZ$66 (U.S. $42.90) single without bath, NZ$76 (U.S. $49.40) single with bath; NZ$85 (U.S. $55.25) double without bath, NZ$95 (U.S. $61.75) double with bath. AC, DC, MC, V.

This charming century-old home on the northern edge of the city center is presided over by Mel and John Ainsworth. The guest rooms are fresh and bright, each with hot and cold running water, electric blankets, and a heater. The substantial breakfast is served buffet style, and an attractive feature here is the availability of tea, coffee, hot chocolate, soup, cheese, crackers, and cookies all day. Local restaurants are within a 10-minute stroll. Complimentary morning and evening local newspapers are available. There's no smoking in the lodge.

$ **Victoria,** 58 Pirie St., Mount Victoria, Wellington. ☎ **04/385-8512.** 3 rms (1 with bath). **Bus:** 2 or 5. **Directions:** Exit from the highway onto Ghuznee Street and take Taranaki Street to Vivian Street and Vivian Street across Kent Terrace, and turn up Pirie Street.

Rates (including breakfast): NZ$40 (U.S. $26) single; NZ$60 (U.S. $39) double. No credit cards.

Elizabeth and Robert McGuigan and their three teenagers live upstairs in this two-story home adorned with lacy cast iron. Downstairs are three guest rooms and two baths, a TV lounge, and a dining room with tea and coffee makings. The cooked breakfast has won raves from our readers, who also like the location, which is convenient to the city center and to Mount Victoria. There's no smoking in the house.

HOSTELS

Maple Lodge, 52 Ellice St., Mount Victoria, Wellington. ☎ **04/385-3771.** 11 rms (none with bath), 2 dormitories.

Rates: NZ$17 (U.S. $11.05) single; NZ$30–NZ$32 (U.S. $19.50–$20.80) double; NZ$13 (U.S. $8.45) dorm bed. No credit cards.

Near the center of the city, the Maple Lodge is perched on one of Wellington's picturesque hillsides in a row of small colonial houses. Recently renovated, most rooms are spacious. There are singles, twins, and doubles, all with hot and cold running water, plus two dormitories. Other facilities include a fully equipped kitchen, dining room, TV lounge, car park (parking lot), and laundry.

$ **Port Nicholson Hostel,** at Wakefield St. and Cambridge Terrace (P.O. Box 24-033), Wellington. ☎ **04/801-7280.** Fax 04/801-7278. 7 rms (5 with bath), 88 dormitory beds.
Rates: NZ$24 (U.S. $15.60) single; NZ$19 (U.S. $12.35) per person double; NZ$17 (U.S. $11.05) dorm bed. Nonmembers pay NZ$4 (U.S. $2.60) additional. MC, V.

This luxurious modern hostel is considered the flagship of the New Zealand Youth Hostel Association. There are 22 four-bed dormitories and five double rooms, all with private bath, plus two single rooms with shared facilities. A mattress cover, a quilt, and clean pillows are supplied free, and there are a limited number of free sleeping sheets (bring your own to be on the safe side). Facilities include a self-catering kitchen, dining room, TV/common room, games room, and well-stocked shop for basic food and toiletries. The hostel is across from a supermarket and in the center of a restaurant/theater area. All your reservations for ongoing ferry, bus, and train services (both domestic and international) can be handled right on the premises, and they can also book ahead in other YHA hostels around the country.

Rowena's Lodge, 115 Brougham St., Mount Victoria, Wellington. ☎ and fax **04/385-7872.** 50 rms (none with bath). **Transportation:** Free pickup and dropoff service to trains, buses, and the Inter-Island Ferry.
Rates (including breakfast): NZ$30–NZ$39.50 (U.S. $19.50–$25.70) single; NZ$49.50 (U.S. $32.20) double. Additional person NZ$10 (U.S. $6.50) extra. No credit cards.

Rowena's has a variety of accommodations: dormitories, singles, doubles, twins, and triples. In addition to the three guest lounges, there's a dining room (cooked or continental breakfasts are available at a small charge), a large guest kitchen, a barbecue, and picnic areas. It's near the city center, on four city bus routes, and drivers will appreciate the off street parking. The staff can make reservations for ongoing travel.

CABINS & CAMPING

Since a few years ago when the Lowe Hutt City Council took over operation of the ★ **Hutt Park Holiday Village,** at 95 Hutt Park Rd., Moera, Lower Hutt (☎ **04/568-5913;** fax 04/568-5914), some 7 miles northeast of the city, great improvements have been made to both the grounds and the cabins. This is a large camp, abundant in native shade trees. There are 53 cabins, many equipped for wheelchair access. They range from two-berth standard cabins with basic furnishings to fully equipped motel apartments; all units with kitchens come with a full range of cutlery and crockery. Bedding and linen are required in most cabins and are available for rent from the office, along with TVs. There are two coin-operated laundries and three facility blocks, each with a kitchen, a dining area, a TV room, showers, and toilets. Rates (for one or two people) for motel apartments, fully equipped, are NZ$65 (U.S. $42.25); tourist apartments with kitchen and toilet are NZ$52 (U.S. $33.80); tourist cabins with kitchens are NZ$39 (U.S. $25.35); and standard cabins are NZ$28 (U.S. $18.20). Powered caravan sites cost NZ$18 (U.S. $11.70) for one or two (NZ$9/U.S. $5.85 for each additional person), and tent sites are NZ$8 (U.S. $5.20) per person. Public transport into Wellington or Lower Hutt is located nearby. Bankcard and Visa are accepted.

WORTH THE EXTRA MONEY

Harbour City Motor Inn, 92–96 Webb St. (P.O. Box 16-125), Wellington. ☎ **04/384-9809.** Fax 04/384-9806. 23 rms (all with bath), 2 suites. MINIBAR TV TEL

Rates: NZ$140 (U.S. $91) single or double weekdays, NZ$105 (U.S. $68.25) single or double weekends; NZ$155 (U.S. $100.75) suite. Best Western discounts available. AE, DC, MC, V.

The Harbour City could justify its rates solely on location—it's convenient to all city-center attractions, major theaters, shopping, and good restaurants—but its merits certainly don't stop there. The guest rooms are attractively furnished, with comfortable sitting areas and excellent lighting. Suites come with kitchens, and there's a covered garage. Other facilities include a guest laundry, dry-cleaning service, and photocopying and fax service for guests. A moderately priced licensed restaurant is on the premises, and there's a spa pool.

James Cook Centra Hotel, The Terrace, Wellington. ☎ **04/499-9500.** Fax 04/499-9800. 260 rms (all with bath). A/C MINIBAR TV TEL

Rates: NZ$253 (U.S. $164.45) single or double. Weekend discounts available. AE, DC, MC, V.

With what has to be the best location in town, this is a "big splurge" well worth considering. It's in the very heart of the city center, and its rooms come with tea- and coffee-making facilities, fridges, and in-house video. There's same-day laundry and dry-cleaning service (except Sunday), business facilities that include secretarial service and copy machines, a first-class restaurant (see "Where to Eat," below), and an inexpensive coffee shop. It's also just steps away from shopping, sightseeing, dining, and entertainment. The normal rate is lowered dramatically for weekend specials.

4 Where to Eat

There's an interesting diversity of cuisine offered in Wellington's 350 restaurants. However, if you'd like to dine with a Wellington family, **Harbour City Homestays,** P.O. Box 14-345, Wellington (☎ **04/385-0408**), can arrange a home-cooked New Zealand dinner—but be sure to give sufficient advance notice. They can also arrange a complete homestay, with bed and breakfast or bed, breakfast, and dinner with a Wellington family.

Backbenchers Pub and Cafe, Molesworth St. and Sydney St. E., opposite Parliament. ☎ **472-3065.**

Cuisine: LIGHT MEALS. **Reservations:** Not required.
Prices: Main courses NZ$9–NZ$16 (U.S. $5.85–$10.40). AE, DC, MC, V.
Open: Lunch Mon–Sat noon–2:30pm; dinner daily 5:30–10:30pm.

A Wellington friend steered me to this terrific pub and eatery. The old building retains the original ceilings from 1917, and its natural brick-and-wood interior creates a sense of history that just can't be reproduced in a more modern edifice. As for the menu, it makes as good reading as the offerings are good eating. Take, for example, Rogers "no tax" chicken—roulade of chicken, pesto, and ham on a grain mustard–cream sauce—"the more you have, the better it gets!" Or you may opt for the "new Labour loaf" (lefter-leaning slices). Most other dishes are also named for New Zealand political figures or events, and the ambience in this popular place is lively and convivial. Fully licensed, of course.

Brooklyn Café & Grill, 1 Todham St., in Brooklyn. ☎ **385-3592.**

Cuisine: NEW ZEALAND. **Reservations:** Not required.

Prices: Appetizers NZ$9 (U.S. $5.85); main courses NZ$23 (U.S. $14.95). AE, DC, MC, V.

Open: Dinner only, daily 6–11pm.

One of the city's most popular eateries, the Brooklyn Café & Grill occupies a corner in this inner-city suburb. Owner Lois Dash (a local food columnist) took over several old shops and created a rather spare but comfortable interior that has won an architectural award. The menu features appetizers that could well serve as a light meal (like the potato cakes with gherkins, sour-cream dressing, and tomato salsa), steaks, lamb, fish, chicken, and vegetarian dishes such as polenta served with charcoal-grilled mushrooms, red-pepper sauce, and arugula. The vegetables are terrific and served with all main courses as well as organically grown leafy salads and steamed baby potatoes. There's limited parking back of the restaurant, and it's BYO as well as licensed.

Chevys, 97 Dixon St. ☎ **384-2724.**

Cuisine: AMERICAN LIGHT SNACKS. **Reservations:** Not required.

Prices: Main courses NZ$14–NZ$18 (U.S. $9.10–$11.70). AE, DC, MC, V.

Open: Mon–Thurs 11:30am–11pm, Fri–Sat 11:30am–midnight.

Anyone tempted by the offer of "two meals for the price of one" should head over to Chevys after 5pm on Monday and Tuesday. You'll see the neon cowboy and his wiggling lasso a few blocks before you arrive at the door. The casual, congenial place has decidedly American fare: BLTs, chicken wings, nachos, barbecued spareribs, Philadelphia steak sandwiches, omelets, seven kinds of burgers, potato skins, and even banana splits. Your final bill will depend entirely on your appetite. Licensed.

Ford's Cafe, 342 Tinakori Rd., Thorndon. ☎ **472-6238.**

Cuisine: MODERN NEW ZEALAND. **Reservations:** Not accepted.

Prices: Small plates NZ$10.50–NZ$12.50 (U.S. $6.85–$8.15); large plates NZ$14.25–NZ$16.75 (U.S. $9.25–$10.90). AE, BC, DC, MC, V.

Open: Mon–Fri 7am–"late," Sat–Sun 9am–"late."

I like this place both for its good food and for its casual café decor. Contemporary paintings hang on pale maize walls. Diners can sit at wooden tables or at a counter. Small plates, which make an adequate light meal, include vegetable crêpes, chicken kebabs with spicy peanut sauce, and several pasta choices. The *really* hungry can have lamb filets rolled in fresh herbs; a pumpkin, tomato, and feta frittata; or pork with paprika and cream sauce. This two-story restaurant serves all three meals, and smoking is not permitted on the ground floor. Licensed.

Greta Point Tavern, 467 Evans Bay Parade. ☎ **386-1065.**

Cuisine: SEAFOOD. **Reservations:** Not required.

Prices: Main courses and vegetables or salad NZ$10–NZ$20 (U.S. $6.50–$13). AE, MC, V.

Open: Lunch Mon–Sat noon–2:30pm, Sun 11:30am–2:30pm; dinner Mon–Sat 5:30–9:30pm, Sun 5:30–9pm.

If you're driving, or happen to find yourself out in the lovely Evans Bay area, 3km (2 miles) from the city center, plan on one meal here. Actually, the walk from downtown along Oriental Bay, Roseneath, and Evans Bay Parade to the tavern is picturesque and well worth doing. The large black building with rose trim sits right on the waterfront and has windows the entire length of its south side, looking out to sweeping views of the bay (often filled with sailboats) and a nearby marina with its forest of masts. The high-ceilinged room, which once housed a commercial laundry, now has a wooden lifeboat suspended from the overhead pipes. There's a nice upstairs Promenade Deck bar, and downstairs you'll find the Anchorage Lounge Bar, as well as the Galley Restaurant, featuring fresh seafoods. The restaurant is self-service and fully licensed, and the long counter will have you drooling while trying to decide between Bluff oysters, roast baron of beef, marinated mussels, baked leg of lamb, and a host of other tempting dishes on display.

Il Casino Restaurant & Piano Bar, 108 Tory St. ☎ **385-7496.**

Cuisine: NORTHERN ITALIAN. **Reservations:** Recommended.

Prices: Appetizers NZ$11.50–NZ$13.50 (U.S. $7.50–$8.80); main courses NZ$18–NZ$26 (U.S. $11.70–$16.90). AE, BC, DC, MC, V.

Open: Lunch Mon–Fri noon–2pm; dinner daily 6pm–"late."

Home to Wellington's first wood-burning pizza oven, this is the place for designer versions of that Italian favorite. Il Casino also offers pasta dishes in two sizes and an extensive menu of fish and meat dishes—all definitely "worth the extra money." If you're ready for a splurge, try the veal escalopes layered with truffles, Parma ham, and Gruyère cheese or the New Zealand scallops sautéed in a sauce of orange, brandy, fresh oregano, diced avocado, and tomato. On the other hand, if you stick to the entree-size portions of pasta and fish or share a pizza, your meal at award-winning Il Casino will fall within our budget guidelines. Look for the Italian street scene painted on the outside of the building. Licensed.

Mexican Cantina, 19 Edward St. ☎ **385-9711.**

Cuisine: MEXICAN. **Reservations:** Not accepted.

Prices: Appetizers NZ$4–NZ$7 (U.S. $2.60–$4.55); main courses NZ$13 (U.S. $8.45). No credit cards.

Open: Lunch Tues–Fri noon–2pm; dinner Tues–Sun 5:30–10pm.

This sometimes-noisy cantina is set in a former warehouse a short walk from the center of the city, and it's such a favorite with locals that you may find yourself waiting in line at lunch. The atmosphere is casual; the decor is south of the border, complete with a Mexican sombrero on the brick walls; and the menu features all those beans, tacos, and tostadas you'd expect. Licensed and BYO.

★ $ **Peppercorn Park,** 1st floor in the Grand Arcade, Willis St. ☎ **472-2255.**

Cuisine: BREAKFAST/PASTRIES/SANDWICHES. **Reservations:** Not accepted.

Prices: Breakfast NZ$11 (U.S. $7.15); sandwiches with salad and fries NZ$8 (U.S. $5.20); dinner NZ$9–NZ$11 (U.S. $5.85–$7.15). AE, DC, MC, V.

Open: Mon–Thurs 7am–4pm, Fri 7am–8:30pm, Sat 9am–1:30pm.

This pleasant upstairs self-service restaurant is one of my favorite drop-in eateries in the city center. Its reputation for the best bagels in Wellington certainly gets my endorsement, and the phyllo pastry filled with smoked salmon, chicken, smoked salmon, or some other delicacy just melts in your mouth. For heartier eating, there's Indonesian lamb rendang, pork in ginger-and-orange sauce, Mexican beef, lasagne, and on Friday nights, traditional roast meals of pork or beef and vegetables. Licensed.

Sala Thai, 134 Cuba St. ☎ **382-8780.**

Cuisine: THAI. **Reservations:** Recommended.

Prices: Appetizers NZ$7.50–NZ$11.50 (U.S. $4.90–$7.50); main courses NZ$11.50–NZ$23.50 (U.S. $7.50–$15.30). MC, V.

Open: Lunch Mon–Fri 11:30am–3pm; dinner daily 5:30pm–"late."

Wellington's original Thai restaurant continues to serve good food in a pleasant atmosphere. Some dishes are characteristically spicy, others not so. Vegetarians have several good choices. You could start with tod mun kad pod (sweetcorn pancake, served with sweet-and-sour sauce) followed by pad med mamuang (stir-fried cashew nuts with chicken, pork, or beef and mushroom, onion, chile, and spring onions) or take your chances with "wild cobra" (fried minced pork with green beans and tons of chiles). Licensed.

The Skyline, 1 Upland Rd., Kelburn. ☎ **475-8727.**

Cuisine: BUFFET. **Reservations:** Recommended for a window table.
Prices: Full buffet lunch NZ$25 (U.S. $16.25); one plate NZ$8.50–NZ$13.50 (U.S. $5.55–$8.80). AE, BC, MC, V.
Open: Lunch only, daily 11am–4pm (buffet lunch noon–2:30pm).

This is a great spot to have morning or afternoon tea or lunch with an expansive view of the city and beyond. It's located steps from the top station of the Kelburn Cable Car, so it's even fun to get to. I don't like midday buffets because I end up feeling like a slug all afternoon, but this place is great because you can opt for a single stroll through the line with either a small or a large plate. Licensed.

WORTH THE EXTRA MONEY

Roxburgh Bistro, 18 Majoribanks St. ☎ **385-7577.**

Cuisine: GERMAN. **Reservations:** Required.
Prices: Average meal NZ$45 (U.S. $29.45). AE, DC, MC, V.
Open: Lunch Tues–Fri noon–2pm; dinner Tues–Sat 6–10pm.

This very pleasant, attractive place is not as expensive as most splurge restaurants. It's in an old, two-story house just off Cambridge Terrace, a short distance from the city center, and the cuisine here is mostly German, with such traditional specialties as Rheinischer sauerbraten, venison and other game, and lamb, along with New Zealand seafood. Friendly service, pink linen napkins, fresh flowers at each table, complimentary sherry, and an open fireplace on cool evenings add the pampered feeling that makes your pricey dinner tab seem more than a bargain. No smoking is allowed in the bistro. BYO.

The Tug Boat on the Bay, Freyberg Lagoon, Oriental Bay. ☎ **384-8884.**

Cuisine: NEW ZEALAND. **Reservations:** Recommended on weekends.
Prices: Appetizers NZ$9.50–NZ$14 (U.S. $6.20–$9.10); main courses NZ$18.50–NZ$24.50 (U.S. $12.05–$15.95). AE, BC, DC, MC, V.
Open: Lunch daily noon–2pm; tea, coffee, drinks from the bar daily 2–6pm; dinner daily 6–10pm.

This really is an old tugboat—restored, of course. It's believed the tug was part of the fleet taking supplies across to Normandy after the D-Day invasion. Later it was used by the British Royal Navy in Singapore before coming to New Zealand in 1947. The *Tapuhi* worked on Wellington harbor for the next 26 years. Today it's the city's only floating restaurant and affords wonderful water and city views. Diners walk a red gangplank from the parking lot to reach the boat. The attractive decor includes marine artifacts and crisp white tablecloths. Dinner main courses include Canterbury rack of lamb, oven-baked baby salmon, Palliser Bay flounder topped with a tangy bacon-and-onion sauce, and vegetarian phyllo strudel. Licensed.

Whitby's Restaurant, in the James Cook Centra Hotel, The Terrace. ☎ **499-9500.**

Cuisine: NEW ZEALAND. **Reservations:** Required.
Prices: Appetizers NZ$10–NZ$13 (U.S. $6.50–$8.45); main courses NZ$18.50–NZ$23.50 (U.S. $12.05–$15.30). AE, DC, MC, V.
Open: Breakfast buffet daily 6:30–9:30am; lunch buffet daily noon–2:30pm; dinner daily 6–10:30pm.

Terrific breakfast and lunch buffets are served in this elegant room on the second floor of the conveniently located hotel, but it's at dinner that chef Grahame Seymours really shines. He offers the option of buffet/grill or à la carte at dinner. The buffet offers a roast of the day, fish, pork, chicken, salads, and rich desserts. From the à la carte menu, there's roast loin of lamb rolled in hazelnuts, with a wild-mushroom center, set on a bed of layered potatoes, finished with truffle jus. Other New Zealand specialties, such as filet of beef, poached salmon, and farm-raised venison, are on the extensive menu. The desserts are fabulous. There's a pianist in the piano bar nightly. Licensed.

SPECIALTY DINING

Wellington's only food court is **Gourmet Lane,** in the BNZ Centre, 1 Willis St. This spot is a dream for dollarwise travelers as most main courses are NZ$5 to NZ$6 (U.S. $3.25 to $3.90). Some of the eateries here include Wellington's Gourmet Pies, Sizzler's BBQ'D Food, Stars & Stripes, and Chinese Wok. Gourmet Lane is open Monday through Thursday and Saturday from 9am to 3pm and Friday (late-night shopping night) from 9am to 9pm. Some, but not all, places accept credit/charge cards. You can buy beer and wine to accompany your meal. This area is particularly popular at lunchtime, when entertainment is often offered. The BNZ (Bank of New Zealand) has a counter adjacent to the food court—handy if you need to make a transaction.

5 What to See & Do

One of my strongest impressions of Wellington lingers from my very first visit—sore feet and sheer exhaustion from climbing up and down its hilly terrain. Of course, I realized later that the blame lay with *me,* not Wellington. This is a city that requires *planned* sightseeing, and to save yourself my own trials and travails, I recommend that you head straight for the **Wellington City Information Centre** (see "Tourist Information" under "City Specifics," earlier in this chapter) and plot your course before taking one step. A good plan is to concentrate on city-center attractions first, then take the cable car up to Kelburn and Mount Victoria, then *plan* how you're going to reach the outlying places, so that you're not backtracking for something overlooked when you're sightseeing in one direction. There are excellent day trips by car or even easier organized tours (see below) that can make your life happier and more relaxed as you take in Wellington's splendors. If you prefer a do-it-yourself tour, pick up the **"Scenic Drive"** booklet and map. Three routes are outlined, and they're color-coordinated with discs on lampposts along each route so you won't go astray. They cover Wellington from top to bottom, traveling southeast on one route, west on another, and north on the third.

You can also do your feet a favor in the city center by taking advantage of the excellent public transport system. The **Daytripper** allows one adult and two children under age 15 to ride all day for NZ$5 (U.S. $3.25). This is a fine way to see the city: Jump on any bus, leap off when you see something interesting; go to the beach (take the Lyall Bay, Island Bay, or Seatoun bus from Willis Street) and stay all day or catch the next bus back. Take bus no. 12 or 14 to one of the hill suburbs, have a cup of coffee in a local café, then catch a bus back and enjoy the views all along the way. You can even use the same bus ticket after dinner for after-hours exploring.

While in the city center, take time to walk down to that magnificent harbor, where the ★ **Lambton Harbour Development Project** is busily lining its shores with park areas and other amenities for residents and visitors alike that will make it truly the focal point of the city.

Wellington is central to many hiking areas, some that afford prime views of the city and harbor. Ask at the information center for the **"Bus & Walk"** brochure, which outlines 16 walks and gives information on getting to them from Wellington and back into town by bus. An easy, educational choice is a visit to the ★ **Otari Open Air Native Plant Museum** (☎ **475-3245**), which offers four hikes of half an hour to an hour, some through 198 acres of native bush and 5 acres of cultivated gardens; take the no. 14 Wilton Route bus to the entrance on Wilton Road. The bus trip takes 20 minutes.

The Top Attractions

Note that the new—and much talked about—**Museum of New Zealand** will open in 1996.

Kelburn Cable Car, Lambton Quay. ☎ **472-2199.**

For the fullest appreciation of Wellington's spectacular setting, take a marvelous 4½-minute ride in a sleek red cable car, which climbs to an elevation of 1,980 feet up Mount Victoria, leaving every 10 minutes from Lambton Quay opposite Grey Street. The beautiful harbor lies at your feet, and it's a great loitering spot to drink in the beauty of that curving shoreline backed by jagged hills.

The **Botanic Gardens** entrance is also at the top of the cable-car ride, open from dawn to dusk, with no admission charge. Stop by the Interpretive Centre for brochures and a full briefing on the gardens. Your downhill stroll through lush greenery can be broken by a stop at the **Begonia House** and its **Tea House** in the **Lady Norwood Rose Gardens** (open from 10am to 4pm) for a look at hundreds of begonias, bush foliage, and ferns. From the foot of the gardens, you can get back to the city on a no. 12 bus.

Admission: Fare, NZ$1.50 (U.S. $1) for adults one way, NZ$2.50 (U.S. $1.65) round-trip; NZ70¢ (U.S. 45¢) children round-trip.

Open: Cable car runs every 10 minutes, Mon–Fri 7am–10pm, Sat 9am–10pm, Sun and public holidays 10:30am–10pm.

Katherine Mansfield Birthplace, 25 Tinakori Rd, Thornton, Wellington. ☎ **473-7268.**

Katherine Mansfield, New Zealand–born short-story writer, poet, and essayist, first saw the light of day in 1888. One of the country's most prestigious writers—and arguably its most famous worldwide—she inspires such veneration that a nonprofit organization was formed to restore the old house to its decor in the year of her birth. There's a shop with books, cards, posters, and souvenirs, and if you order in advance, you can enjoy a light lunch or morning/afternoon tea on the premises.

Admission: NZ$4 (U.S. $2.60) adults, NZ$2 (U.S. $1.30) senior citizens and students, NZ$1 (U.S. 65¢) children.

Open: Tues–Sun 10am–4pm.

★ **National Art Gallery and National Museum,** Buckle St. ☎ **385-9609.**

The art gallery emphasizes both New Zealand and international art, and on most Sundays at 2:30pm there's a free music recital, theatrical performance, film, or lecture. Artifacts of South Pacific, New Zealand, and Maori history are featured at the museum.

Admission: Free.

Open: Daily 9am–5pm. **Closed:** Good Friday and Christmas Day. **Bus:** 11 to Buckle Street; or 1 or 3 to Reserve Basin, then a five-minute walk.

★ **Wellington Maritime Museum,** in the Wellington Harbour Board Building, Queens Wharf. ☎ **472-8904.**

Those interested in things of the sea will want to visit this museum, where Wellington's close association with seafarers and their vessels is well documented, with displays of ship models, paintings, flags, bells, photographs, ships' artifacts, and a reconstructed captain's cabin.

Admission: By donation; suggested amounts, NZ$2 (U.S. $1.30) adults, NZ$5 (U.S. $3.25) family group.

Open: Mon–Fri 9:30am–4pm, Sat–Sun and public holidays 1–4:30pm. **Closed:** Good Friday and Christmas Day.

Wellington Zoo, Newtown. ☎ **389-8130.**

This zoo dates back to 1906 and its collection includes kangaroos, wallabies, monkeys, lions, tigers, chimpanzees, and tamarin. There's also a nocturnal **Kiwi House** (open daily from 10am to 4pm), featuring kiwi, tuatara, and giant weta. In fine weather on weekends and holidays there are miniature railway rides from noon to 4pm, for minimal charges.

Admission: NZ$7.50 (U.S. $4.90) adults, NZ$3.50 (U.S. $2.30) children 5 and above, free for children under 5.

Open: Daily 9:30am–5pm. **Bus:** 10 (Newton Park) from the railway station.

More Attractions

You can tour **Parliament** any weekday free of charge (☎ **471-9457** Monday through Friday or **471-9999** Saturday and Sunday for tour times). The ★ **Beehive,** completed in 1981, is the executive wing of the Parliament buildings. And if by this time you're hooked on New Zealand history and culture, spend some time at the **National Library of New Zealand,** across the road from Parliament at 70 Molesworth St. You can browse in the **National Library Gallery,** bookshop, and the New Zealand collection of books, all on the ground floor. The **Alexander Turnbull Library,** in the same building, is the research wing of the National Library, specializing in New Zealand and the Pacific. Books, serials, sound recordings, manuscripts, and archives are researched on the first floor, and newspapers on the ground floor. On the second floor, visitors can peruse files of photographs, and drawings, paintings, and maps are available for research by appointment. It's open Monday through Friday from 9am to 5pm, and 9am to 1pm on Saturday for nonpictorial materials.

To bring this city's history sharply alive, keep an eye out for the **12 shoreline plaques** that have been embedded in footpaths to show the sites of early Wellington: You'll find them at Pipitea Point, on the south side of Davis Street and Thorndon Quay; at the top of the steps leading to Rutherford House; on Mason's Lane, on the north side; on Lambton Quay, north of Woodward Street; on the Lambton Quay footpath near Cable Car Lane; at Steward Dawson's, on the west side of the Lambton Quay corner; at Chews Lane, on the east side of the Willis Street footpath; on Mercer Street, outside George Harrison Ltd. on the Willis Street corner; on Farrish Street, on the southeast side of Farrish and Lombard streets; on Cuba Street outside Smith and Smith Ltd.; on Taranaki Street outside the Caltex Service Station; and on Wakefield Street next to the Schaffer Street bus stop.

★ **Old St. Paul's Church,** on Mulgrave Street, in the suburb of Thorndon (☎ **473-6722**), is a marvelous Early English Gothic–style wooden church much beloved by Wellingtonians. Using the native timbers of totara, matai, rimu, and kauri, the softly lit church with its dark timbers, soaring wooden arches, and brilliant stained glass radiates peace and calmness. A relaxing stop in your sightseeing itinerary. There's no admission charge (donations are welcome), and it's open to the public Monday through Saturday from 10:30am to 4:30pm and Sunday from 1 to 4:30pm; closed Good Friday and Christmas Day.

Organized Tours

BUS TOURS

The best possible way to get an in-depth look at the city itself and its immediate environs is to take the escorted ★ **Wally Hammond's Wellington City Scenic Tours bus tour** (☎ **472-0869** for information and reservations), which leaves from the Visitor Information Centre on Wakefield Street every day at 10am and 2pm. For the bargain price of NZ$20 (U.S. $13) for adults (children ride for half price), you'll be driven some 49km (30 miles), with 2$^1/_2$ hours of informative narrative as you see the financial and commercial center, take a look at government buildings and Parliament's unique Beehive building, visit the lookout on Mount Victoria (with a stop for picture taking), skirt the bays, stop for afternoon tea, then reenter the city via View Road, a scenic drive, which does full justice to Wellington's headlands, hills, bays, and beaches. The information center can also furnish details on a wide variety of other city and area tours available such as the **Harbour Capital Tours** (☎ **499-1281**).

HARBOR CRUISES

There's no doubt about it—that spectacular harbor exerts an irresistible pull to see Wellington from the water. The bargain way to accomplish this is via the ★ **Trust Bank Ferry** (☎ **499-1273** for timetable information), which crosses the harbor from Queens Wharf in Wellington to Days Bay. The 25-minute ride on the Trust Bank Ferry costs NZ$6.50 (U.S. $4.25) for adults each way, and NZ$3.50 (U.S. $2.30) for children, or NZ$33 (U.S. $21.45) for a round-trip family excursion ticket that covers two adults and up to four children. The ferry has a full bar and also serves coffee. At Days Bay, you can enjoy the park, have afternoon tea in the pavilion, or take the three-minute stroll around to Eastbourne for galleries, gift shops, and the Cobar Restaurant on the waterfront, recommended if you arrive at mealtime.

Other, more costly cruises are offered by **Harbour City Cruises** (☎ **386-2740**) and **Bluefin Harbour Cruises** (☎ **569-8203**); both offer day and nighttime cruises, with or without food and beverage.

Incidentally, if the Wellington–Picton **Inter-Island Ferry** (☎ **498-3999,** or toll free **0800/658-999** in New Zealand) is not on your travel itinerary, ask about their excursion special that lets you pay one way and return the same day free. It's one of Wellington's special experiences, so don't miss it. For details, see "Crossing Between the North and South Islands," at the end of this chapter.

6 Sports & Recreation

Many of the city's **gymnasiums** welcome drop-in guests. An aerobics or stretching class or a weightlifting session costs about NZ$6 or NZ$7 (U.S. $3.90 or $4.55). The information center can provide details.

The **Wellington Regional Aquatic Center,** in the suburb of Kilbirnie (☎ **387-8029**), has four heated pools: a lap pool, learner's pool, and adjoining junior and toddlers' pools with an access ramp for the disabled. There are also diving facilities, spa pools, saunas, a sun deck, café, and YMCA fitness center. You can rent swimsuits and towels; goggles are for sale. The no. 2 bus to Miramar takes you to the door.

The **Wellington Renouf Tennis Centre,** on Brooklyn Road at Central Park (☎ **384-6294**), has 14 outdoor and 4 indoor courts available for rent at about NZ$28 (U.S. $18.20) per hour. It's open Monday through Friday from 6am to 11pm and Saturday and Sunday from 8am to 11pm. Practice or hitting partners can be arranged on short notice, and there's a café on the premises.

Horse racing is a popular sport in Wellington, and its **Hutt Park Racecourse** is classified as all-weather. For recorded racing information, call **473-8800** (24-hou service).

7 Savvy Shopping

Much of Wellington's best shopping is along **Lambton Quay.** Don't miss **Capital on the Quay,** three linked arcades at 250 Lambton Quay.

For window-shopping and browsing, you might also like to stroll the ★ **Manners and Cuba pedestrian malls,** which are particularly fun on Friday night when the buskers are out. You'll find crafts and secondhand shops on Cuba Street near Ghuznee Street.

The **Wakefield Market** is held on Friday, Saturday, and Sunday, and is filled with clothing, leather goods, and jewelry. Antiques shops are in the suburb of Brooklyn.

The **Great New Zealand Shop,** 13 Grey St. (☎ **472-6817**) is a good souvenir shop. For splurge shopping, head to ★ **Vibrant Handknits,** Lee Andersen's Designer Gallery, Shop 5, Sun Alliance Centre, 280 Lambton Quay (☎ **472-8720**); it's next to Cable Car Lane. **Mainly Tramping,** 39 Mercer St. (☎ **473-5353**), will help you get outfitted for the bush.

The **duty-free shop** in central Wellington is at the DFC Centre, on Grey Street, with a branch out at the airport.

8 Evening Entertainment

Check the current issue of the ***Capital Times*** and ***What's On,*** available at tourist information centers, for entertainment.

THE PERFORMING ARTS

The **Downstage Theatre,** in the Hannah Playhouse on Cambridge Terrace (☎ **384-9639**), presents first-rate theater in an exciting theater structure that provides for flexibility in staging in the main auditorium and a smaller cabaret in the bar. The Downstage is a year-round enterprise, staging classics and contemporary drama, musicals, and comedies, and works of New Zealand playwrights. Check the newspapers for current showings. Reserve as far in advance as you possibly can, however, for Downstage productions are very popular. Ticket prices are about NZ$27 (U.S. $17.55) for the auditorium and NZ$20 (U.S. $13) for the gallery. Students, senior citizens, and groups of 10 receive a ticket discount. **Bats Theatre,** at 1 Kent Terrace (☎ **802-4175**), presents new and experimental plays and dance that attract a young audience, as well as folks who are not traditional theatergoers. Tickets are NZ$15 (U.S. $9.75).

Check the newspapers to see what's doing at the **Wellington Festival & Convention Centre** (incorporating the distinctively shaped **Michael Fowler Centre** and the elegant **Town Hall**) in Civic Square on Wakefield Street (☎ **801-4242**). The Michael Fowler Centre was completed in 1983; the Town Hall dates from 1904. There are concerts and other events scheduled there throughout the year.

THE CLUB & BAR SCENE

The **James Cook Centra Hotel** has a piano bar nightly and a classical string quartet on Saturday and Sunday; **Paisley Park,** upstairs at 24 Taranaki St. (☎ **384-1525**), is open daily from 7pm to 1am for live music (the cover charge varies) or for recorded music, along with Dutch-style food, drinks, and an inviting atmosphere; the ★ **Greta Point Tavern,** Evans Bay Parade (☎ **386-1065**), has live entertainment Friday and Saturday nights; and ★ **Old Bailey Bar & Café,** at the corner of Lambton Quay and Bailance Street (☎ **471-2021**), has sing-along nights Wednesday through Friday. You might also like to have a drink at **Molly Malones** or one of the other Courtenay Place nightspots.

Note: If you're a night owl, be aware that upper Cuba Street is *not safe* after dark.

9 An Easy Excursion from Wellington

Northeast of Wellington, a little less than two hours' drive from Wellington, the Wairarapa region is well worth a day trip from the city—even better, an overnight stay in order to explore all the riches of the region.

En route to Masterton, the region's chief town, plan your first stop in Featherston to visit ★ **Kahutara Canoes,** R.D. 1, Featherston (☎ **06/308-8453**). Owner John McCosh, also known as "Tuatara Ted" and often called New Zealand's Crocodile Dundee, and his wife, Karen, have put together a fascinating taxidermy museum. In a spacious Canadian log structure, the museum houses more than 350 mounted animals from around the globe. John is a friendly, colorful character, always happy to show you around and talk about all the specimens. He's also enthusiastic about the small animal park he was just getting started when I visited.

The museum, however, is only a small part of what the McCoshes get up to. They and their staff of expert guides operate a variety of canoe trips on the scenic Ruamahanga River. The canoes range from large, stable Canadian craft down to fast one- and two-person kayaks, and the river trips are designed to appeal to all ages, from toddlers to grandparents. Some are as short as two to three hours, others for three or more hours. You'll have to call ahead for hours, charges, and reservations. But no matter if you only plan to visit the museum (NZ$3/U.S. $1.95 for adults, NZ$1/U.S. 65¢ for children; open daily from 10am to 5pm), be sure to allow extra time here—it's *very* hard to pop in and right back out! Barbecue facilities are available.

In Carterton, a stop at the **Paua Shell Factory Shop,** 54 Kent St. (☎ **06/379-6777**), can yield unique gifts, jewelry, and souvenirs, and there are free factory tours. It's open Monday through Friday from 8am to 4:30pm and Saturday and

Sunday from 10am to 5pm. Carterton is also a good place to look for New Zealand leather products—**Jeffrey Chandel Leathers,** 69–73 Nelson Crescent (☎ **06/379-8927**), makes an extensive line of ladies' and men's jackets and coats, as well as a wide range of other leather products, all at competitive prices. It's open Monday through Friday from 9am to 5pm, Saturday from 9am to 3pm, and most Sundays from 10am to 2pm (call in advance to see if it's open).

The **Tourism Wairarapa Visitor Information Centre,** 5 Dixon St., Masterton (☎ **06/378-7373;** fax 06/378-7042), should be your very first stop. The bright, modern building houses loads of literature on attractions in the region, the many nature walks, and sporting opportunities. The friendly staff can also furnish information on accommodations (everything from luxury motels to farmstays) and places to eat.

This is one of the best regions in the country in which to explore New Zealand's native bush country. Ask at the visitor center for the **"Wairarapa Walks"** booklet, which details all manner of walks, trails, and tracks. A great wilderness experience.

About 17 miles north of Masterson on State Highway 2, the ★ **Mount Bruce National Wildlife Centre** (☎ **06/375-8004**) is one of the most moving wildlife experiences I've run across. Its 15 different aviaries; nocturnal complex inhabited by a small population of kiwi, morepork owls, and lizards; and outside paths that wind through native bush are a world apart and one seldom accessible to the likes of you and me. They do a lot of work with New Zealand's rare and endangered species. I also like the fact that paths have been made wheelchair friendly. In the Visitor Centre at the entrance there's an audiovisual exhibit, a souvenir shop, and tearooms overlooking the natural splendors just beyond wide picture windows. It's open daily from 9am to 4pm (closed Christmas Day), and there's a NZ$6 (U.S. $3.90) admission fee for adults, NZ$1.50 (U.S. $1) for children, and NZ$12 (U.S. $7.80) for a family ticket. Don't miss this one!

About 21km (13 miles) south of Masterton, the little townland of Martinborough is home to Wairarapa's best **wineries.** Most welcome visitors.

10 Crossing Between the North & South Islands

A special tip to those who won't be going on to the South Island (poor souls!): A marvelous day trip is the round-trip on **the Inter-Island Ferry** operated by New Zealand Rail. You can take either of the morning departures, enjoy a sea voyage, and have five full hours in Picton before returning on the 6:40pm ferry from Picton (see "Harbor Cruises" under "Organized Tours," in "What to See and Do," earlier in this chapter). I highly recommend it.

From Wellington's Aotea Quay (north of the city center), the Cook Strait ferries depart several times daily for Picton, across on the South Island. The earliest sailing is 5:40am; the latest, 5:50pm. All tickets must be reserved, and sailing times can be affected by weather conditions, so be *sure* to check current sailing times and book by calling **04/498-3999,** or toll free **0800/658-999** in New Zealand, between 6am and 8pm daily. City buses for the terminal leave from Platform 9 at the railway station 35 minutes before sailing time and meet arriving vessels. Also, since crossings can become quite crowded during summer months and holiday periods, it's a good idea to make your reservations as early as possible (through Visitor Information Centres or by calling the numbers given here). Fares for the 3¹/₃-hour, 83km (52-mile) trip are NZ$38 (U.S. $24.70) for adults, NZ$19 (U.S. $12.35) for children, and NZ$114 to NZ$150 (U.S. $74.10 to $97.50) for cars. Ask about off-peak fares, weekend specials, and seasonal price changes. If you're going on to Christchurch, an express train leaves for Christchurch at 2:15pm (connects with the 9:30am sailing from Wellington), and for a small charge your luggage can be through-checked at the luggage office at the Wellington Railway Station. Also, buses to and from Blenheim, Nelson, and Christchurch connect with some ferry arrivals and departures.

You'll travel on the Interislander on either the *Arahura* or the *Aratika,* each of which has a licensed bar, cafeteria, TV lounge, information bureau, and shop. They also have a family lounge with toys to keep young children amused during the voyage, video and movie theaters, a recliner lounge, and a work room. Crossings generally take on a jovial air, with passengers strolling the decks (whatever you do, don't go inside until you've viewed the departure from Wellington's lovely harbor from the rail—a sight you'll long remember) or congregating happily in the lounges, passing the time over friendly conversation and mugs of beer.

Warning: Someone once spoke of Cook Strait's "vexed waters," and in truth the swells can be a little unsettling. If you're subject to a queasy stomach at sea, best pick up something from the pharmacy before embarking. Another tip: If you don't want to miss one minute of the magnificent views or the company of friendly schools of dolphins, take along a picnic lunch to eat outside under the sky and the curious glances of seagulls wheeling overhead.

Note: As I write this, two faster Cook Strait ferry services have just been launched. One is the ★ **Sea Shuttle** (☎ **03/573-8100,** or toll free **0800/104-210** in New Zealand) and the other is **The Lynx,** operated by NZ Rail: The crossing takes about 1½ hours and costs about NZ$46 (U.S. $29.90). Both make three round-trips a day. You can also fly across Cook Strait on **Soundsair** (☎ **04/388-2594** or **03/573-6184**) and **Float Air** (☎ **04/236-6870** or **03/573-6433**).

10 Marlborough, Nelson & the West Coast

SO DIFFERENT ARE NEW ZEALAND'S TWO ISLANDS THAT CROSSING COOK STRAIT IS akin to crossing an international boundary. This is not really surprising because both geography and history are quite different on the two sides of that stretch of water.

On the South Island the majestic Southern Alps raise their snowy heads along the diagonal Alpine Fault that forms its craggy backbone. Along its West Coast are the lush, mysterious rain forests, while to the east of the Alps the broad Canterbury Plains stretch to the sea. It was on those plains that prehistoric moa hunters lived in the greatest numbers, roaming the tussocklands in search of giant birds that grazed there. When waves of Maori began arriving, it was to the North Island that they gravitated, since its climate was more suitable for growing *kumara* and to their agrarian lifestyle. Thus, there were relatively few Polynesian settlements along the fringes of the South Island. It was the waters of the South Island that first lured sealers and whalers, although whalers found the northern Bay of Islands a more hospitable base for their land operations. Then when Europeans began arriving in great numbers and fierce land wars raged on the more populated North Island, the South Island Maori faced those conflicts only when tribes pushed from their lands in the north crossed the strait to battle southern tribes for territory. Because one tribe after another obliterated those who came before them, little evidence was left of South Island Maori culture, legend, and tradition.

The discovery of gold in Central Otago and on the West Coast brought miners pouring onto the South Island in vast numbers. They came from Australia, from Europe, and from the goldfields of California to this new "promised land," and the South Island's tranquillity and isolation gave way to a booming economy, which for a time saw it leading the country in terms of both population and prosperity. Inevitably, the goldfields were mined beyond profitability, but then came the advent of refrigeration, which meant that meat could be exported on a large scale, and the South Island's grasslands became gold mines of a different sort. Thus, it's on this side of the strait that you'll see the most of these woolly four-legged creatures busily eating their way to the butcher. As a tourist, you can give them a tip of the hat as you pass, for it's their need for widespread grazing land that accounts for the fact that today only a little more than one-quarter of New Zealand's population lives on the South Island. This means that you'll find uncrowded roadways, unhurried city lifestyles, and unspoiled scenic grandeur.

1 Picton

29km (18 miles) N of Blenheim, 146km (91 miles) E of Nelson

GETTING THERE • By Plane Air service to Picton from Wellington is provided by Soundsair (☎ **04/388-2594** or **03/573-6184**). Float Air (☎ **03/573-6433**) provides float-plane service, and Ansett and Air New Zealand Link fly into nearby Blenheim.

• **By Train** The Coastal Pacific provides daily rail service between Picton and Christchurch.

• **By Bus** Coach service is provided by InterCity and Mount Cook Landline. The trip from Christchurch takes five hours; from Nelson, two hours. Southern Link Shuttles (☎ **03/573-6378** or **573-6855**) also offers bus service to Christchurch.

• **By Ferry** See "Crossing Between the North and South Islands," in Chapter 9.

What's Special About Marlborough, Nelson & the West Coast

Scenic Splendors

- Abel Tasman National Park, on the coast northwest of Nelson, with wonderful hiking trails and water views.

Historic Buildings

- Christ Church Cathedral, set on a hillside overlooking Nelson's Trafalgar Street, a magnificent gothic structure with a beautiful stained-glass window.

Natural Spectacles

- Fox and Franz Josef glaciers, twin rivers of ice reaching out to the sea.
- Farewell Split, a slender sandbar surrounding Golden Bay.

Crafty Creations

- South Street, in Nelson, with its artistic population and restored colonial homes that hold all manner of craft workshops and sales rooms.
- Hokitika, where visitors watch greenstone become jewelry.

Ace Activities

- Boating amid the labyrinth of coves and inlets in the Marlborough Sounds.
- Tasting Marlborough vintages at wineries in and around Blenheim.

• **By Car** Most car-rental companies request that you turn in the car in Wellington and pick up a new one in Picton. However, you can take cars and campers on the ferry, should the need arise.

ESSENTIALS • Orientation Picton faces Queen Charlotte Sound whence cometh ferries and fishing boats—with great regularity. The shopping area is small and centered around High Street. London Quay runs along the foreshore, with the ferry terminal at one end and the town wharf at the other. The Book and Stationery Centre, 28 High St. (☎ **03/573-6107**), is handy for postcards and reading material.

• **Information** The **Picton Information Centre** is on Auckland Street near the ferry terminal (☎ **03/573-8838;** fax 03/573-8858).

• **Telephone** The telephone area code (STD) for Picton is **03.**

GETTING AROUND Picton doesn't have a local bus system, but **water taxis** of the Cougar Line (☎ **03/573-7925**) will take you to the inlet of your choice. **Float Air** seaplanes (☎ **03/573-6433**) are another option.

Picton sits at the head of Queen Charlotte Sound, ready to receive the ferryloads of visitors who arrive daily. It's a quiet community that's foolishly overlooked by many who disembark the ferry and head straight through town and onto the southbound highway or onto the Queen Charlotte Drive leading to Havelock and Nelson. In their haste these folks miss one of New Zealand's most wonderful playgrounds, because Picton is the jumping-off point for the glorious Marlborough Sounds.

Savvy New Zealanders have vacation homes on the tree-clad fingers of land that protrude into the green waters of the sound, and on holiday weekends they can be seen in their dinghys or on the water taxi heading out to their little patches of paradise. The area is ideal for sailing, kayaking, and bush walking, as well as for kicking back on one of the area's hundreds of secluded bays and tiny beaches. Because it's sparsely populated, pollution is practically unheard of. Dolphins, whales, and occasionally seals are seen here, and the fishing is great.

Picton, (pop. 3,300), actually lies *north* of Wellington, so the ferry curiously sails north to reach the South Island. The town was named by Captain Cook in 1770 for George III's wife. He found it "a very safe and convenient cove," and indeed used it as an anchorage for much of his later Pacific exploration. He can also be credited for bringing the first sheep to New Zealand, when he put ashore a ram and a ewe in 1773—prophetic, even though that particular pair survived only a few days, and thus the good captain cannot lay claim to having furnished the fountainhead of today's millions of woolly creatures.

What to See & Do

It's not a question of *whether* you'll go out on the water in the Marlborough Sounds, but rather *which* vessel you'll be on. The ferry from Wellington provides a good introductory view as it makes its way toward Picton, though for a closer look you'll need to go out on a smaller boat. The Cougar Line (☎ **03/573-7925**) operates a water taxi on Queen Charlotte Sound and offers **three-hour cruises** covering about 80km (50 miles) of coastline (NZ$35/U.S. $22.75). You can go out on the morning cruise, be dropped off at one of the resorts on the sound, and then return on the afternoon excursion. Another option is to join the **mail run** operated by Beachcomber Cruises (☎ **03/573-6175**) and cruise around the sound on the mail boat. This trip departs at 11:15am on Monday, Tuesday, Thursday, and Friday and, depending on how much mail needs to be delivered, returns between 4:30 and 6pm (NZ$45/U.S. $29.25). **Sea kayaking** is another popular activity. The Marlborough Sounds Adventure Company (☎ **03/573-6078;** fax 03/573-8827) offers one-day guided trips for NZ$60 (U.S. $39) per person, including morning tea and lunch. These excursions are accompanied by a naturalist interpreter. The MSAC also offers a twilight paddle and barbecue (NZ$45/U.S. $29.25) and fully catered four-day trips for groups of six (NZ$500/U.S. $325, including meals and camping gear). The four-day kayaking trip is very popular so be sure to book early. The Marlborough Sounds Adventure Company was awarded the 1993 New Zealand Tourism Award for Best Visitor Activity. For those who like **sailing,** the 16-meter yacht *Te Anau* (☎ **03/573-7726**) cruises along the coastline (NZ$25/U.S. $16.25 for two hours). While passengers on any of these vessels may see dolphins, **Dolphin Watch** (☎ **03/573-8040**) makes these lovely creatures the focus of their naturalist tours. Trips of 3½ to 4 hours cost NZ$50 (U.S. $32.50) for adults and NZ$30 (U.S. $19.50) for children; those under 6 free. You might even be able to swim with them for an additional NZ$20 (U.S. $13) per person equipment hire.

OTHER ACTIVITIES

Walking is nearly as popular as boating in the sounds. While there are numerous tracks (trails) near Picton (ask for the "Picton Walkways" brochure at the information center), the hands-down favorite is the **Queen Charlotte Walkway** (also see "Hiking" in Chapter 4). Under the watchful eye of the Department of Conservation (☎ **03/573-7582;** fax 03/573-8362), this 67km (42-mile) track offers wonderful water views, adventurous activity, and a taste of natural New Zealand. The trail stretches from Ship Cove to Anakiwa, and walking from one end to the other takes four days. However, you needn't walk the whole track. The Queen Charlotte offers two unusual options: the possibility of walking only part of the trail and accommodation in cabins, rustic lodges, and homestays along the way. (Read about Craglee Homestay

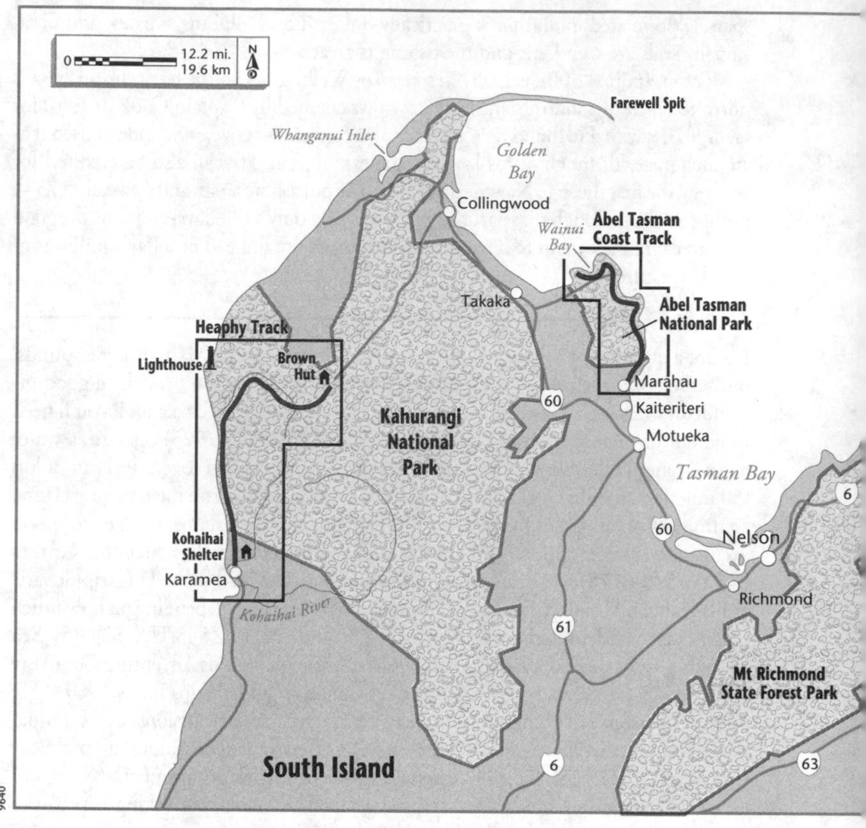

under "Where to Stay," below.) Access is by boat or float plane, and you can start or finish the walk at many different points along the way. You can do the walk with friends or with a guide. And—this is the best part—you don't have to carry your pack. It can be transported by boat from one point to another while you enjoy an unweighted walk. The Marlborough Sounds Adventure Company (☎ **03/573-6078;** fax 03/573-8827) offers a **One-Day Queen Charlotte Sound Walking Adventure** that includes boat transfers, a knowledgeable guide, morning tea and a picnic lunch, and a guided walk on the Queen Charlotte Walkway between Resolution Bay and Ship Cove (NZ$85/ U.S. $55.25). This company also offers a **Four-Day Guided Walk** for NZ$550 (U.S. $357.50) per person, which includes bunk-bed accommodation, good meals, and hot showers. If you want to go it alone, contact the Cougar Line (☎ **03/573-7925**), which will drop you off, transfer your pack, and pick you up when you want to return.

IN NEARBY BLENHEIM

While water is the focus of attention in Picton, wine is the big draw to nearby Blenheim. Here in the heart of the Marlborough District, some of the country's finest **wineries** are open for visitation. Three of my favorites are listed below, but I recommend that before you start out you pick up a copy of the *Wine Trail Guide* from the **Blenheim Information Centre,** Main Street (☎ **03/578-9904;** fax 03/577-8084).

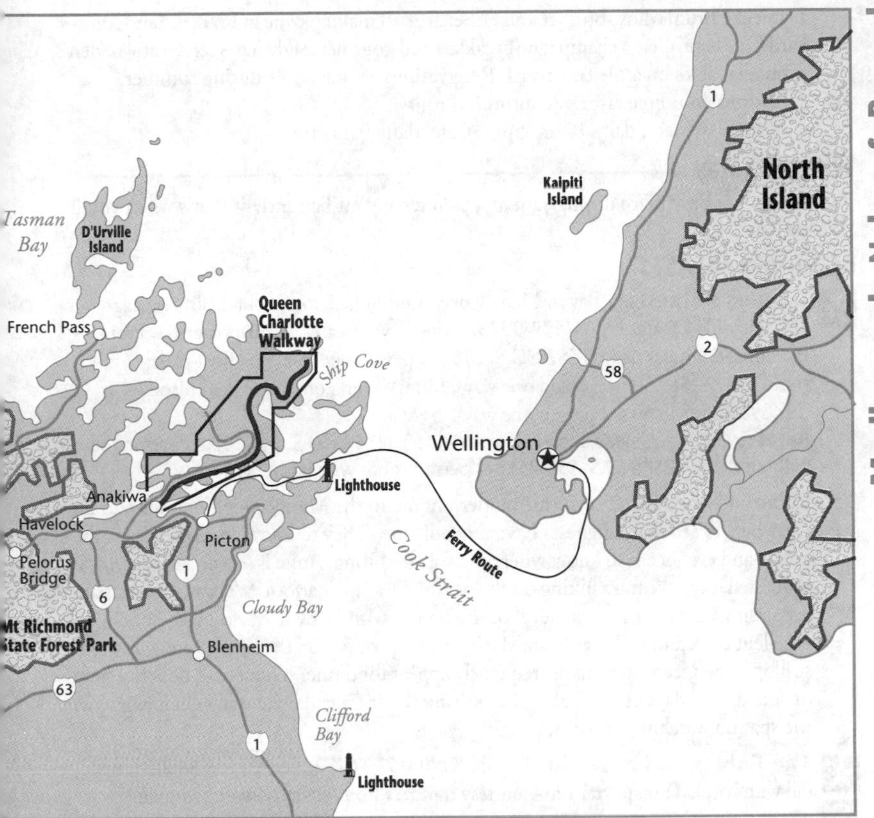

Hunter's Winery, Rapaura Rd. ☎ **03/572-8489.**

The *London Sunday Times* wine critic called Jane Hunter one of the world's top five women winemakers, and you'll understand why when you taste her wine. The Vintners Restaurant on the premises specializes in Marlborough produce, including seafood, lamb, venison, rabbit, freshwater trout, and salmon. Diners can sit out next to the swimming pool and enjoy the garden; an open fire warms in winter.

Admission: Free tasting (no tours).

Open: Winery, Mon–Sat 9:30am–4:30pm, Sun 11am–3:30pm. Restaurant, lunch daily noon–2:30pm; afternoon tea daily 2:30–4pm; dinner daily 6–9:30pm.

Cloudy Bay, Jacksons Rd. ☎ **03/572-8914.**

One of my favorite Christmas presents this year was a bottle of Cloudy Bay Sauvignon Blanc—a gift from a Kiwi friend who managed to find it for sale in San Diego. The *Wine Spectator* calls it "wild and exotic"—who am I to disagree?

Admission: Free tasting (tours by arrangement).

Open: Daily 10am–4:30pm.

Cellier Le Brun, Terrace Rd., Renwick. ☎ **03/572-8859.**

Cellier Le Brun produces four *méthode champenoise* wines as well as a still chardonnay and a pinot noir. The winery was established more than a decade ago by champenois

Daniel Le Brun, whose brother and father are still making wine in France. The Courtyard Cafe here offers a champagne breakfast and gourmet sandwiches served at wooden umbrella tables on a tile courtyard. Reservations are advisable during summer.

Admission: Free tasting (continuous tours).

Open: Winery, daily 10am–5pm. Café, daily 9am–4pm.

Where to Stay

Picton is a busy place during January, so reserve your bed early if that's when you'll be here.

BED-&-BREAKFASTS

Craglee Homestay, Bay of Many Coves, Queen Charlotte Sound (Private Bag 407, Picton). ☎ and fax **03/579-9223.** 4 rms (1 with bath). **Transportation:** From Picton, take a water taxi (NZ$20/U.S. $13 per person one way) or a float plane (NZ$30/U.S. $19.50 per person one way); from Wellington, take a float plane (NZ$90/U.S. $58.50 per person one way).

Rates (including all meals and wine with dinner): NZ$70 (U.S. $45.50) per person room without bath, NZ$85 (U.S. $55.25) per person room with bath. BC, MC, V.

Robin and Anne Perret own this modern home in the Marlborough Sounds and do their best to see that all guests have a good time. They're knowledgeable about the area—and even seem to know where the fish are biting. Anne is a keen walker and, if requested, can take folks hiking on the nearby Queen Charlotte Walkway. Guests are accommodated on a separate level of the house, with its own TV lounge. Anne is an excellent cook and includes fresh Marlborough produce on the menus; fresh salmon, scallops, and green-lip mussels frequently appear for dinner. Guests can be active here or spend their days on the balcony admiring the spectacular view and their nights in the spa tub watching the stars.

The Gables, 20 Waikawa Rd., Picton. ☎ **03/573-6772.** Fax 03/573-8860. 3 rms (all with bath). **Transportation:** Courtesy transfers from the ferry, bus, and train.

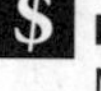

Rates (including breakfast): NZ$40 (U.S. $26) single; NZ$75 (U.S. $48.75) double. BC, MC, V.

What a treat you're in for if Ann and Dick Smith are going to be your hosts. I'm not a random hugger, but I must say I felt compelled to give each of them a squeeze after my last stay. Words like *kind, thoughtful,* and *caring* just don't seem adequate to describe these two. The house that holds their little inn was built in 1924, and they're in the process of restoring it. Already there are fine bed and bath linens, toiletries in the bath, chocolate pillow treats, an open fire in the lounge, and attractive touches everywhere. Complimentary before-dinner drinks and snacks are offered. Ann's breakfasts are legendary: seafood crêpes are a specialty, as are scrambled eggs with Marlborough salmon, fresh fruit, homemade muffins, and freshly brewed coffee. A queen-size room and a single have attached baths, and the other room has a private bath across the hall.

A HOSTEL

The Villa Backpackers Lodge, 34 Auckland St., Picton. ☎ and fax **03/573-6598.** 4 rms (none with bath), 5 dormitories. **Transportation:** Courtesy shuttle from the ferry.

Rates (including breakfast): NZ$17 (U.S. $11.05) per person twin or double; NZ$15 (U.S. $9.75) dorm bed. Discounts to VIP and GOOD cardholders. No credit cards.

Carolyn and Rob Burn own and operate this out-of-the-ordinary hostel in a

100-year-old villa on the main street. They provide—free of charge—blankets and quilts for all beds (if required), the use of mountain bikes and 10-speeds, herbs and spices for cooking, storage, and tea and coffee. On the premises are a well-equipped kitchen, a coin-op laundry, shower and bathroom facilities for the disabled, indoor/outdoor living areas, a barbecue, fax facilities, and a cardphone. I don't know of another hostel that offers so much at this price.

A MOTEL

Aldan Lodge Motel, 86 Wellington St., Picton. ☎ **03/573-6833.** Fax 03/573-6091. 11 units (all with bath). TV TEL

Rates: NZ$79 (U.S. $51.35) single or double. Lower winter rates. AE, BC, DC, MC, V.

All units here have cooking facilities, and one is specially equipped for the handicapped. There are also laundry facilities, a pool, spa, and playground. Units sleep up to six: All upstairs quarters have a double and a single bed on one level and a spiral staircase leading to three singles. Everything is neat and clean, the beds have electric blankets, and the management is friendly.

A MOTOR CAMP

Blue Anchor Holiday Park, 70–78 Waikawa Rd., Picton. ☎ and fax **03/573-7212.** 2 units, 1 suite, 20 cabins, caravan and tent sites.

Rates: NZ$48 (U.S. $31.20) unit for two; NZ$68 (U.S. $44.20) suite for two; NZ$28–NZ$38 (U.S. $18.20–$24.70) cabin; NZ$18 (U.S. $11.70) powered site for two.

I was impressed with how clean everything was when I visited this caravan park. Besides lots of housing, there's a playground with a trampoline, a pool, a barbecue area, and a games room. The units and suite sleep five, and five of the cabins sleep six.

IN NEARBY BLENHEIM

A Motel & More

Vintner's Rest Motor Lodge, 161 Middle Renwick Rd., Blenheim. ☎ **03/577-7711.** Fax 03/577-7712. 4 rms (all with bath), 12 units (all with bath). TV TEL

Rates: NZ$50 (U.S. $32.50) single; NZ$65 (U.S. $42.25) double; NZ$80 (U.S. $52) apartment for one or two. AE, BC, DC, MC, V.

I saw this hostelry only partially completed on my last trip to New Zealand and can only hope it'll be finished by the time you get there. Allan and Jan Graham started with a large house on a good site and are adding 12 motel units. Each of the four attractive, spacious rooms upstairs in the house has coffee- and tea-making facilities, a small fridge, and electric blankets; 4 of the 12 motel units have cooking facilities. Everyone uses the outdoor pool, enclosed spa room, and licensed restaurant. Cooked and continental breakfasts are available.

If you need more space than Vintner's Rest can provide, Allan and Jan have two self-contained units, each sleeping four, adjacent to their home 4 miles away. **Chardonnay Lodge** (☎ and fax **03/570-5194**) costs NZ$80 (U.S. $52) for two, plus NZ$10 (U.S. $6.50) for each additional person. Guests are welcome to use the large pool, tennis court, and spa. Allan also runs Straits Air, a charter airline, and will be happy to take you anywhere you want to go in New Zealand.

Where to Eat

In addition to the places mentioned here, don't overlook the possibility of dining at Hunter's Winery or Cellier Le Brun in Blenheim. See "What to See and Do," above.

 **Stokers Bar & Cafe,** in the Picton Railway Station, 5 Auckland St. ☎ **573-8311.**

Cuisine: NEW ZEALAND. **Reservations:** Recommended.

Prices: Appetizers NZ$8–NZ$11 (U.S. $5.20–$7.15); main courses NZ$15–NZ$26 (U.S. $9.75–$16.90); lunch NZ$4–NZ$10 (U.S. $2.60–$6.50). DC, MC, V.

Open: Lunch daily 10am–8pm; dinner daily 5–10pm.

This is a cute place with delicious food. There's a mock train engine over the bar, and the real train tracks are right outside the window. An old-world ambience is created by hanging plants, lace curtains, and an open fire. Lunch options include "soup of the moment," "snack by the track" (pâté, cheese, and crackers), and "Stokers tatie" (baked potato with sour cream, coleslaw, and cheese). The dinner menu includes lamb or pork filet, scallops, and whitebait, crayfish, and paua when available. Licensed, with a nice selection of Marlborough wines.

 **Toot 'n' Whistle Inn,** Auckland St., next to the railway station. ☎ **573-6086.**

Cuisine: MODERN NEW ZEALAND/PUB. **Reservations:** Not required.

Prices: Lunch NZ$5–NZ$13.50 (U.S. $3.25–$8.80); dinner NZ$13–NZ$16.50 (U.S. $8.45–$10.75). AE, BC, DC, MC, V.

Open: Summer, daily 8am–3am. Winter, Mon–Fri 10am–3am, Sat–Sun 8am–3am.

The chalkboard menu here lists such offerings as tandoori chicken; burritos; steak, egg, and, chips; and a stuffed potato with salad. There's usually some pretty good music playing, and the pub atmosphere is lots of fun. A 12-ounce beer will set you back NZ$2 (U.S. $1.30). There's also a separate area for families and seating on a wooden deck outside. Breakfast, lunch, and dinner are served all day, and they even offer tea, coffee, and scones. Licensed.

WORTH THE EXTRA MONEY

Neptunes Seafood Restaurant, upstairs in the Waikawa Marina, Waikawa Bay. ☎ **573-7060.**

Cuisine: SEAFOOD. **Reservations:** Recommended.

Prices: Appetizers NZ$7.50–NZ$11 (U.S. $4.90–$7.15); main courses NZ$18.50–NZ$25 (U.S. $12.05–$16.25). BC, MC, V.

Open: Sept–May, dinner only, daily 6:30–9pm. June–Aug, dinner only, Thurs–Mon 6:30–9pm.

Diners here sit at Formica tables, and a few blue fish nets are strewn around for atmosphere. However, the food is really good, and the view overlooking the marina is pleasant. For an appetizer you could have peppered mackerel, Kenepuru Sound mussels, or smoked eel. Main courses include sole filets, king prawns, and a seafood medley of shrimp, mussels, scallops, calamari, and fish filet. The house specialty is crayfish, although it isn't available year round. The restaurant is located less than 3km (2 miles) out of town. Licensed.

En Route South

If you follow Highway 1 south along the coast for the leisurely 2½-hour drive to **Kaikoura**—almost midway between Christchurch and Picton—you'll have arrived at a place whose name means "crayfish food," and the only place on New Zealand's east coast where the mountains (the Kaikoura Range) meet the Pacific. It is also fast gaining an international reputation for the animal and marine life that calls it home: seals, dolphins, whales, and numerous seabirds, including albatross, terns, penguins, and petrels. Sperm whales are most often seen between April and August; dolphins, between August and April. Seals and birds are always on hand. **Whalewatch Kaikoura Limited,** in the Kaikoura Railway Station (☎ **03/319-5045,** or toll free **0800/655-121** in New Zealand), organizes daily 3-hour ★ **whale-watching cruises**—they must surely be the highlight of any Kaikoura visit, and to avoid disappointment, you should book as far ahead as possible. The fare runs about NZ$85 (U.S. $55.25); check schedules when booking; and remember that you'll see the most whales between April and August. If you plan to wander on your own, just follow the **Shoreline Walk** along the coast to the tip of the peninsula and you should see seals and a variety of birds; the walk is almost 3 miles long and takes 1½ hours. Or you could opt for the ★ **Cliff-Top Walk,** which affords panoramic views; it's 3 miles long and takes an hour.

Where to Stay & Eat

About 6km (4 miles) south of Kaikoura on State Highway 1, **Fyffe Gallery and Restaurant** (☎ **03/319-6869**)is a great place to stop for a meal or snack—or even overnight accommodation. Breakfast is served from 8 to 10am, and lunch is from noon to 3pm. Dinner is daily from 6pm during January; Friday, Saturday, and Sunday during the other summer months; and Saturday night only during winter. Morning and afternoon tea are offered daily year round. The restaurant serves New Zealand specialties and seafood and is fully licensed. Three pretty rooms upstairs offer fluffy duvets, window boxes, TVs, and baths. They share the restaurant's view of black-and-white dairy cows and pretty gardens against a backdrop of snowcapped mountains. These quarters cost NZ$95 (U.S. $61.75) for two, including continental breakfast. Be sure to say hello to congenial hosts Jan and Graeme Rasmussen. She's the resident artist; he's the gardener. (Ask them about their all-natural interior and exterior wall finishes.) They accept all major credit/charge cards.

En Route to Nelson

The **Queen Charlotte Drive** affords wonderful vistas of the Marlborough Sounds. The narrow road climbs high over the water and forested extensions of land to reveal beautiful beaches and tiny coves. Allow plenty of time for this trip. Even if you're a saturated sightseer, I think you'll want to stop and survey this view. After passing the township of Havelock, you'll come to Pelorus Bridge where there are nice tearooms, picnic spots, and walking tracks.

2 Nelson

110km (68 miles) W of Picton, 290km (179 miles) NE of Greymouth

GETTING THERE • By Plane Service between Nelson and all major New Zealand cities is provided by Air New Zealand Link and Ansett. The airport shuttle (☎ **547-5782**) operates regularly between the airport and the city center for NZ$6 (U.S. $3.90) one way.

• By Bus InterCity and Mount Cook Landline coaches service Nelson. During the 2¼-hour trip from the ferry at Picton, buses stop at the tearoom near Pelorus Bridge—they don't travel the scenic Queen Charlotte Drive route.

• **By Car** From Picton it's a pretty drive to Nelson—110km (70 miles) along Route 6—filled with clifftop views, seascapes glimpsed from bush-lined stretches of the road, and rolling farmlands: a pleasant, picturesque journey you may want to break with a stop by the giant totara tree in picnic grounds near Pelorus Bridge.

ESSENTIALS • Orientation Two landmarks will keep you oriented in Nelson: Trafalgar Street (the main street) and Church Hill, crowned by Christ Church Cathedral and surrounded by lush lawns and plantings that are a local gathering point. The post office is at the corner of Halifax and Trafalgar streets, diagonally opposite the Visitor Information Centre.

• **Information** You'll find the **Nelson Visitor Information Centre,** on the corner of Trafalgar and Halifax streets (☎ **03/548-2304;** fax 03/546-9008). It's open in summer, daily from 7am to 6pm (with longer hours in December and January); in winter, Monday through Friday from 7:15am to 5pm and Saturday and Sunday from 9am to 5pm. The *Tourist Times* and the *Nelson Visitors' Guide,* available from the Visitor Information Centre and local hotels and motels, will give you an update on what to see and do. The **Department of Conservation** counter in the Visitor Information Centre is staffed only October to Easter.

• **Telephone** The telephone area code (STD) for Nelson is **03.**

GETTING AROUND Taxis pick up riders outside the Majestic Theatre on Trafalgar Street and on Bridge Street opposite the Suburban Bus Company, or you can call **Bluebird Taxis** (☎ **546-6681**).

Nelson sits on the shores of Nelson Haven, sheltered by the unique 11km (7-mile) natural wall of Boulder Bank. Its 2,500 hours of annual sunshine, its tranquil waters, and its golden sand beaches make it perhaps the South Island's most popular summer resort. That wonderful climate, combined with the fertile land hereabouts, also makes it an important center of fruit, grapes, hops, and tobacco growing (although tobacco is being phased out). And maybe all that sunshine has something to do with an easygoing, tolerant outlook that makes it a haven for those of an artistic bent. Potters are here in abundance, drawn by a plentiful supply of fine clay and the minerals needed for glazing; weavers raise sheep and create natural-wool works of art; artists spend hours on end trying to capture on canvas the splendors of a Nelson sunset or the shifting light on sparkling water.

Colonel William Wakefield hoisted the New Zealand Company flag on Britannia Heights in December 1841 and placed a 9-pound cannon there as a signal gun (it's there today for you to see), and settlers began arriving on February 1, 1842, a day still celebrated annually in Nelson. They named the new town Nelson to honor that great British seafaring hero, since the company's first New Zealand settlement, Wellington, had been named for Britain's most famous soldier. Lord Nelson's victories, ships, and fellow admirals are commemorated in street names like Trafalgar, Vanguard, and Collingwood. Graves of some of those early settlers lie under the trees at Fairfield Park (at the corner of Trafalgar Street South and Brougham Street), and many of the gabled wooden houses they built still cling to Nelson's hillsides and nestle among more modern structures on midtown streets. Some have become the homes and studios of the artistic community.

Nelson has two distinctions of which it is equally proud: It's known as the "cradle of rugby" in New Zealand, first played here in 1870 (although Christchurch's Football Club is older than Nelson's, it didn't adopt the national sport until some five years after its introduction at Nelson's Botanical Reserve); and a native son, Baron

Central Nelson

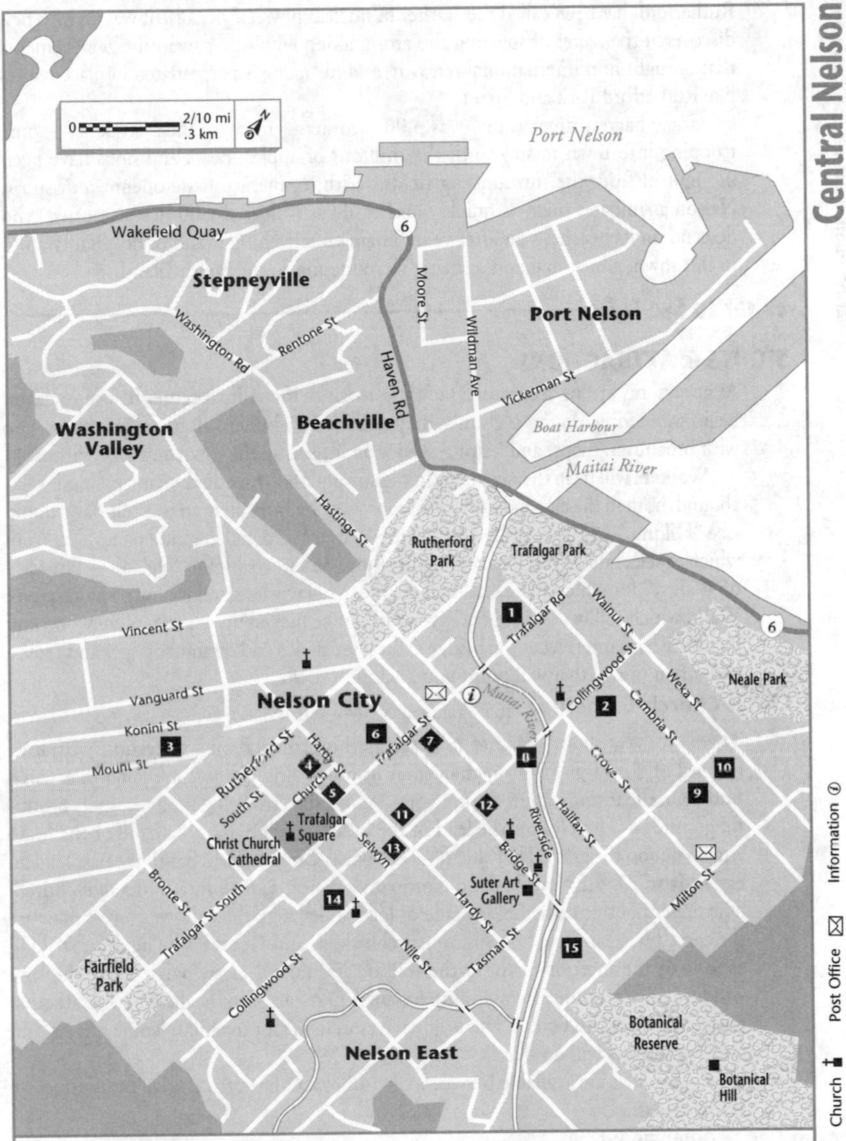

ACCOMMODATIONS

California House Inn 2
Club Nelson 3
Collingwood House 14
Mid-City Motor Lodge 6
Palm Grove Guest House 9
Sussex House 15
Trafalgar Autolodge 1
Waimarie Motel 8
YHA Hostel 10

DINING

Broccoli Row 11
Chez Eelco Coffee House 5
Faces Cafe Bar 4
Juniper's 13
La Bonne Vie 7
Little Rock Cafe Bar 12

Church · Post Office · Information

Rutherford, has been called the "father of nuclear physics" because it was he who first discovered the secret of splitting the atom, along with other scientific achievements that brought him international renown, and his name is perpetuated in place names like Rutherford Park and Street.

Come harvest time, as many as 3,000 workers—many of them students—come trooping into town to stay until the millions of apples, pears and hops have been brought in from the surrounding fields. With its characteristic openness of spirit, Nelson assimilates them as quickly and easily as it does the hordes of tourists who descend on its beaches year after year. There's a refreshing brand of hospitality afoot in this town, which makes it a fitting introduction to the South Island.

What to See & Do

SIGHTS & ATTRACTIONS

As always, my strong recommendation is a visit to the visitors center before you even begin wandering around Nelson—they're a friendly bunch, all too eager to arm you with brochures, maps, and helpful advice about seeing the town and its environs.

Walkers will be in their element in Nelson and the immediate vicinity. Good walks abound, both in the city and in the environs, varying from an hour to a full-day's tramp (see "Hiking," in Chapter 4). The visitors center has detailed guide pamphlets from which to select those you'll have time to enjoy. Be sure to ask for **"Nelson—The City of Walks,"** for which there's a small charge. My favorite stroll is along **Shakespeare Walk,** which follows the Maitai River and can be picked up where Collingwood and Halifax streets intersect at the bridge. You'll see ducks and quaint cottages and cross a pedestrian bridge that will point you back into town.

Christ Church Cathedral, 365 Trafalgar St. ☎ **548-8574.**

There's no way you're going to miss seeing this cathedral on a splendid elevation at the end of Trafalgar Street in the center of town. And chances are good that you'll find yourself, at some point during your Nelson stay, stopping for a rest in its beautiful grounds—if you follow the lead of the locals, you'll bypass the handy benches to stretch out on the grass. That site, now known as **Church Hill,** has in the past held an early Maori *pa,* the New Zealand Company's depot, a small fort, and a tent church. The present gothic cathedral is made of local Takaka marble; above its west door are the carved heads of five bishops, one archbishop, and George V. The most striking aspects of the interior of the cathedral are its stained glass, particularly the rose window, and its unique freestanding organ. A message from the dean of the cathedral to the readers of this book: "The original Maori name for the hill is 'come higher' and we hope visitors will do that."

Tour guides are available between Christmas and Easter and at all other times by arrangement.

Admission: Free.

Open: Daily 7am–4pm (extended hours in summer).

★ **Suter Art Gallery,** Bridge St. ☎ **548-4699.**

Nelson's affection for the arts is exemplified in this excellent museum in the town center. Works by a bevy of important New Zealand painters are on display, and there's an outstanding collection of works by master painter John Gully, who lived here for a time—if they're not on display, they can be seen by appointment. The gallery also has a craft shop selling prints, pottery, and weaving, plus a good restaurant overlooking the Queen's Gardens. Its multifunctional theater seats 160 people and offers an extensive program of film, theater, music, and dance; to find out what's on, check the local newspaper. The restaurant offers lunches, snacks, and dinner. BYO.

Admission: NZ$1 (U.S. 65¢).

Open: Daily 10:30am–4:30pm.

Founder's Park Historical and Craft Village, 87 Atawhai Dr. ☎ **548-2649.**

This turn-of-the-century city in miniature is a true celebration of Nelson's commercial and industrial development. Old St. Peter's Church, built in 1874, has been moved here. There's a 17-minute audiovisual show and a gift shop with reasonable prices. The unique visitors center, by the way, is a replica of an old mill that used to stand in Nelson where the visitors center is now. Among all the exhibits, my favorites are the Newmans coaches from 1923, 1947, and 1952, which actually saw years of service.

The **Andrés** restaurant, in a building dating from 1853 (entry either from the complex or from the parking area), is open for lunch from 11:30am to 3:30pm and for tea until 4pm. Its award-winning cuisine is based on traditional New Zealand dishes, and they stock a good selection of Nelson wines and ales. The complex is located on the edge of town.

Admission: NZ$5 (U.S. $3.25) adults, NZ$2 (U.S. $1.30) children, NZ$13 (U.S. $8.45) for a family, NZ$4.50 (U.S. $2.95) for members of the YHA, AA or AAA.

Open: Daily 10am–4:30pm. **Closed:** Good Friday and Christmas Day.

Nearby Attractions

A map detailing **scenic drives** from Nelson is available at the visitor center, all of which pass points of historical significance as well as natural beauty. There are three **national parks** within driving distance, sheltered **sandy beaches** all along the coast (one of the best is ★ **Tahuna Beach,** 5km (3 miles) to the south, or if it's too crowded, the beach at Rabbit Island), and several **wineries** open to the public (ask at the visitor center for "A Guide to Nelson's Wineries"). If you don't relish being behind the wheel yourself, several bus tours and scenic flights are available—get current details from the visitor center.

One place you should definitely plan to visit is the suburb of **Stoke,** where you'll find the two attractions listed below:

Nelson Provincial Museum, Isel Park, Stoke. ☎ **03/547-9740.**

Filled with artifacts and displays depicting the area's Maori and European history, the museum also boasts the largest collection of historical photographs in New Zealand, with more than a million images, as well as a large historical reference library. The gardens here, especially the rhododendrons, are lovely.

The museum sits directly behind **Isel House,** an elegant 19th-century stone house with dormer windows and an ornate veranda, situated in manicured grounds set back from Main Road. The house, with its collections of early porcelain, pottery, and furniture, is open only on weekends from November to March, but the park itself is well worth a stroll to relax beneath nature trees, which came to New Zealand from worldwide origins as seeds or mere saplings in the 19th century.

Admission: Museum, NZ$2 (U.S. $1.30) adults and children, to a maximum family charge of NZ$5 (U.S. $3.25); Isel House, NZ$1 (U.S. 65¢) adults, NZ50¢ (U.S. 35¢) children.

Open: Museum, Tues–Fri 10am–4pm, Sat–Sun and holidays 2–5pm; Isel House, Sat–Sun 2–4pm in Nov–Mar.

Broadgreen House, 276 Nayland Rd., Stoke. ☎ **03/546-0283.**

This marvelous old cob house (thick walls made of packed earth) was built in 1855 and has been authentically restored and furnished by dedicated volunteers. Their care and attention to detail are evident all through the house, from the drawing room with its slate mantelpiece and original French wallpaper to the upstairs nursery with wicker carriages and antique dolls. All that work has earned the house a New Zealand Tourism Award. Outside, the rose garden holds more than 2,500 plants, with some 250 varieties represented. The house is in town, near Nayland pool.

Admission: NZ$3 (U.S. $1.95) adults, NZ50¢ (U.S. 35¢) children.

Open: May–Oct, Wed, Sat–Sun, and public holidays 2–4:30pm. Nov–Apr, Tues–Fri 10:30am–4:30pm, Sat–Sun and public holidays 1:30–4:30pm. **Closed:** Good Friday and Christmas Day.

Farther Afield

Abel Tasman National Park.

Anyone who appreciates natural beauty, especially those who like to hike, should put this park high on their New Zealand agenda. Abel Tasman National Park, named for the 17th-century Dutch explorer, covers 56,333 acres between Tasman Bay and Golden Bay. **Marahau,** the southern gateway, is 67km (42 miles) northwest of Nelson. The park encompasses beautiful beaches and coastal forest. The 51km (32-mile) **Coast Track** (see "Hiking," in Chapter 4) can be walked independently or with a guided group in three to five days. (Backpacks are transferred by boat from one overnight stop to the next.) There are also several shorter options for those with less time. One popular alternative is to take a bus from Nelson to **Kaiteriteri,** on Tasman Bay, and then a launch to **Bark Bay.** From here it's an easy 2½-hour walk to **Torrent Bay,** where the launch collects hikers for the return trip to Kaiteriteri and Nelson. You can also stay on the launch for the whole 6½ hours as it cruises from Kaiteriteri to Totaranui and back. Each of these options costs NZ$42 (U.S. $27.30) for adults and NZ$14 (U.S. $9.10) for children for the boat, plus the bus fare of NZ$17 (U.S. $11.05) per person. The **Department of Conservation,** King Edward Street (P.O. Box 97), Motueka (☎ **03/528-9117**), provides huts along the way, and there are lodges at Awaroa and Torrent Bay. **Abel Tasman National Park Enterprises,** Old Cederman House (R.D. 3), Motueka, Nelson (☎ **03/528-7801;** fax 03/528-6087), operates the buses, launches, lodges, and guided walks. The Homestead Lodge at Awaroa Bay offers rooms with baths, wood decks with great views, and good meals. The three-day guided walk costs NZ$550 (U.S. $357.50) for adults and NZ$350 (U.S. $227.50) for children 8 to 14. The five-day guided walk costs NZ$850 (U.S. $552.50) for adults and NZ$595 (U.S. $386.75) for children.

SPORTS & RECREATION

If you've ever cast a line or dropped a hook, the South Island's fishing waters are bound to be a temptation to try your luck. The only problem is knowing just where, when, and how to fish all those rivers, lakes, and streams. Fishing guides cost an arm and a leg, but if you want to spend your money this way, go into the **Rod & Gun Shop,** Montgomery Square, near Trafalgar Street (☎ **03/548-1840;** fax 03/548-2150), and talk to Tony Entwhistle.

Vern Brabant, of the **Nelson River Guides,** P.O. Box 469, Nelson (☎ **03/548-5095**), is also highly regarded locally as a guide. He offers excellent trout-fishing forays, with a maximum of two anglers at a time. He'll take you into remote places—using combinations of helicopters and planes—and camping is in tents. You could also fish with Graeme Marshall of **Motueka River Guides** (☎ **03/526-8800**).

SHOPPING FOR ARTS & CRAFTS

One of the great pleasures of a stop in Nelson is visiting some of its many resident artists and artisans. The visitor center can give you a brochure of names and addresses of those who welcome visitors to their studios and suggested tour itineraries. It's interesting to talk with painters, weavers, potters, and other craftspeople about the subject dearest to their hearts—and fun to browse their wares for sale.

I suggest you spend an hour or two along ★ **South Street** with its artistic population. It's lined with small colonial homes, which have been creatively restored, and the street gives you a sense of what early Nelson must have been like. At the corner of Nile and South streets, visit the **South Street Gallery** in an old two-story house to see some of Nelson's finest pottery. It's open from 10am to 5pm daily. ★ **Art of Living** at 20 Nile St. is my favorite. It's next door to **Painted Pots Partnership,** 14 Nile St.

The **Nelson Community Potters,** 136 Rutherford St., is the hangout of talented amateur potters, and there are regular day schools and night courses (just in case you're an aspiring potter yourself). There's usually someone at work there, and many of their finished products are for sale. Drop by **Seven Weavers Gallery,** 36 Collingwood St., for prime examples of weaving from natural wools. You can see weavers at work Monday through Friday from 10am to 4pm.

Other interesting craft shops are the **Glass Studio,** 276 Hardy St., which also stocks small sculptures, paintings, pottery, and jewelry; and **Jens Hansen,** a cooperative gold- and silversmith workshop and sales room at 320 Trafalgar Sq.

Still farther south, on the Richmond By-Pass (Salisbury Road), Paul Laird runs **Waimea Pottery Ltd.** (☎ **544-7481**) as part of the **Craft Habitat,** a collection of quality craft workshops and a coffee shop and gallery. His ovenproof stoneware and lusterware are sold in the Richmond showroom and throughout New Zealand, as are the unique hand-printed tiles by Collen Laird.

If you like beautiful glass pieces, you won't want to miss ★ **Höglunds Glassblowing Studio** at Korurangi Farm, Landsdowne Road, Richmond (☎ **544-6500**). Ola and Marie Höglund worked at Orrefors and Kosta Boda before emigrating from their native Sweden. There's a nice café on the premises.

EVENING ENTERTAINMENT

Nelson isn't known for its nightlife, but it's worth remembering that nightly there's music, Hogs Head Ale, Weiss Beer, and lots of other fun stuff on tap at the **Little Rock Cafe Bar,** 165 Bridge St. (☎ **546-8800**). You also might want to check out the ★ **Victorian Rose,** 281 Trafalgar St. (☎ **548-7631**). This Old English–style pub is also open "until late" and offers entertainment. Ten beers are on tap here, including Guinness, and a good selection of local and imported wine. **Faces** and **Chez Eelco** (see "Where to Eat," below) are other good gathering spots.

Where to Stay

It is true of Nelson, as of most beach resorts, that accommodations are hard to come by during the summer holidays (December through January), and many Kiwi families book here from year to year. While it's not impossible to arrive roomless and find a place to lay your head, you might be better off booking before arrival. Or plan to come in fall (March and April) or spring (October and November) when things are not so crowded and the weather is still fine.

As is also true of most resorts, Nelson has a wide variety of accommodations. You'll find them in the city proper and at the beachside suburb of **Tahunanui,** which is 4 miles away, but served by city buses.

The rates given below include GST.

MOTELS

Courtesy Court Motel, 30 Gulf Rd., Tahunanui, Nelson. ☎ and fax **03/548-5114.** 15 units, 1 suite. TV TEL

Rates: NZ$83–NZ$89 (U.S. $53.95–$57.85) unit or suite for one or two. Additional person NZ$15 (U.S. $9.75) extra. Best Western discounts available. AE, DC, MC, V.

Several factors make this a good motel: its proximity to the beach (a short walk), pretty grounds (with well-tended, colorful flowerbeds), and comfortable accommodations. I also like the arrangements of the units around an inner court away from street noises and facing the attractive heated swimming pool. There are bed-sitters, one-bedroom units that sleep as many as four, and two-bedroom units that will sleep six; all have complete kitchen, soft carpets, electric blankets and heaters, radio, and a complimentary morning paper; one "honeymoon unit has a water bed and spa bath. A luxury "executive suite" is also available, with space for six. A guest laundry, spa pool, and children's play area are additional conveniences. Owner Tony Hocking welcomes children and will gladly provide a cot and highchair as well as arrange for babysitters. The Courtesy Court Motel is 2½ miles from the town center, near Tahuna Beach. The entrance to Golf Road is at Kentucky Fried Chicken in the Tahunanui shopping area.

Mid-City Motor Lodge, 218 Trafalgar St., Nelson. ☎ **03/546-9063.** Fax 03/548-3595. 15 units (all with bath). TV TEL

Rates: NZ$72 (U.S. $46.80) single; NZ$83 (U.S. $53.95) double. NZ$5 (U.S. $3.25) discount to readers who present this book. AE, DC, MC, V.

Hosts Chris Rye and Colin Ashworth welcome guests to their city-center property. Restaurants, bars, parks, and shopping are all only minutes away. Some units have full kitchens, others only limited cooking facilities. All quarters have TVs and in-house video. Decors are in soft pastel shades. Cooked and continental breakfasts are a specialty, and lunches and evening meals are available on request.

Waimarie Motel, 45 Collingwood St., Nelson. ☎ and fax **03/548-9418.** 6 units (all with bath). TV TEL

Rates: NZ$69 (U.S. $44.85) apartment for one; NZ$79 (U.S. $51.35) apartment for two. AE, DC, MC, V.

I particularly like this motel's setting on the bank of the Maitai River, one block from the bus depot and Visitor Information Centre and a few minutes' walk from downtown. There are only a few units, but each has a separate bedroom (some have two), a fully equipped kitchen, and video. One, called the "executive suite," has a sun balcony with a view of the river.

A MOTEL/BED-&-BREAKFAST

Trafalgar Autolodge, 46 Trafalgar St., Nelson. ☎ and fax **03/548-3980.**

5 B&B rms (none with bath), 6 motel units (all with bath). TV

Rates: NZ$35 (U.S. $22.75) single B&B; NZ$55 (U.S. $35.75) double B&B; NZ$55 (U.S. $35.75) unit for one; NZ$65–NZ$70 (U.S. $42.25–$435.50) unit for two. DC, MC, V.

In addition to bed-and-breakfast accommodations, the Trafalgar offers motel units that are bright, clean, and attractively furnished. Each motel unit sleeps up to four, and all have fully equipped kitchens, radios, and electric blankets. Off-street parking and laundry facilities are available. Rosemary and John Waterson are the friendly, helpful owners. It's a two-minute walk to the city center.

BED-&-BREAKFASTS

In addition to the inn and guesthouse below, I want you to know about two homestays in Nelson. Charming Ida Hunt offers three rooms at **Sussex House,** 238 Bridge St. (☎ **03/548-9972**), and Cecile and Alan Strang have three rooms at **Collingwood House,** 174 Collingwood St. (☎ **03/548-4481**).

$ **Palm Grove Guest House,** 52 Cambria St., Nelson. ☎ **03/548-4645.**

6 rms (none with bath). **Transportation:** Courtesy car from the bus depot.

Rates (including breakfast): NZ$40 (U.S. $26) single; NZ$65 (U.S. $42.25) double. No credit cards.

There may not be a palm grove on the premises, but two 50-foot palm trees do dominate the landscaped gardens of this guesthouse. Host Richard Tidmarsh emphasizes service, comfort, and cleanliness and provides a cooked Kiwi breakfast. Most rooms have sinks, and bathrobes are supplied for the trip down the hall to showers and a "ladies' bath." Off-street parking, laundry facilities, tea and coffee facilities, and a TV lounge are other positive points. Palm Grove is a short walk from the town center. Smoking is not permitted in the house.

★ **Willowbank Guest Lodge,** 71 Golf Rd., Tahunanui, Nelson. ☎ **03/548-5041.**

Fax 03/548-5078. 6 rms (none with bath). TV **Transportation:** Courtesy car pickup is available.

Rates (including breakfast): NZ$49 (U.S. $31.85) single; NZ$67 (U.S. $43.55) double. MC, V.

This gracious two-story house is set back from the road on shaded lawns and just a short walk from the beach; it's $2^1/_2$ miles from the center of town. There's a pretty outdoor pool, a spacious TV lounge with pool table, laundry facilities, and off-street parking. The rooms are attractively done up and comfortable, and have hot and cold running water, electric blankets, and thermostatic heaters. You can have a full cooked breakfast or continental breakfast in the spacious dining room. Guests share three bathrooms. The hosts are Cecily and Ron Mayes.

WORTH THE EXTRA MONEY

★ **California House Inn,** 29 Collingwood St., Nelson. ☎ and fax **03/548-4173.**

4 rms (all with bath).

Rates (including breakfast): NZ$95 (U.S. $61.75) single; NZ$125–NZ$150 (U.S. $81.25–$97.50) double. MC, V.

Near the center of town, this charming yellow historic villa has a flower-trimmed walkway, a wraparound porch, leaded-glass trim, a guest sitting room complete with open fire, games, and library, a country kitchen, and delightful rooms. The guest rooms are furnished with antiques, memorabilia, fluffy quilts, and fresh flowers. The home-cooked breakfasts are well known for fresh fruit and berries, juices, and home-baked muffins. Owners Shelley and Neil Johnston couldn't be nicer, and their daughter, Grace, is adorable. No smoking in the inn.

"FREE" ROOM & BOARD

Todd's Valley Farm, c/o G. R. Roberts, R.D. 1, Nelson. ☎ and fax **03/545-0553.**

Well, it isn't exactly "free"—it's room and board in exchange for daily farm and domestic work averaging four or more hours a day. For that, you'll be getting three healthy meals, rather basic accommodations, and a rich learning experience in the practice of conservation. If that has an appealing ring, read on.

This is the home, farm, dream, and ecological laboratory of G.R. (Dick) Roberts, a graduate of Cambridge University, teacher of biology and geography, and documentary photographer. After some few years of teaching, Dick decided in 1969 that the time had come to translate ideas into action, and he bought a beautiful, but uneconomical, 200-acre valley farm 10km (6 miles) north of Nelson. Only about 15 acres are flat land—the rest rise as high as 1,400 feet above the valley floor. Dick does not claim to be 100% "organic" in his farming methods, but he has nurtured the flourishing vegetable garden with none of the dubious benefits of insecticides. On the slopes, he is working out an integrated approach to biological control by mixing many species of fruit and nut trees according to microclimates. Rough hill pastures are grazed by about 200 sheep and 40 acres have been converted to plantation forestry.

Dick welcomes visitors who are genuinely interested in conservation, willing to work at it, and ready to take instruction and suggestion. Although the farm is not by any means a commune, he believes that the cooperative efforts of like-minded people contributing toward a constructive alternative way of life provide an important contribution to society as a whole. "Dropouts, unproductive people, and those not willing to accept responsibility," he says, "are not part of that plan." Please do apply unless you can stay a minimum of two weeks (brief visits may be arranged, however, for those with an avid interest in ecological land use). At Todd's Valley, conservation is a way of life: You are expected to recycle all wastes, and to refrain from smoking in the house or using drugs. You are heartily invited, however, to enjoy the warm, sunny valley 2 miles from the sea in all its natural beauty, gorge yourself on varied fruits, and become intimately involved with the land and its problems. When you've contributed what you can and are ready to move on, Dick may be able to put you in touch with others with similar concerns in New Zealand—an entree into a circle of involved, concerned, vitally interesting people.

If you'd like to stay at Todd's Valley, write or telephone Dick in advance. He can only give beds to a few people at a time, although those who wish to camp are also welcome. Be aware, however, that occasionally the farm is closed to visitors.

HOSTELS

Club Nelson, 18 Mount St., Nelson. ☎ **03/548-3466.** 5 rms (none with bath), 12 cubicles and dormitories. **Transportation:** Courtesy transfers to and from the airport and bus station.

Rates: NZ$17 (U.S. $11.05) per person in shared room; NZ$19.50 (U.S. $12.70) per person double; NZ$16 (U.S. $10.40) dorm bed. No credit cards.

Hosts Linley Rose and Peter Richards describe their property as a "boutique" backpackers' hostel—this is an out-of-the-ordinary place. Formerly Kirkpatrick House, a private home and later a girls' boarding house, this hostel is set on 2½ acres and has a pool and tennis court. The house was built in 1902 by Samuel Kirkpatrick, who made his fortune manufacturing jam. Free tea and coffee are supplied, as is bed linen, and there's a lounge with a TV and a good music system, as well as a large communal kitchen. There's no phone or fax for guest use, but there's a pay phone nearby. There's no smoking in the house, though Samuel's Rest is a little converted garden shed out back where smoking is permitted.

YHA Hostel, 42 Weka St., Nelson. ☎ and fax **03/548-8817.** 34 beds (no rooms with bath).

Rates: NZ$14 (U.S. $9.10) seniors; NZ$9 (U.S. $5.85) juniors. MC, V.

This inviting yellow house with a green tin roof and a huge front yard has 34 beds in seven rooms, hot showers, and a kitchen. All facilities are open all day, and the hostel managers have extensive travel experience, in both the United States and New Zealand. It's located a short walk from the center of town.

CABINS & CAMPGROUNDS

The ★ **Tahuna Beach Holiday Park,** 70 Beach Rd. (Private Bag 25), Tahunanui, Nelson (☎ **03/548/5159;** fax 03/548-5294), is the largest motor camp in New Zealand, regularly handling several thousand travelers per night during summer months. Spread over 55 acres, the camp is a three-minute walk to the beach, and local bus service is at the corner. The well-kept grounds hold a large selection of vacation accommodations as well as tent, caravan, and campervan sites. If you're not traveling with your own linens, they may be rented for a small charge. Amenities include good shower-and-toilet blocks, kitchens and laundries, ironing boards, car wash, TV lounge, children's playgrounds, and miniature golf. A large food shop on the grounds is open every day. This is a beautifully maintained place, with all accommodations kept freshly painted, carpeted, and comfortably furnished. The accommodations are "star graded" for quality and price: four-star units (top-quality, fully self-contained) are NZ$65 (U.S. $42.25), three-star-plus and three-star units (self-contained and semi-self-contained) are NZ$44 and NZ$38 (U.S. $28.60 and $24.70), and two-star-plus and two-star units go for NZ$30 and NZ$25 (U.S. $19.50 and $16.50). Sites are NZ$17 (U.S. $11.05). All rates are double occupancy, and American Express, Diners Club, MasterCard, and Visa are accepted.

READERS RECOMMEND

Kimi Ora Holiday & Health Resort, Kaiteriteri Beach (☎ **03/527-8027;** fax 03/527-8134). *"This place is great. It's only a short walk from where the boats leave for Abel Tasman National Park, and the chalets have a view of the beach. The restaurant serves vegetarian food, and lots of health treatments—including Kneipp water treatment, therapeutic baths, and Fibrosaun body conditioner—are offered. There's also a pool, a sauna, a gym, a fitness trail, and tennis courts."*—Viktor Hauke, Lindenberg, Germany.

IN NEARBY RICHMOND

Bed-&-Breakfasts

In addition to the inn detailed below, partners Bernie Kirk and Louis Balshaw provide bed and breakfast at **Kirshaw House,** 10 Wensley Rd., Richmond (☎ **03/544-0957**). Richmond is 15 minutes by car from Nelson.

Mapledurham, 8 Edward St., Richmond, Nelson. ☎ and fax **03/544-4210.** 3 rms (all with bath). **Transportation:** Courtesy transfers are provided to and from the airport and bus station.

Rates (including breakfast): NZ$95 (U.S. $61.75) single; NZ$135 (U.S. $87.75) double with private bath, NZ$140 (U.S. $91) double with en suite bath. Dinners (by prior arrangement) NZ$30 (U.S. $19.50) extra. MC, V.

Gracious is the word that comes to mind when I think of hosts Deborah and Giles Grigg. The house was built in 1910 by "a man with pretentions" and is fronted by a large lawn where guests are welcome to play croquet. Each room is appointed with fresh flowers and fruit, tea- and coffee-making facilities, and a little tin of delicious almond cookies. Giles is a fourth-generation New Zealander who grew up on a large Canterbury sheep station; Deborah is English (so, of course, the gardens are lovely). Both are well traveled. Breakfasts include homemade marmalade and jam, as well as such items as scrambled eggs with smoked venison and omelets with mushrooms or fresh strawberries.

Where to Eat

Broccoli Row, 5 Buxton Sq. (near Hardy St.). ☎ **548-9621.**

Cuisine: SEAFOOD/VEGETARIAN. **Reservations:** Recommended.
Prices: Appetizers NZ$7 (U.S. $4.55); main courses NZ$13.50–NZ$14.50 (U.S. $8.80–$9.45). AE, DC, MC, V.
Open: Mon–Sat 9:30am–9:30pm (lunch Mon–Sat 11:30am–2pm; dinner Mon–Sat 7–9:30pm). **Closed:** June and Christmas–New Year's Day.

This is an appealing little place with a chalkboard menu that changes daily. You might be offered snapper filets baked with ginger, grapefruit, and spring vegetables or fresh pasta tossed with artichokes, sun-dried tomatoes, olives, and spinach. The service is a little slow, but the food is superb. Focaccia bread is made on the premises, and I could see huge containers of olive oil, a large pepper mill, and big jars of sun-dried tomatoes when I looked into the open kitchen. Lunch is self-serve, and you can eat in the large outdoor courtyard. There's table service for dinner, which is best enjoyed in front of the open fire. Warm colors make the place feel Mediterranean. Mississippi mud pie is a favorite dessert. BYO.

★ $ **Chez Eelco Coffee House,** 296 Trafalgar St. ☎ **548-7595.**

Cuisine: SNACKS/LIGHT MEALS. **Reservations:** Not required.
Prices: NZ$1.70–NZ$19 (U.S. $1.10–$12.35). MC, V.
Open: Mon–Sat 7am–11pm, Sun 7am–9pm.

Chez Eelco is just about the most popular meeting place in town for students, artists, craftspeople, townspeople, and tourists. In fine weather there are bright umbrella tables on the sidewalk out front. Inside are red-and-white café curtains, matching ruffled lampshades, and candles in wine bottles after dark. Eelco Boswijk (a Dutchman who came to New Zealand over 30 years ago) has owned the high-ceilinged, cavernous place since 1961 and has always run it much like one of New York City's Greenwich Village coffeehouses. There's the buzz of contented conversation, table-hopping regulars, a back room whose walls are a virtual art gallery, a piano for the occasional pianist, and paper place mats that give names and addresses of local artists. The extensive menu includes toasted sandwiches, hamburgers, scones, omelets, yogurt, salad plates, steaks, chicken, Marlborough mussels, Nelson scallops, native cheeses, and sweets that include fresh cream cakes. In short, it's a place to drop in for coffee or tea and a snack, enjoy a light meal, or order your main meal of the day. Incidentally, my favorites are also quite popular with locals—the truly superb mussel chowder and salad bowl with hot roll, each at NZ$5 (U.S. $3.25). The filet steak, at NZ$19 (U.S. $12.35) is the most expensive item on the menu, and most main courses are well under NZ$10 (U.S. $6.50). Breakfast is available. Licensed.

Faces Cafe Bar, 136 Hardy St. ☎ **548-8755.**

Cuisine: ITALIAN. **Reservations:** Recommended, especially weekends.
Prices: Appetizers and light meals NZ$6–NZ$8.50 (U.S. $3.90–$5.55); main courses NZ$8.50–NZ$16 (U.S. $5.55–$10.40). AE, BC, DC, MC, V.
Open: Lunch Mon–Sat noon–2pm; dinner daily 6–10pm; brunch Sun 11am–1pm. (Bar, daily 11am–"late.")

This is a handy spot to know about because of its long hours and flexible menu. The posted all-day snack menu features an antipasto platter, lasagne, canneloni, or—for your sweet tooth—a slice of fresh-baked gâteau with whipped cream. (No one in New Zealand seems to have heard of cholesterol.) Faces has a light, airy ambience and serves a wide selection of coffees and teas. Licensed.

Little Rock Cafe Bar, 165 Bridge St. ☎ **546-8800.**

Cuisine: MODERN NEW ZEALAND. **Reservations:** Not accepted.
Prices: Appetizers NZ$4–NZ$8.50 (U.S. $2.60–$5.55); main courses NZ$10–NZ$18.50 (U.S. $6.50–$12.05). AE, BC, DC, MC, V.
Open: Lunch daily noon–2:30pm; dinner daily 5:30–10pm (closes earlier in winter). (Bar, daily 11am–"late.")

I was experiencing a rare moment of homesickness when I stopped in here for lunch, and my heart rejoiced at the sight of a quesadilla on the menu and the place's unusual recycled decor. "Save our rock" is the theme here, and the "little rock" in question is New Zealand. The floors of the dining and bar areas were formerly the cafeteria walls in an old slaughterhouse in Christchurch; the matai bar top was a roof beam supporting the Southland Malting Works. The informal, industrial look works well in this building—once an automotive repair garage. Specials on the chalkboard, "created by the chef in secret and solitude," change every Wednesday. Beefy boulder burgers are

READERS RECOMMEND

La Bonne Vie, 75 Bridge St. (☎ **548-0270**). *"It's on Bridge Street, just left of Trafalgar, and has a quiet, relaxing ambience, good background music, and excellent food."* —Virginia Wright, Gig Harbor, Wash., U.S.A. [**Author's Note:** These sentiments were echoed by Martha Anamosa of Seattle, Wash., who liked "the warm and cozy atmosphere" and the "excellent meal of sautéed mussels and a salad." La Bonne Vie is a licensed and BYO seafood restaurant open daily for lunch and dinner.]

popular, as are the focaccia sandwiches. The recorded music was a little loud, but I didn't care. My chicken-and-mushroom quesadilla was great. It's licensed, with 11 beers on tap and a good selection of New Zealand and Australian wine.

WORTH THE EXTRA MONEY

 **Juniper's,** 144 Collingwood St. ☎ **548-8832.**

Cuisine: CONTEMPORARY/NEW ZEALAND. **Reservations:** Recommended.
Prices: Appetizers NZ$10 (U.S. $6.50); main courses NZ$18–NZ$22 (U.S. $11.70–$14.30). AE, BC, DC, MC, V.
Open: Dinner only, Mon–Sat 6:30pm–midnight.

The house that is now home to Juniper's was built for a vicar, then inhabited by a commune. Today it houses Nelson's top restaurant, which boasts soft pink walls, black tablecloths, and fresh flowers and candles on all the tables. There's also a small bar with a fireplace for before-dinner drinks. Entrees include garlic mussels and duck dim sum, and main dishes feature seafood fettuccine, apricot chicken, venison médaillons, quail Chartreuse, and rack of lamb. The menu changes regularly to offer season specials. Hosts Glenn and Pamela Dentice are most welcoming. Juniper's is a winner of the Taste New Zealand Lamb Cuisine Award. Licensed and BYO.

Easy Excursions

A side trip to **Golden Bay** affords a good look at some of New Zealand's most spectacular scenery, especially long, wide empty beaches. This is not a drive for the faint-hearted, however, as the road up and over Takaka Hill, also known as Marble Mountain, is a series of switchbacks. Your journey will take you along Highway 60 to **Motueka** (pop. 4,700), the heart of a major hops- and tobacco-growing region, and past lots of apple and kiwifruit orchards. The area around Motueka is popular with craftspeople and devotees of alternative lifestyles (whatever that means today).

After "Mot," perhaps make a short diversion to **Kaiteriteri** and go up to ★ **Kaka-pah Point** for one of the best beach–and–blue water views in the country. After Kaiteriteri, it's through Riwaka Valley and over **Takaka Hill/Marble Mountain.** (Try soda crackers; they help me a lot.) **Abel Tasman National Park** will be on your right until you get to **Takaka** (pop. 1,238), the main business-and-shopping center for Golden Bay. You'll see signs along the road directing you to craft shops and people who sell crafts from their home. Another possible diversion: Beautiful beaches stretch out along the coast from here to Totaranui in the national park, but parts of the road are pretty rough.

From Takaka, it's an easy 28km (17 miles) to **Collingwood** and another 26km (16 miles) from Collingwood to the visitor center at the base of ★ **Farewell Spit.** The sandspit is about 35km (22 miles) long and 800 meters (about 1/2 a mile) wide. All along its length are sand dunes as high as seven- or eight-story buildings. The bird life is amazing: Over 90 species have been recorded, including many migratory waders. The spit has been the site of several mass whale strandings, and the rescue attempts have brought caring people from all over the area. The Visitor Centre (☎ and fax **03/524-8454**) can give you information on four-wheel-drive nature tours. It's open daily from Labour Day Weekend in October to the end of the May school holidays.

The **Heaphy Track,** one of New Zealand's best-known hiking trails, starts southwest of Collingwood and ends at Karamea on the West Coast. It can be walked in four days, but it's better to allow five or six. For more information on the Heaphy, contact the Department of Conservation Office in Takaka (☎ **03/525-8026**) and see "Hiking" in Chapter 4.

WHERE TO STAY

Northwest Lodge, Totara Ave., Pakawau, Collingwood. ☎ **03/524-8108.**
3 rms (2 with bath).

Rates (including breakfast): NZ$80 (US$52) double without bath, NZ$120 (U.S. $78) double with bath. Three-course dinner (with wine) NZ$35 (U.S. $22.75) extra. MC, V.

This homestay is probably one of New Zealand's most remote and also probably one of its nicest. Angela (an amazing cook) and Philip (a potter) England designed this contemporary timber-and-glass house with the idea of accommodating travelers. It's built on a sandspit overlooking an estuary, and the birdlife is amazing. When I was last there, they served whitebait omelets for breakfast with homemade muffins, fresh fruit, and delicious homemade yogurt. The dinner main course of local scallops was accompanied by organic vegetables and salad. The guest rooms have tea- and coffee-making facilities and wood decks. If you want absolute quiet and privacy, this the place to stay, 12km (8 miles) north of Collingwood, about 2½ hours' drive from Nelson.

WHERE TO EAT

In addition to the suggestion below, keep in mind that there's a licensed café at the Farewell Spit Visitor Centre (open daily from late October through mid-May).

The Mussel Inn, Hwy. 60, Takaka. ☎ **03/525-9241.**

Cuisine: NEW ZEALAND. **Reservations:** Not accepted.

Prices: Snacks NZ$2.50–NZ$6 (U.S. $1.65–$3.90); dinner NZ$10–NZ$13 (U.S. $6.50–$8.45). MC, V.

Open: Mid-Oct to mid-Apr, daily 11am–"late" (dinner daily 6–8pm), snacks all day.

The folks who frequent this place would've been happy at Woodstock. There's nothing mainstream about it, not even the beer, which is from boutique breweries around New Zealand. Hosts Jane and Andy Dixon welcome all who gather here—mostly locals, including families. The menu includes mussel chowder, quiche, pizza, and fresh steamed mussels. Everyone shares big wooden tables inside and out. Darts, horseshoes, backgammon, cards, and chess are provided, and there's live music most weekends. Licensed.

En Route South

The choice is up to you: A day's driving—4½ to 5 hours will get you to **Greymouth** or **Hokitika** via Highway 6; or you can proceed at a more leisurely pace and stop off at **Westport,** which is emerging as a center for outdoor-adventure activities and a place that, though fiercely noncommercial, makes a real effort to make visitors feel welcome. You can stop for lunch in **Murchison** or in Westport if you can hold out that long, where there's a wider choice of eateries.

If you're traveling by InterCity coach, your driver's interesting narrative will fill you in on the history of most of the terrain you'll be covering along a road that's steep and winding at times, drops through heavily wooded mountain gorges at others, touches the sea, then turns south along a dramatic coastline, sometimes seen from high bluffs along which the road passes. If you're driving, look for these key landscape notes:

Between Murchison and Westport, you'll be following the **Buller River** much of the way. Those jagged gaps and high scarped bluffs above the wall of the gorge between Murchison and Lyell are the legacy of a disastrous earthquake in June 1929. Passing through the gold-mining ghost town of **Lyell,** you'll see little left to suggest the thriving, bustling town of gold-rush days. Its last surviving building, the Lyell Hotel, burned in 1963, leaving only a few faint vestiges of those turbulent times. Descending to the lower gorge, you'll be driving through flatlands, then under **Hawkes Crag,** where the road has been hewn from a sheer face of solid rock above the river, and on to a stretch of road between bush-clad walls and rocky ravines.

3 Westport

101km (62 miles) N of Greymouth, 226km (140 miles) SW of Nelson

GETTING THERE • By Plane Air New Zealand Link flies in from Wellington.

• By Bus Westport is served by daily InterCity and Mount Cook Landline coaches via Highway 6 from the northeast and via the coast road from the south.

• By Car Westport can be reached on Highway 6 from Nelson or Greymouth.

ESSENTIALS The **Buller Information Centre,** 1 Brougham St. (☎ and fax **03/789-6658**), opposite the post office, is open from 9am to 5pm Monday through Friday, and also Saturday and Sunday from October to March. The **telephone area code** (STD) for Westport is **03.**

Far too many people zip past Westport on their way to Greymouth or Hokitika rather than bothering to turn off Highway 6 onto Buller Gorge Road and drive to the coast. Westport is fast becoming known as the "Adventure Capital" of the West Coast. Its mild climate and coastal and subtropical mountain scenery provide an ideal setting for such outdoor activities as white-water rafting, jet boating, horse trekking, caving, underworld rafting through caves, and rock climbing. The information center can fill you in on just where to go to indulge any of these that suit your fancy. For the not-so-adventurous, this region offers excellent sea and river fishing, gold panning, and a good variety of scenic and history walkways.

The town of Westport (pop. 4,600) found relative prosperity as a coal-mining center after weathering the gold bust. ★ **Coaltown,** on Queen Street South (☎ **03/789-8204**), is a mining museum that provides wheelchair access, with a walk-through coal mine and a multiscreen audiovisual presentation. A new wing holds displays on maritime and pioneering history. It's open daily from 9am to 4pm, with admission of NZ$5 (U.S. $3.25) for adults, NZ$4 (U.S. $2.60) for students, and NZ$2 (U.S. $1.30) for children.

Where to Stay

Westport is a small place, but its accommodations are adequate. The rates quoted below include GST.

A MOTEL

Buller Bridge Motel, on the Esplanade (P.O. Box 187), Westport. ☎ **03/789-7519,** or toll free **0800/500-209** in New Zealand. Fax 03/789-7165. 11 units (all with bath). TV TEL **Directions:** Take the first left turn off the bridge on the outskirts of town.

Rates: NZ$70 (U.S. $45.50) single; NZ$82 (U.S. $53.30) double. Additional person NZ$15 (U.S. $9.75) extra. AE, MC, V.

This genuine retreat, under the friendly management of Pat and Sylvia Bradley, offers self-contained motel apartments in a spacious garden setting close to all town amenities. Each unit has a complete kitchen and video, and some have water beds. I particularly like the large grassy courtyard; kids like the play area with trampolines and swings. There's a guest laundry, as well as a luxurious spa pool.

HOSTELS

Marg's (formerly Dale's) Hostel, 56 Russell St., Westport. ☎ **03/789-8627,** or toll free **0800/808-627** on the South Island. Fax 03/789-8396. 34 beds (no rooms with bath). **Transportation:** Courtesy pickup from the bus stop on request.

Rates: NZ$35 (U.S. $22.75) double; NZ$16 (U.S. $10.40) per person sharing. Off-season discount May–Sept. No credit cards.

This hostel offers a modern communal kitchen, laundry, and showers. Margaret Broderick welcomes guests and provides central heating, an undercover garden, a barbecue area, lock-up bike storage, off-street parking, and bike rental—all in a central location. Twin and double rooms are provided with bed linen and a TV.

Tripinns, 72 Queen St., Westport. ☎ **03/789-7367.** Fax 03/789-6419. 40 beds in 18 rms (none with bath).

Rates: NZ$34 (U.S. $22.10) double; NZ$14.50 (U.S. $9.45) in shared room. AE, MC, V.

Maurice and Beverley Tipping's hostel is in a centrally located home built during the gold-rush era. They also offer newer units, all surrounded by spacious lawns and trees. Linen and blankets are provided free. Guests share the fully equipped kitchen, large dining room, TV lounge, barbecue, and laundry. There are also tent sites, luggage storage, bike rental, cycle lock-up, and off-street parking.

En Route to Greymouth

Turning sharply south at Westport to follow the coastline, you'll pass **Mitchell's Gully Gold Mine** only 22km (14 miles) along your way. It's a fascinating place, not a tourist attraction but a real working mine, open from 9am to 4pm daily except Christmas. It has been in the Mitchell family since 1866, and Ian and Helen McKinnon are the friendly miners. Back on the road, you'll soon pass through Charleston, where gold was discovered in 1866, leading to a population boom, with dance halls, stores, and some 92 hotels—few reminders remain today.

About halfway between Westport and Greymouth, you'll come to one of the West Coast's most unusual natural formations, the ★ **Punakaiki Pancake Rocks.** (InterCity and Mount Cook Landline coaches stop here so passengers may walk down to see them.) At the top of a steep headland, a simple tearoom, restroom, and shop are on the inland side of the road, along with space for parking to allow you to leave your car and follow the track across the road through native bush to the sea, where limestone structures, which look for all the world like a gigantic stack of pancakes, jut out into the water. When the seas are high and rough, water comes surging into the deep caverns below and is spouted up some 20 to 30 feet into the air, accompanied by a tremendous whoosh of sound. The surrounding area has been kept as a scenic reserve.

From the Punakaiki Rocks, the road is almost continually within sight of the sea until you turn to cross the **Grey River** and drive into Greymouth.

4 Greymouth

290km (180 miles) SW of Nelson, 101km (62 miles) SW of Westport, 45km (28 miles) N of Hokitika

GETTING THERE • By Plane The closest air service is in nearby Hokitika (see Section 5 of this chapter).

• By Train The *TranzAlpine Express* runs daily between Christchurch and the Greymouth railroad station on MacKay Street. This is New Zealand's best train experience (see Chapter 14).

• By Bus InterCity and Mount Cook Landline buses reach Greymouth from Christchurch, the Fox and Franz Josef Glaciers, Nelson, and Westport.

• By Car Greymouth is reached via Highway 6 from the north and south.

ESSENTIALS The **Visitor Information Network Centre,** in the Regent Theatre Building on the corner of Herbert and MacKay streets (☎ **03/768-5101**), is open in summer daily from 9am to 6pm. They can furnish information about the area and book accommodations at no charge. They are also the Department of Conservation agency for the region. The **telephone area code** (STD) for Greymouth is **03.**

At Greymouth, it's decision-making time: whether to stop here or push on another 45km (28 miles) to Hokitika. Greymouth offers a wider choice of accommodations; Hokitika has more attractions. Greymouth does have Shantytown, a reconstructed gold-mining town, but there's no local transportation to it, and it's quite possible to double back to see it from a Hokitika base. In the final analysis, your decision may rest chiefly on just how tired and hungry you are when you reach Greymouth, erstwhile "Heart of the Coast."

New Zealand's West Coast is a rugged stretch of country whose incomparable beauty has been molded and shaped by the elements—and its inhabitants are perhaps the most rugged and individualistic of a nation of individuals. Lured by nature's treasures, they have from the beginning seemed to revel in its challenges, and along with a resilient toughness have developed a rollicking sense of fun, a relaxed acceptance of the vicissitudes of West Coast life, and a brand of hospitality that's recognized (and even boasted of) by Kiwis in every other part of the country. "Coasters" are a hardy, good-hearted breed who will welcome you warmly to this unique region.

The coast's beauty and hidden wealth were entirely lost on Captain Cook when he sighted it from the sea, remained offshore, and described it in his journal as "wild and desolate and unworthy of observation." Of course, his sea-based observation could not possibly reveal the presence of nuggets of gold strewn about those "unworthy" beaches. That discovery was left for 1864, when it precipitated an influx of prospectors and miners from as far afield as California (along with a goodly number from Australia), many of whom would remain after the goldfields played out in 1867 to form the basis of a permanent population who take fierce pride in their particular part of New Zealand.

Greymouth, with a population of 11,000, keeps busy these days with coal and timber exports and the import of tourists who come to roam the beaches in search of gemstones and greenstone, fish in the clear streams nearby, and perhaps pan for gold.

What to See & Do

The star attraction at Greymouth is **Shantytown,** a replica West Coast gold-mining town dating back to the turn of last century. It's set amid native bush, and a steam train operates hourly and threads its way through this picturesque setting. Horse-and-buggy rides are also available, and the stagecoach will rattle you over an old bush road. Visitors can also pan for gold.

Shantytown (☎ **762-6634**) is open October to March (except Christmas Day), daily from 8:30am to 7pm; April to September, daily from 8:30am to 5pm. Admission (which includes steam-train rides) is NZ$7 (U.S. $4.55) for adults and NZ$2 (U.S. $1.30) for children. To find Shantytown, drive 8km (5 miles) south of Greymouth to Paroa, make a left turn, and drive another 3km (2 miles) inland. The route is well signposted. If you're carless, a taxi from Greymouth will set you back NZ$8 (U.S. $5.20) per person (minimum two people) each way.

Where to Stay

Greymouth is blessed with many good accommodations at reasonable rates. Motel and guesthouse operators are also very cooperative, helping you find a vacancy if your choice is filled.

The rates given below include GST.

MOTELS

Aachen Place Motel, 50 High St., Greymouth. ☎ **03/768-6901.** Fax 03/768-6958. 10 units (all with bath). TV TEL **Directions:** Drive about 1km (1/2 a mile) south of the town center on Highway 6.

Rates: NZ$72 (U.S. $46.80) single; NZ$84 (U.S. $54.60) double. Additional person NZ$12 (U.S. $7.80) extra. Best Western discounts available. AE, DC, MC, V.

This well-kept Best Western offers 10 units that sleep one to three, all with full kitchen facilities. All have radios, electric blankets, and heating, and some are smoke-free; full laundry facilities are available. It's handy to a restaurant and supermarket and about a 10-minute walk from the center of town. Cooked and continental breakfasts are available.

South Beach Motel, 318 Main South Rd., Greymouth. ☎ **03/762-6768.** Fax 03/762-6748. 11 units (all with bath). TV TEL

Rates: NZ$65 (U.S. $42.25) single; NZ$72–NZ$85 (U.S. $46.80–$55.25) double. Additional person NZ$14 (U.S. $9.10) extra. Best Western discounts available. AE, DC, MC, V.

Across from the beach, this motel has a quiet location only a 5km (3-mile) drive from town. Each unit comes with complete kitchen, video, a radio, and electric blankets. There's one unit for the disabled, a waterbed unit, and one "executive suite." Amenities include a guest laundry, children's playground, barbecue area, and spa. Breakfast is available.

Willowbrook Motor Lodge, Hwy. 6 (P.O. Box 260), Greymouth. ☎ **03/768-5339.** Fax 03/768-6022. 5 units and suites. TV TEL

Rates: NZ$55 (U.S. $35.75) single; NZ$60 (U.S. $48.75) double; NZ$75 (U.S. $48.75) one-bedroom suite for one or two. AE, MC, V.

Located 3km (2 miles) north of town on the Greymouth–Westport highway, this motor lodge offers modern studios and suites, all nicely furnished right down to potted plants. All units have been given old West Coast hotel names like Welcome Nugget, Diggers Home, and Plough Inn by hosts Lois and Ted Gutberlet, one Greymouth's most gracious couples, who delight in making their guests feel at home—they ask that you let them know you're a Frommer reader. The suites are spacious and airy, with slanted roofs and paneled walls; bed-sitters (studios) are more modest but have full kitchens and electric blankets. There's a heated indoor swimming pool and a spa pool, as well as a guest laundry. The one-bedroom suite boasts a spa bath, full kitchen, hairdryer, lounge, and tea-and-toast breakfast served in your suite. Cooked or continental breakfast available at an additional charge.

A BED-&-BREAKFAST

Golden Coast Guest House, 10 Smith St., Greymouth. ☎ **03/768-7839.** 4 rms (none with bath), 1 bed-sitter (with bath).

Rates (including breakfast): NZ$45 (U.S. $29.25) single; NZ$66 (U.S. $42.90) double; NZ$60 (U.S. $39) bed-sitter (studio) for two. V.

Gladys Roche is the hostess at this B&B on Highway 6 above the railroad station, five minutes from the town center. The red-roofed house is set in a sloping, flower-bordered lawn. The guest rooms are bright and clean, with heaters and electric blankets. The bed-sitter has its own kitchen and bath. There's a TV lounge with a pretty rock fireplace, where you're welcome to make tea and coffee whenever you wish.

HOSTELS

Formerly the Blackball Hilton, Hart St., Blackball. ☎ **03/732-4705.** Fax 03/732-4111. 18 rms (none with bath). No credit cards.

Rates: NZ$16 (U.S. $10.40) per person double or twin; NZ$14 (U.S. $9.10) dorm bed. Dinner, bed, and breakfast NZ$40 (U.S. $26).

Jane Wells and Linda Osborn, owners of this hostel since 1994, offer budget lodging, as well as meals and drinks from their bar. You might want to seize this opportunity to try Miner's, a natural West Coast brew. A sample three-course dinner might start with pumpkin soup, followed by beef Stroganoff accompanied by salad and vegetables, followed by Jamaican banana treat with snowflake ice cream for dessert. The kitchen is also freely available for guests to fix their own meals. This no-smoking place isn't posh, but it's homey and cozy and located 24km (15 miles) northeast of Greymouth.

YHA Hostel, "Kainga-Ra," 15 Alexander St. (P.O. Box 299), Greymouth. ☎ and fax **03/768-4951.** 34 beds in 10 rms (none with bath).

Rates: NZ$20–NZ$25 (U.S. $13–$16.25) single; NZ$16 (U.S. $10.40) per person double or twin; NZ$14 (U.S. $9.10) per person shared room; NZ$12 (U.S. $7.90) dorm bed. Nonmembers pay NZ$4 (U.S. $2.60) extra. No credit cards.

This hostel is close to town in a historical building, the ex–Marist Brothers' home, and is surrounded by nice gardens. There are numerous rooms, but the former chapel holding 10 beds is probably the most interesting. Everyone uses the fully equipped kitchen, dining room, living room with open fireplace, and TV/video room. There are also a laundry, bicycle shed, barbecue, and partially covered veranda.

CABINS & CAMPING

Greymouth Seaside Holiday Park, Chesterfield Street, Greymouth (☎ **03/768-6618;** fax 03/768-5873), is, as its name implies, situated by the sea. On level, sheltered sites on the beachfront at the southern edge of town there are 50 tent sites, 72 caravan sites, 10 on-site caravans, 28 cabins, 10 tourist cabins, six tourist units, and a backpackers' bunkhouse with 20 beds. Chesterfield Street is just off the Main South Road, and the camp is signposted. There's a modern TV lounge, kitchen, washing machines and dryers, hot showers, linen for rent, and a camp store. Grounds and all accommodations are well kept, and a courtesy car is available to and from public transport. Double-occupancy rates are NZ$16.60 (U.S. $10.75) for tent sites, NZ$18 (U.S. $11.70) for caravan sites, NZ$34 (U.S. $22.10) for on-site caravans, NZ$32 (U.S. $20.80) for cabins, NZ$39 (U.S. $23.35) for tourist cabins, NZ$56 (U.S. $36.40) for tourist units, and NZ$62 (U.S. $40.30) for a motel suite; backpackers pay NZ$11 (U.S. $7.15) per person. Children pay half price in each case.

Where to Eat

Bonzai Pizzeria & Restaurant, 31 Mackay St. ☎ **768-4170.**

Cuisine: PIZZA/STEAK. **Reservations:** Not required.
Prices: Appetizers NZ$6.50 (U.S. $4.25); main courses NZ$16–NZ$18 (U.S. $10.40–$11.70). DC, MC, V.
Open: Daily 9am–"late."

The Bonzai serves no less than 16 types of pizza, including vegetarian. You can also get soups, sandwiches, omelets, and steaks, all at reasonable prices. The Dutch owner has shellacked European newspapers on the walls as a unique covering. BYO and licensed. It's located near the information center.

WORTH THE EXTRA MONEY

Cafe Collage, 115 Mackay St. ☎ **768-5497.**

Cuisine: NEW ZEALAND. **Reservations:** Recommended.
Prices: Average meal NZ$35 (U.S. $22.75). MC, V.
Open: Dinner only, Mon–Sat 6pm–"late." **Closed:** Occasionally Mon.

If you want a bit of dining elegance in Greymouth's town center, best reserve a table here. The dining room is lovely, with an art deco ceiling and lamps. Dishes on the constantly changing menu focus on fresh local products. BYO and licensed.

En Route to Hokitika

The 45km (28-mile) drive south follows the coastline closely along mostly flat farmland. But look to your left and the snowcaped tips of the Southern Alps become clearer and clearer, sharply defined against the sky, as though painted on the horizon, a teasing glimpse of the mountain scenery that awaits in a few days when you turn away from the Tasman Sea.

About 32km (20 miles) from Greymouth you'll cross the **Arahura River.** This is where Maori found a great quantity of the greenstone they so highly prized for making weapons, ornaments, and tools. Another 8km (5 miles) and you reach Hokitika, where you can see artisans still working that gemstone into a multitude of items, some of which you'll no doubt take along when you depart.

En Route to Christchurch

If your time on the South Island is limited, you can drive from Greymouth to Christchurch (allow the better part of the day in order to enjoy the drive to its fullest) by way of **Arthur's Pass** and some of New Zealand's most spectacular scenery. Just south of Greymouth, turn left onto Highway 73. Opened in 1866, this road was one of the last in the country to be used by horse-drawn Cobb & Co. coaches. If you come in winter, Mount Temple Basin offers a full range of winter sports; in summer, the wild mountain landscape is a marvel of alpine flowers. Regular coach service is also available from Greymouth to Christchurch and this is the route of New Zealand's best train trip: the *TranzAlpine Express.*

5 Hokitika

45km (28 miles) S of Greymouth, 147km (91 miles) N of Franz Josef

GETTING THERE • By Plane There is air service via Air New Zealand Link between Hokitika and Christchurch.

• By Train The nearest rail service is in Greymouth (see Section 4 in this chapter).

• By Bus Hokitika is on InterCity's and Mount Cook Landline's Franz Josef–Greymouth route.

• By Car Hokitika can be reached via Highway 6.

ESSENTIALS The **Westland District Council Information Centre,** on Weld Street, Hokitika (☎ **03/755-8322;** fax 03/755-8026), is open December to March, daily from 8:30am to 6pm; April to November, Monday through Friday from 8:30am to 5pm and Saturday from 10am to 1pm. The center's friendly staff can furnish detailed information on the area's attractions, and make reservations for transportation and accommodations. The **post office,** on Level Street at Weld Street, is open Monday through Friday from 9am to 5pm. The **telephone area code** (STD) for Hokitika is **03.**

GETTING AROUND For taxi service, call Gold Band Taxis (☎ **755-8437**).

As you drive into quiet, peaceful little Hokitika, you'll find it hard to believe that this was once the boisterous, rowdy "Goldfields Capital," where more than 35,000 miners and prospectors kept the dance halls roaring and filled some 102 hotels. And because it was more accessible by sea than overland, ships poured into its harbor, even though the entrance was so hazardous that people would gather on the shore to watch unlucky ships go around. Even so, there were as many as 80 at one time tied up at Hokitika wharfs, many of them waiting to transport the gold that poured out of the area at the rate of half a million ounces a year. It turned out not to be the endless supply they all dreamed of, and when the gold was gone, Hokitika's fortunes took another turn—this time, decidedly downward.

Today, you'll see only rotting remnants of those once-busy wharfs, and almost no vestiges of all those hotels. Still, Hokitika has more attractions than any other West Coast town, and its present-day prosperity rests on farming, forestry, and tourism—likely to be much more lasting than the glittering gold. The major airport of the West Coast is located here, there's good coach service, and you'll find it an ideal base for exploring this part of the South Island.

What to See & Do

One of the primary reasons for making Hokitika your base on the West Coast is to be there after dark so you can see the **glowworms**—this is the largest outdoor group in the country—in a charming dell at the edge of town, right on the main road. The 40-foot-and-higher wooded banks are filled with sparkling clusters of thousands of glowworms, a truly awe-inspiring sight. And as interesting as the more touristy Waitomo displays are, there's something about walking down a dirt path under a natural archway of treetops and standing alone in absolute silence that makes for a more enjoyable personal experience. There's no charge, but there's a donation box at the entrance and all contributions are appreciated by the town, which keeps this wondrous place available for us all. Best bring a flashlight for the first part of the path, but remember to turn it off when you begin to see the glowworms or they'll turn their lights off.

One of the best ways to gain an immediate insight into this fascinating little town is to pick up the **Hokitika Historic Walk** brochure from the information center or the West Coast Historical Museum. In less than a half hour, you'll have learned about the historical buildings and sites and the part each played in the town's history. As you walk the town's tiny streets, your invisible companions are bound to be the ghosts of those early gold miners, merchants, and sailors who once walked here.

The ☆ **West Coast Historical Museum,** on Tancred Street (☎ and fax **03/755-6898**), features reconstructions and artifacts of the 19th-century "Alluvial placer" gold-mining era on the West Coast. Hastily built canvas and slab dwellings display cooking utensils and furnishings, with equipment represented by pit-sawing and a blacksmith's forge for servicing the tools needed to open up cemented wash concealing the golden treasure. In direct contrast to this sort of hardship and poverty, there are church fittings and elaborate furniture from a merchant's home, along with a typical hotel bar. There are horse-drawn vehicles on display, and pictorial records of the rich maritime trade of the river harbor. In addition, a marvelous meccano model gold dredge is operated on request, and there's a 20-minute audiovisual presentation of Westland's goldfields history. Early Maori occupation is represented by authentic artifacts and jade workings. Displays also feature decorative jade craft works. Gold panning is an all-weather attraction in the miner's hut built just for panning; the cost is NZ$5 (U.S. $3.25) per person. The museum is open daily from 9:30am to 5pm. Admission is NZ$3 (U.S. $1.95) for adults, NZ$1 (U.S. $65¢) for children, NZ$7 (U.S. $4.55) for a family group. A treasure hunt is available for children at no extra charge.

Hokitika's Rotary Club has provided an excellent orientation base at the **lookout point** just off the road to the airport. From there you can look over valley farmland to the towering peaks of the Southern Alps (each one identified by a revolving bronze pointer, which stands on a stone base) or across the town to the glistening Tasman Sea. It's a spectacular view, within easy walking distance of the center of town.

There are excellent **scenic flights** from Hokitika over the glaciers—not landing on them as some others do, but the flight is longer. The plane flies south from Hokitika to the Main Divide, over the Tasman Glacier, skirts Mount Cook, over the Fox and Franz Josef Glaciers, over Okarito Lagoon (nesting place of the white heron) and large stands of New Zealand native timber. It's quite a flight. There's no regular schedule at this writing, but inquire at the information office about times and current prices.

For **canoeing, rafting,** and **heli-rafting** information, contact Alpine Rafts, 57 Tramway St., Ross (☎ **03/755-8322** or **755-4077**).

★ NEARBY LAKE KANIERE SCENIC RESERVE

This beautiful nature reserve, centered around one of the South Island's largest lakes, is just 18km (11 miles) from Hokitika—drive inland from the main road to Kaniere township, and drive straight ahead instead of turning right and going over the Hokitika River. If time is too short for a stop, there's a lovely 58km (35-mile) circular scenic drive past the lake and back through Kikatahi Valley farmlands. Loitering, however, will be rewarded by beautiful, peaceful vistas of the lake ringed by unspoiled forests with a backdrop of distant mountains. You'll find an information kiosk and toilets at the Landing, where the road first comes to the lake's edge, and there are picnic tables, fireplaces, and toilets at Sunny Bight. Pick up advance information on lake and bush walks at the Information Centre in Hokitika, or contact the Department of Conservation, on the corner of Gibson Quay and Sewell Street, Hokitika (☎ **03/755-8301**). Needless to say, this exquisite bit of South Island scenery should be treated with due respect.

SHOPPING

★ **Westland Greenstone Company Ltd.,** Tancred St. between Weld and Hamilton sts. ☎ **755-8713.**

You really shouldn't miss this place. The piles of rocks you see show their true color (and value) as the diamond-tipped wheels spin, cutting off slices. The workroom is open for you to wander through, watching talented artisans carving tikis and meres, fitting earrings and pins, and shaping a hundred other souvenirs from the gemstone. Then back to the showroom to consider which of their handiwork to buy (you're under no obligation to make a purchase). There's also an extensive range of lovely paua and pink mussel-shell jewelry from which to choose. Open daily from 8am to 5pm.

Mountain Jade, 41 Weld St. ☎ **755-8007.**

Here you can see some intricately carved pieces from greenstone, real collector's items. Carving is done on the premises. Open daily from 8am to 9pm.

The Gold Room, Tancred St. ☎ **755-8362.**

Rhett and Liz Robinson have put together a marvelous selection of handmade pendants, rings, bracelets, earrings, necklaces, tie tacks, and much more, including some beautifully set opals. Many of the items are fashioned from natural gold nuggets that come from the local mines. It's worth a visit even if you don't plan to buy anything. The shop, which also sells greenstone jewelry, is open daily from 8am to 7pm.

★ **Hokitika Craft Gallery,** 25 Tancred St. ☎ **755-8802.**

This cooperative displays and sells the work of 19 top West Coast artists and craftspeople. There are lovely contemporary works in fiber, pottery, wood, art, jade, and bone. Open daily from 9am to 5pm, the gallery will mail worldwide.

★ $ **Revelations,** 18 Weld St. ☎ **755-7649.**

A Dutch couple, Hans and Lida Schouten, display their considerable talents here. Hans works with wood and specializes in spinning wheels, coffee tables, and stools, all made from local recycled timber. A weaver, Lida creates lovely woolens. You'll find exceptionally nice hand-knit sweaters of natural hand-spun wool and mohair, shawls, leather goods, and pottery. The Schoutens are happy to mail packages overseas to lighten your load. Open daily from 9am to 5pm (until 8pm in summer). Lida and her daughter, Myrian, manage the shop.

Brent Trolle's Studio, 13 Whitcombe Terrace. ☎ **755-7250.**

Some of the best paintings of the South Island's West Coast are done right here in Hokitika by Brent Trolle, whose work is known throughout the country. You can visit at his home, which also serves as gallery and studio, by calling for an appointment. I can't think of a nicer way to keep New Zealand memories alive than with one of Brent's paintings. His paintings are also on show at the House of Wood, Tancred Street (☎ **755-6061**).

Where to Stay

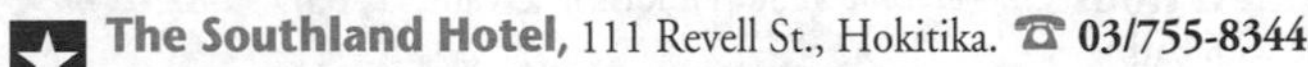

Accommodations are limited, but I bet you'll be pleased with the ones that are here. Hokitika has no youth hostel, but there's backpacker lodging at the Hokitika Holiday Park (see below); the nearest YHA hostel is in Greymouth. The rates below include GST.

A LICENSED HOTEL

The Southland Hotel, 111 Revell St., Hokitika. ☎ **03/755-8344.** Fax 03/755-8258. 15 rms (10 with bath). TV TEL

Rates: NZ$32 (U.S. $20.80) single without bath, NZ$80 (U.S. $52) single with bath; NZ$42 (U.S. $27.30) double without bath, NZ$90 (U.S. $58.50) double with bath. AE, DC, MC, V.

This small hotel near the river in the town center has a range of accommodations—all first class. The rooms are nicely appointed, with attractive decor and comfortable furnishings, and there are units designed for the handicapped. Facilities include in-house video, a launderette, and spa baths. Some readers wrote recently to comment on the good dinner they had here. Reservations can be made through Flag Inns.

MOTELS

Goldsborough Motel, 252 Revell St. (P.O. Box 201), Hokitika. ☎ and fax **03/755-8772** or **755-8773.** 14 units (all with bath). TV TEL

Rates: NZ$60 (U.S. $39) single; NZ$78 (U.S. $50.70) double. Additional person NZ$14 (U.S. $9.10) extra per adult, NZ$10 (U.S. $6.50) extra per child. Best Western discounts available. Continental breakfast NZ$5 (U.S. $3.25) extra. AE, DC, MC, V.

Top billing in Hokitika's motels goes to the Goldsborough, across from the Tasman Sea and a short walk from the glowworm dell. The hosts at this Best Western member are Katie and Leo McIntyre. All units—bed-sitters (studios) and two-bedroom

READERS RECOMMEND

Pete's Place, 40 Fitzherbert St., Hokitika (☎ **03/755-8845**). *"This is a great hostel. Pete is really friendly, and I had a nice room to myself for NZ$20 (U.S. $13)."*—H. Irvine, Christchurch, New Zealand.

Farm Stay Duindam, Evans Creek, Hari Hari (Private Bag 763, Hokitika) (☎ **03/883-3028**). *"Joanne and Jon Duindam are great hosts, and their dairy farm is the best place I stayed in the 18 days I visited New Zealand."*—Ted Wilson, Walnut Creek, Calif., U.S.A. [**Author's Note:** Hari Hari is 80 km (50 miles) south of Hokitika.]

apartments—have fully equipped kitchens, central heating, and electric heaters. There's a guest laundry, a pretty swimming pool, a spa pool, and a children's playground. A seven-day food store is within walking distance. The motel is a mile from the town center.

Hokitika Motel, 221 Fitzherbert St., Hokitika. ☎ **03/755-8292.** Fax 03/755-8485. 3 studios, 16 units. TV TEL **Transportation:** Courtesy car available.

Rates: NZ$60 (U.S. $39) single; NZ$65–NZ$75 (U.S. $42.25–$48.75) double. Additional person NZ$12 (U.S. $7.80) extra per adult, NZ$10 (U.S. $6.50) extra per child. AE, DC, MC, V.

The Hokitika is just across from the glowworm dell. There are one- and two-bedroom apartments with full kitchens, as well as three bed-sitters (studios) with only electric tea/coffee pot, toaster, teapot, crockery, and fridge. All units have central and electric heating, electric blankets, and radios. There's a ministore for essential provisions, a car wash, a laundry, and a courtesy car to the airport.

A BED-&-BREAKFAST

★ **Central Guest House,** 20 Hamilton St., Hokitika. ☎ and fax **03/755-8232.** 8 rms (none with bath).

Rates (including continental breakfast): NZ$39 (U.S. $25.35) single; NZ$59 (U.S. $38.35) double. MC, V.

As its name implies, this guesthouse is centrally located, with banks, restaurants, attractions, and the bus station nearby. All bedrooms are heated and have electric blankets, and the lounge has a TV and tea- and coffee-making facilities. Laundry facilities and a telephone are also available. Owners Russell Wenn and Julie Collier are happy to provide information on dining and outdoor activities. A cooked breakfast can be ordered. There's no smoking in the house.

CABINS & CAMPGROUNDS

The $ **Hokitika Holiday Park,** 242 Stafford St., Hokitika (☎ and fax **03/755-8172**), has accommodations to suit many needs. Tent sites are NZ$7.50 (U.S. $4.90) per person; power caravan sites, NZ$8.50 (U.S. $4.40) per person; bunkhouse for up to 12 people, NZ$10 (U.S. $6.50) per person; backpacker cabins with double or twin beds, NZ$24 (U.S. $15.60) for two; and additional people are NZ$10 (U.S. $6.50) extra. Tourist cabins with hot and cold running water, kitchen, and toilet cost NZ$38 (U.S. $24.70) for two. Tourist flats with kitchen and bathroom are NZ$49 (U.S. $31.85) for two; an additional person is NZ$11 (U.S. $7.15) extra for adults, half price for children under 16.

Where to Eat

★ $ **Gold Strike Sandwich Bar,** 23 Weld St. ☎ **755-8315.**

Cuisine: SANDWICHES/ICE CREAM. **Reservations:** Not required.

Prices: NZ$5 (U.S. $3.25) light meal. No credit cards.

Open: Daily 8am–5pm.

Try not to miss at least one stop by the Gold Strike. In the Regent Theatre building, it offers a variety of light meals, made-to-order sandwiches, and luscious ice cream in 16 flavors. With plenty of seating for foot-weary sightseers, this eatery (run by Myrna Peterson) offers a comfortable rest stop combined with nutritious food and lots of friendly conversation. There's always a brisk business at the ice-cream bar, but take my advice and sample at least one of their unusual sandwiches. All come on hearty fresh-baked bread; you might like the venison (which, with a bowl of homemade soup, makes a satisfying meal). A local favorite is the honey, walnuts, and raisins combination, with cheese and corn also very popular. Pork, salami, and beef are also available.

Preston's Bakery & Restaurant, 105 Revell St. ☎ **755-8412.**

Cuisine: BREAKFAST/SANDWICHES/STEAKS/PASTRIES. **Reservations:** Not required.
Prices: Under NZ$10 (U.S. $6.50). No credit cards
Open: Mon–Fri 8am–5pm (bakery closes at 6pm), Sat 9am–1pm.

A breakfast tradition in Hokitika is to congregate at this restaurant, which has a perfect small-town decor. Eggs, toast, and bacon or sausage costs NZ$6.50 (U.S. $4.25); poached eggs and toast, NZ$3.30 (U.S. $2.15); fruit and cereal, NZ$3 (U.S. $1.95). You can also get sandwiches, steaks, roast chicken, stew, fresh vegetables, and sweets, and this is a great place to load up your campervan before driving farther along the West Coast.

★ **Tasman View Restaurant,** in the Southland Hotel, 111 Revell St. ☎ **755-8344.**

$ **Cuisine:** SEAFOOD/NEW ZEALAND. **Reservations:** Recommended.
Prices: Appetizers NZ$7.50 (U.S. $4.90); main courses NZ$20 (U.S. $13). AE, DC, V.
Open: Dinner only, daily 6–9pm.

The Tasman View scores high on its seafood and its view of the Tasman Sea. I enjoy their lightly sautéed whitebait (only when it's in season, of course), but they also have great dishes you're not likely to encounter elsewhere, such as chili venison balls served with a plum compote or wild pork with port and juniper berries. Crystal and flowers are on the tables and the wood beams are rimu. Licensed.

En Route to Franz Josef & the Glaciers

Author's Travel Tip: There's no pharmacy, supermarket, or bank between Hokitika and Wanaka, although you'll find a small country hospital and a doctor in Whataroa. Be sure to stock up in advance.

About 31km (20 miles) south of Hokitika is the historic little town of **Ross,** well worth a drive over from Hokitika or a stop on your way to Franz Josef Glacier. Look for the information center in a restored miner's cabin.

Next stop is Franz Josef, 147km (91 miles) down the road.

6 The Glaciers

Glaciers are pretty impressive no matter where in the world you encounter them—tons and tons of snow crystals that have, over thousands and thousands of years, been subjected to such enormous pressures that they fuse into a solid mass of clear ice, which even greater pressures cause to move at an invisible, but inexorable, rate. What makes the Fox and Franz Josef Glaciers so unforgettable (sure to be one of your most memorable New Zealand experiences) is their descent well below 1,000 feet above sea level, framed by valley walls of deep-green bush, until they terminate in luxuriant rain forests. Nowhere else in the world outside arctic regions do glaciers reach such low altitudes. Fox is the longer of the two glaciers and has a more gradual slope.

On equal footing with your memories of these giant rivers of ice, however, will be those of the sunsets in these parts. From your motel lawn or window, you'll be treated to a show of great beauty. Julius von Haast, the great explorer who was the first

European to explore this region, wrote of the sunsets, "New changes were every moment effected, the shades grew longer and darker, and whilst the lower portion already lay in the deep purple shade, the summits were still shining with an intense rosy hue."

ORIENTATION

The small townships of Franz Josef and Fox Glacier are only 24km (15 miles) apart, a 30-minute drive. InterCity has daily **bus service** between the two townships.

The two glaciers are only a small part of the 284,000-acre **Westland National Park,** an impressive park of high mountain peaks, glacial lakes, and rushing rivers. The park is popular for tramping, mountain climbing, fishing, canoeing, hunting, and horse trekking.

There are **visitor centers** at both glacier townships (☎ **03/752-0796** in Franz Josef; **03/751-0807** in Fox Glacier), and their displays, literature on the park, and visitor activities are essential to a full appreciation of the area.

The only local transportation is by **taxi** (ask locally about telephone numbers), but for travel between the two townships, InterCity coaches provide dropoff service year round.

What to See & Do

Check with the two visitor centers about the schedule for ★ **nature lectures, slide presentations,** and **guided walks** conducted by conservation officers. These cost about NZ$4 (U.S. $2.60) per adult, less for children, which makes it possible for budgeteers to enjoy all the park has to offer with a minimal effect on the pocketbook. They also administer the alpine huts and tramping huts available for overnight hikers, and keep track of trampers and mountain climbers (you must check conditions and register your intentions with the officers before setting out).

Your sightseeing at the glaciers can be as costly or as inexpensive as your budget dictates. There are, it must be said, several sightseeing experiences that can put a large hole in that budget—and they are among the most spectacular travel experiences in the world, worth every cent of their cost. Yet it's quite possible to enjoy Mother Nature's free display and leave with an equally soul-satisfying experience that has cost you nothing. Either visitor center can give you literature outlining self-guided walks, and for just pennies you can buy detailed information sheets on each. For less than a dollar there are booklets that give you a complete rundown on how the glaciers were formed, the movement of the ice, the mountains, the history of the region, and much, much more.

GLACIER TRIPS

Now, about those expensive glacier experiences. You can do three very special things at the glaciers: Take a **skiplane ride,** take a **helicopter ride,** and go for a **glacier walk.**

If this is where you decide to go all out and splurge on one of the finest of all international travel experiences, take the **Mount Cook Airline's skiplane flight** from Franz Josef or Fox to the top of the icefields of Fox or Franz Josef Glacier. The six-seater Cessna 195 or Pilatus Porter whisks you over lush forests and glacial moraines, with vistas of sea and ice and spectacular views of Mount Cook and Mount Tasman. You'll actually land on one of the glaciers, put your feet on the soft, deep snow covering, and perhaps have the pilot take your picture before skiing off into the horizon. The views are all the more magnificent as the sun is beginning to set when you return. Admittedly, it's expensive, but it's an experience that will live with you the rest of your days.

The hour-long flight is NZ$130 (U.S. $84.50) for adults, NZ$98 (U.S. $63.70) for children. Flights without a snow landing are also available, at NZ$100 (U.S. $65) for adults and NZ$75 (U.S. $48.75) for children.

There are several shorter flights for less, as well as a wide range of other choices, and the choice may not turn out to be as agonizing as you think—weather can make it for you. It's very unpredictable, and especially if your time is short, my best advice is to take the first one available. Of course, if the weather is fine, it's agonizing time again. But even if weather really closes in and neither is available, not to worry—you'll have another opportunity at Mount Cook.

There are Mount Cook Airline **flightseeing centers** at both townships (☎ **03/752-0714** in Franz Josef, **03/751-0812** in Fox). You can also book flights through both the Franz Josef Glacier Hotel and the Fox Glacier Hotel, and most motels.

There are a number of ★ **helicopter flights** to the glaciers every day, including those that make a snow landing, and generally they're shorter and less expensive than the skiplane trips. The trips last 10 to 40 minutes and cost NZ$70 to NZ$185 (U.S. $45.50 to $120.25). Take my word for it, it's a thrilling way to get close to nature, but the fixed-wing planes have a better safety record. For details and reservations, contact **Alpine Guides** (see below) or **Glacier Helicopters,** Main Road, Franz Josef (☎ **03/752-0755**), or Main Road, Fox Glacier (☎ **03/741-0803**).

There's another great way to experience the Franz Josef Glacier that's far less expensive than the flights and—in my opinion—actually complements them. That's the **glacier walk,** with an expert guiding you along the surface of the ice. If you're in reasonably good shape you'll be able to do the walk, regardless of age. Guides chip steps in the ice, which during warm weather is granular instead of glass-slick. You'll go up into the ice fall, walk among the crevasses, listen to the deep-throated grumble of the moving glacier. Hobnailed boots, a waterproof parka, heavy socks, and a walking stick are provided, and walks are scheduled at 9:30am and 2pm in summer, mornings only at other times. And the walk goes regardless of the weather! The cost of the three-hour trip is NZ$34 (U.S. $22.10).

At Fox, in addition to a glacier walk like the above, there's a half-day ★ **heli-hike,** when you fly by helicopter to about 1km (1/2 a mile) up the glacier and walk to Victoria Falls before being picked up. All equipment is provided. The cost of the heli-hike is NZ$145 (U.S. $94.25) per adult. Other tours, including overnights, are offered.

For details on all the glacier experiences described above, contact **Alpine Guides (Westland) Ltd.,** P.O. Box 38, Fox Glacier (☎ and fax **03/751-0825**).

If you're reading this book at home and the glaciers have you hooked, or if you were hooked already and are coming to New Zealand primarily to spend time at the glaciers, you might like to know that Alpine Guides also offers several **mountaineering courses,** varying in length from seven days to two weeks. These are the guides who conduct the walks just described (check with them for schedules and prices), and their experience covers mountain and ice climbing from the Himalayas to Antarctica. Write ahead for details on physical requirements, enrollment, and prices.

OTHER ACTIVITIES

If **fishing trips** are a big lure, contact Stan Peterson, Westland Guiding Services, P.O. Box 163, Hokitika (☎ **03/755-8203**). He'll have you out on Lake Mapourika (the name means "Flower of the Dawn") in no time, and you might just come back with a 12- or 15-pound trout or salmon. Stan charges about NZ$50 (U.S. $32.50) per hour for up to four people in a boat and a minimum of 1 1/2 hours. He'll also take you on

minibus tours, including trips to the glaciers; Lake Matheson, with its scenic reflections of Mount Cook and Mount Tasman, and the gold-mining area of Okarito.

★ **Lake Matheson,** 5km (3 miles) from the Fox Glacier Hotel, shows up on all the postcards, but **Lake Mapourika,** 9km (5½ miles) north of Franz Josef and the largest lake in Westland National Park, deserves attention for its own arresting reflections and setting. You can swim in the lake, as well.

In Franz Josef, take a few minutes to visit **St. James Anglican Church,** the Tudor-style church whose east window frames a spectacular alpine view behind the altar. Watch for the sign just south of the visitor center. If you'd like to do an hour-long **hike,** follow the sign opposite St. James Church and you're on your way.

If you managed to miss the **glowworm dells** in Waitomo or Hokitika, you can at least get the idea, on a smaller scale, in Franz Josef. Day or night, follow the sign- and rock-lined path to the helipad (it's across the street from the gas station). The path will tunnel through some trees and lead you down 11 steps to where you see the roots of a tree overhanging the path at a height of about 4 feet. Stoop down and take a peak—it's like looking at a starry night in an underground world.

Where to Stay

During peak season, accommodations are woefully short, with a greater choice at Franz Josef than at Fox Glacier. Each township has a licensed hotel; however, both are out of reach of budget travelers. My best advice is to book well ahead for this popular part of the West Coast.

The rates listed below include GST.

IN FRANZ JOSEF

Motels

$ **Bushland Court Motel,** Cron St. (P.O. Box 41), Franz Josef. ☎ **03/752-0757.** 14 units (all with bath). TV TEL

Rates: NZ$55 (U.S. $35.75) single; NZ$65–NZ$85 (U.S. $42.25–$55.25) double. MC, V.

This centrally located motel has appealing units with beamed ceilings incorporating warm rimu wood. Sleeping two to six people, all are immaculate and have central heating, kitchens, videos, radios, and covered parking areas. Smaller units are available in the Alpine Lodge Wing. There's a laundry, barbecue area, and children's playground on the premises. Proprietors Owen and Maggie Morris take great pains to accommodate and will even provide hairdryers and Exercycles on request.

★ **Glacier Gateway Motor Lodge,** State Hwy. 6 (P.O. Box 1), Franz Josef. ☎ and fax **03/752-0776.** 23 units (all with bath). TV TEL

Rates: NZ$70 (U.S. $45.50) single; NZ$85 (U.S. $55.25) double. Additional person NZ$13 (U.S. $8.45) extra. AE, DC, MC, V.

Brian and Gilly Jenkins's attractive motel, totally refurbished in 1994, has studio as well as some units that sleep as many as six; two have spa baths. The facilities include a spa pool, sauna, guest laundry, and children's playground. There's also off-street parking. The hostelry is on the outskirts of the township, just south of the bridge, opposite Glacier Access Road. Cooked or continental breakfasts are available. No smoking is permitted inside.

Glacier View Motel, State Hwy. 6 (P.O. Box 22), Franz Josef. ☎ **03/752-0705.** Fax 03/752-0761. 14 units (all with bath). TV TEL

Rates: NZ$80 (U.S. $52) one-bedroom unit for two; NZ$85 (U.S. $55.25) two-bedroom unit for two. Additional person NZ$12 (U.S. $7.80) extra. AE, DC, MC, V.

There's a small shop on the premises here, plus a spa pool in a natural setting. The hosts offer courtesy transfers to the bus stop, and breakfasts are available. The motel is 2km (1¼ miles) north of the township.

Motel Franz Josef, State Hwy. 6, Franz Josef (Private Bag 766, Hokitika). ☎ **03/752-0742.** Fax 03/750-0760. 8 units (all with bath). TV TEL

Rates: NZ$80 (U.S. $52) single or double. Additional adult NZ$12 (U.S. $7.80) extra. AE, DC, MC, V.

Quiet, trim, and tidy, the Franz Josef has one- and two-bedroom units, all with private patios facing a view of the distant hills. The guest rooms are centrally heated, and there's a spa pool. Mr. and Mrs. Trevor Gibb, the friendly owners, also have a small canteen with canned and frozen foods. The motel is located 5km (3 miles) north of the township.

Rata Grove Motel, Cron St. (P.O. Box 3), Franz Josef. ☎ and fax **03/752-0741.** 10 units (all with bath). TV TEL

Rates: NZ$65–NZ$85 (U.S. $42.25–$55.25) single or double. AE, DC, MC, V.

Just behind the grocery store, souvenir shop, and tour operator, this accommodation is as close to the bus stop and town center as you can get. The motel units are in a quiet location with glacier and mountain views.

A Hostel

Franz Josef YHA Hostel, 2–4 Cron St. (P.O. Box 12), Franz Josef. ☎ and fax **03/752-0754.** 60 beds (no rooms with bath).

Rates: NZ$16 (U.S. $10.40) per person double or twin; NZ$14 (U.S. $9.10) dorm bed for members, NZ$18 (U.S. $11.70) dorm bed for nonmembers. MC, V.

This modern hostel, with a spacious kitchen, new owners, and 60 beds in 10 rooms, is convenient to shops and the bus stop in the town center and close to the rain forest. Double and family rooms are available; all rooms have heaters and quilts. Facilities include TV and video, a laundry and drying room, a hostel shop, bikes, and a pool table. Advance reservations are always advisable, especially November to April and during holiday periods.

Camping

The ★ **Franz Josef Holiday Park,** on the main road (☎ and fax **03/752-0766**), is set in attractive grounds of bush and hills. There are tent sites, powered sites, and eight basic cabins sleeping two to four people on bunks, all with good, comfortable mattresses. The 24-room lodge has private bedrooms, each with hot and cold running water, central heating, and internal access to shared baths and kitchens. The bedrooms sleep two to five people, and there are family rooms. Four tourist cabins, sleeping two to five, have hot and cold running water, stoves, refrigerators, crockery, cutlery, cookware, blankets, and heaters. Three tourist flats sleep two to four people, all with kitchens, showers, toilets, blankets, and heaters. Other facilities include kitchens with microwaves, showers, an automatic laundry, a TV, a recreation room, a barbecue, and a children's playground. Bedding can be rented, and there's a bus stop near the entrance. Dormitory bunks are NZ$10 (U.S. $6.50), cabins are NZ$24 (U.S. $15.60) for two people (additional people are charged NZ$10/U.S. $6.50), and lodge rooms are NZ$15 (U.S. $9.75). Tourist flats run NZ$50 (U.S. $32.50) for two, plus NZ$11 (U.S. $7.15) for each additional person. Tent sites cost NZ$7.50 (U.S. $4.90) per person.

Worth the Extra Money

Westland Motor Inn, Main St. (P.O. Box 33), Franz Josef. ☎ **03/752-0729.** Fax 03/752-0709. 100 rms (all with bath). TV TEL

Rates: NZ$147–NZ$200 (U.S. $95.55–$130) single or double. AE, DC, MC, V.

By far the prettiest motel in Franz Josef township, the Westland is centrally located on the main street. It has a licensed restaurant (see "Where to Eat," below) and lounge bar, plus a beautiful guest lounge with huge glass windows and one entire wall covered by a native-stone fireplace. The grounds are beautifully planted, and just at the entrance is an old cobble cart planted with native ferns. The rooms include video, tea and coffee facilities, and central heating. Facilities include two spa pools, a games room, and a guest laundry.

IN FOX GLACIER

Motels

A1 Motel, Lake Matheson Rd. (P.O. Box 29), Fox Glacier. ☎ **03/751-0804.** Fax 03/751-0706. 10 units (all with bath). TV TEL

Rates: NZ$75 (U.S. $48.75) single or double. Additional person NZ$12 (U.S. $7.80) extra. AE, DC, MC, V.

This motel sits in a valley about 2km (1 mile) from the township down Lake Matheson Road and is managed by Pat and Tony Clapperton and Brian and Jean Mather. The units, nicely designed and attractively furnished, sleep two to five. Other amenities include a laundry, barbecue facilities, a swimming pool, a nine-hole putting green, a squash court, a spa pool, and a children's playground. A continental breakfast is available.

★ **Golden Glacier Motor Inn,** State Hwy. 6 (P.O. Box 32), Fox Glacier. ☎ **03/751-0847.** Fax 03/751-0822. 51 rms (all with bath).

$ **Rates:** NZ$90 (U.S. $58.50) single; NZ$115 (U.S. $74.75) double. AE, DC, MC, V.

In the township center, the Golden Glacier's serviced rooms are enhanced by such amenities as the licensed restaurant, house bar, and open log fire that's a focal point for sociability in the evening. The rooms are well located, and there's a laundry and drying room.

READERS RECOMMEND

Glow-worm Forest Lodge, Fox Glacier (☎ **03/751-0888**). *"This is a brand-new all-wood homestead with high ceilings. There are five bedrooms upstairs with large bathroom and a kitchen downstairs for use of the people in bedrooms and the camper spots. Our corner room had a lovely view of the mountains, and we paid NZ$55 (U.S. $35.75). It's right next door to the glowworm grotto. I would have liked to have spent more time in Fox Glacier because of all the walks through the rain forest and to the glacier."*—Beverly Carr, Toronto, Ont., Canada.

A Hostel/Camping

About 1/2 km (1/4 mile) from Fox Glacier township, you'll find the **Fox Glacier Motor Park** (☎ **03/751-0821;** fax 03/751-0813), with six motel units, four tourist flats, 20 cabins, 14 lodge cabins, a backpacker's bunkhouse, 65 tent sites, and 65 powered sites. There are two kitchen blocks with dining rooms, three shower blocks, and a coin-operated laundry. Linens may be rented, and canned and frozen goods are available at the camp store. Double-occupancy rates are NZ$17 (U.S. $11.05) for tent sites, NZ$20 (U.S. $13) for caravan sites, NZ$32 (U.S. $20.80) for cabins, NZ$36 (U.S. $23.40) for lodge rooms, and NZ$54 (U.S. $35.10) for tourist flats. A bed in the bunkhouse is NZ$12 (U.S. $7.80).

Where to Eat

There are not a great many places to eat in either township, and this may be where you do more home-cooking than anywhere else in New Zealand. However, some of the following are quite good.

IN FRANZ JOSEF

Clematis Room, In the Westland Motor Inn, State Hwy. 6. ☎ **752-0729.**

Cuisine: NEW ZEALAND. **Reservations:** Recommended in summer.

Prices: Appetizers NZ$8 (U.S. $5.20); main courses NZ$23 (U.S. $14.95). AE, DC, MC, V.

Open: Summer, dinner only, daily 6–8:30pm. Winter, dinner only, daily 6–7:30pm.

This attractive restaurant, on the northern edge of the township, has slanted-beam ceiling and gaslight-style fixtures overhead, with wide windows that look out to the mountains. The à la carte menu lists many local specialties; it's fully licensed and has a nice lounge bar for before or after meals, where you're likely to meet a local or two.

Glacier Store and Tearooms, Main Rd.

Cuisine: LIGHT LUNCHES/TEAS. **Reservations:** Not required.

Prices: Under NZ$10 (U.S. $6.50). AE, MC, V.

Open: Daily 7:45am–6:30pm (until 9:30pm in summer).

The Glacier Store and Tearooms, in a beautifully designed building in the township center, serves light fare for lunches and teas. Select from assorted sandwiches, quiche, filled rolls, soup, croissants, and pastries. The upstairs tearooms offer fantastic views of the snowcapped Southern Alps and the luxuriant west-coast rain forest. Within the same building you can shop for food, hardware, and clothing, and adjacent to the building is the **Fern Grove Souvenir Shop,** which carries a wide range of quality souvenirs, film, and a wide selection of woolen knitwear.

IN FOX GLACIER

The **grocery store** sells foodstuffs, hot meat pies, and sandwiches right along with camping supplies, hardware, boots, heavy jackets, and polyester shirts. The **Tea Rooms** have inexpensive grills and snacks. Readers recommend **Saddle Saloon** for ribs, salad, nachos, and beer. All are open daily, and hours vary. Meals in the licensed restaurant at the **Golden Glacier Motor Inn** are quite good, with moderate prices.

Note: For picnics while you're in the area, pick up supplies at the store. You can get a hearty snack at the bus stop café in Makarora.

En Route to Queenstown

Author's travel tip: This is a stretch that I have driven and enjoyed, but if you aren't comfortable on mountain roads, do yourself a favor and let InterCity do the driving from here on to Queenstown, leaving your eyes free to drink in some of the world's most spectacular natural beauty. Tall trees line the road, which twists from one breathtaking view to the next. A final word: If you *are* driving, exercise caution all the way.

This is a day-long drive along a 413km (256-mile) route that takes you through some of New Zealand's most striking terrain: cool green ferns; secluded sea coves; deep-walled gorges; high, steep bluffs; alpine lakes; lagoons alive with white herons; and valleys filled with grazing sheep. Before this road was built, the only passage from east to west was an old bridle path, and at the very top of the Haast Pass there's a signpost that will point you to that path, a pretty walk back into the past. The road itself took 40 years to build, and in fact work still goes on in sections as rock slides occur. Some portions are gravel, though most are paved and a good surface. There are steep climbs and sharp descents, hairpin curves and stretches of one-lane travel. At 1,847 feet above sea level, the Haast Pass is actually the lowest pass through the Southern Alps, very seldom blocked by snow, but peaks on either side rise as high as 10,000 feet.

If you wish to linger in Haast, a reader recommends the **World Heritage Hotel** (☎ **03/750-0828**).

A picnic lunch is ideal, as there are any number of places to stop and let your senses ramble as you eat. It's a good excuse, too, to loiter at any scenic spot that especially takes your fancy. There are roofed outdoor tables (and restrooms) at a public picnic area about 197km (122 miles) into the journey at Pleasant Flat Bridge. If you're picnicking, save a bit for a tea break when you reach Lake Wanaka—the view, with 9,975-foot Mount Aspiring in the distance, begs a lingering look.

WANAKA

A popular resort with New Zealanders, Wanaka offers many sports activities, as well as smashing scenery. If you arrive there utterly exhausted, it makes a good overnight stopping place before going on to Queenstown.

Mount Aspiring National Park has its park headquarters in Wanaka, although the park is some 45km (27 miles) to the northwest. If you plan to spend time here, drop by the **Mount Aspiring National Park Visitor Centre,** on the corner of Ballantyne Road and Highway 89 (☎ **03/443-7660** or **03/442-9937**), for information on park activities.

How to get lost and found—and totally bewildered!—in Wanaka? Head for ✪ **The Puzzling Place and Great Maze** on the main highway (☎ **03/443-7489**). Behind tall fences are pathways that lead somewhere and passageways that lead nowhere. The fun comes in finding your way through without becoming hopelessly lost. But there's *much* more to this unique place that has been some 21 years in the making: a display of holograms and an exhibition of illusion pictures. Take my word for it, adults and youngsters will be intrigued and entertained. A tilted house should be completed by the time you get here. Admission is NZ$6 (U.S. $3.90) for adults, half price for children.

Where to Stay

Best Western Manuka Crescent Motel, 51 Manuka Crescent (off Beacon Point Rd.), Wanaka. ☎ **03/443-7773.** Fax 03/443-9066. 10 units (all with bath). TV TEL

Rates: NZ$67.50–NZ$81 (U.S. $43.90–$52.65) single or double. Additional person NZ$12 (U.S. $7.80) extra. AE, DC, MC, V.

Set in a peaceful garden about 2km (1 mile) from town, the Manuka Crescent has marvelous views of the mountains in the distance. The units have full kitchens, radios, and parking spaces at the door. There's a guest laundry, barbecue area, trampoline, and children's play area, and, in addition to cooked and continental breakfast, there are frozen TV meals available.

YHA Hostel, 181 Upton St., Wanaka. ☎ **03/443-7405.** 36 beds.

Rates: NZ$16 (U.S. $10.40) per person double or twin; NZ$14 (U.S. $9.10) dorm bed for members. No credit cards.

This hostel is well located for activities on the lake and skiing at Treble Cone or Cardrona. Mount Aspiring National Park is nearby. The hostel offers bike storage and ski-tuning facilities.

Where to Eat

In addition to the restaurants below, **Aspiring Takeaways,** 68 Ardmore St. (☎ **443-7803**), has burgers, ice cream, milkshakes, and sandwiches at low prices and is open daily from 8am to 9pm.

Ripples, Pembroke Village Mall. ☎ **443-7413.**

Cuisine: NEW ZEALAND. **Reservations:** Not required.

Prices: Lunch NZ$3–NZ$14 (U.S. $1.95–$9.10); dinner NZ$30–NZ$40 (U.S. $19.50–$26). AE, DC, MC, V.

Open: Summer, lunch daily noon–2pm; dinner daily 6–10pm. Winter, dinner only, Mon–Sat 6–10pm.

It's hard to say if the setting or the food is more agreeable at this cozy little place in town. In summer, you can dine outside on the veranda with those wonderful views of the mountain in the distance; other times, inside is just as pleasant. The menu offers some truly innovative dishes, and it changes from month to month. A sampling includes pan-fried lamb noisettes dipped in egg and rosemary, wild pork and venison

READERS RECOMMEND

Cliffords Hotel, Ardmore St., Wanaka (☎ **03/443-7826**). *"I got a discounted rate and enjoyed a very comfortable room. I was practically frightened out of bed by the spectacular scenery I woke up to."*—Amelia Conrad, Wilkes, Conn., U.S.A. [**Author's Note:** My guess is that this was a winter rate.]

Archway Motels, Hedditch St., Wanaka (☎ **03/443-7698**). *"Our unit with bath and kitchen was NZ$65 (U.S. $42.25), and the hostess was very pleasant. Her son works in the bistro next door, which has tremendous food—and cheap."*—Valerie, Stanley, and Renata Vicich, Bateman, Western Australia.

combo, smoked chicken and Camembert triangles wrapped in phyllo pastry, and an avocado, crab, and prawn plate. BYO.

FROM WANAKA TO QUEENSTOWN

You have a choice here, with two routes you could follow to reach Queenstown, one not open to trailers and not recommended to inexpert drivers. That 71km (44-mile) stretch of Highway 89 crosses the **Crown Range** and opens up fantastic panoramic views of the entire **Wakatipu Valley,** then descends into the valley in a series of sharp curves until it reaches the aptly named "Foot of Zig Zag," where you make a sharp right turn and level out to drive through farmlands all the way to Lake Wakatipu and Queenstown. Some rental-car companies don't permit their cars on this road.

The other route (the one I recommend unless you're stout of heart and a whale of a driver) is via Highway 6 and is good traveling all the way. You'll drive alongside artificial **Lake Dunstan,** which was formed behind the **Clyde Dam.**

Whichever route you choose, you may want to stop in historic **Arrowtown,** although it's just a short drive back from Queenstown if you're ready to push on to dinner and bed after a long day behind the wheel (and there are good coach tours from Queenstown to Arrowtown, so you won't have to miss it).

Where to Eat en Route

★ $ **Cardrona Hotel Restaurant & Bar,** Hwy. 89, 24km (15 miles) south of Wanaka. ☎ **03/443-8153.**

Cuisine: NEW ZEALAND/APRES-SKI. **Reservations:** Recommended but not required.
Prices: Snacks under NZ$10 (U.S. $6.50); lunch NZ$6–NZ$13.50 (U.S. $3.90–$8.80); dinner NZ$13.50–NZ$16.50 (U.S. $8.80–$10.75). MC, V.
Open: Daily 9am–"late."

Sited at the base of two ski fields, this building was born as an inn back in 1865 at the height of the gold-rush era—it's now primarily a restaurant/bar. The decor is one of hardwood floors, antique oak tables and chairs, and patchwork cushions on the chairs. It has long been one of the area's most popular après-ski spots, where slopes-weary skiers relax with mulled wine before a blazing log fire. In summer there's dining in lovely sheltered gardens. The menu features local lamb, game, and seafood. Fully licensed. The Cardrona also offers accommodations if you want to stay over before pushing on the last 45km (28 miles) to Queenstown.

Queenstown & Environs

11

QUEENSTOWN IS THE JEWEL OF SOUTH ISLAND RESORTS—PRONOUNCED BY GOLD prospectors to be "fit for any queen," after which they promptly christened it with the present name on a very unqueenly blacksmith's anvil. The city is nestled at the foot of mountains called the Remarkables, on the northeastern shore of Lake Wakatipu, a 86km (53-mile) long, 1,280-foot-deep beauty encased in a glacial bed. Its shape vaguelyresembles that of a reclining figure with its knees drawn up. Maori legend will tell you that's because at the bottom of the lake lies the heart of a great *tipua* (giant) named Matau, who captured a beautiful girl who caught his fancy and took her back to his mountain home. Her valiant lover, however, came to her rescue and set fire to the giant as he lay sleeping on a bed of fern. As the flames flared higher and higher, fed by the fat from his enormous body, he was suffocated by the smoke and sank deep into the earth to form a vast chasm. Only his heart was not reduced to ashes. As the rains fell and mountain snows melted with the heat of the fire, the chasm filled with water to form a lake in the shape of the giant, his knees drawn up in agony. His head, they say, is at Glenorchy, his knees at Queenstown, and his feet at Kingston. His heart beats on from far below, and that, they say, explains the fact that the surface of the lake rises and falls 3 inches every five minutes. Of course, scientists have another explanation—they call the phenomenon seiche action. But, then, what do *they* know about giants and beautiful girls and valiant lovers!

Sheepherders were the first settlers in this district, and they endured the onslaught of hundreds of gold miners when the Shotover River, which feeds Lake Wakatipu, was proclaimed "the richest river in the world." The claim was well founded, for as much as £4,000 was dredged by the discoverer of gold in his first two months. When the gold played out in fairly short order the sheep men came into their own once more, and today the Wakatipu district is filled with vast high-country sheep stations, a source of less spectacular, but certainly more reliable, riches.

1 Queenstown

404km (250 miles) SW of Franz Josef, 172km (107 miles) NE of Te Anau, 263km (163 miles) SW of Mount Cook

GETTING THERE • By Plane There's air service via Mount Cook Airlines, Air New Zealand National, and Ansett New Zealand between Queensland and Auckland, Rotorua, Palmerston North, and Wellington on the North Island, and Christchurch, Milford Sound, Mount Cook, Te Anau, and Wanaka on the South Island. The airport shuttle (☎ **03/442-9803**) runs to and from the airport regularly and will drop you off or pick you up at your hotel for about NZ$5 (U.S. $3.25). A taxi (☎ **03/442-7788**) from the airport to the town center costs about NZ$15 (U.S. $9.75).

• By Bus Service is offered by InterCity and/or Mount Cook Landline between Queenstown and Christchurch, Dunedin, Fox Glacier, Franz Josef, Invercargill, Milford Sound, Mount Cook, Te Anau, and Wanaka. The InterCity depot is in the Visitor Centre, at the corner of Camp and Shotover streets (☎ **03/442-8238**), and the Mount Cook depot is on Church Street (☎ **03/442-4640**). Southern Link Shuttles (☎ **03/442-6666**) runs a daily budget service to and from Christchurch, Dunedin, Picton, Timaru, and Queenstown.

• By Car Queenstown can be reached via Highway 6.

SPECIAL EVENTS Queenstown wears a perpetual festive air, but if you happen to get here during the last week in July, you can join the annual ✪ **Winter Festival**

What's Special About Queenstown

Scenic Splendors

- The splendid mountains called the Remarkables, especially at sunrise and sunset, when the play of light is quite spectacular.
- The legendary Lake Wakatipu, a beauty in the shape of a fatally wounded giant.

Adrenaline Rushes

- Skiing at Coronet Peak, Cardrona, Treble Cone, and the Remarkables.
- Bungee jumping, from the Kawarau Bridge or from a helicopter.
- White-water rafting on the Shotover or Kawarau River.
- Jetboating on the Shotover River.

Ace Attractions

- A lake cruise on the TSS *Earnslaw.*
- A gondola ride to the top of Bob's Peak.

Special Events

- The Winter Festival, in July, a week of nonstop fun events.

fun. There's something going on all day and into the night every single day, and some of the goings-on are downright hilarious. Take, for example, the Dog Derby (when dogs and their masters descend the slopes any way they can except on skis), or the dog barking contest, or … well, you can imagine. There are other, really spectacular, events, such as the **Otago Goldfields Heritage Trail** for 10 days in November, the **Arrowtown Autumn Festival** for 8 days in April, and the annual **Queenstown Easter Sports Festival,** when expert skiing performers display ballet skiing and breathtaking acrobatic feats. There are Ski Bunnies, a Miss Snowbird, visiting celebrities, children's ski events, and fancy-dress (costume) competitions, a Mardi Gras night, and all sorts of other activities, some a bit on the madcap side, others real tests of skill.

The lifeblood of Queenstown, with a year-round population of only 3,500, is tourism, and no matter what time of year you come, you'll find visitors from all over the world here to enjoy the lake, the river, and the mountains. Many also come to get the adrenaline rush promised by the area's attractions, and at times the town feels a little like Disneyland. Many travelers, disappointed with the commercialism, favor Wanaka—which is much like Queenstown was before it became so touristy.

From late June through September an international skiing crowd flocks to ski the slopes of Coronet Peak, whose dry, powdery snows are said to be the best in Australasia. Then, this pretty little town, far from being provincial, has a decidedly cosmopolitan air.

City Specifics

ORIENTATION

The lakefront is the hub of Queenstown, and the street fronting the sheltered horseshoe bay is Marine Parade. On the northern edge, at Beach Street, are the jetty, pier, and wharf. To the south are lovely public gardens. The Mall, reserved for pedestrians only, runs from Rees Street for one bustling block. It's a busy concentration of activity: shops, booking agencies, and restaurants.

INFORMATION

The **Queenstown Travel & Visitor Centre** in the Clocktower Centre, at Shotover and Camp streets (☎ **03/442-4100**), is open Monday through Friday from 7am to 7pm and Saturday and Sunday from 7am to 6pm. It sells stamps, sends faxes, operates a currency exchange, and makes reservations for accommodations and activities. The **Mount Cook Travel Office** is on Camp Street (☎ **03/442-4600**). The **Fiordland Travel Centre** is on the Steamer Wharf, Beach Street (☎ **442-7500**). The **Department of Conservation Information Centre,** at 37 Shotover St. (☎ **03/442-7933**), is the place to go for information on walking trails, tramping in national parks, and conservation souvenirs.

FAST FACTS

The **telephone area code** (STD) for Queenstown is **03**. The **Thomas Cook Bureau de Change,** in the Mall at Camp Street (☎ **442-8600**), is open daily from 8am to 7pm in winter and from 8am to 8pm in summer. The **BNZ bureau de change** on Rees Street (☎ **442-7325**) is open daily from 9am to 8pm. The **post office** (for *Poste Restante* mail) is on the corner of Camp and Ballarat streets. The **American Express** representative in Queenstown is located at 59 Beach St. (☎ **442-7730**).

GETTING AROUND

The **Shopper Bus** provides transportation to town from outlying lodgings for NZ$1 (U.S. 65¢) each way. To call a **taxi,** phone **442-7888** or **442-6666.**

What to See & Do

There's always so much going on in Queenstown, as well as so many things to see and do, that your first order of business should be to go by the Travel & Visitor Centre and pick up the **"Queenstown Today and Tonight"** brochure, which lists all current attractions, prices, hours, and reservations details. The free booklet **"Queenstown A to Z"** is also a useful directory for public services, accommodations, restaurants, sightseeing, and a host of other details. Look also for the free tourist newspaper ***The Mountain Scene,*** available at most accommodations and at the Travel & Visitor Centre. Armed with all that information, your dilemma becomes one of setting priorities.

One thing you won't want to miss, no matter what time of year you come to town, is the ✪ **gondola ride** (☎ **442-7860**) up to Bob's Peak, and don't forget your camera. The view is breathtaking, and if you go at lunch or dinner you can stretch your viewing time by eating at the buffet restaurant or brasserie (see "Where to Eat," below). The gondola operates from 10am until the restaurant closes at midnight, with a

READERS RECOMMEND

Southern Cross Car Rental, 37 Stanley St., Queenstown (☎ **03/442-7399**). *"We called from Hawaii and arranged a car rental through this company. 'Kevin' couldn't have been nicer. He met us at the airport and spent about an hour giving us directions, maps, and suggestions. When we returned the car in Christchurch (no drop charge), the fellow there was just as nice!"*—Meg Barth Gammon, Kailua, Hawaii, U.S.A.

Scotty's Network Rentals, Queenstown (☎ **03/442-6497**). *"When our rental car from a North Island company died in Queenstown, we found Scotty's was very responsive in arranging for another car at reasonable rates for the rest of our trip."*—William R. Svirsky, Longwood, Fla., U.S.A.

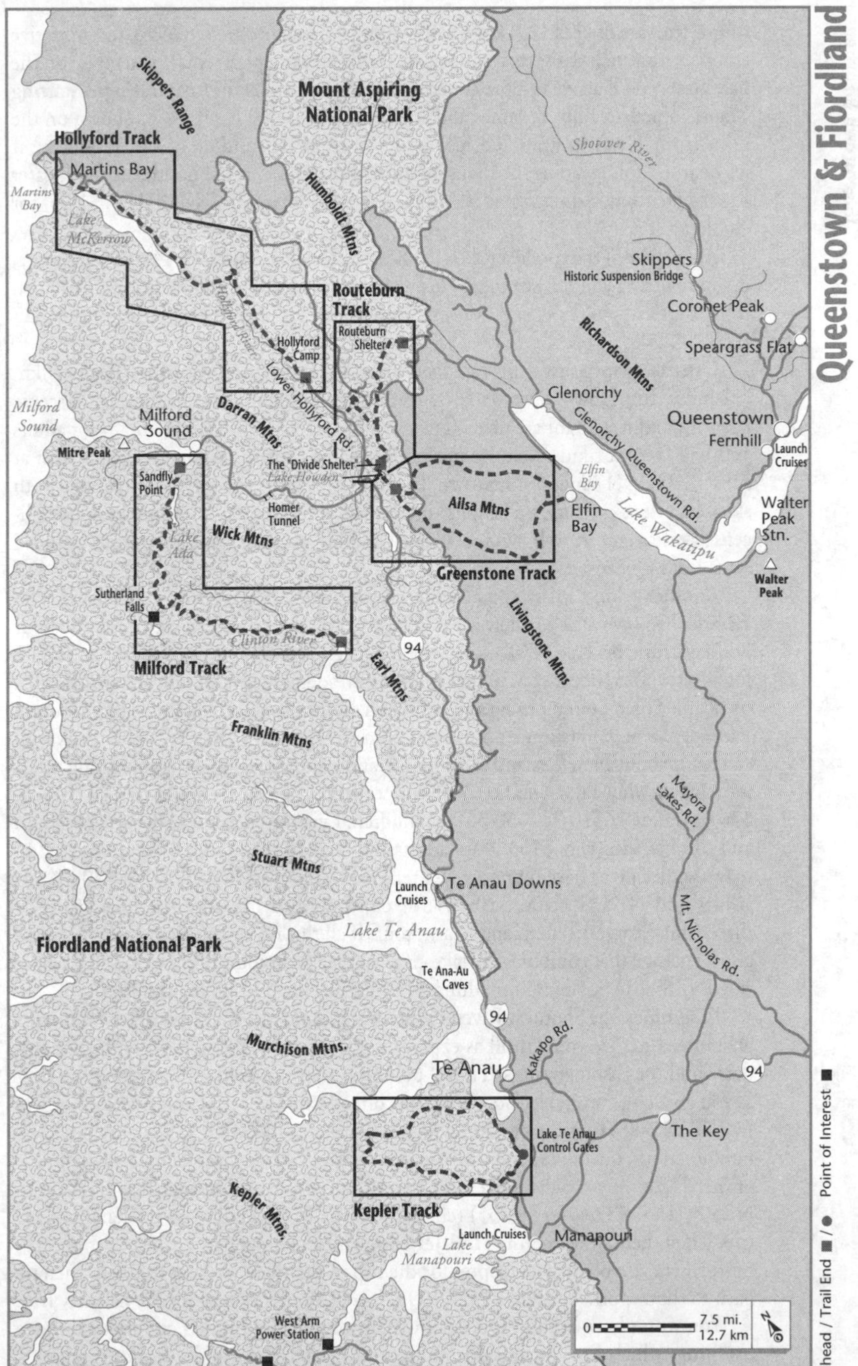
Queenstown & Fiordland
Mount Aspiring National Park
Skippers Range
Hollyford Track
Martins Bay
Martins Bay
Lake McKerrow
Humboldt Mtns
Hollyford River
Hollyford Camp
Lower Hollyford Rd.
Routeburn Track
Routeburn Shelter
Shotover River
Skippers
Historic Suspension Bridge
Coronet Peak
Speargrass Flat
Richardson Mtns
Glenorchy
Glenorchy Queenstown Rd.
Queenstown
Fernhill
Launch Cruises
Milford Sound
Milford Sound
Mitre Peak
Darran Mtns
The "Divide Shelter"
Lake Howden
Homer Tunnel
Sandfly Point
Lake Ada
Wick Mtns
Ailsa Mtns
Elfin Bay
Elfin Bay
Lake Wakatipu
Walter Peak Stn.
Walter Peak
Greenstone Track
Sutherland Falls
Clinton River
Milford Track
94
Earl Mtns
Livingstone Mtns
Franklin Mtns
Mavora Lakes Rd.
Stuart Mtns
Launch Cruises
Te Anau Downs
Lake Te Anau
Fiordland National Park
Te Ana-Au Caves
Mt. Nicholas Rd.
94
Murchison Mtns.
Kakapo Rd.
Te Anau
94
The Key
Lake Te Anau Control Gates
Kepler Track
Kepler Mtns.
Launch Cruises
Manapouri
Lake Manapouri
West Arm Power Station
Wilmot Pass
0
7.5 mi.
12.7 km
Trailhead / Trail End ■/● Point of Interest ■

round-trip fare of NZ$12 (U.S. $7.80). Completely renovated in 1994, the attractive complex now includes several shops and a large viewing platform. If you go up on the half hour, you'll arrive in time to see the thrills-and-spills film ***Kiwi Magic,*** starring Maori comedian Billy T. James and American actor Ned Beatty—it's shown on the hour from 11am to 9pm. To feel as if you're in the middle of the action, be it jet-boating, tobogganing, or flying in a small plane, sit in the middle of the theater toward the front. Admission is NZ$7 (U.S. $4.55) for adults, NZ$3 (U.S. $1.95) for children.

At the base of the gondola ride is the **Kiwi & Birdlife Park** (☎ **442-8059**), where, if you're lucky, you can see those elusive kiwi birds feeding and fossicking. It's open from 9am to 5pm daily, and evenings during the summer. The admission is NZ$7 (U.S. $4.55).

Queenstown has two top-rated **ski areas** at its doorstep. **Coronet Peak,** 18km (11 miles) from town, operates five lifts during winter months. In summer, a scenic chair lift and restaurant are open. The chair lift costs NZ$10 (U.S. $6.50) for adults and half price for kids. **The Remarkables** (named for the colors the peaks turn at sunset), 28km (17 miles) from town, has three lifts and a self-service restaurant. Both ski areas offer ski rental, ski lessons, and fast-food restaurants. Coronet Peak has a licensed restaurant as well. Mount Cook Landline operates shuttle buses to both ski areas from Queenstown.

Another "don't miss" is a ★ **lake cruise** on the 1912 vintage steamship TSS *Earnslaw.* Known affectionately as the "Lady of the Lake," the *Earnslaw* does a one-hour midday cruise on Lake Wakatipu, which departs at 12:30pm (NZ$21/U.S. $13.65 for adults, NZ$10/U.S. $6.50 for children). Moderately priced lunches are available on board. Three-hour morning and afternoon excursions to Walter Peak High Country Farm depart at 9am (summer only) and 2pm (year round). Once at Walter Peak, you can learn about New Zealand farming life and enjoy complimentary morning or afternoon tea while taking in the wonderful scenery. The cost for adults is NZ$41 (U.S. $26.65), and NZ$10 (U.S. $6.50) for children. Evening lake cruises depart at 5:30pm and cost NZ$26 (U.S. $16.90) for adults and NZ$10 (U.S. $6.50) for children. You may also decide to have dinner at Walter Peak. This costs NZ$62 (U.S. $40.30) for adults and NZ$31 (U.S. $20.15) for children and includes the lake cruise, a three-course carvery buffet, and a farm tour. If all this isn't confusing enough, there's also a package that combines the lake cruise with a farm tour, horse trek, and jet-boat ride (NZ$99/U.S. $64.35 for adults, NZ$49.50/U.S. $32.20 for children).

In summer, the Shotover River's white-water rapids are the scene of **jet-boat trips** guaranteed to give you a thrill as expert drivers send you flying between huge boulders amid the rushing waters. They'll point out traces of gold mining along the river as you go along. Several jet-boat operators offer a variety of trips and prices. Shotover Jet (☎ **442-8570**) is the best known; Wilderness Jet (☎ **442-9792**) provides a less rambunctious, quality experience. You can drive out to the river (allow half an hour), or there's courtesy-coach service from town. The jet-boat rides range from NZ$36 to NZ$99 (U.S. $23.40 to $64.35) (children pay half), depending on the length of the trip. Then there's the exciting **Heli-Jet trip,** which takes you by coach out to the airport, where you board a helicopter for the trip to the river, jet-boat through, then fly back to the airport. The fare is NZ$199 (U.S. $130) per person for the half-day trip.

You won't have been in Queenstown for long before finding out about **bungee jumping,** which I'm convinced is more fun to watch than to do. It means taking a 43-meter (143-foot) head-first plunge off the world's first bungee site, the Kawarau Suspension Bridge with A. J. Hackett Bungy (☎ **442-7100**). There's a super-strong and long bungee cord attached to your ankles so you actually stop just shy of the water (or after you've dunked your head—you can decide). You then swing back and forth about five times. You'll pay about NZ$89 (U.S. $57.85) for this moment of madness that some people consider "fun." The fall at Skippers Canyon is 70 meters (229 feet) (NZ$120/U.S. $78). Or you can watch the videos for free at the A. J. Hackett station, at the corner of Shotover and Camp streets. **River rafting** is another popular spills-'n'-thrills Queenstown activity. Danes Shotover Rafts (tel **442-7318**) offers several options. The **"Awesome Foursome"** combines rafting, a helicopter flight, bungee jumping, and jet-boating.

If you're a motoring enthusiast, go by the **Queenstown Motor Museum,** on Brecon Street just below the gondola (☎ **442-8775**). Opened in 1971, the modern museum houses 35 vehicles in two hangarlike wings, and is managed by John and Glenys Taylor, who are happy to chat away about any of the displays. There's a 12-horsepower 1903 De Dion, and other fascinating reminders of automobile travel as it has evolved over the years. Admission is NZ$6 (U.S. $3.90) for adults, half price for kids; hours are 9am to 5:30pm daily.

Out on the wharf down at the end of the Mall, **Underwater World,** Main Town Pier (☎ **442-8437**), provides an intimate look at what goes on under the lake's surface. In a viewing lounge lined with panoramic windows, you are brought face to fin with rainbow and brown trout, longfin eels, and scaup duck (that quite often take an underwater dive to feed with the trout). Admission is NZ$6 (U.S. $3.90) for adults, half price for kids; hours are 9am to 5:30pm daily.

The lake is great for **fishing,** and the Travel & Visitor Centre can help you get gear and guides together. Jeff Jones (☎ **442-6570**) is a good guide. **Golfers** will want to head for the 18-hole Queenstown Golf Club, Kelvin Heights (☎ **442-9169**), or the 9-hole Frankton Golf Club (☎ **442-3584**). Greens fees are NZ$30 (U.S. $19.50) at Queenstown and NZ$9 (U.S. $5.85) at Frankton.

Right in town—and free for everyone—is the 11-acre ✪ **Queenstown Gardens,** across the water from the Parkroyal. There are tennis courts and lawn bowls to use at no charge, and the park is always open. Also, go by the **Maori Arts and Crafts Center** on Brecon Street to see a Maori carver at work.

Believe it or not, all the above is just a sample of things to do and see in Queenstown. There are scads of tours taking in many of the above and a whole lot more. For example, there's **paraflying** in a twin-seat chair or harness some 250 feet above the lake as a launch tows your parachute; and the **"Grape to Glass"** tour of three regional wineries; and **horse trekking** at Moonlight Stables; and flying in a DC-3 with **Pionair** (☎ **442-9732**) and. . . . But best go by the Travel & Visitor Centre and check over the complete list. They can make any reservations you need, and they'll also assist with onward accommodations and transportation arrangements.

SKIING

Despite the treasure trove of attractions listed above, it is skiing that brings Queenstown most alive. Skiers from around the world congregate to take to the slopes of this part of the Southern Alps from mid-June through September. All have good trails for beginner, intermediate, and expert skiers, and there's good public transport to each from town.

The nicest thing about skiing in Queenstown is that you don't have to be an expert to enjoy the sport. In fact, if you fall captive to the town's ski excitement and have arrived *sans* either equipment or experience, you can rent skis and take advantage of the excellent instruction offered at all four peaks. Coronet Peak, in fact, has a beginner's slope just waiting for you, and you'll pay about NZ$32 (U.S. $20.80) per adult and NZ$20 ($13) per child for class instruction, NZ$72 (U.S. $46.80) per hour for private lessons. Ski rental runs about NZ$28 (U.S. $18.20) for adults, NZ$18 (U.S. $11.70) for children. Lift fees average NZ$54 (U.S. $35) for adults and NZ$27 (U.S. $17.55) for children for a full day, less for a half day, and even less for learner lifts. Costs can be cut by taking advantage of ski packages offered by Mount Cook Line. Be sure to check for any specials offered during your stay.

WALKS

The **Department of Conservation Information Centre,** 37 Shotover St. (☎ **442-7933**); is the place to go for information on all walking tracks. They can furnish details and brochures on short walks around Queenstown as well as those farther afield. It's open daily from 8am to 8pm.

There are several excellent walkways through the **Wakatipu Basin,** some well formed and suitable for the average amateur walker, others that require a bit more physical fitness, and still others that should be attempted only by experienced and well-equipped trampers. Before setting out, consult the Department of Conservation and follow its advice.

Ask, also, about the **Otago Goldfields Heritage Trail** that runs throughout Otago.

The Routeburn Walk

Queenstown and Te Anau are the starting points for this famous walk, a three-day/two-night, 39km (24-mile) trek that takes you right into the heart of unspoiled forests, along river valleys, and across mountain passes. It's a soul-stirring experience, and suitable for ages 10 and up (and they won't say how high is "up")—a good level of physical fitness is the only requirement.

The Greenstone Valley Walk

This walk also takes you through scenes of natural beauty that will form lifetime memories. It follows an ancient Maori trail used by tribes who passed through the valley en route to rich greenstone lodes near Lake Wakatipu. The trail you'll walk, however, was actually cut by Europeans in the late 1800s as they opened up a route between Lake Wakatipu and Martins Bay on the Fiordland coast. Since the track passes through a valley, it is somewhat less demanding than the Routeburn Walk, but certainly no less beautiful. You'll pass Lake Howden and Lake McKellar and follow the Greenstone River through deep gorges and open valley land to Lake Wakatipu.

Independent walkers *must* check with the Department of Conservation (see above), which maintains a backcountry-huts system on both routes.

Guided Walks

For those less eager to rough it, guided walks are a terrific way to enjoy these scenic delights. For **Routeburn Walk** tours, you'll be bused from Queenstown to "The Divide" (on Milford Road), then walk to Lake McKenzie, across the Harris Saddle,

READERS RECOMMEND

Farm Scene Queenstown, Arthur's Point (☎ **442-7813**). *"This is an absolutely first-class operation, a wonderful overview of farming in New Zealand. We spent half a day there, and it was one of the highlights of our trip."*—Marilyn Farquhar, Santa Fe, N.M., U.S.A. [**Author's Note:** More than one reader has written to rave about this agricultural attraction.]

past the Routeburn Falls, and on to meet the coach that returns you to Queenstown. Along the way, comfortable lodges are provided for overnight stops, and you'll be treated to some of the most spectacular views in New Zealand. Treks run regularly from November through April every year, and cost NZ$820 (U.S. $533) for adults, NZ$710 (U.S. $462) for children under 15. Costs include all transport, meals, and accommodation. And you should reserve as far in advance as possible, since this trek is very, very popular with New Zealanders and groups are limited in size.

If the **Greenstone Valley** is your choice, comfortable lodges provide overnight accommodation, and as you relax at night there are books on hand to tell you about many of the plants and wildlife you've seen during the day's walk. Your expert guides can also relate tales of the Maori and how they once lived when they walked this valley. The three-day/two-night walk costs NZ$720 (U.S. $468) for adults, NZ$610 (U.S. $397) for ages 10 to 15; children under 10 not allowed. You can book through any Visitors Information Centre, travel agent, or Routeburn Ltd., P.O. Box 568, Queenstown (☎ **03/422-8200;** fax 03/442-6072).

It's also possible to combine the two walks in a six-day/five-night excursion called **"The Grand Traverse"** that follows the Routeburn Track northbound for three days and the Greenstone Walk for three days. Costs are NZ$1050 (U.S. $683) for adults, NZ$950 (U.S. $618) for children, including GST. This option is available only between November and April each year.

For information on the **Milford Track,** see Te Anau, later in this chapter.

NEARBY ATTRACTIONS IN ARROWTOWN

For an enjoyable outing, drive 20km (12 miles) northeast to Arrowtown. It was a boom town during the gold-mining days back in the 1860s when the Arrow River coughed up a lot of glittery stuff. Many of the original stone buildings remain, along with a stunning avenue of trees that were planted in 1867. To get a better understanding of the history of the town, go to the fine ★ **Lakes District Museum** on Buckingham Street, the town's main street (☎ **442-1824**), for an admission charge of NZ$3 (U.S. $1.95) for adults and NZ50¢ (U.S. 35¢) for children, and to the **Reconstructed Chinese Camp** (don't miss Ah Lum's General Store) on Bush Creek at the northern end of town. Other places to explore are the **Royal Oak Hotel,** the oldest licensed hotel in central Otago (you can still have a drink there); **Hamilton's General Store,** which has been in business since 1862; the **Old Gaol; St. John's Presbyterian Church,** dating from 1873; and the **post office,** where the staff dress in period costumes. The **Opal & Jade Factory** on Buckingham Street is a great place to buy jewelry.

Plan to have lunch or Devonshire tea at the **Stone Cottage,** Buckingham Street beside the museum (☎ **442-1860**).

If you're driving from Queenstown, come via Arthur's Point and return via Lake Hayes and Frankton for the maximum in scenery. A red **double-decker bus** (☎ **422-6067**) that escaped from London makes the round-trip from Queenstown twice a day for NZ$30 (U.S. $19.50); it leaves from the top of the Mall at 10am and 2pm.

SHOPPING

Surely Queenstown has more shops per capita than anywhere else in New Zealand. Whether you want to buy souvenirs or sweaters, sheepskin rugs or spinning wheels, you can do it here. The **Steamer Wharf,** which opened at the end of 1994, houses Polo Ralph Lauren, Tiffany, Benetton, and so forth. I'm not sure it makes sense to buy these items in New Zealand, but obviously someone must want to or the stores wouldn't be there. On the other hand, I love the beautiful sweaters at **Sheeps,** 75 Beach St. (☎ **442-7064**). They're almost all made in New Zealand, and about 60% are handcrafted. Sheeps is open daily from 9am to 10pm. **Aotea Souvenirs,** across from the Steamer Wharf, is also open daily.

The best value on books, calendars, and cards will be found at **Paper+Plus,** on Beach Street (☎ **442-9739**), open Monday through Friday from 9am to 9pm and Saturday and Sunday from 10am to 9pm. Look for toiletries and such at **Wilkenson Pharmacy,** on Rees Street, open daily from 8:30am to 6pm and 7 to 9pm. **Camera House,** 39 Beach St. (☎ **442-7644**), sells film and other supplies and offers one-hour processing. **The Mountaineer Shop,** on the corner of Beach and Rees streets (☎ **442-7460**), sells leather coats by Knights of New Zealand, oilskin coats, greenstone jewelry, and Coogi sweaters. They're open daily from 9am to 11pm. (The long shopping hours found in these stores and others are one of the reasons I contend that Queenstown is *not* New Zealand. It's sort of a "down under" Disneyland.)

Every other Saturday, the **Queenstown Art Council Craft Market** takes place in Earnslaw Park near the Steamer Wharf. On **The Mall,** you can buy casual clothing, spinning wheels, art supplies, and sheepskin rugs at **Alpine Artifacts** (☎ **442-8649**). The **Shopper Bus** will bring you to The Mall from outlying motels for NZ$1 (U.S. 65¢) each way.

EVENING ENTERTAINMENT

Eichardt's Tavern, at the water end of The Mall, is sort of the Old Faithful of Queenstown's nightlife, and the **Vilagrad** above it is the current hot dance spot. If there's going to be live entertainment in town, it will be at the Vilagrad. **Wicked Willie's,** the pub at the Hotel Queenstown, is also popular, as is the **Casbah,** a dance spot at 34 Shotover St. Live music is featured regularly at the **Skyline Restaurant** on Bob's Peak, accessible only by gondola. Most folks who go up for dinner—and the fantastic view—stay and make a night of it. A couple of places described above and in "Where to Eat," below, also qualify as nighttime entertainment: the cultural show and hangi dinner mentioned in a reader recommendation and the dinner cruise on the ***Earnslaw.*** Of course, the stores are open at night, so you could shop, or drop into the **Naff Caff** for a lattè.

Where to Stay

IN QUEENSTOWN

Queenstown is filled with accommodations, many in the budget range despite the fact that, on the whole, prices are higher here than in other places. However, it's also filled with visitors vying for these lower-cost lodgings. That means you should try to reserve before you come. If you arrive *sans* reservations, the Travel & Visitor Centre can help you find a place to lay your head.

The rates given below include GST.

READERS RECOMMEND

Queenstown Nightlife. *"Don't forget to include the 'jumping' Red Rock Café, where all the 'high' bungee jumpers go to trade in their free Speights beer coupons in the evenings. We also found a cozy 'greenstone' tavern, McNeill's, which serves great micro-brewed ales."* —Sue and Frank Thorn, Fallbrook, Calif., U.S.A.

Central Queenstown

ACCOMMODATIONS
Alpine Village Motor Inn 28
Amity Lodge 23
Autoline Motel 24
Bumbles 19
Creeksyde 6
Garden Court Motor Lodge 25
Goldfields Motel and Guest House 26
Mountain View Lodge 27
Queenstown House 7
Stone House 8
Wakatipu YHA Lodge 20

DINING
Avanti Restaurant and Bar 14
The Cow Pizza and Spaghetti House 15
The Fishbone Bar and Grill 10
Gourmet Express 17
HMS Britannia 13
Minami Jujisei Restaurant 16
Naff Caff 18
Pot au Feu 12
Skyline Restaurant 1
Solera Vino 11

ATTRACTIONS
Department of Conservation 9
Kiwi & Birdlife Park 4
Maori Arts and Crafts Centre 5
Queenstown Gardens 29
Queenstown Motor Museum 3
Skyline Gondola 2
Steamer Wharf/TSS *Earnslaw* 21
Underwater World 22

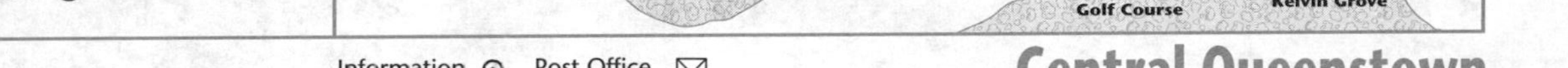

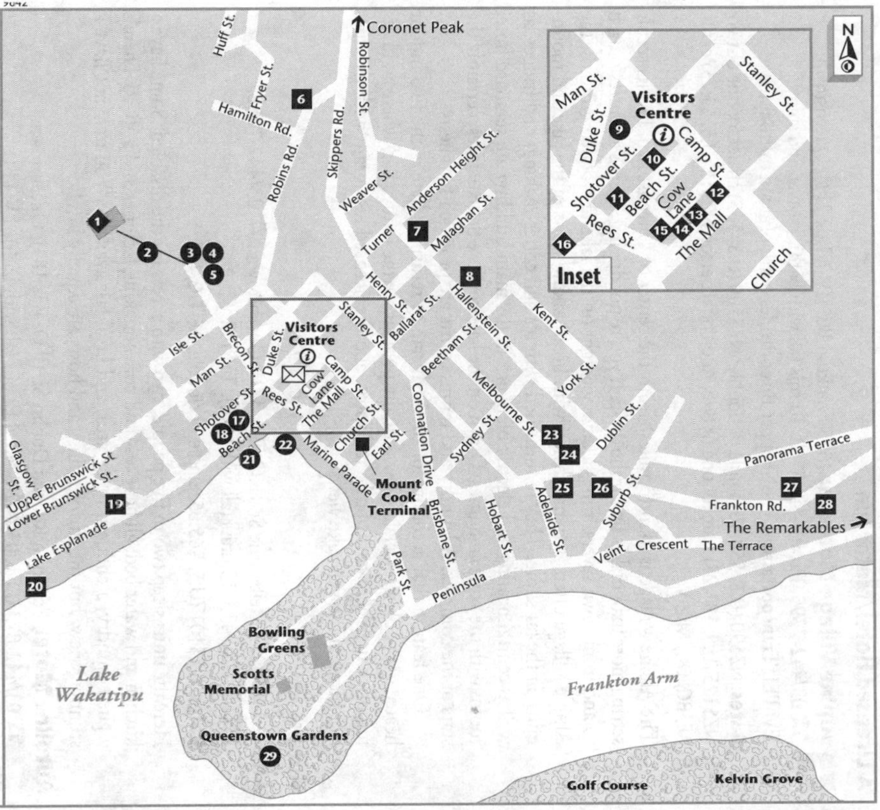

Information ⓘ Post Office ✉

A Licensed Hotel/Motor Inn

Alpine Village Motor Inn, 325 Frankton Rd. (P.O. Box 211), Queenstown. ☎ **03/442-7795.** Fax 03/442-7738. 50 rms (all with bath), chalets, and suites. TV TEL **Transportation:** The Shopper Bus provides transportation to/from town.

Rates: NZ$90 (U.S. $58.50) single or double; NZ$100 (U.S. $65) chalet for one or two; NZ$125 (U.S. $81.25) suite for one or two. Additional person NZ$15 (U.S. $9.75) extra. AE, BC, DC, MC, V.

The Alpine Village is 5km (3 miles) from the center of Queenstown, but its scenic setting more than makes up for the drive. If you're not driving, there's a courtesy coach to and from town several times a day. Set right on the lake in wooded grounds, the Alpine Village offers A-frame chalets with breathtaking views of the lake and mountains on the far shore. They're furnished with tea and coffee makings and fridges, as well as central heating and electric blankets. In the main building are standard hotel rooms with the same amenities. Down on the lakefront are deluxe suites, certainly the stars of the complex. A laundry and tennis courts are provided for guests.

One feature that accounts for the high rate of returnees here is the two indoor heated spa pools with a lake view. Equally popular are the lounge bar, where an inviting brick fireplace warms body and spirit, and the licensed restaurant with its superior menu and lovely lake view.

Motels

Amity Lodge, 7 Melbourne St. (P.O. Box 371), Queenstown. ☎ **03/442-7288.** Fax 03/442-9433. 13 units (all with bath). TV TEL

Rates: NZ$101 (U.S. $65.65) single or double. AE, DC, MC, V.

Here the units sleep two to five people, two with access for the disabled. Some have a kitchen and water bed; all have tea- and coffee-making facilities and a VCR. There's a guest laundry, a children's play area, and breakfast available. You may not have a stunning view, but the surroundings and hosts are equally lovely.

Autoline Motel, Frankton Rd. and Dublin St. (P.O. Box 183), Queenstown. ☎ **03/442-8734.** Fax 03/442-8743. 11 units (all with bath). TV TEL **Transportation:** Courtesy-car service from the bus depot by arrangement.

Rates: NZ$86 (U.S. $55.90) apartment for one or two. Additional person NZ$15 (U.S. $9.75) extra. AE, DC, MC, V.

This two-story motel has spacious one- and two-bedroom units sleeping two to six. All have nice views from their sun deck, but the end unit, no. 6, has the best lake view. Kitchens are fully equipped and have complete ranges. There's a radio, central heating, and electric blankets in each unit. Additional facilities include an automatic laundry with dryer, a hot spa pool, a children's play area, a car wash, and covered off-street parking. The apartments are serviced daily. The Autoline is a short walk from shopping and even closer to the gardens.

Earnslaw Lodge, 53 Frankton Rd., Queenstown. ☎ **03/442-8728.** Fax 03/442-7376. 19 units (all with bath). TV TEL

Rates: NZ$90 (U.S. $58.50) single; NZ$102 (U.S. $66.30) double. Additional person NZ$15 (U.S. $9.75) extra. AE, DC, MC, V.

This is one of the most inviting places you'll happen upon as you drive into town, and the congenial host is Barry Ellis. It's modern, with a skylight in the inviting lobby/bar area. Five of the spacious units have a small kitchen; 14 have bay views (for the best views, ask for the upper level). There's also a laundry and dining room, with breakfast available on request, tea and coffee facilities, and a unit accessible to wheelchairs.

Garden Court Motor Lodge, 31 Frankton Rd. (P.O. Box 572), Queenstown. ☎ **03/442-9713.** Fax 03/442-6468. 15 studios, 8 units (all with bath). TV TEL

Rates: NZ$105–NZ$145 (U.S. $68.25–$94.25) studio or apartment for one or two. Best Western discounts available. AE, DC, MC, V.

The Garden Court offers eight two-level units, each with balconies, two TVs, and alpine views courtesy of picture windows. There are also 15 studios with kitchenettes. You can walk into town from here in five minutes. The hosts are Pauline Kelly and Ken Chisholm.

Goldfields Motel and Guesthouse, 41 Frankton Rd., Queenstown. ☎ and fax **03/442-7211.** 4 rms (3 with bath), 8 units (all with bath). **Transportation:** The airport shuttle bus and the Shopper Bus stop at the gate.

Rates: NZ$45 (U.S. $29.25) single or NZ$65 (U.S. $42.25) double (including continental breakfast); NZ$70 (U.S. $45.50) motel unit for one or two without kitchen, NZ$75 (U.S. $48.75) motel unit for one or two with kitchen. Additional person NZ$10 (U.S. $6.50) extra. AE, BC, DC, MC, V.

At Goldfields, Bev Cooper offers units that sleep two or three; four have a full kitchen. All motel quarters are heated and have radios, TVs, showers, and electric blankets. Three of the four rooms in the modest guesthouse have private baths. Guesthouse guests share a lounge where there are a TV and tea- and coffee-making facilities, and a continental breakfast is included in the guesthouse tariff. There's plenty of off-street parking and a guest laundry. This property is a 15-minute walk from town, and there's a great lake view.

A Motel with Bunkrooms

Mountain View Lodge, Frankton Rd., Queenstown. ☎ **03/442-8246.** Fax 03/442-7414. 57 units, 10 bunkrooms (all with bath).

Rates: NZ$90 (U.S. $58.50) units for one or two without kitchen, NZ$100 (U.S. $65) unit for one or two with kitchen; NZ$45 (U.S. $29.25) bunkroom for two; NZ$65 (U.S. $42.25) bunkroom for four. AE, DC, MC, V.

In a wooded hillside setting about a 15-minute walk from town, this lodge offers a wide range of accommodations, all of which have stunning lake and mountain views. There are nice motel units that sleep two to four and come with full kitchen, TV, radio, heater, and electric blankets. Other accommodations come with everything except the kitchens (tea and coffee facilities only). A two-story building farther up the hill houses 10 rooms with heaters, each room with four bunks or a double bed with two bunks, bath, carpeting, and a table and four chairs in front of a window with a lovely view. A fully equipped kitchen is shared by all, and there's a TV lounge/bar,

READERS RECOMMEND

McFee's Waterfront Lodge, Shotover Street, Queenstown (☎ **03/442-7400**). *"Our motel was definitely 'the friendliest place in the center of town'—if maybe a little too noisy. But for NZ$75 (U.S. $48.75), with all facilities including laundry, it was fine for us."* —Sue and Frank Thorn, Fallbrook, Calif., U.S.A.

laundry, and children's playground. You supply cooking and eating utensils; they supply bedding. The Mountain View Lodge also has a licensed family-style restaurant on the premises. There are candles at night, windows look out to mountains and lakes, and main-course prices are in the NZ$15 to NZ$25 (U.S. $9.75 to $16.25) range.

One of the Mountain View's structures, the **Bottle House,** built in 1956, is known throughout New Zealand. Constructed entirely of 14,720 glass bottles set in sand-and-cement mortar, it serves as the motel office. The builder (whose identity is not revealed) says that there's not a single beer bottle included—he got the bottles from a dealer, and he emptied not one himself.

Bed-&-Breakfasts

Queenstown House, 69 Hallenstein St., Queenstown. ☎ **03/442-9043.** Fax 03/442-8755. 8 rms, 1 unit (all with bath).

Rates (including continental breakfast): NZ$95 (U.S. $61.75) single; NZ$125 (U.S. $81.25) double; NZ$149 (U.S. $96.85) family room. MC, V.

The big draw here is the lounge with its open fire and TV. Adjacent to it is the dining area where breakfast (fresh fruit, homemade jams, coffee, and a variety of teas) is served. All rooms have their own bath and lake view, and there's also a laundry. King-size beds are available. From Queenstown House it's a short downhill walk into town and a short uphill walk back. A cooked breakfast and an evening meal are available on request. No smoking permitted in the house.

★ **The Stone House,** 47 Hallenstein St., Queenstown. ☎ and fax **03/442-9812.** 3 rms (all with bath).

Rates (including breakfast): NZ$102 (U.S. $66.30) single; NZ$154 (U.S. $100.10) double. MC, V.

Happily removed from the hubbub, the Stone House sits on a hill above central Queenstown, providing a restful haven. Hosts Deb and Grant Alley, both former Air New Zealand flight attendants, have lovingly restored their home, which was built in 1874. The interiors are very appealing: Laura Ashley and other English chintzes are featured on draperies, doonas (comforters), and shams, and the collections of ceramic mugs, jugs, and teapots are colorful and inviting. Two rooms have attached baths and one room has its bath across the hall. Grant and Deb will take guests fishing, walking, or picnicking for an extra charge. They also know the operators of many of the local attractions and are in a good position to make recommendations. Breakfast features homemade muffins and a great lake view. Sherry or wine is served in the parlor at "6-ish."

★ **Trelawn Place,** P.O. Box 117, Queenstown. ☎ **03/442-9160.** 4 rms (all with bath), 1 cottage.

Rates (including breakfast): NZ$110–NZ$140 (U.S. $71.50–$91) double; NZ$165 (U.S. $107.25) cottage. BC, MC, V.

Sitting on a spectacular bluff overlooking the Shotover River on the outskirts of town, this is the private home of Nery Howard. She provides not only double-occupancy rooms but also a very personal, friendly welcome that has won raves from our readers, as has Nery's cooking. Very popular with guests is the fishing trip and picnic lunch she arranges to what she says is "some of the best trout and salmon fishing in New Zealand." The self-contained stone cottage with roses around the door is perfect for honeymooners.

Hostels

Bumbles, 2 Brunswick St. (at Lake Esplanade), Queenstown. ☎ **03/442-6298.** 70 beds (no rooms with bath).

Rates: NZ$20 (U.S. $13) per person double or twin; NZ$16 (U.S. $10.40) dorm bed. MC, V.

This lakeside hostel enjoys great views and a friendly atmosphere. There's room for 70, and everybody shares the big "self-cooking" kitchen (open from 7:30am to 10:30pm), the TV lounge, and laundry. Linens are available for rent. The hostel is a five-minute walk from the bus station and town center.

★ $ **Wakatipu YHA Lodge,** 80 Lake Esplanade, Queenstown. ☎ **03/442-8413.** Fax 03/442-6561. 8 rms (2 with bath), 76 dormitory beds.

Rates: NZ$18 (U.S. $11.70) per person double or twin; NZ$16 (U.S. $10.40) dorm bed. Dinner NZ$8 (U.S. $5.20) extra. No credit cards.

This hostel is across the street from the lake, a 10-minute walk from The Mall. The two-story lodge-type building is designed with many windows to take advantage of the beautiful view. There are 100 beds in 17 rooms, including 4 twin rooms and 4 family rooms, two with private facilities. The hostel provides good evening meals nightly year round, and there's a large communal kitchen. Other amenities include a laundry, drying room, and TV room. The hostel stays open all day.

Cabins & Campgrounds

★ **Creeksyde Campervan Park,** Robins Road (P.O. Box 247), Queenstown (☎ **03/442-9447;** fax 03/442-6621), definitely the Mercedes of campgrounds, was blessed by the Wizard of Christchurch when it opened in 1988. In another life it was a plant nursery, so there are plenty of trees around and room for 50 campervans, all with power outlets and water and waste hookups. The reception area is in a striking 12-sided building; there's complimentary tea and coffee in the lounge in the evenings, a spa bath (great if you've spent the day skiing), bright baths (women get a hairdryer), a bath for the disabled, kitchen, dining area, and complete laundry facilities. The charge is NZ$20 (U.S. $13) for two; tent sites cost NZ$10 (U.S. $6.50) per person. Cottage and lodge rooms are also available at NZ$35 to NZ$55 (U.S. $22.75 to $35.75) for two adults.

READERS RECOMMEND

Adelaide Street Guest House Bed & Breakfast, 15 Adelaide St., Queenstown (☎ **03/442-6207**). *"Stunning views of snowcapped peaks and blue water. Noela runs it for its absent owners. It's reasonable and a room with a view."*—Meg Barth Gammon, Kailua, Hawaii, U.S.A.

Larch Hill Bed & Breakfast, 16 Panners Way, Queenstown (☎ **03/442-7126**). *"We stayed at this B&B in Queenstown. The accommodation, host and hostess, and location were five-star quality."*—Paul and Micky Mathews, Overland Park, Kans., U.S.A.

The Queenstown Lodge, Sainsbury Road, Fernhill (☎ **03/442-7107**). *"In Queenstown I was very impressed with the Queenstown Lodge. It was sort of like a backpackers' place—four beds to a room, with no sink, but linens were supplied. That was NZ$20 (U.S. $13) per night (with a restaurant and bar on the premises). Rooms with baths also were available for NZ$45 (U.S. $29.25). My backpackers' room had a great view of the lake. One note: There are lots of steps, so it's not a place for the disabled. I also liked the lodge because it was slightly out of town and away from the tourist-trap hubbub of Queenstown."*—P. A. McCauley, Baltimore, Md., U.S.A.

The **Queenstown Motor Park,** Main Street (P.O. Box 59), Queenstown (☎ **03/442-7252;** fax 03/442-7253), is about 1km (1/2 mile) from the post office and set on well-kept wooded grounds overlooking the lake. Mountain and lake views greet the eye on every path, and the camp itself sparkles with fresh paint on its airy kitchen, dining, and recreation blocks. There's a TV lounge, a provisions shop/take-out bar, a laundry with dryers, and a children's playground. Basic cabins—carpeted and heated, sleeping three or four in beds or bunks, and with a table and chairs—rent for NZ$30 (U.S. $19.50) for one or two people. Tourist apartments—with toilet, shower, and tea- and coffee-making facilities—cost NZ$56 (U.S. $36.40) for one or two. The 200 campsites are NZ$9 (U.S. $5.85) per adult, NZ$4.50 (U.S. $2.95) per child under 14; and 300 caravan sites go for NZ$10 (U.S. $6.50) per adult, NZ$5 (U.S. $3.25) per child under 15. Be sure to reserve ahead if you're coming between December 24 and January 10.

IN NEARBY ARROWTOWN

Motels

Lake Hayes Motel, Lake Hayes Rd. (R.D. 1), Queenstown. ☎ and fax **03/442-1705.** 7 apartments. TV TEL

Rates: NZ$96 (U.S. $62.40) apartment for one or two. Additional person NZ$17 (U.S. $11.05) extra. AE, DC, MC, V.

Its location—5km (3 miles) from Arrowtown, 13km (8 miles) from Queenstown—makes this an ideal base for exploring both those towns. On the peaceful shores of Lake Hayes, there's a relaxing country air that takes full advantage of the scenic surroundings. The apartment units have full kitchens, radios, and both electric and down blankets. Laundry facilities are available. In the garden is a children's playground with a trampoline and barbecue. The lake at the bottom of the garden is good for swimming and fishing for brown trout, and there's a fishing boat available without charge for guest use. Also convenient is their Travel Desk, which can book sightseeing attractions for you.

Mace Motel, Oak Ave., Arrowtown. ☎ and fax **03/442-1825.** 6 apartments. TV TEL

Rates: NZ$60 (U.S. $39) apartment for one. NZ$75 (U.S. $48.75) apartment for two. Additional person NZ$15 (U.S. $9.75) extra. BC, MC, V.

Located on Arrowtown's famous Oak Avenue near the town center, this motel is surrounded by lawns planted with shrubs. Units have two or three bedrooms, and with convertible divans in the wood-paneled lounges they'll accommodate up to eight. All have kitchens, videos, electric blankets, central heating, and radios. There's a heated spa pool, children's play area, laundry, and provision store on the premises. It's within walking distance of licensed restaurants and convenient to skifields.

A Bed-&-Breakfast

Speargrass Lodge, Speargrass Flat Rd. (R.D. 1), Queenstown. ☎ and fax **03/442-1417.** 4 rms (all with bath).

Rates (including breakfast): NZ$75 (U.S. $48.75) single; NZ$105–NZ$125 (U.S. $68.25–$81.25) double. Three-course dinner NZ$28 (U.S. $18.20) extra. AE, BC, DC, MC, V.

Michael and Raewyn Fleck live on 8 acres of green hills from which there's a view of snowcapped Coronet Peak. They've arranged their 5,500-square-foot house so they can accommodate guests without impacting their family life. Each attractive room has an exterior door, electric blankets, and underfloor heating. One room has a bathtub; the rest, showers. Guests gather around a big round table for the evening meal; wine is available for purchase. (The hosts eat separately.) There are also a games rooms with a pool table and bar, a lounge with an open fire, and guest laundry. Speargrass Lodge is very close to Arrowtown and a 20-minute drive from Queenstown. There's no smoking in the lodge.

Where to Eat

You won't lack for a place to eat in Queenstown, in any price range you choose. The food court on the ground floor of O'Connell's Shopping Centre, at the corner of Beach and Camp streets, is a thrifty place to dine, and I really like the inexpensive take-out items at the Jazz Bar on Camp Street—especially the frozen yogurt. Moderate prices for full meals are easy to come by, and I'll tell you about just one of the several places that qualify for a "big splurge."

Avanti Restaurant & Bar, 20 The Mall. ☎ **442-8503.**

Cuisine: ITALIAN. **Reservations:** Not required.
Prices: NZ$5–NZ$16 (U.S. $3.25–$10.40). AE, DC, MC, V.
Open: Daily 7am–11pm.

Fresh pasta is featured daily for lunch and dinner, and there's fresh fish on Wednesday. Any day's a good day for continental breakfast. The bistro atmosphere is inviting, and in warm weather there's courtyard dining with a view of the gondolas. Avanti is located in the town center. Licensed.

The Cow Pizza and Spaghetti House, Cow Lane. ☎ **442-8588.**

Cuisine: PIZZA/PASTA. **Reservations:** Not accepted.
Prices: Most pizzas and main courses under NZ$15 (U.S. $9.75). AE, BC, DC, MC, V.
Open: Daily noon–11pm.

This cozy little stone building in the town center is at the end of a lane that got its name from the fact that cows were once driven this way each day to be milked. Inside, this place probably hasn't changed a whole lot since those early days—there's a smoke-darkened fireplace, wooden beams, lots of old farm memorabilia, and wooden benches and tables. It's a friendly gathering spot for locals, many of whom you'll rub elbows with at those long tables.

As for the menu, it was *designed* for budget travelers! I counted eight varieties of pizza (including a vegetarian version) and six spaghetti dishes—and the highest price on the menu is NZ$14.95 (U.S. $9.70), unless you go for the extra-large pizza (don't, unless you're ordering for two or have an extra-large appetite), which can cost as much as NZ$21.95 (U.S. $14.25). Soup, salad, homemade whole-meal bread, and ice-cream desserts are also offered. It's BYO. Take-out is available, but I strongly recommend that you eat right here—the Cow is a delightful experience.

The Fishbone Bar & Grill, 7 Beach St. ☎ **442-6768.**

Cuisine: SEAFOOD. **Reservations:** Not accepted.
Prices: Appetizers NZ$9.50–NZ$14.50 (U.S. $6.20–$9.45); main courses NZ$16.50–NZ$24.50 (U.S. $10.75–$15.95); "kiddies' meals" NZ$7.50–NZ$8.50 (U.S. $4.90–$5.55). AE, DC, MC, V.
Open: Lunch daily noon–3pm; dinner daily 5:30–10pm or later.

The colorful fish mobiles hanging from the ceiling and an open kitchen are part of the casual decor here, and daily specials are written on a chalkboard. These might include garlic-steamed mussels, oysters (natural or Kilpatrick), whitebait, prawns, or scampi. The scallops are sometimes poached and served with a Cointreau-cream sauce. Dollarwise diners might choose the fish and chips main course for only NZ$9.95 (U.S. $6.45). Seating is at half a dozen booths and a dozen or so tables. Licensed and BYO.

$ **Gourmet Express,** in the Bay Centre, Shotover St. ☎ **442-9619.**

Cuisine: AMERICAN. **Reservations:** Not required.
Prices: Appetizers NZ$5.25–NZ$8.75 (U.S. $3.40–$5.70); main courses NZ$7.50–NZ$15.50 (U.S. $4.90–$10.10). AE, DC, MC, V.
Open: Daily 6:30am–9pm. **Closed:** Christmas Day and Boxing Day.

The Gourmet Express bills itself as an American-style restaurant and coffee shop, and indeed you'll find a very Americanized menu. Hamburgers, cheeseburgers, and baconburgers; club sandwiches; pancakes; hash browns; omelets; and chili are among the lighter fare, with heartier offerings of steak (in several varieties), fish, chicken-in-the-basket, lamb chops, lamb filets, and venison. In the center of town, it's a large, bright, and cheerful place with booth and counter seating. Licensed and BYO.

★ $ **Giuseppe's Gourmet Pizza and Pasta Bar,** 155 Fernhill Rd., Richard's Park Lane, Fernhill. ☎ **442-5444.**

Cuisine: CREATIVE ITALIAN. **Reservations:** Recommended. **Transportation:** If you don't have a car, you'll need to pay NZ$5 (U.S. $3.25) for a taxi or NZ$1 (U.S. 65¢) bus fare from town.
Prices: Appetizers NZ$4–NZ$10 (U.S. $2.60–$6.50); main courses NZ$11–NZ$16 (U.S. $7.15–$10.40). AE, BC, DC, MC, V.
Open: Dinner only, daily 6–10:30pm (later in summer).

This spot is the favorite of many locals. It's in an unlikely location: a suburban shopping center, where you'd expect to see a fish-and-chips shop or a dairy—in fact, there's a dairy next door. The food here is—in short—*superb.* I'd start with the traditional bruschetta, followed by pasta topped with sun-dried tomato and fresh asparagus. You might, however, prefer Gino's bruschetta, with pickled eggplant, garlic, olive oil, and parsley. My favorite pizza is generously sprinkled with marinated lamb and fresh mushrooms. Giuseppe's is fully licensed, with many wines from Australia, Italy, France, and New Zealand available by the glass or bottle. You can also BYO and pay a small corkage fee. No smoking.

HMS *Britannia,* The Mall. ☎ **442-9600.**

Cuisine: NEW ZEALAND. **Reservations:** Required.
Prices: Appetizers NZ$6–NZ$16 (U.S. $3.90–$10.40); main courses NZ$17.50–NZ$30 (U.S. $11.40–$19.50). AE, DC, MC, V.
Open: Dinner only, daily 6:30–10pm.

This local favorite in the town center is designed like the interior of an 18th-century sailing ship, with nets and ropes hanging from the ceiling and lanterns and dripping candles giving off a warm glow. There may be more elegant restaurants in Queenstown, but none is more pleasant than this. Owner Doug Champion and his staff go overboard to provide painstaking service and a meal prepared to order. The menu features fresh lobster, mussels, fish, steak filet, and vegetarian dishes.

 **Minami Jujisei Restaurant,** 45 Beach St. ☎ **442-9854.**

Cuisine: JAPANESE. **Reservations:** Required.

Prices: Appetizers NZ$5–NZ$17 (U.S. $3.25–$11.05); main courses NZ$19–NZ$50 (U.S. $12.35–$32.50). AE, DC, MC, V.

Open: Lunch daily noon–2pm; dinner daily 6–10pm.

If you have a yen for something Japanese, try this marvelous restaurant. The upstairs setting is a serene room with traditional decor; its kitchen is under the direction of Koji Honda, a chef of distinction, and manager Tony Robertson will be happy to help you with your selection if you're not too sure about the dishes. Specialties include selections from the South Island's only sushi bar and ise-ebi (crayfish). There's a large choice of Japanese snacks and soups, plus three fixed-price meals of six courses and tea (tempura, sashimi, or steak). Licensed.

 **Naff Caff,** 62 Shotover St. ☎ **442-8211.**

Cuisine: CAFE. **Reservations:** Not accepted.

Prices: Coffee NZ$2–NZ$3.50 (U.S. $1.30–$2.30); lunch NZ$4–NZ$5 (U.S. $2.60–$3.25). No credit cards.

Open: Daily 8am–10:30pm (lunch daily 11am–2pm).

Coffee drinkers rejoice! Whether you want Vienna, borgia, lattè, mega mucho, mella bella, flat white, double espresso, cappuccino, long black, or macchiato—you'll find it here. The Naff Caff is known to coffee drinkers New Zealand–wide because they roast and grind their own beans, serve the lattès in large bowls, and perform all the other rituals that devotees require. The casual atmosphere is also appealing: There's indoor and outdoor seating, and CDs provide background music. Besides the entrance on Shotover Street, another door faces Beach Street. No smoking.

Pot au Feu, 24 Camp St. ☎ **442-8333.**

Cuisine: MEDITERRANEAN. **Reservations:** Recommended.

Prices: Appetizers NZ$5–NZ$15 (U.S. $3.25–$9.75); main courses NZ$18–NZ$26 (U.S. $11.70–$16.90). AE, MC, V.

Open: Dinner only, daily 6–10pm.

The ambience here is colonial: The restaurant consists of two rooms in what might have been an old house, and an interesting plate collection hangs on the walls. The food, however, is a Mediterranean treatment of fresh New Zealand produce. You might start with seafood soup flavored with sumac and coriander and follow with hogget (mature lamb) loin roasted and served with a ratatouille of potatoes, courgettes (zucchini), mushrooms, and mint. Another popular main course is monkfish roasted with garlic, tomato, and fennel. The cervena (venison) medallions on a mustard-soy sauce are also popular.

 **Solera Vino,** 25 Beach St. ☎ **442-6082.**

Cuisine: MODERN NEW ZEALAND. **Reservations:** Recommended.

Prices: Appetizers NZ$4–NZ$18.90 (U.S. $2.60–$12.30); main courses NZ$17–NZ$21 (U.S. $11.05–$13.65). AE, BC, MC, V.

Open: Dinner only daily 5pm–"late."

I felt as if I'd walked into a Spanish bodega when I crossed the threshold at Solera Vino. With the rough plaster walls, wooden tables, and rustic fireplaces, all that was missing was a flamenco guitarist. However, diners here don't think they're missing a thing, because the food is truly great! South Island salmon is prepared with fresh tomato, seasonal green vegetables, and fresh basil. Oven-baked rack of lamb is served on provençal vegetables with a capsicum (green-pepper) rouille and marjoram part jus. Homemade vegetarian ravioli is served with a purée of root vegetable, nut pesto, and sun-dried tomatoes in a coriander-lemongrass broth. The restaurant is licensed and offers nine beers as well as an extensive wine list. There are seven tables downstairs and eight upstairs. Ask to be seated with nonsmokers if that's important to you.

WORTH THE EXTRA MONEY

★ **Skyline Restaurant,** Bob's Peak. ☎ **442-7860.**

Cuisine: NEW ZEALAND. **Reservations:** Recommended for lunch, required for dinner.
Transportation: Take the Skyline Gondola up Bob's Peak.
Prices (including access by gondola): Buffet lunch NZ$36 (U.S. $23.40); dinner buffet NZ$48 (U.S. $31.20). AE, BC, DC, MC, V.
Open: Lunch daily noon–2pm; dinner daily 6–9pm.

Spend at least one of your Queenstown meals at the Skyline Restaurant, where the wraparound windows give you a fantastic panoramic view of the town and lake. The restaurant is accessible by Skyline Gondolas. The star attraction is the carvery buffet, which features lamb, seafood, and other New Zealand specialties. The tariff includes your gondola round-trip fare, meal, and entertainment (usually a band that plays for dancing). Licensed.

Other dining choices in this lofty location include a coffee shop (open daily from 10am to 6pm) and a brasserie.

Easy Excursions from Queenstown

MILFORD SOUND

As you'll see from the sections of this chapter that follow, I heartily recommend that you spend at least one day in Te Anau and go from there to Milford Sound. If, however, time or budget prevents that, you're not condemned to miss that very special part of New Zealand. InterCity, Mount Cook Line, and Fiordland Travel have day-long coach trips that include launch trips on the sound and the option of flying one or both ways to Queenstown. Fiordland Travel's coach trip to the sound, launch trip, and plane trip back to Queenstown comes with a bonus free ticket for the TSS *Earnslaw* cruise of your choice.

Taking the coach in and flying out gives you an opportunity to see the scenery from two different perspectives while saving some time as well. Should weather conditions ground the plane at Milford, you can always take the coach back. The

READERS RECOMMEND

Queenstown Maori Cultural Restaurant, Man Street (☎ **442-8878**). *"In Queenstown there's an absolutely delicious hangi feast and Maori cultural show done by a large Maori family. They were so gracious, made us feel very welcome, shared much insight into their culture, and performed fascinating songs and dances. It was an evening I'll never forget."*—Jackie Plusch, Phoenix, Ariz., U.S.A.

Saguaro, upstairs in the Trust Bank Arcade, Beach Street (☎ **442-8240**). *"We were given a recommendation of a Mexican restaurant in town. . . . We found it to be reasonable and had the best Mexican food I've eaten in a long time. I also sampled a delicious local wine: Gibbston Valley Chardonnay."*—Meg Barth Gammon, Kailua, Hawaii, U.S.A.

cost of this trip is NZ$265 (U.S. $172.25) for adults and NZ$159 (U.S. $103.35) for children; flying both ways is a few dollars less. Pionair offers a round-trip flight on a DC-3 and a cruise for NZ$235 (U.S. $152.75).

You can book through the Travel & Visitor Centre, the Fiordland Travel Centre at the Steamer Wharf, or the Mount Cook Travel Centre on Camp Street. I, personally, am quite fond of the Fiorland trip, because of their superior (luxury-class) coaches, comfortable cruisers, and wonderfully informed drivers. They also furnish commentary tapes in four languages other than English, with a four-channel music system to soothe the return trip. It's a long day, but a memorable one, from a Queenstown base.

All coach excursions to Milford Sound leave Queenstown between 7am and 8am, returning around 8pm, and fares average NZ$135 (U.S. $87.75) for adults, NZ$67.50 (U.S. $43.90) for children, inclusive of the launch trip. Lunch is available on most launch trips, but you're free to bring your own.

Fiordland Travel also offers a two-day adventure from Queenstown beginning with a cruise across Lake Wakatipu aboard the TSS *Earnslaw,* followed by a coach trip to Milford Sound and an overnight stay on the *Milford Wanderer.* This excursion allows time for a walk in Fiordland National Park and costs NZ$176 (U.S. $114.40).

★ DOUBTFUL SOUND

Captain Cook was doubtful that it *was* a sound when he first saw it, thus the name, Doubtful Sound. And the name alone is intriguing enough to make you want to go there. It's not as famous as its neighbor to the north, Milford Sound, but where Milford is majestic, Doubtful is mysterious. Both are undeniably serene. Doubtful Sound is 10 times bigger than Milford, and while it can't boast Mitre Peak, its still waters mirror Commander Peak, which rises 4,000 feet in vertical splendor.

While the round-trip overland to Milford is pretty tiring (fly one way if you can); getting to and from Doubtful is less so. Yet getting to Doubtful Sound does require four modes of transportation (all organized by the tour operator): a bus to Te Anau, a van to Lake Manapouri, a boat across that pristine lake, and another bus to Deep Cove in Doubtful Sound—through lush forest and over Wilmot Pass, 2,208 feet above sea level, stopping along the way at the Manapouri Power Station, spiraling downward 750 eerie feet to view the seven immense underground turbines. It's like delving into the underworld and is absolutely fascinating.

Deep Cove Village, where you pick up the boat to explore the sound (another mode of transport on this trip), has a population of one—the Fiordland National Park conservation officer. A highlight of the boat trip through the sound comes at its end when the captain shuts off the engine in Hall Arm and you can hear how incredibly silent it is here. You return to Te Anau and Queenstown the way you came, without the stop at the power station. Another high point is crossing Lake Manapouri again (especially at sunset) and watching as what looks like a wall created by the many islands in the lake magically opens as the boat draws near.

Fiordland Travel is the only operator in Doubtful Sound. The price of the "Triple Trip" described here is NZ$170 (U.S. $110.50), half that for children.

Another difference between Milford and Doubtful sounds is that at Milford you know civilization is nearby, with the airstrip and the THC hotel near the boat harbor. Doubtful Sound is definitely more remote. If you've never done either trip, I'd recommend Milford Sound for its sheer majesty and save Doubtful Sound as the highlight of your next trip.

En Route to Te Anau

It's a 167km (104-mile) drive from Queenstown, on good roads all the way. You'll follow Highway 6, then take Highway 94 over the summit of **Gorge Hill,** along the **Mararoa River** and through sheep and cattle country to **Te Anau,** the largest lake on the South Island.

2 Te Anau

167km (104 miles) SW of Queenstown, 116km (72 miles) S of Milford Sound

GETTING THERE • By Plane Mount Cook Airline provides daily service from Mount Cook and Queenstown.

• By Bus There is daily coach service between Te Anau and Christchurch, Dunedin, and Invercargill via InterCity and Mount Cook Landline; both lines also have daily service to Te Anau and Milford Sound from Queenstown.

• By Car From Queenstown, take Highway 6, then Highway 94.

ESSENTIALS • Orientation Te Anau's main street is actually Highway 94 (called Milford Road within the township). Stretched along each side you'll find the post office, restaurants, grocery stores, and most of the township's shops. At the lake end of Milford Road sits the Fiordland Travel office, ready to make your reservations for all launch trips. Just opposite the lake, on Highway 94 before it turns westward to become Milford Road, is the Ta Anau Travelodge Hotel.

• Information A visit to the **Fiordland National Park Visitor Centre,** on Lakefront Drive (P.O. Box 29), Te Anau (☎ **03/249-7921;** fax 03/249-7613), is a must for those contemplating any of the celebrated walks, and is highly recommended for anyone headed to Milford Sound. It has a museum and audiovisual display, and does all the bookings for the independent Milford Track. The center is open daily from 8am to 6pm; the Milford Track booking office (☎ **03/249-8514**) is open daily from 9am to 4:30pm.

Visitor information is also dispensed at **Fiordland Travel,** on Lakefront Drive (P.O. Box 1), Te Anau (☎ **03/249-7419;** fax 03/249-7022), open daily from 8am to 6pm.

• Telephone The telephone area code (STD) for Te Anau is **03.**

Lake Te Anau spreads its south, middle, and north branches like long fingers poking deep into the mountains that mark the beginning of the rugged and magnificent three-million-acre World Heritage **Fiordland National Park,** New Zealand's largest and, indeed, one of the largest in the world. Within its boundaries, which enclose the whole of the South Island's southwest corner, lie incredibly steep mountain ranges, lakes, sounds, rivers, magnificent fjords, and huge chunks of mountainous terrain even now unexplored. In fact, one large section has been closed off from exploration after the discovery there in 1948 of one of the world's rarest birds, the wingless takahe. It had not been seen for nearly a century before, seldom even then, and was thought to be extinct. When a colony was found in the Murchison Mountains, the decision was made to protect them from human disturbance. What other wonders remain to be discovered within the vast park, one can only speculate.

Lake Te Anau itself presents a wonder of a sort, with its eastern shoreline (that's where Te Anau—its name means "to arrive by water"—township is located) virtually treeless with about 30 inches annual rainfall, its western banks covered by dense forest nurtured by more than 100 inches of rain each year. To visitors, however, the attractions of this second-largest lake in New Zealand consist of a variety of water sports and its proximity to Milford Sound, 116km (72 miles) away. That sound (which is actually a fjord) reaches 22½km (14 miles) in from the Tasman Sea, flanked by sheer granite peaks traced by playful waterfalls that appear and disappear depending on the amount of rainfall. Its waters and the surrounding land have been kept in as nearly a primeval state as man could possibly manage without leaving it totally untouched. In fine weather or pouring rain, Milford Sound exudes a powerful sense of nature's pristine harmony and beauty—a visit there is balm to my 20th-century soul.

What to See & Do

★ **Lake cruises** are the main attraction in Te Anau, and **Fiordland Travel,** Lakefront Drive (P.O. Box 1), Te Anau (☎ **03/249-7419;** fax 03/249-7022), can give you their latest brochure with current times and rates on trips. The most popular is to the Te Ana-au Caves, which runs year round. The tour includes an underground boat ride into the glowworm grotto in the "living" cave, so called because it's still being formed. A crystal-clear river cascades down the cave tiers at the rate of 55,000 gallons per minute, creating frothy white falls. On the second level of the waterbed you'll see the glowworm grotto. In my opinion, the day trip is preferable to the evening, since the scenic 10-mile lake cruise begs to be enjoyed in daylight. The cost for adults is NZ$33 (U.S. $21.45) and for children NZ$10 (U.S. $6.50).

In most cases, the primary reason for coming to Te Anau is to go on to **Milford Sound** and **Doubtful Sound.** You can drive, fly, or take a coach tour to Milford Sound. Fiordland's half-day coach trip includes cruise fares and costs NZ$80 (U.S. $52), half price for children. There's no way you can get to Doubtful Sound on your own. Fiordland's Doubtful Sound trip costs NZ$150 (U.S. $97.50) for adults.

Waterwings Airways Ltd., Lakefront Drive (P.O. Box 222), Te Anau (☎ **03/249-7405;** fax 03/442-3050), operates floatplane flights between Te Anau and Milford Sound. Their one-hour 10-minute ★ **scenic flight** is a real delight, at a cost of NZ$154 (U.S. $100.10) per adult, NZ $92 (U.S. $59.80) per child. For NZ$131 (U.S. $85.15) per adult, NZ$92 (U.S. $59.80) per child, they'll take you on a 35-minute flight to Doubtful Sound. In addition, there's a 20-minute scenic flight around Te Anau, at NZ$66 (U.S. $42.90) and NZ$40 (U.S. $26), and one for 10 minutes that costs NZ$36 (U.S. $23.40) and NZ$22 (U.S. $14.30), respectively. One of their best offerings is the one-hour combination Fly 'N Boat trip at a cost of NZ$84 (U.S. $54.60) per adult, NZ$51 (U.S. $33.15) per child; they'll take you down the Waiau River to Manapouri via jet boat, then bring you back by floatplane to Te Anau by way of the Hidden Lakes.

Other activities include Fiordland **helicopter flights, raft trips on the Waiau River, jet-boat rides,** and **fishing** with any one of the experienced guides available. Check with Fiordland Travel for these or other activities, and with the Department of Conservation for nature walks and tramping tracks. Then, head for glorious Milford Sound.

WALKS

Most dedicated trampers consider the world-famous ★ **Milford Track** the finest anywhere in the world. Four days are required to walk the 51km (32 miles) from Glade Jetty at Lake Te Anau's northern end to Sandfly Point on the western bank of Milford Sound. To walk the pure wilderness is to immerse yourself in the sights, sounds, smells,

"Waltzing" on the Track at Christmas

As the launch glided across Lake Te Anau toward the head of the Milford Track, those of us on board sipped tea and tried to eye one another without being too obvious. My Kiwi friend Donald and I sat together amid our companions: a Kiwi family (a husband and wife, their 13-month-old daughter and 7-year-old son, and the husband's teenage brother) and seven Australian university students.

What am I doing here? Tomorrow's Christmas and I'm 7,000 miles from home and about to start a four-day hike with 12 strangers and someone I know only slightly.

The plans for walking the Milford Track had been made five months earlier when I'd visited New Zealand during my summer vacation. I'd met Donald on that trip, and he'd convinced me I wouldn't have really seen his country until I'd spent some time "in the bush." Being a red-blooded Kiwi, Donald had thought we should hike independently, not in an organized group: "Groups have running hot and cold water in all their lodges and clean beds every night. You wouldn't want that, would you?"

"Oh, no, of course not," I'd assured him. Then I'd wondered, *How do I tell this guy I've never walked farther than from one end of a shopping mall to the other?*

I'd prepared for the trip by trekking up and down the hills around my home in California in a pair of borrowed hiking boots. By the time Christmas vacation had come, I'd felt like John Muir. But now I was having misgivings.

Our first hut, Clinton Forks, was 5 miles from the boat landing, and it began raining as we disembarked. The Australians took off at a jog and were quickly out of sight. We crossed the bridge over the Clinton River and followed a "bush track" through a beautiful beech forest. It stopped raining, and sunlight glittered on the leaves.

We walked and talked, then stopped for a "brew up" (a trailside tea party) and for taking lots of photos, so it was mid-afternoon before we arrived at the hut. If I'd seen our spartan lodgings before the forest beauty had mellowed me I might've been upset. As it was, I hesitated a moment—then began unloading my pack.

That night we dined on sausages and pooled our food supplies—Donald had loaded up on dehydrated Surprise brand peas, and there were plenty to go around. The Aussies, however, preferred a diet of Fosters Lager and generous portions of whisky. About halfway through their first case of beer they broke into song: traditional carols, tunes from *Godspell,* and an occasional chorus of "Waltzing Matilda." Other Christmas Eves had been more elegant, but none more enjoyable.

In the morning we watched in delight as the 13-month-old girl presented her parents with a unique gift by taking her first steps across the hut. (Since then, the Department of Conservation has prohibited children under 10 from the Track.)

We walked the 8 miles to Mintaro Hut, passing from the light greens of beech and fern to darker trunks resembling a scene from a gothic fairy tale. We picnicked near some rapids, with waterfalls cascading over granite cliffs.

Except for a few brief showers, the weather held during the day, but rain that turned to hail started about the time we sighted the hut. We dressed for Christmas dinner in hiking gear and feasted on rehydrated beef stroganoff and more Surprise peas accompanied by a fine New Zealand wine. Near the end of dinner, one of the Aussies stepped outside and returned with the news that it was snowing.

Thousands of miles from home, I was in an isolated wilderness hut on Christmas night and was sure I'd never been happier. Donald scattered the rest of the peas on the hut's steps for the birds, and we climbed into our sleeping bags. The last thing I remember hearing was a faint chorus of "Waltzing Matilda."

and feel of nature left to itself—it's utterly impossible to emerge without a greater sense of the earth's rhythms. It's a walk closely regulated by park authorities, both for the safety of hikers and for the preservation of this wilderness area, yet there is no intrusion on individual response to nature once you begin the journey.

You set out from Te Anau Downs, 27½km (17 miles) north of Te Anau township, where a launch takes you to the head of the lake. You'll sleep in well-equipped lodge/huts with bunk beds, cooking facilities, and toilets, but you must carry your own sleeping bag, food, and cooking utensils. Overnight huts are manned by custodians, should you need any assistance along the way. At Sandfly Point, another launch ferries you across Milford Sound. Upon arrival, you may elect to spend the night at Milford or to return to Te Anau, but reservations are a must, whichever you choose.

You must be over 10 years of age, an experienced tramper, and apply to the **Department of Conservation,** Milford Track Booking Office, P.O. Box 29, Te Anau (☎ **03/249-8514**). Reservations are accepted from early November to mid-April for the following tramping season, which runs from mid-October to mid-April. No more than 24 people are booked to start the walk on any given day, and applications begin coming in early for specific days.

There are two ways to walk the Milford Track: as a member of an organized group or as independent walker. The Te Anau Travelodge Hotel offers an excellent **guided walk,** which includes guides, cooked meals at the overnight huts, and accommodations at each end of the trek. Fees run about NZ$1,412 (U.S. $918). As an independent, you take care of all these details yourself, at a cost of about NZ$188 (U.S. $122.20).

Other popular walks in this area are the **Hollyford Valley** and the **Kepler.** The Hollyford is a relatively flat track that takes you out to the coast at Martins Bay. It can be walked round-trip, or one way with an optional fly out to Milford Sound. Another option is to use a jet boat to avoid the "Demon Trail" section. This is one of the few Fiordland trails that can be walked year round (there are no alpine crossings).

The 67km (42-mile) **Kepler Track** is a circular trail starting and ending at the Lake Te Anau outlet control gates. It takes four days to complete, and en route trampers pass through beautiful forests and along the edges of Lakes Te Anau and Manapouri. For further information on this walk and others in the vicinity, see "The Best Hikes: Queenstown and Fiordland," in Chapter 4.

Where to Stay

Between Christmas and the end of February, accommodations are tightly booked in Te Anau (most are occupied by the week by holidaying Kiwi families), and you should reserve as far ahead as possible or plan to stay outside the township. Other times, there are usually ample accommodations available.

The rates given below include GST.

MOTELS

Amber Court Motel, 68 Quintin Dr., Te Anau. ☎ **03/249-7230.** Fax 03/249-7486.

9 units (all with bath). TV TEL **Transportation:** Courtesy-car service available.

Rates: NZ$79–NZ$109 (U.S. $51.35–$70.85) single or double. Additional person NZ$15 (U.S. $9.75) extra. AE, DC, MC, V.

This hostelry is in a quiet in-town location, with one- and two-bedroom units that sleep two to eight. There's a guest laundry and—most unusual—a car wash. The hosts can arrange sightseeing reservations and will furnish a cooked breakfast at an extra charge.

Redwood Motel, 26 McKerrow St. (P.O. Box 161), Te Anau. ☎ **03/249-7746.** Fax 03/249-7607. 6 units (all with bath), 1 house. TV TEL **Transportation:** Courtesy-car service available.

Rates: NZ$60 (U.S. $39) unit for one; NZ$75–NZ$85 (U.S. $48.75–$55.25) unit for two; NZ$80 (U.S. $52) house for two. Additional adult NZ$15 (U.S. $9.75) extra; additional child NZ$10 (U.S. $6.50). AE, MC, V.

Some of Te Anau's nicest motel units are presided over by friendly hosts Shirley and Allan Bradley. The Redwood is centrally located on a quiet residential street. The units are nicely furnished, sparkling clean, and beautifully equipped. All have central heating, and four even have their own washing machines (guest laundry on the premises for others). There's also a three-bedroom house on the grounds with full kitchen, bath and shower, and private garden—ideal for families. A children's playground is also on the premises. A continental breakfast is available at a small charge.

A BED-&-BREAKFAST

Matai Lodge, 42 Mokonui St., Te Anau. ☎ and fax **03/249-7360.** 7 rms (none with bath).

Rates (including breakfast): NZ$54 (U.S. $35.10) single; NZ$72 (U.S. $46.80) double; NZ$99 (U.S. $63.35) triple. AE, DC, MC, V. **Closed:** June–Aug.

The Matai Lodge is only one block from the lakefront and has its rooms in a long block, with toilet and showers at one end. The rooms all have hot and cold running water, are tastefully decorated, and have heaters as well as electric blankets and comforters. The lounge is spacious, with comfortable seating, and there's a separate TV lounge. You're given several choices on the menu for the fully cooked breakfast. Host Richard Bevan is very helpful: He knows the area well and enjoys sharing sightseeing information with guests and booking tours, cruises, and the like. He will also store baggage for trampers, and there is off-street parking for drivers. No smoking is permitted in the lodge.

A HOSTEL

YHA Hostel, 220–224 Milford Rd., Te Anau. ☎ **03/249-7847.** 42 beds (no rooms with bath).

Rates: NZ$17 (U.S. $11.05) per person double or twin; NZ$15 ($9.75) dorm bed. MC, V.

This is a real standout, one of the most attractive hostels in the country. It adjoins a sheep meadow in a very central location and has 42 beds in six pine-paneled rooms with central heating, with plans to add more beds in the near future. There's a nicely equipped kitchen, a lounge (with a pot-belly stove), dining room, and laundry; in January, overflow accommodation is available. This is the ideal place to begin and

READERS RECOMMEND

Manapouri Glade Motor Park & Hotel, Murrell Avenue, Manapouri (☎ **03/249-6623**). *"I highly recommend this place to your readers, especially if they are going on the all-day Doubtful Sound trip. It's at the end of the road, across the street from the water, and it's incredibly beautiful and peaceful. Also in Manapouri, I recommend the Hays Store and Restaurant—Mrs. Hays's home-cooking is not to be missed."*—Meg Barth Gammon, Kailua, Hawaii, U.S.A. [**Author's Note:** Manapouri (pop. 278) is about 12km (7 miles) from Te Anau.]

end your Milford Track, Routeburn, Hollyford, Dusky, or Greenstone Track walks. They can also arrange discounted tours and sightseeing fees for YHA members.

CABINS & CAMPGROUNDS

If you want to do some tramping in the Fiordland National Park on a lesser scale than the Milford Track, conservation officers will supply a map of trails and overnight hut locations. The park huts are basic shelters that provide a place to bunk down and cook simple fare. The overnight fee is NZ$6 to NZ$14 (U.S. $3.90 to $9.10) per person.

WORTH THE EXTRA MONEY

★ **Te Anau Travelodge Hotel,** 64 Lakefront Dr. (P.O. Box 185), Te Anau. ☎ **03/249-7411.** Fax 03/249-7947. 112 rms (all with bath), 15 villa suites. MINIBAR TV TEL

$ **Rates:** NZ$112.50 (U.S. $73.15) single or double; NZ$208 (U.S. $135.20) villa suite for one or two. AE, BC, DC, MC, V.

This resort hotel on the lakefront is *the* superior accommodation in this area. Guest rooms all have tea and coffee facilities, and hairdryers are available from reception. The villa suites consist of a lounge, bedroom, kitchen, and bath. On-premises amenities include two restaurants, three bars, a pool, spas, saunas, and two guest laundries.

Where to Eat

In addition to the places mentioned below, the café in the **Kiwi Country Complex,** on Milford Road, is a good choice for a quick pick-me-up.

Bailey's, in the Luxmore Resort Hotel, Milford Rd. ☎ **249-7526.**

Cuisine: NEW ZEALAND. **Reservations:** Recommended.
Prices: Appetizers NZ$7.95–NZ$9.50 (U.S. $5.15–$6.20); main courses NZ$15–NZ$17 (U.S. $9.75–$11.05). AE, MC, V.
Open: Daily 7:30am–9:30pm.

Right in the center of town, Bailey's offers a range of food—from all-day breakfasts to morning and afternoon teas, to lunches of sandwiches, pies, and casseroles, to full à la carte dinners in the evenings. Fully licensed.

$ **Henry's Family Restaurant,** in the Te Anau Travelodge Hotel, 64 Lakefront Dr. ☎ **249-7411.**

Cuisine: NEW ZEALAND. **Reservations:** Not required.
Prices: Main courses NZ$15–NZ$23 (U.S. $9.75–$14.95); lunch NZ$8–NZ$15 (U.S. $5.20–$9.75). AE, DC, MC, V.
Open: Lunch daily noon–2pm; dinner daily 5:30–9pm.

The lakefront setting is rustic and the food reasonably priced. The atmosphere is much like that of a frontier saloon, with a pot-belly stove and bare wooden tables. New Zealand specialties include Milford Sound crayfish, Fiordland venison, Steward Island salmon, and lamb. Fully licensed.

READERS RECOMMEND

Jintz Restaurant, in the Te Anau Motor Park, Te Anau–Manapouri Road, Te Anau (☎ **249-7457**). *"Such a wonderful surprise! The food was excellent in preparation and seasoning. There was one young man in the kitchen whose only job was to arrange the fresh flower and herb decorations on the plates. My pavlova was almost too pretty to eat."* —Pauline Cooper, Westminster, Calif., U.S.A.

For more elegant (and expensive) dinners, reserve at the Travelodge's **MacKinnon Room,** which specializes in local delicacies, including fresh crayfish. The Te Anau Travelodge Hotel can pack a very good **picnic lunch** for your Milford Sound day trip or tramping, if you notify them the night before.

Pop-in Catering, in the Waterfront Merchants Complex, 92 Lakefront Dr. ☎ **249-7807.**
Cuisine: ICE CREAM/LIGHT MEALS. **Reservations:** Not required.
Prices: NZ$5–NZ$9 (U.S. $3.25–$5.85). No credit cards.
Open: Summer, daily 7am–8:30pm. Off-season, daily 7:30am–6pm.

Diagonally across from Fiordland Travel is this window-lined restaurant serving light meals at very moderate prices in a setting that overlooks the lake. A glass-walled conservatory affords 180° views. Everything is home-cooked and baked right on the premises. Sandwiches, meat pies, salad plates, barbecue, Kiwi-style chicken, venison, beef, and baked-on-the-premises pastries can meet just about any size hunger attack. Licensed.

The Milford Road

You'll be driving (or riding in a coach) through fascinating geographical, archeological, and historical country, through the **Eglinton and Hollyford valleys,** the **Homer Tunnel,** and down the majestic **Cleddau Gorge** to Milford Sound. To open your eyes to just what you're seeing, beyond the spectacular mountain scenery, take a tip from this dedicated Milford lover and contact the **Fiordland National Park Visitors Centre,** Lakefront Drive (P.O. Box 29), Te Anau (☎ **03/429-7921;** fax 03/249-7613), for information on **Fiordland National Park,** and ask specifically for their pamphlet **"The Road to Milford,"** which illuminates each mile of the way. It's a good idea, too, to arm yourself with insect repellent against sand flies, which can be murderous at Milford.

Highway 94 from Te Anau to Milford Sound leads north along the lake, with islands and wooded far shores on your left. The drive is, of necessity, a slow one as you wend your way through steep climbs between walls of solid rock and down through leafy glades. Keep an eye out for the keas, sometimes perched along the roadside trying to satisfy their insatiable curiosity about visitors to their domain. **Homer Tunnel,** about 101km (63 miles) along, is a major engineering marvel: a three-quarter-mile passageway first proposed in 1889 by William Homer, begun in 1935, and finally opened in 1940. It was, however, the summer of 1954 before a connecting road was completed and the first private automobile drove through. Incidentally, during winter months take those NO STOPPING—AVALANCHE ZONE signs very seriously. No matter how much you may want to stop for a photo, *don't!*—it could cost you your life.

Some 6km (4 miles) past the tunnel you'll see **"The Chasm"** signposted on a bridge (the sign is small, so keep a sharp eye out). By all means take the time to stop and walk the short trail back into the forest, where a railed platform lets you view a natural sculpture of smooth and craggy rocks along the riverbed of the **Cleddau River.** As the river rushes through, a sort of natural tiered fountain is formed by its waters pouring through rock apertures. Well worth the time and the short walk.

WHERE TO STAY & EAT EN ROUTE

Te Anau Downs Motor Inn, Hwy. 94 (P.O. Box 19, Te Anau). ☎ **03/249-7811,** or toll free **0800/500-805** in New Zealand. Fax 03/249-7753.
28 B&B rms, 24 motel units (all with bath). TV

Rates: NZ$38 (U.S. $24.70) per person B&B room; NZ$89–NZ$109 (U.S. $57.85–$70.85) apartment for one or two. Additional person in apartment NZ$17 (U.S. $11.05) extra. Best Western and AA discounts available. AE, DC, MC, V. **Closed:** June Aug.

Dave Moss, president of Best Western NZ, owns and operates this outstanding property on the road between Te Anau and Milford Sound. There are B&B rooms with private facilities and one-bedroom motel apartments that are neat and modern, with cooking and eating utensils, fridge, electric rangette, and color TV. There's a laundry available to all guests. Dave also runs a licensed restaurant with a local reputation for serving the largest and best roast dinner in the area at reasonable prices. It's located about 30km (19 miles) from Te Anau.

3 Milford Sound

119km (74 miles) NE of Te Anau, 286km (177 miles) NW of Queenstown

No matter what time of year you arrive or what the weather is like, your memories of Milford Sound are bound to be very special. Its 14 nautical miles leading to the Tasman Sea are lined with mountain peaks that rise sharply to heights of 6,000 and 7,000 feet. Forsters fur seals sport on rocky shelves, dolphins play in waters that reach depths up to 2,000 feet, and its entrance is so concealed when viewed from the sea that Captain Cook sailed right by it without noticing when he was charting these waters some 200 years ago.

It rains a lot in Milford—some 300 inches annually, more than in any other one place in New Zealand. I personally don't mind the rain, for the sound (which is actually a fjord carved out by glacial action) shows yet another side of its nature under dripping skies—the trip out to the Tasman in the rain is as special in its own way as one when the sun is shining. Ah, but on a fine day, when the sky is blue, the water reflects varying shades of green and blue and dark brown, the bush that flourishes even on sheer rock walls glows a deep, shiny green—that day is to be treasured forever.

In summer, coaches pour in at the rate of 30 or more each day for launch cruises. That tide slows in other months, but the launches go out year round, rain or shine. As is the custom at some of New Zealand's isolated beauty spots, the THC hotel is the center of things, and in the case of the THC Milford, that continues a tradition that began in 1891, when Elizabeth Sutherland (wife of the sound's first settler) built a 12-room boardinghouse to accommodate seamen who called into the sound.

What to See & Do

To be fully appreciated, Milford Sound must be seen from the deck of one of the launches, with the skipper filling you in on every peak, cove, creature, and plant you pass. Both the THC and Fiordland Travel run ★ **cruise excursions.** The 2½-hour cruise takes you out into the Tasman where you see the shoreline close and understand how it is that the sound's entrance escaped Captain Cook's keen eye. Even in warm weather, a jacket or sweater will likely feel good out on the water, and if it should be raining, you'll be glad of a raincoat.

I've been out on Milford Sound in many different boats over the years, and my conclusion is that Fiordland Travel's *Milford Wanderer* is my favorite vessel. It's the only motor-sailor on the run and costs NZ$40 (U.S. $26) for adults and NZ$10 (U.S. $6.50) for children. It operates from October through April. Fiordland's *Milford Haven* and *Milford Monarch* operate year round, and their excursions cost NZ$38 (U.S. $24.70) for adults and NZ$10 (U.S. $6.50) for children.

If you can stay over long enough, there are some marvelous ★ **walks** from Milford Sound. Some climb into the peaks, others meander along the shore or up close to waterfalls. Ask at the Fiordland National Park Visitor Centre in Te Anau (see above) or at the reception desk of the THC Milford Sound. It's worth the effort to know this timeless place from the land as well as the water.

I find the tiny (2,650-foot-long) ★ **airstrip** a constant source of fascination on every trip. The air controller here talks in by radio more than 5,000 planes every year, and that without the help of such safety devices as lights or radar. The perfect safety record is accounted for by the fact that pilots must be rated specifically for this airfield, so they know what they're about as they zoom down, dwarfed by those stupendous mountain peaks. I rather suspect, also, that careful monitoring of weather conditions and a watchful eye on all air traffic within radio range have a lot to do with that record. Among the clientele are scenic flights and farmers who drop down in their private planes. The airfield is a short (less than five-minute) walk from the THC.

On the other side of the airstrip, another short walk will bring you to the **fishing facilities** on the Cleddau River, an interesting and colorful sight, since there are nearly always a few of the fishing boats tied up in this safe anchorage.

Where to Stay

It's possible to overnight on the water from October to April, for the ★ ***Milford Wanderer*** sleeps up to 70. Sleeping bags are provided, and dinner and breakfast are included in the package: NZ$118 (U.S. $76.70) for adults and NZ$59 (U.S. $38.35) for children.

Milford Sound Lodge, Hwy. 94 (Private Bag, Te Anau), Milford Sound, Fiordland. ☎ and fax **03/249-8071.** 23 rms (none with bath).

Rates: NZ$20 (U.S. $13) single; NZ$45 (U.S. $29.25) double; NZ$16 (U.S. $10.40) dorm bed; NZ$9 (U.S. $5.85) campervan site. AE, MC, V.

This is the only accommodation at Milford Sound other than the THC Milford Sound (below). In it, you'll find a simple, dormitory-type lodging in gorgeous surroundings just a short, beautiful mile from the sound. Basic rooms mostly hold four beds—nothing more in the way of furnishings—and the toilet-and-shower block is immaculate. There's also a big lounge with a fireplace, cooking facilities, a restaurant, and laundry facilities. Many hikers who walk the Milford Track stay here on their first night back—perhaps to prolong a too-rare close communion with nature in the wooded site. You'll get an early night's sleep—power is shut off at 10pm.

WORTH THE EXTRA MONEY

★ **THC Milford Sound Hotel,** Private Bag, Milford Sound, Fiordland. ☎ **03/249-7926,** or toll free **0800/657-444** in New Zealand. Fax 03/249-8094. 35 rms (all with bath), 1 suite. TV TEL

Rates: NZ$135–NZ$214 (U.S. $87.75–$139.10) single or double; NZ$340 (U.S. $221) suite. Occasional off-season special packages available. AE, BC, DC, MC, V.

This is the one "big splurge" I would hate to miss in New Zealand. The historic hotel faces the waterfront, amid lawns and shrubs that have grown twisted into stylized shapes. To watch the sun set and darkness descend over Mitre Peak from the glass-walled lounge is a memorable experience. There's a comfortable patina overlaying the lounge, convivial bar, and dining room. The bedroom furnishings are tired, but tea and coffee makings and TVs are provided; video is available each evening in the lounge. The rooms in front have wall-width windows to take advantage of the striking view ("economy rooms" face the back). And it's the view and the atmosphere that make this place worth the extra money. Periodic off-season specials are real bargains.

Where to Eat

You can eat very inexpensively in the nearby **Public Bar,** which serves pub grub. Or you can bring a **picnic lunch** with you from Te Anau.

The Lobster Pot, in the THC Milford Sound Hotel, on the waterfront. ☎ **249-7926.**

Cuisine: NEW ZEALAND. **Reservations:** Recommended.

Prices: Breakfast buffet NZ$14 (U.S. $9.10); lunch buffet NZ$27 (U.S. $17.55); dinner NZ$30 (U.S. $19.50) for two courses, NZ$36 (U.S. $23.40) for three courses. AE, DC, MC, V.

Open: Breakfast daily 7–9am; lunch daily 11:30am–2pm; dinner daily 6–9pm.

Treat yourself and dine in the THC Milford Sound, next to a window looking out on the sound and Mitre Peak. The menu features the freshest of New Zealand produce, along with soup, dessert, and coffee. You might add another bit to the tab for a glass of wine and dine happily in anticipation of the launch cruise ahead.

En Route to . . .

DUNEDIN

The drive to Dunedin from Te Anau takes about 4½ hours over good roads. Take Highway 94 across Gorge Hill into Lumsden, across the **Waimea Plains** to the milling center of **Gore,** through farmlands to **Clinton,** and across rolling downs to **Balclutha.** As you approach Balclutha, look for ★ **Peggydale** (☎ **03/418-2345**), an ideal stopping point for tea, scones, sandwiches, or salad plates in the lovely Tea Kiosk. Peggydale handles a wide range of handcrafts—leather goods and sheepskin products (some made in their leathercraft shop), hand-knits, etc.—even paintings by local artists. They're open daily from 8:30am to 5pm and will send you a mail-order catalog on request. From there, it's Highway 1 north along the coast past **Milton** to **Lookout Point,** where you'll get your first look at Dunedin. Along the way, you may want to stop in **Mossburn,** where **Wapiti Handcrafts Ltd.,** on the main street, makes and sells deerskin fashions.

INVERCARGILL

If Invercargill is your destination, you'll take Highway 94 only as far as **Lumsden,** then turn south on Highway 6 to ride through rolling farm and sheep country all the way down to Invercargill, 157km (102 miles) from Te Anau.

MOUNT COOK

If Mount Cook is your next destination after exploring Fiordland, you'll need to head north on State Highway 6, turn east at **Frankton** (just outside Queenstown), and then pick up State Highway 8 at **Cromwell** and go north. The distance from Te Anau to Mount Cook is 433km (268 miles); the drive will take about 6½ hours. If you start in Queenstown, you'll be covering 263km (163 miles), and the trip will take about 4 hours.

Cromwell's identity completely changed in 1992 when **Lake Dunstan** was formed by the massive Clyde Dam on the Clutha River. The original commercial center of the town is now under the new lake, as are more than 2,500 acres of productive orchards. The folks at **Cromwell & Districts Information Centre,** 47 The Mall, Cromwell (☎ **03/445-0212;** fax 03/445-1649), can fill you in on the details.

Where to Stay en Route

$ **The Briars,** Ahuriri Heights (P.O. Box 98), Omarama. ☎ **03/438-9615.** 2 rms (neither with bath).

Rates (including breakfast): NZ$35 (U.S. $22.75) single; NZ$65 (U.S. $42.25) double. No credit cards.

The Briars, about 2km (1 mile) north of Omarama and an hour from Mount Cook, is the perfect place to overnight en route to Mount Cook, especially if you leave Te Anau or Queenstown later than you expected. Marylou and Don Blue have a very attractive modern house high on a hill just off State Highway 8. From their living-room window and the veranda is a good view of the Ben Mor Range. The decor includes some lovely antiques, lots of books, paintings of MacKensie Country scenery, and an impressive porcelain collection. The Blues have retired from farming and now enjoy gardening and tramping. The guest quarters are on a separate level, where two twin-bedded rooms share one bath. Wise travelers will arrive at this rural homestay by 5pm so they can enjoy afternoon tea with their congenial hosts.

4 Mount Cook

263km (163 miles) NE of Queenstown, 331km (199 miles) SW of Christchurch

GETTING THERE • By Plane With regularly scheduled service, Mount Cook Airline has flights between Mount Cook and Queenstown and Te Anau.

• By Bus There is daily coach service via Mount Cook Landline and InterCity between Mount Cook and Christchurch, Queenstown, and Timaru.

• By Car Mount Cook can be reached via Highway 80.

ESSENTIALS • Orientation A T-intersection at the end of the highway marks the entrance to Mount Cook Village. Turn left and you pass the Mt. Cook Travelodge, a modern, moderately priced motor hotel, and the youth hostel, post office, grocery shop, Alpine Guides Mountain Shop, and finally the DOC Visitor Information Centre. Turn right at the intersection and you pass Mount Cook Chalets before reaching the elegant, peak-roofed internationally famous Hermitage Hotel.

• Information At the **Department of Conservation Visitor Information Centre** (☎ **03/435-1818**), open daily from 8am to 5pm, conservation officers can give you the latest information on weather and road conditions, and it's a strict requirement that trampers into the wild check in with them and sign the intentions register. They can also fill you in on high-altitude huts, picnic grounds, and recommended walks in the area. **Alpine Guides (Mount Cook) Ltd.,** P.O. Box 20, Mount Cook (☎ **03/435-1834**) can also provide a wealth of information on alpine activities, schedules, and fees.

• Telephone The telephone area code (STD) for Mount Cook is **03.**

Tiny Mount Cook Village is known the world over for its splendid alpine beauty and its remoteness. It sits within the 173,000 acres of **Mount Cook National Park,** some

2,510 feet above sea level and surrounded by 140 peaks over 7,000 feet high, 22 of which are over 10,000 feet. Most famous of all the Southern Alps is **Mount Cook/ Aoraki,** which soars 12,316 feet into the sky (it lost 60 feet in a 1991 avalanche). A full third of the park is permanent snow and ice, and the famed **Tasman Glacier** is the longest known outside of arctic regions—29km (18 miles) long and 3km (2 miles) wide. More difficult to get onto than either Fox or Franz Josef, it's still accessible for exhilarating downhill swoops on skis.

The park's most noted plant is the mountain buttercup, known as the Mount Cook lily, a pure-white blossom with thickly clustered petals and as many as 30 blooms to a stalk. There are, however, more than 300 species of native plants growing within park boundaries. Many have been marked by park staff so you can identify them as you walk. Bird sounds fill the air, most notably that of the mischievous kea, that curious little native parrot, which has clearly earned the nickname "Clown of the Snowline," and I strongly advise you to heed the "Do Not Feed" advice from park staff. Most animal life has been introduced—Himalayan thar and chamois. Hunting permits are issued by park staff.

What to See & Do

No need to tell you what to see—it's all around you! And if you missed the ★ **skiplane scenic flights** at Fox and Franz Josef, you'll have another chance here. The planes lift off some 2,000 feet above sea level to begin an hour-long flight, which includes glimpses of Fox and Franz Josef and a 5-minute snow landing; the less expensive 40-minute flight surveys the Tasman Glacier only; and there are other options as well, with fares ranging from NZ$88 to NZ$283 (U.S. $57.20 to $183.95) for adults, NZ$66 to NZ$212 (U.S. $42.90 to $137.80) for children. Book through Mount Cook Airline (☎ **435-1849** locally, or toll free **0800/800-737** nationwide).

Alpine Guides (☎ **03/435-1834**) conducts two-hour **coach excursions** to the Tasman Glacier for about NZ$28 (U.S. $18.20) per person.

Skiers will undoubtedly head for the Tasman during the June-to-October ski season, but you should know in advance that **skiing** is neither inexpensive nor for those whose expertise leaves anything to be desired. Skiing on the glacier involves two runs of about 11km (7 miles) each, with skiplanes returning you to the top after the first run and flying you out at the end of the day. Before you embark on the great adventure, you'll have to convince the Alpine Guides that you're reasonably good on skis. The price for this glorious day to add to your ski tales will run about NZ$550 (U.S. $357.50). That's if *the weather is right*—it could run considerably higher if you have to wait for the weather to break, which could be a few days, and that means additional lodging, eating, and drinking expenses. Book through Mount Cook Airline or Alpine Guides.

All those high-priced activities (and in my opinion, they're worth every penny if you have the pennies) do *not* mean there are no budget activities at Mount Cook. First of all, the sheer grandeur of the place costs nothing and is there for all. Park conservation officers will furnish a map of **easy walks,** which take anywhere from half an hour to half a day—no charge, and you'll commune with Mother Nature all the way. Individual booklets are available to explain the flora you'll be seeing.

Alpine Guides rents ski and climbing equipment and can furnish guides to take you **mountain climbing.** There's a four-day hike, which leaves you at Fox Glacier via a transalpine crossing; a range of climbing experiences for those from novice to expert level; and special guided expeditions to the top of Mount Cook itself. These are *not,* however, budget activities. Alpine Guides can give you full details and make reservations.

If you're here in late September or early October, you'll be able to enjoy the annual **Mt. Cook Alpine Festival.**

EVENING ENTERTAINMENT

The liveliest spot after dark is the **Tavern** in the village, as campers and hostelers come crowding in after a day on the slopes in all that mountain air. The **Snowline Bar** in the Hermitage Hotel is more elegant and features a wonderful mountain view. The house bar at the Mt. Cook Travelodge is the **Chamois Bar and Lounge.** That's most of Mount Cook Village's nightlife—and after a day amid so many of Mother Nature's wonders, it's likely to be enough!

Where to Stay

Most accommodations—at any price level—are owned by Southern Pacific Hotels, and the pickings are poor in the budget range. One alternative, if you're driving, is to stay at nearby locations: Twizel, Fairlie, Tekapo, Omarama, and Kurow are under a two-hour drive and have motels aplenty. Glentanner Park, 14 miles from Mount Cook Village, is a well-equipped motor camp. Needless to say, with such a scarcity of rooms, advance reservations are an absolute necessity!

The rates listed below include GST.

CHALETS

Mount Cook Chalets, Mount Cook Village (Private Bag, Mount Cook N.P.).
☎ **03/435-1809.** Fax 03/435-1879. 18 chalets (all with bath). TV

Rates: NZ$113 (U.S. $73.45) chalet for up to four. AE, DC, MC, V. **Closed:** Winter.

These chalets are A-frame prefab structures but are attractive, comfortable, and convenient, with several bright chairs in the felt-floored living area. There's a hotplate, fry pan, small fridge, bathroom facilities, and electric heaters. Two curtained-off sections hold two small bunks in each, and linen is provided. It's an efficient use of space, which manages to be pleasing to the eye as well. The complex, located in the village, includes parking space and a laundry with washers, dryers, and irons.

A LODGE

Mt. Cook Travelodge, Mount Cook Village (Private Bag, Mount Cook N.P.).
☎ **03/435-1879.** 57 rms (all with bath). TV TEL

Rates: NZ$191 (U.S. $124.15) single or double. AE, DC, MC, V.
Closed: Winter.

The Mt. Cook Travelodge is an attractive block of 57 rooms with nice decor, plus a convivial house bar that serves as a magnet for après-ski or après-sightseeing/flightseeing gatherings. One reader even ranks the Travelodge above the Hermitage Hotel (below). The Wakefield Restaurant serves a buffet dinner for NZ$30 (U.S. $19.50).

A HOSTEL

YHA Hostel, Bowen and Kitchener drives (P.O. Box 26), Mount Cook 8770.
☎ **03/435-1820.** 5 rms (none with bath), 52 beds.

Rates: NZ$19 (U.S. $12.35) double or twin for members; NZ$17 (U.S. $11.05) dorm bed for members. Nonmembers pay an additional NZ$4 (U.S. $2.60). MC, V.

There are four twin rooms, one double room, one four-bed room, and eight six-bed rooms at this pretty alpine-style hostel in the village. Cooking facilities are good, and there are a large common room, a shop, and a sauna. Best of all, the large peaked window wall frames a fair share of that gorgeous snowcapped mountain scene. Reservations are essential during summer.

CAMPING

Camping and caravaning are permitted in the park, but only at designated sites (*not* in the bush), which have water and toilets. If you use these facilities, remember that lighting fires is prohibited within park boundaries. Check with the park visitor information center for locations and conditions. Hikers and mountaineers have the use of 12 huts in the park, most of which have stoves, cooking and eating utensils, fuel, blankets, and radios with emergency lines. Only two of these are within reach of the casual tramper—the others are at high altitudes and you'd need to be an experienced, expert climber to reach them. Fees for overnight use of the huts are about NZ$14 (U.S. $9.10) per person, and arrangements and payment must be made at the Department of Conservation Visitor Information Centre.

WORTH THE EXTRA MONEY

★ **THC Hermitage Hotel,** Mount Cook Village (Private Bag, Mount Cook N.P.). ☎ **03/435-2809,** or toll free **0800/801-111** in New Zealand. Fax 03/435-1879. 104 rms (all with bath). MINIBAR TV TEL

Rates: NZ$214–NZ$276 (U.S. $139.10–$179.40) single or double. AE, DC, MC, V.

Rooms at the world-famous Hermitage Hotel can only be classified as a "big splurge," but in this isolated wonderland, this may be the place to do it. The rooms qualify in every sense as "premium," the views are magnificent, and there are good restaurants and bars as well as a spa and sauna, a tennis court, and an activities desk.

NEARBY PLACES TO STAY

Because of the scarcity of accommodations at Mount Cook, Twizel (less than an hour's drive away) makes a good base.

High Country Holiday Lodge, P.O. Box 16, Twizel. ☎ **03/435-0671.** 100 rms (some with bath), 9 motel units (all with bath).

Rates: NZ$48 (U.S. $31.20) single or double without bath, NZ$58 (U.S. $37.70) single or double with bath; NZ$70 (U.S. $45.50) single or double motel unit; N$15 (U.S. $9.75) backpacker's bed. MC, V.

The High Country Holiday Lodge is set amid lawns and shade trees just minutes away from shops, a skating rink, tennis courts, squash courts, a golf course, and pools. Nearby Lake Ruataniwha offers boating, jet skiing, windsurfing, and picnic areas. Incidentally, this area has some of the best fishing in the country, as well as excellent mountain tramping. The lodge holds single and double rooms and motel apartments, all serviced daily; the comfortable backpacker beds are in rooms with hot and cold running water, with centrally located bathroom facilities and a self-catering kitchen. The licensed restaurant/café is open all day.

MacKenzie Country Inn, Ostler Rd., Twizel. ☎ **03/627-0869.** Fax 03/627-0857. 80 rms and motel units (all with bath). TV TEL

Rates: NZ$110 (U.S. $71.50) single, double, triple, or apartment for one, two, or three. AE, DC, MC, V.

This attractive in-town hostelry offers serviced rooms and motel units with tea and coffee facilities and a communal kitchen. On the premises are a licensed restaurant, a bistro, bars, a games room, and a guest laundry. Readers have commented on the "spacious rooms with fantastic views of Mount Cook."

Where to Eat

In Mount Cook Village, budgeteers will gravitate to the **Mount Cook General Store,** which stocks grocery items.

At the **Hermitage Hotel,** the least expensive option is the **coffee shop,** which offers light meals and snacks and closes at 6pm. The **Alpine Room** serves an extensive buffet lunch for NZ$29.25 (U.S. $19), as well as à la carte dinners featuring New Zealand specialties for about NZ$30 (U.S. $19.50) for two courses. The **Panorama Room** serves up fantastic sunset views and gourmet fare. You'll spend about NZ$60 (U.S. $39) per person if you decide to endulge in a mega-splurge here. You might be wiser to buy the beautifully illustrated *Mount Cook Book* for NZ$35 (U.S. $22.75) and prepare the recipes back home.

At the **Wakefield Restaurant** in the **Travelodge,** buffet dinners cost NZ$30.50 (U.S. $19.85).

En Route to Christchurch

Christchurch is about a five-hour drive. Follow Highways 80 and 8 to **Fairlie,** about 150km (93 miles). At **Lake Tekapo,** take a minute to visit the **chapel,** whose altar is made from a large block of Oamaru stone and features a carved shepherd. The chapel was built of rock, wood, and stone from the area, and is dedicated to early settlers.

From Fairlie, Highway 79 takes you through **Geraldine,** and if it's lunchtime or teatime as you pass through, consider **Plums,** on the main road. Then it's back to Highway 1, through Canterbury Plains filled with grazing sheep, and across the level terrain you'll see the spires of Canterbury's capital, **Christchurch,** long before you arrive.

WHERE TO STAY EN ROUTE

A Bed-&-Breakfast & More

Kimbell Park Homestead and Colonial Cottages, State Hwy. 8, Kimbell (R.D. 17, Fairlie). ☎ and fax **03/685-8170.** 2 rms (all with bath), 2 cottages.

Rates (including breakfast): NZ$180 (U.S. $117) single in homestead; NZ$200 (U.S. $130) double in homestead; NZ$150 (U.S. $97.50) Laurel Cottage for two; NZ$130 (U.S. $84.50) Walnut Cottage for two. Dinner NZ$15–NZ$30 (U.S. $9.75–$19.50) extra delivered to cottage, NZ$55 (U.S. $35.75) extra for four courses in the homestead. AE, MC, V.

Ron and Kay Collyer live on 400 acres (1½ hours from Mount Cook and 2 hours from Christchurch) where almost 2,000 sheep graze and pretty gardens surround their homestead. They've restored their 1915 house as well as two nearby cottages. If you opt for Walnut Cottage, on the main road next to the pub, you'll find yourself in an 1877 colonial house. One bedroom has a double bed, the other a double and a single. The property also enjoys an herb garden and a trout stream. Kay leaves breakfast ingredients, and guests prepare their own meals in the full kitchen. The same breakfast routine is followed for Laurel Cottage, dating from 1878 and located on Perambulator Lane. Here, one room has a double bed, the other a single. The homestead quarters are more luxurious: one room has a king-size bed and bathroom with a shower; the other has a queen-size bed and a bathtub. Both open onto the garden. Occupants are treated to the finest bed and bath linens, terry robes, toiletries, an early-morning "cuppa" in bed, an elaborate cooked breakfast, and before-dinner drinks. And what else makes this place special? Did I mention that it's also a truffle plantation? Children are not accepted, and smoking is not permitted in the homestead.

12 Southland

INVERCARGILL IS NEW ZEALAND'S SOUTHERNMOST CITY, THE "CAPITAL" OF Southland, a region you entered when you turned south at Lumsden, extending as far northwest as Lake Manapouri and as far east as Balclutha. It is the country's coolest and rainiest region, yet the even spread of its rainfall is the very foundation of its economy, the raising of grass and grass seed, which in turn supports large numbers of sheep stations.

Its coastline saw settlements of Maori (in limited numbers) and whalers, with frequent visits from sealers. From its waters have come those succulent Bluff oysters and crayfish (rock lobsters) you've devoured in your New Zealand travels. In fact they account for about 90% of the value of fish landed in this area.

1 Invercargill

187km (116 miles) S of Queenstown, 221km (137 miles) SW of Dunedin

GETTING THERE • By Plane Both Air New Zealand and Ansett have service between Invercargill and Auckland and Wellington on the North Island; and Christchurch and Dunedin on the South Island.

• By Train The *Southerner* serves Invercargill and Christchurch, Dunedin, and Timaru Monday through Friday. The railway station is on Leven Street.

• By Bus Both Mount Cook Landline and InterCity have coach service between Invercargill and Christchurch, Dunedin, Queenstown, Te Anau, and Timaru. The bus depot is also on Leven Street.

ESSENTIALS • Orientation Invercargill's streets are laid out in neat grid patterns. Main thoroughfares are Tay Street (an extension of Highway 1) and Dee Street (an extension of Highway 6). Many of the principal shops and office buildings are centered around their intersection, and the post office is on Dee Street. Queens Park is a beautiful green oasis (200 acres) right in the center of town and the site of many activities.

• Information You'll find the **Invercargill Visitor Centre** in the Southland Museum and Art Gallery, Victoria Avenue (☎ **03/218-9753**).

• Telephone The telephone area code (STD) is **03.**

The first thing you'll notice about Invercargill is its flatness—a bump is likely to take on the dimensions of a "hill" in these parts! Actually, that flatness is due to the fact that a large part of the city was once boggy swampland. In its reclamation, town planners have turned what might have made for a dull city into a distinct advantage by creating wide, level thoroughfares and great city parks. Invercargill is a *spacious* city. Many of its broad, pleasant streets bear the names of Scottish rivers, revealing the home country of many of its early settlers.

Among its many attractions, perhaps primary, is its proximity to Stewart Island, the legendary anchor of Maui's canoe (which became, of course, the South Island, with the North Island seen as the huge fish he caught). Day trips to Stewart Island are possible any day by air and several times a week by the ferry that runs from nearby Bluff.

What's Special About Southland

- The Southland Museum and Art Gallery, the only place in the country you can view tuataras in a natural setting and a fossilized forest from the Jurassic era.
- Queens Park, a green retreat for the senses in the heart of Invercargill.
- The "Glory Walk," in Bluff, passing through native bush and trees that form a shady canopy overhead.
- The Sterling Point–Ocean Beach Walk, following the coastline around Bluff Hill while the surf breaks against rocks below.
- The Curio Bay Fossil Forest, a sea-washed rock terrace that's 160 million years old.

What to See & Do

Allow at least a full hour to visit the ★ **Southland Museum and Art Gallery,** on Gala Street by the main entrance to Queens Park. The collections inside the Southern Hemisphere's largest pyramid include a multitude of exhibits that'll bring alive much of the history and natural resources of this area. In addition, there's a tuatarium, the only place in the country you can view live tuataras in a simulated natural setting. You can also see a multi-image audiovisual program on New Zealand's subantarctic islands. In front of the museum, examine the section of fossilized forest from the Jurassic era some 160 million years ago. The museum is open Monday through Friday from 9am to 5pm and Saturday, Sunday, and public holidays from 1 to 5pm. Admission is free.

Two minutes from the city, ★ **Queens Park** is just one (the largest) of Invercargill's parklands (a total of 2,975 acres) and might well keep you occupied for the better part of a day. Within its 200 acres are a rhododendron walk; an iris garden; a sunken rose garden; a grove of native and exotic trees; a wildlife sanctuary with wallabies, deer, and an aviary; a duck pond; a winter garden; an 18-hole golf course; tennis courts; and—perhaps most of all—a cool, green retreat for the senses. A very special thing to look for is the beguiling children's fountain encircled by large bronze animal statues. Over the years this beautiful botanical reserve has seen duty as grazing land, a racecourse, and a sporting ground. The entrance is from Queens Drive at Gala Street. There's a delightful café for light refreshments.

Drive out to **Bluff,** Invercargill's port, some 27km ($16^1/_2$ miles) to the south. This is the home port for the Stewart Island ferry, and the site (on the other side of the harbor at Tiwai Point) of the mammoth Tiwai Aluminum Smelter (the only one in the country) whose annual production is 259,000 tons. If you'd like to tour the complex (a fascinating experience), contact **Tiwai Smelter Tours,** NZ Aluminum Smelters Ltd., Private Bag, Invercargill (☎ **03/218-5999**). You must be at least 12 years of age and wear long trousers or slacks, heavy footwear, and clothing that covers your arms. There's no charge, but usually tours are limited to one each day, so it pays to reserve well in advance.

There are two great ★ **walks** in Bluff (ask the Visitor Centre in Invercargill for the "Foveaux Walk, Bluff" pamphlet). The **"Glory Walk"** (named for a sailing vessel, *England's Glory,* which was wrecked at Bluff) is about $1^1/_2$km (1 mile) long and passes through native bush and trees, which form a shady canopy overhead. Ferns and mosses add to the lush greenery. The **Sterling Point–Ocean Beach Walk** begins where Highway 1 ends at Foveaux Strait. It's almost 7km ($4^1/_2$ miles) long, following the coastline around Bluff Hill, with marvelous views of beaches, offshore islands, and surf breaking against coastal rocks. Parking facilities are provided at both ends of the walk, and you are asked to follow the signposts and to leave no litter in your footsteps.

Where to Stay

You should have no trouble finding a place to lay your weary head in Invercargill. There are good budget accommodations in ample quantity, as well as more upmarket motels and hotels.

The rates given below include GST.

A LICENSED HOTEL

Ascot Park Hotel, Tay St. and Racecourse Rd., Invercargill. ☎ **03/217-6195.** Fax 03/217-7002. 54 rms (all with bath), 23 motel units (all with bath). TV TEL

Rates: NZ$143 (U.S. $92.30) single or double room; NZ$90 (U.S. $58.50) single or double motel unit. AE, DC, MC, V.

This is Invercargill's top spot, with hotel rates out of the reach of budget travelers; however, the motel units are affordable. Everyone shares the heated indoor pool, spa, two saunas, and solarium. A licensed restaurant is open daily. The complex is 4km ($2^1/_2$ miles) from the center of town.

MOTELS

Colonial Motor Inn, 335–339 Tay St., Invercargill. ☎ **03/217-6058.** Fax 03/217-6118. 10 units (all with bath). TV TEL

Rates: NZ$70 (U.S. $45.50) single; NZ$78 (U.S. $50.70) double. Additional adults NZ$14 (U.S. $9.10) extra. AE, DC, MC, V.

There are one- and two-bedroom units with dining areas and fully equipped kitchens at the Colonial, five minutes from the city center. Other facilities include a guest laundry, room service, and off-street parking. Continental breakfast is available on request.

Tayesta Motel, 343 Tay St., Invercargill. ☎ **03/217-6074.** Fax 03/217-7075. 12 units (all with bath). TV TEL

Rates: NZ$80 (U.S. $52) apartment for one or two. Additional person NZ$12 (U.S. $7.80) extra. Best Western discounts available. AE, DC, MC, V.

This attractive one-story blue-and-white motel has one- and two-bedroom apartments, each with large picture windows in the lounge, a fully equipped kitchen, central heating, video, and a radio. There's a laundry, plus a play area with swings and sandpit. Continental or cooked breakfasts are available for a small charge. The Tayesta is located a mile from the city center.

READERS RECOMMEND

Montecillo Lodge, 240 Spey St., Invercargill (☎ **03/218-2503**). *"In Invercargill, we took the information office's recommendation and stayed at Montecillo Lodge, which has been lovingly furnished by friendly hosts James and Aileen Horn. Our peach room at the B&B was charming, the breakfast table a picture of propriety, and the price very reasonable."*—Sue and Frank Thorn, Fallbrook, Calif., U.S.A.

A BED-&-BREAKFAST

Gerrards Railway Hotel, 1 Leven St. (at Esk St.), Invercargill. ☎ **03/218-3406.** Fax 03/214-4567. 21 rms (12 with bath).

Rates: NZ$40–NZ$70 (U.S. $26–$45.50) double without bath and with breakfast; NZ$75–NZ$90 (U.S. $48.75–$58.50) double with bath but without breakfast. AE, MC, V.

This interesting 1896 B&B hotel, across from the rail and bus stations, has a rosy-pink brick facade with white trim; the facade has had a face cleaning and the rooms have been redone, thanks to owners Keith and Margaret Gerrard. Though not fancy accommodations, they are comfortable, clean, and centrally located. Showers and toilets are conveniently located for those that share. Rooms with bath also have telephones and TVs. There's a guest TV lounge, cocktail bar, and moderately priced restaurant.

A HOSTEL

YHA Hostel, 122 North Rd., Waikiwi, Invercargill. ☎ **03/215-9344.** 44 beds (no rooms with bath).

Rates: NZ$14 (U.S. $9.10) dorm bed. No credit cards.

The 44 beds here are in six rooms, and other facilities include showers and a kitchen. There's a barbecue/picnic area available for use during the day, and the resident manager can arrange reduced fares to Stewart Island on a standby basis. He can also advise about hostel-type accommodations on the island (there are tentative plans for a YHA hostel, but no timetable yet). The hostel is located on an extension of Dee Street, before it becomes Highway 6.

CABINS & CAMPGROUNDS

The **Invercargill Caravan Park,** 20 Victoria Ave., Invercargill (☎ **03/218-8787**), has two chalets and 21 cabins that sleep one to six people. On the premises are a kitchen, showers and toilets, a laundry, store, car wash, vehicle-storage area, and play area. There are facilities for the disabled, plus 50 campsites and 40 caravan sites. Rates for bunks are NZ$10 (U.S. $6.50) per person; cabins are NZ$22 to NZ$28 (U.S. $14.30 to $18.20) for two; caravan sites run NZ$16 (U.S. $10.40) for two, and tent sites, NZ$7 (U.S. $4.55) per person. It's in a central location, two minutes from McDonald's.

Where to Eat

Invercargill has numerous coffee shops offering good value. The coffee lounge in the **D.I.C. Department Store** has good morning and afternoon teas as well as light lunches, all inexpensive.

Gerrards, in Gerrards Railway Hotel, 1 Leven St., at Esk St. ☎ **218-3406.**

Cuisine: NEW ZEALAND/CONTINENTAL. **Reservations:** Recommended.
Prices: Appetizers NZ$10 (U.S. $6.50); main courses NZ$20 (U.S. $13); average lunch NZ$12 (U.S. $7.80). AE, DC, MC, V.
Open: Lunch Mon–Fri noon–2pm; dinner daily 6:30–9pm.

There's a bright café air about this restaurant, which is a great favorite with locals. The menu is a mixture of native New Zealand and continental dishes and includes coquilles St-Jacques and escalope de porc with mushrooms and brandy-cream sauce, local Bluff oysters, and fresh blue cod in a lemon-and-wine sauce. Service is friendly, and it's fully licensed. Gerrards is in the city center, opposite the rail and bus stations.

The Grand Hotel, 76 Dee St. ☎ **218-8059.**

Cuisine: NEW ZEALAND. **Reservations:** Recommended.
Prices: Appetizers NZ$6–NZ$9 (U.S. $3.90–$5.85); main courses NZ$14 (U.S. $9.10). AE, DC, MC, V.
Open: Dinner only, daily 6–9:30pm.

This elegant hotel in the city center is a joy to go into, even if you don't eat. The lovely formal dining room serves seasonal dishes of mostly local ingredients, using many traditional recipes. If oysters are on the menu in any form, let that be your order—they'll be from Bluff and superior to any you've tasted before. Fully licensed.

$ **Joy's Gourmet Kitchen,** 122 Dee St. ☎ **218-3985.**

Cuisine: LIGHT MEALS/SNACKS. **Reservations:** Not required.
Prices: Average lunch under NZ$8 (U.S. $5.20); less for snacks. No credit cards.
Open: Sat–Thurs 7:30am–6pm, Fri 9am–9pm.

This is the place for quiche, baked potatoes with a variety of fillings, many different salads, nutritious hot meals, light lunches, carrot cake, muesli munch, soups, and cakes—all made daily on the premises and all very good. Try one of their traditional Kiwi roast meals. They also have take-out. Incidentally, owner Peter Breayley and his staff are only too pleased to give advice on sightseeing in the city. It's located in the city center.

A CARVERY TREAT

Friday night in Invercargill means a carvery treat at the ★ $ **Ascot Park Hotel**—to residents as well as visitors—so reservations are a very good idea (in fact, I heard about this feast way up on the North Island when I mentioned coming to Invercargill). The Ascot Park, on the corner of Racecourse Road and Tay Street (☎ **217-6195**), is a modern hotel of the first order, and the carvery is presented in an enormous room with different levels for tables. The spread is just about as enormous as the room, with every kind of seafood currently available, fresh salads, great roasts for non-seafood lovers, and luscious desserts. You'll see parties of locals chatting away with visitors, and there's a party atmosphere all through the place. The price is NZ$29 (U.S. $18.85), for which you get full value, indeed.

En Route to Dunedin

You can drive from Invercargill to Dunedin in a little over three hours by way of Highway 1, through Gore, past farmlands and mile after mile of grazing sheep. It's a pleasant drive, and one I think you'll enjoy.

However, if you have a day to spend on the road, let me urge you to follow the Southern Scenic Route along Highway 92 and allow a full day to loiter along the way, rejoining Highway 1 at Balclutha. If you make this drive, the leaflet **"Drive New Zealand's Southern Scenic Route"** from the Visitor Centre in Invercargill is quite helpful as it details the reserves through which you'll pass.

The **Southern Scenic Route,** as it's known, takes you through a region of truly unusual character. There are great folds in the land covered with such a diversity of native forests that from Chaslands on you'll be in one national forest reserve after the other. Short detours will take you to the coast and golden sand beaches, prominent headlands, and fine bays.

Highway 92, let me hasten to add, is not paved its entire length—however, even unpaved portions are in good driving condition, albeit at a slower speed than the faster

Highway 1. Picnic spots abound, so you can take along a packed lunch from Invercargill, or plan to stop in the country pub in Owaka's only hotel for lunch (stop for refreshments even if you lunch elsewhere—it's an experience you wouldn't want to miss). One very special detour you might consider follows.

Just beyond Fortrose, follow the Fortrose–Otara road to the right, and when you pass the Otara School, look for the turnoff to **Waipapa Point.** The point is the entrance to Foveaux Strait, a treacherous waterway that has scuttled many a sailing vessel and that is now marked by a light, which was first used in 1884. Follow the Otara–Haldane road to Porpoise Bay, then turn right and drive a little over half a mile to the ★ **Curio Bay Fossil Forest,** which is signposted. This sea-washed rock terrace dates back 160 *million* years and is the original floor of a Jurassic subtropical forest of kauri trees, conifers, and other trees that were growing at a time when grasses had not even evolved. At low tide, you can make out low stumps and fallen logs that have been petrified after being buried in volcanic ash, then raised when the sea level changed. You can then retrace your way around Porpoise Bay and follow the signs to Waikawa and continue north to rejoin Highway 92 and travel on to Chaslands.

If you'd like more information about this lovely part of a lovely country, contact the **Department of Conservation,** Otago Peninsula Trust, P.O. Box 492, Dunedin (☎ **03/478-0499**; fax 03/478-0575).

2 Stewart Island

30km (19 miles) SW of Bluff, across Foveaux Strait

GETTING THERE • By Plane The major transport to Stewart Island is via Southern Air, which is based in Invercargill (☎ **03/218-9129,** or toll free **0800/658-876** in New Zealand; fax 03/214-4681), and during the 20-minute flight, the nine-seat Britten-Norman Islander gives you breathtaking views of the coastline, changing colors of the waters below (which mark the passage of an oceanic stream flowing through the strait), bush-clad islands, and Stewart Island itself, where you land on a paved runway and are minibused into Oban. Southern Air flies daily, almost every hour in the summer; there's a minimum of four flights a day, and extra ones are added upon demand. The airline schedules even allow for a day visit if you're pressed for time. The adult fare is NZ$67.50 (U.S. $43.90) one way, NZ$118 (U.S. $76.70) round-trip; children pay half. The Golden Age fare for those over 60 is NZ$104 (U.S. $67.60) round-trip; and students can go standby for NZ$33.75 (U.S. $21.95) round-trip. Southern Air can also help you plan and book your entire Stewart Island holiday. They know the island well and are happy to arrange things to suit your preferences.

• By Boat You can go aboard the *Foveaux Express,* operated by Stewart Island Marine. During the winter it sails from Bluff on Monday, Wednesday, and Friday at 9:30am and 4pm and Sunday at 4pm. From late August to late May the boat departs Bluff Monday through Saturday at 9:30am and 5pm and Sunday at 5pm. The crossing takes one hour, and there is connecting bus service from Invercargill to Bluff. The round-trip fare is NZ$74 (U.S. $48.10) for adults and NZ$37 (U.S. $24.05) for children. For more information, call **03/212-7660** or fax 03/212-8377.

ESSENTIALS The town of **Oban** is located on Halfmoon Bay and consists of a general store, post office, travel office, craft shop, hotel, forestry office, a small museum, and the pier at which the ferry docks. The **Stewart Island Visitor Centre** is on the main road (☎ **219-1218**; fax 03/219-1555). The **telephone area code** (STD) for Stewart Island is **03.**

Seen on the map, Stewart Island is not much more than a speck; but seen from the deck of the *Foveaux Express* or from the air, its magnitude will surprise you. There are actually 1,600km (975 miles) of coastline enclosing 1,680km^2 (625 square miles) of thick bush (most of it left in its natural state), bird sanctuary, and rugged mountains. Only a tiny stretch of that long coastline has been settled, and it's the little fishing town of **Oban** that will be your landfall. There are about 12 miles of paved road on the island, which are easily covered by the minibus tour, and many of the houses you see are the holiday "batch" or "crib" of Kiwis from the South Island who view Stewart Island as the perfect spot to escape the pressures of civilization. The population of Stewart Island is 690.

The pace here is quite unhurried—few cars, friendly islanders more attuned to the tides and the running of cod and crayfish than to commerce—and the setting is a botanist's dream. The Maori called the island Rakiura, "heavenly glow," a name you'll find especially fitting if you are lucky enough to see the southern lights brighten its skies or to be here for one of its spectacular sunsets.

While its beauty and serenity can be glimpsed in the few hours of a day trip, you might want to consider at least one overnight to explore its beaches, bush, and people so as to savor this very special place to the fullest. Incidentally, should you hear yourself or other visitors referred to as "loopies" by the islanders, not to worry—it'll be said with affection.

What to See & Do

On the island, the only thing you really must not miss is the hour-long ★ **minibus tour** given by Lloyd Wilcox at Stewart Island Travel (☎ **03/219-1269**). Lloyd will not only cover every one of those 20km (12 miles) of paved road, he'll give you a comprehensive history of Stewart Island—the whalers who settled here, the sealers who called in (it was, in fact, the mate of a sealer who gave his name to the island), the sawmill and mineral industries that came and went, and the development of the fishing industry—and will point out traces they left behind scattered around your route. He also knows the flora of the island (you'll learn, for instance, that there are 17 varieties of orchids on the island) and its animal population (no wild pigs or goats). You'll see many of the 18 good swimming beaches and hear details of the paua diving, which has proved so profitable for islanders (much of the colorful shell that went into those souvenirs you've seen around New Zealand came from Stewart Island). From **Observation Point** right to the road's end at **Thule Bay,** Lloyd gives you an insider's view of his home. And questions or comments are very much in order—it's an informal, happy hour of exchange: a perfect way to begin a stay of several days, an absolute essential if the day trip is all you will have. Check when booking for schedule and fare.

The **Rakiura Museum** in Halfmoon Bay features photos and exhibits that follow Stewart Island's history through its sailing, whaling, tin-mining, sawmilling, and fishing days. It also has shell and Maori artifact exhibits. It's open Monday through Saturday from 10am to noon and Sunday from noon to 2pm, with extended hours during the summer holidays (see the local noticeboard). Admission is NZ$1 (U.S. 65¢) for adults and NZ50¢ (U.S. 35¢) for children.

Visit the small **deer park** just across from Stewart Island Travel. Small Virginian (whitetail) deer are right at home in the enclosure and seem delighted to have visitors.

Next to the deer park is the office of the ★ **Department of Conservation,** P.O. Box 3, Stewart Island (☎ **03/219-1130**), which has an interesting display of island wildlife in a small exhibition room. More important, the staff there can supply details on many beautiful **walks** around Oban and farther afield. If you're interested in spending a few days on the island tramping, I suggest that you write ahead for their informative booklets on just what you'll need to bring and what you can expect. There are recently upgraded tramping huts conveniently spaced along the tracks (ranging in size from 6 to 30 bunks), but they're heavily used during summer. A two-night stay is the maximum at any one hut. The DOC office is open from Christmas to the end of February, daily from 8am to 7pm; the rest of the year, daily from 8:30am to 5pm. If you find it closed, just ask locally—the conservation officer may well have just popped out for a short spell.

Popular **short walks** around Oban are those to Golden Bay, Lonneckers, Lee Bay, Thule, Observation Point, and the lighthouse at Acker's Point. Ringarina Beach is a mecca for shell hounds (I have New Zealand friends who serve entrees in paua shells they've picked up on the beach here), but your finds will depend on whether the tides are right during your visit. If you're here on a day trip, be sure to check locally to be certain you can make it back from any walk you plan in time for the ferry or air return.

You can engage local boats for **fishing** or visiting nearby uninhabited islands at prices that are surprisingly low. Contact Stewart Island Travel.

Where to Stay

Stewart Island Travel, P.O. Box 26, Halfmoon Bay, Stewart Island (☎ **03/219-1269**; fax 03/219-1293), can send you a complete list of accommodations and prices, and can help you make reservations. If you write from overseas, be sure to enclose return postage. Accommodations are extremely limited, and in summer they're booked months in advance, so if your plans include a visit here, write or call just as soon as you have firm dates for your visit. It's sometimes possible to rent one of the holiday homes not currently in use, and Beryl Wilcox is the one to contact.

A LICENSED HOTEL

South Sea Hotel, P.O. Box 52, Halfmoon Bay, Stewart Island. ☎ **03/219-1059.** Fax 03/219-1120. 18 rms (none with bath).

Rates: NZ$28–NZ$57 (U.S. $18.20–$37.05) single; NZ$45–NZ$85 (U.S. $29.25–$55.25) double or twin; NZ$85 (U.S. $55.25) triple. MC, V.

Stewart Island's only hotel sits in the curve of Halfmoon Bay, in the village center across from the water. Its public bar, bar/lounge (whose windows overlook the bay), and licensed restaurant are the center of much island activity, and even if you lodge elsewhere you're likely to find yourself in and out of the South Sea many times during your stay. The rooms all share the bath and toilet facilities down the hall, and there are six singles, two doubles, eight twins, and two triples. This is the kind of charming, old-fashioned inn that seems exactly right for this island—the guest lounge, for example, has an open fire glowing on cool days, and the staff takes a personal interest in all guests (and casual visitors, too).

Captain Crayfish's South Sea Saturday Night

Of all the good times I've had in country pubs in New Zealand, one particularly enjoyable night in the public bar of the South Sea Hotel on Stewart Island stands out in my mind.

It was a Saturday evening and the pub was crowded with fishermen wearing their traditional patched overalls, heavy sweaters, and Stewart Island slippers (white gumboots). The local band, Captain Crayfish and the Wekas, was composed of a piano, an accordion, a trombone, and a tea chest (an instrument similar to a wash-tub bass, made of a carton box with a piece of rope attached to a broom handle). The musicians played simultaneously, but it didn't always seem as if they were playing the same tune—and no one seemed to mind.

The band took a break while the Kiwis' rugby match against Australia was broadcast on television. The home team won and the crowd went wild.

Toward the end of the evening the trombone player conducted a sing-along—"Alouette" was the favorite, with "You Are My Sunshine" a close second. There was no dance floor, but that didn't stop a slippered local and a chubby woman in Nikes from doing a waltz.

I had planned to go to bed early, but halfway through the evening I realized I wouldn't have been able to sleep anyway. My room was right over the bar.

When the pub closed, I went upstairs and had the pleasure of drifting off to sleep with the sound of waves breaking on the beach directly across the road from the hotel.

The South Sea Hotel sounds like a place one would discover in Fiji, but only the name suggests a Polynesian resort. It never gets very warm on Stewart Island, and pesky sand flies often make sitting on the beach uncomfortable.

The rugged island is inhabited by commercial fishermen and their families. They live a basic existence and depend heavily on supplies and personnel that come by boat from Bluff. On a recent visit I noticed that the community bulletin board outside the general store carried news of the impending arrival of a hairdresser from Invercargill.

The South Sea Hotel is the social center of the island. Birthdays are celebrated in the dining room, and the problems of the world are solved over a pint in the bar; cards and darts tournaments are held regularly to raise money for the local primary school. . . .

The two-story weatherboard hotel was built in 1927; its predecessor on the same site dated from the early 1900s. When the present hotel activated its liquor license in 1955, it broke a "drought" that had been in effect since the 1880s. It's hard to believe that Stewart Island was ever "dry," and there are plenty of stories about home-brewed beer and a secret whisky still.

I can only imagine the sigh of relief that issued from thirsty locals on the day the public bar opened its doors.

MOTELS

The **Shearwater Inn** complex (below) has single, double, and family rooms in addition to its backpacker accommodations, as well as a bar and licensed restaurant.

Rakiura Motels, P.O. Box 96, Stewart Island. ☎ **03/219-1096.** 5 units (all with bath). TV

Rates: NZ$40 (U.S. $26) single; NZ$70 (U.S. $45.50) double. Additional person NZ$15 (U.S. $9.75) extra per adult, NZ$10 (U.S. $6.50) extra per child under 12. MC, V.

Elaine Hamilton offers self-contained motel units located about a mile from Oban. The units sleep up to six, are heated, and have kitchens and private baths.

A HOSTEL

$ **Shearwater Inn,** Ayre St. (P.O. Box 25), Halfmoon Bay, Oban, Stewart Island. ☎ **03/219-1114.** Fax 03/214-4681. 80 beds (no rooms with bath).

Rates: NZ$28 (U.S. $18.20) single; NZ$52 (U.S. $33.80) double; NZ$56 (U.S. $36.40) family room; NZ$20 (U.S. $13) dorm bed. Additional child NZ$10 (U.S. $6.50) extra. MC, V.

When the Shearwater Inn complex opened in conjunction with Southern Air in 1989, it was the first major new accommodation on the island in 50 years. Situated right in the heart of Oban, near the post office, shops, and beach, it's an associate YHA hostel, and also has single, double, and family rooms. The 80 beds are in two- to four-bed rooms; there's a communal lounge with an open fireplace and TV; a kitchen (all utensils furnished); a licensed restaurant for moderately priced à la carte meals; and a courtyard used for barbecues. The inn provides wheelchair facilities.

Where to Eat

In addition to the listings below, the **Shearwater Inn** (see "Where to Stay," above) has a good à la carte restaurant serving breakfast from 8 to 9am, and dinner from 6 to 9pm daily at reasonable prices. The South Sea Hotel can pack a **picnic lunch** if notified in ample time, and there's a **general store** where you can pick up picnic makings for a day in the bush. For light lunches, morning and afternoon teas, or take-aways, it's the **Travel Inn Tearooms,** adjacent to Stewart Island Travel in the village center.

$ **Annie Hansen's Dining Room,** in the South Sea Hotel, Oban, Halfmoon Bay. ☎ **219-1059.**

Cuisine: SEAFOOD/NEW ZEALAND.

Prices: Average lunch NZ$15 (U.S. $9.75); average dinner NZ$25 (U.S. $16.25). MC, V.

Open: Lunch daily noon–1pm; dinner daily 6–7pm.

One of the best seafood meals I've had in New Zealand was in this large, pleasant waterfront dining room, named for a longtime owner of the hotel back in the early days of this century. My fish was truly fresh and cooked to perfection, the salad bar was more extensive than I would have expected on an island where so much must be imported, the dessert was very good, and the service included a friendly chat about how best to spend my time on Stewart Island. Other main courses included beef, lamb, and chicken, and the manager tells me that they are constantly trying out traditional recipes, many of them brought by early Stewart Island settlers.

13 Dunedin

YOU WON'T FIND PIPERS IN THE STREETS OF DUNEDIN—AND THE CITIZENS OF "NEW Edinburgh on the Antipodes" are quick to tell you they're *Kiwis,* not Scots. Still, one look at the sturdy stone Victorian architectural face of the city with its crown of upreaching spires will tell you that the 344 settlers who arrived at the beautiful Upper Harbour in March 1848 could have come only from Scotland. And when you learn that Dunedin is the old Gaelic name for Edinburgh, that the city produces New Zealand's only domestic whisky and has the only kilt store in the country, and that the strains of a pipe band are common here, you surely won't be able to mistake its Scottish nature!

The other aura that's impossible not to notice is created by the University of Otago. The 15,000 students and faculty members at this learned institution (which was patterned after Glasgow University) are much in evidence—giving the community an appealing academic/college-town atmosphere. The university's slate-roofed bluestone buildings hint of serious cerebral endeavors, but anyone who has visited Dunedin's pubs will assure you that these students know how to have fun, too.

Dunedin (pop. 110,000) is the South Island's second-largest city. The community's economy boomed in the 1860s when gold was discovered in central Otago, and the city's (and the country's) future was forever impacted by the shipment of frozen meat that was sent to Britain from nearby Port Chalmers in 1882. Throughout its history, Dunedin has held on to its priorities of education, conservation of natural beauty, and humanitarian concerns.

A reader wrote recently, "Dunedin has a quiet charm.... It's one of New Zealand's best-kept secrets." I couldn't agree more!

SPECIAL EVENTS Dunedin is fun to visit anytime of the year, but you'll be doubly blessed if you arrive during one of its special events. Probably the highlight of them all is the late-March ✪ **Scottish Week,** when the city breaks out with kilts, bagpipes, Scottish country dancing, and a host of other activities that reflect its heritage.

You might also enjoy its annual ✪ **Festival Week** in early February, with art and craft displays, a vintage-car rally, a family fun run, a street carnival, and—the highlight—a Festival Procession that features decorated floats, clowns, and bands. Then in early March there's the one-day **Food and Wine Festival,** first celebrated in 1990, held outdoors in the Woodhaugh Gardens. A large variety of Dunedin restaurants set up stalls and sell a selection of dishes from their menus; there's live music and entertainment, and cooking demonstrations. And the third week of October each year, **Rhododendron Week** celebrates the city's most famous floral asset by decking out just about every public space with the lovely blooms and hosting tours of private and public gardens in and around town.

IMPRESSIONS

We are in another country/Scotitanga/Where brass bands play, people fling to Scottish music in Moray Place, ladies of the Salvation Army palm ribboned tambourines, and smiles shiver and snap in the cold.

—Witi Ihimaera, *Deep South/Impressions of Another Country,* 1975

Dunedin is a place where it is front page headline if someone has a fire in their wardrobe.

—Dennis McEldowney, *Full of the Warm South,* 1983

What's Special About Dunedin

Museums

- Otago Settlers Museum, a fascinating collection of exhibits that depict the lives of Dunedin's first residents.
- Otago Museum, with displays relating to New Zealand's natural history.

Historic Buildings

- The railway station, a splendid Flemish Renaissance-style edifice, built of bluestone and boasting a colorful mosaic floor.
- Olveston, one of the country's best-known stately homes, Jacobean in style.
- Larnach Castle, a magnificent neo-gothic mansion dating from 1871.

Ace Attractions

- The Octagon, an eight-sided park in the heart of town.
- Cadbury's factory tours, where chocolate is the center of attention.

Gardens

- Glenfalloch Woodland Garden, a 30-acre estate whose grounds hold native bush, ancient English oaks, rhododendrons, and azaleas.

Wildlife

- The Royal Albatross Colony at Taiaroa Head, the world's only known mainland nesting ground of the magnificent royal albatross.
- Southlight Wildlife, a fascinating colony of the rare and dignified yellow-eyed penguin.

1 City Specifics

ARRIVING

BY PLANE Both **Air New Zealand** and **Ansett** provide air service between Dunedin and Auckland, Hamilton, and Wellington on the North Island; and Christchurch and Invercargill on the South Island.

The minibus **airport shuttle** (☎ **479-2481**) provides service for all flights, with hotel pickup and delivery, for a fare of NZ$10 (U.S. $6.50). The airport is a full 30 minutes from the city, which makes a **taxi** prohibitive at fares of about NZ$45 (U.S. $29.25).

BY TRAIN/BUS The ***Southerner*** train runs between Dunedin and Christchurch and Invercargill. The railway station (a sightseeing attraction; see "What to See and Do," later in this chapter) is at the foot of Stuart Street.

InterCity and Mount Cook Landline provide coach service between Dunedin and Christchurch, Invercargill, Picton, Queenstown, Te Anau, and Timaru. The two lines have separate **bus terminals:** InterCity is at 599 Princes St. (☎ **477-8860**), and Mount Cook, at 205 St. Andrew St. (☎ **474-0674**). Shuttle-bus transportation is provided by **Southern Link Shuttles** (☎ **543-6549**) to Christchurch, Kaikoura, Picton, and Queenstown.

BY CAR Dunedin can be reached via Highways 1 and 87. It's 336km (208 miles) south of Christchurch and 220km (136 miles) northeast of Invercargill.

CITY LAYOUT

Most cities have a public square, but Dunedin has its eight-sided **Octagon,** a green, leafy park right at the hub of the city center that was totally remodeled in 1989 (be sure to notice the Writer's Walk on the upper side). Around its edges you'll find St. Paul's Anglican Cathedral and the City Hall. Within its confines is a statue of Scotland's beloved poet Robert Burns (whose nephew was Dunedin's first pastor) and park benches for foot-weary shoppers or brown-bagging lunchers. The Octagon divides the main street into **Princes Street** to the south, **George Street** to the north.

The city center, at the head of **Otago Harbour,** is encircled by a 500-acre strip of land, the **Green Belt,** that has been, by edict of the founders, left in its natural state, never to be developed regardless of the city's growth. Thus it is that when driving to any of Dunedin's suburbs, you pass through forestland from which there are glimpses of the harbor.

TOURIST INFORMATION

The staff at the **Dunedin Visitor Centre,** 48 The Octagon (☎ **03/474-3300**; fax 03/474-3311), will be happy to answer your questions. The office is normally open Monday through Friday from 8:30am to 5pm and Saturday, Sunday, and public holidays from 9am to 5pm, with extended hours in summer. They can make lodging reservations and book all your sightseeing excursions and onward travel arrangements.

2 Getting Around

BY BUS Most **city buses** (☎ **477-2224**) leave from the vicinity of The Octagon. There's frequent bus service during the week, a little spotty on weekends. The fares are by zone and range from NZ$1.10 to NZ$1.80 (U.S. 70¢ to $1.15) per section, less for children. If you buy a packet of 10 tickets, you essentially get one ride free. The **Shopper Special** operates from 10am to 3pm and costs NZ$1.10 (U.S. 70¢).

BY TAXI Taxi stands can be found at The Octagon, at all terminals, and near the Chief Post Office (☎ **477-7777** or **477-1771**).

BY CAR A one-way street system makes driving easier than in most cities, all central streets have metered parking, and there's a municipal parking building near City Hall. The **Automobile Association** office is at 450 Moray Place (☎ **477-5945**). Central **gas (petrol) stations** include the Shell Kaikorai, 433 Stuart St. (☎ **477-8391**), and Everedi Service Station, opposite the Oval (☎ **477-5566**), which also sells groceries.

Fast Facts: Dunedin

Airlines There is an Air New Zealand (☎ **477-5769**) ticket office at the corner of The Octagon and Princes Street. The Ansett office is at The Octagon and George Street (☎ **477-4146**).

American Express This is represented by Brooker Travel, 369 George St. (☎ **477-3383**).

Area Code The telephone area code (STD) for Dunedin is **03**.

Automobile Association The AA is at 450 Moray Place (☎ **477-5945**) and is open Monday through Friday from 8:30am to 5pm.

Emergencies For police, fire, and/or ambulance service, dial **111**.

Photographic Needs Camera House, 115 George St. (☎ **479-2200**), provides one-hour processing and other camera-related services.

Post Office The Chief Post Office is at 283 Princes St. and there's another at 233 Moray Place.

Shopping Hours Stores are open Monday through Thursday from 9am to 5:30pm, Friday from 9am to 9pm, and Saturday from 10am to 1pm.

Taxis See "Getting Around," earlier in this chapter.

3 Where to Stay

Dunedin has many fine accommodations in all price ranges. It also has, however, a large student population (with lots of visitors!), so you'll need to reserve in advance if your visit coincides with graduation or another campus event.

The rates given below include GST.

In Town

A LICENSED HOTEL

Leviathan Hotel, 65–69 Lower High St., Dunedin. ☎ **03/477-3160.** Fax 03/477-2385. 77 rms (all with bath), 6 suites. TV

Rates: NZ$49–NZ$84 (U.S. $31.85–$54.60) single; NZ$55–NZ$84 (U.S. $35.75–$54.60) double; NZ$108 (U.S. $70.20) suite. AE, DC, MC, V. **Parking:** Free.

This three-story triangular hotel is a Dunedin landmark dating back to 1898. It's on a corner across from the Otago Settlers Museum, one block from the railway station and within walking distance of the bus depot. The old building is in excellent condition and offers a high standard of central budget accommodations, plus fully equipped suites. The rooms are attractively decorated and furnished with built-in wardrobe, chest of drawers, and overbed lights; all have electric heaters. Two family units sleep five. There's a games room with a pool table and two TV lounges. The elegant dining room serves meals in the moderate range. There's an elevator, hall telephones for guests, and off-street parking.

MOTELS

Aaron Lodge Motel and Holiday Park, 162 Kaikorai Valley Rd., Dunedin. ☎ **03/476-4725.** 7 units (all with bath). TV

Rates: NZ$31 (U.S. $20.20) per person. Additional person NZ$13 (U.S. $8.45) extra per adult, NZ$8 (U.S. $5.20) extra per child. AE, DC, MC, V.

Near Brockville Road, the Aaron Lodge offers one-bedroom units with heaters, radios, and electric blankets. All are nicely carpeted and well maintained. See "Cabins and Campgrounds," below, for a complete description.

$ **Aberdeen Motel,** 46 Bank St. (at George St.), Dunedin. ☎ **03/473-0133.** Fax 03/473-0131. 18 units (all with bath). TV TEL

Rates: NZ$65 (U.S. $42.25) single; NZ$75 (U.S. $48.75) double. Best Western discounts available. AE, DC, MC, V.

Jen and Graham Richardson are the thoughtful Aberdeen hosts who provide such little extras as a complimentary morning newspaper, a video on Dunedin attractions plus three Sky TV channels, and a collection of Dunedin restaurant menus. The attractive

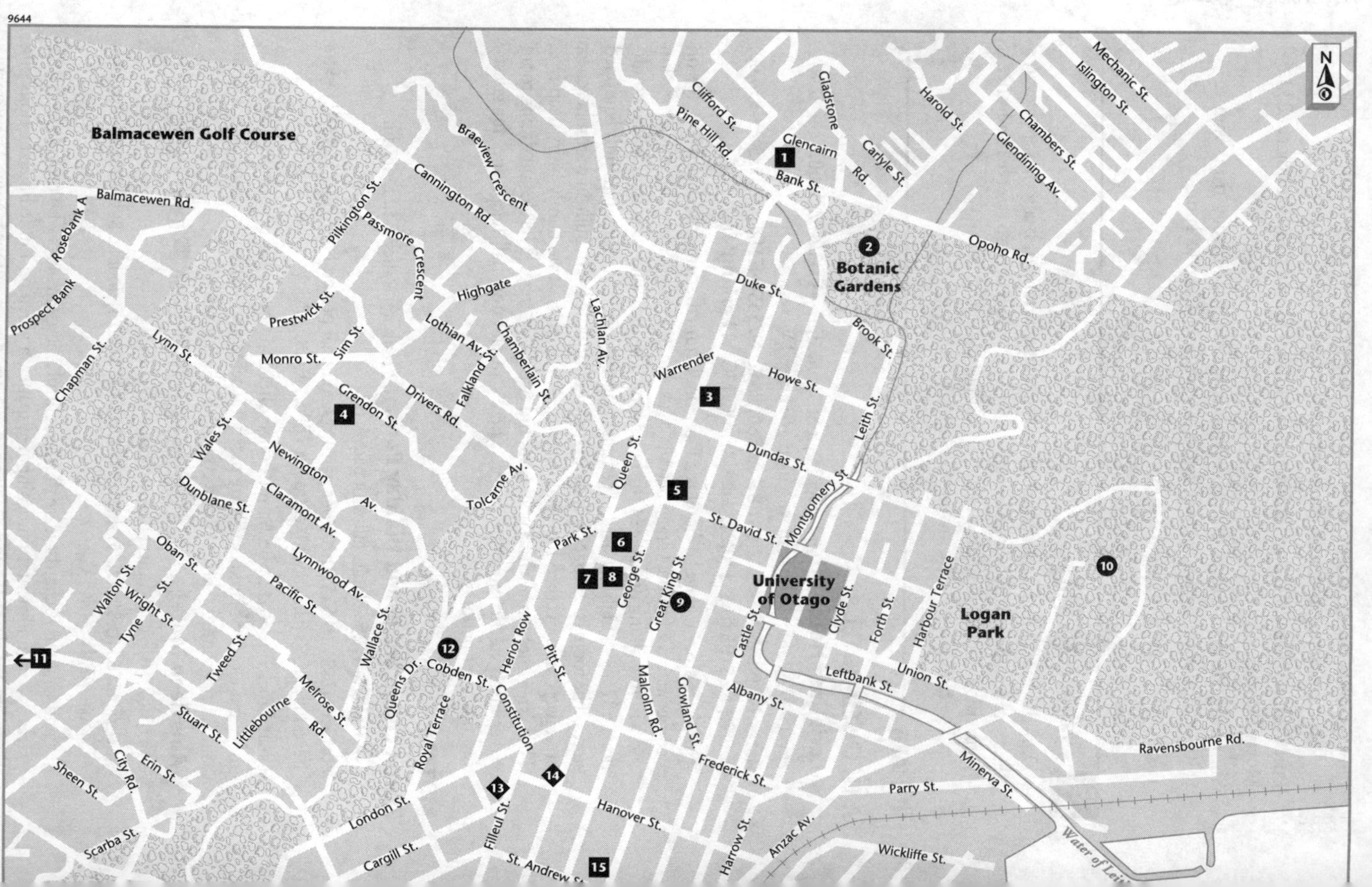

9644
N
Balmacewen Golf Course
Balmacewen Rd.
Rosebank A
Prospect Bank
Chapman St.
Lynn St.
Prestwick St.
Monro St.
Sim St.
Pilkington St.
Passmore Crescent
Cannington Rd.
Braeview Crescent
Highgate
Lothian Av.
Falkland St.
Chamberlain St.
Lachlan Av.
Grendon St.
Drivers Rd.
Wales St.
Newington Av.
Dunblane St.
Claramont Av.
Tolcarne Av.
Lynnwood Av.
Oban St.
Walton St.
Wright St.
Tyne St.
Pacific St.
Wallace St.
Tweed St.
Melrose St.
Littlebourne Rd.
Stuart St.
City Rd.
Erin St.
Sheen St.
Scarba St.
Queens Dr.
Cobden St.
Royal Terrace
Heriot Row
Constitution
Pitt St.
London St.
Filleul St.
Cargill St.
Hanover St.
Park St.
Queen St.
George St.
Great King St.
Malcolm Rd.
Gowland St.
Frederick St.
Harrow St.
Anzac Av.
Wickliffe St.
Parry St.
Minerva St.
Warrender
Howe St.
Dundas St.
St. David St.
Montgomery St.
Castle St.
Albany St.
University of Otago
Clyde St.
Forth St.
Harbour Terrace
Leftbank St.
Union St.
Logan Park
Ravensbourne Rd.
Duke St.
Brook St.
Leith St.
Botanic Gardens
Clifford St.
Pine Hill Rd.
Glencairn Rd.
Bank St.
Gladstone
Carlyle St.
Harold St.
Opoho Rd.
Glendining Av.
Chambers St.
Islington St.
Mechanic St.
1
2
3
4
5
6
7
8
9
10
11
12
13
14
15

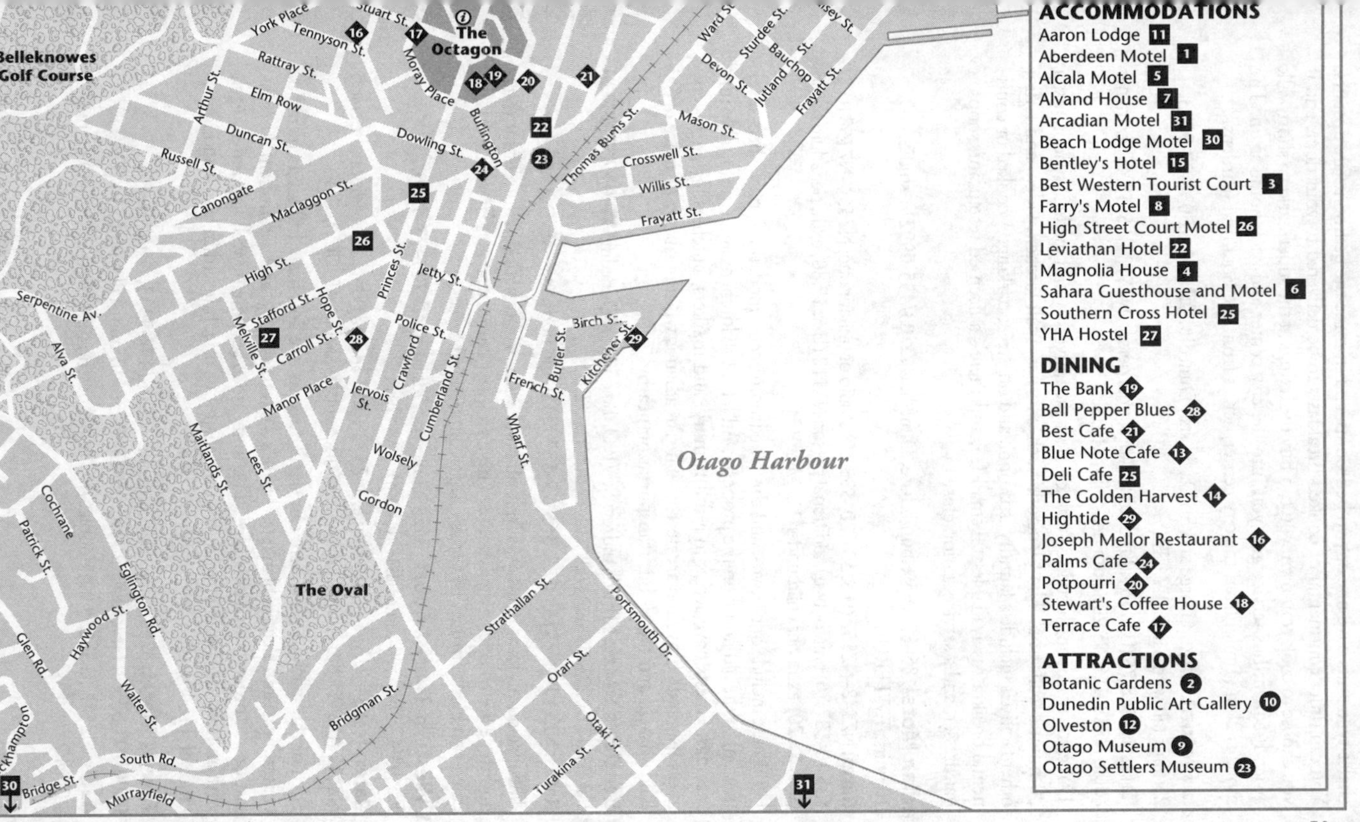
ACCOMMODATIONS
Aaron Lodge 11
Aberdeen Motel 1
Alcala Motel 5
Alvand House 7
Arcadian Motel 31
Beach Lodge Motel 30
Bentley's Hotel 15
Best Western Tourist Court 3
Farry's Motel 8
High Street Court Motel 26
Leviathan Hotel 22
Magnolia House 4
Sahara Guesthouse and Motel 6
Southern Cross Hotel 25
YHA Hostel 27
DINING
The Bank 19
Bell Pepper Blues 28
Best Cafe 21
Blue Note Cafe 13
Deli Cafe 25
The Golden Harvest 14
Hightide 29
Joseph Mellor Restaurant 16
Palms Cafe 24
Potpourri 20
Stewart's Coffee House 18
Terrace Cafe 17
ATTRACTIONS
Botanic Gardens 2
Dunedin Public Art Gallery 10
Olveston 12
Otago Museum 9
Otago Settlers Museum 23
Belleknowes Golf Course
The Octagon
Otago Harbour
The Oval
York Place
Stuart St.
Tennyson St.
Rattray St.
Elm Row
Arthur St.
Duncan St.
Russell St.
Canongate
Maclaggon St.
Moray Place
Burlington
Dowling St.
Thomas Burns St.
Ward St.
Sturdee St.
Devon St.
Bauchop St.
Jutland St.
Frayatt St.
Mason St.
Crosswell St.
Willis St.
Fravatt St.
High St.
Serpentine Av.
Alva St.
Stafford St.
Hope St.
Melville St.
Carroll St.
Princes St.
Jetty St.
Police St.
Crawford
Jervois St.
Manor Place
Cumberland St.
Birch St.
Butler St.
Kitchener St.
French St.
Wharf St.
Maitlands St.
Lees St.
Wolsely
Gordon
Cochrane
Patrick St.
Eglington Rd.
Haywood St.
Glen Rd.
Walter St.
Strathallan St.
Portsmouth Dr.
Orari St.
Otaki St.
Turakina St.
Bridgman St.
Leckhampton
South Rd.
Bridge St.
Murrayfield
Information
Railroad

Dunedin

chalet-type units have one or two bedrooms, and in some the bedrooms are upstairs. You can order continental or cooked breakfasts to be delivered to your door, and if you choose to cook your own, you can buy the fixings at the supermarket a short walk away. Frequent bus service gets you into the city center and back home again. The motel is 2km (1mile) from the city center, across from the Botanical Gardens.

Alcala Motor Lodge, George and St. David sts., Dunedin. ☎ and fax **03/477-9073.** 23 units (all with bath). TV TEL

Rates: NZ$78.75 (U.S. $51.20) double. Additional person NZ$13 (U.S. $8.45) extra per adult, NZ$8 (U.S. $5.20) extra per child. MC, V.

This attractive Spanish-style complex is near the university and medical school, just a 20-minute walk from The Octagon. Each unit has a full kitchen, video, and radio; other facilities include a laundry, spa pool, and off-street parking. A cooked or continental breakfast is available at a small fee, and there's a licensed restaurant, shops, a hairdresser, and a service station close by.

Arcadian Motel, 85–89 Musselburgh Rise, Dunedin. ☎ **03/455-0992.** 1 studio, 10 units. TV TEL

Rates: NZ$48–NZ$52 (U.S. $31.20–$33.80) studio or unit for one; NZ$54–NZ$58 (U.S. $35.10–$37.70) unit for two. Additional person NZ$12 (U.S. $7.80) extra per adult, NZ$8 (U.S. $5.20) extra per child under 12. MC, V.

Units here include one-, two-, and three-bedroom accommodations, plus a bed-sitter (studio) in the old house on the property. All have full kitchens and comfortable furnishings. Guests have access to a full laundry, and markets, butchers, greengrocers, and a fish-and-chips shop are nearby. The Arcadian is within walking distance of St. Kilda Beach, and there's bus transportation nearby.

★ **Bentley's Hotel,** 137 St. Andrew St. (P.O. Box 5702), Dunedin. ☎ **03/477-0572.** Fax 03/477-0293. 39 units (all with bath). TV TEL

Rates: NZ$101–NZ$135 (U.S. $65.65–$87.75) single or double. AE, DC, MC, V.

The spacious units at Bentley's Hotel all come with private bath (bathtub or shower), and three are wheelchair-accessible. There's a guest laundry and a restaurant. It's located two blocks from The Octagon, at Cumberland Street.

Best Western Tourist Court, 842 George St., Dunedin. ☎ **03/477-4270.** Fax 03/477-6035. 9 units (all with bath). TV TEL

Rates: NZ$64 (U.S. $41.60) single; NZ$73 (U.S. $47.45) double. Additional person NZ$12 (U.S. $7.80) extra. Best Western discounts available. AE, DC, MC, V.

Each of the spacious units here can sleep three to five and has a full kitchen, radio, central heat, and electric blankets. There's a guest laundry, and a continental breakfast can be ordered for a small fee. The units are exceptionally well appointed, each with an iron and ironing board. It's on a main bus line, but within easy walking distance of The Octagon.

★ **Farry's Motel,** 575 George St., Dunedin. ☎ **03/477-9333,** or toll free **0800/109-333** in New Zealand. Fax 03/477-9038. 15 units (all with bath). TV TEL

Rates: NZ$86 (U.S. $55.90) double. Additional person NZ$16 (U.S. $10.40) extra. AE, DC, MC, V.

The apartments are tastefully furnished, with large picture windows in all lounges. Each unit is centrally heated and has a fully equipped kitchen, in-house video, Sky TV, and a radio. Standard units sleep up to four and special "executive suites" have private spa baths and videocassette movies. There's a guest laundry, a children's play area with swings and trampolines, and off-street parking. A continental or cooked breakfast is available for a small charge. The motel is near city bus transportation, the university, and shopping.

High Street Court Motel, 193 High St., Dunedin. ☎ **03/477-9315,** or toll free **0800/509-315** in New Zealand. Fax 03/477-3366. 9 units (all with bath). TV TEL

Rates: NZ$75 (U.S. $48.75) single; NZ$83 (U.S. $53.95) double. Additional person NZ$16 (U.S. $10.40) extra. AE, MC, V.

With the same ownership and management as Farry's (above), this pretty place has a white-stucco facade with black wrought-iron trim. See the Farry's entry for the description of the rooms and facilities. A continental breakfast is available for a small charge. If you're on foot, it's an uphill hike from the city center. There's city bus transportation nearby.

BED-&-BREAKFASTS

Alvand House, 3 Union St., Dunedin. ☎ **03/477-7379.** Fax 03/477-6638. 6 rms (none with bath). TV

Rates (including breakfast): NZ$48 (U.S. $31.20) single; NZ$68 (U.S. $44.20) double. Additional person NZ$17 (U.S. $11.05) extra. Dinner NZ$20 (U.S. $13) extra. MC, V.

One of my favorite finds is this B&B perched at the top of a hill, with tidy white shingles and red trim and a carnation- and rose-trimmed walkway leading to the red front door and lace-curtained windows. There are six bedrooms, with high ceilings, carpeted floors, tall windows with stained-glass touches, electric blankets, and coffee- and tea-making facilities. Guests have the use of a washing machine and clothesline, and they often linger on the sunny porch reading the newspaper that the gracious hostess, Farah Jamali, leaves out. She will prepare an evening meal, including wine, by special arrangement. Alvand House is near the university and Botanic Gardens; there's city bus service nearby.

Magnolia House, 18 Grendon St., Maori Hill, Dunedin. ☎ **03/467-5999.** 3 rms (none with bath). TV TEL

Rates (including breakfast): NZ$45 (U.S. $29.25) single; NZ$70 (U.S. $45.50) double. No credit cards.

The suburban home of George and Joan Sutherland, Magnolia House is set on half an acre of sloping lawns and gardens, surrounded by native bush. The Victorian house, framed by a white picket fence at the lawn's edge, is quite spacious and graciously decorated, with a welcoming sitting room and a drawing room that holds a piano and opens onto a sun balcony. There's central heating throughout, and the bedrooms have fireplaces and antique furnishings. There are also two cats in residence and a no-smoking rule. The Sutherlands, who have lived in Dunedin for almost 30 years, are gracious hosts who enjoy helping guests plan their time in the city for the utmost enjoyment and provide a courtesy car upon request. There's city bus transportation nearby.

Sahara Guesthouse and Motel, 619 George St., Dunedin. ☎ **03/477-6662.** Fax 03/479-2551. 10 rms (2 with bath), 10 units (all with bath).

Rates: NZ$45–NZ$55 (U.S. $29.25–$35.75) single B&B; NZ$74–NZ$79 (U.S. $48.10–$51.35) double B&B; NZ$59 (U.S. $38.35) unit for one; NZ$69 (U.S. $44.85) unit for two. AE, DC, MC, V.

This gabled brick guesthouse sports elaborate iron grillwork, is just a five-minute walk from The Octagon, and is on major bus routes. Built as a substantial family home back in 1863, it now holds nice-size rooms with hot and cold running water, with one to three twin beds, all immaculate and cheerful. Room 12 is especially bright, with a stained-glass window. Behind the house is a block of motel apartment units, four of which sleep up to five, all with kitchens, baths, telephones, color TVs, and use of laundry facilities. The home-style breakfast is a hearty one.

A HOSTEL

YHA Hostel, Stafford Gables, 71 Stafford St., Dunedin. ☎ and fax **03/474-1919.** 60 beds (no rooms with bath).

Rates: NZ$14 (U.S. $9.10) for members, NZ$18 (U.S. $11.70) for nonmembers. No credit cards.

Dunedin's YHA hostel is housed in a grand old early-1900s mansion located right in the city center, near the Chief Post Office. It's also near food stores and a large supermarket. There are 60 beds in 21 rooms with high ceilings, carpeting, and attractive wallpaper, and ranging in size from twins, doubles, triples, and family rooms to dormitories. Three common rooms include a pool table and smoking room, and a TV and music room, and there are two dining rooms, a kitchen, and a coin-operated laundry. There is 24-hour access to the hostel for guests, off-street parking, and a resident ghost (if you believe in such things).

CABINS & CAMPGROUNDS

The **Aaron Lodge Motel and Holiday Park,** 162 Kaikorai Valley Rd. (near Brockville Road), Dunedin (☎ **03/476-4725**), is a whole complex of powered sites, tent sites, cabins, cabin blocks, and motel units on a main artery with a grassy hill out back. Seven motel units are in front (see "Motels," above), and there are 15 family rooms in two large red-and-gray concrete cabin blocks. Four- or five-berthed, all are spacious, and have carpets, large wardrobes, a table and chairs, and electric heater. Beds can be curtained off for privacy. There are two modern kitchens with TVs, showers, and a laundry with dryer. Across a grassy lawn and up the hill are eight two-berth cabins with built-in beds, a shelf, and a chest of drawers; a kitchen (crockery and cutlery provided), toilets, and showers are adjacent. There's a children's playground on the premises, and a supermarket adjacent. Rates for all cabins are NZ$29 to NZ$32 (U.S. $18.85 to $20.80) per adult couple, NZ$5 (U.S. $3.25) per child, NZ$10 (U.S. $6.50)

READERS RECOMMEND

Portobello Village Tourist Park, 27 Hereweka St., Portobello, Dunedin (☎ **03/478-0359**). *"We were traveling the delightful Otago Peninsula just north of Dunedin in our campervan. We didn't want to return to Dunedin to camp and the locals told us about this friendly, clean place. Hosts Kevin and Sherryl Charles were very helpful."*—Tom and Jackie Prevost, Holly, Mich., U.S.A.

per extra adult. Tent and caravan sites are also available. The Aaron Lodge is owned and managed by Margaret and Lindsay McLeod and may be reached via the Bradford or Brockville bus from The Octagon. GST is included in all rates.

WORTH THE EXTRA MONEY

Southern Cross Hotel, 118 High St., Dunedin. ☎ **03/477-0752.** Fax 03/477-5776. 134 rms (all with bath), 8 suites. A/C MINIBAR TV TEL

Rates: NZ$141 (U.S. $91.65) standard single or double; NZ$169 (U.S. $109.85) premium single or double; NZ$197 (U.S. $128.05) superior single or double; NZ$281 (U.S. $182.65) suite. Lower weekend and corporate rates. Reservations can be made through Flag Inns. AE, DC, MC, V.

The Southern Cross is Dunedin's top hotel: It's got a great city-center location, attractive rooms, and an unusually personable staff. When I last stayed here, the Exchange Wing (formerly the adjacent State Insurance Building) had just opened, and I was impressed with its standard rooms (I liked these quarters more than the premium rooms). The Carlton Restaurant offers a full à la carte menu and flambé cooking. The Ports O' Call Bar & Grill is more casual, and the Deli Cafe is conveniently open very long hours. Four rooms are equipped for the handicapped.

On the Otago Peninsula

Larnach Lodge and Hostel, Larnach Castle, Otago Peninsula (P.O. Box 1350, Dunedin). ☎ **03/476-1616.** Fax 03/476-1574. 12 rms (all with bath), 40 beds (no rooms with bath).

Rates: NZ$20 (U.S. $13) single in hostel; NZ$30 (U.S. $19.50) double in hostel; NZ$120 (U.S. $78) double in lodge. Three-course dinner in castle NZ$40 (U.S. $26) extra. AE, BC, DC, MC, V.

Larnach Castle dates from 1871, but when Margaret Barker bought it in 1967 it was in a sorry state. Now many years and much hard work later, it has been restored to its original glory; in addition to planting beautiful gardens, she and her family have converted the stables into a hostel and added a 12-room lodge to the grounds. Lodge rooms have heaters, telephones, and coffee- and tea-making facilities, and by the time you get there they'll all have bathrooms. My favorite room is upstairs in the corner, but all quarters here have spectacular views over lush green hills rolling all the way down to the harbor. Guests can dine in the castle and eat breakfast overlooking the grounds. House guests tour the castle for half price. Remember, it's chilly on this windswept peninsula, so wear your woolies. It's 13km (8 miles) east of Dunedin.

4 Where to Eat

Dunedin is literally broken out with good places to eat—name your price range and you're sure to find half a dozen or more that fit the bill.

A LOCAL INSTITUTION

Stewart's Coffee House, 12 Lower Octagon. ☎ **477-6687.**

Cuisine: SPECIALTY COFFEES/SANDWICHES/PASTRIES. **Reservations:** Not required.
Prices: Under NZ$10 (U.S. $6.50). AE, MC, V.
Open: Mon–Thurs 9am–5pm, Fri 9am–6:30pm.

Dunedin residents have long treasured this coffeehouse for its fresh-roasted coffee, espresso, and cappuccino (you'll love the smell!); its cozy basement location—also very central—and sandwiches, which far surpass those in most such places, in both quality and selection. For example, the plain old egg sandwich becomes a curried egg sandwich at Stewart's. There's soup and a nice array of cakes and other sweets. You can, of course, get tea, but it's the coffee that's a standout, and you can buy it by the pound to enhance meals back in your motel kitchen.

RESTAURANTS

★ $ **The Bank,** 12 The Octagon. ☎ **477-4430.**

Cuisine: MODERN NEW ZEALAND. **Reservations:** Not accepted.
Prices: Lunch about NZ$6 (U.S. $3.90). AE, BC, DC, MC, V.
Open: Mon–Thurs 11:30am–11pm, Fri–Sat 11:30am–midnight.

Until 1993 this really was a bank—the ANZ Bank. Now it's a really attractive spot to have a light meal, afternoon tea, or a drink. Large windows overlook the comings-and-goings in The Octagon, and banknotes decorate the walls. Lunch choices include quiche and salad, phyllo parcels, nachos with chiles, pita-bread basket with salad, or a Kiwi version of a traditional ploughman's. The same buffet menu is in effect all during the day until 9pm; after that only drinks, coffee, and desserts are offered. Licensed (with Guinness on tap).

The Best Cafe, 30 Stuart St. ☎ **477-8059.**

Cuisine: SEAFOOD/STEAK. **Reservations:** Not required.
Prices: Main courses NZ$12–NZ$15 (U.S. $7–$9.75). BC, MC, V.
Open: Mon–Fri 11:30am–7pm.

This friendly family-run café in the city center specializes in seafood served in down-home surroundings, complete with plastic tablecloths and a linoleum floor. Steaks and grills are also on the menu, and it has been welcoming families with children since 1937.

Blue Note Cafe, 95 Filleul St. ☎ **477-7233.**

Cuisine: MODERN NEW ZEALAND. **Reservations:** Required Fri–Sat.
Prices: Appetizers NZ$8–NZ$10 (U.S. $5.20–$6.50); main courses NZ$19–NZ$22 (U.S. $12.35–$14.30). Bar and lunch menu less expensive. AE, MC, V.
Open: Lunch Wed–Fri noon–2:30pm; dinner Mon–Sat from 5:30pm.

Owner Adrienne Malloy presides over this attractive dining spot, with its rimu bar at one end, high ceiling, double-hung kauri windows, and blue walls. Jazz and blues accompany such delicious main courses as chicken breast crusted in nibbed almonds, served on bitter greens with a ginger-and-sherry sauce; tripe simmered in a fresh herb, onion, and tomato sauce with black olives; and grilled beef filet with mushrooms, garlic, and bacon, set on a leek-and-potato rosti and served with a port sauce. There's occasional live entertainment early in the week. They may be offering Sunday brunches by the time you get there. Licensed.

$ **Deli Cafe,** in the Southern Cross Hotel, 118 High St. ☎ **477-0752.**

Cuisine: DELI/ROASTS. **Reservations:** Not required.
Prices: Appetizers NZ$2–NZ$3 (U.S. $1.30–$1.95); main courses NZ$6.50–NZ$9 (U.S. $4.25–$5.85). AE, DC, MC, V.
Open: Daily 6am–1am.

This luxury hotel (see "Where to Stay," earlier in this chapter) has a very good budget eatery at street level—it's bright, casual, and open long hours. It has the feel of a late-night diner, even in the afternoon. Food is served cafeteria style and there's a smoking room upstairs. You can get a snack for under NZ$5 (U.S. $3.25), as well as roasts and other hot dishes. Licensed.

Golden Harvest Restaurant, in the Harvest Court Mall, 218 George St. ☎ **477-8333.**

Cuisine: CHINESE. **Reservations:** Not required.
Prices: Appetizers NZ$5–NZ$8.50 (U.S. $3.25–$5.55); main courses NZ$13.50–NZ$35 (U.S. $8.80–$22.75). AE, DC, MC, V.
Open: Lunch daily 11:30am–2:30pm; dinner daily 5:30pm–"late."

My cardinal rule for finding really good Chinese restaurants is to go where the Chinese go—and the large Chinese clientele at the Golden Harvest attests to its excellence in ambience, food, and service. It's a pleasant place done in muted reds and greens, with an attractive lounge and bar, Chinese lanterns, and soft Chinese music. Specialties include pork filet Peking style on a sizzling plate, crispy chicken, sweet-and-sour choices, and other spicy dishes of the Orient. Le Ah Sew Hoy is the hostess and owner. Licensed and BYO.

High Tide, 25 Kitchener St. ☎ **477-9784.**

Cuisine: NEW ZEALAND. **Reservations:** Recommended.
Prices: Appetizers NZ$7 (U.S. $4.55); main courses NZ$18.50 (U.S. $12). AE, BC, DC, MC, V.
Open: Dinner only, Mon–Sat 6pm–"late."

If you have a penchant for sitting by the water and gazing out to sea, you'll feel right at home at this L-shaped restaurant in a former heliport building with a dozen large windows looking onto the harbor. Ceiling fans gently stir the air in this peaceful spot, where the chalkboard menu tempts with chicken, sirloin steak, lamb, pasta, fish, and seafood. BYO. The High Tide is a short drive from the city center in an unlikely industrial area.

Joseph Mellor Restaurant, at the Otago Polytechnic, Tennyson St. at Upper Stuart St. ☎ **477-3014.**

Cuisine: NEW ZEALAND. **Reservations:** Recommended.
Prices: Three-course lunch NZ$9.50 (U.S. $6.18); four-course dinner NZ$17 (U.S. $11.05). BC, MC, V.
Open: Lunch Tues–Thurs at noon; dinner Tues–Thurs at 6pm. (Call to confirm.) **Closed:** All school vacations.

This is Dunedin's best-kept dining secret (I wouldn't know about it if long-time locals hadn't told me). The food is prepared by catering students under the watchful eye of their instructors. It's really good, but they keep their prices low because they need a constant flow of people to practice on. There's only one sitting for each meal, and I suggest you ring (phone) in advance to make sure there isn't a school holiday in effect. In addition to a good meal, you'll enjoy a harbor view and excellent service. Licensed and BYO.

The Palms Cafe, 84 Lower High St., at Dowling St., Queens Gardens. ☎ **477-6534.**

Cuisine: NEW ZEALAND. **Reservations:** Recommended Sun–Fri, required Sat.
Prices: Appetizers NZ$8.50 (U.S. $5.55); main courses NZ$18–NZ$20 (U.S. $11.70–$13). AE, BC, DC, MC, V.

Open: Dinner only, Mon–Fri from 5pm, Sat–Sun from 6pm.

This has got to be one of Dunedin's prettiest eateries. Its window walls, ornate ceiling, and two intimate dining rooms make it romantic as well. The chalkboard menu usually lists an excellent chowder, and main dishes might include lamb satay, vegetable quiche, or pan-baked flounder. There's a budget fixed-price menu on Monday through Friday from 5 to 6:30pm. It's strictly no-smoking and BYO.

Potpourri, 97 Lower Stuart St. ☎ **477-9983.**

Cuisine: VEGETARIAN. **Reservations:** Not accepted.
Prices: Appetizers/light lunches NZ$4–NZ$5 (U.S. $2.60–$3.25); main courses NZ$6–NZ$8 (U.S. $3.90–$5.20). No credit cards.
Open: Mon–Fri 9am–8pm, Sat 11am–3pm. **Closed:** Three weeks at Christmas.

Make Potpourri (locals pronounce it "Pot-*pour*-ee") one of your first choices for a meal because you'll probably want to return again and again. If you've been neglecting your vegetables, this is your chance to make up for it. Check the chalkboard for the quiche and main dish of the day or choose salads (you can order half portions), open-face sandwiches that come with three small salads, fresh scones and muffins, spanakopita with a half salad, and tacos. Good news for frozen yogurt lovers—it's available here. Not licensed and not BYO.

★ $ **Terrace Cafe,** 118 Moray Place. ☎ **474-0686.**

Cuisine: MEDITERRANEAN/ETHNIC. **Reservations:** Recommended.
Prices: Appetizers NZ$4.50–NZ$8.50 (U.S. $2.95–$5.55); main courses NZ$14–NZ$17.50 (U.S. $9.10–$11.40). MC, V.
Open: Dinner only, Tues–Sat 6pm–"late."

This little place is a real gem! By that, I don't mean that this is a spit-and-polish, take-yourself-seriously little gem—on the contrary, it's a down-to-earth, as-casual-or-as-dressy-as-you-feel sort of place that looks like a Victorian parlor. On cool nights, the fireplace glows with yet another inducement to relax as you enjoy a menu composed of great homemade soups (if they have pumpkin, you're in luck), main courses that might include deviled kidneys with bacon and mushrooms, fish curry, veal, chicken cooked in any one of a number of inventive ways, at least one vegetarian dish, Mediterranean and ethnic cuisine, crisp salads, and homemade desserts like carrot cake or chocolate gâteau. Everything is fresh and the service is friendly (as are your fellow diners—this has long been a Dunedin favorite). It's across from the Fortune Theatre. BYO.

Worth the Extra Money

Bell Pepper Blues, 474 Princes St. ☎ **474-0973.**

Cuisine: MODERN NEW ZEALAND. **Reservations:** Recommended.
Prices: Appetizers NZ$11–NZ$14 (U.S. $7.15–$9.10); main courses NZ$20–NZ$25 (U.S. $13–$16.25); less expensive at lunch. AE, BC, DC, MC, V.
Open: Lunch Wed–Fri noon–2pm; dinner Mon–Sat 6:30–9pm.

Try to arrive here early enough to have a before-dinner drink in front of the open fire. Bell Pepper Blues has an inconspicuous exterior and an understated interior, but chef Michael Clydesdale offers this city's highest haute cuisine. Sample main courses include roast lamb rump flavored in olive oil with kaffir lime leaves and garlic, served with crisp polenta and potato rosti; grilled fresh Marlborough salmon on linguine and wilted spinach; and baked tartlet of roast aubergine (eggplant) purée, avocados, and spinach under a feta-and-cornbread crust. Licensed (no BYO).

5 What to See & Do

If you find yourself in the vicinity of Water and Princes streets, diagonally across from the Chief Post Office, you'll be standing on what was the waterfront back when the first settlers arrived in Dunedin and what had been a Maori landing spot for many years. Look for the **bronze plaque** that reads: "On this spot the pioneer settlers landed from a boat off the *John Wickliffe* on the 23rd day of March, 1848, to found the city and province." It's a good jumping-off point for your exploration of the city as it is today.

Now, for any **bagpipe** fanatics, let me suggest that you try to arrange to hear the lovely instruments while you're in this little bit of transported Scotland. You may be in town for a scheduled event at which they're featured, but if not, just take yourself to the **Dunedin Visitor Centre,** 48 The Octagon, or call 474-3300. They'll do their best to get you to a pipe-band rehearsal, if nothing else (which could turn out to be more fun than a formal performance!). Also ask about attending an **evensong choral service** at St. Paul's Cathedral or a **welcoming haggis ceremony.**

In any case, your first order of business should be a stop by the visitor center; consider watching their half-hour color video ***Dunedin Discovered,*** which will give you a good overview of the region and of Dunedin's attractions. Also, pick up a sightseeing map and look for the ★ **"Walk the City"** brochure (NZ$2.50/U.S. $1.65) to guide you around the streets.

There are terrific **scenic drives** around the city and on the peninsula, so request the relevant brochures.

There are three very good lookout points from which to view the city and its environs: ★ **Mount Cargill Lookout,** 8km (4³/₄ miles) from the city center (turn left at the end of George Street, then left on Pine Hill Road to its end, then right onto Cowan Road, which climbs to the summit); **Centennial Lookout,** or Signal Hill (turn onto Signal Hill Road from Opoho Road and drive 3km (1³/₄ miles), to the end of Signal Hill Road); and **Bracken's Lookout** (at the top of the Botanic Gardens).

According to the *Guinness Book of World Records,* Dunedin has the ★ **steepest street in the world,** beating out San Francisco and alpine Switzerland. Just minutes from the city center, the little street begins gently, then rears skyward dramatically to come to a dead end on the hillside. It's quite an experience to walk up, and for the hale and hearty, there's a footpath with a railing on one side of the street, while on the opposite side, no fewer than 270 steps take you to the top. Steps or footpath, walking is your best way up—residents on the street groan when they see (or more likely, hear) a car attempting to climb the hill. Cars stall when you try to change gears; braking power is so much less when the car rolls backward that cars often careen backward down the hill, completely out of control; and gas tanks leak if a car is parked with fuel tanks pointed downward. So, as you *walk* up, remember that the view from the top of the city and harbor goes beyond spectacular. Just where will you find this hilly highlight? Its name is Baldwin Street, and you get there by taking the Normandy bus to North Road, and Baldwin is the 10th street on the right past the Botanic Gardens.

Tours, Cruises & Train Rides

Dunedin is blessed with excellent tour operators who provide enjoyable ways to do sightseeing the easy way. One word of advice, however: If possible, telephone or fax ahead to book, since—especially during summer—the tours are very popular, and if your time in town is limited, you may miss out on the one you most want.

COACH TOURS

Newtons Coach Tours, P.O. Box 2034, Dunedin (☎ **03/477-5577**), conducts excellent tours of varying durations, all with knowledgeable guides providing valuable insight into the city's sightseeing highlights, along with the occasional human-interest anecdote to liven things up. All tours may be booked directly with Newtons or with the visitor center—*be sure to check exact departure times,* since they can vary from time to time. If requested, they will pick up and drop off at your hotel, motel, motor camp, or hostel.

If you book all three tours there's a 10% discount.

Tour 1, with a morning departure, leaves from the visitor center for a guided tour of Olveston House, Queens Drive Scenic Reserve, the city's historic buildings, Otago University campus, and other city sights. The fare (including all admissions) is NZ$21 (U.S. $13.65) for adults; children are charged NZ$11 (U.S. $7.15).

Tour 2 departs the visitor center shortly after noon for the Travel Summit Road, Otago Peninsula, guided tour of Larnach Castle, and a visit to Glenfalloch Woodland Gardens. Fares, including all admissions, are NZ$25 (U.S. $16.25) for adults, NZ$13 (U.S. $8.45) for children.

★ **Tour 3,** an early-afternoon tour, takes you from the visitor center departure point along a 45-mile coastal drive of scenic beauty, a tour of the yellow-eyed penguin conservation project and a cruise to the Royal Albatross Colony. Adults pay NZ$62 (U.S. $40.30); children are charged half price.

Wild South, P.O. Box 963, Dunedin (☎ **03/474-3300;** fax 03/474-3111), runs an unusual ★ **Twilight Wildlife Conservation Experience,** with a maximum of 12 people. This is a six-hour day trip that includes an introduction to Dunedin's history and visits to the Otago Peninsula Ornithological Section, peninsula beaches, and albatross, seal, and penguin colonies. The tour includes a two-hour visit to the Yellow-Eyed Penguin Conservation Reserve, a self-funded project for the world's rarest penguin. Viewing is from specially designed holes 5 to 10 meters (15 to 30 feet) away, which provides good photo opportunities. You'll have to call for exact departure times and for reservations. The fare is NZ$46 (U.S. $29.90) per person.

TOURS FOR A TERRIBLE THIRST

★ **Wilsons Distillery Whisky Tours** take you behind the scenes in New Zealand's only whisky distillery (incidentally, while all other such spirits are "whiskey," in the case of scotch, it's always "whisky"). The tour begins with a short video describing the history of whisky making in Dunedin, with a detailed description of the distilling process from the original grains right through to the bottled product. You're then taken through the distillery to see that process in action, after which you're treated to a tasting in the distillery's visitor center, which has a number of whisky products, including crystal decanter sets and cherries in whisky, for sale. Each tour takes about 1½ hours and costs NZ$5 (U.S. $3.25). All bookings must be made through the Dunedin Visitor Centre, 48 The Octagon (☎ **474-3300**), which can also provide more detail and tour times.

Tours of **Speights Brewery,** 200 Rattray St. (☎ **477-9480**), run only in the morning, usually at 10:30am, for the very good reason that the brewing process occurs only in the morning and an afternoon tour would be far less interesting. You're taken through the entire brewing process of Speights beer, "The Pride of the South," then presented with a sample of the end product. Tours run Monday through Thursday, take about 1½ hours, and cost NZ$5 (U.S. $3.25). Book directly with the brewery.

TOURS FOR A SWEET TOOTH

The factory of ★ **Cadbury Confectionery Ltd.** in Dunedin is among the very few in the world in which the complete chocolate-making process is performed under one roof. The tour begins with a 10-minute video on the company's history, which dates back to the early 1800s. As you're taken through the factory, you'll see the manufacturing process of several different chocolate products, with samples of each. Unfortunately, if one or more of those samples sparks off an appetite for more, you'll have to buy them through retail outlets, since the factory has no showroom or shop. The tours run Monday through Friday at 1:30pm and 2:30pm. There's no charge, and because of their immense popularity and a limit of 24 people per tour, *early booking is essential.* Children under 5 and the wearing of sandals are not permitted. To reserve, contact Cadbury Confectionery Ltd., 280 Cumberland St. (☎ **467-7800**).

CRUISES

To see Dunedin and the Otago Peninsula wildlife from the water, check with **Monarch Otago Harbour Cruises Ltd.** at their waterfront office at the corner of Wharf and Fryatt streets (☎ **03/477-4276**; fax 03/477-4216) to see what they have on offer while you're there. They run a variety of interesting cruises, including viewing albatross, seals, and more. To see the yellow-eyed penguin, take their "Cruise & Penguin" (offered October to March) or "Cruise 'n Coach" (offered August to June). Fares range from NZ$20 to NZ$69 (U.S. $13 to $44.85), and there are discounts for senior citizens, students, and YHA members. For more details and reservations, contact the company directly or inquire at the visitor center.

A TRAIN EXCURSION

The small excursion train to the **Taieri Gorge** is a terrific way to spend an afternoon. The spectacular Taieri Gorge has scenery easily on a par with the famed Silverton–Durango train in the U.S. state of Colorado. There are stops for picture taking and a fine commentary is provided all along the way. Afternoon tea and snacks are available in the snack-bar car, as well as beer, wine, and spirits. Departures for the 4- to 5½-hour trips are from the Dunedin Railway Station, with varying schedules (for days of the week and times) throughout the year. The fare to Middlemarch is NZ$47 (U.S. $30.55) for adults, and one schoolage child rides free with each adult. The fare to Pukerangi is NZ$43 (U.S. $27.95). Students get a 20% discount. Buy tickets at the railway station or the visitor center. Readers recommend riding in the "adults-only" car.

City Sights

Dunedin's ★ **railway station** is a marvelous old Flemish Renaissance–style edifice, designed by George A. Troup. He won the Institution of British Architects Award for his efforts and was later knighted, but never climbed to any position lofty enough to leave behind his affectionate local nickname, "Gingerbread George." Built of Kokonga basalt, with Oamaru limestone facings, the station's most prominent feature is its large square clock tower, but equally impressive are the Aberdeen granite pillars supporting arches of the colonnade across the front, the red Marseilles tiles on the roof, and the colorful mosaic floor in the massive foyer depicting a "puffing billy" engine and other bits of railroad life (more than 725,000 Royal Doulton porcelain squares). Look for a replica of Dunedin's coat-of-arms, stained-glass windows above the balcony (the engines on both look as if they're coming straight at you, no matter where you stand), and the plaque honoring New Zealand railway men who died in the 1914–18 war.

Dunedin's lovely **Botanic Garden** is at the northern end of George Street. Established in 1869, it's noted for masses of rhododendrons and azaleas (at their best from October to December). The rock garden, winter garden, and native kohai and rata trees are also noteworthy. Morning and afternoon teas, as well as hot snacks and buffet lunches, are available in the kiosk restaurant on the grounds. No matter how rushed your schedule, you owe yourself a stroll through this lovely, peaceful spot.

★ **Otago Settlers Museum,** 220 Cumberland St. ☎ **477-5052.**

This museum provides a look back into the lives of Dunedin's first residents and follows the development of the city and province right up to the present. It's just down from the railway station in the city center. Look for the sole surviving gas streetlamp outside, one of many used on the city's major streets circa 1863. Inside are an exhibition on the Kai Tahu communities of Otago; a transport collection; three period rooms; *Josephine,* a double Fairlie steam engine, which pulled the first Dunedin–Port Chalmers express; a Penny Farthing Cycle you can actually ride (although you won't go anywhere since it's held by a frame and mounted on rollers—still fun, though); and all sorts of other relics of life in these parts many years ago. There are other hands-on exhibits, such as toys and mechanical musical instruments, and life in the 20th century is also vividly portrayed. In the Furniture Room, faded sepia photographs of early settlers peer down with stern visages at visitors—one has to wonder what they think of their progeny who wander through. The Archives and Research Department holds records of thousands of Otago families, and is open Monday through Friday for a charge of NZ$10 (U.S. $6.50), which includes admission to the museum.

Admission: NZ$4 (U.S. $2.60) adults, NZ$3 (U.S. $1.95) senior citizens, free for children. Additional charges for special exhibitions.

Open: Mon–Fri 10am–5pm, Sat–Sun and public holidays 1–5pm.

Otago Museum, Great King St. ☎ **477-2372.**

Established in 1868, this is one of New Zealand's most important museums, containing large ethnographic, natural history, and decorative-arts collections. Exhibits in the Maori Gallery focus on the culture of the southern Maori, as well as on Oceania in general. There's even a display showing a moa, the extinct giant bird of New Zealand. The hands-on science center, Discovery World, is definately cool for kids. There are a museum shop and a café on the premises.

Admission: Museum, free; Discovery World, NZ$6 (U.S. $3.90) adults, NZ$3 (U.S. $1.95) children, NZ$11–NZ$14 (U.S. $7.15–$9.10) families.

Open: Mon–Fri 10am–5pm, Sat–Sun 1–5pm. **Closed:** Good Friday and Christmas Day.

Olveston, 42 Royal Terrace. ☎ **477-3320.**

Olveston is a "must see" of any Dunedin visit. It's one of the country's best-known stately homes, fully furnished, open to the public—and it's magnificent. The double brick house is Jacobean in style, faced with Oamaru stone and Moeraki gravel, surrounded by an acre of tree-shaded grounds. A much-traveled and very prosperous couple, the Theomins, built the 35-room home in 1904–6 as a 25th-anniversary gift for each other, and it's as much a work of art as the multitude of art works within its walls. The house was bequeathed to Dunedin in 1966, and has been carefully maintained in virtually its original state. There are more than 250 pictures in a variety of media in Olveston, including those of some 37 New Zealand artists. The dining room's Regency table and Chippendale chairs are graced by a range of table settings allowing the variety of glass, porcelain, and silver, also seen in the butler's pantry, to be enjoyed by visitors. At every turn there is evidence of the comfort and convenience, as well as visual beauty, built into this home. Although reservations are not essential, they are given preference, and you can view the house only on a guided tour.

Admission: NZ$10 (U.S. $6.50) adults, NZ$3 (U.S. $1.95) children.

Open: Guided tour, daily at 9:30 and 10:45am, noon, and 1:30, 2:45, and 4pm.

Dunedin Public Art Gallery, in Logan Park. ☎ **477-8770.**

Don't miss a visit to this art gallery, which holds a special collection of more than 40 works by Frances Hodgkins, Dunedin born and considered the finest painter ever produced by New Zealand. In addition, there's a fine collection of old masters that includes Gheeraerdts, Landini, Lorrain, and Monet, which was given to the gallery by the de Beer family, who have a long connection with Dunedin. It's presently located at the end of Anzac Avenue, but may have moved to The Octagon by the time you get here.

Admission: Free (donations encouraged).

Open: Mon–Fri 10am–5pm, Sat–Sun and holidays 2–5pm.

The Otago Peninsula

You really shouldn't leave Dunedin without exploring the 33km (20-mile)-long peninsula that curves around one side of the beautiful Otago (Oh-*tah*-go) Harbour. You can take one of the tours mentioned above, or head out Portobello Road, which runs along the harbor. In addition to the places listed below, other sights you may want to visit include a **Maori church at Otakou** and an **aquarium** at the Portobello Marine Laboratory operated by the University of Otago near Quarantine Point (it's open on Saturday, Sunday, and holidays from noon to 4:30pm). The Visitor Centre can supply details.

You will also quite possibly be interested in the **yellow-eyed penguins** that can be seen at Southlight Wildlife near the Royal Albatross Colony. Admission is NZ$5 (U.S. $3.25) for adults, free for children. Late afternoon is a good time to go; make arrangements through the visitor center.

Royal Albatross Colony, Taiaroa Head. ☎ **478-0499** or **478-0498.**

The magnificent royal albatross, perhaps with an instinctive distrust of the habitations of humankind, chooses remote, uninhabited islands as nesting grounds. With the single exception, that is, of this mainland colony 33km (20 miles) from Dunedin. The first egg was found here in 1920; today the colony consists of more than 20 breeding pairs, as well as several nonbreeding juvenile birds, each year. While the Albatross Gallery here is open daily throughout the year, the observatory is open only from late November to mid-September (the dates vary slightly from year to year) and is closed during the approximately nine weeks when the birds are choosing their nesting sites. Tours include an informative presentation on the birds, a video, a visit to the observatory, and a tour of the tunnel complex of the old Fort Taiaroa. These tours are popular during the late November to April period, so I *strongly* suggest that you reserve in advance (either with the Visitor Centre on The Octagon or by calling the Albatross Colony directly).

Admission: Albatross Gallery, free. Two-hour tours, late Nov to the end of Mar, NZ$25 (U.S. $16.25); early Apr to mid-Sept, NZ$20 (U.S. $13); mid-Sept to late Nov, NZ$15 (U.S. $9.75) (dates are approximate, depending on birds' activity). Children are charged about half price; family discounts available.

Open: Albatross Gallery, daily (hours vary seasonally). **Closed:** Christmas Day.

Glenfalloch Woodland Garden, 430 Portobello Rd. ☎ **476-1006.**

A good morning or afternoon tea stop on your Otago Peninsula excursion, Glenfalloch provides a microclimate on its grounds that allows plants to grow even in winter. At the 30-acre estate, allow time to wander through native bush, under English oaks (some as old as 200 to 300 years), and among magnificent and unusual rhododendrons and azaleas not to be found anywhere else in the country, fuchsias, and primroses. Full lunches as well as teas are available in the fully licensed Garden Chalet Restaurant with strolling peacocks occasionally fanning their glorious plumage just outside.

Admission: Donation requested.

Open: Daily dawn–dusk.

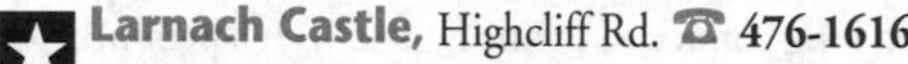

Larnach Castle, Highcliff Rd. ☎ **476-1616.**

This neo-gothic mansion is right out of an old English movie, but much more grand than anything you've ever seen on film. William Larnach came from Australia in the late 1860s to found the first Bank of Otago. He began building the grandiose home (which he called "The Camp") in 1871 for his French heiress wife. It took 200 workmen 3 years to build the shell and a host of European master craftsmen another 12 years to complete the interior. Total cost: £125,000. Larnach's concept was to incorporate the very best from every period of architecture, with the result that the hanging Georgian staircase lives happily with Italian marble fireplaces, English tiles, and colonial-style verandas. One of the most magnificent examples of master craftsmanship is the exquisite foyer ceiling, which took three craftsmen $6^{1}/_{2}$ years to complete.

After rising to the post of M.P. but suffering a series of personal misfortunes, Larnach committed suicide in his typically dramatic fashion in the Parliament Buildings in Wellington. (Larnach's first two wives died, and his younger third wife dealt him a fatal emotional blow by dallying with his son.) After his death, the farm around the castle was sold off and the Crown used the castle as a mental hospital. It is now the private home of the Barken family, who found it in a thoroughly dilapidated condition in 1967 and have spent the intervening years lovingly restoring it to its original glory. Pick up a printed guide at the reception area and wander as you choose, climbing the spiral staircase to battlements that look out onto panoramic views, and strolling through gardens and outbuildings. The stables now house hostel-type accommodations, and there are also comfortable accommodations in the lodge. Lunch and teas are available.

Admission: NZ$9.50 (U.S. $6.20) adults, NZ$3.50 (U.S. $2.30) children.

Open: Daily 9am–5pm. **Closed:** Christmas Day. **Directions:** Take Portobello Road 2 miles north of Glenfalloch Woodland Garden and follow the signs inland.

A Drive North of the City

Half an hour's drive from the city on the northern shore of Otago Harbour lies historic **Port Chalmers.** It was from here in 1884 that a ship sailed for England with the country's first shipment of frozen meat, creating an important new industry for New Zealand. A bit of an artists' colony today, Port Chalmers has a visitor center and a small seafaring museum. This area is popular for salmon and trout fishing from October to April. Drive over by taking Oxford Road out of Dunedin through the rolling hills to Port Chalmers and return via the harbor road for completely different scenery. While you're in the town, drop into **Carey's Bay Pub,** where all the fisherpeople go.

6 Sports & Recreation

When the time comes for a break in all that sightseeing, the **Moana Pool,** at the corner of Littlebourne Road and Stuart Street (☎ **474-3513** for pool information, **477-7792** for water slides, **477-6592** for the café), can provide a refreshing hour or two. There's a 50-meter, eight-lane swimming pool, a diving pool, a learner's pool, and water slides. Those slides are fully enclosed tubes, and you can choose a leisurely ride in the slow tube or a more adventurous one in the fast tube. Other watery options are scuba instruction, aqua-fitness classes, underwater hockey, and water polo. On the less wet side, you can take advantage of the poolside circuit gym, sunbeds, and sauna. Plan lunch at the café, or in summer bring a picnic on the sun terrace, where there are barbecues, trampolines, and a children's play area. There's also Flippers Poolside Crèche (day-care center) for children under 5, which is open daily to give parents a bit of time off to enjoy all the above. Hours vary, so call ahead, and fees depend on the activities you choose.

If you play **golf,** you might like to play at the St. Clair Golf Club (☎ **487-9201**). And if **cycling** is an interest, rent a bike from Browns, Lower Stuart Street (☎ 477-7259).

7 Savvy Shopping

Dunedin offers excellent shopping. Stores are generally open Monday through Thursday from 9am to 5:30pm, Friday from 9am to 9pm, and Saturday from 10am to 1pm.

If the need arises, there are good public restrooms on Municipal Lane on the upper Octagon.

The **Golden Centre,** 251 George St., between St. Andrew and Hanover streets, is a glass-enclosed concentration of shops specializing in everything from leather to woolens to women's fashions to cosmetics to gifts to books to … well, whatever you want, you'll probably find it here, including the **Golden Food Centre Court,** with a variety of eateries. The **Carnegie Centre,** 110 Moray Place, was built in 1908 as the city's public library, and the impressive building now houses the **Carnegie Gallery,** featuring New Zealand contemporary art exhibits, the Abbey Road Bar & Cafe, and assorted craft shops and cultural service organizations.

Some of the cheapest spirits on sale can be purchased at the **Robbie Burns Shoppe,** 374 George St. (☎ **477-6355**). The markup is slight on New Zealand wines. Open Monday through Saturday from 9am to 10pm.

Dunedin has more than its fair share of **gift shops,** but one I can recommend is the ✪ **New Zealand Shop,** on The Octagon (☎ **477-3379**) next to the visitor center (in the Civic Centre), with a fine collection of quality wool sweaters and other items, along with a large selection of T-shirts, gifts, and souvenirs; it's open daily in summer (normal shopping hours in winter) and will open just for you if you give them a call. Also worth a visit are the **Scottish Shop,** 187 George St. (☎ **477-9965**), which sells tartan ties as well as clan crest items; and **Helean Kiltmakers,** 8 Hocken St., Kenmure (☎ **453-0233**). For leather and lambskin items, **Glendermid Limited,** 192 Castle St. (☎ **477-3655**), is the leading specialist, with a wide selection of both.

The **Moray Gallery,** 32 Moray Place (☎ **477-8060**), has an excellent selection of paintings, glassware, and pottery by New Zealand artists and craftspeople.

☒ **Hyndman's Ltd.,** 17 George St., in the Civic Centre (☎ **477-0174**), was established back in 1906 and today stocks specialty books not readily found elsewhere, as well as a wide range of general-interest books. It's open Monday through Wednesday and Friday from 9am to 5:30pm, Thursday from 9am to 9pm, and Saturday from 10am to 1:30pm.

Daniels Jewellers Ltd., 72 Princes St. (☎ **477-1923**), has a wide variety of quality gifts, crystal, silverware, wooden items, leather items, pottery, Marlestone, diamond rings, gold, and silver. It's open Monday through Friday from 9:30am to 5pm.

8 Evening Entertainment

As you might imagine, students from the University of Otago keep Dunedin's pub life lively—except, maybe, during exam week. The community also has two good live theaters and a multiscreen movie theater. For current schedules, check the *Otago Daily Times.*

The Performing Arts

Fortune Theatre, at Stuart St. and Upper Moray Place. ☎ **477-8323.**

The Fortune, the world's southernmost professional live theater, is housed in a century-old bluestone building that was formerly Trinity Methodist Church. This theater presents the best of contemporary New Zealand and international plays in a nine-play season running from February to December.

Admission: Tickets, NZ$22 (U.S. $14.30) adults, NZ$12 (U.S. $7.80) students with ID.

Regent Theatre, on the Lower Octagon. ☎ **477-8597.**

Another venue for live entertainment, the Regent Theatre hosts shows by international and New Zealand performers. Check the local newspaper for current schedules of concerts and plays.

Admission: Tickets, NZ$10–NZ$45 (U.S. $6.50–$29.25).

The Bar Scene

PUBS & A WINE BAR

In addition to the places listed below, The Bank (see "Where to Eat," earlier in this chapter) is open Monday through Thursday until 11pm and Friday and Saturday until midnight.

The Albert Arms Tavern, 387 George St. ☎ **477-8035.**

This is Dunedin's "local"—popular with students and budget travelers for its cheery atmosphere and good-value pub meals. Monday night is Irish Band Night. The interior is Scottish tartan: Upstairs the decor includes a red-plaid rug, red upholstery on the chairs and booths, and green walls and ceiling. This upper level is where meals are served. The menu has been the same since 1971: chicken, or fish, or steak with chips for NZ$10 (U.S. $6.50). The Albert Arms, which dates from 1862, is across the street from the Robbie Burns (see below), so it's convenient to stop at both places. It's open daily from 11am to 11pm.

Bacchus Winebar, on the 1st Floor, 12 The Octagon. ☎ **474-0824.**

British, Australian, and New Zealand readers will know that the "first floor" referred to in the address of this wine bar means one level above ground. However, since "first floor" is synonymous with "ground floor" in American English, I need to point out to my compatriots that they'll have to climb a flight of stairs to find this spot. (I'm not sure where Canadians stand on this issue.)

This is a great place for a glass of wine or a light meal overlooking The Octagon. Domestic and imported wines are available by the glass or bottle. It's open Monday through Saturday from 11am to 11pm. Lunch is served Monday through Saturday from 11am to 3pm; dinner is Tuesday through Saturday from 6 to 9pm. Smoking is not allowed.

Clarendon Hotel, 28 MacLaggon St. ☎ **477-9095.**

While pubs traditionally close at 11pm, the Clarendon Hotel stays open later. Here you'll find the upstairs Shamrox and Karaoke Bar open from 5pm until "late." Downstairs there's dance music and plenty of high spirits.

Heffs, 244 King Edward St., South Dunedin. ☎ **455-1017.**

I personally found this pub too smokey to be enjoyable, but it's very popular as a venue for live music and budget meals. If you go there, you'll find collections of spoons and mugs on display, as well as about 500 whisky jugs and Jim Beam bourbon bottles.

Robbie Burns Pub, 370 George St. ☎ **479-2701.**

This is one of the oldest pubs in Dunedin, with a license dating from 1859. The "Poets Corner" near the door honors its namesake. There's a painting of Robbie Burns and friends and another of the poet at the opposite end of the bar. This attractive spot is popular with the university crowd. It's open Monday through Saturday from 11am to 11pm, and—as in most pubs—a "handle" (500ml) of beer will set you back NZ$3 (U.S. $1.95).

More Entertainment

Hoyts 6, 33 The Octogon. ☎ **477-7019.**

There are six big screens at the Hoyts Cinema on The Octagon. You may even be able to see a recently released New Zealand film before it's shown overseas. My friends had talked about *Once Were Warriors* for more than a year before I could see it in California.

Admission: Tickets, NZ$8.50 (U.S. $5.55).

9 En Route to Christchurch

The 366km (227-mile) trip from Dunedin to Christchurch can be completed in about five hours, but it's probably a good idea to slow down and look at a few things along the way.

MOERAKI

At Moeraki, about an hour's drive north of Dunedin, there's an unusual natural phenomenon that's worth looking at. On the beaches around this picturesque fishing village just south of Hampden, huge rounded boulders are scattered around as though some prehistoric giant had used them for a game of handball. The curious rocks were, according to scientists, formed by the gradual accumulation of lime about 60 million years ago, but the Maori have a different story. According to legend, one of the great migration canoes capsized nearby and large gourds and kumara seeds scattered on the beach and were turned to stone; they are known as *te kai-hinaki,* "the food baskets." Now, maybe rocks don't sound like a sightseeing attraction to you, but some people find them fascinating. Incidentally, if you travel from Dunedin to Christchurch by rail or bus, you'll get a good view. If you happen to arrive shortly after noon, you may be able to buy fish straight from the fishing boats coming in about that time.

You may well be tempted to linger in this pleasant setting, and it can easily be arranged by contacting **Walter and Theresa Kiener,** R.D. 2, Palmerston (☎ **03/439-4759**), who can provide a variety of accommodations, including flats, cabins, and caravan or sheltered tent sites—all at modest rates. Ask about the nearby penguin and seal colonies, which can be seen for free.

WAIANAKRUA

Some 85km (53 miles) north of Dunedin, you might want to stop at the **Mill House,** in Waianakrua (☎ **03/439-5515**), a handsome three-story stone building that was once a flour mill but is now a handsome restaurant-and-motel complex. The colonial-style dining room is beamed and attractively furnished, and the meals are reasonably priced. There's a wine license, and it's open Wednesday through Monday.

OAMARU

Oamaru, 116km (72 miles) north of Dunedin, is another good place to stop. In the 1870s it claimed 8 hotels, 30 grog shops, and 14 brothels, but the importance of Oamaru today is its **architecture.** Rightfully known as the "White Stone City," it's filled with impressive buildings made of gleaming-white limestone quarried in Weston, 6$^{1}/_{2}$km (4 miles) away (you can visit the **quarry** on Monday through Friday from 9am to 5pm—well worth the mini-excursion). Once you've walked along the main street and admired the architecture of the courthouse, bank, post office, and the fine Forrester Art Gallery, walk a little farther to the Harbour–Tyne Street **historic precinct** that the preservation-minded citizens of Oamaru have fought to save.

The **Oamaru Information Centre** is open Monday through Friday from 9am to 5pm and Saturday and Sunday from 10am to 4pm. The helpful staff can provide a map and show you how to get to the **basilica** and the **Waitaki Boys' School** to see more impressive examples of how the local limestone has been put to good use; and the local **Museum and Art Gallery,** which often features displays by local artists of the beautiful North Otago scenery. Ask at the information center about **architectural walks,** which can sometimes be organized for parties of two or more upon request, and about visits to the nearby colonies of yellow-eyed and blue penguins. You might want to save some time during your visit to Oamaru to stroll through the **Public Gardens,** especially Wonderland. For a quick bite, drop by one of the many coffee shops along the main street.

ASHBURTON

In Ashburton, 87km (54 miles) south of Christchurch, the Mill House Cafe in the **Ashford Craft Shop** makes a good lunch or tea stop. The shops in this complex are interesting too. It's on the west side of State Highway 1 and open Monday through Friday from 9am to 5pm and Saturday from 10am to 4pm. The café closes at 4pm during the week and at 3:30pm on Saturday.

READERS RECOMMEND

Penguin Watching. *"In Oamaru there's a small section where the little blue penguins come in to shore for the night. I'm told they arrive at dusk and leave an hour before daybreak. A couple of people have fenced off the area and just recently built bleachers for the spectators. They are adorable, noisy little critters and well worth a night's stay in Oamaru to see."*—Lois Churchill, Elkland, Penna., U.S.A.

Christchurch

14

CHRISTCHURCH IS AS ENGLISH AS DUNEDIN IS SCOTTISH—IN FACT, IT'S EVEN MORE so. Gothic buildings built of solid stone are everywhere, modern glass-and-concrete buildings scattered among them like afterthoughts. London's red buses are emulated here. English trees, brought out by settlers as a bit of home, flourish along the banks of the Avon River. A primary preoccupation of its citizenry is with private gardens of the English variety. And cricket, that most English of all sports, is played by all Christchurch boys. One of its most prized appellations is that of the "Most English City Outside England."

It is also a prosperous city—New Zealand's third largest after Auckland and Wellington, with a population of 307,000—staunchly conservative, with much to be proud of. An equitable climate (2,120 hours of sunshine annually), an airport considered to be one of the finest in the country, civic centers and sports arenas that outshine all those in other New Zealand cities—all are factors in Christchurch's 20th-century image.

For the visitor, Christchurch offers a variety of restaurants and entertainment, as well as excellent accommodations and plenty of sightseeing attractions. Seattle and Christchurch are sister cities, by the way, so if you hail from Seattle, be sure to sign the Sister City Visitors Book at the information center.

1 City Specifics

ARRIVING

BY PLANE Christchurch has frequent air service via Air New Zealand National, Mount Cook Airlines, Air Nelson, and Ansett. On the North Island, there's service to/from Auckland, Hokitika, Palmerston North, Rotorua, Taupo, and Wellington; on the South Island, to/from Dunedin, Invercargill, Mount Cook, Nelson, Queenstown, Te Anau, and Timaru.

Christchurch International Airport is 10km (6 miles) from Cathedral Square, out Memorial Avenue. The **Info-Service Centre,** in the domestic terminal, will book accommodations and transportation at no charge. There's a cafeteria and fully licensed (expensive) restaurant, car-rental desks, a bank with money-changing desks, a bookshop, gift and souvenir shops, a flower shop, hairdressers for both men and women, showers, and a large duty-free shop.

The **airport coach** to Worcester Street (opposite Noah's Hotel) costs NZ$3 (U.S. $1.95); the **express bus** to the airport from hotels, motels, and backpacker lodgings costs NZ$7 (U.S. $4.55). The **airport shuttle bus** runs regularly and picks up travelers from hotels, motels, and backpacker lodgings, for a fare of NZ$7 (U.S. $4.55). Call **365-5655** anytime.

BY TRAIN There's train service to/from Christchurch via the ***Southerner*** (Dunedin, Invercargill), the ***TranzAlpine*** (Greymouth), and the ***Coastal Pacific*** (Picton). The **railway station** is on Moorhouse Avenue, south of the city center. For train information, call **0800/802-802** toll free in New Zealand.

BY BUS Two bus companies—**InterCity** and **Mount Cook Landline**—offer service between Christchurch and Dunedin, Fox and Franz Josef Glaciers, Greymouth, Invercargill, Mount Cook, Nelson, Picton, Queenstown, Te Anau, Timaru, and Wanaka. **Southern Link Shuttles** (☎ **379-9991**) also provides service. InterCity buses arrive at and depart from the corner of Fitzgerald and Moorhouse avenues; the Mount Cook terminal is at 40 Lichfield St. (☎ **379-0690**). For bus information, call **379-9020.**

What's Special About Christchurch

Museums

- The Canterbury Museum, a one-stop look at Antarctica memorabilia, New Zealand birds, Oriental art, Maori culture, and a re-creation of a 19th-century Christchurch street.
- The International Antarctic Centre, which re-creates the current life, landscape, and scientific activity on that icy continent.

Gardens

- The Botanic Gardens in Hagley Park, recognized around the world as one of the best.
- Private gardens on Royds Street, and at the Sanitarium Health Food Company in Papanui.

Public Spaces

- Cathedral Square, in the city center, with its collection of such "eccentrics and nutters" as the colorful Wizard of Christchurch.

Walks

- The two-hour guided walk from the Visitor Centre that explores the city center and provides an in-depth commentary on its history.

Cathedrals

- Cathedral of the Blessed Sacrament, on Barbados Street, with its magnificent classic revival architecture.
- Christchurch Cathedral, on Cathedral Square, with its 120-foot tower affording splendid panoramic views.

Crafts

- The Arts Centre, on Worcester Boulevard, a workplace and showcase from some of New Zealand's best craftspeople.

Day Trips

- The *TranzAlpine*, New Zealand's best train, makes daily round-trip excursions to Greymouth.

BY CAR If you're coming from the north, you'll arrive on State Highway 1. If you're driving up from Dunedin, via Ashburton, you'll also be on State Highway 1. However, if your approach is from the southwest, via Lake Tekapo and Geraldine, I suggest you take Highway 79 to Highway 77 to Highway 73; this will bring you into Christchurch through Mt. Hutt and over the scenic Rakaia River. Christchurch is 366km (227 miles) north of Dunedin, 350km (217 miles) south of Picton, and 254km (157 miles) southeast of Greymouth.

CITY LAYOUT

The center of things is **Cathedral Square,** the point from which to get your bearings. Above it rise the spires of Christchurch Cathedral, from whose gothic tower you can look out over the flat, neatly laid out city. The **Avon River** runs lazily through the heart of the city, spanned by no fewer than 37 bridges as it wends its 24km (15-mile) course from Ilam (west of Christchurch) to the sea. The graceful willows that line its banks are said to have come from Napoleon's gravesite on St. Helena. **Colombo Street** bisects Cathedral Square north to south and is the city's main thoroughfare.

TOURIST INFORMATION

The **Christchurch-Canterbury Visitor Centre,** at the corner of Oxford Terrace and Worcester Boulevard (☎ **03/379-0629;** fax 03/377-2424), occupies a lovely 1886 red-brick building that was the first home of the Christchurch City Council. It's open Monday through Friday from 8:30am to 5pm and Saturday, Sunday, and holidays from 8:30am to 4pm (longer hours in summer). Be sure to pick up a copy of the ***Christchurch and Canterbury Visitor's Guide,*** a gold mine of information that's published by the Canterbury Tourism Council and distributed through hotels and the Visitor Centre. It not only gives up-to-date information on goings-on in the city, but also includes the surrounding area.

The Visitor Centre can also provide sightseeing advice, and arrange transportation, accommodations, and sightseeing reservations. There's a well-stocked gift shop that may be just the place to pick up craft items, maps, postcards, etc.

2 Getting Around

There are **local buses** that leave from the square, with zoned fares ranging from NZ80¢ to NZ$4 (U.S. 50¢ to $2.60). From 9am to 4pm, fares are reduced by half (get details from the bus information center in Cathedral Square or phone **366-8855**), and a 10-ride concession ticket is available.

In February 1995, Christchurch's **tramway** started running from Cathedral Square down Worcester Boulevard, along Rolleston Avenue, Armagh Avenue, New Regent Street, then back to the square.

You'll find **taxi** stands at Cathedral Square and all terminals. To call a cab, phone **379-9799, 377-5555,** or **379-5795.**

Getting behind the wheel of a car and **driving** isn't difficult; you only need to master the city's one-way street system. And since all on-street parking is metered, one of the following centrally located municipal parking buildings is your best bet: on Oxford Terrace near Worcester Boulevard, on Manchester Street near Gloucester Street, and on Lichfield Street near Durham. Check locally for the location of others.

Bikers will find the city ideal cycling country, since most of the terrain is dead flat. Traffic may frighten the life out of you in the city center, but move out a bit and the bike will do just fine.

As for seeing the city **on foot,** that's the way to go as long as you're concentrating on the city center near the square. To ramble through other, more far-flung sections, best take a public bus and then hoof it.

Fast Facts: Christchurch

Airlines The Air New Zealand ticket office is at 702 Colombo St.; Mount Cook Airline, at 91 Worcester Blvd.; Ansett, at 78 Worcester Blvd., and Qantas, at 119 Armagh St.

American Express The American Express agency in Christchurch is Guthreys Travel Centre, 126 Cashel St. (☎ **03/379-3560**). They accept mail for cardholders, issue and change traveler's checks, and replace lost or stolen traveler's checks and American Express cards.

Area Code The telephone area code (STD) is **03.**

Babysitters There's a child-care center (crèche) at 161 Tuam St. (☎ **365-6364**), open Monday through Friday from 8am to 5:30pm. Many hotels can furnish evening babysitters.

Currency Exchange The ANZ Bank bureau de change, at the corner of Hereford and Colombo streets, in Cathedral Square (☎ **371-4714**), is open Monday through Friday from 8:30am to 4:30pm.

Disabled Services Contact Disabilities Information Service, 314 Worcester St. (☎ **366-6189**), open Monday through Friday from 9am to 5pm.

Doctors For emergency referrals, contact After Hours Surgery, 931 Colombo St., at Bealey Avenue (☎ **365-7777**).

Emergencies For police, fire, and/or ambulance emergency service, dial **111.**

Hospitals Christchurch Hospital is at Oxford Terrace and Riccarton Avenue (☎ **364-0640**); ask for the Accident and Emergency Department.

Libraries The public library is on the corner of Gloucester Street and Oxford Terrace (☎ **379-6914**), open Monday through Friday from 10am to 9pm and Saturday, Sunday, and holidays from 10am to 4pm.

Post Office There's a large, centrally located post office in Cathedral Square.

Telegram/Fax All telegrams are sent through the post office, either by telephone or in person. The cheapest rate is "Letter Rate," which takes about 24 hours for delivery; rates for telegrams sent after regular post office hours can be as much as double.

Fax facilities are offered at the post office and at many hotels and motels. There's a commercial fax service at 148 Manchester St. (☎ **366-4829**).

3 Where to Stay

Christchurch has an abundance of good accommodations in all price ranges. Most are convenient to public transportation, a boon to those not driving.

The rates cited below include GST.

MOTELS

★ **Alexandra Court Motel,** 960 Colombo St., Christchurch. ☎ **03/366-1855.** Fax 03/379-8796. 9 units (all with bath). TV TEL **Bus:** 4.

Rates: NZ$88 (U.S. $57.20) single; NZ$93 (U.S. $60.45) double. Best Western discounts available. AE, DC, MC, V.

Units at the Alexandra Court are spacious and nicely decorated and have outside patios. Bonus facilities here are in-room video, Sky TV, phones, and electric blankets. Also available are wakeup-call service, hairdryers, continental breakfasts and fax service. One-bedroom units have both bathtub and shower, with an iron, ironing board, and radio. The guest laundry also holds a dryer. One-bedroom units can sleep up to four, those with two bedrooms will sleep six, and all have complete kitchens. There's at-your-own-door parking, with covered carports, at all except four units (there's covered parking space for them across the courtyard). Nearby are a golf course and a pool. The motel is a 15-minute walk to the city center.

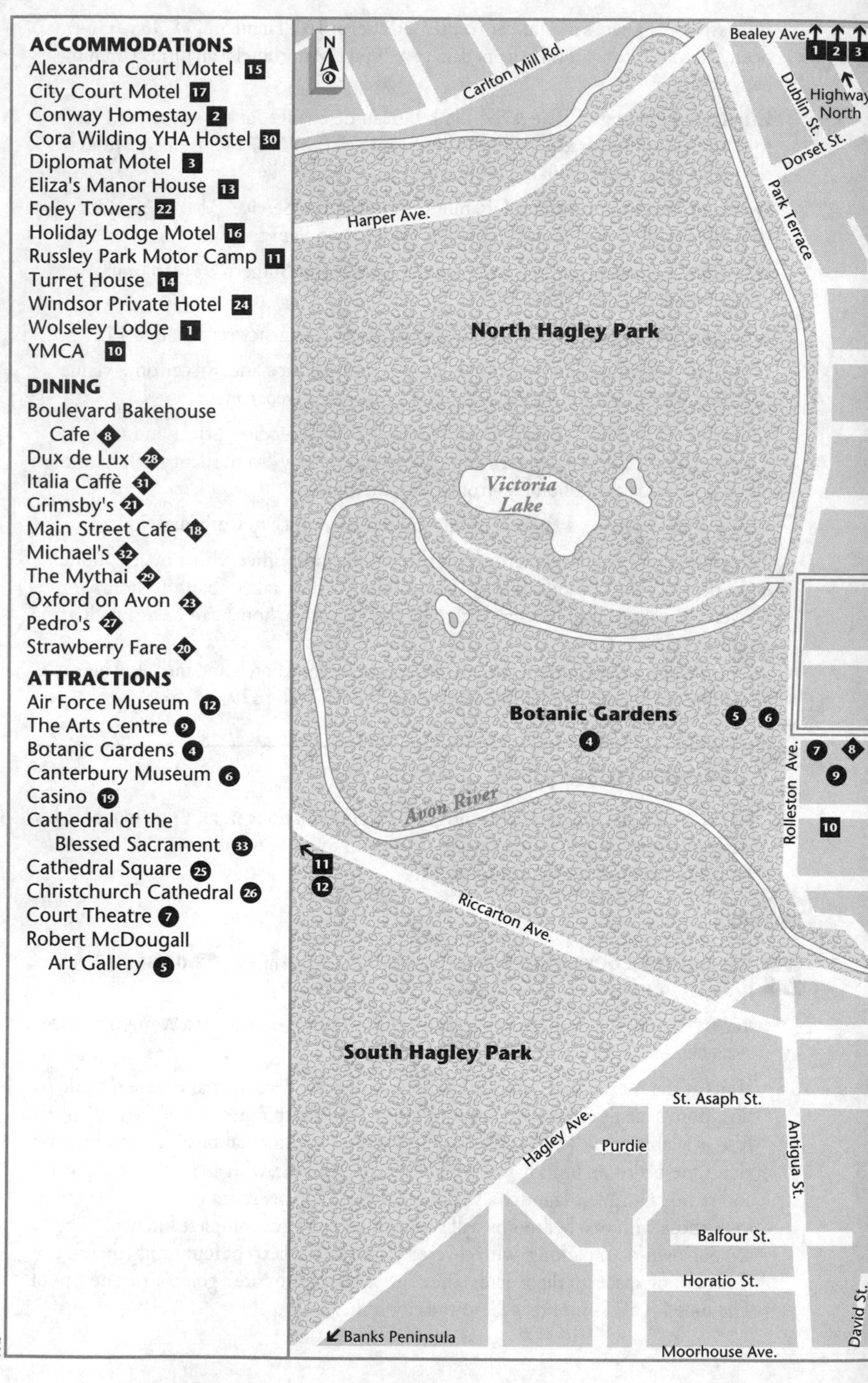
ACCOMMODATIONS
Alexandra Court Motel 15
City Court Motel 17
Conway Homestay 2
Cora Wilding YHA Hostel 30
Diplomat Motel 3
Eliza's Manor House 13
Foley Towers 22
Holiday Lodge Motel 16
Russley Park Motor Camp 11
Turret House 14
Windsor Private Hotel 24
Wolseley Lodge 1
YMCA 10
DINING
Boulevard Bakehouse Cafe 8
Dux de Lux 28
Italia Caffè 31
Grimsby's 21
Main Street Cafe 18
Michael's 32
The Mythai 29
Oxford on Avon 23
Pedro's 27
Strawberry Fare 20
ATTRACTIONS
Air Force Museum 12
The Arts Centre 9
Botanic Gardens 4
Canterbury Museum 6
Casino 19
Cathedral of the Blessed Sacrament 33
Cathedral Square 25
Christchurch Cathedral 26
Court Theatre 7
Robert McDougall Art Gallery 5
N
Bealey Ave.
Carlton Mill Rd.
Highway North
Dublin St.
Dorset St.
Park Terrace
Harper Ave.
North Hagley Park
Victoria Lake
Botanic Gardens
Rolleston Ave.
Avon River
Riccarton Ave.
South Hagley Park
St. Asaph St.
Hagley Ave.
Purdie
Antigua St.
Balfour St.
Horatio St.
David St.
Banks Peninsula
Moorhouse Ave.

9645

Christchurch

Tramway ═ Pedestrian Mall ⦀ Post Office ✉ Information ⓘ

City Court Motel, 850 Colombo St. (at Salisbury St.), Christchurch. ☎ and fax **03/366-9099.** 8 units (all with bath). TV

Rates: NZ$60 (U.S. $39) single or double. Additional person NZ$12 (U.S. $7.80) extra. AE, MC, V.

The City Court Motel welcomes families with children. There's one studio, one one-bedroom unit, and six with two bedrooms (two of them large enough to sleep eight). The immaculate units all have kitchens, separate sitting areas, electric heaters, and electric blankets, and six have a bathtub as well as a shower. There's a guest laundry on the premises, and a seven-day food store just across the street. The motel is six blocks from Cathedral Square and one block from the casino and City Hall.

Diplomat Motel, 127 Papanui Rd., Christchurch. ☎ **03/355-6009.** Fax 03/355-6007. 12 studios, 4 units. TV TEL

Rates: NZ$92 (U.S. $59.80) studio for one or two; NZ$111 (U.S. $72.15) apartment for one or two. Low-season and Best Western discounts available for direct bookings. AE, DC, MC, V.

Johanna and Peter Cunningham are the friendly and helpful hosts at the Diplomat. The attractive units have cathedral ceilings with timbered rafters and are surrounded by landscaped grounds. Artwork in each unit is by New Zealand artists and represents a wide range of styles. These two-bedroom apartments are spacious, with complete kitchens, queen-size beds, and a personal safe for your valuables. There's a nice spa, also in a landscaped garden setting, as well as a guest laundry. Both cooked and continental breakfasts are available. Located about a mile from the city center on a city bus route, the Diplomat is a three-minute walk from the Merivale Mall. French and German spoken.

$ **Holiday Lodge Motel,** 862 Colombo St., Christchurch. ☎ **03/366-6584.** Fax 03/366-6822. 15 units (all with bath). TV TEL

Rates: NZ$60 (U.S. $39) single; NZ$65 (U.S. $42.25) double. AE, MC, V.

The spacious and clean two-bedroom units at the Holiday Lodge are housed in two blocks on either side of a parking lot. Those in a yellow stucco building are all duplexes with bedrooms and a glassed-in sun porch upstairs. All units have Sky TV, radio, electric blanket, electric heater, and bath with both tub and shower. There's daily maid service, a sauna, laundry, and children's play area; a bus stop is nearby.

BED-&-BREAKFASTS

Conway Homestay, 11 Clissold St., Christchurch. ☎ **03/355-4806.** 1 rm (with bath).

Rates (including breakfast): NZ$40 (U.S. $26) per person. No credit cards.

Roberta Conway is a charming woman who welcomes guests in her private home on a quiet residential street close to Hagley Park and within walking distance of the city.

Family-Friendly Accommodations

City Court Motel (see above) The two-bedroom units with kitchens here are ideal for traveling families.

YMCA (see p. 374) The Y's location adjacent to the Botanic Gardens makes it a good choice for families with rambunctious children. There's plenty of room to run and nice grassy areas for playing games.

Guests are made to feel part of the family, with a good deal of personal attention (lots of help on what to see and do). There's a bus stop nearby.

★ **Eliza's Manor House,** 82 Bealey Ave., Christchurch. ☎ **03/366-8584.** Fax 03/366-4946. 11 rms (9 with bath).

Rates (including breakfast): NZ$75–NZ$150 (U.S. $48.75–$97.50) double. Lower rates in winter. AE, DC, MC, V.

This splendid old two-story mansion, approached by a curved driveway, has been completely restored. The carved kauri staircase is magnificent. There's lots of carved woodwork, plus colored leadlight (stained-glass) windows, antique pieces, and bits of Victoriana scattered about all add to the charming interior of this 1860s inn. All the rooms are comfortably furnished. One wing of the house holds a restaurant (open weekends only). Buses stop nearby.

Turret House, 435 Durham St. N., Christchurch. ☎ **03/365-3900.** Fax 03/365-5601. 10 rms (all with bath). TV TEL

Rates (including continental breakfast): NZ$65 (U.S. $42.25) single; NZ$85–NZ$100 (U.S. $55.25–$65) double. AE, DC, MC, V.

Turret House, built in 1885, has been renovated to the same style as Eliza's Manor House, next door. The rooms all have private facilities, and there's a nice guest lounge. Owners Glenda and Graham Weavers can provide fax service, laundry service, and babysitting. There's a nearby bus stop and it's a five-minute walk from the town center, park, and casino.

$ **Windsor Hotel,** 52 Armagh St., Christchurch. ☎ **03/366-1503.** Fax 03/366-9796. 40 rms (none with bath).

Rates (including breakfast): NZ$55 (U.S. $35.75) single; NZ$84 (U.S. $54.60) double. Discounts for groups of three or four; children are charged half price. AE, DC, MC, V.

Don Evans and Carol Healey, the charming—and caring—hosts, have built a devoted following over the years, primarily because of their personal interest in all guests. The carefully renovated, rambling old brick home has nicely decorated rooms (some with hot and cold running water). The hallways are heated for the trip to the conveniently placed bathrooms. The TV lounge holds lots of chairs and stacks of magazines. The outstanding breakfast often includes omelets or some other special item. Off-street

READERS RECOMMEND

Ashford Motor Lodge, *35 Papanui Rd.* (☎ **03/355-3416**; fax 03/355-3414). *"It was sparkling clean and comfortable, offered modern kitchen appliances, free automatic washer, swimming pool, and luxurious bathroom—and two quiet bedrooms cost us only NZ$130 (U.S. $84.50). They also have smaller units for NZ$88 (U.S. $57.20)."*—Patricia J. Powers, Kailua-Kona, Hawaii, U.S.A.

Latimer Lodge, 30 Latimer Sq. (☎ **03/379-6760;** fax 03/366-0133). *"I found this a lovely, yet homey place to stay. The staff went out of its way to assist me in locating an unusual item I wanted to buy. The rooms are nicely done and have all those little items that travelers need. The lodge has a cute pub and excellent restaurant. The rate is NZ$99 (U.S. $64.35)."*—Melissa Sistrhart, Templeton, Calif., U.S.A.

Cokers Hotel, 52 Manchester St. (☎ **03/379-8580;** fax 03/379-8585). *"At NZ$65 (U.S. $42.25) a night in the heart of Christchurch, this was a great find, even if slightly faded in glory."*—Sue and Frank Thorn, Fallbrook, Calif., U.S.A.

parking is available. The guesthouse, centrally located off Cranmer Square, is located near a bus stop and on the tramway line.

Wolseley Lodge, 107 Papanui Rd., Christchurch. ☎ **03/355-6202.** Fax 03/355-6180. 12 rms (none with bath). TV

Rates (including breakfast): NZ$35 (U.S. $22.75) single; NZ$65 (U.S. $42.25) double. Additional person NZ$20 (U.S. $13) extra. Discount for children. AE, MC, V.

This 92-year-old home is set in a tree-shaded lawn. Guest rooms in the two-story house come with hot and cold water and nice furniture, plus electric blankets and reading lamps. The lounge has overstuffed chairs and tea- and coffee-making facilities, and the dining room overlooks the lawn. There's a guest laundry with washer, dryer, and ironing board. The Wolseley is a 10-minute walk to the city center and casino, and there's bus service at the gate. Hosts Ray and Evelyn Upston are helpful.

HOSTELS & A YMCA

Cora Wilding YHA Hostel, 9 Evelyn Couzins Ave., Avebury Park, Richmond, Christchurch. ☎ **03/389-9199.** 40 beds (no rooms with bath). **Bus:** 10.

Rates: NZ$14 (U.S. $9.10) for members, NZ$18 (U.S. $11.70) for nonmembers. MC, V.

This lovely old white mansion is on a tree-shaded residential street about 1½ miles from Cathedral Square. It has stained-glass panels in the front door and is crowned by turrets and cupolas. There are six rooms sleeping 40 people, all bright and cheerful, plus a comfortable lounge. To one side is a large parking area, and in the rear, a children's playground. The laundry has coin-operated washers and dryers.

Foley Towers, 208 Kilmore St., Christchurch. ☎ **03/366-9720.** Fax 03/379-3014. 70 beds in 28 rms (7 rooms with bath).

Rates: NZ$14 (U.S. $9.10) per person double without bath, NZ$17.50 (U.S. $11.90) per person double with bath; NZ$10–NZ$14 (U.S. $6.50–$9.10) dorm bed. MC, V.

This comfortable two-story house is a short walk from Cathedral Square in the city center. Most rooms have underfloor heating, and there are two lounges, kitchens, and dining rooms, plus off-street parking and laundry facilities, at this privately owned hostel. It's strictly no-smoking and no children.

YMCA, 12 Hereford St., Christchurch. ☎ **03/365-0502.** Fax 03/365-1386. 40 dorm beds, 147 rms (25 with bath), 2 units.

Rates: NZ$33–NZ$52 (U.S. $21.45–$33.80) single; NZ$45–NZ$70 (U.S. $29.25–$45.50) double; NZ$90 (U.S. $58.50) one-bedroom unit for four; NZ$110 (U.S. $71.50) two-bedroom unit for six; NZ$15 (U.S. $9.75) bunk. AE, BC, DC, MC, V.

READERS RECOMMEND

Christchurch B&Bs. *"We have just spent a month in New Zealand staying at B&Bs, and we can recommend in the highest terms, for comfort, convenience, and company, two in Christchurch:* ***Fendalton House,*** *50 Clifford Ave., Fendalton, Christchurch (☎* ***03/355-4298****); and* ***Wairere,*** *55 Fendalton Rd., Fendalton, Christchurch (☎* ***03/355-5661****)."*—Prof. Irving Massey, Buffalo, N.Y., U.S.A.

Gothic Heights Motel, 430 Hagley Ave. (☎ **03/366-0838;** fax 03/366-0188). *"They picked us up at the airport and took us to the train; when we returned they picked us up at the bus station and took us to the train. What service! All free! Plus a newspaper at your door. The rate is NZ$91 (U.S. $59.15)."*—Beverly Carr, Toronto, Ont., Canada.

This Y was the best find of my most recent visit to Christchurch. The location couldn't be better—across from the Arts Centre and steps from the Botanic Gardens. Each person in a 4-, 6-, or 10-bunk room gets a locker with a key. The more expensive singles and doubles have baths, telephones, TVs, and tea- and coffee-making facilities. Only the units have kitchens. Rooms in this five-year-old building have contemporary decors, and the bathrooms are modern; half the rooms overlook the gardens, and 34 have balconies. There are both a dining room and a café on the premises. (I heard the food left something to be desired, but so what? There are several great places to eat in the Arts Centre.) The Y's gym, sauna, and aerobics class are available to guests at a discount.

CABINS & CAMPGROUNDS

Russley Park Motor Camp, 372 Yardhurst Rd. (on State Highway 73), Christchurch (☎ **03/342-7021**), is only 2 miles from the airport, close to Riccarton Racecourse, and about 6 miles west of Cathedral Square. Ten chalets in a green, grassy setting are all individual dark-timber structures with slanted roofs and natural light-wood interiors. All have foam mattresses, floor mats, coffee/tea pot, toasters, stove, dishes and cutlery, cooking utensils, and electric heaters. Small chalets sleep three in two single beds and one upper bunk. The large ones will sleep five in two singles, one double, and one upper bunk, and have dividing curtains for privacy, as well as a small front porch. Also available are three deluxe chalets (same as the large, but with hot and cold running water and fridge).

Three tourist chalets sleep five, with two separate rooms plus kitchen, lounge, shower, toilet, two-ring rangette, electric fry pan, and blankets (linen is for rent). Amenities include a kitchen, TV lounge and leisure room, spa pool, children's play area, and a laundry with automatic washing machines and dryer. There's a food shop close by. Caravan and campsites are also available. Rates for chalets range from NZ$30 to NZ$39 (U.S. $19.50 to $25.95). The tourist chalets are NZ$50 (U.S. $32.50). Camp and caravan sites are NZ$16 to NZ$19 (U.S. $10.40 to $12.95). Sheets and blankets can be rented. Take the Yardhurst Road bus from the city.

WORTH THE EXTRA MONEY

★ **Cashmere House,** 141 Hackthorne Rd., Cashmere Hills, Christchurch. ☎ and fax **03/332-7864.** 5 rms (3 with bath).

Rates (including breakfast): NZ$110 (U.S. $71.50) single; NZ$140 (U.S. $91) double without bath, NZ$190 (U.S. $123.50) double with bath. BC, MC, V.

What a wonderful place! This 9,000-square-foot hillside mansion was built in 1928 and has more leadlight windows than I've ever seen in one place. There are also a charming conservatory with grand piano, a full-size billiard table in its own room, a lovely parlor with a fireplace, and a dining room with an expansive view of the whole city. Hosts Monty and Birgit Claxton couldn't be nicer or more helpful (Birgit speaks Swedish and German; Monty is a classic car buff). The five bedrooms vary in size, and occupants of the White and Rose rooms use private, but not attached, bathrooms. My favorite is East, where there's an antique king-size bed. Cashmere House is about a 15-minute drive from the city center, surrounded by lawn and gardens. The historic Sign of the Takehe is nearby. Smoking is not permitted in the house, and Cashmere House is not suitable for children.

4 Where to Eat

★ **Dux de Lux,** Montreal and Hereford sts. ☎ **366-6919.**

Cuisine: VEGETARIAN/SEAFOOD/SALADS. **Reservations:** Not required.
Prices: Appetizers NZ$6–NZ$9 (U.S. $3.90–$5.85); main courses NZ$12 (U.S. $7.80) at lunch, NZ$15 (U.S. $9.75) at dinner. AE, DC, MC, V.
Open: Daily 11:30am–11pm.

Dux de Lux, a favorite eating and meeting spot among Christchurch locals, is housed in one of the atmospheric old stone buildings that once comprised the University of Canterbury. It calls itself a gourmet vegetarian restaurant and serves such creative dishes as phyllo pastry stuffed with mushrooms, cottage cheese, and spinach or pumpkin-and-kumera roulade. For nonvegetarians, there's also a seafood bar. Hot main dishes come with a choice of salads and hot vegetables. There are two congenial dining rooms and a tree-filled courtyard with picnic tables. Service is cafeteria style, and if there's a line, it's worth the short wait. There's music on Thursday through Saturday nights. It's located in the Arts Centre. Licensed.

Italia Caffè, in the Guthrie Centre, Cashel Mall. ☎ **365-5349.**

Cuisine: ITALIAN. **Reservations:** Accepted but not required.
Prices: Light meals NZ$3–NZ$16 (U.S. $1.95–$10.40). AE, BC, DC, MC, V.
Open: Mon–Thurs 8:30am–6:30pm, Fri 8:30am–10pm, Sat 8:30am–5pm.

This pleasant little café in one of Christchurch's best city-center shopping malls is fully licensed and serves quite nice wines (as well as mixed drinks, of course) to go with their terrific Italian dishes. The heaping portions of meats, cheeses, and salads were so delicious that I went back to sample the pasta. Freshly made, it came with a selection of napoletana (tomato, basil, and garlic), bolognese (spicy beef and tomato), or carbonara (bacon, onion, cream, egg, and parmesan cheese) sauce. To top it all off, there was one of the best cups of coffee of my entire trip. Cappuccino, espresso, and other specialty coffees are also available. This one's a real delight for a lunch break or dinner at the end of a shopping or sightseeing foray in the city center. Everything on the menu is available as a take-away.

★ $ **Main Street Cafe & Bar,** 840 Columbo St., at Salisbury St. ☎ **365-0421.**

Cuisine: VEGETARIAN.
Prices: Light meal NZ$6.50 (U.S. $4.25); main courses NZ$12–NZ$14 (U.S. $7.80–$9.10). AE, BC, DC, MC, V.
Open: Daily 10am–10:30pm.

This is my kind of place. It has healthy, wholesome food served in relaxed surroundings—and it's licensed, so you can have a beer with dinner. The procedure is to order at the counter: They usually offer half a dozen really interesting salads, such as cold rice with veggies, chick pea, carrot and sprout, and hummus. Typical main courses include cheesey bean casserole, chile yogurt vegetables, and spinach-and-mushroom lasagne. The homemade soups are especially tasty. The decor includes pastel-green walls with lavender trim hung with modern art. The bar stays open after food service stops. Licensed and BYO. No smoking.

★ $ **The Mythai,** 84 Hereford St. ☎ **365-1295.**

Cuisine: THAI. **Reservations:** Required for dinner Fri–Sat.
Prices: Appetizers NZ$6–NZ$7.50 (U.S. $3.90–$4.90); main courses NZ$13–NZ$17 (U.S. $8.45–$11.05). AE, DC, MC, V.
Open: Dinner only, daily 5–11pm.

You could walk right past this unpretentious little place in the city center, but that would be a real mistake if you like authentic Thai food. There's an extensive menu of chicken dishes (try the pad gai benjarong, chicken with vegetables in peanut sauce), pork, beef, lamb, seafood, and vegetarian choices. The spicy fish cakes with a sauce of cucumbers sweet chiles are outstanding among appetizers, as is the traditional dessert of mythai gluay ghium (banana with coconut sauce).

The Mythai is popular with office workers at lunch, but don't be put off if the place is crowded—there's a larger back dining room and you seldom have to wait very long. It's a different story, however, for dinner on Friday and Saturday, when you could well be disappointed if you don't book ahead. It's BYO, and everything on the menu is available take-out.

Oxford on Avon, 794 Colombo St., on Oxford Terrace. ☎ **379-7148.**

Cuisine: BISTRO/NEW ZEALAND. **Reservations:** Not accepted for dinner.
Prices: Appetizers NZ$5.50–NZ$7.50 (U.S. $3.60–$4.90); main courses NZ$12–NZ$16 (U.S. $7.80–$10.40); roast meal NZ$10.95 (U.S. $7.20). AE, BC, DC, MC, V.
Open: Daily 6:30am–midnight.

This fully licensed restaurant is in a 125-year-old building that for many years was a hotel and tavern. Nowadays it houses a complex of bars and a large restaurant that serves fish, roasts, grills, and salads at prices that make it truly one of Christchurch's best buys. Recent renovations have given birth to a tasteful garden bar built out onto the banks of the Avon—a terrific place to while away a sunny afternoon at the umbrella tables. Breakfast, lunch, dinner, and supper are served. The roast meals are especially good value.

In the upstairs bar is a disco. A bottle shop is also located on the premises. It's located near the city center.

Pedro's, 143 Worcester St. ☎ **379-7668.**

Cuisine: SPANISH. **Reservations:** Recommended.
Prices: Appetizers NZ$9 (U.S. $5.85); main courses NZ$23 (U.S. $14.95). AE, MC, V.
Open: Dinner only, Tues–Sat 6:30–11pm.

Pedro's has been called the country's best Spanish restaurant. It's also very attractive: No bullfighter-poster-studded walls in this city-center eatery—instead, its tasteful decor is accented by an old Spanish sideboard and the crockery is imported from Spain. Specialties include traditional paella (outstanding!), grilled king prawns (langostinos a la plancha), and pork medallions in a sauce of tomatoes red beans (cerdo a la Navarra). Save room for lemon mousse or crema Catalana for dessert. BYO.

Strawberry Fare Dessert Restaurant, 114 Peterborough St. ☎ **365-4897.**

Cuisine: DESSERTS/SAVOURIES. **Reservations:** Not required.
Prices: Desserts NZ$10–NZ$14 (U.S. $6.50–$9.10); savoury meals NZ$10–NZ$16.50 (U.S. $6.50–$10.75). BC, MC, V.
Open: Daily 10am–midnight.

Family-Friendly Restaurants

Strawberry Fare (see above) Kids love this dessert restaurant where they have lots of options for satisfying their sweet tooth.

Oxford on Avon (see above) The roast dinners here have a homecooked taste that children enjoy. This is also a good spot for breakfasts with kid appeal.

For a dip into decadence, rush to Strawberry Fare and order a luscious dessert or a light meal. Desserts are their specialty, of course, but they also have an interesting selection of savory meals. Assuage that sweet tooth with such temptations as Death by Chocolate, Chocolate Mud Pie, or Devil's Dream Cake—or settle for a savory such as salmon in phyllo or crunchy-topped chicken. Strawberry Fare is just off Colombo Street, set back from the street.

WORTH THE EXTRA MONEY

Grimsby's Restaurant, Cranmer Court, at the corner of Kilmore and Montreal sts. ☎ **379-9040.**

Cuisine: NEW ZEALAND. **Reservations:** Recommended.

Prices: Appetizers NZ$10–NZ$12 (U.S. $6.50–$7.80); main courses NZ$19–NZ$26 (U.S. $12.35–$16.90). AE, BC, DC, MC, V.

Open: Dinner only, daily 7–9:30pm.

You'll be dining in gothic splendor at Grimsby's. It's a marvelous stone building opened in 1876 as Christchurch Normal School, which operated until 1954, when it became the Post Primary Department of Christchurch Teacher's College until 1970; it lay vacant and was severely vandalized until developers took it in hand in 1980 to create co-op apartments in one wing and this elegant restaurant on the ground floor. You enter through heavy wooden doors into a medieval hall, thence into a high-ceilinged dining room beautifully furnished with tables set with crisp white linen, exquisite china, crystal, and silverware. Classical music plays softly in the background. Service is as elegant as the surroundings, and the food is well presented. Main courses include rack of lamb, seasoned filet of pork studded with prunes and walnuts, and slices of medium-rare venison resting on a chestnut custard. Licensed. Be sure to request the nonsmoking section if that's important to you. Grimsby's is located in the city center.

★ **Michael's,** 178 High St. ☎ **366-0822.**

Cuisine: MODERN NEW ZEALAND. **Reservations:** Recommended.

Prices: Appetizers NZ$9–NZ$12 (U.S. $5.85–$7.80); main courses NZ$19–NZ$24 (U.S. $12.35–$15.60). AE, BC, DC, MC, V.

Open: Dinner only, Mon–Sat 6–10pm.

Michael's is spoken of very highly by Christchurch's "foodies," many of whom have taken one of his cooking classes or belong to the Canterbury Gourmet Society, which gathers under his roof. Sample main courses include lamb with sun-dried tomato and summer basil served on arugula salad with red-pepper dressing, wine-poached fish with julienne of vegetables, and smoked salmon with lemon herb-and-vermouth sauce. Licensed and BYO.

SPECIALTY DINING

The **Boulevard Bakehouse Cafe,** in the Arts Centre on Worcester Boulevard, is a great spot to pick up sandwiches or other goodies for a picnic in the nearby Botanic Gardens. Or you could take your lunch up to Cathedral Square and eat while you listen to the Wizard rant and rave. This "beautiful-baking, great-coffee" spot is open daily from 8am to midnight, so you can go there after a play at the nearby Court Theatre, too.

Speaking of coffee, there are several cafés on the Cashel Street Mall. You might try **Bardellis, Cafe Bleu,** or **Espresso 124.** In the same area is one of Christchurch's best **food courts:** look for it upstairs in Shades Arcade.

One of the loveliest places for morning or afternoon tea is the **Sign of the Takahe,** a historic stone building on Dyers Pass Road overlooking the city in the Cashmere Hills. Devonshire tea is served from 10 to 11am and 2:30 to 4pm and costs NZ$6 (U.S. $3.90). Buffet lunches in this impressive setting cost NZ$23 (U.S. $14.95), and prices for à la carte dinners are off the charts.

There are four **McDonald's** in Christchurch—yes, the golden arches. The most central is at 689 Columbo St.

Breakfast isn't a meal that many Kiwis eat outside their homes, so it's sometimes hard to find places that serve interesting ones. In Christchurch, you'll find good morning fare at **Oxford on Avon,** opposite the City Hall. It's served from 6:30 to 11am.

5 What to See & Do

Your first stop should be the **Christchurch-Canterbury Visitor Centre,** at the corner of Oxford Terrace and Worcester Boulevard (☎ **03/379-9629**). They have an extensive supply of brochures on Christchurch and all of Canterbury. Be sure to pick up the **City Walk** brochure. The center can also book you on a two-hour ★ **guided city walk** (costing NZ$8/U.S. $5.20) that leaves from their office at 9:45am and 1:45pm daily from October through April and 15 minutes later from the kiosk in Cathedral Square. From May through September, the tours are at 1pm.

THE TOP ATTRACTIONS

The hub of the city center is ★ **Cathedral Square**—it will almost certainly be your orientation point, and it's great people-watching territory. If you happen to be in that area around 1pm, look for the **Wizard of Christchurch,** a colorful character (and actually a very learned individual) with very definite ideas about almost everything in the universe. If the Wizard's in town, you're in for some unusual entertainment, for which you won't be charged a cent. Christchurch treasures its "eccentrics and nutters," as the plaque outside the post office on the square attests. It's in memory of another local character, the Bird Man.

More imposing architecturally than Christchurch Cathedral, below, is the magnificent **Cathedral of the Blessed Sacrament,** also called the basilica, on Barbados Street, about a 15-minute walk from Cathedral Square (or take bus no. 3J or 3K). Its classic revival architecture features colonnades, galleries, and an Italian mosaic floor, embellished with tapestries and bronzes. It's open daily from 8am to 4pm.

Christchurch Cathedral, Cathedral Sq. ☎ **366-0046.**

Begun in 1864, just 14 years after the first settlers arrived, it was completed in 1904. The cathedral choir sings a half-hour choral evensong at 5:15pm on Tuesday and Wednesday and the service is sung by the Boy Choristers on Friday at 4:30pm (except during school holidays). The cathedral is open for prayer weekdays, and holy communion is also celebrated daily. Climb the 133 steps in the 120-foot tower for a splendid panoramic view of the city and its environs.

Admission: Cathedral (and guided tours), free; tower, NZ$3 (U.S. $1.95) adults, NZ$1 (U.S. 65¢) children.

Open: Mon–Sat from 8:30am, Sun from 7:30am. Guided tours given at 11am and 2pm.

★ **Canterbury Museum,** Rolleston Ave. ☎ **366-8379.**

The Canterbury Museum has an excellent permanent Antarctica exhibit, along with the Hall of New Zealand birds and a prize-winning exhibit "Iwi Tawhito-Whenua

Hou" on New Zealand's early Maori settlers. A new gallery of Asian art opened in October 1994, and a series of new exhibits is planned through the year 2000.

Admission: Free.

Open: Daily 9am–4:30pm. Free guided tours at 10:15 and 11:30am and 1:15 and 2:30pm. **Closed:** Christmas Day.

★ **Botanic Gardens,** Rolleston Ave. ☎ **366-1701.**

The world-renowned Christchurch Botanic Gardens are most easily accessed from Rolleston Avenue, but the 75 acres of trees, flower beds, and lawns spread out across Hagley Park and can also be approached via Riccarton Avenue. The gardens are encircled by a loop of the Avon River, and this peaceful stream, with its duck population, enhances the beauty of the plantings. Even if horticulture isn't of particular interest to you, this is a great place for a stroll among large majestic trees—many are more than 100 years old. And if you're a plant person, you'll want to visit the various special gardens and the conservatories (Cuningham House, Townend House, and Foweraker House). Twenty-minute guided tours on the "Toast Rack" tram leave from the Botanic Gardens Restaurant (☎ **366-5076**). An information center is adjacent.

Admission: Free; guided tours, NZ$4 (U.S. $2.60).

Open: Grounds, daily 7am until one hour before sunset; conservatories, daily 10:15am–4pm; information center, Sept–Apr daily 10:15am–4pm, May–Aug daily 11am–3pm.

Robert McDougall Art Gallery and Art Annex, access via the Botanic Gardens. ☎ **365-0915.**

Displays here include early and contemporary European, British, and New Zealand works—including two Rodins. There are also regular visiting and special-interest exhibitions from other places in New Zealand and abroad. The Art Annex presents the work of contemporary Canterbury artists.

Admission: Free.

Open: Daily 10am–4:30pm.

Closed: Good Friday and Christmas Day.

★ **The Arts Centre,** bounded by Worcester Blvd., Rolleston Ave., Hereford St., and Montreal St. ☎ **366-0989.**

There's no way I can write about the Arts Centre without letting my prejudice show, so I might as well tell you up front that I love this place. Even if the wonderful old stone buildings were vacant, I'd like roaming among the gothic arches and arcades and standing in the quadrangles that feel as if they're part of a "Masterpiece Theatre" set. The buildings were once the site of the University of Canterbury. They were constructed from 1876 to 1926 and coordinated by Samuel Hurst Seager's "grand design." The university left the space in 1975, and it now is home to several good eating spots (Dux de Lux and the Boulevard Bakehouse Cafe are described in "Where to Eat," earlier in this chapter; Le Cafe is also very popular) and craft workshops. In addition, the **Court Theatre** is housed in the original Engineering Building and Hydraulics Lab; the **Academy Cinema** is in the old Boys' High Gym; and the **Southern Ballet** occupies the Electrical Engineering Lab and the Mechanical Engineering Lab. You may also be interested in seeing Rutherford's Den, which acknowledges Nobel Prize winner Ernest Lord Rutherford, who studied here from 1890 to 1894. Not surprisingly, the Arts Centre won a 1994 New Zealand Tourism Award.

Admission: Free.

Open: Most craftspeople and retailers, daily 10am–4pm; market and Food Fair, Sat–Sun 10am–4pm; restaurant and café hours vary.

★ **International Antarctic Centre,** Orchard Rd., adjacent to the Christchurch International Airport. ☎ **358-9896.**

I hope you won't be like me and allow only a short time for this fascinating center. Christchurch has long been the gateway to Antarctica, and finally there's a place where the public can share the experience of life on the frozen continent. Displays and sophisticated audiovisuals here tell about daily routines, the difficulty of access, the weather, the wonderful wildlife, and the ongoing scientific studies. They also tell of the various nations that maintain bases in Antarctica and the efforts to keep politics out of science. My spouse and I spent several hours and left wishing we had more time. There's a gift shop and a café on the premises. (Several readers have written to say how much they liked this attraction, and at least one has raved about the good food in the café.)

When you come out of the center, look across the street and note the **Operation Deep Freeze Base** on the edge of the airport. It is from here that the Antarctica-bound planes depart.

Admission: NZ$10 (U.S. $6.50) adults, NZ$6 (U.S. $3.90) children 5–15; NZ$25 (U.S. $16.25) family ticket. Free for children under 5.

Open: Oct–Mar, daily 9:30am–8:30pm; Apr–Sept, daily 9:30am–5:30pm. **Closed:** Christmas Day. **Transportation:** The center is a 20-minute drive from central Christchurch—I suggest that you take the airport bus.

Ferrymead Historic Park, 269 Bridle Path Rd., Heathcote. ☎ **384-1970.**

The 100-acre, 15,000-square-foot Ferrymead Historic Park holds a collection of things from the past, including Moorhouse Township (an Edwardian township complete with a church, a schoolhouse, a jail, an operating bakery, a print shop, a cooperage, and a livery stables), Hall of Fame, Hall of Wheels, working exhibits, and lots more. There's a 1 1/2 km (1-mile) tramway link between the two main areas of the park, with restored electric trams from Dunedin and Christchurch, an 1881 Kitson steam tram, and a horse-drawn tram.

Admission: NZ$7 (U.S. $4.50) adults, NZ$3.50 (U.S. $2.75) children, free for children under 5; NZ$19 (U.S. $12.35) family ticket.

Open: Daily 10am–4:30pm. **Closed:** Christmas Day. **Bus:** 3 from Cathedral Square. **Directions:** Take Ferry Road south and make the first right turn after Heathcote Bridge (near the Mount Cavendish Gondola).

Willowbrook Wildlife Reserve, 60 Hussey Rd. ☎ **359-6226.**

This delightful natural park includes a zoo of exotic animals and a farmyard of endangered breeds, but it's the New Zealand Experience, featuring native birds, including the kiwi, that's of particular interest. Visitors who eat dinner here can see kiwis in their natural nighttime environment (floodlights help you). The fully licensed restaurant also serves morning and afternoon teas and lunch.

Admission: NZ$8 (U.S. $5.20) adults, NZ$3.50 (U.S. $2.30) children; free (including a guide) with purchase of an evening meal costing NZ$20 (U.S. $13) or more.

Open: Daily 10am–10pm. **Directions:** Take Harewood Road, turn right onto Gardiners Road, and right again into Hussey Road; it's a 15-minute drive from the city.

MORE ATTRACTIONS

Christchurch **gardens** are known throughout the country, and there's fierce competition every year between neighborhoods. To view some of these glorious gardening achievements, visit **Royds Street,** opposite Boys' High, which has won the competition for many years running. In the business community, it's the exquisite garden at the **Sanitarium Health Food Company,** 54 Harewood Rd., Papanui, which comes out on top time and time again. However, just about any street you stroll down will display garden patches of exceptional beauty, and if you express your delight in seeing them the nearest gardener will have you deep in conversation in no time flat. In February there are bus tours of the award-winning gardens.

Farther afield, **Air Force World,** Main South Road, Wigram, Christchurch (☎ **343-9532**), is a must for aviation buffs. It's located in Wigram Aerodrome, a 15-minute drive south of the city via Riccarton Road or Blenheim Road (both of which merge into Main South Road), where the Royal New Zealand Air Force was established in 1923. The aviation history of the country is depicted in dramatic re-creations, videos, and comprehensive displays of planes; exhibits such as the Bomber Command and Battle of Britain exhibits; and memorabilia. There's also a cafeteria overlooking the airfield, still in use by the RNZAF. It's open daily from 10am to 5pm (closed Christmas Day), and you'll probably want to spend an hour or even two. Admission is NZ$9 (U.S. $5.85) for adults and NZ$4 (U.S. $2.60) for children. To get here, take bus no. 8 or 25 from Cathedral Square.

Another really great way to spend a day is to take the scenic ★ ***TranzAlpine*** train trip to Arthurs Pass or Greymouth. You can make the journey round-trip by train or come back by bus for completely different views.

In either case, you'll cross the Canterbury Plains, go through the gorges of the Waimakariri River, and travel up into the beautiful Southern Alps. The day-excursion fare is NZ$66 (U.S. $42.90) to Arthurs Pass and NZ$97 (U.S. $63.05) to Greymouth. If you take the Arthurs Pass option, you'll have five hours there before the train returns. If you go to Greymouth, you can take a short bus tour (NZ$5/U.S. $3.25) before heading back to the east coast. For reservations and further information, call New Zealand Rail (☎ toll free **0800/802-802** in New Zealand).

You may also be interested in going up on the **Mount Cavendish Gondola,** which provides a 360° view of Christchurch and Lyttelton Harbour. The top station of the cable car is 500 meters (1,500 feet) above the city, and you can stay and enjoy a meal before starting your descent. You can also mountain-bike down. The gondola is 15 minutes from town, but there's regular bus service from the visitor center. Phone **329-9699** for information on the mountain-bike adventure, **384-4645** for Ridge Restaurant bookings, and **384-4914** for general information. The gondola operates Monday through Thursday from 10am to 11pm, Friday and Saturday from 10am to midnight, and Sunday from 10am to 10:30pm. The cost is NZ$12 (U.S. $7.80) for adults and NZ$5 (U.S. $3.25) for children (less after 5pm), with discounts for families, seniors, and students.

ORGANIZED TOURS

There are many good **coach tours** for seeing the city and its surroundings, all of which may be booked through the visitor center, your lodging, or directly with the tour operators. One of the best is that given by Gray Line Tours (☎ **343-3874**). It covers city highlights, and the afternoon tour takes the spectacular Summit Road to Lyttleton Harbour, with panoramas of snowcapped Alps, plains, and sea, and makes a stop at the baronial Sign of the Takahe for tea on the way back. The fare for adults is NZ$32 (U.S. $20.80), half price for children.

Gray Line also has day tours to **Akaroa** (adults pay NZ$54/U.S. $35.10; children are charged half fare).

Daily bus tours to **Kaikoura** from Christchurch are also offered by Mount Cook Landline (☎ **379-0690**) and Gray Line (☎ **343-3874**); for more information on Kaikoura, see "En Route South" under "Picton" in Chapter 10. There is also a **rail excursion;** book at the railway station on Moorhouse Avenue in Christchurch (☎ **379-9020**).

6 Sports & Recreation

BICYCLING Christchurch's flat terrain invites cycling, and bike lanes are marked off in several parts of the city, including parks. Parking lots even provide bike racks. Join the bikers by renting from **Rent-a-Cycle,** 141 Gloucester St. (☎ **365-7589**), opposite the Coachman Inn. The price is NZ$2 (U.S. $1.30) per hour or NZ$10 (U.S. $6.50) per day for a single-speed bike, NZ$3 (U.S. $1.95) per hour or NZ$15 (U.S. $9.75) per day for a 3- or 10-speed bike, and NZ$5 (U.S. $3.25) per hour or NZ$20 (U.S. $13) per day for mountain bikes; discounts are given for weekly rentals, and cycle helmets are supplied. It's open daily from 10am to 6pm. There are other bike-rental shops, and the visitor center can supply a list of names and addresses, as well as brochures on cycling in Christchurch and its environs.

BOATING You won't be in Christchurch long before you notice the ★ **punts,** maneuvered by young men in straw hats, on the Avon River. The way to get from the bank into one of those boats is to reserve a ride through the Visitor Centre. A 45-minute ride costs NZ$15 (U.S. $9.75) per person or NZ$10 (U.S. $6.50) for 20 minutes.

You can also take matters in hand and paddle your own canoe down the lovely Avon River. Canoes are for rent from **Antigua Boatsheds,** 2 Cambridge Terrace (☎ **366-5885**), as they have been from this same company for over a century. Prices for canoes are NZ$4 (U.S. $2.60) per person per hour; for paddleboats, NZ$4 (U.S. $2.60) per person per half hour. It's open daily from 9:30am to 6pm.

SKIING & OTHER OUTDOOR SPORTS About 92km (57 miles) southwest of Christchurch and 34km (21 miles) north of the agricultural center of Ashburton, Methven lures those afflicted with downhill fever. It's the gateway to the **Mount Hutt** ski field, which is blessed with a long season, often from late May through early December. Lift tickets cost NZ$46 (U.S. $29.90) for adults and NZ$24 (U.S. $15.60) for children; equipment rental runs NZ$25 (U.S. $16.25) per day for adults and NZ$17 (U.S. $11.05) per day for children. For further information, call Mount Hutt (☎ **302-8811**); for a snow report, call **302-8605.**

Other outdoor activities in the region include mountaineering, fishing, boating, trekking, and golf.

WALKING If you prefer walking, Christchurch is the perfect place to do it; the Visitor Centre can supply pamphlets mapping out scenic strolls, or simply follow the river or wander through the Botanic Gardens.

READERS RECOMMEND

Country Golf Tours, located in the Kingsgate Hotel, 776 Colombo St., Christchurch (☎ **03/366-4653**). *"We found a great way to play golf in the Christchurch area is with this company. They escort you to your choice of ten affordable courses and furnish clubs if needed."*—Maynard & Eloise Raffety, Grinnell, Ia., U.S.A.

7 Savvy Shopping

There's good shopping in Christchurch, and I find prices here among the most reasonable in the country. For some of the best buys in New Zealand woolens and crafts, go by the **Arts Centre,** on Worcester Boulevard (☎ **366-0986**), where the **Galleria** houses most of the permanent craft shops under one roof; it's open daily from 10am to 4pm. And don't forget about the **Public Market** held at the Arts Centre on Saturday and Sunday.

I also really like **Applied Arts,** in Cashel Plaza, on Cashel Street near High Street (☎ **377-2898**), a gallery that sells the work of New Zealand–only artists. There's a **Regency Duty-free Shop** at 736 Colombo St. (☎ **379-1923**), and **Ballantyne's Department Store,** on the corner of Colombo Street and City Mall (☎ **379-7400**), is a good source for quality souvenirs. **Jumpers,** in the Shades Arcade, sells cute sweaters. Auto nuts are sure to find a trinket they'll need at **Fazazz, the Motorists Shop,** 82 Lichfield St. (☎ **365-5206**).

8 Evening Entertainment

For the latest news on nightlife, consult the "What's On" section of the ***Tourist Times.***

THE PERFORMING ARTS

In addition to the venue described below, concerts, plays and musical performances are often held in the **Town Hall,** on Kilmore Street (☎ **377-8899**).

★ **Court Theatre,** in the Arts Centre, Worcester Blvd. ☎ **366-6992.**

This is quite possibly New Zealand's best theater. I've seen many plays here—ranging from Tom Stoppard to Shakespeare—and never been disappointed in the quality. As I write this, the shows being considered for future production are *She Stoops to Conquer, The Dining Room, Medea, Charley's Aunt,* and *I Hate Hamlet.* Performances are Monday through Wednesday and Friday and Saturday at 8pm, and Thursday at 6pm. The theater offers standby tickets on Monday, Tuesday, and Wednesday evenings (all unsold tickets are sold at a reduced price). Box office hours are Monday through Friday from 9am to 8:15pm and Saturday from 1 to 8:15pm. Highly recommended.

Admission: Tickets, NZ$23 (U.S. $14.95) adults, NZ$18 (U.S. $11.70) students, seniors, YHA cardholders, NZ$10 (U.S. $6.50) children.

THE CLUB, MUSIC & BAR SCENE

If you want to dance, the **Palladium Niteclub,** on Gloucester Street opposite the library and near Cathedral Square (☎ **379-0572**), is a good choice. It's open nightly from 9pm until very late and live bands play Thursday, Friday, and Saturday. Admission is free, except Thursday, Friday, and Saturday after 11pm when it's NZ$3 (U.S. $1.95).

Jazz fans will want to head to **Kickin Jazz,** 633 Colombo St. (☎ **366-4662**), a lively spot that also serves good pizza.

New Zealand's answer to the Hard Rock Café is **Coyotes,** 126 Oxford Terrace, near the Bridge of Remembrance (☎ **366-6055**). This very popular place is known for its great music.

The **Finn Bar,** 144 Gloucester St., has an Irish band and is a great place to dance and meet the locals.

A SPECIALTY BAR If your idea of a good night out involves drinking beer in a convivial atmosphere, get yourself over to the **Dux de Lux,** in the Arts Centre on the corner of Hereford and Montreal streets (☎ **366-6919**). They brew five beers in-house, including De Lux Lager, Nor'wester Pale Ale, Blue Duck Draught, Hereford Bitter, and Sou'wester Dark Strout. The Dux is also a great place to eat (see "Where to Eat," earlier in this chapter).

MORE ENTERTAINMENT

CITY SPECTACLES Don't overlook the opportunity to combine sightseeing and nightlife: You can ride to the top of the **Mount Cavendish Gondola** and have dinner with a knockout view, or you can have dinner and a guided tour of the habitats of nocturnal animals at **Willowbank Wildlife Reserve.**

MOVIES The **Academy Cinema,** in the Arts Centre (☎ **366-0167**), shows international and national art films. There's a **Hoyts Multiscreen Theatre** at 392 Moorhouse Ave. (☎ **366-6367**). Tickets cost NZ$9 (U.S. $5.85).

CASINOS Christchurch is home to **New Zealand's first casino,** which opened at the end of 1994. This is a particularly attractive one, and features over 350 gaming machines, as well as blackjack, baccarat, minibaccarat, Caribbean stud poker, American roulette, keno, and sic bo. There's a buffet restaurant called the Grand Cafe and a bar, the Canterbury Room. You must be 20 to enter the Christchurch Casino, Victoria Street (☎ **365-9999**), and the dress code prohibits wearing jeans, thongs, T-shirts, or active sportwear. It's open Monday through Wednesday from 11am to 3am, and continuously from Thursday at 11am to Monday at 3am.

9 An Easy Excursion from Christchurch

I went to ★ **Akaroa** and the Banks Peninsula at the suggestion of a friend from Christchurch, and I agree with her that it's a lovely spot. This area has a beauty and charm all its own and I urge you to experience it for yourself. You can drive or take a bus 84km (52 miles) from Christchurch to Akaroa (sit on the right-hand side for the best views). Once there, take the mail-run bus and experience the beauty of the Eastern Bays (the bus departs Akaroa at 8:45am and returns at 1:15pm); be assured that the driver will point out places of interest, in between delivering mail, milk, and passengers. En route you'll pass **Lake Ellsmere,** 111 square miles but only 6$^1/_2$ feet deep at its deepest part, and home to the Australian black swan, and **Lake Forsyth,** New Zealand's dramatic easternmost lake (you'll find an information center and restrooms at Little River). Stop at the **Hilltop Tavern** for a view of Akaroa across the harbor. The town, with a population of a scant 800, is the southernmost French settlement in the world, and New Zealand's only French inroad. In 1840 the French tried to establish a colony here, but England had just laid claim to the country in the Treaty of Waitangi. The original 63 French settlers loved the area so much, however, that they stayed on at the north end of town; French was spoken in that area until 1890. The English colonists who arrived in 1850 lived in the southern end, and to this day the street names reveal the dichotomy.

The Maori word *akaroa* means "long harbor," and the water is very much a constant reality here. And if you spend any time at all, seduced by the delicate play of light and shadow on water and land alike, you may be overcome by an irresistible urge to try your hand at watercolors. At the very least, you'll feel as if you've wandered into one. No wonder so many artists gravitate here.

Akaroa is known for its walnuts—it was the French who first brought the trees here. You can get a sense of much of Akaroa's character by wandering along **rue Lavaud** and **rue Balgueri.** Admire the winsome wooden buildings and houses dating from the 19th century, and by no means miss the cottages at the junction of Bruce Terrace and Aubrey Street (behind the Village Inn motel). The old **French cemetery** is just off rue Pompallier.

What to See & Do

Experience Akaroa Harbour firsthand on the ★ ***Canterbury Cat,*** which departs daily at 1:30pm year round from the main wharf (☎ **03/304-7641**). From November through March, there's also an 11am cruise. During the two-hour cruise you'll spot penguins and dolphins (they're in residence November to April) and visit a salmon farm. Fares are NZ$23 (U.S. $14.95) for adults, NZ$10 (U.S. $6.50) for children, NZ$56 (U.S. $36.40) for the family ticket. The booking office is on the main wharf.

Akaroa's land-side attractions include its fine **museum,** the best place to start your visit, especially since it doubles as the town's **information center** and can provide a good map; the **Langlois-Eteveneaux House,** part of the museum and probably the oldest in Canterbury; and the ★ **lighthouse,** which was in service from 1880 to 1980.

If you want to buy a book on the area or perhaps a woolen souvenir, go to ★ **Pot Pourri,** on rue Lavaud, open from 10am to 5pm daily. I also like the **Picturesque Gallery,** on rue Lavaud.

Where to Stay

For a little place, Akaroa has an impressive array of accommodations, including some of New Zealand's finest offerings of bed-and-breakfast and backpacker accommodation. No matter where you stay, you'll want to linger. The rates quoted below include GST.

A MOTEL

L'Hotel, 75 Beach Rd., Akaroa. ☎ **03/304-7995.** Fax 03/304-7455. 5 units (all with bath). TV TEL

Rates: NZ$90 (U.S. $58.50) single or double. AA discount available. AE, BC, MC, V.

This is no ordinary motel. All five units are no-smoking; have spacious, contemporary decors; and offer such thoughtful amenities as fresh flowers, heated towel rods, and pretty doonas (comforters). Each has cooking facilities and a private balcony, and it overlooks the harbor from its first-floor (second-floor, to Americans) location. Downstairs there's a wine bar with an open fire and a sidewalk café, and room-service meals are provided. One unit is designed for handicapped travelers. Owner Mike Smith couldn't be nicer.

A BED-&-BREAKFAST

Glencarrig, 7 Percy St., Akaroa. ☎ and fax **03/304-7008.** 3 rms (1 with bath).

Rates (including breakfast): NZ$50 (U.S. $32.50) single; NZ$95 (U.S. $61.75) double without bath, NZ$120 (U.S. $78) double with bath. No credit cards.

Picturesque Glencarrig was built in 1853 by the first Anglican vicar in Akaroa for his wife and six children. You'll love the original timberwork and the large farmhouse kitchen with its drying rack and Rayburn wood-burning stove that also runs the central heating. The lovely single room and two doubles all sport country decor, and two sitting rooms come with open fireplaces. The property, which sits prettily on $1\frac{1}{2}$ acres a short drive from the town center, even has a stream and mill wheel on it, as well as a pool. Hosts Bob Parker and Sally Omond plan to add a second bathroom—maybe by the time you get there.

A RUSTIC RETREAT

Mount Vernon Lodge, at the end of rue Balgueri, Akaroa. ☎ **03/304-7180.**

6 rms (all with bath), 1 chalet, 2 cabins, 1 flat. **Transportation:** Courtesy transfers provided from Akaroa.

Rates: NZ$40 (U.S. $26) double; NZ$60 (U.S. $39) cabin for two; NZ$60 (U.S. $39) chalet for two; NZ$70 (U.S. 45.50) apartment for two. NZ$13 (U.S. $8.45) bunk. Additional person NZ$8 (U.S. $5.20) extra. No credit cards.

Put on your hiking shoes, for Mount Vernon Lodge has a premier site overlooking Akaroa Harbour, and it's no mean feat to get to it if you're on foot. The reward is a beautiful farmyard setting with well-maintained accommodations. Each room in the lodge has two levels with two beds on each level. There is a communal kitchen, lounge, barbecue area, and swimming pool. The lodge also has self-contained cabins and a cottage, as well as an A-frame chalet perfect for a couple who want to retreat from the world or for a family. It has a double bed looking out at the hills, three more beds upstairs, a tub and washing machine, a kitchen, and a TV. Horseback riding is available, and hiking is a given. This is a great place for families.

A FARMSTAY

Kawatea Farmstay, Okains Bay, Banks Peninsula. ☎ **03/304-8621.**

3 rms (1 with bath).

Rates (including dinner and breakfast): NZ$75 (U.S. $48.75) per person. No credit cards.

Judy and Kerry Thacker are genuinely nice people and great hosts. Kerry is a fourth-generation New Zealander, and his family has been on the Banks Peninsula since 1850. Their 1,250-acre property provides an opportunity for guests to see a real working farm, with 1,000 sheep and 600 beef cattle. Depending on the time of year, you might be able to watch shearing or feed a lamb with a bottle. The historic homestead, built at the turn of the century, is another plus. Also within a couple of kilometers are a beach, a Maori museum, and a seal colony. My favorite room is upstairs, with its own bathroom.

Where to Eat

A popular place to sit and have breakfast or a "cuppa" is the **Akaroa Bakery,** on Beach Road.

La Rue Restaurant, 6 rue Balgueri. ☎ **304-7658.**

Cuisine: SEAFOOD/NEW ZEALAND. **Reservations:** Recommended.
Prices: Appetizers NZ$9.50–NZ$12 (U.S. $6.20–$7.80); main courses NZ$10–NZ$11 (U.S. $6.50–$7.15) at lunch, NZ$17.50–NZ$24 (U.S. $11.35–$15.60) at dinner. AE, DC, MC, V.
Open: Lunch Tues–Sun noon–2pm year round; dinner daily from 6:30pm in summer, Tues–Sun in winter.

Overlooking Akaroa Harbour, La Rue is undoubtedly one of the best restaurants in town, and it has been a Taste New Zealand Award winner for six years running. The menu changes seasonally, always featuring seafood, with crayfish and Bluff oysters appearing in season. Lamb, venison, and pork dishes are also on the menu. Licensed and BYO.

★ **Astrolabe Cafe & Bar,** 71 Beach Rd., Akaroa. ☎ **304-7656.**

Cuisine: ITALIAN/MODERN NEW ZEALAND. **Reservations:** Recommended.

Prices: Appetizers NZ$10.50– NZ$11.50 (U.S. $6.85–$7.50); main courses NZ$14.50–NZ$18.50 (U.S. $9.45–$12.05); lunch NZ$10–NZ$16.50 (U.S. $6.50–$10.75). AE, BC, MC, V.

Open: Daily 10:30am–8pm (later in summer). **Closed:** Wed in winter.

The name of this restaurant comes from the first French ship to sail into the harbor here, but neither the cuisine nor the decor has a Gallic flavor. Lunchtime options include pizza, calzone, focaccia sandwiches, and some interesting salads. Sample dinner main courses include grilled beef filet, Akaroa salmon filet, and lamb kebabs on couscous. The attractive modern decor is part of the reason for its popularity: Three walls are yellow, one is orange, and the high wood ceiling is green. Diners have the choice of sitting at the counter or at a table (the ones near the windows have a view). Focaccia is served on a wooden cutting board and the soup arrives in huge white china bowls. It's licensed, so you can enjoy a Mac's Gold or DB Natural or choose from the wine list.

Appendix

A Kiwi/Yankee Lexicon

air conditioning refers to both heating and cooling the air
All Blacks New Zealand rugby team
bach North Island term for vacation house (plural: baches)
bath bathtub
bathroom where one bathes; bath
big bickies high salary
Biro ballpoint pen
biscuits/bickies cookies
bludge borrow
bonnet hood of car
boot trunk of car
Boxing Day the day after Christmas
bursary scholarship
bush forest
chemist shop drugstore
chilly bin Styrofoam cooler (U.S.), esky (Aus.)
Christmas crackers cylindrical party favors (U.S.), bon bon (Aus.)
cocky farmer
college high school
crib South Island term for holiday house
cuppa cup of tea
dairy convenience store
doona comforter, quilt
duvet comforter, quilt
electric blankets in New Zealand they're found under the bottom sheet
en suite facilities attached bath
entree smallish first course, appetizer

Parlez-vous Kiwi?

My lessons in Kiwi English began on my first trip to New Zealand, even before my plane had landed in Auckland.

"How about going to a hotel with me after we get into town?" queried my Kiwi seatmate.

"Would I *what?*" I shot back. I started giving him a piece of my mind, but, luckily, a nearby passenger intervened.

"If you'll excuse me," he said in a tone laced with détente, "I'm fluent in both Yank and Kiwi and I think I can straighten this out." He explained to me that in New Zealand *hotel* is synonymous with *pub* and my seatmate was only proposing we stop and have a drink. I accepted—both the drink and my first lesson in Kiwi.

My lesson continued as the gentleman and I drank our Lion Browns in Auckland's Albion Tavern: I learned that "to shout" has nothing to do with raising one's voice. "Hey, mate, it's your shout" is an invitation for your fellow guzzler to open his or her wallet, not mouth. I also learned that *blokes* often drink pints, handles, or scooners, but *birds* who request a 20-ounce mug of beer might get some sidelong glances.

Future lessons have helped me build my Kiwi vocabulary: When visiting friends at their home in Christchurch, I asked to use the bathroom. My hostess graciously showed me the way, but after I'd closed the door I realized the one piece of plumbing I urgently required was nowhere in sight. How was I to know that in New Zealand a *bathroom* is for bathing only and I should've asked for the *toilet*?

I expanded my vocabulary further during my brief career as a fruit picker on a South Island farm. When I was told it was time for a *smoko,* I replied, "Thanks, but I don't smoke." That brought peals of laughter from my Kiwi co-workers. Had they called it a coffee break I would've understood. It was on this same farm that I realized a *fine* day is one without rain and the small cottage I was living in was called a *crib.* (Had I been on the North Island it would've been called a *bach.*)

Unfortunately, not all my learning experiences have been pleasant. The farmer I was working for owned sheep as well as apple trees. One day he asked if I'd like to assist the shearer who was coming the next day. He said I could "pick dags." Though I had no idea what he was talking about, I happily jumped at the chance to pick something besides apples. I felt like a real fool when I realized what I'd agreed to do: The dictionary says a *dag* is a "dung-caked lock of wool around the hindquarters of a sheep"—but that isn't nearly descriptive enough.

While working as a waitress in one of Auckland's licensed restaurants, I had to master more Kiwi. When a customer ordered a *lemonade,* I correctly delivered a 7-Up. When someone requested *silverbeet,* I brought Swiss chard. I already knew that a diner ordering *chips* wanted french fries, but I added *kumara* (sweet potato), *silverside* (corned beef), *capiscum* (bell pepper), and *courgette* (zucchini) to my verbal repertoire.

However, I'll never forget the look on the face of one pompous businessman when I asked him if he needed a fresh napkin. While his dinner guests howled, one of the other waitresses explained that a *napkin* is what a baby wears (and *mums* change) and what I should've offered him was a fresh *serviette.*

It's been many years since that embarrassing incident, and now *I'm* the one who intervenes to smooth out potential international crises. Such was the case at a B&B in Napier when the proprietor asked a female compatriot, "Shall I knock you up in the morning?" As salacious as this sounded, he was only offering to wake her.

fanny female genitalia; you'll shock Kiwis if you call the thing you wear around your waist a "fanny pack"
freezing works slaughterhouse
gallops thoroughbred horse racing
get stuck in get started
as good as gold everything's OK
grizzle complain
grog booze
gumboots waterproof rubber boots (U.S.), Wellingtons (Britain)
homely homey
hooker front-row rugby player
hotties hot-water bottles
housie Bingo
jandals thongs (Aus.), flip-flops (Britain)
jersey pullover sweater (U.S.), jumper (Aus.)
judder bars speed bumps
jug electric kettle or a pitcher
Kiwi person from New Zealand; native bird of New Zealand
knickers underwear, undies
knock up wake up
LSZ low-speed zone
lift elevator
loo toilet
lounge living room
main course entree
mate friend
nappy diaper
Pakeha anyone of European descent
panel beaters body-repair shop
private facilities private bath
pushchair baby stroller
queue line, waiting in line
rates property taxes
return ticket round-trip ticket
rug blanket
serviette napkin
shout treat someone (usually refers to a meal or a drink), buy a round
single bed twin bed
singlet sleeveless undershirt
sister nurse
smoko morning or afternoon break
strides trousers
ta thank you
tea beverage, also colloquial for "dinner"
to call to visit
to ring to phone
togs swimsuit (U.S.), cozzie (Aus.)
track trail
trots harness racing
uplift pick up

varsity university, college
wop wops remote location, boondocks
Yank American

B Kiwi/Yankee Menu Savvy

Afghans popular Kiwi cookies made with cornflakes and cocoa
ANZAC biscuits cookies named for the Australia New Zealand Army Corps; they contain rolled oats and golden syrup
bangers sausages
beetroot beets
biscuits cookies
blue vein bleu cheese
capsicum green or red bell pepper
chips french-fried potatoes
chook chicken
courgette zucchini
Devonshire tea morning or afternoon tea, plus scones with cream and jam
entree appetizer
grilled broiled
hogget year-old lamb
jelly gelatin dessert
kumara Kiwi sweet potato
lemonade 7-Up
lollies candy
main course entree
milk shake flavored milk
meat pie a two-crust pie filled with stewed, cubed, or ground meat (usually beef) and gravy
Milo a hot drink similar to Ovaltine
muesli granola
pavlova popular meringue dessert named after prima ballerina Anna Pavlova, served with whipped cream and fruit
pikelets small pancakes served at tea time
pipis clams
pudding dessert in general, not necessarily pudding
roast dinner roast beef or leg of lamb served with potatoes and other vegetables that have been cooked with the meat
rock melon cantaloupe
saveloy a type of wiener
scone a biscuit served at tea time
silverbeet swiss chard
silverside corned beef
takeaway take-out
tamarillos tree tomatoes
tea the national beverage; also, colloquially, "dinner"
thick shake milkshake

tomato sauce ketchup
water biscuit cracker
whitebait very tiny fish, served whole without being cleaned
white tea tea with milk

C The Metric System

Length

1 millimeter (mm)	=	.04 inches (*or* less than 1/16 in.)
1 centimeter (cm)	=	.39 inches (*or* just under 1/2 in.)
1 meter (m)	=	39 inches (*or* about 1.1 yards)
1 kilometer (km)	=	.62 miles (*or* about 2/3 of a mile)

To convert kilometers to miles, multiply the number of kilometers by .62. Also use to convert speeds from kilometers per hour (kmph) to miles per hours (m.p.h.).
To convert miles to kilometers, multiply the number of miles by 1.61. Also use to convert speeds from m.p.h. to kmph.

Capacity

1 liter (l)	=	33.92 fluid ounces	=	2.1 pints	=	1.06 quarts	=	.26 U.S.gallons
1 Imperial gallon							=	1.2 U.S. gallons

To convert liters to U.S. gallons, multiply the number of liters by .26.
To convert U.S. gallons to liters, multiply the number of gallons by 3.79.
To convert Imperial gallons to U.S. gallons, multiply the number of Imperial gallons by 1.2.
To convert U.S. gallons to Imperial gallons, multiply the number of U.S. gallons by .83.

Weight

1 gram (g)	=	.035 ounces (*or* about a paperclip's weight)		
1 kilogram (kg)	=	35.2 ounces	=	2.2 pounds
1 metric ton	=	2,205 pounds	=	1.1 short ton

To convert kilograms to pounds, multiply the number of kilograms by 2.2.
To convert pounds to kilograms, multiply the number of pounds by .45.

Area

1 hectare (ha)	=	2.47 acres		
1 square kilometer (km^2)	=	247 acres	=	.39 square miles

To convert hectares to acres, multiply the number of hectares by 2.47.
To convert acres to hectares, multiply the number of acres by .41.
To convert square kilometers to square miles, multiply the number of square kilometers by .39.
To convert square miles to square kilometers, multiply the number of square miles by 2.6.

Temperature

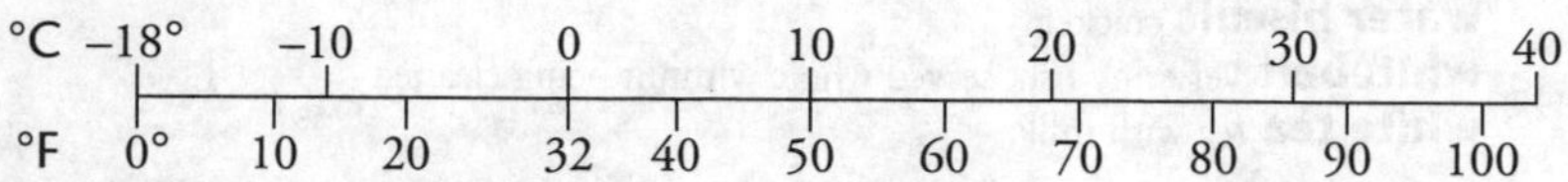

To convert degrees Fahrenheit to degrees Celsius, subtract 32 from °F, multiply by 5, then divide by 9 (example: 85°F − 32 × 5 ÷ 9 = 29.4°C).

To convert degrees Celsius to degrees Fahrenheit, multiply °C by 9, divide by 5, and add 32 (example: 20°C × 9 ÷ 5 + 32 = 68°F).

Index

Please send me the books checked below:

FROMMER'S COMPREHENSIVE GUIDES

(Guides listing facilities from budget to deluxe, with emphasis on the medium-priced)

	Retail Price	Code
☐ Acapulco/Ixtapa/Taxco, 2nd Edition	$13.95	C157
☐ Alaska '94-'95	$17.00	C131
☐ Arizona '95 (Avail. 3/95)	$14.95	C166
☐ Australia '94'-'95	$18.00	C147
☐ Austria, 6th Edition	$16.95	C162
☐ Bahamas '94-'95	$17.00	C121
☐ Belgium/Holland/ Luxembourg '93-'94	$18.00	C106
☐ Bermuda '94-'95	$15.00	C122
☐ Brazil, 3rd Edition	$20.00	C111
☐ California '95	$16.95	C164
☐ Canada '94-'95	$19.00	C145
☐ Caribbean '95	$18.00	C148
☐ Carolinas/Georgia, 2nd Edition	$17.00	C128
☐ Colorado, 2nd Edition	$16.00	C143
☐ Costa Rica '95	$13.95	C161
☐ Cruises '95-'96	$19.00	C150
☐ Delaware/Maryland '94-'95	$15.00	C136
☐ England '95	$17.95	C159
☐ Florida '95	$18.00	C152
☐ France '94-'95	$20.00	C132
☐ Germany '95	$18.95	C158
☐ Ireland, 1st Edition (Avail. 3/95)	$16.95	C168
☐ Italy '95	$18.95	C160
☐ Jamaica/Barbados, 2nd Edition	$15.00	C149
☐ Japan '94-'95	$19.00	C144
☐ Maui, 1st Edition	$14.00	C153
☐ Nepal, 2nd Edition	$18.00	C126
☐ New England '95	$16.95	C165
☐ New Mexico, 3rd Edition (Avail. 3/95)	$14.95	C167
☐ New York State '94-'95	$19.00	C133
☐ Northwest, 5th Edition	$17.00	C140
☐ Portugal '94-'95	$17.00	C141
☐ Puerto Rico '95-'96	$14.00	C151
☐ Puerto Vallarta/ Manzanillo/Guadalajara '94-'95	$14.00	C135
☐ Scandinavia, 16th Edition (Avail. 3/95)	$19.95	C169
☐ Scotland '94-'95	$17.00	C146
☐ South Pacific '94-'95	$20.00	C138
☐ Spain, 16th Edition	$16.95	C163
☐ Switzerland/ Liechtenstein '94-'95	$19.00	C139
☐ Thailand, 2nd Edition	$17.95	C154
☐ U.S.A., 4th Edition	$18.95	C156
☐ Virgin Islands '94-'95	$13.00	C127
☐ Virginia '94-'95	$14.00	C142
☐ Yucatan, 2nd Edition	$13.95	C155

FROMMER'S $-A-DAY GUIDES

(Guides to low-cost tourist accommodations and facilities)

	Retail Price	Code
☐ Australia on $45 '95-'96	$18.00	D122
☐ Costa Rica/Guatemala/ Belize on $35, 3rd Edition	$15.95	D126
☐ Eastern Europe on $30, 5th Edition	$16.95	D129
☐ England on $60 '95	$17.95	D128
☐ Europe on $50 '95	$17.95	D127
☐ Greece on $45 '93-'94	$19.00	D100
☐ Hawaii on $75 '95	$16.95	D124
☐ Ireland on $45 '94-'95	$17.00	D118
☐ Israel on $45, 15th Edition	$16.95	D130
☐ Mexico on $45 '95	$16.95	D125
☐ New York on $70 '94-'95	$16.00	D121
☐ New Zealand on $45 '93-'94	$18.00	D103
☐ South America on $40, 16th Edition	$18.95	D123
☐ Washington, D.C. on $50 '94-'95	$17.00	D120

FROMMER'S CITY $-A-DAY GUIDES

	Retail Price	Code		Retail Price	Code
☐ Berlin on $40 '94-'95	$12.00	D111	☐ Madrid on $50 '94-'95	$13.00	D119
☐ London on $45 '94-'95	$12.00	D114	☐ Paris on $50 '94-'95	$12.00	D117

FROMMER'S FAMILY GUIDES

(Guides listing information on kid-friendly hotels, restaurants, activities and attractions)

	Retail Price	Code		Retail Price	Code
☐ California with Kids	$18.00	F100	☐ San Francisco with Kids	$17.00	F104
☐ Los Angeles with Kids	$17.00	F103	☐ Washington, D.C. with Kids	$17.00	F102
☐ New York City with Kids	$18.00	F101			

FROMMER'S CITY GUIDES

(Pocket-size guides to sightseeing and tourist accommodations and facilities in all price ranges)

	Retail Price	Code		Retail Price	Code
☐ Amsterdam '93-'94	$13.00	S110	☐ Montreal/Quebec City '95	$11.95	S166
☐ Athens, 10th Edition (Avail. 3/95)	$12.95	S174	☐ Nashville/Memphis, 1st Edition	$13.00	S141
☐ Atlanta '95	$12.95	S161	☐ New Orleans '95	$12.95	S148
☐ Atlantic City/Cape May, 5th Edition	$13.00	S130	☐ New York '95	$12.95	S152
☐ Bangkok, 2nd Edition	$12.95	S147	☐ Orlando '95	$13.00	S145
☐ Barcelona '93-'94	$13.00	S115	☐ Paris '95	$12.95	S150
☐ Berlin, 3rd Edition	$12.95	S162	☐ Philadelphia, 8th Edition	$12.95	S167
☐ Boston '95	$12.95	S160	☐ Prague '94-'95	$13.00	S143
☐ Budapest, 1st Edition	$13.00	S139	☐ Rome, 10th Edition	$12.95	S168
☐ Chicago '95	$12.95	S169	☐ St. Louis/Kansas City, 2nd Edition	$13.00	S127
☐ Denver/Boulder/Colorado Springs, 3rd Edition	$12.95	S154	☐ San Diego '95	$12.95	S158
☐ Dublin, 2nd Edition	$12.95	S157	☐ San Francisco '95	$12.95	S155
☐ Hong Kong '94-'95	$13.00	S140	☐ Santa Fe/Taos/ Albuquerque '95 (Avail. 2/95)	$12.95	S172
☐ Honolulu/Oahu '95	$12.95	S151	☐ Seattle/Portland '94-'95	$13.00	S137
☐ Las Vegas '95	$12.95	S163	☐ Sydney, 4th Edition	$12.95	S171
☐ London '95	$12.95	S156	☐ Tampa/St. Petersburg, 3rd Edition	$13.00	S146
☐ Los Angeles '95	$12.95	S164	☐ Tokyo '94-'95	$13.00	S144
☐ Madrid/Costa del Sol, 2nd Edition	$12.95	S165	☐ Toronto '95 (Avail. 3/95)	$12.95	S173
☐ Mexico City, 1st Edition	$12.95	S170	☐ Vancouver/Victoria '94-'95	$13.00	S142
☐ Miami '95-'96	$12.95	S149	☐ Washington, D.C. '95	$12.95	S153
☐ Minneapolis/St. Paul, 4th Edition	$12.95	S159			

FROMMER'S WALKING TOURS

(Companion guides that point out the places and pleasures that make a city unique)

	Retail Price	Code		Retail Price	Code
☐ Berlin	$12.00	W100	☐ New York	$12.00	W102
☐ Chicago	$12.00	W107	☐ Paris	$12.00	W103
☐ England's Favorite Cities	$12.00	W108	☐ San Francisco	$12.00	W104
☐ London	$12.00	W101	☐ Washington, D.C.	$12.00	W105
☐ Montreal/Quebec City	$12.00	W106			

SPECIAL EDITIONS

	Retail Price	Code		Retail Price	Code
☐ Bed & Breakfast Southwest	$16.00	P100	☐ National Park Guide, 29th Edition	$17.00	P106
☐ Bed & Breakfast Great American Cities	$16.00	P104	☐ Where to Stay U.S.A., 11th Edition	$15.00	P102
☐ Caribbean Hideaways	$16.00	P103			

FROMMER'S TOURING GUIDES

(Color-illustrated guides that include walking tours, cultural and historic sites, and practical information)

	Retail Price	Code		Retail Price	Code
☐ Amsterdam	$11.00	T001	☐ New York	$11.00	T008
☐ Barcelona	$14.00	T015	☐ Rome	$11.00	T010
☐ Brazil	$11.00	T003	☐ Tokyo	$15.00	T016
☐ Hong Kong/Singapore/ Macau	$11.00	T006	☐ Turkey	$11.00	T013
☐ London	$13.00	T007	☐ Venice	$ 9.00	T014

Please note: If the availability of a book is several months away, we may have back issues of guides to that particular destination. Call customer service at (815) 734-1104.